Business Information Systems

2nd edition

Paul Beynon-Davies

Professor of Organisational Informatics,
Cardiff Business School, Cardiff University, UK

Consultants:

Bob Galliers, *The University Distinguished Professor and*
former Provost, Bentley University, USA

Chris Sauer, *Senior Tutor, Green Templeton College,*
University of Oxford, UK

palgrave
macmillan

First published 2009
Second edition published 2013 by
PALGRAVE MACMILLAN

Palgrave Macmillan in the UK is an imprint of Macmillan Publishers Limited, registered in England, company number 785998, of Houndmills, Basingstoke, Hampshire RG21 6XS.

Palgrave Macmillan in the US is a division of St Martin's Press LLC, 175 Fifth Avenue, New York, NY 10010.

Palgrave Macmillan is the global academic imprint of the above companies and has companies and representatives throughout the world.

Palgrave® and Macmillan® are registered trademarks in the United States, the United Kingdom, Europe and other countries

ISBN 978–1–137–26580–7

This book is printed on paper suitable for recycling and made from fully managed and sustained forest sources. Logging, pulping and manufacturing processes are expected to conform to the environmental regulations of the country of origin.

A catalogue record for this book is available from the British Library.

A catalog record for this book is available from the Library of Congress.

Also by the same author and published by Palgrave Macmillan:

Database Systems (*3rd edition*)
eBusiness (*2nd edition*)
Significance: exploring the nature of information, systems and technology

Short contents

Contents

1 Introduction: the domain of business information systems   1

Part I   Key concepts   33

2 Organisations and systems   35

13 Successful informatics practice

Figures

Tables

Case studies

There is a huge range of case studies both integrated into and as an additional resource for this book:

- Specially written cases highlighted in the book and featured in full at the end of the book (pp. 424–465).
- Mini cases in the book only.
- Cases from the *Journal of Information Technology* (JIT) and *Journal of Information Technology Teaching Cases* (JITTC) with cross-chapter relevance summarised at the end of the book (pp. 466–470).
- Further online author-written cases (see p. 471).
- Further JIT and JITTC cases accessible free online (see p. 472).

For mapping the cases against the learning goals of IS2010 curriculum see p. xxvii.

Specially written cases

These case studies are featured in full at the end of the book. Short sections (CASE CHECK boxes) are often also integrated at relevant points in the text.

	CASE CHECK boxes integrated into chapters	Case mentioned here	Full case in the Case Studies section, pp. 424-465	Additional lecturer notes available online
Amazon	240, 246, 250, 255, 256		424	Y
Apple	144		426	
Arab Spring and social media	253		427	
Cisco	–	158	428	
Citizens Advice Bureau	267		430	
Dell	–	158, 336	430	
dotCYMRU	153		432	
eBay	162		435	Y
Facebook	253		436	
Failure in government ICT systems	284, 294		438	
Google	159		440	
Hollerith electronic tabulating machine	–	130	442	
Indian identity number	–	–	444	
Inka Khipu	76, 93		445	
Microsoft	337		449	
Music industry	–	–	451	
Offshoring in Bangalore	344		452	
Open source software	186, 375		453	
SAP	190		455	
Tesco	38, 52, 59, 230, 286, 341		455	Y
Twitter	–	260	459	
UK Revenue and Customs	320		460	
Victorian railway clearing house	–	92	462	
Wikipedia	159		464	

Mini cases

These cases appear as CASE CHECK boxes in the chapters only.

Cases from the *Journal of Information Technology* and the *Journal of Information Technology Teaching Cases*

Specially selected case studies with cross-chapter relevance. These case studies are summarised at the back of the book, including brief case descriptions, an author commentary and some issues for consideration. The full case studies are downloadable as PDFs from www.palgrave.com/business/beynon-daviesbis2e/.

	CASE CHECK boxes integrated into chapters	Summary of the case in the Case Studies section, pp. 466–470	Additional lecturer teaching notes available by request online
Fixing the payment system at Alvalade XXI: a case on IT project risk management	–	467	
Modernisation of passenger reservation system: Indian Railways' dilemma	–	467	Y
Crafting and executing an offshore IT sourcing strategy: GlobShop's experience	–	468	Y
Infosys Technologies: improving organisational knowledge flows	–	468	
Constructing an e-Supply Chain at Eastman Chemical Company	–	469	
Lessons learned from the development and marketing of Mozilla Firefox 1.0	–	469	Y
Finding the process edge: ITIL at Celanese	356	470	Y
Peak experiences and strategic IT alignment at Vermont Teddy Bear	321	470	Y

Online case study resource bank

Further specially written cases

Additional case studies written by the author are available at www.palgrave.com/business/beynon-daviesbis2e. See also p. 471 for mapping against Learning goals of IS2010 curriculum.

	Additional lecturer notes available online
Beer distribution game	
Business motivation modelling	
Easyjet	Y
HiCar	
IKEA *Written by Sharon Cox, Birmingham City University*	Y
MySpace	Y
OGC gateway process	
Research information system	
UK electoral system	
UK stock market	
YouTube	

Further cases from the *Journal of Information Technology* and the *Journal of Information Technology Teaching Cases*

The full case studies are downloadable as PDFs from the www.palgrave.com/business/beynon-daviesbis2e. See also p. 472 for mapping against Learning goals of IS2010 curriculum.

	Additional lecturer notes available by request online
Managing the Internet Payment Platform project	Y
Challenges in delivering cross-agency integrated e-services: the OBLS project	
Wireless technologies at Agriculture ITO	Y
The ultimate bluff: a case study of partygaming.com	Y
E-business transformation at the crossroads: Sears' dilemma	Y
DCXNET: e-transformation at DaimlerChrysler	
Addressing the new regulatory landscape: IT compliance and E-Discovery at KMCO Gaming	

About the author

Paul Beynon-Davies is Professor of Organisational Informatics at Cardiff Business School, Cardiff University. He received his BSc in Economics and Social Science and PhD in Computing from University of Wales College, Cardiff. Before taking up an academic post he worked for several years in the informatics industry in the United Kingdom both in the public and private sectors. He still regularly acts as a consultant to public and private sector organisations and has been consistently rated as one of the top scholars in his area worldwide.

He has published widely in the field of information systems and ICT and has written 12 books, including *Information Systems*, *Information Systems Development* and *Database Systems*. He has also published over 80 academic papers on topics including the foundations of information systems, electronic business, electronic government, information systems planning, information systems development, database development and artificial intelligence.

Paul Beynon-Davies has engaged in a number of government-funded projects related to the impact of ICT on the economic, social and political spheres. He was involved in an evaluation of electronic government in Wales and was seconded part-time to the National Assembly for Wales (NAfW) as an evaluator of its Cymru-ar-Lein/Information Age strategy for Wales. From 2006 to 2008 he was Director of the eCommerce Innovation Centre at Cardiff University, which also included the Broadband Observatory for Wales.

His recent research work has focused on the foundations of informatics. This involves an attempt to build a more coherent and unified conception of informatics as an interdisciplinary area focused on the accomplishment of organisation through the entanglement of signs, patterns and systems. A summary of this work to date is published by Palgrave Macmillan in the book *Significance: Exploring the Nature of Information, Systems and Technology*.

Acknowledgements

My thanks to Professor Bob Galliers and Dr Chris Sauer for their valuable guidance on the content and structure of this book. Thanks also to the long list of reviewers who contributed comments on both the first and second editions of the book, including:

Reviewers of the first edition:

Colin Ashurst, *University of Durham*, UK
Vladlena Benson, *Kingston University*, UK
Laura Campoy, *University of the West of England*, UK
Julian Coleman, *University of Bolton*, UK
Gordon Harris, *University of Exeter*, UK
Ulf Höglind, *Swedish Business School, Örebro University*, Sweden
Ghulam Musa, *London Metropolitan University*, UK
Martin Rich, *Cass Business School*, UK

Reviewers of the second edition:

Jyoti Bhardwaj, *Edinburgh Napier University*, UK
Clare Branigan, *University College Dublin*, Ireland
Per Flensburg, *University College West*, Sweden

Stephen Gulliver, *University of Reading*, UK
Jonas Hedman, *Copenhagen Business School*, Denmark
Ulf Höglind, *Swedish Business School, Örebro University*, Sweden
Alexander Mädche, *University of Mannheim*, Germany
Irena Spasic, *University of Cardiff*, UK
Irene Vanderfeesten, *Eindhoven University of Technology*, Netherlands
Jason Whalley, *University of Strathclyde*, UK

Thanks also to the Association for Information Technology Trust, for permission to use cases from the *Journal of Information Technology* and the *Journal of Information Technology Teaching Cases*. Finally, I wish to thank Ursula Gavin, Ceri Griffiths and Leo Goretti at Palgrave Macmillan for their support in the production of this work.

Message to students

Why it is important to read this book

This book introduces both the current and the aspiring business professional to three topic areas that are critical to their working life.

First, **information** is so important to the modern world that some have even referred to it as the global information society. In this book we help the reader unravel the ways in which information underpins business activity of many forms. We shall demonstrate that information underlies the work not only of managers but also of shop-floor workers.

Second, organisations establish **information systems** in order to control their current activities and also as the basis for changing and improving their ways of doing things. We describe a number of typical information systems within businesses which drive their operations. We also describe the ways in which information systems are now critically important for managing activities and relationships with customers and suppliers.

Third, **information and communication technology** (ICT) has been used to increase the efficiency and effectiveness of both information systems and business practice. Much of the way modern business works is embedded or encoded in its ICT. Without ICT systems many organisations would cease to function.

But these topics are not isolated areas of concern for the modern business. For instance, the modern business organisation may have the aim of improving its performance through the collection and use of better information. But in order to do this the business must develop an efficient information system, which is likely to require the use of ICT. This book provides a guide to best practice in each area, as well as an understanding of the relationships between these areas.

This book is based on my experience of teaching various undergraduate, postgraduate and commercial courses in the area; it is has also been enhanced by my consulting and professional practice. Hence, the concepts and frameworks described in this textbook have been field-tested, not only in an educational context but also in practical work.

Why this book is different

My aim in writing this book has been to create a coherent path through the subject of business information systems which addresses some of the needs I have identified during over three decades of experience in the field. This textbook has been tested at a number of academic institutions around the world and we have taken the opportunity in this second edition to include a number of improvements suggested by users of the book; both teaching staff and students.

The book covers essential core material in the area of business information, systems and technology. Care has been taken to ensure that only material that is critical for the student is included.

Many business information systems textbooks consist of a collection of interesting but disconnected topics. This book is different in that we consider the material as an integrated and seamless web of ICT application in organisations. This book therefore makes it easier for you to make sense of the subject as a whole. It also makes it easier for you to see how different elements of the subject inter-relate.

The book provides a balanced coverage of both theory and practice. The aim is to use precise definitions of a number of foundation concepts to provide an understanding of the place of information, information systems and ICT within business. This understanding then makes it possible to show you some practical uses and applications of information systems. It identifies and explains a number of key skills that are important to business professionals of many kinds.

So what you will get from this book is a *rounded* but *grounded* conception of this important area of business. The book will equip you with knowledge which will enable you to better perform as a business professional in the modern, complex organisational world.

In the psychologist Edward De Bono's words, creativity involves '*breaking out of established patterns in order to look at things in a different way*'. Most of all this book is designed to get you to think differently; not only about organisations of all forms, but particularly about the place of information and information technology within such organisations. After all, thinking differently is a necessary pre-condition for any successful innovation.

For more details on the book's structure, learning features and companion website please see the 'About the book' section.

Message to lecturers

Mission

My aim in writing this book has been to create a coherent path through the subject area which addresses some of the needs I have identified during over three decades of experience in the area. *Business Information Systems* includes the following distinctive characteristics:

- **Coverage of core material**. The book covers essential core material in the area of business information, systems and technology which will be useful not only for academic but also for commercial courses. As such, we have taken care to exclude material present in other texts in the area that is not critical for a relevant, introductory exploration of the subject. However, we have taken great care to ensure that the material provided covers all the core topic areas defined in standard, international curricula: particularly that detailed in the IS2010 curriculum (see below).

- **Use of clear terminology**. The book uses a more precise set of terms than competing texts for explaining the area. For instance, the field of study is described not with the conventional term *Information Systems*, but with the less confusing label *Organisational Informatics* throughout. The book also also makes great play of the distinction between an information and communication technology (ICT) system, an information system and an activity system.

- **Integrated account**. It is unfortunate that many textbooks in this area appear to consist of a collection of interesting but disconnected topics. This book presents a much more integrated and holistic account. We believe that organisational informatics is not a series of interesting but independent organisational and technological issues; rather, it is a seamless web of ICT application in organisations. This book enables students to make sense of this as a whole and to gain an appreciation of the inter-relationship between elements of the subject. This approach has been tried and tested a number of times, not only in my own teaching but in the teaching of many others. Feedback from students suggests that they find such an approach provides a more rounded and lasting educational experience. They are able to better appreciate the inter-connectedness of different topics within the subject area and their critical importance to all forms of organisation.

- **Based in theory**. Over the last two decades, organisational informatics has achieved a greater degree of coherence as a discipline. However, most introductory and intermediate texts on the subject tend to de-emphasise the coverage of theory. Here, the aim is to provide a stronger theoretical foundation than competing texts. Foundation concepts discussed in earlier chapters are used throughout the book to provide coherence to the description of current practice. For example, the distinction between an ICT system, an information system and an activity system is not simply a matter of convenience: we believe it has practical implications in the sense that the design and use of an ICT system is affected very much by the context of communication (the information system) in which it is placed and the activity system it is meant to support.

- **Broad nature of application**. This book pays great attention to the way in which concepts discussed have a much broader application than just purely digital computing technology. We deliberately introduce what may appear at first glance as 'strange' cases such as that of the Inka Khipu and the Royal Air Force's warning network during the Battle of Britain. These cases are designed to get students to think differently about our current 'information technology' and how it relates to other technologies used historically and by other cultures. It also establishes the usefulness of applying the lens of 'information' to help bring into better focus the nature of organisation.

- **Practical emphasis**. Having stronger theory does not mean less relevance to practice. In fact, I would argue the opposite; as the American sociologist Kurt Lewin once said '*nothing is as practical as a good theory*'. Theory, hence, guides good practice in organisational informatics. Throughout the book we have highlighted good practice of relevance to organisational practitioners who are aiming to improve the adoption of ICT, as well as those more generally who are attempting to innovate organisational activity through better management of information and information systems within organisations.

- **Design emphasis**. Some see organisational informatics as very much a 'design science', in the sense that it is interested in the effective design and construction of organisational systems of various forms. This book takes the position that it is no good just teaching students what they should know: it is equally important to show them how to do things with this knowledge. Therefore, this book provides coverage of a number of key analysis and design skills of importance. The emphasis is very much on modelling systems and using such models as the basis not only for understanding current issues within organisations but also for describing possible futures for organisational life.

- **Field-tested**. As well as being based on my experience of teaching various undergraduate, postgraduate and commercial courses in the area, the book has also been enhanced by my consulting and professional practice. Hence, the concepts and frameworks described here have been field-tested, not only in an educational context but also in practical work. The first edition of the book was also adopted as a core teaching text at a number of institutions around the world. Adopters of the text kindly provided much feedback on their experiences of using it, which has helped improve this second edition.

Using the book as part of a course or module

The coverage in this book emphasises the inter-connected nature of the subject and presents material in a deliberate sequence: later concepts are based upon concepts covered in earlier chapters. It is therefore ideally suited for an intensive undergraduate or postgraduate course or series of modules on business information systems.

Since the coverage is necessarily broad, there are a number of ways in which this material might be used within educational courses or modules at different levels:

- The book deliberately attempts to demonstrate the importance of considering business information and information systems in isolation from ICT. Hence, it is possible to use the first three chapters of the book to build a coherent account of **business information management**.

- A module on **electronic business** or **electronic commerce** can be built around the content in the *environment* and *eBusiness* chapters. The two chapters on *ICT infrastructure* supporting contemporary business may also be used for this purpose.

- A module on **information systems and ICT management** would use the chapters on *planning and management*, *service and operations* and possibly *use and impact*.

- The chapter on *information systems development* acts as an introduction to this area and, together with the two *ICT infrastructure* chapters, could be used within a module on **business ICT**.

- This book introduces various modelling techniques that form core activity within **business analysis**. A module on this subject could therefore usefully rely upon a considerable amount of material provided in this text.

For more details on the book's structure, learning features and companion website, please see the 'About the book' section.

Coverage of IS2010 core curriculum   **IS2010**

IS2010 is the latest in a series of model curricula for undergraduate degrees in Information Systems developed by the Association for Information Systems (AIS) and the Association for Computing Machinery (ACM). This curriculum specifies seven core courses and a number of elective courses. The material presented in this book provides a systematic introduction to the learning outcomes as specified in the seven core courses of IS2010. The relationship between the various chapters and the seven core courses of the IS2010 curriculum are illustrated in Figure L.1.

IS2010 CORE COURSES

Part	Chapter	IS2010.1 Foundations of information systems	IS2010.2 Data and information management	IS2010.3 Enterprise architecture	IS2010.4 IS project management	IS2010.5 IT infrastructure	IS2010.6 Systems analysis and design	IS2010.7 IS strategy, management and acquisition
I	1 Introduction: the domain of business information systems	✓	✓	✓	✓	✓	✓	✓
	2 Organisations and systems	✓					✓	
	3 Data, information and knowledge	✓	✓				✓	
	4 Information systems and organisational infrastructure	✓		✓				
II	5 Communication infrastructure			✓		✓		
	6 ICT infrastructure		✓			✓		
III	7 The business environment	✓						
	8 Electronic business, commerce and government	✓				✓		
	9 Assessing the use and impact of information systems				✓			✓
IV	10 Planning, strategy and management				✓			✓
	11 Service, projects and operations			✓				✓
	12 Information systems development		✓	✓	✓		✓	
	13 Successful informatics practice	✓	✓	✓	✓	✓	✓	✓

Figure L.1 *The relationship between book chapters and the IS2010 core curriculum*

The IS2010 also provides a set of core capabilities, or competencies, that its curriculum should provide to students. These are

- improving organisational processes
- exploiting opportunities created by technology innovations
- understanding and addressing information requirements
- designing and managing enterprise architecture
- identifying and evaluating solution and sourcing alternatives
- securing data and infrastructure
- understanding, managing and controlling IT risks.

 The places where these capabilities are covered in the book are indicated with an icon next to the appropriate section.

Relationship to the AACSB learning standards and to the AMBA model curriculum

The Association to Advance Collegiate Schools of Business (AACSB) is a not-for-profit corporation devoted to the promotion and improvement of higher education in business administration and accounting. Any higher education institution wishing to gain AACSB accreditation must provide courses which meet a number of learning standards as far as the student experience is concerned. These include communication, ethical reasoning, analytical skills, use of IT, multiculturalism and diversity, and reflective thinking. The reflective section placed at the end of each chapter takes a number of these standards and suggests how the material presented can be addressed in such an experience.

The Association of MBAs (AMBA), as part of its specification for its model Master of Business Administration curriculum, stresses that MBA students should have *knowledge of the concepts and applications of management information systems, including IT applications.* This book provides a sound introduction to the knowledge, understanding and skills required in this subject area.

Changes to the second edition

A number of changes have been made to the second edition in response to feedback received from users and reviewers of the first edition:

- Chapters 2, 3 and 4 have been completely rewritten. The discussion of organisations, information, data, knowledge and infrastructure is retained, but great care has been taken to introduce these foundation concepts gradually, with many more examples.
- Chapter 6 includes a section on cloud computing.
- The structure of Chapter 7 has been re-worked to focus upon the concept of value and the value network.
- Chapter 8 now includes sections on mobile eCommerce and eGovernment.
- Chapter 11 now includes a section on green ICT.
- A critical reflection section has been added to the end of each chapter.
- A number of updates have been made to all chapters. Some sections in chapters have been extended and a small number of sections have been dropped.
- A number of 'Careers in IS' video interviews with IS/IT practitioners have been conducted especially for this book. They are available online and are referenced throughout the book.
- The appendix features nine new case studies, including wider coverage of non-European countries. All the cases from the first edition have been consistently updated.
- Referencing has been reduced within the text of each chapter to avoid detracting from the reading experience. Key texts are now highlighted in the further reading section.

About the book

Chapter 1 Introduction: the domain of business information systems

The material in this book is organised in 13 chapters. The opening chapter considers how important an understanding of information systems is to the effective performance of organisations of various kinds. It then introduces a model of the domain, which is used to emphasise the necessary multifaceted and inter-connected nature of information systems in business. This model is useful in helping demonstrate that the successful adoption and application of ICT in organisations relies on the positive interaction between different elements. These elements range from the effective planning and management of information through to the successful development, implementation and use of information systems.

Each element of this domain model is considered in a separate chapter. It is also used as a device in the final chapter to help structure and summarise good practice in information systems or organisational informatics. By the final chapter readers should therefore have a clear conception of good practice for use in their future careers.

Part I Key concepts

Chapter 2 Organisations and systems

The purpose of ICT can only be considered in terms of human activity within organisations. This chapter examines what an organisation is, and uses this as a basis for considering the relevance of information, information systems and ICT to organisations. The concept of system is used to relate to each other many of the issues seen as critical to the modern organisation, such as strategy, management and performance. The chapter concludes with coverage of the issues of process modelling and design.

Chapter 3 Data, information and knowledge

The concept of information is much taken for granted. This chapter argues that an understanding of the multifaceted nature of information is essential. It uses the concept of a sign to help explain the crucial relationship between data, information, decision and action. It also considers the practical importance of modelling data, information and knowledge in organisations.

Chapter 4 Information systems and organisational infrastructure

This chapter defines the concept of an information system as a communication system used to support a given activity system, sometimes through the use of technology. It therefore argues for its place as a sociotechnical system in that it covers both activities and ICT. The chapter also examines the place of information systems infrastructure within the wider infrastructure of modern business.

Part II Understanding ICT

Chapter 5 Communication infrastructure

The adoption of ICT is promoted within both the public and the private sector as a means of improving the efficacy, efficiency and effectiveness of the delivery of services and goods to internal and external stakeholders. Modern organisations therefore rely on effective ICT or technical infrastructure. This book considers technical infrastructure in two parts. Chapter 5 examines key elements that make up the communication infrastructure supporting such changes to organisational activity. This includes access devices and channels, communication networks, the Internet and the World Wide Web. It also considers the importance of such networks for carrying business transactions and the on-going attempts to develop various standards in this area.

Chapter 6 ICT systems infrastructure

This chapter begins by considering the component elements of an ICT system and how their processing is now distributed across communication networks. This leads to a discussion of front-end ICT systems and the important role that websites and Web content play in such systems. It then considers the place of the business tier and the concept of business rules. This is followed by a discussion of back-end ICT systems and the critical place of data management in modern ICT infrastructure. The chapter concludes with a discussion of the integration of front-end and back-end infrastructure and of the importance of securing data both within ICT systems and across the communication infrastructure connecting ICT systems.

Part III Applying information systems to business

Chapter 7 The business environment

In this book an organisation is seen primarily as an activity system (or more accurately, a collection of interacting activity systems) that is affected by forces in its environment. Organisations are not isolated entities, they are open systems. This means that the success of any organisation will depend on how well it integrates with aspects of its environment. This chapter focuses primarily on the economic environment of the organisation and describes ways in which organisations can be considered as systems producing value that travels within and between them. Hence, activity systems provide supportive mechanisms for the customer, supply and internal value-chains of organisations. The chapter outlines the key elements of these value-chains and describes how they act as conduits within a wider value network and serve to coordinate the flow of goods, services and transactions.

Chapter 8 Electronic business, electronic commerce and electronic government

Much of the global economic environment now relies on ICT infrastructure for effective operation, so many modern businesses are 'electronic' businesses to a greater or lesser extent. This chapter considers the use of ICT, using the concept of the value network to help distinguish between various forms of electronic business. The term eBusiness as used here incorporates eCommerce. Intra-business eBusiness involves the use of ICT to support the internal value-chain. Business to consumer (B2C) eCommerce is concerned with the place of ICT in the customer-chain. Business to business (B2B) eCommerce particularly focuses on the place of ICT in the supply-chain. Consumer to consumer (C2C) eCommerce covers the application of ICT in the community-chain. Lastly, partner to partner (P2P) eBusiness concerns the use of ICT in support of collaboration networks.

Chapter 9 Assessing the use and impact of information systems

After an information system is introduced, it begins to have effects on that organisation. There are both first-order effects, concerning use, and second-order effects, which concern the impact of the system on individuals, groups and the organisation as a whole. Both use and impact are critical to the assessment of the success or failure of an information system. This chapter considers the relationships between use, impact and success, and concludes with a consideration of the ways in which the worth of information systems can be established.

Part IV Managing information systems in business

Chapter 10 Planning, strategy and management

This chapter considers two of the critical processes that affect an organisation's informatics infrastructure: management and planning. It looks at the importance of informatics planning to the effective coupling of informatics strategy with general business strategy, and then moves on to discuss the management activities associated with both current and future informatics infrastructure.

Chapter 11 Service, projects and operations

This chapter considers the structure of the informatics industry and service, which might be either in-house or outsourced to a vendor organisation. It looks at two critical activities of an informatics service: the essentials of project management and the neglected topic of operating the ICT infrastructure for organisations, now often described as ICT services management.

Chapter 12 Information systems development

This chapter considers information systems development as a key organisational process. Since it is a process, development can be considered as a system in itself. The key inputs into the process are ICT resources and developer resources, including a toolkit of methods, techniques and tools. The development process is normally organised in terms of projects and divided into defined phases of activity. Each of these phases is discussed.

Chapter 13 Successful informatics practice

The final chapter synthesises the material from previous chapters using the domain model from Chapter 1. It then applies the domain model to a well-known case study – the London Ambulance Services Computer Aided Despatch (LASCAD) System. This helps to summarise some of the key elements of the body of knowledge for the discipline and area of practice. The chapter also considers the likely future for informatics in both organisations and the wider environment.

Pedagogical features

This book contains a range of carefully thought out features designed to enhance learning, engage student interest and provide the lecturer with a variety of sources for discussion and case study analysis.

At the start of each chapter

A set of features is designed to orient the reader and prepare them for what follows:

- **Learning outcomes** set out what the student can expect to gain. Each is linked to a core principle which can be applied to business, so students can see how each piece of knowledge is relevant.
- **Chapter outlines** give an overview of the content of the chapter and highlight the key skills sections (see below).
- A brief **introduction** sets the scene.

Throughout each chapter

Throughout the text, the following are used to aid learning:

- Regular **recap features** appear at the end of each main section, to remind students of the key issues and how they relate to the previous and subsequent information.

- **Did you know?** features to highlight interesting or intriguing facts related to the subject to inform and entertain readers.
- **Reflect** comments and questions to encourage students to consider how the subject relates to real-world issues
- **Key skill** sections provide students with an appreciation of crucial skills and how they apply to business (for example, modelling, evaluation, eMarketing)
- Regular **case** sections, encourage students to relate a number of different issues discussed throughout the book to real-world examples. Case studies in the appendix are identified with < 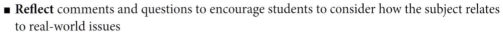 >, those on the website are identified with the icon < W >.
- The **careers in IS** boxes link to video interviews with IS practitioners talking about their jobs and the role of information systems in private and public sector organisations. The interviews have been especially recorded for this textbook and are fully integrated with the chapter contents.
- Brief **examples** highlight the concepts just discussed and an **on-page glossary** is provided for quick reference.

At the end of each chapter

A **focus on value** feature demonstrates how the material in the chapter relates to the central concept of value, while the main points discussed in the chapter are highlighted in the **chapter summary**. This is followed by an extensive section of activities consisting of a review test, a series of exercises and suggestions for student projects:

- The **review test** questions are designed to test understanding and the ability to recall appropriate answers. Answers can be obtained by re-reading the chapter.
- **Exercises** are opportunities for the reader to take what has been learnt and extend knowledge, or apply it to some other situation. They are deliberately open-ended and may be used in tutorials or other learning opportunities to structure more extensive learning about a topic.
- **Student research projects** outline a larger piece of work (in both effort and duration) than a student exercise. Typically they involve:
  - independent investigation, including formulating a project proposal
  - production of a plan of work
  - data collection
  - analysis and presentation of the results.
- Ideally, a student research project should display elements of independent and critical thinking. It should be noted that what are provided here are outlines of interesting research questions; they will demand much further work to develop into a working project proposal.
- A critical reflection section which invites the reader to challenge conceptions and debate effectively on the nature of business information systems in particular, as well as the developing nature of business and indeed all forms of organisation.

At the end of the book

A series of specially-written **case studies** provide more detail on the application of the concepts discussed to real-word experience. Each describes an organisation, project or technology relevant to the topic. The case studies are deliberately written as independent, but rich, resources of educational content. This means they can be used as sources of consolidation and for discussion across a range of chapters and topic areas. They are referred to throughout the book and each is supported by a list of issues for discussion. Further case studies are available online.

At the end of the book, a **glossary** and **index** make it easier to skim search for coverage of particular topics.

For information on how the material in this book can be used to support a range of information systems-related courses, please see the 'Message to lecturers'.

Website

ONLINE
RESOURCES
AVAILABLE

Business Information Systems is accompanied by extensive online materials, accessible to lecturers and students at **www.palgrave.com/business/beynon-daviesbis2e/.** This companion website is packed with valuable features to aid teaching and learning, including **free access to selected articles from the** *Journal of Information Technology* **and the** *Journal of Information Technology Teaching Cases*. These are supported by a list of issues to discuss in the **case studies** section of the book itself.

In addition to the unique journals zone, the following password-protected online materials have been carefully designed to support lecturers in delivering their course:

- **PowerPoint lecture slides** for each chapter (including relevant diagrams, charts and figures; the slides can be customised by lecturers to suit module needs)
- **Lecturer manual** including
  - lecture outlines and teaching tips
  - suggested answers and discussion guidelines for questions in the book
  - sample course outline giving suggested course structure for a range of courses
  - sample end-of-module exam paper and guideline answer.
- **Additional in-depth case studies** for classroom use, supported by
  - suggestions, role-play, activities and links to multimedia resources
  - teaching notes.
- **Selected additional content** from other textbooks by the author
- **Test bank** to use as a resource for creating end-of-module assessments.

Students will be able to check and expand their learning using the following features. Many of these materials are stored in an access database that is available to lecturers and can be mined in flexible ways.

- **Multiple choice questions** for each chapter to self-test and check understanding
- **Searchable glossary** of key terms for quick reference
- **Annotated weblinks** to relevant sites and articles, including news articles that emphasise the contemporary relevance of business information systems
- **Careers in IS video interviews** with IS professionals talking about their jobs and the role of information systems in private and public sector organisations
- **Career and learning section,** including student case studies and links to advice on study skills.

Careers in IS videos

As you will learn from reading this book, information systems are key to business success and therefore play a crucial role in many business and management jobs. Information systems managers, systems analysts and IT consultants work to help companies meet their goals more efficiently and more successfully. This is why this book includes video interviews with IS/ICT professionals who talk about their *Careers in IS*. The interviewees are high-profile managers working for private companies: Proxima and Schuh; and in public sector organisations: the BBC and the National Archives. Our interviewees talk about their educational and professional background, answer a few questions on some of the key themes of this book and give some advice to students who wish to pursue a career in IS.

The Careers in IS videos are fully integrated with the book contents. Each interview is presented with a box in the relevant chapter of the book; these boxes include a few discussion questions that students might try to answer after having watched the videos. There are four of these interviews in the book:

Chapter 5: Interview with John Linwood, Chief Technology Officer for the BBC, who talks about how important the Internet has become for the digital delivery of content, the use of mobile devices within the BBC, green ICT and cloud computing.

Chapter 8: Interview with David Thomas, Director of Technology and Chief Technology Officer at the National Archives, UK, who points out how ICT and information systems help in the delivery of public services to citizens.

Chapter 8: Interview with Stuart McMillan, Deputy Head of e-Commerce at Schuh, who explains the benefits, and the challenges, of B2B and B2C eCommerce and m-commerce for a company selling physical goods, such as shoes.

Chapter 11: Interview with Katherine Coombs, Chief Information Officer at Proxima Group, who talks about her experience of working as a woman in the IS/ICT sector, and the way in which ICT can contribute to business success.

ONLINE RESOURCES AVAILABLE

The videos can be accessed online in the companion website to this book: **www.palgrave.com/business/beynon-daviesbis2e/**

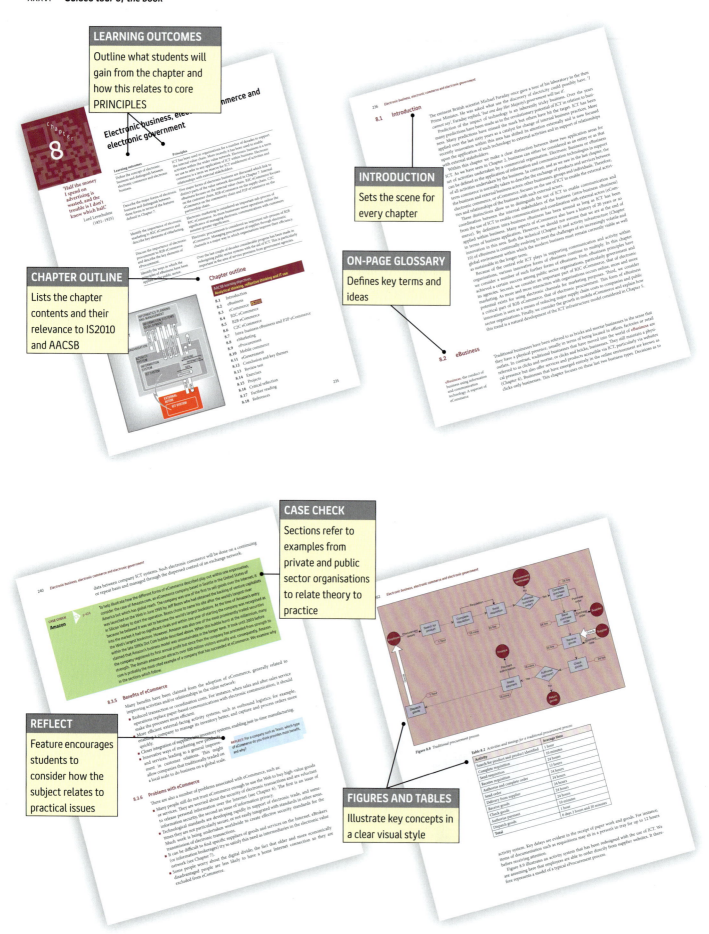

LEARNING OUTCOMES
Outline what students will gain from the chapter and how this relates to core PRINCIPLES

CHAPTER OUTLINE
Lists the chapter contents and their relevance to IS2010 and AACSB

INTRODUCTION
Sets the scene for every chapter

ON-PAGE GLOSSARY
Defines key terms and ideas

CASE CHECK
Sections refer to examples from private and public sector organisations to relate theory to practice

REFLECT
Feature encourages students to consider how the subject relates to practical issues

FIGURES AND TABLES
Illustrate key concepts in a clear visual style

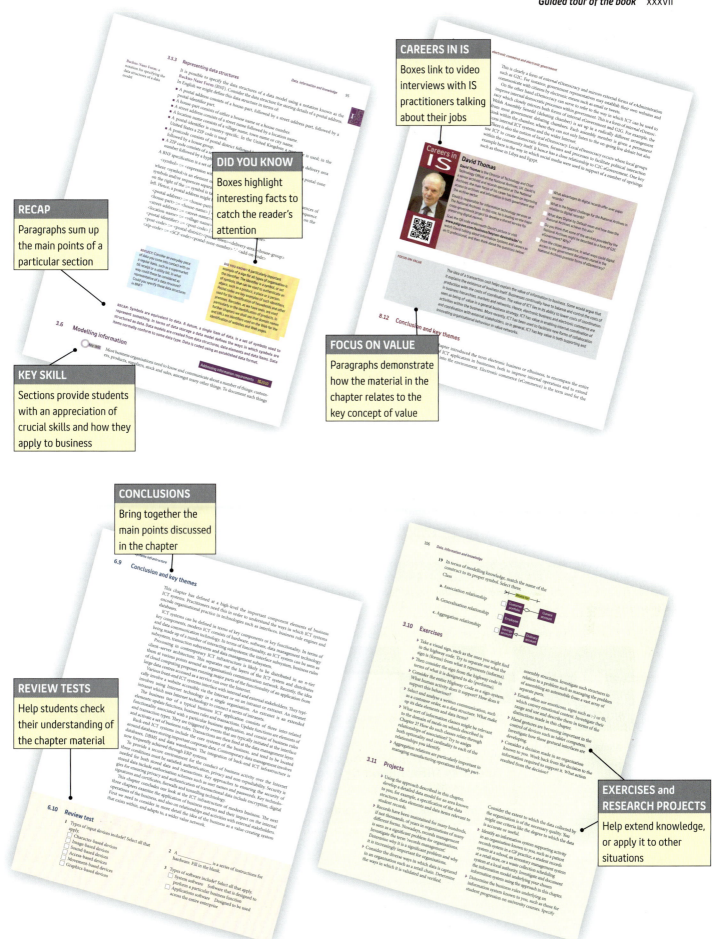

RECAP
Paragraphs sum up the main points of a particular section

DID YOU KNOW
Boxes highlight interesting facts to catch the reader's attention

KEY SKILL
Sections provide students with an appreciation of crucial skills and how they apply to business

CAREERS IN IS
Boxes link to video interviews with IS practitioners talking about their jobs

FOCUS ON VALUE
Paragraphs demonstrate how the material in the chapter relates to the key concept of value

CONCLUSIONS
Bring together the main points discussed in the chapter

REVIEW TESTS
Help students check their understanding of the chapter material

EXERCISES and RESEARCH PROJECTS
Help extend knowledge, or apply it to other situations

CRITICAL REFLECTION

Sections invite the reader to challenge conceptions

FURTHER READING

Identifies key texts for further research

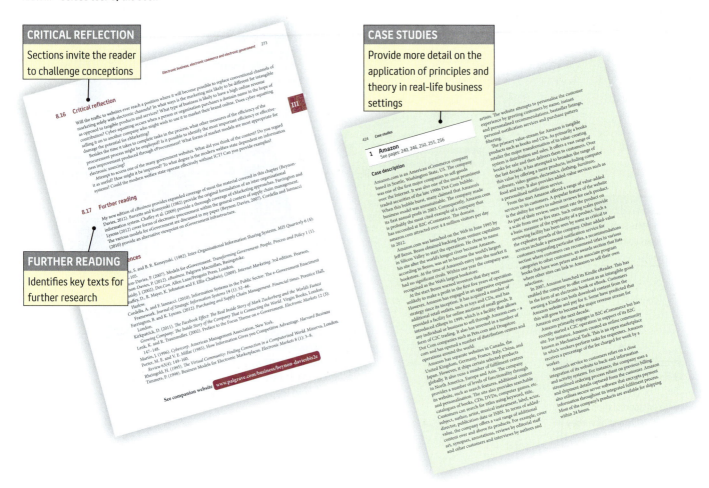

CASE STUDIES

Provide more detail on the application of principles and theory in real-life business settings

COMPANION WEBSITE

Visit our companion website at **www.palgrave.com/business/beynon-daviesbis2e** to find an extensive range of extra materials, exercises and the Careers in IS videos

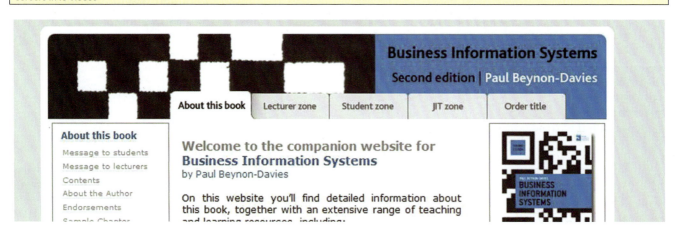

Introduction: the domain of business information systems

'When I use a word',
Humpty Dumpty said
in a scornful tone, 'it
means what I choose it
to mean – neither more
or less.'

Lewis Carroll (1832–1898),
Through the Looking Glass
(1871), chapter 6

This chapter provides a high-level overview of the material covered in more depth in separate chapters.

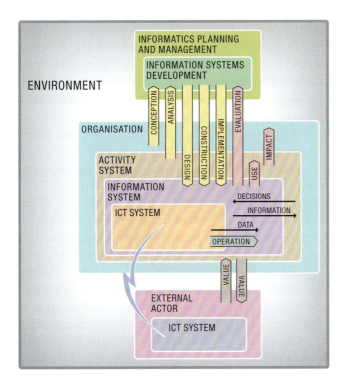

Chapter outline

1.1   Why study business information systems?

You, the reader, will be engaging with the topic area of this book probably every waking hour of your life. You may be using your mobile phone to text or email friends, or to access your page on a social networking site. You might use your personal computer at home to order goods online, or pay your taxes to government as a banking transaction, or apply for a job using a company website. You might use your interactive digital television to download and watch a movie. You might use your netbook or tablet or eBook reader on the train to read the latest crime thriller, or perhaps even a textbook.

Information and communication technology (ICT) is constantly present as it underpins so many aspects of our modern daily life. But you probably have never pondered on the way in which such technologies actually work, or how they support the activities we pursue. Why should you? The very presence and contribution of ICT frequently only comes to attention when there is a breakdown in its appropriate use or a malfunction in the technology itself.

So when you find that you cannot access the Internet because your broadband connection has failed, you are likely to feel frustrated. When your personal details have been accessed on your social networking profile by a potential employer, you might feel somewhat uncomfortable. When you are sent targeted emails by companies who have analysed your Web surfing activities, you might feel somewhat aggrieved. When someone steals your online identity to pilfer funds from your bank account, you might feel very angry.

So it may be that, when things are running smoothly, ICT is effectively 'invisible' to all but ICT professionals. But, in order for such smooth running to be achieved, it is crucial that businesses are able to anticipate future needs, plan and implement the relevant developments and continuously seek to protect their customers. To do this, they need employees and managers who are able to understand and reconcile the needs of the market and the organisation with the ever-evolving capability of ICT.

1.1.1   Why information systems are important for business

It's often said that information is power. In business there's certainly truth in that, all over the world, information is critical to the competitiveness of the private sector. The modern business organisation demands information about, for example, its customers, orders, sales, stock and inventory. It needs this information to be integrated, and it needs it to be accurate and up to date. As a result the management of information is critical to business success.

Companies collect significant amounts of transactional data about their own activities, and about the behaviour of their suppliers and customers (Burnham, 1983). Transactional data are data that record events that take place between individuals, groups and organisations. They are essential to monitoring the performance of organisations in competitive markets. For example, Tesco collects vast amounts of information about what people buy in its supermarkets. It uses this both to find out how well particular stores are performing, and to discover which product lines sell best to which types of customer.

Today we often hear terms like eBusiness (electronic business), eCommerce (electronic commerce) and eGovernment (electronic government), which show how important ICT and information systems are to modern organisations. Although these are relatively new terms, ICT has been used to transform internal and external business processes for at least three decades. But it can be argued that the role it plays has become larger and more central over time, as technology has developed and led to new business techniques, both internally and, more recently, externally. For instance, although Tesco has used ICT for many years, it is only relatively recently that it was able to offer customers the ability to order their groceries online.

As individuals we also need an increasing range of information, in order to live our lives effectively at work, at home and in our leisure time. For example, we need an increasingly large range of identity information: passports, driving licences, credit cards, debit cards, library cards, employee identity cards and so on.

ICT has also caused changes to the way work is carried out. One significant change has been the degree to which individuals work from home or on the move. Now they can use ICT to keep in contact with an 'organisational hub' wherever they are.

So we can say with confidence that information underpins modern society. In the 1970s Daniel Bell, a US sociologist, made a series of predictions about the state of Western societies in his influential book *The Coming of Post-Industrial Society* (Bell, 1972). He claimed that they were becoming information societies, and it is now generally accepted that this has happened. The same is true in much of Asia. Bell's argument was that just as there was an industrial revolution in the nineteenth century, in the latter part of the twentieth century there was an information revolution. This has led some commentators to suggest that whereas in the twentieth century we lived in an industrial society, our twenty-first century society will be best described as an **information society** (Castells, 1996).

> **Information society:** A term very loosely used to refer to the effect of ICT, information systems and information generally on modern society

One key indicator of an information society is the way in which information is increasingly regarded as an important economic 'commodity'. For instance, it underpins news media, the music industry and the entertainment industry. These so-called 'content' industries are experiencing some of the most rapid growth in Western economies. Also, many organisations in other sectors now devote most of their time to information-related activities, so they can be described as information corporations. One of the clearest examples is Google, the market leader in the Web search sector.

Many people expect this trend to continue. ICT forms critical infrastructure for modern organisations; they are converging around common standards, and this is leading to increased integration and interoperability of electronic devices and systems. For example, we can now access pretty much the same material from our smartphone or tablet computer as we can from our Internet-enabled personal computer.

However, the picture is not entirely rosy. Many people are worried that this type of convergence could enable governments (or other groups) to take greater control over people; and about the dangers if information falls into the wrong hands. In many countries there is continuous debate and negotiation over what information the government, or other bodies, should be allowed to collect about individuals, what purposes this information can be used for, and how its integrity can be protected.

1.1.2 How business information systems relate to other academic disciplines

Not surprisingly, since information systems are essential in so many ways for modern organisations and individuals, this area is very interdisciplinary in nature. Business students, in particular, will be familiar with some of the disciplines with which it overlaps from other modules in their courses.

To understand how business information systems relate to other disciplines, we can view it as being made up of a number of interdependent areas of interest. We look at all of them in this book, and they are also shown in Figure 1.1.

> **Environment:** Anything outside the organisation with which the organisation interacts and which influences the behaviour of the organisation

- **Environment**. To understand the value of information systems to organisations we need to understand the economic, social, political and physical environment within which the organisations using them operate.
- **Organisations**. One of the main focuses of the book is on how modern information systems contribute to organisational performance: by supporting traditional organisational forms, and leading to new ones being introduced.

> **Management:** The process through which organisations are controlled

- **Management**. The promise of the technology is only achieved when managers find effective ways of managing information, information systems and ICT in their organisations.
- **Technology**. Of course, those studying this field need to know something about the technology involved. This includes both its use and the principles that underlie it.
- **Development**. This concerns appropriate ways of constructing information systems that support human activity, particularly decision-making.

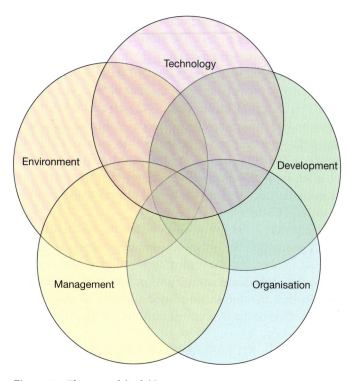

Figure 1.1 *Elements of the field*

This way of dividing the subject area enables us to consider more clearly how business information systems overlaps with five other established disciplines (Figure 1.2). These are known as reference disciplines (Keen, 1980), since they provide us with major frames of academic reference.

- **Economics**, **politics** and **sociology** overlap with the subject through its emphasis on context, particularly the social and economic effects of information systems and ICT.
- **Organisational theory** (and particularly **organisational behaviour**) overlaps with the subject through its emphasis on organisational issues.
- **Management science** and **operations management** overlap with the subject through its interest in appropriate management.
- **Computer science** overlaps with the subject because of the need for knowledge about the workings of contemporary ICT.
- **Software engineering** overlaps with the subject through its interest in the process of developing information systems.

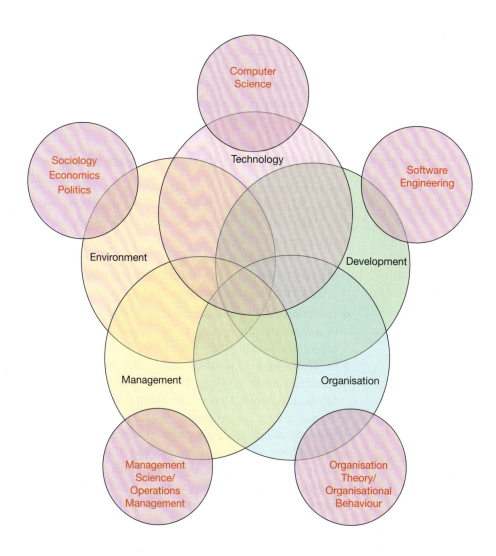

Figure 1.2 *Reference disciplines*

Information: Data interpreted in a meaningful context

System: An organised set of interdependent components that exists for some purpose, has some stability, and can be usefully viewed as a whole

Within the area of business and management itself (see Chapters 4 and 5), the concepts of **information** and **system** are both integral and integrating. This means that information systems are critical to understanding contemporary operational practices in marketing, sales, customer relations, production, finance, human resources, procurement and distribution. An understanding of information, information systems and ICT is particularly important to management practice in these areas, so there is a strong argument for placing an understanding of this area at the heart of operating and managing the modern business.

1.1.3 Information systems and value

Value: A general term used to describe the worth of something such as the output from some organisation or ICT system

The idea of **value** is critical to the study of information systems. We can map some of the many shades of meaning of the term 'value' onto the different contexts we have just outlined:

- the concept of value as the essence of economic systems
- the organisation as a value-creating system embedded within a wider value network
- the human values embedded within information systems (meaning that the design of such systems is a value-laden activity).

Taking value and ICT together leads to questions such as:

- What is the value of ICT to business?
- How do we ensure the value of ICT to business?
- How do we improve the value of ICT to business?

In one sense, these questions are relatively easy to answer. If modern organisations switched off their ICT systems they would fail to operate effectively; many would fail to operate at all. In another sense, the questions are more difficult to answer. Chief executives in many global companies have continually asked questions about the value of ICT. Many billions of dollars have been invested globally in ICT, but companies still find it difficult to put an accurate monetary value on the return to the organisation from this investment.

Typically, this is because of the way in which ICT is considered by both business managers and technologists. Both groups tend to focus more on the technology itself than on its application. But all the value lies in the application, the most advanced and brilliantly networked computer system is worthless (except to companies that make or sell the equipment) unless the organisation has a worthwhile use for it.

ICT is translated into value through the mediating force of information. This means that to ensure that ICT systems have value, organisations must ensure that their ICT infrastructure matches their information needs, which involves activities both inside and outside the individual organisation. Chapter 9 discusses some of the many examples of information systems that have failed in organisations. Sometimes the failure was so bad that it brought down the entire organisation, as happened, for example with the UK Child Support Agency.

Throughout this book we argue that to improve the value of ICT, organisations need to employ good practice in the planning, management, development and operation of their ICT infrastructure. Businesses (and non-profit organisations) operate in increasingly volatile environments, within which their needs often change; they need to be skilled in adapting the ICT infrastructure to these changing needs.

1.1.4 How this book will help

To summarise, information systems are critical to the modern world: in business, in other sectors, and to individuals. It's important to appreciate their importance and to understand their founding principles. This book shows you how to use best practice to ensure that you and your organisation get the most value out of your ICT investment, now and in the future.

The focus here is on the application of information systems in organisations, and because this is so intimately tied up with other aspects of organisational management, we look at some of those as well. We introduce a number of key skills that are important, not only for information systems professionals but for general business management. These are intended to provide an appreciation of important approaches, frameworks and techniques in the area.

Models are useful to help us understand what is going on and plan how to change it. A number of modelling techniques are used throughout the book. Together, they provide a good grounding in the applications of modelling, especially for the analysis and design of many kinds of business systems.

Overall, this book should enable you to develop an understanding and practical appreciation of information systems. It will serve you well, both in the study of related disciplines and in your working career.

1.2   Organisational informatics

The term 'information systems' is used in a number of different ways. It can refer to:

- A **product**: a system of communication between members of a group of people. (These days many communication systems involve technology, although there are ways of communicating without technology too, of course, and have been for thousands of years. But an information system as a product really refers to a technological information system.) For example, an orders and sales processing system is an information system, used to communicate between members of the selling organisation, and between them and their customers.
- An **academic field of study:** some of the first courses in information systems were run in Stockholm in the 1960s. Over the last three decades particularly the field of information systems has become established in many centres of higher education around the world, in both teaching and research.
- An **area of industrial practice:** many organisations across the world work in planning, managing and developing information systems for other organisations. Many of the largest and best-known business consultancies do a lot of their work in this field. Some organisations in other fields, which originally developed their expertise in setting up their own systems, also sell their know-how to others.

Information system: a system of communication between people

ICT system: a system of data representation and processing

Informatics: The study of information, information systems and ICT applied to various phenomena

It can be confusing, though, to use the same term in each of these different contexts, so in this book we use a set of terms with distinctive meanings:

- Here, **information system** refers to a system of communication between people, within and between organisations.
- **ICT system** is the term we use for technology: hardware, software, data and communication technology designed to support an information system.
- **Informatics** is our term for the related academic discipline and area of professional activity.

The term *informatics* began to be used in the US in the early 1960s, around the same time that the term *informatique* started to be used in France. In France the name took on the meaning of '*the modern science of electronic information processing*' and was eventually accepted by L'Academie Française as an official French word. The word informatique has now been adopted and adapted in various European languages: Informatik in Germany, and Informatica in Spain and Italy.

Informatics is a particularly useful term. It covers a much broader area of interest than simply information systems. It considers the place of information in communication and action, and the use of various artefacts or technologies as tools within this process. In short, it takes in information systems, ICT systems, the processes that concern them and the information that flows between them. It's also a term that is often used in relation to specific applications. For instance, health informatics, bio-informatics and chem-informatics are the terms for the application of information, information systems and ICT systems to processes within the health sector, biology and chemistry respectively.

Organisational informatics: the application of informatics within and between organisations

The main focus of this book is on applications in organisations, by which we mean not just businesses, but the entire range of private sector, public sector and voluntary sector organisations. The study of applications in this context is known as **organisational informatics** (Kling and Allen, 1996). This is a wider term than the related **business informatics**.

So from now on, 'informatics' is used as shorthand for organisational informatics, which is broadly used as a synonym for the discipline of information systems.

Informatics is very much a systemic discipline. It is interested not in ICT, information systems, information and organisations in isolation, but in their interaction and its effects. To make sense of systems of any kind it is useful to create models which illustrate the interactions of their components, interdependencies, and their effects. This book is structured around a core model (which we shall encounter shortly) which captures the key elements of informatics as well as the interaction between these elements. In essence, this model provides a map of the entire area, which we call here the informatics domain.

Our model is founded on the premise that the effects of an information system on an organisation emerge over time, as the result of interaction between the system and its organisational context. We need to understand these effects in order to design and run systems that provide benefits for the organisation, and avoid the hazards that information systems are sometimes prone to (Silver et al., 1995).

The informatics domain model forms the basic structure for the book. Each of the component elements contained in the model is covered in much more detail in one chapter of the book. So you might not understand all the concepts introduced here right away, but you can explore them throughout the book, and follow links to further chapters at any time if you want to delve into one particular aspect. This chapter not only introduces the model, it acts as a summary and reference for it.

1.2.1 Introducing the informatics domain model

Organisation: a social system consisting of activity, communication and representation

Activity system: a coherent collection of interrelated and coordinated activities performed by some group of people

The model begins with the key context for the application of information systems, the **organisation** itself (see Figure 1.3). Any organisation is considered as a series of interdependent **activity systems**. Hence, we nest the activity system box within the box labelled *organisation* on the domain model. When activity systems are combined in action within an organisation they produce value of some form (see Chapter 2). **Value** is the key flow between an organisation and actors in its environment (see Chapter 7). Hence, we express value as a broad arrow on the domain model flowing from the organisation to an external actor or from an external actor to the organisation.

The value produced by a business organisation is typically the products or services it provides for its customers. (Of course, non-profit organisations have value too, although in different forms.) The organisation also receives value from other actors in its environment, such as its suppliers or partners. Hence, a business organisation is a value-creating system which interacts with a wider value network that makes up its environment.

Any activity system relies on an information system. Therefore, on the domain model we nest the box labelled *information system* within the box labelled *activity system*. An **information system** (see Chapter 4) is a system of communication between a group of people, which is used by the group to coordinate its members' actions. On the basis of information supplied by the information system, people within the group decide what actions to take (see Figure 1.4). So information is essential to the effective control of organisational action. Hence, to represent this relationship on the domain model we draw a narrow arrow with the label *information* flowing from the information system into the activity system. We also draw a narrow arrow labelled *decisions* flowing from the activity system into the information system.

Data: symbols used to represent something

Datum: A unit of data

Information is **data** interpreted in some context (see Chapter 3). The context that enables the proper interpretation of business information is the wider activity system. A **datum** – that is, a unit of data – is one or more symbols used to represent something. **Data** is supplied to the information system by its ICT system (see Chapters 5 and 6). The **ICT system** processes

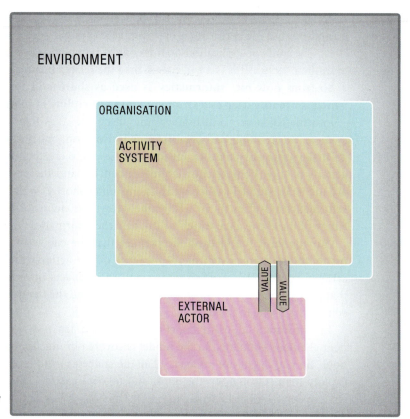

Figure 1.3 *Organisation, activity systems and environment*

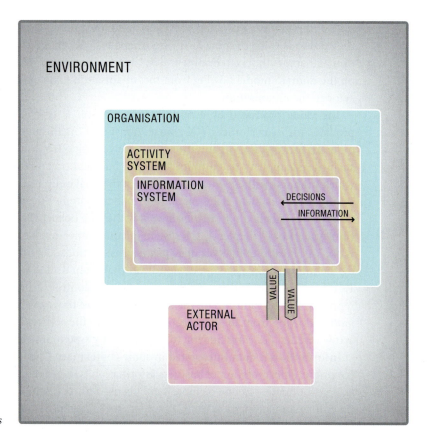

Figure 1.4 *Information systems*

business data, such as records of sales orders, and produces information, such as the total number of sales orders received in the last quarter, for the purpose of business decision-making (see Figure 1.5). Therefore, upon the domain model we nest the box labelled *ICT system* within the box labelled *information system*. We also have a narrow arrow labelled *data* flowing from the ICT system into the information system.

ICT (see Chapters 5 and 6) consists of hardware, software, data and communication technology used in support of an information system. Traditionally, ICT has been used to improve the operation of internal activity systems in organisations. More recently, it has also been used to improve activity systems between the organisation and its wider value network. Central to this is electronic business (eBusiness) and electronic commerce (eCommerce, see Chapter 8). **eCommerce** refers to the use of ICT to enable activities within the wider value network. We use **eBusiness** as a term for the use of ICT to enable both internal and external activities (see Figure 1.6). To represent the electronic interchange of data upon which eCommerce relies we have a communication symbol connecting the ICT system of the external actor with the ICT system of the organisation.

Business systems have to be developed. By this we mean that a clear case has to be made for their creation, the key requirements of the system have to be determined and represented, a design has to be produced for the system, and the system has to be built and implemented. Since the focus of this book is business information systems, we focus on these activities in a business context. All these activities (see Figure 1.7) are stages within what we refer to as the **information systems development process** (see Chapter 12). Therefore, upon the domain model we have a box labelled information systems development with a series of arrows representing the key stages of the development process interacting with other aspects of the domain model. Conception flows from the organisation in the sense that it involves constructing the key business case for some information system. Analysis flows from the activity system because it involves determining the key activities to be supported by the new information system. Design, construction and implementation flow into the information system since design involves creating a blueprint which is used to construct the information system and implement it into the organisation.

After an information system is implemented or introduced, it begins to have effects on the organisation (see Figure 1.8). We can divide these into first-order effects, which concern issues of use, and second-order effects, which concern the impact of the information system on the activities of individuals, groups and the organisation as a whole (see Chapter 9). Hence, we have the broad arrow of use flowing from the information system into its encompassing activity system. Likewise, we have the broad arrow labelled impact flowing from the activity system into the surrounding organisation.

The broad arrow labelled evaluation is meant to represent the process of evaluating not only the issues of use and impact but also the information system's successful development. Hence, it is represented as a broad arrow on the domain model flowing from the information system into the box labelled *information systems development*.

eCommerce: The conduct of business commerce using ICT

eBusiness: The conduct of any business activity using ICT

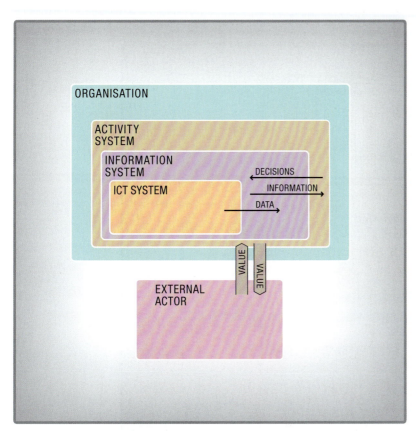

Figure 1.5 *Data, information and decisions*

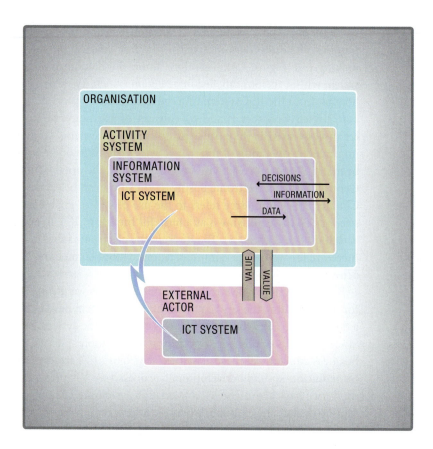

Figure 1.6 *ICT systems and infrastructure*

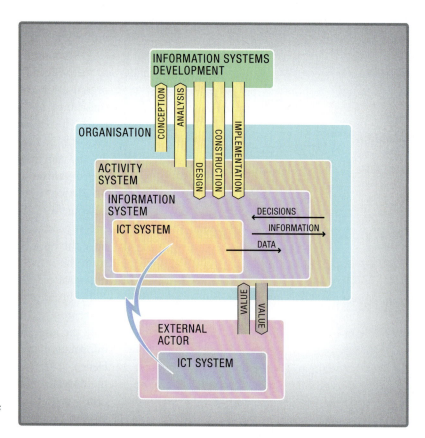

Figure 1.7 *Information systems development*

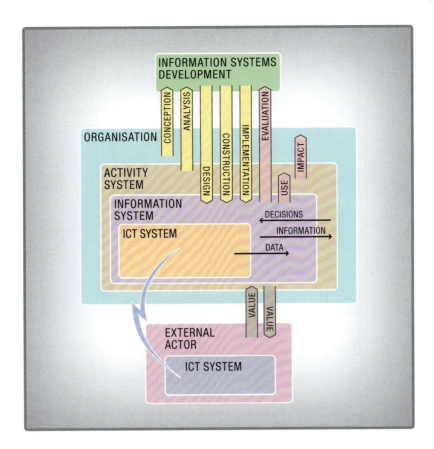

Figure 1.8 Use, impact and evaluation

Peter Drucker's (Drucker, 1994) *Theory of the Business* attributes organisational success to three factors: businesses understanding their external environments, businesses undertaking missions (developing strategies) consistent with their external environments, businesses developing core competencies needed to accomplish their missions.

Since information is central to the modern organisation, organisational success depends not least on information systems success, and this calls for effective informatics planning and management. Planning and management (see Figure 1.9) are necessary to ensure that information systems are aligned with organisational **strategy** (see Chapter 10).

Therefore, upon the domain model we re-introduce the surrounding environment encompassing everything else. We also introduce a box labelled informatics planning and management and surround the information system development box with this. This is to indicate that development is controlled by wider processes of planning and management. Both these boxes are placed outside rather than inside the organisation box to indicate that nowadays planning, management and development of information systems infrastructure is frequently done by, or outsourced to, other organisations.

The rest of this chapter introduces key elements from this model, and shows its relevance by applying it to a case study of a small manufacturing company that is part of a multinational organisation. Manufacturing is particularly chosen as the focus for this case because of the way in which a particular type of ICT system, known as an enterprise resource planning system, has impacted upon the activities of such organisations over two decades.

First, we describe the position the organisation found itself in during the mid-1980s, with little use of ICT. Then we consider how and why the organisation developed its first ICT system, and what form this took. It had some early success with the system, and this led to the gradual rollout and extension of an integrated **informatics infrastructure** throughout its parent organisation. But that was less easy, and there are still management problems with which it is grappling today.

Strategy: The process of directing future activity

Informatics infrastructure: The sum total of information, information systems and ICT resources available to an organisation at any one time

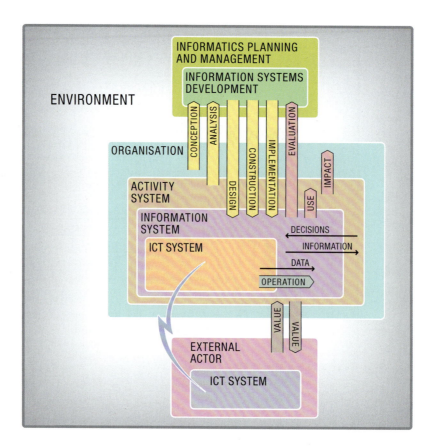

Figure 1.9 *Planning, management and operations*

1.3   Organisation and environment: an illustrative case

Goronwy Galvanising is a small company which specialises in treating steel products such as lintels (beams), crash barriers and palisades (fence-posts) produced by other manufacturers. It is a subsidiary of a large multinational, Rito Metals, whose primary business includes the extraction and processing of base metals such as zinc and the production of various metal alloys. Rito Metals has ten galvanising plants similar to Goronwy across Europe. The Rito Metals head office coordinates administrative activities such as finance and human resources, but each plant manages its own operational activities in areas such as sales and logistics.

Put simply, galvanising involves dipping steel products into baths of molten zinc to provide a rustproof coating. In the trade, untreated steel products are known as 'black' and treated ones as 'white'. The galvanising process causes a slight gain in weight.

As much as 80% of Goronwy's business (in the mid-1980s, when this case study starts) was with one major regular customer, Blackwalls Steel, with the rest coming from other customers on a more irregular basis.

Goronwy's staff comprises a plant manager, a production controller, an office clerk, three shift foremen and 50 shop-floor workers. The plant remains open 24 hours per day, seven days a week, so most of the production workers, including the foremen, work shift patterns.

We can think of Goronwy Galvanising as a system, as indeed we can of any organisation. A system can be defined as a coherent set of interdependent components that exists for some purpose, has some stability, and can usefully be viewed as a whole. Systems of interest to informatics are generally referred to as open systems. These are systems that interact with their environment. So we can model them, using an input–process–output model of the organisation within its environment.

■ By the environment of a system we mean anything outside the system that has an effect on the way the system operates. We usually identify a number of actors with which the system interacts, to help define this environment.

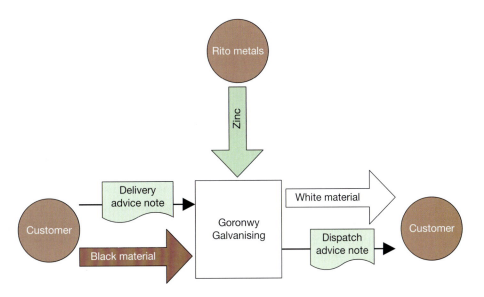

Figure 1.10 *Goronwy Galvanising as a system*

Input: The things that a system takes from its environment

Output: The things that a system provides to its environment

Process: a set of activities that transform inputs into outputs

- The **inputs** to the system are the resources it acquires from actors in its environment.
- The **outputs** from the system are those things that it supplies back to actors in its environment.
- The **process** of the system is that set of activities that transform system inputs into system outputs.

Figure 1.10 illustrates at a high level the component, physical elements of Goronwy Galvanising as an open system. Its main inputs are black products and its main outputs white products. Both these physical flows are represented as broad arrows on the diagram. The process, or transformation, is the galvanisation. Along with the physical flow of steel products there is a corresponding information flow, consisting of documents which detail deliveries and dispatches of material. These are represented on the diagram as narrow arrows with document symbols.

The main actors in Goronwy's environment are its suppliers and customers. There are two kinds of supplier: one is also its customer, the steel fabrication firms – Blackwalls and the smaller customers – that provide black goods to be galvanised; the other is Rito Metals, which supplies zinc as raw material for the galvanising process.

From this perspective, we can see the overall purpose of the organisation as being to create value, through the process or transformation at its core. For commercial organisations that value becomes concrete when they sell their products or services and make a profit. We can also think of the organisation as part of a **value network**, in which there are flows of value between the organisation and the actors in its environment (its customers and suppliers). So as well as creating value itself, Goronwy adds value to the outputs of other actors in its value network. Steel producers, steel fabricators and zinc producers are all part of Goronwy's value network.

Value network: The network of actors within which an organisation sits and with which the organisation exchanges value

We shall encounter the concept of system in a number of different ways in this book. In a sense, it acts as a unifying theme. For example, we discuss and make distinctions between:

- a system of activity (an activity system)
- a system of communication (an information system)
- a system of technology (an ICT system).

In the sections that follow we investigate each of these in turn.

1.4   Activity systems

We can view an organisation as a number of interdependent human activity systems (or activity systems for short). An activity system is a social system, sometimes referred to as a 'soft' system. It consists of a collection of activities, processes or tasks performed by a group of people in pursuit of a goal. The precedence or order of activities is normally critical, as this determines the flow necessary for the coordination of work.

For Goronwy, the main activity systems consist of processes for:

- receiving unfinished products
- galvanising these products
- dispatching finished products back to customers.

The 'black' material – steel fabricated products of various forms – is delivered to Goronwy on large trailers in bundles referred to as batches. It is unpacked by an inbound logistics operative and checked for discrepancies or problems that would make it unsuitable for galvanising. If satisfactory, the products are then galvanised and left to dry. The white material is then checked again, and any unsatisfactory material is re-galvanised. Satisfactory white material is bundled on trailers and dispatched back to the customer. The activity system is shown in Figure 1.11, with dotted lines indicating the precedence of each activity in the system. In other words, the dotted lines indicate the workflow through the activity system.

In any activity system there will also be some form of embedded control. Control is the idea that any system (including social systems such as organisations) needs to be regulated in some way, and must also be able to adapt to changes in its environment. Regulatory **control** is typically implemented through a process known as **feedback**, in which information is collected from a monitored process and is compared against defined levels of performance for the system. This information then triggers actions designed to maintain the system's performance within given bounds. Environmental control also depends upon monitoring and acting on the information obtained.

Figure 1.11 includes two regulatory control processes. Each one consists of a sensing or monitoring activity, a decision-making activity (represented by a triangle) and an effecting activity. The first control process checks to see that black material is of a suitable form to be processed. If the material is satisfactory it is passed on to galvanisation. If it is not satisfactory, it is returned to the customer un-galvanised. The second control process checks to see that galvanisation has operated effectively on particular batches of steel products. Therefore, in both control processes, information and decisions will trigger appropriate action to ensure

Control: The process that implements regulation and adaptation within systems

Feedback: The way in which a control process adjusts the state of some system being monitored to keep it within defined limits

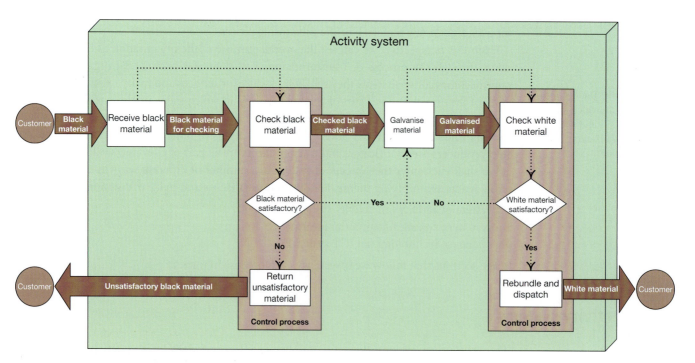

Figure 1.11 *The activity system at Goronwy*

that the organisation performs effectively, such as returning damaged, unfinished products to the customer or re-galvanising steel products before dispatch.

1.5 Information systems

Manual information system: A term used to refer to an information system relying upon the technology of paper-based forms and other types of business documentation

Every activity system relies on an associated information system; that is, a system of communication between people. Information systems are systems involved in the gathering, processing, distribution and use of information. In this way they support activity.

By way of example, let's look first at the information system Goronwy Galvanising used in the 1980s, before mass computerisation. It was a **manual information system** in the sense that it relied on the flow of documents to inform the coordination of activity.

A trailer arriving from a customer might be loaded with a number of different types of steel product. These were divided into batches, and each batch was labelled with a unique order number. Each trailer was given a delivery advice note detailing all the associated batches on it.

Since Blackwalls was Goronwy's major customer, the delivery advice note system was designed to dovetail with Blackwalls' own internal system. Blackwalls itself generated the order numbers. Figure 1.12 shows a typical delivery advice note from Blackwalls detailing all the black material on a particular trailer. The information about each particular batch is referred to as an order line.

On arrival at the galvanising plant the black material was unpacked by an inbound logistics operative and checked for discrepancies with the information on the delivery advice note. There are two major types of discrepancy:

- A count discrepancy, between the number of items delivered and the number indicated on the delivery advice note.
- A non-conforming black discrepancy arises when some of the material is unsuitable for galvanising. For instance, a steel lintel might be bent or the material might be of the wrong type.

The operative would note both kinds, by making a comment in the appropriate box on the delivery advice note.

When all the material had been checked, the delivery advice note was passed on to the production controller who, with the office clerk, copied by hand all the details on the delivery advice note, including any discrepancies, to a job sheet. A separate job sheet was filled in for each order line on the delivery advice note (a sample is shown in Figure 1.13).

Blackwalls steel products **Delivery advice**

Advice No.	Date	Customer name	Instructions
A3137	20/01/1988	Goronwy Galvanising	Galvanise and return

Order No.	Description	Product code	Item length	Delivery Qty	Weight (Tonnes)
13/1193G	Lintels	UL150	1500	20	145
44/2404G	Lintels	UL1500	15000	20	1450
70/2517P	Lintels	UL135	1350	20	130
23/2474P	Lintels	UL120	1200	16	80

Haulier	Received in good order
International 5	√

Figure 1.12 Sample delivery advice note

Job sheet

Job No:	2046

Order no.	Description	Product code	Item Length	Order Qty	Batch weight
13/1193G	Lintels	L150	1500	200	145

Count discrepancy	Non-conforming black	Non-conforming white	Non-conforming no change		

Galvanised	Dispatch no.	Dispatch date	Qty returned	Weight returned	
Y					

Figure 1.13 Sample job sheet

The job sheet was passed down to the shop floor of the factory, where the shift foreman used it to record details of processing. Most jobs passed through the galvanising process smoothly. The steel items were placed on racks, dipped in the zinc bath and left to cool. The site foreman then checked each job. If all items had been galvanised properly he put a Y for yes in the box on the job sheet, and passed it back to the production controller.

Occasionally, some of the items were not galvanised properly. They were classed as non-conforming white, and also noted on the job sheet (and typically scheduled for re-galvanising).

When the shop floor had treated a series of jobs, the production controller issued a dispatch advice note and sent it the outbound logistics section. Workers in this section used the information on it to stack the white material on trailers – one trailer to a dispatch advice note – ready to be returned to the manufacturer.

The discrepancies meant there was not a one-to-one correspondence between the delivery advice notes and the dispatch advice notes, so the production controller needed to record the separate dispatches associated with a delivery on the job sheet. You can see how this worked from the typical dispatch advice in Figure 1.14, where the final order, 23/2474P, had not yet been delivered in full.

Goronwy Galvanising   **Dispatch advice**

Advice No.	Date	Customer name
101	22/01/1988	Blackwalls

Order No.	Description	Product code	Item length	Order Qty	Batch weight	Returned Qty	Returned weight
13/1193G	Lintels	UL150	1500	20	145	20	150
44/2404G	Lintels	UL1500	15000	20	1450	20	1460
70/2517P	Lintels	UL135	1350	20	130	20	135
23/2474P	Lintels	UL120	1200	16	80	14	82

Driver	Received by

Figure 1.14 Sample dispatch advice

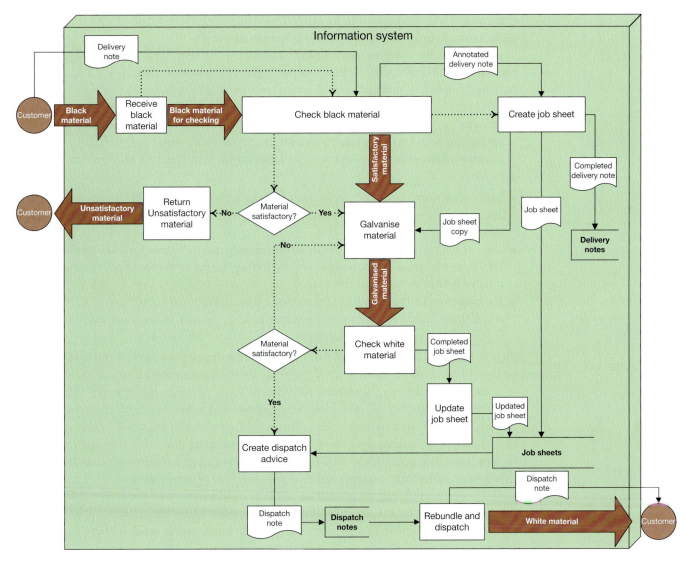

Figure 1.15 *Information system at Goronwy*

Figure 1.15 is a diagram of the entire information flow through the system. This information or document flow parallels the flow of work or activity through the system, so it shows both physical transformation processes and information-handling activities. The open boxes represent data stores, places where records such as delivery notes were kept.

1.6   Information

After this first introduction to information systems, let's step back and take a look in more detail at the idea of information itself.

Delivery notes, dispatch notes and job sheets are all information elements within the information system; they flow through the system. Employees use the information on these documents to make decisions, in Goronwy's case, for example, what material to galvanise. They then act on the basis of their decisions. If the information is incorrect, the wrong decisions will be made, and the process will not perform effectively. Information – and more particularly, good-quality information – is therefore essential for the effective coordination of activity. Without the information recorded on delivery notes, dispatch notes and job sheets it would prove difficult to coordinate the work of inbound and outbound logistics staff with shop-floor staff galvanising the material. The same is true of the relationship between information and systems on a more general level; all systems rely on the provision of accurate information in order to operate control processes effectively.

Information therefore supports human activity, in the sense that it enables decisions to be made about appropriate actions in particular circumstances. Decisions and decision-making lie between information and action, and are a critical aspect of any activity system. In this sense, management can be seen as a control process in organisations. Management is an activity system that controls other operational activity systems. The primary activity of management is making decisions concerning organisational action.

Effective management decision-making relies on three interrelated information-handling activities:

- Effective definitions of the performance of an activity system. This means turning the defined purpose or purposes of the activity system into a defined set of performance measures.
- The construction of effective performance management systems for managerial activity. This means establishing clear ways of establishing the performance of operational activity systems against performance measures.
- The collection and processing of information from operational activity systems. This means establishing effective information systems to capture and manipulate the information required for performance management.

To stay with the Goronwy example, one definition for the performance of this system might be to achieve efficient throughput of materials for the galvanising process. Goronwy could measure this efficiency in a number of different ways. For example, it might measure the amount or proportion of non-conforming black and white material identified over a particular period, such as one month. This would involve keeping track of the amount of non-conforming material, and the total amount of material processed, perhaps categorised by type using product codes, as well as the date of processing. So Goronwy needs an effective information system that captures and processes this type of information.

Information model: A model of the things of interest relevant to some area of business

In defining an information system we not only need to represent the flow of information, we also need to model the structure of information, particularly the information of relevance to decision-making. For this purpose we need an **information model**. There is a sample information model for Goronwy Galvanising in Figure 1.16.

Information class: A category that defines something of interest. A key element of an information model

The boxes on this diagram indicate individual classes of information, things of interest to a business domain. The connecting lines between **information classes** indicate that particular things are associated with other things. Hence, within this domain we know that a customer produces a delivery advice note and receives a dispatch advice note.

The symbols attached to each line represent a number of rules governing the behaviour of the association between classes: this is explored in more detail in Chapter 3. For example, a fork or crow's foot on the end of a line indicates a one-to-many relationship. So a delivery advice note (class) contains (association) many order lines (class). Each order line corresponds to a row or record of information on the delivery advice note in Figure 1.12. An order line represents information about one particular order, such as the product to be galvanised and the quantity of the product in the batch. Therefore, the order line directly corresponds to a batch on an inbound trailer. It also directly corresponds to a job sheet, which may also indicate the non-conforming black material that is returned because of identified discrepancies.

1.7   ICT systems

ICT: Information and communication technology consists of hardware, software, data management and communications technology

As the Goronwy example has shown, information systems do not need to use modern **ICT**. But modern ICT makes systems work better and faster and, in today's complex global world, most information systems use it to at least some degree. We can see why by looking at some of the problems with the system Goronwy used in the 1980s:

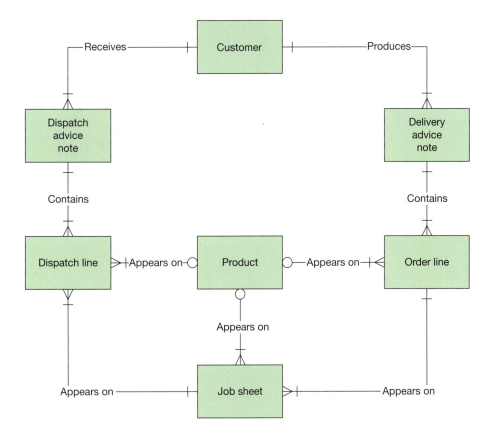

Figure 1.16 *An information model for Goronwy Galvanising*

- Information needs to be shared among a number of people, for Goronwy they include inbound logistics operatives, production controllers, shift foremen and outbound logistics operatives. So copies of it are needed, and making manual copies is slow and therefore expensive.
- A lot of time was taken transferring information from one type of form to another, for instance, from delivery advice notes to job sheets.
- Every transfer stage is an opportunity for human error to creep in and this can lead directly to processing errors, which are costly and time-consuming to correct.
- It is difficult to analyse information held manually. Even if it works well for production purposes, it does not provide a good resource for managers who want to collate and analyse it to determine trends such as the throughput of the plant or the productivity of the workforce.

As a result, Goronwy and its parent company looked at moving to an ICT-based system for basic administrative functions. Let's consider what this means in practice.

Technology amounts to a set of artefacts for doing things. ICT is the term for any type of technology used to support data gathering, processing, distribution and use. ICT systems consist of hardware, software, data management technology and communication technology:

- **Hardware** is the term for the physical aspects of ICT: processors, input devices such as keyboards and output devices such as monitors.
- **Software** is the term for the non-physical aspects of ICT, essentially this means programs or sets of instructions for controlling computer hardware. Types of software include operating systems (such as Windows Vista), programming languages (such as Java) and office productivity packages (such as Microsoft Word).
- **Data management technology** consists of artefacts for storing data on peripheral devices such as hard disks. Data are normally stored in databases managed by a database management system (such as Microsoft Access).

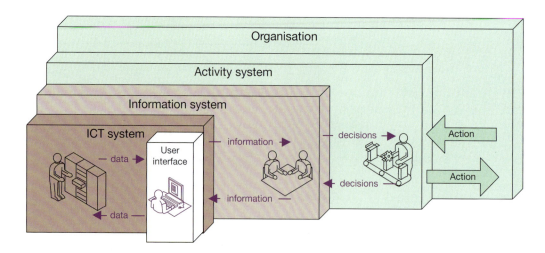

Figure 1.17 *Three types of business system*

- **Data communication technology** consists of programs and devices used to manipulate and transmit data. Communication technology forms the interconnective tissue of ICT, and includes cabling, transmitters and routers. Communication networks between computing devices are essential elements of the modern ICT infrastructure of organisations (see Chapter 8).

ICT systems are technical systems. They are frequently referred to as 'hard' systems in the sense that they consist of an assembly of designed artefacts. But an **ICT system** is not just made up of hardware; it is an organised collection of hardware, software, data and communication technology designed to support aspects of an information system. It takes data as input, manipulates the data as a process, and outputs manipulated data for interpretation within a human activity system. The relationship between these three types of system is shown in Figure 1.17. An ICT system forms part of an information system, which in turn forms part of an activity system. Activity systems are the key component elements of organisations.

1.7.1   Data, information and sociotechnical systems

A datum is, as we said earlier, a symbol (or group of symbols) that is used to represent something. (Data is its plural.) Since an ICT system deals with manipulating and transmitting data, it is therefore more accurately referred to as a data processing system.

Information is interpreted data; it consists of data placed within a meaningful context. The use of the term 'information' therefore implies a group of people doing interpretation (for more on this, see Chapter 3). Consider the string of symbols UL150. Taken together these symbols form a datum, but by themselves they are meaningless. To turn these symbols into information we have to supply a meaningful context. We have to interpret them. In the Goronwy Galvanising information system, this group of symbols is a product code identifying a type of steel lintel of a particular length.

Let's look at how Goronwy Galvanising might set up an ICT system. Staff would enter (or input) data that describe the properties of orders on delivery advice notes (such as product codes and quantities). This data is then manipulated, by linking it to other data collected (such as discrepancies identified at inbound logistics), to provide information on processed orders. This part of the ICT system then supports human activities and actions concerned with the effective quality control of raw material into the production process. For instance, the ICT system might identify that two pieces of data do not match. But it would take a human being to interpret this information, and come to the conclusion that a lintel has been lost from a particular order. Then it's down to human beings to take action, perhaps to return a batch to the customer. So the organisation introducing an ICT system really needs two things: first, a good data and ICT system; second, human beings that effectively and efficiently make use of the system to ensure that the organisation meets the needs of its customers.

The key lesson to be drawn from Figure 1.17 is therefore that many systems in organisations are examples of **sociotechnical systems**. A sociotechnical system is a system of technology used within a system of activity. Information systems are primary examples of sociotechnical systems; they consist of ICT used within an activity system. They therefore span ICT and activity. Part of the human activity will involve the use of ICT systems through an interface. The information provided by the information system will also drive decision-making, leading to further action within the organisation.

Sociotechnical system: A system of technology used within a system of activity

1.8   Information systems development

Information systems development: That activity system devoted to the creation of a new information system or the maintenance of an existing information system

In order to justify the investment required to develop a new information system, an organisation must make a business case for it. It evaluates the investment strategically and assesses its feasibility. The organisation also attempts to estimate the degree of risk associated with the development project. This phase of information systems development is known as the conception phase.

Generally speaking there are three ways in which human activity and ICT can be used in combination within a new information system:

- ICT can be used to **support** aspects of an existing information system. This implies that some aspects of the information system are computerised but that the activity system supported remains largely unchanged.
- ICT can be used to **supplant** aspects of an existing activity system and its associated information system. This implies that certain aspects of both the activity system and the information system are automated, in the sense that the logic of the ICT system replaces some aspect of human decision-making and action.
- ICT can be used to **innovate**, creating new activity systems for organisations. This is the most radical use of technology.

Let's go back to Goronwy Galvanising. Its managers drew up a business case for a new ICT system which outlined many of the problems with the existing manual information system. They decided to keep the existing activity system much as it was, and to base the design of the associated ICT system closely on it. They chose this support option because there was a low risk of failure in the development effort.

If the business case for a new information system is made successfully, then the development process progresses to the systems analysis phase. This involves identifying and specifying requirements for the new information system. These typically describe the **functionality** of the information system; that is, they concentrate on what an information system should be able to do.

Functionality: what an ICT system is able to do

For instance, a core part of the functionality for Goronwy's system involved capturing, storing and manipulating data associated with the receipt of orders from customers. Another part was a function for reporting regularly on the number of orders from particular customers and the amount of non-conforming material returned.

Once the required functionality has been identified, the next development phase is systems design. This is the process of planning the shape of the information system to meet the requirements established by the earlier analysis. If the aim is to use ICT to supplant an existing system or to innovate, then it is necessary to jointly design an ICT system and its associated activity system. In other words, the designer does not only need to consider the shape of software, hardware, data and communication, they also need to design new forms of work to be used with the new ICT. But, when the aim is to use ICT to support existing ways of doing things, the focus of design is primarily on the shape of the ICT system alone. This is what we focus on in the rest of this section.

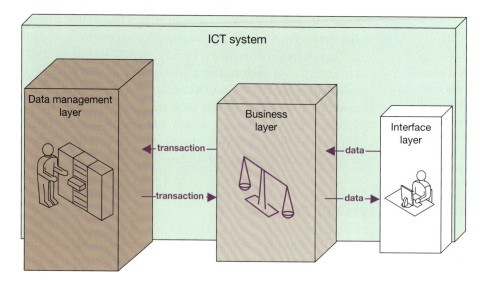

Figure 1.18 *Layers of an
ICT system*

We can think of an ICT system as consisting of three interdependent subsystems, or layers, for which designs need to be formulated (see Figure 1.18):

- a data management layer
- a business layer
- an interface layer.

1.8.1 The data management layer

Data management layer:
That part of an ICT system
involved with the storage and
maintenance of data

Since ICT systems are essentially data processing systems, they rely on a core repository, somewhere to keep the data used in the system. This repository is normally referred to as a database, and is controlled by the data management layer. The design for the structure of the database at the heart of the ICT system is referred to as a data model. Essentially, this data model defines what data is stored within the system and in what form.

For Goronwy, the structure of data might be defined as:

Customers (Customer name, Customer address, Customer telephone no.)
Dispatch advices (Dispatch no., Dispatch date, Customer name)
Delivery advices (Delivery no., Delivery date, Customer name)
Jobsheets (Job no., Order no., Count discrepancy, Non-conforming black, Non-conforming white, Non-conforming no change)
Products (Product code, Product description, Item length)
Order lines (Order no., Delivery no., Product code, Order qty, Order weight)
Dispatch lines (Order no., Dispatch no., Returned qty, Returned weight).

These definitions are derived directly from the information model represented in Figure 1.16. They act as a design-shorthand for specifying data structures in this database, such as Customers and Dispatches. Each data structure is a collection of data elements, and each data element consists of a set of data items. A sample of the data that might be entered into 'Order lines' is shown in Figure 1.19. In this example, Order no. and Delivery no. are examples of data items. Each row of the table represents a data element. Each data element is identified by a key data item. In this example, the key is the value associated with an Order no., and such keys are underlined in the data structure definitions above.

1.8.2 The business layer

Business layer: That part of
an ICT system involved with
the management of update
functions, transactions and
business rules

The **business layer** of a typical business ICT system or application consists of three inter-related elements: transactions, business rules and update functions.

Data structure				
Order No.	**Delivery No.**	**Product code**	**Order Qty**	**Order Weight**
13/1193G	A3137	UL150	20	145
44/2404G	A3137	UL1500	20	1450
70/2517P	A3137	UL135	20	130
23/2474P	A3137	UL120	16	80

Data element

Data item

Figure 1.19 *Order-lines data structure*

Transactions

A transaction changes a database from one state to another. There are four major types of transaction activities associated with a database, collectively referred to as CRUD:

- **Create** transactions create new data elements within the data structures of a database (more on this in Chapter 6). For example, in Goronwy's new ICT system, a 'create' transaction might be used to enter a new order line against a particular delivery advice.
- Retrieval (or **Read**) transactions access data contained within the data structures of a database, and are often called query transactions. In Goronwy's new ICT system a 'read' transaction might be used to assemble a list of the order lines appropriate to a particular delivery advice.
- **Update** transactions cause changes to values held within particular data items of data elements in a database. In Goronwy's new ICT system an 'update' transaction might be used to change the value Order weight associated with a particular order line.
- **Delete** transactions erase particular data elements. In Goronwy's new ICT system, a delete transaction might be used to remove a particular order line from the database.

Business rules

A considerable amount of the functionality of an ICT system is taken up with business rules. These are found in both the business layer and the data management layer. They ensure that the data held in the data management layer remain an accurate reflection of the activity system they represent. In other words, the data held in an ICT system should display integrity; they should accurately reflect the state of the activity system. For instance, in the case of Goronwy, the data stored in the data structure *jobs* should accurately represent batches of material that either have been successfully processed by the company in the past or are in the process of undergoing galvanisation. Likewise, in a university the data structure of a student record should store data about either existing or past students of the university.

Update functions

Update functions represent units of functionality associated with a particular ICT system. They include both business rules and transaction types. Update functions are triggered by events, which are typically activated from the interface or from other update functions. When an update function is activated, transactions are fired at the data management layer of the ICT system and cause changes to the database.

Hence, in an ICT system at a university a typical update function might be *create student* or *enrol student on module*. Alternatively, in the case of the Goronwy ICT system we might have an update function named *create order line*. When activated, this function would first check that a dispatch advice existed for the order line. Then it would check to see that the order line had not already been entered and that the data to be entered was in the correct format; for instance, that the order number is unique and a correct product code had been entered. If all these checks within business rules proved satisfactory, a transaction would be formed which would create a new row within the order-lines table.

1.8.3   The interface layer

The **interface layer** is responsible for managing interaction with the user, and is generally referred to as the user interface, or sometimes as the human–computer interface. User interfaces are typically designed by creating mock-ups of menus and screens.

■ Menus enable the user to navigate between different elements of the interface.

■ Screens are normally concerned with data maintenance or data retrieval. Data maintenance screens allow the user to enter new data into the system or amend existing data, and trigger update functions, which handle create, update or delete transactions as described above. Data retrieval screens allow the user to extract data from the system, and trigger update functions which handle retrieve transactions.

Figure 1.20 shows a proposed design for a menu and data entry screen associated with the Goronwy Galvanising system. The data entry screen permits the user either to enter a new Jobs record or amend an existing Jobs record.

The design or system specification acts as a blueprint for systems construction. Once the ICT system has been designed, the systems construction phase can begin. This involves building the three layers of the ICT system (data management, business and interface) using development tools such as programming languages and database management systems (which are discussed in Chapter 9).

Systems **construction** may be undertaken either by a team internal to the organisation or by an outside contractor (a form of construction known as outsourcing). Many information

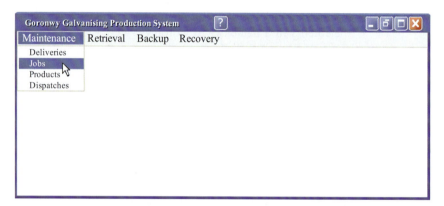

Figure 1.20 *Part of the proposed interface for the Goronwy ICT system*

systems are now also bought in as packages and tailored to organisational requirements. In the case of Goronwy there were no internal technical staff in the organisation and staff could find no external package covering all the desired functionality, so they outsourced construction to an external vendor.

The final phase in the development process is systems **implementation**. This involves the delivery of the system into its context of use. It can be done in a confident manner by immediately moving from the old to the new system. Alternatively, it can be approached in a cautious way in which the old and new systems are run in parallel for a period to ensure that there is a fall-back position. Because Goronwy was new to innovations of this form, it decided to run the manual system in parallel with the new ICT system for two months. At the end of this period it had had no significant problems with the technology, so the plant moved over entirely onto the ICT system.

1.8.4 Enterprise systems

The bespoke system produced for Goronwy worked successfully for a number of years. However, a number of problems were experienced in integrating the bespoke system with other ICT systems produced for the owning company. This was particularly true of the financial ICT system, the human resources ICT system and the procurement ICT system. Eventually a decision was made to purchase a package from an external vendor known as an enterprise resource planning (ERP) system, sometimes known as an enterprise system. An ERP system effectively provides an ICT infrastructure for a company,– integrating the data required by a number of different organisational functions under one umbrella. This ICT infrastructure system commonly consists of a series of packaged software modules feeding off a central database. Many of these packages were developed from manufacturing resource planning (MRP) systems and hence are ideally suited for manufacturing organisations such as Goronwy. However, nowadays ERP systems are applied in many different industrial sectors.

1.9 Operation, use, impact and evaluation

Once an information system is built and implemented it has to be operated and used. The information system will then impact upon its activity system.

1.9.1 Operation

The process of operation not only involves using the ICT system for data entry, retrieval and processing, it also involves enacting procedures to ensure that the system is continuously available as a safe service to use by workers. This means ensuring that security procedures and technologies are in place to protect against unauthorised access to data. It also means ensuring that both the availability and continuity of the system are assured. Hence, for example, suitable procedures have to be put in place for backing up data and recovering it in the event of system failure.

1.9.2 Use and impact

Evaluation: assessing the worth of something

Obviously, once an information system is introduced into an organisation, it begins to be used and to have effects on that organisation. It is important to **evaluate** closely how it is used and what impact it has, in order to ensure that the objectives for introducing it in the first place are achieved.

Two questions need to be asked:

- Is the system actually being used? In reality many systems do not get used; they may be abandoned instead.
- How is it being used, and is this in line with what was intended in its original design? If not, is the unintended use positive or negative? For example, a system supporting decision-

making might also be used as a tool for improving customer relations. Alternatively, a system designed for use by management executives might be used to intimidate subordinates and stifle creativity and innovation.

In order to evaluate impact, we must consider the effect of the information system on individuals, groups and the organisation as a whole (this is examined in greater depth in Chapter 9). For example, it could lead to shifts in the power and influence of certain groups or individuals.

Goronwy tried to minimise the risk associated with the introduction of its new ICT system, but it still led to a number of changes, many of which were unintended. For example, inbound logistics and outbound logistics staff began to assume more responsibility for correct entry of data. The production controller gradually began to assume more of a supervisory role, especially in quality control, and the office clerk did much of the data entry associated with production.

1.9.3   Evaluation

On the surface at least, business organisations invest in information systems for one of three reasons: to do things more efficaciously, to be more efficient or to be more effective. Each type of gain can lead to improved profitability.

- **Efficacy** relates to the core competencies of the organisation. For example, appropriate application of ICT can improve output from those activities that the organisation has to do well.
- **Efficiency** relates to ways in which ICT can enable better utilisation of resources, for example increased worker productivity. Efficiency measures relate the inputs to the activity system to its outputs. Hence, improvements in efficiency mean doing the same thing with less resource or doing more with similar resource.
- **Effectiveness** in organisational terms means improving the contribution an activity system makes to the organisation as a whole. This normally involves attempts to increase market share or competitiveness (Checkland, 1999).

In order to evaluate the performance of a new information system, a business should assess whether or not the efficiency, efficacy or effectiveness of the business has been enhanced as a result. If it has, the next question is whether this has led to a financial return greater than the initial investment in the system.

When Goronwy introduced its new system, it found staff were identifying much more non-conforming black and white material, because more quality checks could be made, both at inbound logistics and after production. This initially caused problems with customers, they were getting more non-conforming material returned to them, and it took more time to return finished goods. However, after a few months customers began to comment favourably; they saw they were getting a better quality of service. Workers seemed to adapt to higher quality control standards, and, over time, production times started to decrease because there were fewer problems with both inbound and outbound material. Higher levels of customer satisfaction tend to lead to more orders, from the satisfied customers themselves or from their recommendations to others. So in efficacy terms, the ICT system seemed to have a good effect. Both satisfaction levels and order levels can be used to measure this effect.

In terms of efficiency, smoother throughput led to greater productivity. This enabled the plant to take on more business, and as a result it became the most profitable galvanising operation within the Rito Metals group for two years running. Hence, Goronwy proved itself to be the most effective galvanising plant in the group.

1.10   eBusiness and eCommerce

The application of informatics to organisational issues in the private sector is known as electronic business (eBusiness) or electronic commerce (eCommerce). The two are not the same.

1.10.1 eBusiness

Value-chain: a collection of interrelated activities that delivers value to the customer

An eBusiness is a business in which the use of ICT is critical to supporting both its internal **value-chain** and its external value network. The internal value chain consists of the series of activity systems by which the organisation delivers a product or service to its customers. The external value network consists of the activities, relationships and flows of value between the organisation and actors in its external environment.

For Goronwy, it is possible to show how the introduction of the new ICT system led to the establishment of its parent company, Rito Metals, as an eBusiness. Goronwy's new ICT system continued in operation for a couple of years, then Rito Metals carried out an evaluation. It concluded that the system had improved the plant's performance in a number of ways, as we have seen. Executives at headquarters made a strategic decision to roll out the ICT system to all ten galvanising plants in the group. As well as wanting to improve the information-handling at the plants, they wanted to see them using standard activity systems.

This rollout took a further two years to complete, as some plants found it difficult to adapt. When it was complete it became possible to create a management information system (MIS) at headquarters, fed with data from the individual plant ICT systems. To enable this, a dedicated wide-area communication network was created, linking each plant with headquarters.

Now Rito Metals could carry out more effective strategic management of its galvanising plants, because it was able to obtain an accurate and up-to-date picture of operations and problems at particular plants, making them easier to identify and rectify. In this sense, the MIS enabled more effective control of the separate business units.

In developing an integrated ICT and information systems infrastructure, Rito Metals moved in the direction of becoming an eBusiness, because the use of ICT became critical to supporting its internal value-chain.

1.10.2 eCommerce

Supply chain: the chain of activities that an organisation performs in relation to its suppliers

Customer chain: the chain of activities that an organisation performs in relation to its customers

eCommerce means the use of ICT in value-chains within the wider value network, such as supply and customer chains:

- The **supply chain** consists of activity systems by which an organisation obtains goods and services from other organisations to enable it to conduct its business.
- The **customer chain** consists of activity systems by which an organisation distributes value to its customers.

The objective of much eCommerce is the redesign of activity systems with ICT to support electronic delivery of products and services. Such joint organisational and technological change typically involves:

Access channel: consists of an access device and associated communication channel

- Investigating and implementing various **access channels** for different organisational stakeholders (such as managers and employees concerned with the internal value-chain and customers and suppliers in the wider value network). An access channel consists of an access device and communication channel.
- Constructing front-end ICT to manage interactions with stakeholders (such as customers and suppliers working in supply and customer chains).
- Re-engineering or constructing back-end ICT.
- Ensuring front-end/back-end ICT systems integration.
- Ensuring secure stored data as well as secure transactions along communication channels.

Back-end systems are those that are used within the organisation, while front-end systems are those that it uses to interface with its stakeholders, such as its customers and suppliers.

Among the commonly used access channels are face-to-face contact and telephone conversations, but channels that use ICT are being introduced more and more in both the public and private sectors. Typical remote access devices are Internet-enabled personal computers (PCs) and a growing range of mobile devices such as tablet computers. Front-end ICT systems include corporate websites. Using these brings a number of advantages to both the organisation and its external stakeholders; for example, customers can log on to the website to access an organisation's services 24 hours a day, 365 days a year.

Goronwy went down this route in the mid-1990s. It started by introducing hand-held devices for inbound and outbound logistics operatives, linked via a plant wireless communication network. The workers could use the devices to access data from the central system, and update it with information on receipt and dispatch.

Goronwy used the Internet and the Web to upgrade its customer chain technology. These are often thought of as the same, but in fact they are distinct:

Internet: a set of interconnected computer networks distributed around the globe that adopt the TCP/IP standard

World Wide Web: a set of standards for hypermedia documentation

- The **Internet** is a set of interconnected computer networks distributed around the globe.
- The **World Wide Web** (www or Web) is an application which runs on top of the Internet. It is basically a set of standards for the representation and distribution of chunks of content (such as text, graphics and images) connected through associative links, known as hyperlinks.

One of the most critical examples of the use of the Web in business is, of course, corporate websites made up of logical collections of web documents normally stored on a computer system referred to as a web server.

Initially, corporate websites were created primarily as an additional promotional tool, to inform customers about the business and provide them with contact details, but many businesses have since invested to increase their levels of interactivity and therefore their applications. Many companies now provide fully transactional websites through which customers can choose and purchase items, track delivery progress, email queries and so on.

Goronwy initially invested in a limited corporate website which merely promoted its services and provided contact details. It then created a companion website specifically for repeat customers such as Blackwalls, so they could enter details of orders and track their progress from receipt, through galvanisation, to dispatch.

To enable fully transactional websites, organisations need to update the information dynamically from back-end databases, and to ensure that information entered by stakeholders updates the company information systems effectively. So, when a customer inputs delivery details, this information needs to be available to all the other systems that need it. This demands integration and interoperability of front-end and back-end systems within the ICT infrastructure. For Goronwy, the back-end ICT infrastructure managed the data model we described above as well as the business rules, update functions and transactions critical to what we referred to as the business layer.

After ten years of operation, Goronwy decided to upgrade its ICT system onto a new hardware and software base, to make it easier to develop web interfaces and integrate them with a central corporate database system. The system was redesigned and rewritten, and the company also invested to ensure the privacy of electronic data held in the system, and the security of transactions travelling both within Goronwy and between Goronwy and the central ICT systems at Rito Metals. This continual investment in the ICT infrastructure is evidence of its growing value to the performance of the business.

1.11   Planning and management

For Goronwy, information systems and ICT infrastructure are central not only for the operation of its individual galvanising plant, but also to the on-going operation of the Rito Metals group. There is also increasing pressure from the competitive environment. Goronwy, like all organisations, needs to match what its competitors do, and to offer some things they do not, to gain a competitive edge. ICT is central to this.

Informatics planning: the process of defining the optimal informatics infrastructure for an organisation

This creates a need for effective planning for, and management of, information, information systems and ICT. We call these collectively the informatics infrastructure. This is known as **informatics planning**.

Informatics service: the organisational function devoted to the delivery of informatics

All this means, of course, that an organisation needs informatics professionals to provide an **informatics service**, which consists of planning, management, development and operation of information systems. It has the choice of employing people to carry out these functions, or of outsourcing them.

Goronwy's choices are dictated in part by the fact that it is one organisation within a larger group. It initiates formal informatics planning and incorporates it into the on-going development of general business strategy. Rito Metals runs a periodic review of its infrastructure in the light of technological developments. Most recently this process led to the rollout of radio frequency identification (RFID) tagging (see Chapter 8). This enables the company to better integrate its information across supply, internal and customer chains.

Initially, Rito Metals took the strategic decision to employ no informatics professionals. It outsourced all the development of its initial systems, but as it came to use more and more ICT and information systems, top-level management decided the group needed an internal workforce devoted to informatics processes. It still uses some outsourcing, however. Much informatics planning and management is tackled in-house by a group of 10 to 20 individuals, but most development and operations work is conducted by external vendors. For instance, provision and operation of its communication network has been outsourced for a number of years.

FOCUS ON VALUE

The concept of value is a common thread that ties together the range of topics considered in this book. The *Oxford English Dictionary* defines value as *the importance or usefulness of something*. Here we are concerned with the value of ICT to organisations. We can only understand it if we consider the layered contexts within which ICT is used and applied.

There is key value in organisational informatics as an academic field of study and an area of organisational practice. In an academic field of study, much new knowledge emerges at the boundaries between established disciplines. Organisational informatics is interdisciplinary in its interest in the interaction between organisational or business systems of many forms. Much current organisational experience relies on the interaction between these systems, so knowledge of organisational informatics is particularly important for the business practitioner in helping to understand and control their performance.

1.12 Conclusion and key themes

This book is about the *interaction* of business systems with information and its wider context. Because our focus is on the application of informatics in organisations, there are a number of themes that run through the book. Each of them relates to the issue of value and ICT.

- An information system need not necessarily be computerised. The processes of gathering, processing, storing and distributing information have been undertaken in human societies for many thousands of years. Technologies based around the digital computer are only the latest form of information and communication technology (ICT).
- Organisational informatics is concerned with information in general, as well as information systems and ICT in particular. It is important to understand what information is, and how it is related to effective decision-making and human action.
- We cannot properly understand information and an information system without understanding the context. This operates at several different levels: the organisation or part of an organisation that uses the systems; markets, societies and economies (for instance, with systems making up a national financial infrastructure); and more recently focus has shifted to the global scale, particularly for information systems such as the Web.
- An information system must fit its context: the organisation, its strategy, its processes and its environment. Information systems that do not fit are likely to be resisted, under-

used, misused, sabotaged and unprofitable. They are likely to have negative effects on organisational performance.

■ The 'value' of ICT in a given organisation relates to ICT's place within its information systems, and the way in which these information systems impact on the organisation, enabling it to remain viable and sustainable.

The next three chapters consider the fundamental bedrock of the issue of value. In Chapter 2 we consider the organisation as a value-creating system. This leads us to consider the place of information in support of value-creation and value-adding activity in Chapter 3. The concepts of system and information are then brought together in our consideration of the place of information systems in organisations, and the role of ICT in those systems, in Chapter 4.

1.13   Critical reflection

Each chapter in this book contains a section such as this in which we would like you, the reader, to question and reflect upon the portrayal of Business Information Systems or Organisational Informatics you will receive from this text. This is an opportunity to challenge conceptions and debate effectively about the nature of business information systems in particular, as well as the developing nature of business and indeed all forms of organisation.

The domain model presented in this chapter received its initial inspiration from an article published in *Management Information Systems Quarterly* (Silver et al., 1995). This model has been refined over the years and has been found useful not only to organise the material in this book but also as a means of emphasising the interdisciplinary nature of the area. However, it is not the only way of parcelling up the field of Business Information Systems. Try looking at an alternative viewpoint such as Steven Alter's Work System Method (Alter, 2006). Does this viewpoint offer a clearer view of the area than the one presented here?

1.14   Further reading

There is substantial literature examining the state of the discipline of information systems from various perspectives. A good place to start is with the three papers by Galliers (Alter, 2006), Hirschheim and Klein (Hirschheim and Klein, 2003) and Benbasat and Zmud (Bell, 1972). Keen (Keen, 1980) provides the original idea of the discipline of Information Systems relying upon a number of reference disciplines. The paper by Kling and Allen (Kling and Allen, 1996) sparked off the idea of using the term organisational informatics as a better label for the domain of study and bears a resemblance to ideas expressed by Kling and Scaachi (Kling and Scaachi, 1982).

1.15   References

Alter, S. (2006). *The Work System Method: Connecting People, Processes, and IT for Business Results*. Work system press, San Francisco.

Bell, D. (1972). *The Coming of the Post-industrial Society*. Addison-Wesley, Reading, Mass.

Burnham, D. (1983). *The Rise of the Computer State*. Random House, New York.

Castells, M. (1996). *The Rise of the Network Society*. Blackwell, Mass.

Checkland, P. (1999). Soft Systems Methodology: A Thirty Year Retrospective. John Wiley, Chichester.

Drucker, P. F. (1994). The Theory of the Business. *Harvard Business Review* 72 (5): 95–104.

Hirschheim, R. and H. Klein. (2003). Crisis in the IS Field? A Critical Reflection on the State of the Discipline. *Journal of the Association for Information Systems* 4 (5): 237–293.

Keen, P. G. W. (1980). *Reference Disciplines and a Cumulative IS Tradition*. First International Conference on Information Systems, Philadelphia.

Kling, R. and J. P. Allen. (1996). Can Computer Science Solve Organisational Problems? The Case for Organisational Informatics. *Computerisation and Controversy: Value Conflicts and Social Choices*. Edited by R. Kling. Academic Press, San Diego.

Kling, R. and W. Scaachi. (1982). The Web of Computing: Computer Technology As Social Organisation. *Advances in Computers* 21: 1–90.

Silver, M. S., M. L. Markus and C. M. Beath. (1995). The Information Technology Interaction Model: A Foundation for the MBA Core Course. *MIS Quarterly* 19 (3): 361–390.

See companion website **www.palgrave.com/business/beynon-daviesbis2e**

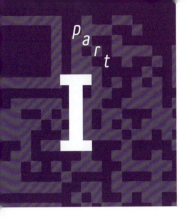

Key concepts

This part examines some of the fundamental, or foundation, concepts of the discipline of information systems or organisational informatics.

Chapter 2 considers what organisations actually are. It looks first to organisation theory for a number of perspectives on organisations. It then use elements of **systems thinking** to distinguish between three forms of system of interest to organisational informatics: activity systems, information systems and ICT systems. The focus of this particular chapter is upon activity systems. It considers the importance of modelling such systems in various ways and introduces ideas of process modelling and process design as practical approaches to engaging with organisations.

Chapter 3 discusses **information,** a concept which is not well-covered in other texts. Here, it is covered in some depth and considered from the perspective of semiotics, which helps us understand its multi-faceted nature. This approach makes it possible to make clear connections between information, data and knowledge, as well as decision-making and action. The chapter also considers the importance of modelling data, information and knowledge and examines some approaches in this area.

In **Chapter 4** the two concepts of *information* and *system* come together in our consideration of the concept of an **information system.** The chapter describes the critical importance of information systems to activity systems throughout history. This leads to a consideration of some generic information systems underlying business activity that form, what we refer to as, the back-end information systems infrastructure of many modern commercial organisations. Around this core a number of front-end information systems interface with the major internal and external stakeholders of the business: managers, employees, customers and suppliers.

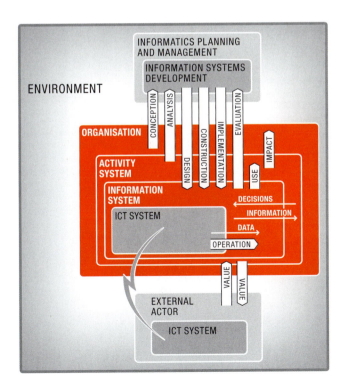

Overview

The chapters in this part cover the following key areas:

- Information
- Systems
- Human activity systems
- Data systems
- Management and decision-making
- Modelling business systems
- Business and informatics infrastructure

Organisations and systems

'Observe how system into system runs, What other planets circle other suns.'

Alexander Pope (1688–1744), *An essay on man* (1733), Epistle 1

Learning outcomes	Principles
Understand the fundamental elements of all systems.	The concept of system is fundamental to the three types of systems considered in this work: activity systems, information systems and ICT systems.
Explain the idea of the organisation as a value-creating system.	An organisation can be considered as an open system interacting with a wider value network making up its environment.
Discuss the place of control in the regulation and adaptation of systems.	Control is essential both to the internal regulation of systems such as organisations, as well as to the ways in which organisations adapt to changes in their external environment.
Explain the importance of modelling to informatics work and construct a simple, rich picture, root definition, activity system model and process model.	Modelling is important both to help managers understand their organisations as well as to provide tools for intervening in organisations. Four types of model are introduced, all relevant to considering the organisation as a system.

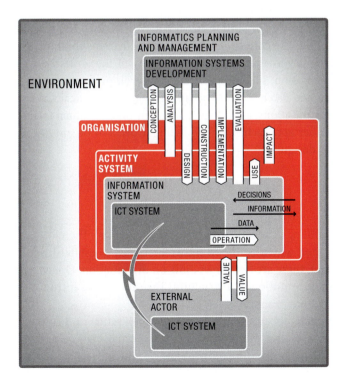

Chapter outline

AACSB learning objectives: Analytical skills, reflective thinking and ethical reasoning

2.1   Introduction

Consider the following question. How much of your life is spent either working within organisations or interacting with organisations in various forms? When given time to reflect, most people would probably answer, 'a lot of time'. People worldwide spend a substantial proportion of their lives either working in or interacting with organisations. Much of modern-day life is therefore organisational life. This explains why, in organisational informatics, we are interested in the ways in which information and communication technology (ICT) is used to support human activity in organisations.

This chapter examines what we mean by an organisation. In the following chapters we consider how information, information systems and ICT are relevant to shaping organisations.

To understand the place of information, information systems and ICT in the modern world we need to look critically at the concept of organisation. For instance, it has become accepted that the success of an organisation is dependent on its information systems, since they can support efficient and effective human activity. The development of information systems also typically contributes in important ways to changes in human activity within organisations. Modern societies and economies therefore rely on information systems to perform effectively. For these reasons, understanding the nature of organisations is critical to understanding the nature of informatics.

The proper place to start is with the theory of organisations. Unfortunately, there is not just one theory; there is a series of useful viewpoints, each offering a partial insight. In this chapter, we consider two perspectives on the organisation: top-down and bottom-up. The top-down perspective emphasises how organisations are institutions that constrain human activity. The bottom-up perspective emphasises how organisations are built by individuals who decide and act.

It is possible to integrate aspects of the top-down and bottom-up perspectives into a view of the organisation as a complex adaptive system. This leads us to define an organisation as a social arrangement which pursues collective goals, which controls its own performance, and which has a boundary separating it from its environment. This conception of both the unit and the process of organisation is important because it allows us to define clearly, and to relate, issues of activity, information and technology.

The word 'organisation' derives from the Greek word organon, meaning a tool. This is useful because it suggests the value of treating organisations as tools for action. The greater part of this chapter explains a number of the core concepts underlying systems thinking, or systemics. We show how these concepts allow us to inter-relate many of the issues critical to management in the modern organisation, including strategy, control, performance and change. A systems view of organisations is also important because it suggests practical ways of analysing the dynamics of existing organisations, and of designing new organisational forms. So, throughout the chapter, we consider approaches for modelling aspects of organisations within processes of both analysis and design.

2.2   What is organisation?

Organisational informatics, by definition, is an organisational phenomenon. Therefore, to understand this form of informatics and why it is important we first need to establish what organisation is (Morgan, 1986). In fact, there are two viewpoints on organisation. One views organisation from the top down, as an institution or a structure. The other views it from the bottom up, as a continuing process of human action.

Institutional perspective: The perspective on organisations that treats them as wholes or units

In essence, the **institutional perspective** focuses on the unit of organisation and is interested in the features of organisations as wholes. The institutional perspective views organisations as entities which exist independently of the humans belonging to them. Human actions are directed or constrained by such larger social structures. Institutions have a life over and above the life of their members.

In contrast, the **action perspective** focuses on the process of organising rather than the unit of organisation. The critical interest here is in how humans generate structures of coordination and cooperation at work. For the action perspective social institutions such as business organisations are fundamentally constructed or produced through actions performed by human beings. This means that organisations do not exist independently of the humans belonging to them.

Action perspective: The perspective on organisations that focuses on the process of organising

2.2.1 A simple example of organisation

To help introduce this idea let us first consider a very simple case of an organisation. A number of people in a particular area are concerned about the growing isolation of the elderly in their local community. Many old people are unable to shop for foodstuffs on a regular basis and are physically incapable of preparing a hot meal for themselves. However, many old persons want to continue to live independently in their own homes. To help enable this, some local councils in the UK provide a service called meals on wheels to the elderly in their immediate area. However, many other areas of the country are not served by such a public sector service but rely instead upon charitable activity. This is the case in the local area in which our group of volunteers live so they decide to set up a meals on wheels service for their area themselves.

But how should they organise themselves? There are clearly a number of activities that must go into providing such a service. First, they need to continuously determine who amongst the elderly population in their area would like a hot meal every day and be willing and able to pay a small fee for it. Then somebody has to source foodstuffs from suppliers. Someone else will have to cook the meals and package them ready to be delivered. Yet others will have to deliver meals to people who subscribe to the service. All these activities, performed by many different people, will have to be coordinated effectively to ensure that the old people who want a hot meal get it on time and that it is of a requisite quality.

Initially, they recruit some twenty elderly people to the scheme and decide to try and provide a hot meal to just these persons, three days a week, for a small weekly charge. A number of volunteers allocate themselves to the task of purchasing foodstuffs and preparing meals at a local community kitchen they are able to rent for this purpose. A group of other volunteers indicate that they are prepared to deliver the hot meals to subscribers in reusable, insulated containers, in their own vehicles. The cooks indicate to the delivery people what they have prepared on any particular day and the delivery people indicate to the subscribers what they can expect each day the scheme operates.

This way of working is successful for a number of months. However, the success of the scheme passes by word of mouth throughout the community and within a short period the number of subscribers trebles. Consequently, the quantity of foodstuff needed rises considerably and the established way of purchasing from high-street supermarkets is no longer viable. Also, a growing number of volunteers are needed to cover gaps in the workforce caused by illness and other circumstances. This makes the task of determining who is, or should be, doing what and when more difficult.

As a consequence, the group of volunteers decide to *organise* themselves more appropriately. They start making records of things such as: member details, including their address and dietary requirements; volunteer details, including contact details and times when they are able to contribute; a rotating monthly menu with a detailed breakdown of foodstuffs required; details of foodstuff suppliers; financial details, such as what money has been collected from which members and how much has been expended on foodstuffs, rent of the kitchen and fuel for deliveries.

Such records help volunteers to coordinate their actions. The rotating menu, for instance, is used by many different volunteers as key to making decisions appropriate to their own activity: volunteers that deal with suppliers use the menu to determine what foodstuffs to buy and when; volunteers that cook the meals use the menu as a guide to food preparation; and volunteers that deliver hot meals use the menu to guide subscribers as to what to expect.

In this simple example we have all of the component elements making up an organisation, which we shall consider in some depth in this chapter. The volunteers are best described as actors in the sense that they perform, on a repeating basis, a set of activities such as cooking meals and delivering them to subscribers. Each volunteer needs to coordinate his or her activities with those of other actors, or volunteers. As a group they also need to coordinate their collective activity with that of further actors such as foodstuff suppliers and of course the subscribers themselves. For such coordination, communication is needed.

Communication relies upon some mutually agreed system of signs between coordinating actors. Statements in a spoken language are clearly acts of communication between two or more actors that rely on such a common sign-system. But statements in a spoken language do not persist beyond the communication in which they take place. Hence, groups of actors that wish to coordinate their performance across time, and possibly space, have to create records. In other words, records ensure that multiple actors are informed of the actions of others some time after such actions have been completed. Records can also be accessed in a different place from where the action took place. Such records are thus, by their very nature, used to do different things such as to make persistent certain assertions about the current state of some organisation, or to direct future actions of group members. In this sense, records are particularly important for making decisions about future courses of action.

So, from an institutional, or top-down, perspective this meals on wheels service exists as an entity greater than any particular individual who participates in the organisation. From an action, or bottom-up, perspective the organisation is constituted from the actions of the individuals who make up the organisation.

CASE CHECK

Tesco   p 455

Tesco plc. is an international grocery and general merchandising retail organisation. From an institutional perspective, Tesco can be seen as a large multinational company, retailing goods, offering services and competing in a number of markets. Other aspects of interest are its strategy and ways of designing its activities to improve performance in areas such as its supermarket operations. This would lead us to examine the place of information in support of activities such as deciding which products to stock, in which stores and at what times.

Looking at Tesco from an action perspective, we would be interested in how its employees perform their work. How, for instance, do they operate checkouts, stock shelves and receive goods into the supermarket? We would look not only at any written instructions directing this activity, but also at what people do in practice, even though it is not formally spelled out for them. We would consider how they acquire this knowledge, how they communicate it to others, and we would need to examine the ways in which they account for their activity to others.

2.2.2   Organisations as complex, adaptive systems

For much of its history the theory of organisation has tended to portray the institutional and action perspectives on organisations as mutually exclusive. In practice, of course, each is a legitimate or valid position. We all act and interact with fellow human beings within organisations and appreciate the fluidity of organisational life. We all also experience the monolithic nature of organisations and the constraints placed upon our actions by these institutional structures.

In this chapter we shall demonstrate how these two viewpoints on organisation are not incompatible. We shall demonstrate how the idea of organisation as structure, or institution, emerges from organisation as process or activity. To do this we shall introduce the idea of structuration, which takes the perspective of an organisation as a complex, adaptive system.

Structuration: The process by which human action both produces and reproduces social structure, and also how social structure both informs and constrains human action

The idea of **structuration** was created by the sociologist Anthony Giddens (Walsham and Han, 1991) as an attempt to reconcile the duality of the action and institutional perspectives on organisation. In this view, organisations are both institutions and collections of action. On the one hand, the structure of social institutions such as organisations is created by human action. Through human interaction, social structures are reproduced but may also change. On the other hand, humans utilise institutional structure as a resource in interpreting their own and other people's action. This means that institutions act as a constraint on human action. Giddens calls this cyclical process the process of structuration.

Figure 2.1 illustrates this process. Social structure both informs and constrains human action. In turn, human action both produces and reproduces social structure.

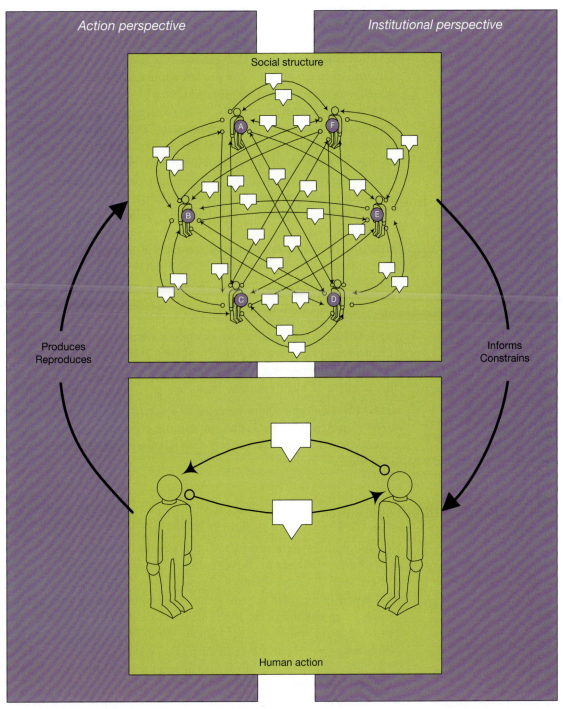

Figure 2.1 The process of structuration

Spoken languages such as English have many similar features with organisations, as we have discussed. A necessary pre-condition for conversation (or speech acts) is that people have a common language. We can talk about the features of a language without talking about specific conversations, for instance, discussing its vocabulary, grammar and syntax (see also Chapter 3). In this sense, English as a spoken language has an existence independent of the people who speak it. However, spoken language is only really evident in actual speech acts. People use language as a resource for communication; they produce and re-produce it through speech acts. Over time speech acts change the structure of a language. New vocabulary, grammar and syntax evolve. For example, the English in Shakespearean plays is recognisably the same language as that spoken today, but many of the words Shakespeare used have fallen out of favour today, and many other words have different meanings in a modern context.

> **REFLECT:** Consider an organisation known to you. In what way can it be considered an institution? Think of an organisation you are a member of (not necessarily a work organisation), and consider what activities you and others engage in. In what way can such actions be said to be the organisation? Reflect on your experience of entering this new organisational setting. How long did it take you to understand how things were done there? How did you acquire this knowledge? In the time that you have been a member, have its practices changed? If so, how and why?

There is a similarity between the notion of structuration, and the idea of considering organisations as complex adaptive systems (Stacey, 2003). Although the system perspective used to be seen as a top-down, institutional perspective (looking at the organisation as a whole and the ways it regulates itself), more recently systems theorists have become interested in how organisation occurs through the complex interaction of multiple individuals. This bottom-up perspective offers a useful insight into how organisations adapt and change.

A systemic conception of organisations is therefore useful in a number of ways (Jackson, 2003). First, it has clear ways of addressing some classic concerns of organisation theory such as decision-making, coordinated action and the place of information. Second, the conceptual tools of systemics offer managers practical ways of engaging with, or intervening in, organisations for which they are responsible; not only so they can ensure operational effectiveness, but also to understand environmental uncertainty, plan strategy and manage change.

Later on in this chapter, for instance, we shall consider how what we mean by organisation is actually accomplished through the interaction of three types of systems: activity systems, information systems and data (ICT) systems. This distinction helps the manager understand more clearly the role that information plays in her decision-making, and how such information is reliant on quality data.

RECAP: There are two major perspectives on organisational life: the institutional perspective and the action perspective. The institutional perspective considers organisations as units that constrain or structure people's behaviour. The action perspective considers organisations as arising out of human interaction.

2.3   Organisational systemics

The concept of system is central to thinking in numerous fields. For instance, in medicine it is seen as important to consider our bodies as being made up of various systems such as a digestive system and a central nervous system. In terms of astronomy we live on a planet that is part of the solar system. From the perspective of the social sciences we engage with people in groups that form social, political and economic systems. In mathematics we are educated in the use of number systems. Modern organisations are systems of activity that would collapse without effective information systems.

At first sight these varied systems appear to have little in common. However, on closer examination we see that all these examples represent what we might describe as a patterning or ordering of things. Systems theory, systems thinking or, as we prefer to call it, **systemics** is the attempt to study the generic features of such patterning.

Systemics: The study of the general properties and behaviour of all systems

As we have seen, any organisation consists of a multitude of business actors. An actor is any entity that can act and we deliberately use the term actor here rather than person because we wish to emphasise that actors include humans, animals and machines. In the past, for instance, animals such as pit ponies were significant actors within industry. Nowadays, machines, such as vans, cranes and even ICT systems, as we shall see, are significant actors within most organisations. From the meals on wheels example it should be apparent that three distinct but inter-related forms of action are undertaken by actors and that these three forms of action serve to accomplish what we mean by organisation. Actors perform instrumental activity, make decisions and communicate about such activity and represent aspects of such activity in records.

However, business actions do not normally occur in isolation. The actions of one business actor are normally entangled with, or bound to, the actions of other actors and as such form coherent patterns of action. A pattern consists of a set of elements that repeat in a predictable manner. Inherent in the idea of a pattern is the idea that it is reproduced across more than one situation. We will argue that what we mean by organisation consists of the patterning of performance, communication and representation by actors. Such patterning produces, or accomplishes, the order characteristic of human organisation and produces its institutional properties. Hence, in the meals on wheels example the business actors reproduce on a weekly basis the delivery of hot meals to designated people. They also regularly communicate about such activity to each other and to facilitate communication between each other and their customers make records of their activities.

These three patterns of activity constitute organisation as a complex adaptive system. But what is a system, why are organisations complex systems and in what sense are they adaptive?

2.3.1 Systemics

The discipline devoted to the study of the general nature of systems is often referred to as systems thinking or systems theory. We prefer to refer to it as systemics because it has become popular in numerous aspects of life to refer to problems as systemic. But what actually underlies a systemic approach to things? Very broadly, a **system** is an organised set of interdependent elements that exists for some purpose, has some stability, and can be usefully viewed as a whole. Five key principles are significant within this definition: holism, identity, organisation, purpose and emergence.

First, one of the fundamental principles of systemics is summed up in the ancient Greek philosopher Aristotle's dictum that *the whole is more than the sum of its parts*. This suggests that when we attempt to investigate and understand complex phenomena, such as how businesses work, we should attempt to do so holistically – in terms of the whole phenomena rather than its parts. Second, a system has an *identity*. By this we mean it can be clearly distinguished from other phenomena. We can draw a boundary around what is inside and what is outside the system. We can also see a system as persisting through time. Third, systems display *organisation*. Systems are different from aggregates or collections of things because in a system we observe the continuous patterning of phenomena. Fourth, to say a system displays organisation implies that a system is organised to do something: it has some explicit or implicit *purpose*. This means that systems are normally seen as organised to achieve some goals. Fifth and finally, a consequence of a system having identity, displaying organisation and achieving purpose is that systems accomplish *emergence*. A system is a complex entity that has properties that do not belong to any of its constituent parts, but emerge from the relationships or interaction of its constituent parts. This is really what is meant by: *The whole is more than the sum of its parts*.

Consider a simple example of a physical system. A road network can be viewed as a system. It is made up of component parts such as roads, road intersections and vehicles which travel along this network. The purpose of a road network is likely to be to convey people and goods between points within a geographical space. In a road network a bottleneck experienced at

System: An organised set of interdependent elements that exists for some purpose, has some stability, and can be usefully viewed as a whole

a road intersection is the result of the interactions between a large body of components or parts (vehicles) coming together in particular ways. A bottleneck is not a property of any one component of a system, such as a vehicle, it is only a property of the system as a whole; it is an emergent effect of the operation of this system.

As we shall see, systemics has been applied to both 'hard' systems such as road infrastructure and 'soft' systems such as organisations. Hard systems are not 'hard' in the sense of being any more complex than soft systems. Instead, they are 'hard' in the physical or technical sense. In such situations it is possible to use system concepts as a means of investigating complex situations and taking rational action with the objective of achieving what are seen to be defined, unquestioned and frequently unproblematic goals. For instance, large integrated manufacturing plants, such as petro-chemical plants, can be treated as hard systems in the sense that designing such plants to achieve production goals is relatively unproblematic. Most technological systems, including, as we shall see, ICT systems, can be considered as 'hard' systems in a similar manner.

In contrast, most human systems are 'soft' systems because they are social in nature. They are collections of people undertaking activities to achieve some purpose. However, within human systems the boundaries or scope of the system may be fluid and the purpose of the system may be problematic and certainly open to interpretation from many different viewpoints. Hence, the purpose of a private, public or voluntary sector organisation may be open to different interpretations depending upon the viewpoints of particular actors who are not only members but also observers of the system. Hence, a university, for instance, might be considered a system for educating students, for conducting research, for engaging with industry or for contributing to the wider community.

2.3.2   Core system constructs

The meals on wheels service described earlier can clearly be regarded as a system. This service has a clear identity in that we can draw a boundary around what forms activity in this area. The activity that accomplishes this service is continuously reproduced in a patterned way and it is through such patterning that this organisation persists through time. The purpose of this organisation is to provide regular hot meals to the elderly. Such purpose is achieved, or emerges from, the complex coordination of the activities of a multitude of different actors.

The term *system* has a Greek origin, derived from *syn* meaning together and *histemi* meaning to set. In very broad terms, and from a static point of view, a system can be seen to consist of a collection of objects that are related or set together. But by setting together it also means that a system is dynamic in the sense that the objects potentially influence each other.

Our very general definition of a system clearly encompasses a vast array of phenomena. For a certain interesting class of systems (open systems) on which we shall focus, a popular way is to specify certain types of objects and relations to be of interest. Systems of this type are generally portrayed in terms of an input–process–output entity existing within a given environment (Figure 2.2). In this view, systems can be seen as being composed of the following elements: one or more operational *processes* or mechanisms of transformation; one or more sets of *inputs* from and *outputs* to actors in the environment; one or more *control* processes.

Processes represent the dynamic elements of systems. A process is a mechanism of transformation. It consists of an inter-connected set of actions (behaviour) necessary to transform some input(s) into some output(s). It is possible to define two major types of process as relevant to any type of system: operational processes and control processes. Operational processes achieve the defined purpose or transformation of a system. Control processes, as we shall see, maintain the behaviour of operational processes in desired directions and hence maintain the overall identity of the system. The *inputs* to a system are the resources it gains

DID YOU KNOW? The systems perspective has had much influence in areas such as ecology. Some have even proposed considering the entire earth as a complex ecological system and even given such a system a name: Gaia. Changes to any part of Gaia, such as deforestation of the Amazon basin, are likely to have knock-on effects on many other parts of system, such as changes to climate. This, in turn, is likely to influence melting of the polar ice caps, which is likely to further exacerbate changes to climate.

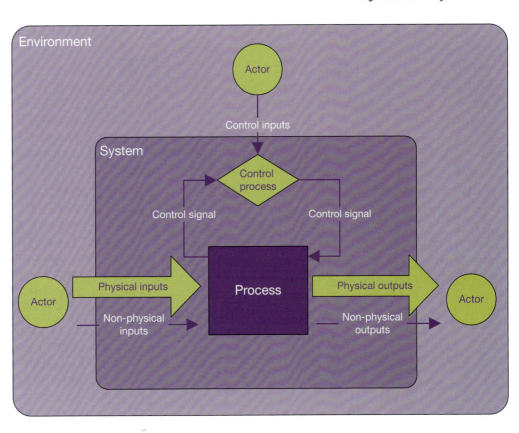

Figure 2.2 *Core system constructs*

from actors in its environment, some of which may be other systems. The *outputs* from a system are those things that it supplies back to actors in its environment.

For example, a manufacturing firm such as Goronwy Galvanising, which we discussed in Chapter 1, can be considered as a system that transforms raw materials (inputs) from its customers (actors) into finished products (outputs) for those customers. Similarly, an organisation such as the meals on wheels service can be considered a system that uses resources such as foodstuffs (inputs) to produce hot meals (output) for its subscribers (actors).

2.3.3 System complexity

Organisations are open systems in the sense that they interact with actors in their environment. Organisations are also complex systems that, as we shall see, need to regulate themselves and adapt to changes in their environment. Two other constructs are useful for specifying and managing the complexity inherent in systems such as organisations: that of variety and the associated idea of a **subsystem**.

The complexity of any system can be defined in terms of the notion of **state**, which is defined by values appropriate to the attributes of the system. At any point in time, a value can be assigned to each of these attributes. The set of all values assumed by the attributes of a system defines a systems' state. **Variety** may be defined as the number of possible states of a system. For many systems, particularly those involving human activity, the variety of the system may be quite large in the sense that the number of possible states may not be precisely countable. Variety is therefore useful as a measure of the complexity of a system.

We can illustrate this idea using a simple example. Consider a collection of actors, each of which we represent as a node labelled A–F in the diagram in Figure 2.3. We assume that each actor within this system can theoretically communicate with each other actor in the group. We draw arrows between actors to represent that communication and draw these arrows in both directions between any two actors to indicate that, for instance, relation A → B is different from B → A. In other words, actor A can make an utterance to actor B and actor B can make an utterance to actor A; each is a separate speech or communicative act. In this sense, each relation

Subsystem: A coherent part of a system that can be treated as a system itself

State: The set of all values assumed by the properties of a system at one point in time

Variety: A measure of the complexity of a system; the number of states a system can assume

Figure 2.3 *A simple dynamic system*

or communication channel in this system is effectively a 'switch' that may be turned on or off, perhaps indicating the effect of one actor in the network on another through communication. Here we have a simple system in which a collection of things now interacts; it operates or behaves.

Hence, we could consider this as a simple model of a human communication network in which, perhaps, we wish to study the movement of communication around the network; perhaps the way in which some particular business communication travels amongst group members. In this system, one state of the system is when one particular communicative act such as A → B takes place. Another state is when B → C as an act of communication takes place, and so on.

As we have seen, using the idea of a system's states, variety may be defined as the number of possible states of a system. Hence, since there are 2 possible communication relations between each of the 6 actors in the network, there are n (n−1) or 6 times 5 possible relations between actors, which is 30 possible relations. If we regard a state of the system as being a particular configuration of active and inactive communication relations then there are over 2^{30} (1,073,741,824) possible states for the entire system. This is a measure of the variety inherent in this comparatively simple system. Hence, for many actual social systems in which there are many more actors and relationships than in our example, the variety or complexity of such systems may be incomprehensibly large.

At first glance, we might conclude that the consequence of this is that it is impossible to understand the workings of any reasonable complex system such as an organisation. But one way of handling the complexity of systems is to apply the notion of hierarchy to understanding and representing them. In this way, systems can be seen as being composed of various levels, each level of which can be conceptualised in terms of a system. Hence, the environment of a system may be viewed as a system in its own right and a process that is part of one system may be treated as a system in turn, and so on. In this way we can build a hierarchy of system, subsystem, sub-subsystem, and so on.

For example, within the meals on wheels case we can identify a number of subsystems of activity. These include ordering foodstuffs, preparing foodstuffs, cooking meals, packaging meals, delivering meals to subscribers, collecting subscriptions, washing containers, and so on. Each of these subsystems can be seen to consist of a number of inter-related processes. Each process, in turn, can be considered a system in itself.

RECAP: The concept of a system is particularly important for managers because of the way it integrates a number of critical issues. Systemics is the study of the nature of systems. Organisational or management systemics concerns the application of the concept of a system to organisation and management problems. This offers a number of lessons for understanding the nature of organisations and the process of management.

A system is an organised collection of things with emergent properties and with a defined purpose. Different stakeholders need to be considered in defining the characteristics of a system. Critical features or components of all systems include subsystems, input–process–output, an environment and control.

2.4   Control

Control: The process by which the order or patterning in some systems is sustained

Regulation: The process of ensuring that a system remains viable

Adaptation: The process of ensuring that a system continues to sustain itself in the face of environmental change

Control is effectively the process by which the order within any system is sustained. We know that something is systemic if it is ordered or organised, if we see evidence of patterning. In other words, we observe a common pattern across situations. Hence, a common pattern of activities is evident in situations such as the meals on wheels or the Goronwy Galvanising examples. These patterns consist of routines through which organisational actors perform work.

Control is the process by which such patterning of order is created and maintained across situations. We recognise something as having a distinct identity – as being a system – through some patterning in the world. *Control* is the process by which a system ensures continuity through time. It is thus the means by which system identity is sustained and the system maintains its viability in terms of changes in its environment. Control is the means by which system behaviour is reproduced. In our terms, control produces the patterning evident in systems of action, communication and representation amongst groups of actors.

Hence, control can be conceived as both a process of regulation and as a process of adaptation applicable to systems. The typical meanings associated with the term *control* are stability and conservation. This side of control is frequently referred to as *regulation* and is typically concerned with the internal operations of a system. In terms of regulation, control ensures that a system will recover some stability after a period of disturbance and maintain its viability over time. For instance, if we were to observe the work of a particular organisation such as the meals on wheels service in close detail for a number of weeks we would see clear evidence of such patterns. Different actors within such settings will reproduce modes of action, communication and record-keeping, time and again.

However, there are alternative meanings associated with the process of organising. This side of control is frequently referred to as *adaptation*. Adaptation is the evolutionary side of control and is concerned with the external relationships between the system and its environment. Systems generally exhibit some form of control that enables the system to adapt to changes in its environment; changing its behaviour to ensure a degree of 'fitness' between system and environment.

Hence, if we consider a manufacturing organisation such as Goronwy as a system then the internal operations of this organisation must be regulated to ensure that it performs effectively and efficiently. But such an organisation also has to adapt to its competitive environment; it must ensure that it produces things demanded by its customers at appropriate prices.

Control can be viewed in terms of a monitoring subsystem, or a hierarchy of such subsystems, that 'steers' the behaviour of other operating subsystems. Hence, this monitoring subsystem is frequently referred to as a control mechanism, subsystem or process.

In terms of systems designed by human beings, such as organisations, control can be considered an imposed process. In the process of designing and constructing a system, necessary processes of control for regulation have to be established. Any coherent element of a system must inherently have a control mechanism, or process, embedded within it. In other words, a system with operational or productive processes must have at least one controller for such processes.

Applying the idea of systems hierarchy, we can refine the idea of a control process within a system as consisting of inputs, outputs and processes (Figure 2.4). For a control process to work effectively it must have three things: resources to deploy to regulate the behaviour of

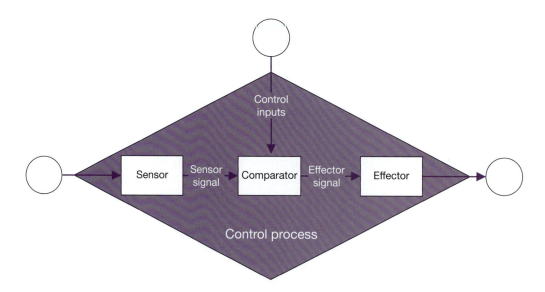

Figure 2.4 *Elements of a control process*

the system in a particular direction; control inputs which implement the purpose of the system; control signals enabling the process to monitor and instruct operational processes.

The control process ensures defined levels of performance for the system through use of a number of control inputs. This sets the key decision strategy for the controller. Such a decision strategy then works in interaction with three other key elements of a control process: sensors, comparators and effectors. *Sensors* are processes that monitor changes in the environment of a system or in the system itself (sensed signals) and send further signals to comparators. *Comparators* compare signals from sensors against a decision strategy and on this basis makes a decision to send signals to effectors. Sometimes referred to as actuators or activators, *effectors* cause changes to a systems' state. In other words, they introduce changes to system variables by sending signals to particular parts of a system.

For instance, in a security system sensors are likely to be placed at points of entry into a building such as windows and doors. If a window is opened when the system is activated, a sensor sends a signal to the control unit. This unit identifies the point of entry, and sends signals to effectors such as alarms.

In the case of Goronwy Galvanising a number of operatives were employed to check incoming steel batches. They effectively acted as sensors and used a set of rules to determine whether a batch was conforming or non-conforming. If a batch was conforming then further operators effected movement of the batch through the galvanisation process. If the batch was non-conforming then it was dispatched back to the customer.

Sensor: A process that monitors changes in the environment of a system

Comparator: A process that compares signals from sensors with control inputs

Effector: Components that cause changes to a systems state

> **DID YOU KNOW?** Much of the literature on organisational adaptation makes an analogy between organisations and biological organisms. In this sense, organisational adaptation is seen as similar to the process of natural selection. Animals evolve to fit their ecological environment; organisations that survive 'evolve' to fit the economic environment. Organisations that do not evolve fast enough to the changes in their environment go out of existence.

> **REFLECT:** Business strategy can be considered as a form of control used in organisations, which might be expressed in a mission statement. Can a mission statement be considered as a control input and, if so, how is it used to regulate or adapt organisational behaviour?

2.4.1   Decision strategy

In these examples there are implicit decision strategies. Consider two other examples of decision strategies within a control process. One is implemented as a physical mechanism; the other as a set of business rules.

Table 2.1 A set of business rules for car rentals expressed as a decision table

Car group	Compact											
Rental period	D				W				M			
Loyalty member	Y		N		Y		N		Y		N	
>3 days in advance	Y	N	Y	N	Y	N	Y	N	Y	N	Y	N
0%			X	X				X				
5%		X					X					X
10%	X					X					X	
15%					X					X		
20%									X			

In a heating system, thermostats normally act as control subsystems. A thermostat is set at a desired temperature (the control input). It then monitors the temperature of its environment, and when this reaches the set level, it activates to switch off the heating components (such as radiators). Once the temperature in the environment drops back below a defined range, the thermostat activates again, to switch the heating components back on.

A **decision strategy** can be modelled in a number of ways. For instance, it could be represented as a series of If–Then statements, or decision rules. For example, these are the decision rules for the decision strategy embedded in a thermostat:

Decision strategy: A set of rules that implement control inputs

IF sensed temperature < desired temperature THEN open heating valve to increase flow of heat.

IF sensed temperature > desired temperature THEN shut heating valve to reduce flow of heat.

Another way of representing a decision strategy is through a decision table or decision tree. For instance, Table 2.1 shows a set of business rules – that is, rules that regulate behaviour in a business process. They control the process of awarding discounts to customers renting compact cars. You can tell what discount is due by following the path from the appropriate type of car group to the status of an advance booking. So someone renting a compact car for a month, with loyalty membership, and booking at least three days in advance is entitled to a 20 per cent discount.

2.4.2 Control and performance

From this discussion it should be evident that the process of control and the concept of information are inherently inter-linked. This is because in order for a control process to work effectively it must continually monitor the state of the system it is attempting to control. Such monitoring occurs through sensing signals from its operating process. The control process must also contain a model of the system it is attempting to control. Critical to this model will be defined measures of performance. Signals transmitted from the monitoring process are compared against this model and interpreted by the decision strategy. On the basis of the interpretation, decisions are made as to appropriate action and further signals are transmitted back to the operational system to maintain the system's performance within defined parameters.

Thus there is an inherent association between control, performance and measurement. In order to control the performance of a system a control process must 'measure' features of its operating system and compare such measurements against its goals. A control process makes decisions about appropriate action by comparing signals from the operating system against its decision strategy. The performance levels will be defined by higher-level systems and consist of control inputs. Such control inputs in the case of an emergency response service to healthcare incidents would amount to response targets, probably expressed in terms of the time expected for an ambulance to arrive at an incident. In terms of a manufacturing plant such as Goronwy Galvanising, a defined level of performance might be productivity level per manufacturing unit. In terms of the meals on wheels example, performance might be judged in terms of the number of satisfied subscribers.

In systems terms the issue of performance can therefore be judged in terms of the central transformation of the system. Three main types of performance measures can be distinguished around this transformation principle: efficacy, efficiency and effectiveness. Efficacy is a measure of the extent to which a system achieves its intended transformation and is fundamentally a check on the output produced by the system. Efficiency is a measure of the extent to which the system achieves its intended transformation with the minimum use of resources. Fundamentally, measures of efficiency involve a check on the resources (inputs) used to achieve an output. Finally, effectiveness is a measure of the extent to which the system contributes to the purposes of a higher-level system and amounts to a check on its contribution as a subsystem to the purpose of the super-system of which it is a part.

We can also see the three Es in terms of how a transformation process might fail. It might fail to produce desired output: this is a problem of efficacy. It could produce the output but consume excessive resources: this is a problem of efficiency. Finally, the output might not make the required contribution to the wider system: this is a problem of effectiveness.

Let's take a sales department. We might measure its efficacy by examining the number of products sold over a chosen time span. To measure its efficiency we could use productivity measures, such as the number of sales per salesperson. Its effectiveness is determined in relation to its contribution to overall company profitability. The key role of the sales department management is to define and operate these measures in order to control the department's work successfully. This example illustrates that specialist performance management systems in organisations are effectively control systems.

There are, of course, other ways of defining and measuring the performance of activity systems. For instance, it is important to consider ethical issues in relation to the performance of organisations. The emerging area of corporate social responsibility can be seen as an attempt to develop baselines of performance for ethical business activity. For example, many clothing companies have been criticised for their use of child labour in the developing world. To address this issue it would be possible to set a control standard below which an organisation would be seen as an ethical failure.

We shall see in Chapter 12 that the design of an information system is inherently an ethical activity, in that the shape of any ICT system is essentially determined by the values embedded within the activity system it is constructed to support. For instance, an ICT system can be designed to support work that is heavily controlled, repetitive in nature and unfulfilling. Alternatively, ICT systems can be designed with the aim of supporting collaboration, variety and enrichment within work.

> **REFLECT:** It is sometimes difficult to specify precise performance measures for an activity system. What difficulties might be experienced in attempting to specify efficacy, efficiency and effectiveness measures for a business? What sort of performance measures might be set for a voluntary sector organisation such as the meals on wheels service?

2.4.3 Control and communication

The management and systems theorist Peter Senge (Senge, 2006) believes that one of the most important and valuable characteristics of systemic thinking is its ability to handle cycles of cause and effect. This is inherently what is meant by *feedback*. Control is normally exercised within a system through some form of feedback. Outputs from the process of an operational system are fed back to the control process. The control process then adjusts the control signals to the operating process on the basis of its interpretation of the data it receives (Figure 2.5).

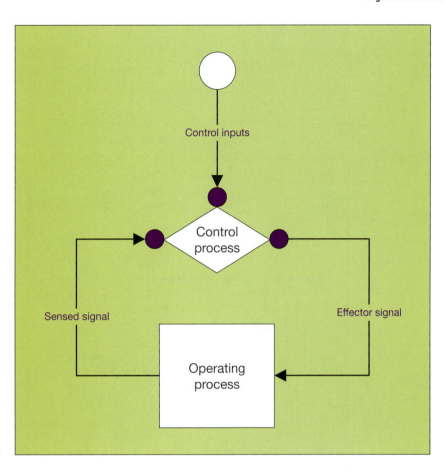

Figure 2.5 *Single-loop feedback*

Negative feedback: A type of feedback in which the control process takes action to reduce the variation between control inputs and sensed inputs

Single-loop feedback: A type of feedback involved in regulating the behaviour of an underlying operational process

Double-loop feedback: A type of feedback which monitors both an underlying control process and the environment and makes adjustments to the control inputs of lower-level controllers if needed

Control is typically exercised through a **negative feedback** loop. Sometimes known as a balancing loop or damping feedback, it involves the control process monitoring the outputs from the operational process through its sensors. The comparators in the monitoring system detect variations from defined levels of performance provided by control inputs. If the outputs vary from established levels then the monitoring subsystem initiates some actions that *reduce* or decrease the variation through its effectors.

For example, a company maintaining cash flow can be conceived of as a system with negative feedback in which the cash balance continually influences company decisions on expenditure and borrowing. Within ambulance control, the deployment of ambulances needs to be continuously adjusted to reflect the location and frequency of emergency incidents.

Negative feedback can be exercised either within a single- or double-loop. **Single-loop feedback** is primarily concerned with regulation. In this type of feedback a single control process monitors variations in the state of an operational process, compares this state against planned levels of performance and takes corrective action to bring performance in line with plan. In single-loop feedback the plans for performance (the control inputs) remain relatively unchanged (Figure 2.5). Sensors only monitor the behaviour of internal processes and effectors only act upon those internal processes.

Double-loop feedback is primarily concerned with adaptation. In this type of feedback the control process must not only monitor variations in the state of an internal process, it must also monitor changes in its environment. Hence, there are two control loops involved and the feedback from the higher-level controller will cause adjustments to the decision strategies of lower-level controllers (Figure 2.6).

Double-loop feedback is consequently a higher-level form of control in that it is essential to ensure that a system adapts effectively to changes in its environment. Double-loop feedback is that form in which the monitoring of lower-level single-feedback control systems as well as

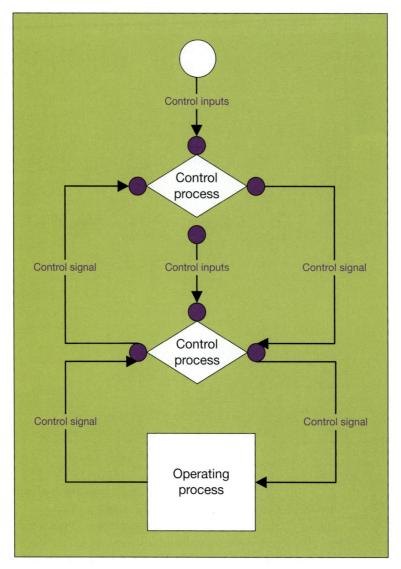

Figure 2.6 Double-loop feedback

monitoring of the environment triggers examination and perhaps revision of the principles on which the control process is established.

Colloquially, double-loop feedback is sometimes referred to as 'thinking outside the box'. At the simplest level, double-loop feedback may cause revisions to the control inputs of lower-level systems. At its most complex, it will involve redesigning the processes and structures on which the lower-level systems are established.

Imagine what would happen if an organisation did not set up double-loop feedback systems for its inventory management. Whatever happened to demand for its products, it would keep on using the same re-order levels and quantities. When demand changed, it would suffer from either excessive levels of stock or stocks running out so that it could not fulfil orders quickly.

Not surprisingly, double-loop feedback is an important characteristic of strategic management in organisations (see Chapter 10). Just as individuals continually learn, organisations also need to continually learn.

RECAP: Control is the process through which a system regulates itself, but also the process by which a system adapts to its environment. Feedback is critical to processes of control. Single-loop feedback implements regulation and double-loop feedback implements adaptation.

2.5   Organisations as systems

Now let us apply the concepts from systemics to the issue of organisations in more detail.

Systems are inherently processes of organisation (order) in a universe of disorganisation (disorder). Systemic thinking is interested in the process of organising as well as the entity of organisation. This entity of organisation (that is, a noun) arises from the process of organising (that is, a verb). Like a river, an organisation as entity is in a continual state of flux. Organisational actions continually recreate the organisation. Organisational action is also the motor for organisational change.

In a typical organisation, actions are to some degree predictable, because they are based on a defined structure of organisational roles and procedures for doing things. In the process of performing their roles and sticking to procedures or routines, organisational actors recreate the organisation. However, there is always a degree of innovation, particularly in times of environmental disturbance, when the organisation has to change or adapt if it is to remain viable. For instance, technological changes evident in the rise of eCommerce (see Chapter 5) have caused some industries (such as the music industry) to totally reassess their actions. In such terms, technological innovation can disrupt the conventional ways in which organisations perform and cause a reassessment of their ways of doing things.

Considered as a whole, an organisation can be seen as a complex system of human activity. Applying the concept of hierarchy, an organisation consists of a collection of inter-related and interdependent subsystems, each of which could also be considered as an organisation in its own right.

Activity systems by their very definition are systems, so we can use the toolkit of systems concepts to help us model existing activity systems and design new ones. We should be able to define the key processes of the system, inputs to each process, outputs from each process and the transformation undertaken by each process. Activity systems in this sense constitute sets of logically related activities by which organisations accomplish goals. For instance, a manufacturing organisation can be considered as a system. It uses inputs (supplies) such as raw materials and labour to produce products which it outputs (sells and distributes). Production as a process consists of a logical set of activities for transforming raw materials into final product.

Open system: A type of system that interacts with its environment

Organisations are **open systems** since they interact with their environment. Business organisations, for instance, interact with a number of actors in the economic environment, including customers, suppliers, partners, competitors and regulators. So organisations are continuously organising – that is to say, they are engaging in a continuous process of interaction with this environment.

To maintain identity an organisation needs to be controlled. This implies that there must be some identifiable control element within each of its activity systems. However, control is not only a process of regulation; it is also a process of adaptation. Control in this dual sense is the essence of the process of organising within activity systems.

For effective control a controller needs a model of the system being controlled, so modelling is useful to deal with the complexity of problem situations. Models make explicit the assumptions underlying the performance in a domain that are normally implicit. Organisational models are useful for management in a number of ways. They help managers better understand the organisation they are responsible for, they aid decision-making and they are useful for managers in learning about the effect of their decisions.

However, managers should not make the mistake of assuming that the model is the system. The model is always an approximation or representation of the system. Generally, it will have much less variety than the system itself. The art of management frequently consists of trying to draw out sufficient essential details of the operation of the system for the purpose of effective control.

Managerial control relies on the effective establishment of organisational sensors, effectors and comparators, which implement performance measurement and monitoring. Information about business processes needs to be compared with the standards set for performance. If there is substantial variation, adjustments need to be made to reduce it. Control within systems relies on feedback, both single-loop and double-loop, so cause and effect in organisational life are frequently circular in nature. Understanding feedback loops is critical, particularly to understanding the unintended consequences of managerial action. This means that organisations need to institute mechanisms not only for single-loop control (focused on regulation) but also for double-loop control (focused on adaptation). Chapter 10 argues that various forms of analysis of the environment are critical to double-loop control.

However, just like the organisation itself, the environment is not a static entity. It is in a state of continual flux, it is a heaving landscape. Actions the organisation takes affect this landscape. In turn the organisation changes to improve its 'fit' with the environmental landscape. For instance, an organisation might pursue a strategy that changes the competitive landscape of its market. Competitors will naturally react, and their actions will cause the organisation to reflect on its strategy, and probably make further changes.

Recently, management theorists have stressed the importance of the speed with which this adaptive process is conducted for organisational survival. They have stressed that business agility is needed in the modern business environment to sense change and respond rapidly to such change. This notion of the agile organisation, sometimes called the agile enterprise, is very much a view of the organisation as a complex, adaptive system.

CASE CHECK

Tesco　　p 455

Tesco plc. can be considered in systems terms. The company originally specialised in food retail. It has now diversified into areas such as discount clothes, consumer electronics, consumer financial services, selling and renting DVDs, compact disks and music downloads, Internet service provision, consumer telecoms, consumer health insurance, consumer dental plans and budget software.

As a food retailer the physical inputs to the organisation are the foodstuffs it receives from its suppliers. Physical outputs consist of foodstuffs sold on to customers. Payments made by customers and to suppliers are examples of data inputs and data outputs respectively. Its key transformation consists of those activity systems involved in supporting the sale of foodstuffs. These activity systems can be considered in a hierarchical fashion. The company will have systems of supply, supermarket operation and financial management that all contribute to the overall purpose of the organisation, which is making a profit for its shareholders. The environment of the organisation consists of the retail industry generally, and supermarket retail specifically. This is illustrated in Figure 2.7.

In terms of the three Es, Tesco efficacy measures are likely to include sales for product groups across different supermarkets. Efficiency measures are likely to include profit margins against product lines, or measures of stock fulfilment against orders in warehouses. Effectiveness measures might include the degree to which new customers are attracted to Tesco supermarkets, old customers continue to come to the stores, and the levels of satisfaction expressed by customers with the level of service they receive.

Tesco operates a number of information systems which contribute to both operational control through single-loop feedback and strategic control through double-loop feedback. For instance, sales of products are recorded at checkouts, and the information updates the data on shelf stock levels, which in turn prompts staff to refill the shelves from the storeroom. This is an example of operational control. Sales to loyalty card holders provide valuable information to the company about which people buy what. This is used for determining which products to sell, at which stores, at which times of the year. This is an example of strategic control.

The idea of a system and the associated concept of control provide two cornerstones for the domain of organisational informatics. This is because the concept of system can be applied both to technology, such as hardware and software ('hard' systems), and to human activity ('soft' systems). The concepts of system and control contributed to the development of modern information and communication technology in the sense that it heavily influenced the design

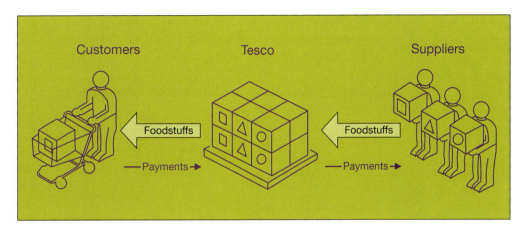

Figure 2.7 *Tesco as a system*

of devices such as the modern computer. Systems thinking also influenced the creation of the communications revolution that underpins the modern Internet. We shall argue that the treatment of organisations as systems underlies much of contemporary thinking within organisational informatics. As a consequence much of the activity in this area is based on the assumption that organisations can be designed by modelling them in system terms and implementing new processes within organisations to improve performance. Within such approaches, ICT is seen as a key agent for organisational change. But we shall argue that an organisation such as a business is not just one system, it is a complex of a least three different types of system: activity systems, information systems and data systems.

RECAP: Organisations can be considered as complex, adaptive systems. Management can be seen to be the process of controlling organisations. Operational management is involved in the regulation of internal processes through single-loop feedback. Strategic management can be seen as concerned with ensuring the adaptation of organisations through a process of double-loop feedback.

2.6 Business action

In a previous section we saw how the term organisation can be treated either as a noun or as a verb. As a noun, the term refers to a social structure or an institution. As a verb, organisation refers to the collection of actions undertaken by people and machines.

We also saw how organisation as institution is created from organisation as action. In systems terms, the properties of an organisation as institution can be seen to emerge from the continuous and complex patterns of activity undertaken by people and machines. It is possible to distinguish between three types of action that inter-relate and help build organisation. We shall call these three types performative, informative and formative action and will demonstrate how these three types of action are critical to the idea of treating organisations as systems.

2.6.1 Performative action and activity systems

Performative action: Action which involves actors transforming objects with tools

Performative acts normally correspond to the 'work' of people in collective interaction, typically using 'tools' to transform 'objects' in the world. Hence, performative acts typically occur in sequences where one performative act is reliant upon the completion of one or more other performative acts. A set of such coherent activities that repeat on a regular basis is sometimes called an organisational routine. We refer to such sets of activities as a performative pattern and suggest that performative patterns are the component elements of an activity system.

Hence, we can describe the primary activity system of the Goronwy Galvanising case we considered in Chapter 1 as consisting of the following performative patterns: receive black material, check black material, galvanise material, check white material, dispatch white material. Each of these patterns can be considered an activity system in itself. Hence, receive black material is likely to consist of the following performative acts: receive delivery, unload batch, prepare batch for checking.

2.6.2   Informative action and information systems

Organisations consist of many different people undertaking many different types of performative action on a continuous basis. To coordinate the performance of a multitude of different actors, communication is needed between them. Hence, along with the patterning of performative activity in organisations there will be a patterning of communication and decision-making and we refer to such a form of order as **informative acts** and informative patterns. Informative patterns are the component elements of information systems.

> **Informative action:** Action involving communication, directed towards coordination

Informative acts involve the transmission and receipt of messages. An informative act is some aspect of performance designed by one actor, the sender of a message, to influence the performance of another actor, the receiver of that message. As we shall see in the next chapter, organisational actors normally communicate in a limited number of ways: they make assertions about how things are; they direct the actions of others; they make commitments about what they intend to do; they express how they feel about particular things; and they declare that something is the case.

For instance, within Goronwy an inbound logistics operative might make the statement to the plant manager, '*15% of all the black material we received over the last year was non-conforming*'. Similarly, the plant manager might request of his production controller, '*Please ensure that all conforming black material is galvanised on its day of delivery*'. He might also make the following commitment to the company's major customer Blackwalls: '*We promise to turnaround all products within a three day period*'. Finally, a production operative might declare, '*That batch Z has been galvanised*'.

2.6.3   Formative action and data systems

Much communication in modern-day organisations still occurs through use of speech. Informative acts consist of spoken statements such as, '*please take this customer order*', '*I will process this customer order*', or '*this customer order has been processed*'. However, there is one big problem with relying upon speech as the medium for communication supporting the coordination of performance, the spoken word does not persist. When someone says something, the sounds he or she makes, dissipate in the air soon after they are spoken.

As we have seen in even the simple case of the meals on wheels service, people soon need to make and maintain records of things. The key purpose of such records is to extend and compensate for the limitations of human memory. Records represent things of interest to a particular information and activity system. They represent things such as what has happened or should happen; they record who has done what and when, or who has indicated that they will do something.

> **Formative action:** Action directed towards representation

The making and maintenance of records is what we shall refer to as **formative action**. Formative action involves the manipulation of data structures such as business forms or database tables. Such formative actions normally occur in patterns such as transactions. We refer to a coherent collection of such formative patterns as a data system.

As we discussed in the previous chapter, Goronwy Galvanising relied upon three critical business forms prior to computerisation in the 1980s: delivery advice notes, job sheets and dispatch advice notes. The flow of such documents served to inform the coordination of activity within this company and constituted the data system at Goronwy. The storage of such forms in files acted as a record, or collective memory, of activity which either had occurred or should occur.

Nowadays of course, many aspects of data systems rely upon ICT to a great extent. For instance, the paper-based data system at Goronwy was the basis on which the company began to develop an ICT system. The data structures of paper-based forms were eventually transformed into the data structures used by a database.

2.6.4   Business organisation

In an operational sense, there are four inter-related questions that all organisations, particularly business organisations, must answer:

- What do we do?
- What do we need to know to do things?
- How do we communicate what we know?
- How do we represent what we do, know and communicate?

These questions correspond to questions about performance, communication and representation. They therefore relate to activity systems, information systems and data systems. Business organisation is accomplished through the inter-related patterning of activity, communication and representation. In this chapter, we focus upon activity systems and demonstrate ways of understanding and modelling activity systems. In further chapters we return to the nature of information and data systems, as well as to the relationships between these three types of system.

2.6.5   Patterns as resources

Pattern: Elements which repeat across situations

An organisation as a complex, adaptive system relies upon the process of structuration which we described in an earlier section. Organisational actors engage in performative, informative and formative action and through these actions produce an organisational structure. They also draw upon the structure as **patterns** of action in creating further action. Therefore such performative, informative and formative patterns act as resources for individuals in building action.

Consider the case of Goronwy Galvanising. A particular organisational actor is normally assigned a role, such as that of an inbound logistics operative. Such roles are part of the organisational structure of Goronwy and define a range of expectations about what this type of actor should do. Specific persons assigned this role draw upon these expectations to help them perform their job. But in performing their job they are actually re-creating or re-producing the role of inbound logistics operative.

Such ideas help to explain how a number of institutional properties of organisations are created: the division of labour, organisational roles, the chain of command and control, and organisational routines.

The division of labour refers to the way in which expected actions are bundled together within defined roles and assigned to particular people. Roles define expected behaviours and responsibilities that cross performative, informative and formative patterns. In other words, a role defines what people should do, how they should communicate about what they do and how they should represent such communication.

The chain of command and control refers to established relationships of power and authority, in other words, who is whose boss. As we shall see, the chain of control is created through the way in which decision-making is located in particular roles and how people in such roles direct the actions of others. Certain aspects of this may be formalised as an organisation chart.

Most medium- to large-scale organisations have explicit rules and procedures which set down expected ways of working. These procedures specify many, but not all, of the routines or patterns of activity that people use to guide their actions. Many patterns of activity within organisations are not written down, they have become established over periods of time as expected ways of doing things.

RECAP: Any organisation clearly consists of a multitude of business actors. Three distinct but inter-related forms of action are undertaken by such actors and these three forms of action serve to accomplish what we mean by organisation. Actors engage in instrumental activity, make decisions and communicate about and represent aspects of such activity in records.

However, business actors do not normally act in isolation. Their actions are normally entangled with or bound to the actions of other actors and, as such, form coherent patterns. What we mean by organisation consists of the patterning of performance, communication and representation by multiple actors. Such patterning produces or accomplishes the order characteristic of human organisation and produces its institutional properties.

2.7   Business analysis and business modelling

Business analysis: The analysis of business systems

To understand business organisation and determine how it should change to adapt to its environment we engage in **business analysis**. Business analysis involves taking a system perspective on organisations and building models of such systems to better understand not only how things are but also how we would like things to be. We therefore undertake business modelling for a number of reasons.

- It allows the modeller to abstract certain features of a situation or phenomenon, and in this sense simplify a business situation.
- It enables the modeller to represent these key features in an agreed formal way.
- The model helps people to communicate and share a set of common understandings about a phenomenon.

A good example is a tube or metro map. The first diagrammatic map of the London Underground was designed by Harry Beck in 1933. Beck was an employee of the London Underground who realised that the exact physical location of stations was irrelevant to travellers who just wanted to know how to get from one station to another. They are interested in the topology of the system, in other words, how the stations are connected. So he drew up a map which was effectively a model of the actual underground railway network. It highlights or abstracts the key features, and represents them as a series of circles (for stations) and coloured line segments (for tube lines). It does not show the distances between stations in proportion, but it does show the features that many users want.

Ontology: A systematic model of an area of existence

Business analysis uses the language of systems to build what artificial intelligence (AI) researchers and software engineers call ontologies. An **ontology** is a term borrowed from philosophy: it means a systematic account or model of an area of existence, which logicians often call the universe, or domain, of discourse. In organisations, for instance, the universe of discourse might consist of employees, products, customers and suppliers, and the relationships and flows between these elements (see also Chapter 3).

There are three main activities of modelling systems in this way:

- First, defining the boundary of a system: what is considered part of the system and what is considered part of its environment.
- Second, defining the hierarchy in the system: assigning structure and behaviour to subsystems, sub-subsystems and so on.
- Third, defining the elements of the system: such as processes, control and flows, as well as the relationships between elements.

Before we consider these issues in the modelling of activity systems, let us consider the relationship between models and reality.

DID YOU KNOW? Business analysis is a significant activity within modern business practice and the term business analysis now appears to have subsumed and somewhat expanded upon the earlier term, *systems analysis*. A number of universities around the world offer modules and courses with the term business analysis as either part of or the whole of their title. There is also now a professional association of business analysts (*International Institute of Business Analysis*). The Institute has produced a handbook documenting what it refers to as a 'body of knowledge', which it uses to accredit business analysis professionals.

2.7.1   Models and reality

There are two alternative positions that define the relationship between a model and reality, which are sometimes called objective and subjective positions.

In an objective position, reality is assumed to be independent of the observer and also to display systemic characteristics. A model in this view is an abstraction of reality, a representation of objective features, that is, features that are agreed on by all observers. The aim for the modeller is to achieve as close a correspondence as possible between the model and reality. We have already described this position as characteristic of the institutional perspective on organisations.

In a subjective position, reality is assumed to be different for different persons. Reality is necessarily subjective, it is argued, because systems do not exist in the world as such; they are a concept, a lens through which we see the world. A system model in this perspective is therefore a tool or lens for debating with reality. The aim is to achieve inter-subjective agreement, mutual understanding and possible joint action. This position is particularly adopted in the action perspective on organisations.

These positions can be appropriate for different forms of reality. Generally speaking, an objective position has proved appropriate for modelling the physical world, and an inter-subjective position for modelling the social world. Since organisations are social constructions, we take a broadly inter-subjective position in this book. So it is assumed here that modelling activity systems, information systems and ICT systems involves negotiation between the differing worldviews (see below) of the stakeholders in the organisation as system.

> **REFLECT:** How important is modelling to the effective management of organisations? Suggest some ways in which having a good model of an aspect of an organisation helps decision-making. What role should managers play in helping form consistent worldviews of problem situations among organisational stakeholders?

2.7.2   Stakeholders

Stakeholder: A person or group that has some claim on an organisational problem and its solution

It follows from this that organisational systems are defined through inter-subjective agreement between **stakeholder** groups (stakeholders, for short). Mason and Mitroff (Mason and Mitroff, 1981) provided one of the earliest definitions of the term stakeholder: '*all those claimants inside and outside the organisation who have a vested interest in the problem and its solution*'. What they call a problem, Peter Checkland (Checkland, 1999) calls a problem situation: a situation in organisational life that is regarded by at least one person as a problem. The French use the term *problematique* to describe a network of inter-related problems, while the systems theorist Russell Ackoff referred to complex **problem situations** as 'messes'. Facing up to the problem situation are some 'would-be improvers' of it: that is, people looking for a solution. These are the stakeholders for the system in question.

Problem situation: A situation in organisational life that is regarded by at least one person as a problem

2.7.3   Worldviews and organisational culture

Defining a system, and deciding what is in it, and what is in its environment, depends on the viewpoint of the stakeholder. Stakeholders are normally groups of people to whom a particular system is relevant. As well as having different ideas about the boundaries of the system, they can also differ about what its key elements and its intended purpose are. These differences tend to reflect their differing worldviews.

Consider a manufacturing enterprise. A customer might see it as a system to meet customer demand for a particular range of products, within resource constraints. A shareholder might see it as a system for transforming business needs into a satisfactory return on investment. A shop-floor employee might describe it as a system to achieve maximum utilisation of resources while maintaining secure employment and acceptable working conditions.

Worldview: A set of underlying assumptions held by a particular stakeholder group

A **worldview** then is a set of underlying assumptions used by individuals and groups in understanding and constructing the world. This has much in common with Vickers' concept of an appreciative system (Vickers, 1965). This is '*the interconnected set of largely tacit standards of judgement by which we both order and value our experience*'. He argues that decision-making depends on the different appreciative systems that decision makers bring to bear on a problem, and that the stability of organisations depends largely on shared appreciative systems.

Appreciative systems in turn have much in common with the concept of organisational culture. A culture is the set of behaviours expected in a social group. We all know that any long-standing social group develops its own set of expected behaviours or norms, and people frequently speak of differences of culture between nation-states or regions. More recently commentators on organisations have suggested that differences in organisational culture are important.

It is also a dangerous simplification to assume that all organisations have a single culture. In practice, medium- to large-scale organisations are likely to feature a number of interacting subcultures. Subculture refers to a subgroup within a broader social unit (such as an organisation), who shares sets of meanings (a worldview) that is not the same as, and distinguishes its members from, the wider group and culture around them. Subcultures can grow up in structural units (such as departments) or within different stakeholder groups (managers, shop-floor employees, shareholders).

For example, in a utility company with which the author was involved two distinct groups of workers displayed quite different subcultures, even though the work performed by both groups was actually very similar and both groups were sited very close together in the headquarters of the utility company. Both groups of people were lines-people, that is, workers with responsibility for inspecting, maintaining and repairing parts of the utility network. However, one group of lines-people serviced low-power electricity lines while the other group serviced high-power lines. The low-power lines people worked as a group with decisions about which lines to service and what maintenance to be conducted made at the centre. In contrast the high-power lines-people worked very much as individuals with maintenance decisions delegated to the lines-people themselves. Part of the rationale provided for such differences in behaviour was the dangerous nature of the high-power line maintenance and the consequent need for a delegation of authority.

> **REFLECT:** What different stakeholders are involved in Tesco as a system? What differing worldviews of the company might these stakeholders hold?

2.7.4   Organisations as soft systems

Soft system: A social system that is designed to meet certain objectives

A human activity system (or activity system for short) is what Checkland refers to as a **soft system**. It is a type of social system that is 'designed' to meet certain defined objectives. Activity systems are soft because:

- their boundaries or scope may be fluid
- their purpose is likely to be open to interpretation, depending on the stakeholder viewpoint or worldview
- the definition of precisely what control (see below) means in the context, and therefore exact measures of performance, depends on the worldviews of stakeholders.

Organisations are different from mere collections of people, or social groups in general, in the sense that they are normally established for a purpose, usually to produce value of some form. Organisations are typically seen as needing clear identities to establish a context for action. However, organisational purpose is a dynamic, not a static, issue. Purpose is continually negotiated, understood and disseminated throughout the organisation by its stakeholders.

The purpose of an organisation is typically formulated in terms of its mission. One popular way to define this is to list the key competencies the organisation needs, that is, those things the organisation must do well. The idea is that these define critical levers for ensuring the viability and sustainability of the organisation.

As should be evident from this, identifying the stakeholders in a system is critical to understanding the system itself. However, building a coherent and inter-subjective worldview (in management-speak, a vision) is important to the organisation.

Let's take a sawmill and consider how different stakeholders might see it. An industrial engineer might view it as a production system, and a management scientist as a profit-maximising system. The industrial engineer will be interested in how it transforms logs into finished products, using resources such as plant and machinery, and will probably be studying it to determine effective control procedures for the production process (to decide where machinery is placed, the way in which products are handled and so on).

The management scientist would probably be less interested in the physical activities of this sawmill than in their financial consequences. They might see it as a series of subsystems, such as a log handling and storage subsystem, a finished goods and warehousing subsystem, a marketing subsystem and a financial control subsystem, and be interested mostly in the way each subsystem communicated its needs to other subsystems, and how the flow of goods and information affected the financial performance of the firm. The system's environment in this case consists of the market for logs, the market for finished wood products and other elements such as the financial, labour and legal environment of the firm.

2.7.5   Equifinality and organisational design

Equifinality: The idea that a system can be designed to fulfil its purpose in a number of different ways

Wright (1989) defines an important property of open systems, such as organisations, as **equifinality**. This means that an open system can achieve its goals or purpose in a number of different ways. So there are likely to be several different ways of designing and organising an activity system to meet defined objectives (in other words to optimise performance against established measures). One consequence is that it should be possible to set objectives (or goals, or targets) for an activity system and establish clear criteria for measuring performance.

The objective in most organisations is to design activity systems to support core organisational competencies. A general assumption is that most organisations consist of a limited number of activity systems which contribute to fulfilling their key mission or strategy. So there is a clear link between the design and operation of activity systems, and the planning of organisational strategy (see also Chapter 10).

Sub-optimisation: The idea that optimising the performance of a particular subsystem will not necessarily optimise the performance of the whole system

But when engaging in any organisational design we must take note of a key principle of systemic thinking, **sub-optimisation**. Optimising the performance of one subsystem within an organisation will not necessarily optimise the performance of the system as a whole; it could even worsen it. ICT, for instance, can be used in the design, or redesign, of business systems. For many years the tendency was to replace existing activity systems, automating them in whole or in part. More recently the emphasis has been on seeing ICT as an agency to innovate new forms of activity system. But improvements in technology do not guarantee improvements in activity. As we shall see in Chapter 9 there are many examples of ICT innovation that have caused organisational failure. This means, importantly, that activity systems, information systems and ICT (data) systems should be designed in parallel to achieve optimal performance (see Chapter 12).

CASE CHECK
Tesco   p 455

Tesco is primarily in the business of selling foodstuffs to customers. Its declared mission is to 'create value for customers to earn their lifetime loyalty'. Its strategy is based on offering a range of different types of stores, understanding its customers and treating its employees well. Tesco introduced its loyalty card for customers a number of years ago. Value for this company might therefore include the additional value services available to loyalty card customers, such as discounting of goods.

We can demonstrate the equifinality characteristic of activity systems by considering two alternative models for food retail. Tesco supermarkets operate a traditional model of supermarket retail designed to manage the flow of physical goods from suppliers to customers. This involves maintaining a large floor-space stocked with products. Customers travel to the supermarket, pick products from the shelves and transport them home themselves (see Figure 2.8). Tesco then introduced online retail. This uses a different design for the activity system. Customers order goods through a website. A picking list is produced for a store operative who walks around a store and picks products to satisfy the customer order. The customer shopping basket is crated and delivered by van to the customer's home, in return for a delivery charge. A limited service is available, whereby customers can avoid the delivery charge by picking up crated goods from the local store themselves.

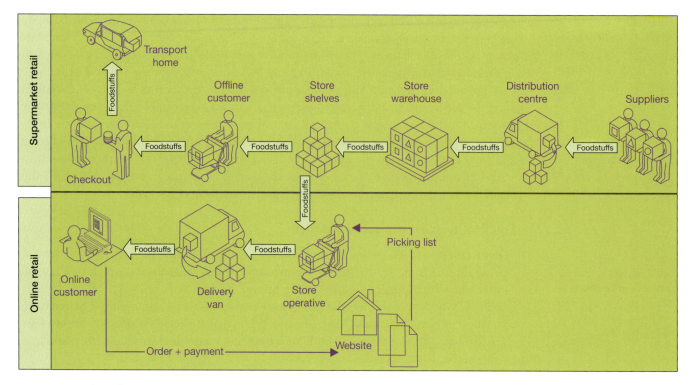

Figure 2.8 *Food retail as two activity systems*

2.7.6   Modelling problem situations and worldviews

Rich picture: A graphical representation of key elements of a problem situation

Checkland suggests that the starting point for modelling activity systems is to consider the problem situation as the context for the system, and represent the environment, stakeholders, concerns and issues in this problem situation as a 'rich picture'. **Rich pictures** are deliberately loose or informal. There is no standard notation for rich pictures, it is up to the modeller. Instead, they attempt to capture the essence of a complex situation within which some stakeholders perceive a problem, and some form of business analysis work needs to take place.

CASE CHECK

UK National Identity Card

In 2002 there was an attempt to introduce a national identity card in the UK. This scheme was eventually abandoned in 2010 after over a decade of planning and implementation. Figure 2.9 presents the identity cards case as a problem situation and helps to make plain some of the reasons why this scheme was abandoned. Within this case there are clear examples of stakeholders holding differing perspectives as to what constituted the 'problem' and whether technologies for personal identity management were an appropriate solution to such problems. The UK government and its agencies saw an identity card as a tool contributing to the battle against terrorism, illegal working and identity fraud. It therefore enacted an Identity Cards Act and produced a scheme to create a national identity management infrastructure for the UK. The private sector and law enforcement agencies were generally supportive of the government's intentions and were keen to use aspects of the identity infrastructure to help combat identity-related crime. The ICT sector saw significant work opportunities in the programme. They also relished the prospect of the proposed infrastructure raising the skills profile of the UK in the area of personal identity management technologies.

Root definition: A way of representing the perspectives of key stakeholders as to the core purpose of some activity system

The ideas that stakeholders hold of a particular activity system can be modelled more precisely using a root definition. This expresses the core purpose of an activity system, in terms of the classic input–process–output model. Checkland has suggested that most useful **root definitions** consist of six elements, which make up the acronym CATWOE:

■ Customers: the victims or beneficiaries of the transformation
■ Actors: those who would do the transformation

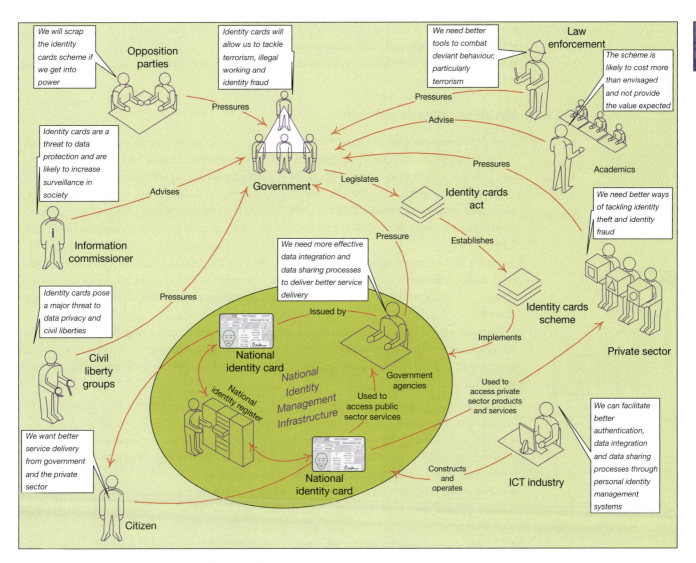

Figure 2.9 *A rich picture of the national identity card situation*

- Transformation: the conversion of input to output
- Worldview: the worldview which makes the transformation meaningful
- Owners: those that could stop the transformation
- Environmental constraints: elements outside the system which it takes as given.

The core of CATWOE is the pairing of transformation with the worldview, which makes it meaningful. There will always be a number of different transformations through which any activity system can be expressed, derived from different interpretations, or worldviews, of its purpose. The other elements of the acronym add ideas of key stakeholder types and their role in the system: someone must undertake the purposeful activity, someone could stop it and someone will be its victim or beneficiary. The system will also take some environmental constraints as a given.

As an example, suppose we built a rich picture of a university in which we identify its key stakeholders as being students, academic staff and administrative staff. Each will potentially hold a different worldview about the purpose of this system. For example, a student's world-view of a university might be:

- Customer = myself as a student
- Actors = other students, academic staff and administrative staff
- Transformation = the process of education: attending modules, achieving satisfactory assessments and getting a degree

- Worldview = that higher education is a passage to better job prospects
- Owners = the academic and administrative staff
- Environment = the higher education system: other universities and higher education institutions.

2.7.7   Modelling activities and control

Root definitions provide the material for constructing conceptual models of purposeful activity for managers. They specify the minimum activities needed to support the key transformation process, and their key relations can be shown graphically, as we shall see.

The modeller starts with the key transformation of the system. Let's use the example of a university once more, where this might be 'the process of education'. This transformation is shown as an activity or process (or a series of activities or processes) in a diagram (see Figure 2.10).

The modeller might then consider in turn the inputs and outputs for each of the processes added. However, a conceptual model at this stage is a high-level model of the activity system. The usual rule is to limit the number of processes or activities shown to a maximum of seven.

We next need to consider the issue of control. This means answering the questions: how do we assess the key purpose of the activity system? and how do we implement this purpose in terms of the three Es of performance? This involves specifying four additional types of activity or process to the model:

- Planning activities: which supply criteria for assessing performance in terms of the resources to be used and how they will be measured (that is, control inputs)
- Control processes (comparators): which need to be in place to assess performance against criteria set; such processes put into practice the decision-making strategies that are necessary to assess the performance of an operational process
- Monitoring processes (sensors): which collect measurements of activities against performance criteria set; these are necessary to supply performance information to control processes
- Change processes (effectors): that are needed to regulate operational activities.

These processes need to be joined together with appropriate dependencies. In our example (see Figure 2.11), each of the main operational activities might need to be controlled. For instance, the university might set recruitment targets for each of the schools or faculties under its umbrella. It will take action if actual levels of recruitment do not match the targets, perhaps with greater investment in recruitment campaigns for particular courses.

The complete model for this example is shown as Figure 2.12. This could be used as the basis for a more detailed process analysis and design exercise (something that is looked at later in the book).

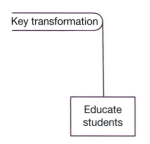

Figure 2.10 *The key transformation*

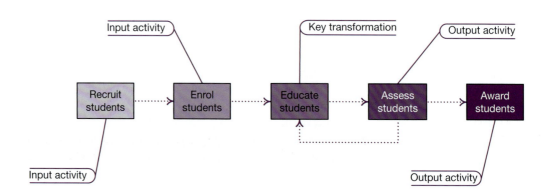

Figure 2.11 *Inputs to and outputs from the key transformation*

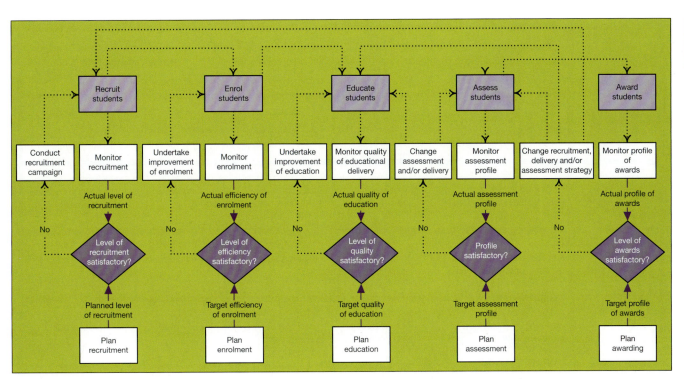

Figure 2.12 *The complete activity model*

2.8   Modelling processes

In a previous section we described how we can consider any system as a hierarchy. An organisation, for instance, can be considered as a series of inter-related activity systems. Each activity system can be considered, in turn, as a series of activities or processes. And further, each process or activity can be considered as a series of inter-related tasks.

It therefore becomes possible to apply the same modelling approach to different levels of the hierarchy. We can attempt to model entire organisations, particular activity systems, or specific processes. Because of issues of complexity we considered earlier, much business analysis work focuses on specific business processes rather than entire organisations.

To reiterate, modelling is important, not only for understanding how organisations work now, but for designing new ways of working. In this section we review the **modelling notation** we have introduced in an informal way in previous sections. In doing so we shall hint at the need to model the role of information systems and ICT in support of business activity. These issues will be considered in more detail in further chapters.

Modelling notation: A way of representing the constructs of a model

2.8.1   Modelling constructs and notation

Any form of modelling needs three elements:

- constructs: the components of the modelling approach
- notation: the way we choose to represent the constructs in the model, which could be textual, graphical and/or mathematical (although it is usually graphical in informatics work because graphics are easy to use and a good way of communicating with others)
- principles: the formal and informal rules for constructing the model correctly.

Although modelling is essential in informatics work, there is no agreement on the most appropriate way of modelling organisational systems. We have hinted at one way of doing it through many of the figures in this chapter, though, and now we shall look at this more closely and completely. It is based loosely on Business Process Modelling Notation (BPMN),

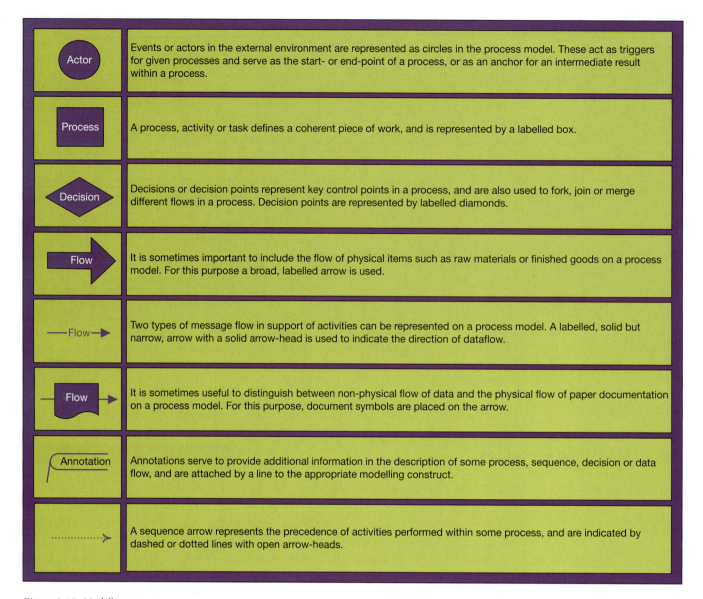

Figure 2.13 Modelling constructs

which was developed by the Business Process Management Initiative and is now maintained by the Object Management Group. Its aim is to provide a standard notation that is readily understandable by a variety of business stakeholders, including business analysts who create and refine business processes, technical developers responsible for implementing the ICT systems they need, and business managers who manage and control them. (The BPMN notation has been modified in this book to fit better with the modelling techniques discussed in other chapters.) It is summarised in Figure 2.13.

2.8.2   Two examples of process modelling

As one example, a possible process for managing inventory is illustrated as a model in Figure 2.14. The entire process is made up of a workflow of defined activities. The control processes are embedded as key decision points. You can see a clear feedback process at the decision point, stock level > re-order level: if false (that is, the answer is no), this generates an order for new stock. It should also be clear that the activities both rely on information and generate information.

But **process modelling** is not just applicable to the private sector. Figure 2.15 is an example of process modelling from the public sector, dealing with the apparently simple issue of

Process modelling:
Specifying how the activity system in some existing area works

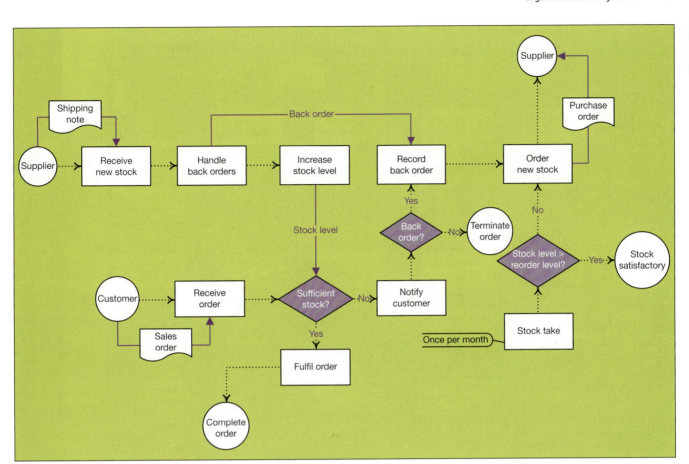

Figure 2.14 Inventory management process

conducting a civil marriage, and showing how it has cross-organisational and inter-organisational consequences. Deciding to get married sets off a train of information-handling and other activities. First, details of the two partners need to be set down on an application form, then this is verified against approved documentation such as birth certificates and passports. Once the application is approved, a ceremony is booked and conducted. After the ceremony, a further train of information-handling takes place. The couple need a marriage certificate, and they are likely to need to update other records because of their change of status, and/or name, and/or residence.

The model is useful because it makes many aspects of this process explicit. First, it details the flow of activity: planning for the ceremony, conducting it, and all the post-marriage formalities. Second, it details the control embedded in the process, by a number of decision points. Third, it highlights the important way in which the input of information is critical. It also shows information outputs at various points.

It is also interesting to note how many organisations are involved in this model. Although a civil registrar (in the UK system) deals with much of the activity, various other public sector organisations are also involved, for example, driver and vehicle licensing (if there is a change of name or address), voting registries and tax collection agencies. So we could use this as a first step in considering how these agencies could better integrate their processes and information systems to provide a more effective public service.

2.8.3 Business patterns

In a previous section we described organisations as being made from three inter-related forms of system. We also discussed how each of these forms of system consists of a set of patterns. Hence, an activity system consists of a set of performative patterns – a set of ways of performing organisational activities to achieve collective goals.

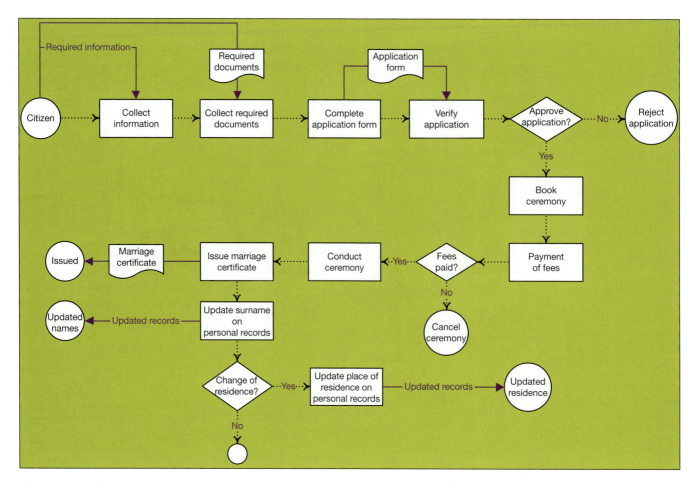

Figure 2.15 *Civil marriage process*

This idea of a pattern has had much influence in other disciplines. For instance, the American architect Christopher Alexander (Alexander, 1964) proposed that architectural design is based on a number of archetypal patterns. These patterns define a number of fundamental principles of building design. Within software engineering design patterns are proposed as general solutions to programming problems.

This way of thinking about organisations as a web of patterns is particularly useful because it suggests that patterns cross organisations; that certain patterns of activity occur time and again in different organisations. Modelling approaches such as the one discussed in this chapter can be used to capture such patterns and these patterns can help guide or direct the design or redesign of activity.

2.8.4   Process design

Process design: Specifying how a new activity system should work for a domain

The mapping of civil marriage in the previous section demonstrates how the analysis of business process using process modelling usually done with the objective of redesigning such processes.

In a typical design process there are five phases: mapping, selection, redesign, specification and implementation. The first three consist of unfreezing activities, in the sense that they involve studying inadequacies in the current system and planning new ways of doing things. The last two stages consist of freezing activities, in the sense that they involve specifying a new process in some detail, then implementing it.

The first stage involves constructing a high-level map of organisational processes and indicating key process boundaries on it; such as the one in Figure 2.12 which represents the high-level processes involved in university teaching. To do this, a form of modelling notation is normally used, such as the one used in this chapter.

From the process map, it should be possible to prioritise processes to be considered for redesign. Three sets of criteria can be used to rank processes in this manner:

- The health of the process: does it work well, or is it dysfunctional? The key question is, which processes are in the deepest trouble? Indicators include extensive information exchange, redundancy of work and information, and unnecessary iteration of tasks.
- The criticality of the process: how important is it to the core competencies of the organisation? The key question here is: which processes have the greatest impact on performance? The aim is to find processes that offer the greatest potential for improving organisational performance.
- The feasibility of redesign: this may involve questions of cost, or issues such as whether redesign is politically and culturally feasible in the organisation.

Having selected a process to redesign then a team of people identify the problems with the existing process, challenge assumptions about ways of doing things, and brainstorm new approaches to organisational activity. Design workshops are held and various system stakeholders participate. Business patterns used by other organisations or industries may be examined and reused.

In the process of redesign the team need to model in detail both the existing processes and specify the design of new ones, using the kind of modelling we discussed earlier.

Finally, the new process needs to be implemented. This is probably the most difficult phase of process redesign, and involves introducing both new work practices and associated technologies. We return to this issue in Chapter 12.

FOCUS ON VALUE

This chapter has shown the value of the concept of systems for considering organisations as both institutions and complex networks of individuals engaging in action. From either perspective, an organisation can be seen as a value-creating system, but how we identify and describe it depends on the worldviews, or different appreciative systems, of stakeholders both within and outside the organisation.

Worldviews or appreciative systems are essentially ways of valuing the world. For instance, our view of the purpose of the organisation-as-system will colour how we assess its performance, and how we design and implement processes of control.

All managers work with models, but these are frequently tacit or implicit. This book argues that it is important to model organisations explicitly. It introduces a number of different techniques or approaches for this. Modelling makes plain our understanding of how organisations work, or should work. This can then be communicated and it can also be criticised.

2.9 Conclusion and key themes

This chapter considered the important context for informatics work, the organisation. It began by considering some classic viewpoints on the organisation, and distinguished between the institutional perspective and the action perspective. It focused on considering organisations as complex, adaptive systems. This unifying perspective allows us to see an organisation as both an institution and a collection of individuals collaborating to achieve a common purpose.

The concept of a system has had a profound influence on informatics. This is seen, for instance, in the label 'information system': the primary bridge between human activity and ICT. The system concept is applied both to technology such as hardware and software ('hard' systems) and to human activity ('soft' systems). Information systems today are key examples of hybrid or sociotechnical systems (Emery and Trist, 1960).

Systems concepts have heavily influenced the design of modern computer technology. Systems thinking also influenced the creation of the communications revolution that underpins the Internet and the World Wide Web.

Systemic thinking underlies much contemporary thinking and work on business organisations, because it offers practical ways of engaging with organisational life. Most organisations can be modelled or analysed in systems terms. The aim of this is to identify deficiencies in current systems, then design new systems that can improve organisational performance. From this perspective, both information systems and ICT are key enablers for organisational change.

In Chapter 3 we consider another of the foundation concepts for informatics, information. We relate this concept to a number of issues arising from our treatment of organisations: the relationship of information to data and knowledge, the role of information in decision-making and action, and the relationship of management to all these issues.

2.10   Review test

1 What are the two major perspectives on organisational life? Select two.
- [ ] Institutional perspective
- [ ] Bureaucratic perspective
- [ ] Action perspective
- [ ] Social perspective

2 Select the two statements that most accurately define the concept of structuration.
- [ ] Social structures never change
- [ ] Through human interaction social structures are reproduced and may also change
- [ ] Social structures do not exist independently of people
- [ ] Social structures constrain and inform human action

3 A _____ is an organised collection of things with emergent properties and some defined purpose. Fill in the blank.

4 Systemics considers things by dissecting things into parts, understanding the way in which parts work, and through this building an understanding of the working of the whole. True or false?
- [ ] True
- [ ] False

5 A bicycle considered as a set of parts would be regarded as a system. True or false?
- [ ] True
- [ ] False

6 Feedback has two major forms: single-loop and _____ feedback. Fill in the blank.

7 The key elements of any system are inputs, outputs and what else? Select one.
- [ ] Process
- [ ] Agent
- [ ] Subsystem

8 Systems can generally be seen to be composed of _____. Hierarchy is an inherent property of any system. Fill in the blank.

9 Variety refers to how flexible a system is? True or false?
- [ ] True
- [ ] False

10 Control enables a system to: Select all that apply
- [ ] Regulate its behaviour
- [ ] Improve its performance
- [ ] Adapt to its environment

11 A control process is composed of: Select all that apply.
- [ ] Sensors
- [ ] Processes
- [ ] Comparators
- [ ] Effectors

12 The UK is a parliamentary democracy and hence is reliant on an effective electoral system. The key inputs into the electoral system are ballot poll cards and ballot papers, provided by the key actors, voters. The key outputs are a set of election results for each constituency in the UK. The key control process is electoral monitoring which establishes guidance on expected electoral practice and monitors any deviation from this practice. The environment of the electoral system is the overall political system in the UK.

On a separate sheet, draw a high-level representation of this system.

13 Organisations are best described as what type of system? Select one.
- ☐ Closed
- ☐ Open
- ☐ Physical

14 Equifinality means that a system can achieve its purpose in a number of different ways? True or false?
- ☐ True
- ☐ False

15 The performance of any system is frequently expressed in terms of the three Es. Select the three most appropriate terms.
- ☐ Efficiency
- ☐ Effectiveness
- ☐ Enabling
- ☐ Efficacy

16 Three types of inter-related business systems typically build organisation. Select three.
- ☐ Information system
- ☐ Data system
- ☐ Accounting system
- ☐ Activity system

17

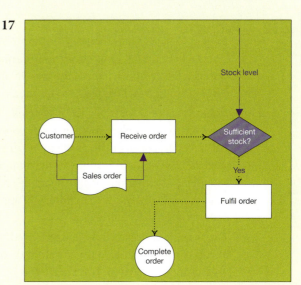

Using the extract from the process model of an inventory management system above, match the modelling construct to its label. Pair each lettered entry with the corresponding numbered entry.

a. Sales order   1. Process
b. Customer   2. Decision point
c. Receive order   3. Document flow
d. Sufficient stock?   4. External actor

18 Process design involves the specification of a new business process? True or false?
- ☐ True
- ☐ False

2.11 Exercises

- ▸ Consider an organisation known to you. Describe it first as an institution and then try to describe it as a series of activities.
- ▸ Identify one activity system known to you, and identify its key components.
- ▸ Investigate the control processes you would expect in an organisation such as a university. What are the appropriate sensors, comparators and effectors in this control process?
- ▸ Consider an educational organisation, such as a school or university, as a system. Try to identify some possible subsystems.
- ▸ There are various ways of classifying systems besides open or closed. Try to identify a number of other system types and give examples of each type.
- ▸ Consider some problem situation in an organisation known to you. What elements would you include in a rich picture of this problem situation?

- ▸ Investigate a process of interest to a university such as the enrolment of students. Develop a simple process model for this process.
- ▸ Consider university teaching as a process and suggest some appropriate measures for assessing its efficacy, efficiency and effectiveness.
- ▸ Negative feedback is frequently used to maintain the homeostasis of a system. Investigate the term homeostasis in greater detail and report on your findings.
- ▸ Look at recruitment adverts in the general press and in specialist publications dealing with ICT. What sort of jobs are advertised for business analysts?
- ▸ Provide an example of the process of structuration (other than those given in this chapter) and discuss its importance.

2.12   Projects

- Examine the literature on business information systems. Determine which of the two perspectives on organisation is most used in this literature.

- Attempt to apply some aspect of systems thinking to a nontrivial problem in business or commerce. For instance, consider the problem organisations such as Tesco have in managing their supplies and suppliers. Attempt to model this supply chain as a system, and analyse the usefulness of applying a systems approach to this area.

- The systems approach has been criticised by a range of authors in the areas of organisation theory and organisation behaviour. Investigate this literature and use it to critically determine the degree to which it is appropriate to use a systems model for describing and understanding organisations.

- The whole is greater than the sum of its parts, or the system is greater than the sum of its subsystems. What do you think is meant by this in terms of the three levels of business systems (activity systems, information systems and ICT systems) examined in this book? Provide some examples of the way in which these principles reflect organisational life.

- Attempt a small project in process redesign within an organisation known to you. For instance, consider the admissions process at a university. How could this process be improved, and how important is ICT to your redesign?

- There are a number of different graphical notations for specifying activity models and process models. Investigate two distinct notations for specifying either activity models or organisational processes. Develop some criteria of comparison (such as number of constructs or ease of drawing) and analyse each approach using these criteria.

- Models are useful as a means of joint understanding, not only within a particular organisation but also between organisations. Some have proposed the development of high-level or generic process models that may be applicable across organisations within the same industrial sector. Suggest some of the benefits and problems of this proposal. Determine to what degree it is possible for organisations to reuse existing generic process models to help in organisational analysis and design.

2.13   Critical reflection

Try reflecting on the nature of organisation in simple settings known to you. For instance, when you go into a coffee shop you probably participate in a performative pattern. You are a business actor – a consumer – and you interact with another business actor – a barista. How would you describe this as a typical pattern of performance? What informative pattern normally accompanies such a performance? In other words, what communication normally occurs between you and the Barista? Is there any formative pattern evident in support of the informative pattern? By this we mean, are there any records involved in supporting this business interaction? Try broadening this idea out from face-to-face interaction to one involving human and machine. What sort of informative and formative patterns support the ordering of goods online via a website?

2.14   Further reading

There are many books on organisational theory and organisational behaviour. Bratton et al. (2010) provide a comprehensive review of the field. Morgan (1986) provides a number of different perspectives on organisation. This chapter has provided an overview of systems theory as applied to organisations, which is particularly designed to act as a foundation to our consideration of informatics. Checkland (1999) provides the definitive account of soft systems work upon which the approach to activity systems described in this chapter is based. Jackson (2003) provides a more general, but comprehensive, overview of the range of systems thinking applied to management practice. Hofstede (1991) provides the classic account of dimensions of culture which has been applied extensively within studies of organisational culture. Unfortunately there is not one central book on process modelling that can be recommended. Yeates et al. (2007) provide a high-level overview of business analysis within which process analysis takes its place. The distinction between activity, information and data systems is explored in my own book (Beynon-Davies, 2011).

2.15 References

Alexander, C. (1964). *Notes on the Synthesis of Form*. Harvard University Press, Harvard, Mass.

Beynon-Davies, P. (2011). *Significance: Exploring the Nature of Information, Systems and Technology*. Palgrave Macmillan, Basingstoke.

Bratton, J., M. Callinan, C. Forshaw and P. Sawchuk. (2010). *Work and Organisational Behaviour*. 2nd edition. Palgrave Macmillan, Basingstoke.

Checkland, P. (1999). *Soft Systems Methodology: A Thirty Year Retrospective*. John Wiley, Chichester.

Emery, F. E. and E. L. Trist. (1960). Socio-Technical Systems. In C.W. Churchman and M. Verhulst (eds), *Management Science, Models and Techniques*. Pergamon, New York.

Hofstede, G. (1991). *Cultures and Organisations*. McGraw-Hill, New York.

Jackson, M. C. (2003). *Systems Thinking: Creative Holism for Managers*. John Wiley, Chichester.

Mason, R. O. and I. I. Mitroff. (1981). *Challenging Strategic Planning Assumptions: Theory, Cases and Techniques*. John Wiley, New York.

Morgan, G. (1986). *Images of Organisation*. Sage, London.

Senge, P. M. (2006). *The Fifth Discipline: The Art and Practice of the Learning Organisation*. Revised edition. Doubleday, New York.

Stacey, R. D. (2003). *Strategic Management and Organisational Dynamics: The Challenge of Complexity*. Pearson Education, Harlow.

Vickers, G. (1965). *The Art of Judgement*. Chapman and Hall, London.

Walsham, G. and C.-K. Han. (1991). Structuration Theory and Information Systems Research. *Journal of Applied Systems Analysis* 18 (1): 77–85.

Wright, R. (1989). *Systems Thinking: A Guide to Managing in a Changing Environment*. Society of Manufacturing Engineers, Dearborn, Michigan.

Yeates, D., D. Paul, T. Jenkins, K. Hindle and C. Rollason. (2007). *Business Analysis*. BCS Publications, London.

See companion website **www.palgrave.com/business/beynon-daviesbis2e**

Data, information and knowledge

'Take care of the
sense, and the sounds
will take care of
themselves.'

Lewis Carroll (1832–
1898), *Alice's Adventures
in Wonderland* (1865),
Chapter 9

Learning outcomes	Principles
Understand the relationship between signs and information and describe the place of information within the process of communication.	The concept of information is difficult to define because of its multi-faceted nature. The concept of a sign provides a useful means for explaining the layered way in which activity, communication and representation inter-relates in any organisation.
Define differences between data, information and knowledge and describe the relationship between information, decision-making and action.	An understanding of the concept of a sign allows us to clearly distinguish between data, information and knowledge in organisations. It also provides a straightforward way of explaining the relationship between business information, business decision-making and organisational action.
Relate the importance of modelling data, information and knowledge to informatics and construct simple data, information and knowledge models for some domain.	The structure of data, information and knowledge is critical to the three major types of business systems making up organisation. It is important to model data, information and aspects of explicit knowledge as preparation for the design, operation and management of such business systems.

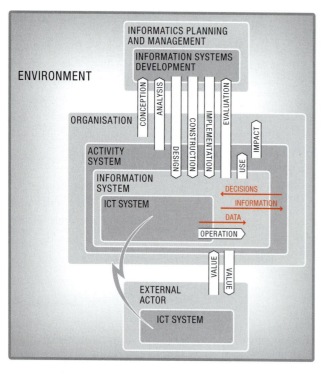

Chapter outline

**AACSB learning objectives:
Analytical skills and communication**

3.1 Introduction

Chapter 1 argued that information is a critical concept for the twenty-first century. Information is vital to the competitiveness of the private sector globally. It is an important 'commodity' in modern economies. It is even developing as an important issue in the natural sciences, particularly physics and biology, causing some to refer to information as the new language of science (Von Baeyer, 2003).

But what is meant by information in these contexts? In the natural sciences it tends to be defined quite narrowly, for example, as the transmission of bits of data. Management writers claim that it is important, but often do not define it at all. Therefore, although information is critical 'stuff', it is extremely difficult 'stuff' to pin down. It is probably not even 'stuff' at all.

Here are some examples to show how difficult it can be to define information.

If information is a commodity it is a very strange commodity. As Ronald Stamper states, *'Information is a paradoxical resource: you can't eat it, you can't live in it, you can't travel about in it, but a lot of people want it'* (Stamper, 2001). If somebody sells information it does not pass from seller to buyer like a traditional commodity, such as food, the seller still retains it. The 'consumption' of information is therefore radically different from the consumption of physical commodities such as food, wine and electronic goods.

Much modern communication is described as information transmission using technology. Take a telephone conversation. When two people talk on the phone, a lot less information is communicated than if they were talking face to face. The electronic signal travelling down the telephone line conveys only a percentage of the sound frequencies of normal human speech, but more importantly, because the people (often) cannot see each other, they cannot read each other's facial expressions and other forms of body language.

Person A looks across at Person B, who is at the opposite end of a room. He holds up a hand and points a finger upwards, clenching his other fingers in a fist. What will B take this to mean? Is it perhaps an insult, a command to provide one of something, or a message that there is something stuck on the ceiling?

We need to consider issues like the ones these examples raise if we are to think seriously about what information is. They highlight that information is particularly associated with human communication, that communication involves signs, and that signs involve human interpretation. They also demonstrate that information is bound closely with language, action, logic and technology, and other phenomena. So, in thinking about the place of information in organisations, we need a multi-layered, or multi-levelled, perspective.

In the last chapter we saw how the term organisation can be treated as either a noun (an institution) or a verb (a continuous process of action). We also saw how these two views of organisation are in fact complementary. It is possible to see organisational structure as emergent from organisational action; indeed, from three inter-related types of action: performance, communication and representation. These three forms of action are linked together through the concept of a sign. As such, signs are closely entangled with all forms of organisation. They help us establish the key value that ICT provides to organisation.

This chapter considers the nature of signs as units of significance and demonstrates how they are crucial building blocks in understanding the role of ICT and information systems in organisations. The concept of a sign helps us relate notions of data, information, decision-making and activity in organisations and connect them to the three types of business system we introduced in the last chapter: activity systems, information systems and ICT systems. These fundamental elements establish the platform upon which organisational informatics is founded.

3.2 Signs: units of business significance

Medical practitioners are prime examples of professionals that use signs to create order. They first diagnose your illness on the basis of signs. In other words, they read your symptoms as a

Sign: a pattern of significance. Something which stands to somebody for something

means of highlighting what may be wrong with you. They then use some strange term (usually with Latin roots) to stand for your illness. On the basis of this **sign** they may prescribe a range of treatment, probably including drugs, again with many weird and wonderful names, some proprietary, some generic.

Take also the example of advertising. Advertising is composed of signs that are used to attempt to influence the actions of consumers. What marketing people attempt to do is to manipulate our responses to products and services in subtle ways through signs. They attempt to affect not only our perceptions of products and services but how we think about them; this is in the hope that they can influence our consumption of those products and services.

But signs are not only critical to activity between producers and consumers, they are also critical for ensuring the effective operation of business organisations themselves. Signs, for instance, are critical to most aspects of management. Managers issue instructions or directives using signs. They also receive reports or assertions of what is happening in their business from other business actors. Signs are thus critical component elements of business communication and such communication is crucial to the control of business operations.

3.2.1   Signs and sign-systems

Sign-system: an organised collection of signs and relations between signs

Very broadly, a sign is anything that is significant. In a sense, everything that humans have or do is significant to some degree. Sometimes not having or doing anything is regarded as significant. The world within which humans find themselves is therefore resonant with systems of signs. For the eminent theorist of signs, Charles Sanders Peirce (1931), signs relate people, objects and ideas: '*A sign is something which stands to somebody for something in some respect or capacity*'. Signs therefore relate for an actor the symbol which stands for a referent: something that is referred to.

Symbol: a pattern of energy or matter used to denote something

Consider Figure 3.1. Here we have the same **symbol**, 434, interpreted in different ways by different business actors. For the business actor in the meals on wheels case, 434 stands for a number – perhaps the number of hot meals delivered in one month to subscribers to the scheme. For the business actor in the case of Goronwy Galvanising, described in Chapter 1, 434 is not a number, it is part of a code; it stands for a particular type of steel girder of a certain length which is treated with a zinc coating by the company.

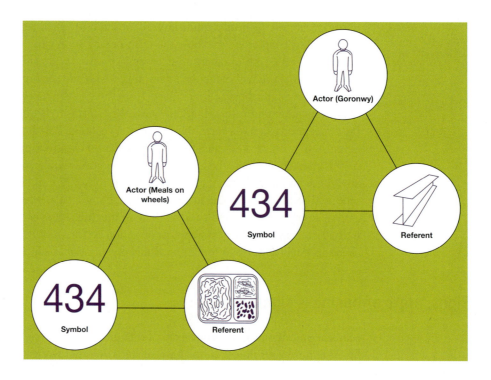

Figure 3.1 Symbols, referents and actors

But signs don't exist in isolation. They normally form parts of an organised system of representation and communication. The cognitive scientist Steven Pinker (2001) argues that our genetic makeup predisposes humans to be excellent manipulators of sign-systems. A sign-system is any organised collection of signs and relations between signs. Everyday spoken human language, such as English, is probably the most readily identifiable example of a sign-system. However, the concept of a sign-system is much broader than spoken human language.

Let us examine briefly two interesting and non-standard examples to help make the point that the idea of a sign-system is much larger than that of spoken language.

3.2.2   Human facial expressions

During his voyage in the HMS Beagle Charles Darwin pondered on how strange it was that he had no difficulty in understanding the facial expressions of the many people he met, even though he could not understand any of their spoken words. Hence, some twenty years after publication of his ground-breaking work *The Origin of the Species*, Darwin published another book of which he was equally proud, *The Expression of the Emotions in Man and Animals*, in which he described his pioneering investigation of emotive facial expressions in humans and their closest evolutionary relatives, the great apes. His key conclusion was that '... *the young and the old of widely different races, both with man and animals, express the same state of mind by the same movements*' (Darwin, 1998).

Figure 3.2 provides six illustrations of the most commonly recognised facial expressions found among humans. Before reading further, try to provide one word which you think aptly describes each illustration. In other words, can you 'read' these illustrations of facial expressions? Can you work out what might be the intention of someone making each of these facial expressions; what does each facial expression stand for?

When people across the Globe are asked what these facial expressions relate to and mean, they frequently come up with similar answers. It appears that facial expressions, such as the ones illustrated, are generally associated with common human emotions and that the making of such faces is a major way in which humans communicate emotion. Facial expression A, for instance, is normally seen to stand for something like 'happiness', while facial expression D is typically seen to stand for something like 'sadness'. Facial expression B stands for something like 'anger', facial expression E stands for 'disgust', C stands for 'fear' and F is a neutral expression – one which is not meant to signify any emotion.

The set of human facial expressions form an important sign-system. A facial expression results from one or more movements of the muscles of the face and these movements seem to be primarily used to convey a mental state, typically the emotional state of the individual to observers. As such, facial expressions are a form of non-verbal communication. They involve signs but do not involve use of the human vocal tract. They are an important means of conveying feelings among humans in social interaction and rely upon the ability of individuals to empathise.

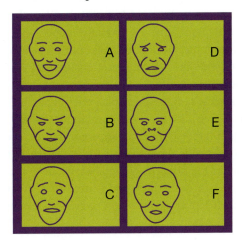

Figure 3.2 Six common facial expressions

REFLECT: Emoticons, such as 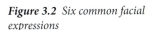, are symbols used to supplement written communication, particularly in messages sent through electronic mail or short messaging services (the formal name for texting) provided in mobile phone networks. Why are emoticons used, and what are they meant to stand for?

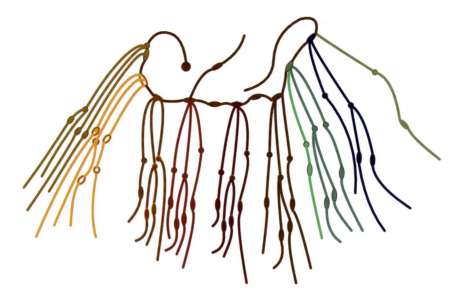

Figure 3.3 *An illustration of a khipu*

CS ⟩ p 445

The Inkas were a sophisticated society which existed in the high Andes of South America for a comparatively short time (c.1200–1572 AD). To administer their large empire the Inka maintained a large and sophisticated administrative organisation. This administration sent and received many messages daily in support of the activity of the empire. Typically such messages contained details of resources such as items required or available in store houses, taxes owed or collected, census data, and the output of mines or the composition of particular workforces. Messages had to be clear, compact and portable. For this purpose a form of artefact known as the khipu (Figure 3.3 illustrates an example) was used, consisting of an assemblage of coloured, knotted cotton or camelid (llama or alpaca wool) cords.

In the spoken language of the Inka the word khipu means to knot and hence specialist personnel known as the khipucamayaq (the keeper of the khipus) were responsible for writing and reading messages contained in khipus. Writing a khipu involved tying together a complex network of cords of different materials and colours, and tying into them a series of different forms of knot. Reading a khipu involved a khipucamayaq both in visual inspection and running his fingers rapidly over the knots, rather like a Braille reader.

Khipu are clearly not examples of written language as we conventionally know it. But they are complex examples of a sign-system and were used for sophisticated forms of record-keeping.

3.2.3   Business signs

Business sign: a sign of interest in a business domain.

Walking down a high street in downtown San Francisco I spotted a sign in a store window. It consisted of a large piece of paper with just three words in large type, 'SIGNS MEAN BUSINESS'. In a sense, those three simple words taken together, sum up what we are trying to achieve within this chapter. Signs are critically important in all forms of activity found within business. Signs are important because without them we could not think, we could not communicate what we think and we could not ensure that we collaborate together successfully in our working activity.

Signs mean business because signs are critical not only to business communication but also to business activity. A sign within business is anything that a business regards as significant; signs are critical things of interest to a business organisation. The American philosopher John Dewey suggested that a word is three things: a fence, a label and a vehicle. The same could be said more generally of the concept of sign. A sign is a 'fence' in the sense that it sets a conceptual boundary around something and is used to distinguish one thing from another. A sign is a 'label' in that it acts as a convenient reference standing for something else. Finally, a sign is a 'vehicle' in the sense that used with other signs as a sign-system it is a means for describing and debating with the world as well as acting upon it.

The arrow, embodied in the idea of the pointing hand, represents these properties of a sign. In other words, a sign 'points'. When a human forms her hand in this way she is using it to direct the gaze of another actor to a particular thing. The act of pointing, which appears unique to our species and our nearest evolutionary cousins, the great apes, serves to highlight an object from its surroundings. That object is normally given a label, both in our spoken and written language. Finally, these labels are used to make records. Such records are in turn crucial for the coordination of business activity.

Figure 3.4 illustrates the importance of signs in business life by using some standard words or terms found within communication by various forms of organisation. For instance, a manufacturing company would be interested in *products*, *orders* and *sales*. In contrast, a service company, perhaps working in the educational sector, would be interested in *courses*, *students* and *bookings*. Finally, a public sector organisation such as a government agency would be interested in *citizens*, *claims* and *benefit payments*.

Semiotics: the discipline devoted to the study of signs

The term *universe of discourse* (UoD), domain of discourse or, more recently, ontology is used to describe the context within which a group of signs is used continually by a group of actors. Take for instance a university. Most universities need to record things to help in the activities of teaching and learning, amongst other things: what students and lecturers

DID YOU KNOW? The discipline devoted to the study of signs is known as **semiotics**. Modern semiotics developed from linguistics and the philosophy of language. Ferdinand de Saussure, one of its founders, wrote a pioneering work on general linguistics in 1916. The American philosopher Charles Morris built on the work of both Saussure and Peirce, mentioned previously, and made it more sophisticated. Claude Lévi-Strauss used semiotic approaches in anthropology in the late 1950s. You may be familiar with some of the discussions of semiotic ideas in popular, as well as in academic, literature; for example, Umberto Eco's *The Name of the Rose* and Dan Brown's *The Da Vinci Code*. Brown's hero, Robert Langdon, is a professor of religious symbology, which (as Brown portrays it) has much in common with semiotics.

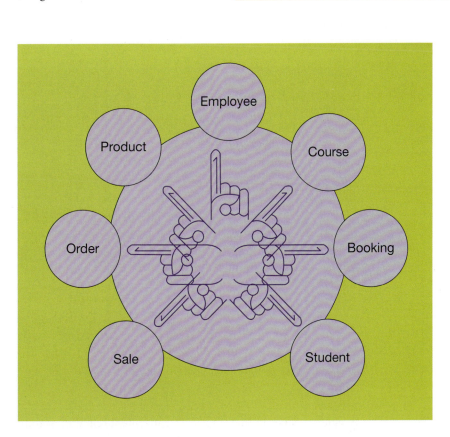

Figure 3.4 *Some typical business signs*

they have; what courses and modules they are running; which lecturers are teaching which modules; which students are taking which modules; which lecturer is assessing against which module; and which students have been assessed in which modules, as well as the grades they receive. All these things form part of the universe of discourse of a typical university. They are all things about which actors within the higher education institution wish to communicate or have discourse about. They are all things about which the university makes records. Finally, on the basis of what they know about such things, actors within the organisation in question take action: they teach students, mark assessments and award grades.

3.2.4   Significant patterns

Forma: the physical representation of signs

Informa: the meaning of signs within communication

Performa: the use of signs in support of coordinated activity

In essence then a sign consists of a significant pattern. Signs are key examples of such repeating patterns treated by two or more actors as significant. It is possible to unpack any sign as a pattern that has three distinct, but inter-related, facets: **forma**, **informa** and **performa**. This distinction serves to link three worlds critical to all business organisation: they link the physical, or technical, world with the social world through the psychological world. Forma constitutes the substance, representation and manipulation of signs and falls within the physical or technical world. Informa constitutes the content of signs and their use within communication and therefore falls within the psychological world. Finally, performa constitutes the use of signs within coordinated, instrumental activity and thus falls within the social world. We shall consider each of these aspects of the sign in more detail in the following sections. In the next chapter we shall then draw together these aspects to review the issue of business organisation, which provides the necessary context for the application of ICT in business.

Take the example of a simple sign used in many modern organisations: a barcode, as illustrated in Figure 3.5. A barcode is a machine-readable representation of a code, typically a product code. Traditionally, barcodes are one-dimensional representations which serve to code data via the widths of lines and spaces between lines.

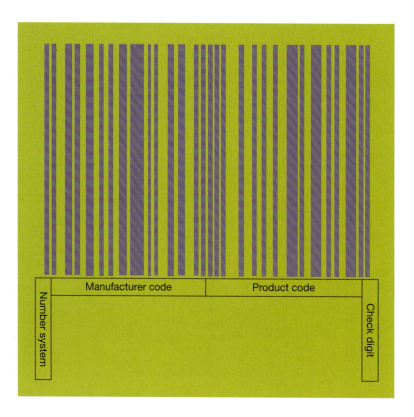

Figure 3.5 *The structure of a barcode*

Barcodes are commonplace in the modern world. Almost every food retail store, from the largest to the smallest, now sell products that contain barcodes. Patients in hospitals are frequently tagged with plastic bracelets containing barcodes. Books and other forms of document are now given barcodes for ease of tracking. Airline luggage is frequently tracked across the world using barcodes.

The relationship, or mapping, between a barcode as forma and what it represents as informa is frequently, and perhaps confusingly, referred to as a symbology. The most common form of symbology is that of standard commodity coding. Most food retail outlets in the UK use a form of commodity coding known as the International Article Number. This is a thirteen digit number used to encode the manufacturer and a product. This sign allows companies to engage in various aspects of performa: track goods from suppliers; control stock in warehouses; manage food displayed within supermarkets; and associate products with sales to customers. So, a simple business sign is critical to a vast amount of organisational communication, decision-making and action.

RECAP: Signs are significant patterns used in organisational communication. Signs form part of sign-systems. Various different types of sign-system might be used in business communication. Human spoken languages form the most readily recognised example of a sign-system, but non-verbal signs such as facial expressions also relate together in sign-systems. A domain of discourse is a term used to describe a group of signs used by a group of actors to describe some situation of interest. Signs can be considered to have three facets: the physical form of the sign (forma);how it is used in communication (informa); and how the sign enables coordinated action (performa).

3.3   Business information

Performative pattern: a coherent collection of related, performative acts

Formative pattern: a coherent collection of related, formative acts

In Chapter 2 we described how an activity system can be considered a set of inter-related **performative patterns**, which in turn consist of a set of inter-related performative acts. Therefore, performa corresponds to the 'performance' of actors in various situations. A performative act amounts to some transformation of the world undertaken by a particular actor, at a particular time and in a particular place, in an attempt to realise a particular goal.

This perspective encourages us to identify the core performative activities critical to an organisation such as Goronwy. In essence, performa relates to the fundamental question, *what does an organisation such as Goronwy do?* The response to such a question normally indicates the central performative activity of the organisation, in this case galvanisation. But galvanisation relies on one set of activities that handle raw material from the customer and yet another set of activities that transport galvanised products back to the customer. Hence, it is possible to think of the activities of Goronwy related by precedence. In other words, to perform one particular activity another activity needs to be performed first and the performance of that activity will normally be a prerequisite for some other activity, and so on ...

Performative acts normally correspond to the 'work' of people in collective interaction, typically using 'tools' to transform 'objects' in the world. Hence, performative acts typically occur in sequences where one performative act is reliant upon the completion of one or more other performative acts. A set of such coherent activities that repeat on a regular basis we refer to as a performative pattern.

Using the principle of system hierarchy discussed in Chapter 2 means that we can take any performative activity and break it down into more detail. Hence, in Figure 3.6 we illustrate how we might provide more detail about the receive and check black material activities, which make up a performative pattern important within the central activity system at Goronwy Galvanising. This form of representation is particularly useful because it highlights the central role of particular business actors in particular performative activities. In the diagram, for instance, we have indicated particular business roles, such as an inbound logistics operative, as being responsible for a particular activity.

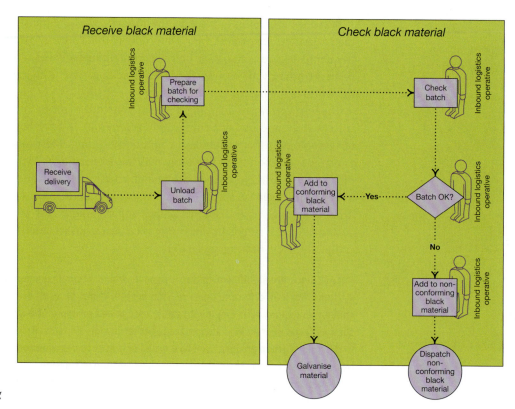

Figure 3.6 *A performative pattern at Goronwy Galvanising*

To refresh, in Figure 3.6 performative acts are the same as processes and are represented as boxes, while the diamond shape represents a decision point. As is evident from this diagram, decisions are choices between alternative courses of performative action – in this case whether the batch is fit for galvanising or not. The choice made by particular business actors has to be communicated in some way to other business actors. This realm of decision-making and communication is the realm of informa. Hence, along with the patterning of performative activity in organisations there will be a patterning of communication and decision-making and we refer to such a form of order as informative acts and informative patterns. An information system, as we have seen, consists of a set of inter-related informative, or communicative, patterns and an informative pattern, in turn, consists of a set of inter-related informative acts.

DID YOU KNOW? In many senses money is information. Money can be seen to act as a proxy for what we shall call in a later chapter, *exchange value*. Within the global economy, money is essentially represented as data within the electronic records of financial institutions. Money is transferred between such systems electronically, as a form of data transfer, and accompanies the exchange of goods and services.

3.3.1   Informative acts

Informative acts are acts of communication. They involve the transmission and receipt of messages. An informative act is some aspect of performance designed by one actor, the sender of a message, to influence the performance of another actor, the receiver of that message.

Consider three examples of informative acts that appear regularly within business organisations: [*Please take the customer order*], [*Will you take the order?*], [*You will take the order*]. The content of these three messages is the same, [*that you will process the customer order*]. However, the intent of these three verbal statements is clearly different: the first is a request, the second a question, the third a prediction.

In any organisational activity business actors normally communicate in five major ways that amount to five major forms of informative act; five major ways in which actors seek to influence the actions of others and, as a by-product, ensure the coordination of their mutual activity.

Hence, it is possible to formulate five key types of communicative, or informative, act in terms of differences in the intentions of the actor performing the communication. The philosopher John Searle refers to these as assertives, directives, commissives, expressives and declaratives. We can thus use the notation I[c] to refer to a communicative act, where I stands for the intent of the communicative act and c to its content. We shall provide a different symbol to designate the intent behind each of these five types and we shall place the content of the informative act between square brackets.

3.3.2 Types of informative act

Assertive: a communicative act that explains how things are in a particular organisational domain

Assertives are communicative acts that explain how things are in a particular organisational domain, such as reports on business activity. Such acts commit the speaker to the truth of the expressed proposition. We express an assertive as ⊢[p]. For instance, within a business organisation a given business actor might make the statement ⊢[*Our orders have fallen by 10% this month*], or in the case of Goronwy an inbound logistics operative might make the statement to the plant manager, ⊢[*15% of all the black material we received over the last year was non-conforming*].

Directive: a communicative act that attempts to influence action

Directives are communicative acts that represent the sender's attempt to get the receiver of a message to perform or take an action, such as requests, questions, commands and advice. We express a directive as ?[p]. Hence, a business actor might ask of another actor: ?[*Please ensure that our production target is met next quarter*], or in the case of Goronwy the plant manager might request of his production controller, ?[*Please ensure that all conforming black material is galvanised on its day of delivery*].

Commissive: a communicative act that commits an actor to some future course of action

Commissives are communicative acts that commit a speaker to some future course of action such as promises, oaths and threats. They are communicative acts that represent a speaker's intention to perform an action some time in the future. We represent a commissive as #[p]. Hence, a business actor might issue statements such as: #[*I promise to write a letter to company X*] or #[*I refuse to pay that invoice from company Y*]. In the case of Goronwy the manager might make the following commitment to its major customer Blackwalls: #[*We promise to turnaround all products within a three day period*].

Expressive: a communicative act that reflects an actor's feelings towards a proposition

Expressives are communicative acts that represent the speaker's psychological state, feelings or emotions such as apologies, criticisms and congratulations. They express a speaker's attitudes and emotions towards some proposition. We represent an expressive as ![p]. Hence, a Facebook user might indicate his feelings towards some content by implicitly communicating ![*I like content X*] or a managerial actor might state, ![*I am unhappy with Joe's overall performance this month*] or, in the case of Goronwy, the production controller might comment, ![*I am pleased with our production over the last quarter*].

Declarative: a communicative act that changes the state of an organisational domain

Declaratives are communicative acts that change the state of an organisational domain through the communication itself. We express a declarative as ≡[p]. Within business settings declaratives are frequently used to represent that some state of performance within an activity system has been achieved, such as in the case of Goronwy, ≡[*Batch Z has been galvanised*] or ≡[*Batch Y has been dispatched back to customer X*].

3.3.3 Informative patterns

Informative pattern: a coherent collection of related, communicative acts

Informative acts form the component elements of **informative patterns** which parallel and support performative patterns in organisations. A coherent collection of such informative patterns we call an information system, which we shall discuss in more detail in Chapter 4.

An informative pattern that occurs frequently in many organisations consists of the sequence: assertive, directive, commissive, declarative. This sequence effectively implements elements of a control process as discussed in Chapter 2. Figure 3.7 illustrates a typical pattern of this nature found in the Goronwy case which supports a performative pattern found within

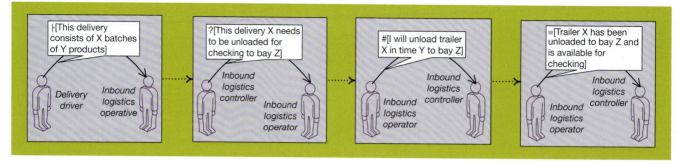

Figure 3.7 An informative pattern

this organisation. Here, an actor fulfilling the role of delivery driver makes an assertion of a delivery to some other actor with the role of an inbound logistics operative. This informative act triggers another actor, namely the inbound logistics controller to issue a directive to unload the trailer. This directive in turn triggers a commitment on behalf of the inbound logistics operator to unload and an eventual declaration by this actor that the trailer has been unloaded.

In this pattern, the assertive implements the sensor of the control process, while the directive implements the effector. The commissive and the declarative implement aspects of feedback, ensuring that the receipt of batches into Goronwy is regulated.

3.3.4   Communication and meaning

Communication: the accomplishment of meaning between actors

Informa is not only about **communication** between two or more actors, it must also involve the way in which actors accomplish collective meaning through both internal and external communication. For example, when one inbound logistics operative speaks to another inbound logistics operative making the utterance, '*Trailer X has been unloaded to bay Z and is available for checking*', both actors must be using a common sign-system for such a statement to be understood. This sign-system clearly consists of a set of coherent sounds forming spoken words, each of which is taken to stand for something. In making this association between what we referred to earlier as symbol and referent, meaning is accomplished. Hence, when one actor speaks the word 'trailer' there is a mutual understanding of what this sound pattern refers to.

Informa is therefore a psychological accomplishment reliant on some collective agreement between actors about symbols and what they stand for. But this agreement about meaning is not inevitable or fixed. Most signs used within human activity and communication are arbitrary in nature. By this we mean that there is no inherent or universal association between symbol and referent. The relation between symbol and referent exists merely through the establishment of some acceptance or expectation amongst a group of actors as to these relations – it is a convention.

This can be illustrated in relation to hand gestures, which are an important part of non-verbal sign-systems we referred to earlier. Six commonly used hand gestures are illustrated in Figure 3.8. What do each of the hand gestures mean to you?

Many of these hand gestures in fact mean different things depending upon the culture of which you are a part. For instance, the upper left-hand sign is generally taken to mean something like OK within a country such as the UK. Hence, a stock market trader on the trading floor of a major investment bank may just use this sign to indicate that she is happy with a particular share deal. However, if you use this sign in social situations within a country such as Tunisia it is likely to be interpreted as: 'I'll kill you'!

Information provided through communicative or informative acts using agreed signs is the basis for making decisions such as whether to buy traded company shares or what material to galvanise. Action is then taken on the basis of decisions made: if the information is incorrect

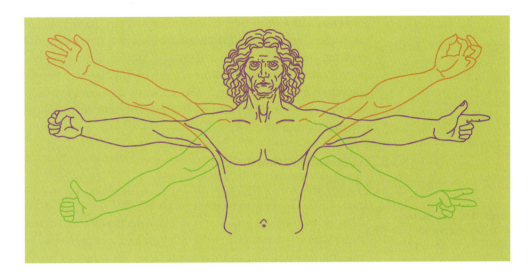

Figure 3.8 *Examples of hand gestures*

or inappropriate, then the wrong decisions will be made and the organisation will not perform effectively. Information – and more particularly, *quality* information – is therefore essential for both the effective coordination of activity within organisations such as Goronwy, as well as to the way in which the overall purpose of this organisation is achieved.

3.3.5　Decision-making

Decision: a selection between alternative courses of action

Decision-making: the process of making decisions

Information therefore supports performative activity in the sense that it enables *decisions* to be made about appropriate actions in particular circumstances. Therefore, **decisions** and **decision-making** mediate between information and action. Such decisions are particularly the responsibility of layers of management within organisations. In other words, the primary activity of management is making decisions concerning organisational action. Decision-making is the activity of selecting an appropriate action from a number of alternative courses of action in particular situations. Decision-making is reliant upon information in the sense that information is seen as reducing uncertainty in decision-making.

Consider the simple case of an individual actor undertaking a sequence of activities (Figure 3.9). In the first scenario there is no uncertainty about the course of activity: the actor performs activity A, then activity B, then activity C. No decisions need to be made about what activity to perform next because each activity is certain. In the second scenario we introduce the simplest form of uncertainty. The actor has performed activity A but there are now two alternative courses of activity open to him: B or C. He now needs to decide or choose what activity to perform next. The key question is, how should such a decision be made? The normal answer to such a question is in terms of information. Information enables the actor to reduce the uncertainty in the situation by directing the choice of future action.

Suppose activity A involves a particular actor checking a batch of steel products that have been delivered to Goronwy Galvanising. The key decision to be made by this actor is whether this batch of black products is fit to be galvanised (activity B) or should be returned to the manufacturer (activity C). This decision is clearly based upon information this actor gleans about the condition of steel products in the batch. The actor communicates with himself about the state of the batch and on this basis decides what to do next. If they are all conforming he chooses action B (sending them on to be galvanised); if some are non-conforming then he separates these products from the batch and returns this non-conforming material to the manufacturer (activity C).

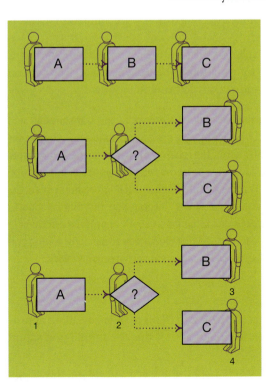

Figure 3.9 *The role of decision-making*

Let us add a small further level of complexity. Rather than one actor performing activities A, B and C and making a decision about each activity, these activities and the act of decision-making are parcelled up in a division of labour: actor 1 performs activity A, actor 3 performs activity B and actor 4 performs activity C. The decision between activities B and C are taken by yet another actor, actor 2. This is clearly an example of social or coordinated action. The various actors in this performative pattern have to coordinate their joint activity through external communication.

3.3.6   Levels of decision-making

Strategic decision-making: making less structured decisions, with summary information about courses of action with a long timescale

We argued in Chapter 2 for thinking of management as a control process in an organisation, in as far as management is an activity system that controls other activity systems. Management's main function is to make decisions about actions that need to be taken in the organisation, particularly at the strategic and tactical levels. Effective management decision-making depends on good information, so the issues of management, decision-making and information are necessarily intertwined.

Any sizeable organisation will have a number of layers of management and although managers at all levels make decisions they are likely to do so in different ways. Three levels of management are often identified: strategic management, tactical management and operational management. They differ in decision-making characteristics, information needs and the time horizon for decisions.

In terms of decision-making characteristics, the higher up the management hierarchy, the less structured problems and decisions become. Structured decisions are known as algorithmic decisions and we can draw up an explicit procedure for making them. Unstructured decisions are known as heuristic decisions, no set procedure can be established, but some rules of thumb can be suggested.

The higher up the management hierarchy, the greater need there is for summary information and information concerned with the external environment. Operational managers need detailed information on operational activities. This can be considered a form of, what we called in Chapter 2, single-loop feedback. Strategic managers need information which summarises aspects of organisational performance and compares it with competitors. This is one form of double-loop feedback.

The higher up the management hierarchy, the larger the time horizon is for both decisions and information. Operational managers need information to help them make decisions on an hour-by-hour basis. Strategic managers are more likely to think in months and years.

RECAP: Information is accomplished through informative acts which involve the transmission and receipt of messages. An informative act is an aspect of performance designed by one actor, the sender of a message, to influence the performance of another actor, the receiver of that message. Informative acts relate together in informative patterns and informative patterns relate together in information systems. Five key types of informative or communicative act are used in such information systems: assertives, directives, declaratives, expressives and commissives. Information therefore supports performative activity in the sense that it enables *decisions* to be made about appropriate actions in particular circumstances. Therefore, decisions and decision-making mediate between information and action and such decisions are the responsibility of layers of management within organisations.

3.3.7   The quality of information

If information supports activity in the sense that it enables *decisions* to be made about appropriate actions in particular circumstances, then we might expect that the more information we have then the better decisions we will make.

In 1967 the management scientist Russell Ackoff (1967) published an influential article which criticised some of the prevailing wisdom about the role of information and information systems in management decision-making. Not least, he claimed it was a myth that more information necessarily leads to better decision-making. Early designers had tended to assume this, and as a result had designed information systems which overwhelmed managers with their volume of information. Ackoff argued that what counts is the *quality* of information. Managers do not need exhaustive information, they need only information that is relevant to the activities being managed or controlled.

So the quality of information relates to the use to which it is put. This suggests that information quality not only relies upon the ways in which supporting data is collected and processed but also factors associated with how communication occurs and through what medium. Information quality is also an issue that can only be judged in terms of the performative activity it is designed to support.

We can sum up these issues by saying that the collection and processing of data needs to focus on providing information that is:

- accurate: that is, free from errors
- complete: sufficiently covering the area for which it is required
- current: reflecting existing and not past circumstances
- timely: available in sufficient time for the processes that need it
- relevant: to the situation in which it is required.

Communication issues involve, for example:

- clarity: so it is easily understood for its intended purpose
- detail: which should be sufficient for its intended use
- medium: for instance a textual report, graph or table, appropriate to the type of information and its use.

3.4   Business data

In the previous section we primarily focused on communication through verbal communication, human speech. We also mentioned another form of communication through non-verbal, or body, language. During the early years of the industrial revolution most business organisations were relatively small, family affairs. To administer and control the performance of activity in such organisations informal communications were generally sufficient. Verbal and non-verbal communication was used for immediate purposes and written letters were used for communications that had to travel some distance or were about events in the future.

By the 1840s in Great Britain large-scale administrative offices had developed to handle the increasing complexity and size of business operations. A new philosophy of management arose around the same time which emphasised the use of standard and formal communications (forms) for numerous purposes, such as the issuing of managerial orders, tracking of worker activity and the production of summary reporting. We tend to forget that the use of the form, as a conventional pattern of forma consisting of a set of defined and named areas for representing things upon paper, is a comparatively recent invention dating back less than two hundred years.

Much communication in modern-day organisations still occurs through use of informal messages created using a verbal sign-system. However, formal communications represented in forms are now part of the essence of what we mean by organisation, even in the modern-day electronic business. Organisations still create such forms on paper but increasingly produce and transfer such documentation as electronic messages.

But why do we represent things in such a manner? The main reasons lie in the limitations of human cognition. Human memory, for instance, is sufficient to support cooperative and simple activities between individuals in small groups. As groups grow, activities, particularly those reliant on economic exchange, need to take place between strangers and generally are more complex in nature, reliant typically on a division of activities amongst a multitude of different actors.

At some point in human development signs started to be used to make persistent, or lasting, records of things. The key purpose of such records is to extend and compensate for the limitations of human memory. Records of economic transactions, for instance, institutionalise the memory of past economic exchanges and the obligations placed upon individuals engaged in such exchanges. Accurate record-keeping is also critical in establishing and sustaining trust between strangers engaging in economic exchange. Economic records account not only for the types and quantities of commodities exchanged, they are also important for supporting social relationships of ownership and debt.

3.4.1   Representation

Representation: the process of denoting something with a physical pattern

Data or forma is about **representation** or, more particularly, the representation of messages as signals or records. At the level of forma we are interested in how a particular message is formed, what medium is used for representation and how signs are formed within this medium. Therefore, forma is concerned with physical patterns used for communication.

In the 1950s two eminent US electronics engineers, Claude Shannon and Warren Weaver, developed a formal model of communication as a process (Shannon, 1949). In this model communication was treated as an 'engineering' problem, not surprisingly given the background of the researchers. As Shannon himself stated, '*the fundamental problem of communication is that of reproducing at one point, either exactly or approximately, a message selected at another point*'. In this model (Figure 3.1), a source is said to generate a message. This message is then encoded and transmitted as a signal along a communication channel. The signal may be subject to what is called 'noise' in the environment, this means that the received signal at the destination may not be identical to that transmitted from the source. Hence, the process of decoding a signal may involve correcting errors introduced by noise to reproduce the original message.

A signal is a physical pattern which travels along a communication channel. Any form of energy propagation can be used for communication through signals. For instance, human speech travels as a signal consisting of a physical pattern of sound waves travelling through the communication channel of air. But the very idea of such a pattern implies that a signal is modulated. **Modulation** is the process by which variation or variety (Chapter 2) is introduced into a signal. If we are unable to modulate the pattern of a signal then no significance can be communicated between sender and receiver along a communication channel. Once we can vary the signal then it becomes possible to code messages using variations in the signal. **Coding** is therefore the translation of a signal from one medium into the same pattern expressed differently in another communication medium.

Modulation: the process of introducing variety into a physical pattern such a signal

Coding: the translation of a signal from one medium into the same pattern expressed differently in some other communication medium

Business actors are the senders or the receivers of communication. The intentions of a sender will be encoded in a message using elements from a particular sign-system. The message, consisting of a series of symbols, will be transmitted by the sender as signals along a communication channel. One, or more, other actor will be a receiver with the ability to decode the signals to reveal symbols and interpret the meaning of the message.

Consider a simple example of a business communication in such terms. Business actor A speaks the words '*our orders have fallen by 10% this month*' to business actor B while at a meeting. In terms of intentions, this message, as we know from Chapter 2, represents an assertion, a report about the state of some 'world', in this case, the performance of some business. The assertion is made using signs from a particular sign-system, in this case a series of spoken English words. As spoken words these signs are encoded as phonemes (elementary pieces of sound that combine to form words), meaning that they travel along a communication channel based on sound transmission. The sounds impinge on the auditory, or hearing, apparatus of actor B. This actor is able to decode these sounds as symbols and is able to understand them as words of English and on this basis to infer the intention of actor A. On the basis of receiving this message he might decide to take appropriate action, such as calling a further meeting with sales staff.

3.4.2   Signals and channels

A signal is a key example of what we referred to in Chapter 2 as business forma: a coherent pattern of differences in matter or energy modulated along a communication channel. Theoretically, any form of matter, whether it be solid, gas or liquid, can be used as forma. Likewise, any form of chemical or physical energy can be used to provide a signal for communication. For instance, as we have seen, human speech travels as a signal consisting of a pattern of sound waves (acoustic energy through air), while hand gestures and facial expressions rely upon the reflectance and transmission of light (optical, reflected, physical energy). In contrast, honeybees communicate through the transmission of particular odours (gases diffusing through air) and through vibrating honeycomb within the hive (manipulation of a solid).

Digital signal: a signal modulated with a limited range of values

Analogue signal: a signal modulated with a continuous range of values

Generally speaking, signals come in two major forms: digital and analogue. A **digital signal** has a small number of possible values, two for a binary digital signal. An **analogue signal** has values drawn from a continuous range. The value of the signal varies over this range. Hence, both light and sound can be considered as a waveform emanating from some source. Sound, for instance, can be considered as a pressure wave travelling through a solid, liquid or gas.

Since a symbol is any aspect of the world that can be modulated and used in communication, the degree of modulation possible determines the variety or complexity of a sign-system. To refresh, the variety of a system refers to the number of states the system may take (Chapter 2). In a sign-system the variety of this system is related to the degree with which signals composed from the sign-system can be modulated. Using Shannon's communication theory this can be used to describe the amount of significance that can be conveyed by the sign-system in communication. The essence of discrimination, or difference, is being able to 'draw' a boundary around something. In doing so an actor distinguishes that which is inside the boundary, hence part of the thing, from that which is outside the boundary, hence not part of the thing. This is in essence a binary distinction and explains why the most basic unit of discrimination, and therefore the most basic way of coding data or forma, is in terms of

Bit: a binary digit

binary digits, otherwise known as **bits**.

Not surprisingly then, Shannon's theory of communication is a theory of forma measured in terms of binary decisions or bits. A statistical measure of the variety in a signal provides an indication of the level of significance being conveyed by a signal. Logarithms to the base 2 are used as a measure of the amount of significance in a message. To calculate this first translate the message into a binary code, then count the binary digits in the message string. This gives you a measure of the significant content of the message. It is therefore no surprise to find that most forms of communication technology nowadays use a form of binary coding (conceived as 0s or 1s similar to the dots and dashes of Morse code) and hence are binary communication channels.

Take an example. During the time of the Napoleonic Wars a communication system was set up by the Royal Navy consisting of a series of flags hoisted on the rigging of warships. The use of a particular sequence of flags was used to code a particular message such as the famous '*England expects...*' message at the battle of Trafalgar. Suppose a sailor wanted to signal a number between 0 and 127 by means of flags. Using a single flag for each number he would need 128 flags to achieve this. If he decides to use a decimal system to code the numbers being transmitted he needs 21 flags – ten for the units, ten for the tens and 1 for the hundreds. Using a binary system he requires just 14 flags – seven ones and seven zeros. 14 bits is therefore a measure of the significance of such messages.

Bandwidth: the number of binary digits that can be transmitted between senders and in a fixed amount of time

The capacity of any communication channel refers to the amount of data or forma that can be transmitted along the channel in a given period of time. The **bandwidth** of a channel refers to the minimum and maximum frequencies allowed along that channel. In a digital communication channel this corresponds to the bit rate, the number of binary digits (bits) that can be transferred per second between sender and receiver. For instance, the bit rate or bandwidth of human speech is around 50 bits/sec, while the typical bandwidth available when connecting a personal computer to the Internet from a UK home is of the order of 2 million (Mega) bits per second.

DID YOU KNOW? Consider two problems which can be solved by treating communication from the perspective of forma. In the search for extra-terrestrial intelligence (SETI) you need some means of identifying whether an alien civilisation is trying to communicate with you using a particular signal. In zoology, scientists need to prove that the clicks and whistles used by dolphins are a form of communication.

George Kingsley Zipf, an American linguist and philologist, studied statistical occurrences in different languages. He noticed that a small collection of elements (such as letters and words) in natural languages are used very frequently, but the vast majority of elements are used infrequently. This insight hints at an appropriate method for determining whether a signal consists of a code based on a language (rather than, say, a series of numbers, or a random succession of states). If you count the number of times particular letters appear in written extracts of English, you get a graph with a -1 (negative) slope. The same is also true of most other human written languages. A random string of letters (not conveying any meaning) appears as a flat slope on the graph (see Figure 3.10).

Interestingly if we plot all the elements of radio signals received from outer space to date, they approximate to the random or flat slope. This implies that, at least in terms of signals received, no alien life form out there has been trying to communicate with us.

In contrast, if we plot the strings of squeaks and whistles produced by dolphins, the line approaches the -1 slope. This is evidence that something is being communicated between these non-human species. But, to know what is being communicated we would need to interpret the signal or decode the message. For this we would need to know the meaning of signs in the dolphin sign-system.

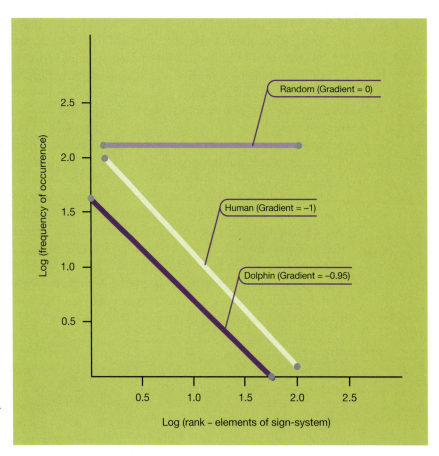

Figure 3.10 *Plotting elements of a sign-system against frequency of occurrence*

3.4.3   Records

Record: an instance of persistent forma or a data element of a file

But communication is not only about the transmission of data as signals, it is also about the persistent storage of such data in **records**. This is fundamentally the difference between persistent and non-persistent forma. When human communication occurs between more than two people and particularly when messages have to be transmitted across time and space, the persistent record is an essential feature of much human communication.

Blackwalls steel products		Delivery advice	

Advice no.	Date	Customer name	Instructions
A3137	20/01/1988	Goronwy Galvanising	Galvanise and return

Order no.	Description	Product code	Item length	Delivery qty	Weight (Tonnes)
13/1193G	Lintels	UL150	1500	20	145
44/2404G	Lintels	UL1500	15000	20	1450
70/2517P	Lintels	UL135	1350	20	130
23/2474P	Lintels	UL120	1200	16	80

Haulier	Received in good order
International 5	√

Figure 3.11 *Delivery advice*

Therefore business forms are clearly artefacts of communication used to represent things. Take three business forms that were used by Goronwy Galvanising in the 1980s, before their mass computerisation. The flow of these documents served to inform the coordination of activity within the company. The storage of such forms in files acted as a record, or collective memory, of activity which either had occurred or should occur. This data infrastructure, as we shall see, was the eventual basis on which ICT systems were developed by the company.

As we have seen in our description of the activity at Goronwy, each trailer arriving from a customer might be loaded with a number of different types of steel product. Each batch of products was therefore labelled with a unique order number. As a whole, each trailer was given its own delivery advice note detailing all associated batches on the trailer.

Since Goronwy mainly processed steel products for Blackwalls, the delivery advice note supplied with Blackwalls products was identified by a delivery advice number (A3137 in Figure 3.11) specific to this manufacturer. Each batch was identified on the delivery advice note by an order number generated by Blackwalls. Figure 3.11 illustrates a typical delivery advice note received from this company detailing all the black material on a particular trailer.

The delivery advice note in Figure 3.11 effectively acts as record of particular batches arriving on a given trailer. Data about a particular batch upon this form was referred to as an order-line. Each order-line effectively served to communicate an assertion from a customer (such as Blackwalls) to a particular business actor (in this case, the inbound logistics controller at Goronwy) about the type of product, its quantity and weight.

3.4.4 Data systems

If we consider an organisation as a system, then the inputs and outputs from such a system may consist of two types of flow: material flows and data flows. Material flows constitute the flow of physical or material things to and from the environment such as plant, machinery and foodstuffs. Since all matter can be described in terms of some energy equivalent, systemic thinkers tend to refer to such physical flows as energy flows. We shall argue in the next chapter that such flows can be considered more generally in terms of the concept of value. Accompanying the flow of physical material there will be a flow of data. Data is used to describe what is currently happening in a system, what has happened in the past, or what is likely to happen in the future.

For example, as we have seen in the case of Goronwy, the physical flow of raw materials from suppliers will normally be accompanied by one or more data flows. These data flows will describe to actors important properties of the physical flow such as the quantity of material, type of material to be or having been processed.

Data system: physical patterns which can be combined into structures and manipulated to produce new structures

Data structure: a collection of data elements

Data element: a collection of data items

Data item: a physical structure which can store some value

Create: a formative act that brings a new data structure, element or item into existence

Update: a formative act that changes the values associated with one or more data items of some data element

Delete: a formative act that removes an existing data structure, element or item from existence

Read: a formative act that decodes the values associated with one or more data items

A coherent set of patterns of data flow we refer to as a **data system**. A data system consists of physical patterns (symbols) that can be combined into structures and manipulated to produce new structures. A data system therefore consists of both data representation and data processing.

Both signals and records are **data structures**, forms for representing data. It is possible to step back from the specifics of a particular case such as Goronwy and consider forma as concerned with the operation of a number of types of formative act upon such data structures. The forms discussed as originally used by Goronwy are examples of such data structures, consisting of a set of **data elements** which in turn consist of a set of **data items**. For instance, as a data structure the Job Sheet used at Goronwy consists of at least three data elements, each consisting of a number of data items: a section which describes the original order with the data items Order No, Description, Product Code, Item Length, Order Qty, Batch Weight; a section which is used to indicate any non-conforming material; and a section which references eventual dispatches from the order.

Four sorts of actions are taken by business actors in relation to data structures such as delivery advices, job sheets and dispatch advices. The first is that we might **create** a new data structure, element or data item. Hence, the production controller might create a new job sheet. The second is that an element or a data item on an existing data structure might be **updated**. Hence, a production controller might place a 'Y' in the count discrepancy box of a particular job sheet. The third is that an existing data structure, element or item might be **deleted**. For example, after a period of a year or so job sheets would be destroyed within the paper filing system of Goronwy. Finally, data structures, data elements and data items will be **read** by business actors. Hence, various business actors within Goronwy will read the data on these forms, interpret what they mean and use this information to make decisions about further action.

3.4.5   Data systems and ICT systems

ICT systems are primarily data systems. However, not all data systems are ICT systems. This conception of information and communication technology allows us to see the clear position such systems play within organisation of all forms.

We have seen that to ensure coordination of business activity, communication is needed through communicative acts. It is perfectly possible for communicative acts to be formed purely as utterances, as speech acts between persons. It is also possible to treat human speech as a data system consisting of the data structure of an utterance. An utterance can be seen as made up of a sequence of morphemes – coherent and meaningful segments of speech – with any given morpheme consisting of a set of phonemes – coherent segments of sound.

But, as we have seen, there are a number of problems involved in using speech as a form of collective communication. The sound signal produced by speech decays rapidly in air, it does not persist. This is why records were invented. They are persistent and hence can be used to represent things through time. In the early office acts of communication were therefore formed as paper-based representation, as data items on paper forms. More recently, organisations such as Goronwy have encoded such acts of communication in the records of an ICT system; perhaps, as we shall see, as the rows of a table within a relational database. As such, the database acts as a form of collective memory for actors working within the organisation, from which decisions can be made.

Such technology not only enables data to be more easily stored and transmitted, it also enables a step-change in the way in which certain aspects of decision-making and communication can be performed within and between organisations. At this stage, let us just consider a simple example. In further chapters we shall demonstrate how ICT systems are now significant business actors, alongside people.

ICT systems use algorithms that operate upon data structures to produce operational decisions. For example, let's take people using their credit cards. A credit card number is typically made up of three elements. The first part of the number codes the card type, the second part identifies the card issuer, and the third part is the owner's account number. The last digit is a check digit, set so that when a particular algorithm is applied to the number, it produces a figure divisible by ten. This is used as a check on whether the number has been entered correctly: if the algorithm does not give a number divisible by ten, the transaction is rejected.

This Luhn algorithm (called after its inventor) works like this:

- Take the original credit card number.
- Reverse the digits in the string.
- Double every second digit.
- Add all three rows of digits together. If any result is more than nine, subtract nine from the number.
- Add together the final string of digits.
- Determine whether the sum divides by 10.

Table 3.1 gives an example. Adding up the final string of digits gives 80, so the number was entered correctly.

Table 3.1 *The Luhn algorithm*

Credit card number	3	7	7	9	5	6	5	7	0	9	4	4	7	2	6
Reverse number	6	2	7	4	4	9	0	7	5	6	5	9	7	7	3
Double every second digit		4		8		18		14		12		18		14	6
Add numbers	6	4	7	8	4	9	0	5	5	3	5	9	7	5	3

RECAP: To refresh, there are four inter-related questions that all organisations, particularly business organisations, must answer: What do we do? What do we need to know to do things? How do we communicate what we know? How do we represent what we do, know and communicate? These questions correspond to questions about performance or performa, communication or informa, and representation or forma.

Any sign such as 23/2474P can be considered merely as forma; in this case as a set of characters. Such forma is only useful for communication when a business actor assigns some meaning to the forma; turning forma into informa. Hence, we know from inspecting, or 'reading', the forms of this company that the symbol 23/2474P stands for a particular product type handled by Goronwy, namely, a steel lintel of 1,200 cms in length and weighing 100 kg. But the purpose of identifying something in this manner is only evident when we consider the context in which the sign is used. This context is defined by the way in which the sign is used in coordinated activity. In this case it serves to identify the appropriate product type of a particular batch and job as it travels through the galvanising process.

REFLECT: Try out the Luhn algorithm on one of your own credit cards. This type of algorithm is known as a data validation check, and is used particularly to make sure that the user of an ICT system enters data correctly. Can you think of any other instances of a validation check?

Think too about decisions that affect your daily life, such as whether you are granted a small loan by a financial institution. How many of these decisions are algorithmic in nature?

3.4.6   Data validation and verification

Data validation: ensuring that data captured and stored remains an accurate reflection of its domain

Data verification: ensuring that data is both entered and transmitted correctly

The quality of information depends upon the quality of data. This leads to some practical considerations for organisations. First, collecting and processing data, as well as ensuring it is in a form for effective communication, takes both equipment and human time and effort, so there is a cost involved. Second, it is important to find ways to ensure that incorrect or invalid data is not entered into a data system. In other words, suitable methods of **data validation** and **data verification** need to be built into the design of such systems.

Data validation is the process of ensuring that data captured and stored in a data system remains an accurate reflection of its domain. Usually, this is done by building a series of validation rules into the data system. These rules will ensure, for instance, that dates are entered in a correct format, if someone enters, say, 30 February 2013, it will be rejected. Or alternatively, they will ensure that data entered in one record matches that in related records. For example, a person might be prevented from ordering from a company until they have supplied a validated contact address and telephone number for the company.

Data verification normally refers to the process of ensuring that data are both entered correctly and transmitted correctly. For instance, many commercial websites ask users when registering to enter their email address twice over. A verification routine checks that the two character strings match before storing customer details. The Luhn algorithm discussed above is actually another example of a data verification algorithm.

> **REFLECT:** What data validation and data verification is required in a general hospital to ensure that the right patients receive the right treatments? How do barcoded tags attached to the wrists of patients ensure this?

3.5   Modelling data

Addressing information requirements   **IS**2010

 key skill

For work in organisational informatics it is important to develop a detailed understanding of the system of signs used within any organisational domain. This is done at two levels: at the level of forma (data) and of informa (information). At the level of forma we need to develop a data model and at the level of informa we need to develop an information model. A data model describes the structure of data used within a data system, while an information model describes elements used in communication within a domain.

3.5.1   Data structures, formats and types

Data model: a model representing the structure of data appropriate to some domain

In general, any **data model** can be built using the constructs of data structures, data elements and data items mentioned in previous sections. A data item is the lowest level of data organisation. It is the atomic construct in any data model, a construct that cannot be divided any further. Hence, data values are stored against data items. A data element is a logical collection of data items, and a data structure is a logical collection of data elements.

The most common data model that has been employed for data storage within organisations is file-based. This data model uses the inter-related constructs of fields, records and files. Fields are data items, records are data elements and **files** are the data structures in this data model.

File: a collection of records

This file-based (sometimes referred to as the records-based) data model has existed for many thousands of years in numerous human civilisations. As discussed previously, records by their very nature involve the use of signs to act as a persistent record of something. For example, in ancient Sumeria small clay tokens were used as signs which signified the amount of certain commodities held in various storehouses.

With the rise of the modern office in the nineteenth century, the technology of filing cabinets, paper folders and paper forms were used to organise data (See Victorian railway clearing house case). Within this data system a typical record consists of a series of data items which serve to represent an instance of something of interest to the organisation. For instance, a business organisation might create a typical record, consisting of a paper form, for each of its customers, with fields such as customer name, customer address and customer telephone number. Such a form might then be placed in a suspension folder for easy access.

Records, in turn, are typically collected into the data structure of a file, perhaps consisting of a filing cabinet, and representing some association between these data elements. For instance, a customer file assembles a series of customer records. Various different customer files might be created, with a specific criterion used to decide which record goes in which file, for instance, customers located in different areas of the country, or handled by different account managers. This file-based model is illustrated in Figure 3.12.

CASE CHECK
Inka Khipu

CS p 445

In terms of the Inka khipu, there is evidence for the knot as being the fundamental symbolic element. The construction and positioning of knots relative to each other upon a pendant cord constituted a datum. A related collection of knots upon a cord – a knot group – constituted a data item. The collection of knots within a knot group serves to value the data item.

The meaning or value assigned to a particular knot group is still much debated amongst scholars of the Inka. Evidence suggests that knot groups tied on pendant cords within certain khipu represent numbers to the base 10 (decimal). Particular types of knots and their positioning upon pendant cords signify distinct numbers. Therefore, within this particular sign-system the relative placement of single knots on a cord could be used to represent units or multiples of ten. The closer the knot is to the top of a cord, the higher the number. At the very top a single knot represented multiples of 10,000, then 1,000, then 100, then 10.

Pendant cords are normally tied together on a khipu in groups. Therefore such a group of pendant cords would constitute a data element and the entire assemblage of cords within a khipu would constitute a data structure. This is illustrated in Figure 3.13.

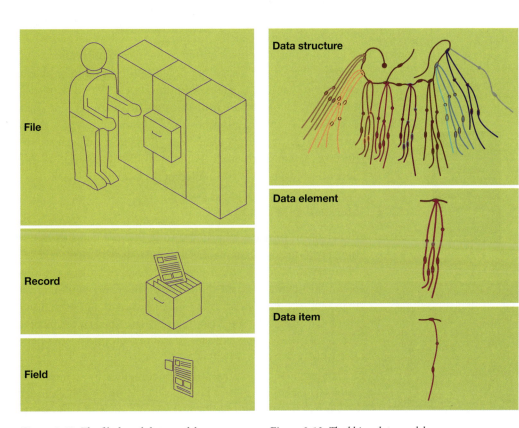

Figure 3.12 *The file-based data model*   **Figure 3.13** *The khipu data model*

Data type: a definition which constrains the data appropriate to a data item

Some of the meaning associated with data is therefore bound together with the way in which data are organised in terms of data structures, data elements and data items. Other aspects of meaning in a data model are represented in the format of the data contained in the data item. This is often called its **data type**. Some of the meaning of a data item is embodied in its data type, since this defines not only the appropriate form of data, but also the range of valid operations on it. For example, one data item within a personal record might be a person's age. At first glance you might think it is merely an integer data type (in other words, it consists of a whole number such as 21 or 43). It is possible to conduct a range of arithmetic operations on integers, although not all of them will necessarily be appropriate in the context of someone's age. Two integers such as 1 and 2 can be added, but it doesn't necessarily make sense to add one customer's age to another, or a customer's age to their house number. In contrast, it not even seem to be an option to add the character A to the character B. So a number data type might allow addition but a text data type will not.

Standard data: data structures using common data types such as text, numbers or unit of time

Most data needed in commercial business systems are what we might call **standard data**. Standard data are defined in terms of a number of standard data types used by most data systems, such as text (strings of symbols made up of characters from the alphabet and a range of other characters), numbers (including integer, decimal and real numbers) and units of time (including dates, seconds, minutes and hours). However, ICT systems are now being used to capture, store and manipulate far more complex data types than these. This is to enable systems to handle different media. Such complex data types include images (such as graphics and photographic images), audio and sound data, and video (forms of moving image).

Complex data: data structures using complex data types such as images, video and audio

These forms of **complex data**, or multimedia data, need different coding schemes, or formats, to enable them to be represented in digital form. For instance, images are coded in pixels, a pixel is a picture element. A high-resolution computer monitor can be considered as a 1,024 by 768 grid in which each cell is a pixel. To represent an image we therefore need to store information about its colour for each pixel in the image. For a complete monitor over 700,000 pixels are needed.

ICT systems are now required to handle complex data structures as well as complex data items or elements. For example, organisations want to be able to define the structure of documentation that they use for communication. A document such as an invoice or a contract is a complex data structure in that it may be made up of text, numeric data and even graphic images. Different organisations may also use different formats for such documents. Hence, there is pressure on organisations in the same industrial sector to develop standards for their documentation, particularly when such documentation is transmitted over communication networks. This issue is considered in Chapter 5.

3.5.2 Standard data coding

In persistent forma symbols have to be represented in some way for storage and manipulation. From the discussion above it is evident why most data can be ultimately coded in terms of binary digital (bit) representation. However, within modern digital computing, the measure of the quantity of data stored is typically expressed in terms of the number of bytes rather than bits. A *byte* consists of 8 bits, the word is a contraction of 'by eight'. The capacity of a particular form of storage can then be described in terms of kilo-bytes (Kbytes, 1 thousand bytes, 10^3), mega-bytes (Mbytes, 1 million bytes, 10^6), giga-bytes (Gbytes, 1 billion bytes, 10^9), or tera-bytes (Tbytes, 1 trillion bytes, 10^{12}).

Byte: a collection of eight bits

Data are actually represented in a computer by strings of characters coded using a character set, a uniform type of coding scheme. The symbols coded are referred to as characters, or words, and in the case of text consist of letters, digits, punctuation and non-printing characters such as control characters. One of the most popular standard character sets is **ASCII** (American Standard Code for Information Interchange). In ASCII the capital A is represented by the binary string or word 10100001.

ASCII: American Standard Code for Information Interchange – a standard coding scheme for characters on computing devices

Persistent forma are an inherent feature of, and a key problem for, the modern world. New measures of the volume of data are becoming required as ICT becomes more and more embedded in modern-day life. For instance, Google's whole data storage was estimated as being 5 peta-bytes (10^{15} bytes) in 2004. At the time of writing Google is now estimated to handle 20 peta-bytes of data per day! It was also estimated in 2002 that print, magnetic and optical storage media produced about 5 exa-bytes (10^{18} bytes) of data, 92% of it stored on magnetic media, mostly on hard disks. 5 exa-bytes is equivalent to the size of data contained in 37,000 new libraries, the size of the Library of Congress book collection. More recently, it has been estimated that 1,200 exa-bytes of digital data was generated in 2010.

3.5.3 Representing data structures

Backus-Naur Form: a notation for specifying the data structures of a data model

It is possible to specify the data structures of a data model using a notation known as the **Backus-Naur Form** (BNF). Consider the data structure for storing details of a postal address. In English we might define this data structure in terms of:

- A postal address consists of a house-part, followed by a street-address part, followed by a postal-identifier part.
- A house-part consists of either a house name or a house number.
- A street address consists of a street name followed by a location name.
- A location name consists of a village name, town name or city name.
- A postal-identifier is country-specific. In the United Kingdom a postcode is used; in the United States a ZIP code is used.
- A postcode consists of postal district followed by postal town followed by a delivery area followed by a house group.
- A ZIP code consists of a sectional centre facility code (SCF code) followed by a postal-zone number followed by a hyphen followed by an add-on code.

A BNF specification is a set of derivation rules, written as:

<symbol> ::= <expression with symbols>

where <symbol> is an element of a sign-system, and the expression consists of sequences of symbols and/or sequences separated by the vertical bar, '|', indicating a choice. The sequence on the right of the ::= symbol is taken as being a possible substitution for the symbol on the left. Hence, a postal address might be defined in BNF as:

<postal-address> ::= <house-part><street-address><postal-identifier>
<house-part> ::= <house-name> | <house-number>
<street-address> ::= <street-name><location-name>
<location-name> ::= <village-name> | <town-name> | <city-name>
<postal-identifier> ::= <post-code> | <zip-code>
<post-code> ::= <postal-district><postal-town><delivery area><house-group>
<zip-code> ::= <SCF-code><postal-zone-number> '-' <add-on-code>

REFLECT: Consider an everyday piece of data you come into contact with on a regular basis, such as a supermarket till receipt or a utility bill. In what way could these be considered as representative of a data structure? Could you specify these data structures in BNF?

DID YOU KNOW? A particularly important example of a sign for all types of organisation is the identifier. The identifier is a symbol, or set of symbols, that can be used to authenticate an object, such as a product, a place or a person. Postal codes are key examples of such identifiers, used for the identification of households and other premises. Barcodes, as we have seen, are used particularly in the identification of products. In further chapters we shall see that domain names and URLs are identifiers used on the Web for the identification of websites and Web pages.

RECAP: Symbols are equivalent to data. A datum, a single item of data, is a set of symbols used to represent something. In terms of data storage a data model defines the ways in which symbols are structured as data. Data models are created from data structures, data elements and data items. Data items normally conform to some data type. Data is coded using an established data format.

3.6 Modelling information

Addressing information requirements **IS**2010

 key skill

Most business organisations need to know and communicate about a number of things: customers, products, suppliers, stock and sales, amongst many other things. To document such things of interest and the relationships between them we need an information model. An information model uses a number of visual signs to stand for things of interest. It thus acts as a representation of the structure of information required by certain business activities. This information is processed within an information system for the purposes of business communication.

3.6.1 Classes, relationships and attributes

Information model: a specification of the things of interest relevant to communication in some organisational domain

Class: a thing of interest in a domain

Relationship: an association between classes

Attribute: a property of some class

An **information model** is built using three major constructs: classes, relationships and attributes.

A *class* may be defined as some 'thing' which an organisation recognises as important and communicates about on a regular basis. Take for instance a university. Universities, as we have seen, need to communicate about a number of things to help in the activities of teaching and learning. These things include students, lecturers, courses and modules. In this example, all these things would be valid classes. We represent such information classes by a labelled rectangle on an information model.

A *relationship* is an association between information classes. Typically these are binary relationships, associations between two classes. For instance, in analysing our business we might express the fact that a customer *places* a sales order or a supplier *handles* a purchase order. Or alternatively, within a university domain we might wish to represent the fact that students *enrol on* modules and that lecturers *teach* modules.

In these phrases customer, supplier, sales order, purchase order, student, module and lecturer are information classes. Places, handles, enrols and teach are labels we might use for the relationships between these classes. We represent relationships on an information model by a labelled line drawn between associated classes.

A class is given shape through its properties or *attributes*. For instance, in a university domain we normally define a class such as Module or Student because we wish to communicate about such things and eventually to record some data about the occurrences of these things. To do this we use the properties or attributes of a class. For instance, students have names, addresses and telephone numbers; modules have titles and credit points. Values assigned to attributes are used to distinguish one instance or object of a class from another. Hence, to distinguish one instance of a student from another we give them a different name, address, and so on. Upon an information model, we represent attributes by adding their names to the appropriate class box.

Figure 3.14 illustrates the graphic notation adopted for classes, attributes and relationships.

DID YOU KNOW? The approach we are describing here is sometimes referred to as entity–relationship–attribute modelling and is based upon some commonly used approaches to database design. It is also important to the idea of information management within organisations, which we shall cover in a later chapter.

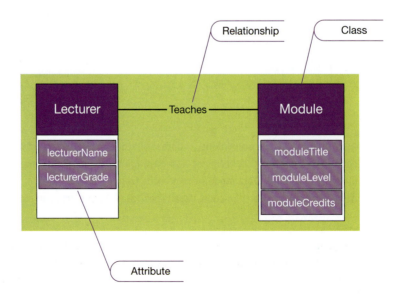

Figure 3.14 Information model constructs

3.6.2 Relationships and constraints

There are various different types of relationship possible between classes. In this section we focus on relationships of association. In a later section we look at relationships of aggregation and generalisation.

In relationships of association, we work typically only with binary relationships, associations between two classes. However, it is possible for more than one relationship to exist between any two classes. For instance, the classes House and Person can be related by ownership and/or by occupation. In theory, if we have a set of say six classes, there could be up to 15 relationships between them. In practice, it will usually be obvious that many classes are not related.

The object of information modelling is to document only direct relationships, that is, relationships between two classes with no intervening class. For instance, there are direct relationships between the classes Parent and Child and between Child and School. The relationship between Parent and School is indirect; it exists only through the Child class.

To each relationship of association we can add two types of business rule or constraint, which expresses for us how a given business works with its associated information classes. One type of rule is known as a **cardinality** rule while the other type of rule is known as an **optionality** rule. These two types of rule help ensure the integrity of the data held about a business domain.

Cardinality establishes how many instances of one class are related to how many instances of another class. Any relationship may be typed as either a one-to-one (1:1), one-to-many (1:M) or many-to-many (M:N) relationship. If we state that the relationship is one to one, then one instance of a class is always associated with one instance of the other class. Specifying a relationship as one to many means that one instance of a class is associated with more than one instance of the other class. If we state that the relationship is many to many, then many instances of one class are associated with many instances of another class.

For example, in terms of the cardinality of the *places* relationship between customer and sales order, we ask ourselves the question: how many sales orders can be placed by one customer and how many customers appear on a particular sales order? If the answer to any of these questions is many, we place a 'crows-foot' symbol next to the respective entity. If the answer to any of these questions is one, we leave the crows-foot off the relationship for the respective entity. Hence, in the case of customer places sales order, customer is likely to have a cardinality of one and sales order a cardinality of many.

In defining this we are actually making two assertions about the business situation we are modelling: that a customer may place many sales orders, but that a particular sale order is placed by at most one customer. On the left-hand side of Figure 3.15 three examples of cardinality are given for the relationship between the classes Lecturer and Module, so there are three sets of two assertions.

- A lecturer may teach at most one module and a module is taught by at most one lecturer.
- A lecturer may teach many modules but a particular module is taught by at most one lecturer.
- A lecturer may teach many modules and a module may be taught by many lecturers.

From these three possibilities the business analyst would choose the one that most readily describes the particular domain being considered.

Optionality establishes whether all instances of a class must participate in a relationship or not. Hence, each class participating in a relationship is either mandatory or optional in that relationship. A zero (O) is used to indicate that a class is optional in a relationship and a vertical line is used to indicate that a class is mandatory. Hence, in the case of customer places sales order the optionality is mandatory both for customer and sales order in the places relationship. This means that we make two further assertions about the business situation: that

Cardinality: rules that specify how many instances of classes are associated with a relationship

Optionality: rules that specify whether all instances of classes participate in a relationship

a customer must place at least one sales order to constitute being a customer of the company and that a sales order must always be associated with an existing customer.

On the right-hand side of Figure 3.15 there are four combinations of optionality for the teaches relationship between Lecturer and Module. Reading from top to bottom these embody the rules:

- Every lecturer must teach at least one module. A module must be taught by at least one lecturer.
- A lecturer need not teach any modules. A module must be taught by at least one lecturer.
- A lecturer need not teach any modules. A module need not have any lecturers assigned to teach it.
- Every lecturer must teach at least one module. A module need not have any lecturers assigned to teach it.

Again, in a specific model the modeller will determine which of these rules should apply.

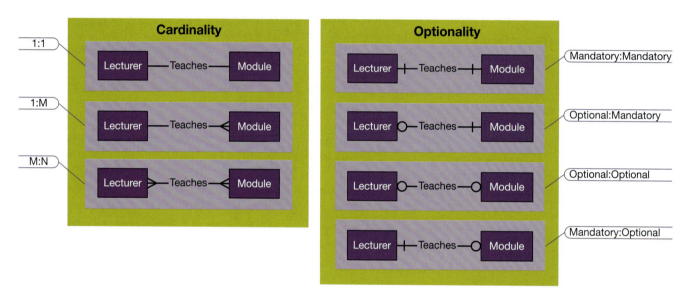

Figure 3.15 *Optionality and cardinality*

Figure 3.16 is a simple information model, again based on a university domain. Take the relationship *registration* between the class Student and the class Course. Its optionality indicates that a course must have at least one student and a student must register on at least one course. The cardinality of the relationship is one to many, indicating that many students take a course, but any given student may register for only one course at one time. The class Module and the class Student are related through two associations: a student may enrol upon many modules and may be assessed on these modules. Finally, the prerequisite class is a link between modules within the curriculum. A module may be the prerequisite for many other modules; meaning that a student has to successfully complete a particular module before being able to take another. Likewise, a particular module may have many prerequisites.

RECAP: An information model is built through classes, attributes and relationships. Classes are things of interest of relevance to some domain. Attributes describe the properties of a class. Relationships define how particular classes relate together. Two types of business rule can be added to a particular relationship. Cardinality refers to how many instances or objects of one class relate to the instances of another class. Optionality determines whether all instances of a class must participate in a relationship or not.

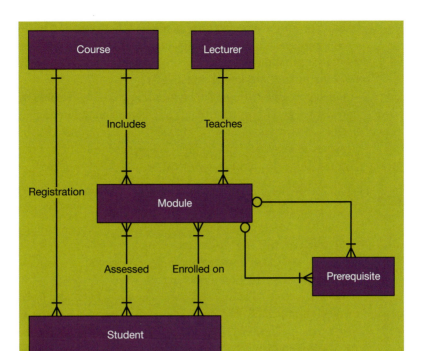

Figure 3.16 *University information model*

3.7   Business knowledge

Unlike data and information, which we have defined and distinguished in previous sections, knowledge is a far more slippery term. The word knowledge is derived from the Ancient Greek word *gignoskein*, which can be roughly translated as to decide upon, determine or decree. Epistemology, or the philosophical theory of knowledge, is at least as old as the term itself, and knowledge, or the problem of knowledge, has been of intensive interest to sociologists and psychologists for centuries. More recently there has been an emphasis on organisational knowledge: how organisations learn and to what degree they can manage their knowledge.

Individuals clearly acquire knowledge that improves their performance in specific fields. But does it make sense to think of groups and organisations as having knowledge, and if so, to what extent? The concept of organisational memory has been suggested to describe what an organisation knows about its internal systems and its environment. This knowledge is a critical resource for business organisations, helping them operate effectively in economic markets. In this section we adopt a practical view of individual and organisational knowledge, which builds upon our previous discussion of data, information and decision-making. This allows us to make the distinction in Chapter 11 between data, information and knowledge management. Knowledge in this view involves building and using patterns of inference from data and information.

3.7.1   Types of knowledge

Knowledge: building and using patterns of inference from data and information

We can categorise types of organisational **knowledge** on three dimensions: accessibility, level of abstraction and purpose.

For accessibility, we can distinguish between explicit and tacit knowledge. Explicit knowledge is readily accessible, documented and organised. Tacit knowledge is implicit and internal. Nonaka and Takeuchi (1995) argue that it is increasingly important to convert internalised tacit knowledge into explicit codified knowledge in order to share it and reduce problems caused by staff turnover. Clearly to make this knowledge explicit it must be translated or converted into data and communicated as information. In other words, mind-stuff must be converted into symbol-stuff.

In terms of purpose, we can distinguish between declarative knowledge (knowing what) and procedural knowledge (knowing how). Declarative knowledge involves being able to recognise something as an instance of something else. Procedural knowledge tells us how to do something in specific circumstances.

Finally, we can distinguish between knowledge applicable to a narrow area of life (domain knowledge) and knowledge that is transferable between domains (generic knowledge). Much business activity relies on workers using domain knowledge, both declarative (such as knowing what an expense claim form is) and procedural (such as the process set down for appraising staff).

3.7.2   Objects and classes

Recent ICT systems incorporate mechanisms for representing or automating certain aspects of both declarative and procedural domain knowledge that is explicit. This section discusses how these aspects of knowledge can be represented in a model, which builds upon the earlier discussion of information modelling.

Object: an instance of something of interest to some domain

We first need to distinguish between an **object** and an object class. As we have seen, one of the key questions for any business organisation is: *what do we need to know about our business to run it effectively?* The answer to this question is business objects and business classes. An *object* is an instance of something of interest to two or more business actors. Objects may be physical, such as customers, products, houses and cars. Objects may also be events, such as a house sale, a customer order, a customer payment or a car service.

An *object class,* or *class* for short, is an abstraction of a group of instances or objects. This means that there are normally many instances of objects that correspond to an object class. If there are not many instances, it is probably not worth thinking of it as an object class.

Generally, a class is something which a group of actors wishes to communicate about. To do this a class must be distinguishable; we must be able to distinguish instances of one class from instances of another class. Therefore, a class is an abstraction from the complexities of a business domain. When we speak of a class we normally speak of some aspect of the domain which can be distinguished from other aspects of the domain, something that makes a difference.

When actually writing of a product such as a steel lintel, or a person such as a lecturer, or an event such as a business visit, we are inherently using signs as classes. To speak or write or generally to communicate about some object we need an identifier to refer to the specific thing we are referring to or identifying. An identifier is a sign. Paul Beynon-Davies is an identifier for me, it is a designator for me as an object of interest. Lecturer, consultant, academic and author are all identifiers for classes which apply to me, they are designators for certain concepts that encapsulate a certain group of objects. We use classes to chunk up the world so that we can communicate about it.

Therefore, an object class is an abstraction of the common features of a group of objects. Such features are defined in terms of relationships between the class, its properties and instances, as well as relationships between that class and others.

3.7.3   Attribution and association

In drawing an information model, described in a previous section, we actually and implicitly used two types of relationships: relationships of attribution and relationships of association.

Attribution: the relationship between an object class and an attribute

When we define the properties of some class, we actually engage in a process of **attribution**. Attribution is the process of defining a class in terms of its properties or attributes. Consider a financial institution which invests money saved by customers in defined savings accounts. Within this domain customers and savings accounts might be two object classes of interest. Typical properties or attributes of customers include names, addresses and telephone numbers. Typical attributes of savings accounts are start dates and current balances. Or, take

Goronwy Galvanising, in this business domain a Product is a class defined by attributes such as product length and product weight.

Information (as we defined it earlier) is interpreted data; data placed in a meaningful context and used within communication. Here the context is defined in terms of two types of relation between classes: the relationship between an object class and its attributes (an attribution relation); or an association between an object class and some other object class. This might be defined in BNF as:

<information-item> ::= <object-class><attribution-relation><attribute>
<information-item> ::= <object-class><association-relation><object-class>

This means that we can either add attributes to the relevant class of a graphic information model, as we have done in previous figures, or we can use a written shorthand using the label HASA to relate the name of the attribute with its class. For example:

Product HASA product Length
Product HASA product Weight

A datum, a unit of data, is used to represent a fact about a domain. We referred to it as a data item earlier. A datum, or data item, can be defined in terms of the constructs introduced, and using BNF, as:

<datum> ::= <object><attribute><value>

A record of details (data element) for a savings account might consist of a set of data items each with a similar structure: an identifier or name for the object; a name for the attribute; a value. Spaces can be used to mark the start and end of these items. Perhaps one savings account is identified as 4324, and we might know its start date is 12 February 2001, which leads to us expressing the data item as:

4324 Start Date 12/02/2001

That the current balance is £500 would produce this data item:

4324 Current Balance 500

The entire collection of assertions about savings accounts corresponds to what we referred to earlier as a data structure.

As we have seen, classes are also defined in terms of their associations with other classes. An **association** is a binary relationship between two object classes. An example from the financial case might be customer *owns* Savings Account. Examples of such binary relationships from the Goronwy Galvanising case are delivery advice *contains* delivery items and delivery item *refers to* product item.

Then we can define the relationships between customers and savings accounts as:

Customer HASA Name
Customer HASA Branch
Customer HASA Tel No
Savings Account HASA Start Date
Savings Account HASA Current Balance
Savings Account HASA Interest Rate
Customer Owns Savings Account

Association: the relationship between instances of one object class and another object class

3.7.4 Classification

The word **inference** is derived from the Latin words *in* and *ferre*, meaning to carry or bring forward. So inference is the process of bringing forward new knowledge from existing knowledge. We can either do this generically by using some established relationships of abstraction or we can write some domain-specific rules for performing inference. Let us first have a look

Inference: bringing new knowledge from existing knowledge

Classification: the relationship between a class and an object or instance

Instantiation: the relationship between an object or instance and its class

at three established relationships of abstraction, the first of which is **classification**, or its opposite, **instantiation**.

An ISA relationship is a relationship between objects and object classes and as such represents processes of classification and instantiation. Thus, when we state that:

Paul Beynon-Davies ISA customer, we are defining a particular object as being a member of the class of customers. In one direction, from object to class (Paul Beynon-Davies to customer), we are classifying an object as being an instance of a class, this is classification. In the other direction (customer to Paul Beynon-Davies), we are engaging in instantiation: instantiating (making an instance of) a given class by listing a particular object that is encompassed by the class. Hence, we might classify business information systems as a course, Paul Beynon-Davies as a patient or LG321 as a product-type relevant to Goronwy Galvanising.

3.7.5   Generalisation

Generalisation: the relationship between a class and a sub-class

Specialisation: the relationship between a sub-class and its super-class

An AKO (A-Kind-Of) relationship is a relationship between an object class (sub-class) and its more general or abstract object class (super-class). As such, an AKO relationship represents processes of **generalisation** and **specialisation**. In one direction, from sub-class to super-class, we are generalising from one level of abstraction to another. In the other direction, from super-class to sub-class, we are reducing the level of abstraction, or specialising a class.

Hence, when we state that:

Ordinary account AKO savings account

we are defining the class of ordinary accounts to be a sub-class of the class of savings accounts. In terms of Goronwy we might declare a lintel is a kind of product.

An AKO, or generalisation relation, can be represented on a diagram as a line terminating in a triangle. This is illustrated in Figure 3.17.

> **DID YOU KNOW?** Classification and generalisation are important to taxonomy, the science of identifying and naming species. Taxonomy is an important sub-discipline of biology where the classification scheme of biological organisms is organised hierarchically in terms of domain, kingdom, phylum, class, order, family, genus and species.
>
> Most libraries also use classification and generalisation schemes for organising the storage and retrieval of publications. For instance the Dewey Decimal scheme organises publications into ten main divisions, which are in turn organised into ten main sections, and so on ...

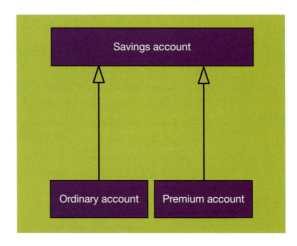

Figure 3.17 *Example of generalisation*

3.7.6   Aggregation

Aggregation: the relationship between a class treated as a part and its containing class

An aggregation relationship occurs between a whole and its parts. An **aggregation** is an abstraction in which a relationship between objects is considered a higher level object. This makes it possible to focus on the aggregate while suppressing low-level detail. For example, in terms of the financial domain we might define a Customer Portfolio class that aggregates together all the financial products making up a given customer's interaction with the financial company. In such terms, a financial Portfolio class can be considered an aggregate of securities, insurance policies, and savings accounts. A country can be considered an aggregate of regions, which are aggregates of counties, which are aggregates of districts, and so on. In the case of the health service a patient record can be considered as a collection of diagnoses, prescriptions and treatments.

Hence, aggregation relationships compose an object out of an assembly or aggregation of other objects. When we state that:

Railway station PARTOF railway

Railway line PARTOF railway

We are declaring that railways are composed of an aggregation of stations and lines.

Decomposition: the relationship between a class treated as a whole and its parts

The opposite of aggregation is **decomposition**. That is, the process of decomposing an object class into its constituent parts. Hence, there is a clear difference between aggregation and generalisation. If two classes are defined in terms of a generalisation relationship then both sub-class and super-class effectively refer to the same thing. In an aggregation relationship the aggregate, the whole, is different from any of its parts.

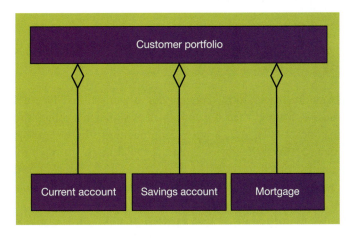

Figure 3.18 Example of aggregation

3.7.7 Business rules

If we add relationships of classification, generalisation and aggregation to an information model we are effectively creating a model of the declarative knowledge relevant to a domain. We can then use some general rules of inference to infer new knowledge from this existing and explicit knowledge.

One particularly important such rule is known as inheritance and takes the form:

IF Object ISA Object Class

AND Object Class Attribute Value

THEN Object Attribute Value

For instance, we know that Paul Beynon-Davies ISA customer and we also know that Customer HASA Branch. From this we can infer that Paul Beynon-Davies HASA Branch.

We can also write domain-specific rules, those that only apply in a particular business domain. For instance, we might write the following rule into our system:

IF Object1 ISA Customer

THEN Object1 Holds Object2

AND Object2 ISA Customer Portfolio

In other words, this rule is that all customers can be assumed to hold a customer portfolio. We can use a rule such as this in a number of ways in an ICT system. For example, when a customer's access details are entered the system could automatically load data on that person's portfolio.

Business rule: a specification of some part of business operation which relates conditions to outcomes

This is an example of a **business rule**, a rule that specifies an aspect of business operation. Business rules have become an important part of the architecture of ICT systems and normally help represent explicit, procedural knowledge. Typically they embed aspects of domain-specific decision-making in them, that is, given a rule that details under which circumstances it must do one thing or another, the system can 'decide' what to do. Domain-specific rules can be used in this way to make changes to the data held in the data system representing the domain. This is the key way in which ICT systems become important actors within business situations.

FOCUS ON VALUE	Information has key value as a mediating force between technology and action or activity. It is the fundamental 'stuff' of communication, and can be understood on a number of different levels. A layered perspective allows us to distinguish between data, information and knowledge, and use this to understand the linkages between technology and activity systems in business organisations. Data consists of 'values' assigned to data items, but the true value of data arises in the use of data in the context of communication and coordinated activity. 'Quality' information has value to decision-making and in support of coordinated activity. Knowledge involves connecting new information with established networks of information and is critical to organisational learning.

3.8   Conclusion and key themes

Information is a central concept for organisational life in the twenty-first century, but, because it is a multi-faceted concept, it is somewhat difficult to define. This chapter used the core concept of signs as a way of approaching a better understanding of information. Signs mediate between the physical and the social world, through the psychological world and can be clearly related to the types of organisational systems discussed in Chapter 2. Signs also allow us to better define related concepts such as data, decisions and knowledge.

A sign consists of a significant pattern treated by two or more actors as significant. It is possible to unpack any sign as a pattern that has three distinct but inter-related facets, which we denote as forma, informa and performa. These distinctions serve to link three worlds critical to all business organisation: the physical or technical world with the social world through the psychological world. Forma constitutes the substance, representation and manipulation of signs and falls within the physical or technical world. Informa constitutes the content of signs and their use within communication. As such, informa falls within the psychological world. Finally, performa constitutes the use of signs within coordinated, instrumental activity and thus falls within the social world.

The three levels of a sign relate directly to the three levels of business system discussed in Chapter 2. Activity systems are social systems. Signs are used in such activity systems to support collaborative and coordinated action. In one direction they are used to encode intentions. In the other direction they are used as key inputs into decisions. An information system is a communication system used to support a given activity system. Information systems use signs to communicate meaning between actors. A data system is a system of symbol representation. It is concerned with the physical representation of signs for storage, transmission and manipulation.

Information therefore supports performative activity in the sense that it enables *decisions* to be made about appropriate actions in particular circumstances. Therefore, decisions and decision-making mediate between information and action

A working definition of knowledge builds on the concepts of data, information and decision-making. A datum, a single item of data, is a set of symbols used to represent something. When symbols are given context and meaning in a situation they become information. Information is therefore data placed in a meaningful context, and is used in organisations to make decisions and take action. Knowledge is derived from information by integrating it with existing knowledge. Declarative knowledge (knowing what) is normally acquired through a process of abstraction. Procedural knowledge (knowing how) typically involves the use of business rules.

Chapter 4 considers the concept of an information system in more detail. It distinguishes more clearly between the three types of business system introduced here. It also introduces the idea of infrastructure to help explain how systems are related in the organisational context. It discusses elements of a typical business information system infrastructure and explains how it supports decision-making and business activity.

3.9 Review test

1 Semiotics is the study of _____. Fill in the blank.

2 Very broadly a _____ is anything that is significant. A _____ is any organised collection of signs and relations between signs.
Fill in the blanks.

3 Why is the concept of a sign useful for understanding what information is? Write two sentences.

4 A datum, a single item of data, is a set of symbols used to represent something. True or false?
☐ True
☐ False

5 Information reduces _____ in decision-making. Fill in the blank.

6 A decision is structured or algorithmic if the decision-making process can be specified in detail before the decision is made. True or false?
☐ True
☐ False

7 There are three levels of managerial decision-making. What are they?
☐ Middle
☐ Strategic
☐ Operational
☐ Tactical

8 A data model consists of? Select all that apply
☐ Data structures
☐ Data elements
☐ Data communications
☐ Data items

9 A data element consists of a number of data items. True or false?
☐ True
☐ False

10 Write down three properties associated with the quality of information.

11 A file is a data structure or a data element?
☐ Data structure
☐ Data element

12 <business-telephone-no>::= <area-code><telephone-no><extension-number>
Write a full sentence that adequately describes this BNF specification.

13 Match the type of communicative act with the appropriate definition. Pair each lettered entry with the corresponding numbered entry.

a. Assertive   1. Communicative acts that attempt to get a receiver to perform some action

b. Directive   2. Communicative acts that commit the speaker to some future course of action

c. Commissive   3. Communicative acts that explain how things are in the world

d. Expressive   4. Communicative acts that aim to change the world through the communication

e. Declarative   5. Communicative acts that represent the sender's psychological state

14 Information modelling consists of using three constructs: _____, relationships and attributes. Fill in the blank.

15 A personal name is a class or an attribute of a class?
☐ Class
☐ Attribute

16 Produce an information model which represents the following domain of criminal court cases. Each judge has a list of outstanding cases over which they will preside. Only one judge presides over each case. For each case one prosecuting counsel is appointed to represent the Department of Public Prosecutions. Cases are scheduled at one Crown Court for an estimated duration from a given start date. A case can try more than one crime. Each crime can have one or more defendants. Each defendant can have one or more defending barristers. If a crime has multiple defendants, each defendant can have one or more defence counsel. Defendants may have more than one outstanding case against them.

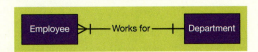

17 Write the assertions associated with the cardinality and optionality of the two classes in the diagram above.

18 Draw the diagram which represents the following statements:
Undergraduate Module AKO module
Postgraduate Module AKO module

19 In terms of modelling knowledge, match the name of the
construct to its proper symbol. Select three.

Class

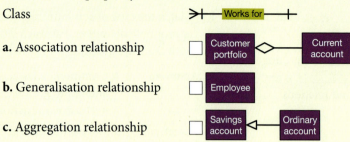

a. Association relationship ☐

b. Generalisation relationship ☐

c. Aggregation relationship ☐

3.10   Exercises

- Take a visual sign, such as the ones you might find
  in the highway code. Try to separate out what the
  sign is (forma) from what it represents (informa).
- Then consider the sign from the highway code in
  terms of what it is designed to do (performa).
- Consider the entire Highway Code as a sign-system.
  What human activity does it support? How does it
  support this behaviour?
- Select and analyse a written communication, such
  as a customer order, as a data structure. What make
  up its data elements and data items?
- What sort of information classes might be relevant
  to the domain of meals on wheels described in
  Chapter 2? How do such classes relate through
  relationships of association? Try to assign
  both optionality and cardinality to each of the
  relationships you identify.
- Aggregation relations are particularly important in
  managing manufacturing operations through part-

assembly structures. Investigate such structures in
relation to a problem such as managing the problem
of assembling an automobile from a vast array of
separate parts.

- Emails often use emoticons, signs such as :-) or ☹,
  which convey emotional content. Investigate their
  range and use and describe them in terms of the
  distinctions made in this chapter.
- Hand gestures are becoming important in the
  control of devices such as tablet computers.
  Investigate how these gestural interfaces are
  developing.
- Consider a decision made in an organisation
  known to you. Work back from the decision to the
  information required to support it. What action
  resulted from the decision?

3.11   Projects

- Using the approach described in this chapter,
  develop a detailed data model for an area known
  to you, for example, a specification of the data
  structures, data elements and data items relevant to
  student records.
- Records have been maintained for many hundreds,
  if not thousands, of years in organisations of many
  different forms. Nowadays, records management
  is seen as a significant problem for organisations.
  Investigate the term 'records management'.
  Determine why it is a significant problem and why
  it is increasingly important for organisations.
- Consider the diverse ways in which data is captured
  in an organisation such as a retail chain. Determine
  the ways in which it is validated and verified.

Consider the extent to which the data collected by
the organisation is of the necessary quality. You
might use criteria like the degree to which the data
is accurate or useful.

- Identify an information system supporting activity
  in an organisation known to you, such as a patient
  records system in a GP practice, a student records
  system at a school, an inventory management system
  at a retail store, or a waste collection scheduling
  system at a local authority. Investigate and document
  the information model underlying your chosen
  information system using the approach in this chapter.
- Determine the business rules underlying an
  information system known to you, such as those for
  student progression on university courses. Specify

the business rules as a decision table or as a set of IF THEN statements.

‣ Claude Shannon's communication theory has had a critical influence on the development of telecommunications, particularly data communications. Investigate the relevance of this theory to ICT. For instance, in what way can Shannon's theory be seen to underlie the modern conception of the Internet?

‣ Electronic mail is a pervasive form of communication in many organisations. Investigate some of the literature in this area. What consequences does its increasing use have for organisational decision-making and action?

‣ Investigate the applicability of the three-layered management model (strategic, tactical and operational) to an organisation known to you. Try to identify who are the strategic, tactical and operational managers. What decisions do they typically take? What information do they use?

‣ Much literature has been published on organisational knowledge and its management. Consider a limited area of an organisation known to you (concerning, for example, the sale of products and services). Try to document some of this knowledge using the approach used in this chapter.

3.12 Critical reflection

Consider accessing two websites. One site is written in English and the other in Russian. Assuming you are not a reader of Russian you can be informed by the English website but not the Russian one. Reflect on why this is the case in terms of the distinction made between information and data considered in this chapter.

Within wider literature the term information system is used in a much looser way than we have used in this chapter to include people, processes and technology. Consider whether the definition applied in this book is better or not in terms of some area known to you.

Much has been published on business decision-making. How do we judge whether decisions are good or not? Does better communication improve decision-making? Is good record management important to decision-making and why?

3.13 Further reading

Stamper (1973) provided the original motivation for considering information in terms of semiotics. It is now out of print but his position is summarised in a more recent book chapter (Stamper, 2001). The theory of informative acts described in this chapter is based on the work of John Searle (1970). For more detail on the distinction between formative, informative and performative acts see my recent book (Beynon-Davies, 2011). Data, information and knowledge modelling are covered in some detail in Beynon-Davies (2004) on database systems. Good further reading on knowledge management and its link to innovation is in Newell et al. (2009).

3.14 References

Ackoff, R. L. (1967). Management Misinformation Systems. *Management Science* 14 (4): 147–156.

Beynon-Davies, P. (2004). *Database Systems*. 3rd edition. Palgrave Macmillan, Basingstoke.

Beynon-Davies, P. (2011). *Significance: Exploring the Nature of Information, Systems and Technology*. Palgrave Macmillan, Basingstoke.

Darwin, C. (1998). *The Expression of Emotions in Man and Animals*. 3rd edition. Oxford University Press, Oxford.

Newell, S. M., M. Robertson, H. Scarbrough and J. Swan. (2009). *Managing Knowledge, Work and Innovation*. Palgrave Macmillan, Basingstoke.

Nonaka, I. and H. Takeuchi. (1995). *The Knowledge-Creating Company*. Oxford University Press, New York.

Peirce, C. S. (1931). *Collected Papers*. Harvard University Press, Cambridge, Mass.

Pinker, S. (2001). *The Language Gene*. Penguin, Harmondsworth, Middx.

Searle, J. R. (1970). *Speech Acts: An Essay in the Philosophy of Language*. Cambridge University Press, Cambridge.

Shannon, C. E. (1949). *The Mathematical Theory of Communication*. University of Illinois Press, Urbana.

Stamper, R. K. (1973). *Information in Business and Administrative Systems*. Batsford, London.

Stamper, R. K. (2001). Organisational Semiotics: Informatics without the Computer? In L. Kecheng, R. J. Clarke, P. BøghAndersen and R. K. Stamper (eds), *Information, Organisation and Technology: Studies in Organisational Semiotics*. Kluwer, Dordecht, Netherlands.

Von Baeyer, H. C. (2003). *Information : The New Language of Science*. Weidenfeld & Nicolson, London.

See companion website   www.palgrave.com/business/beynon-daviesbis2e

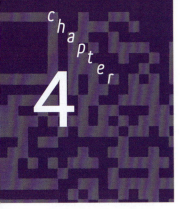

Information systems and organisational infrastructure

'Knowledge is of two kinds. We know a subject ourselves, or we know where we can find information upon it.'

Samuel Johnson (1709–1784). Quoted in the *Life of Johnson* (1791), by James Boswell.

Learning outcomes	Principles
Explain the distinction between an activity system, information system and ICT system and in this process define in more detail the essence of what an information system means.	An information system is a sociotechnical system – a communication system using artefacts (ICT) in support of a given activity system. It therefore spans the concepts of data, information, decision-making and action discussed in Chapter 3.
Describe the concept of business infrastructure and distinguish between back-end and front-end information systems infrastructure.	The activity infrastructure of any organisation relies on a corresponding information systems and ICT infrastructure. In terms of information systems infrastructure, which is the focus of this chapter, it is possible to distinguish between those information systems that directly interface with different organisational stakeholders (front-end information systems) and those which form the core information-handling systems of the organisation (back-end information systems).
Describe the high-level functionality of the key back-end and front-end information systems in the typical enterprise and construct a simple information systems model based on an understanding of such systems.	Organisations in the private sector rely typically on a core set of back-end information systems. Around these core systems a range of front-end information systems are normally constructed. It is important to represent the functionality of this information systems infrastructure as an aid to better management. For this purpose, information systems models are critical.
Describe the relationship between data systems infrastructure and information systems infrastructure and identify some of the key information classes relevant to the enterprise.	The information systems infrastructure of any organisation is reliant on an integrated information infrastructure. High-level information models are therefore important in recognising and managing the interdependencies between information systems within organisations.

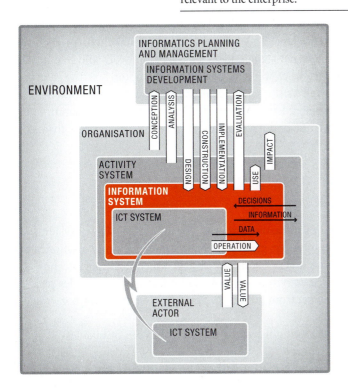

Chapter outline

AACSB learning objectives:
Use of IT, communication and ethical issues

4.1   Introduction

Chapter 2 showed how the concept of a system is core to organisational informatics. This is such a useful concept because it allows us to relate systems of activity to systems of communication and systems of representation. The relationships between these three levels of system are critical anchor points for any consideration of organisational informatics.

Chapter 3 considered the importance of the concept of information. Information arises in the process of communication, is different from data, and is critical in support of decision-making and coordinated activity within organisations. This chapter brings the understanding of systems and information together, and uses it to help explain the place of information systems in organisations.

In Chapter 2 we spent some time discussing the idea of an activity system and came to the conclusion that organisations can be considered as a complex of inter-related activity systems. In Chapter 3 we examined the nature of information and came to the conclusion that any coordinated activity relies upon information, the effective communication between organisational actors. In this chapter we examine the nature of information systems in much more detail and describe the place of such information systems in, what we shall refer to as, the wider organisational infrastructure. We also expand upon the important distinction between an information system and a data or ICT system. This sets the scene for our exploration of ICT infrastructure in further chapters.

We shall demonstrate in this chapter that whereas information systems have existed in support of human organisation for many thousands of years, the application of information and communication technology as data systems in support of information systems is relatively recent, at least in the form of digital computing technology.

Modelling continues to be used in this chapter as a tool to help understand and represent the nature of systems. This leads us to a consideration of diagramming as a tool for modelling information systems. The diagramming approach is built upon that described in previous chapters and is used to help define some of the core information systems found in business, what we shall call the organisation's back-end information systems infrastructure. This provides the bedrock for contemporary business because it supports some of the key activity systems of modern business.

The core back-end information systems infrastructure is also typically the platform for many front-end information systems, which are critical to maintaining effective relationships with key organisational stakeholders. This includes external stakeholders such as suppliers and customers, as well as internal stakeholders such as employees and managers. So these information systems support what we shall describe in Chapter 7 as the internal value-chain of the organisation as well as the wider external value network within which an organisation works. As we shall see, a key challenge for the modern organisation is to successfully integrate back-end and front-end information systems to support new forms of activity (see Chapter 8).

4.2   Business infrastructure

Infrastructure: Systems of activity, communication and technology that create organisation

Organisation in whatever form requires infrastructure. **Infrastructure** consists of systems of activity, communication and technology that generate what we mean by organisation. For example, a road infrastructure is both a supporting social and a technical (sociotechnical) infrastructure for travel, the associated activity system. A road infrastructure enables people driving automobiles, vans or lorries to get from point A to point B using motorways, carriageways and major or minor roads.

In both Chapters 2 and 3 we have distinguished between three types of business system that inter-relate to form the infrastructure of organisation: activity systems, information systems and data systems. This means that there are three layers of infrastructure: activity

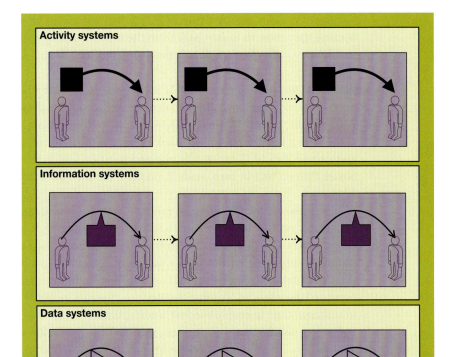

Figure 4.1 *Business infrastructure*

systems infrastructure, information systems infrastructure and data systems or ICT systems infrastructure (Figure 4.1). Each of these layers is critically dependent on the layer below it.

Activity systems, as we have seen, are social systems, so they are sometimes referred to as 'soft' systems. They consist of people engaging in coordinated activities in fulfilment of a goal or purpose. In contrast, data systems are technical systems. They are often called 'hard' systems because they consist of an assembly of artefacts, which are designed to manipulate data and thus to support aspects of an information system. In the modern organisation, as we shall see, data systems primarily consist of digital computing and communications technology.

Information systems clearly mediate between 'hard' technical systems and 'soft' social systems. When people communicate in organisations they frequently use technologies to store and transmit the data which represent the messages being communicated. Such messages, as we have seen, are used to coordinate people's activities. In this sense, some people think information systems are key examples of what are called **sociotechnical systems**; they involve communication using technology, directed at the coordination of activity.

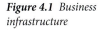

Sociotechnical system: A social system that utilises technology

4.2.1   The warning network

We have deliberately used the term data system rather than ICT system in the previous section because we want to emphasise a number of things. First, that information and communication technology comes in various forms and that modern digital computing and communications technology is the latest in a long line of innovations in data technology. Second, focusing on the technology of data systems allows us to better define the concept of an information system and see its key role in support of performance. Third, this better enables us to understand the value of infrastructure to organisations of all forms.

Historical cases are particularly useful for helping us make these points more clearly, because they allow us to step back from the modern setting and explore the data, information and activity systems of a different time. So let us look at an interesting case from the Second World War.

During the summers of the late 1930s, the Royal Air Force (RAF) Fighter Command created an early warning network which played a part in a decisive battle against the German Luftwaffe, the Battle of Britain in 1940 (Holwell and Checkland, 1998a). Hitler needed control of the skies if he was to invade Britain by sea, but the Battle of Britain gave control to the RAF, and caused him to abandon the planned invasion and turn his attention eastwards to the Soviet Union. This in turn made it possible for the Allies to invade continental Europe in 1944.

During the early 1930s accepted military strategy for air defence was to fly, so-called, standing patrols on flight paths likely to intercept bombing raids by an enemy. This constituted an extremely expensive military strategy in that aircraft had to be kept permanently in the skies. Not surprisingly, this strategy was eventually replaced with the use of interceptor flights that could take-off quickly and attack incoming bomber raids. However, the key question remained, how was an air force to determine the precise position of incoming enemy aircraft in sufficient time to enable effective interception?

The key solution to this problem involved the utilisation of radio technology to detect aircraft, a technology that became known as RADAR. Both the Germans and British had access to this technology and indeed German radar was technically superior to its British equivalent at the time. The crucial difference was that the British were better able to utilise the technology in action.

To do this British Fighter Command constructed a chain of radar stations around the British coast. This was supplemented with a chain of posts manned by persons observing incoming aircraft known as the Observer Corps. There were actually two chains of radar station, one for detecting high-flying aircraft and one for detecting low-flying aircraft. Over a thousand observer posts and fighter airfields were also connected to headquarters by dedicated Post Office teleprinter and telephone lines.

The next crucial step was the creation of effective systems of both activity and communication in which the technology could be utilised. During the summers between 1936 and 1939, teams made up of physicists, engineers and RAF personnel engaged in a series of practical exercises with the aim of solving the fundamental problem of turning raw data from radar and observer posts into information for pilots to fly to the precise point at which to intercept enemy raids. The eventual infrastructure of activity, information and data systems that was created allowed an initially under-strength RAF to successfully compete with a numerically greater force of enemy aircraft.

The main elements of this infrastructure are illustrated in Figure 4.2. Let us examine how this infrastructure worked in more detail. The organisation of Fighter Command was divided into four geographical groups covering major parts of the country. Each group was in turn divided into sectors with a sector HQ at each of the airfields. Group HQ had tactical control within their area and sector HQ had control of pilots when airborne.

Data from the two chains of radar stations were telephoned to Fighter Command HQ. This data went first to a filter room where the quality of the data was assessed. Filtered data was then passed next door to the Fighter Command Operations Room. Filtered data and classified plots were recorded by members of the Women's Auxiliary Air Force (WAAF) with the movement of wooden blocks or counters on a large-scale map of the UK. These counters indicated the height, strength and direction of enemy raids. In addition a display (a slotted blackboard), called the tote, recorded enemy raids and the state of readiness of RAF squadrons (available 30 minutes, five minutes, take-off readiness two minutes or in the air), indicated by a series of lights. Changes to the positioning of counters and updates to the tote were conducted simultaneously at headquarters, group and sector level. Elements from the operations room are illustrated in Figure 4.2.

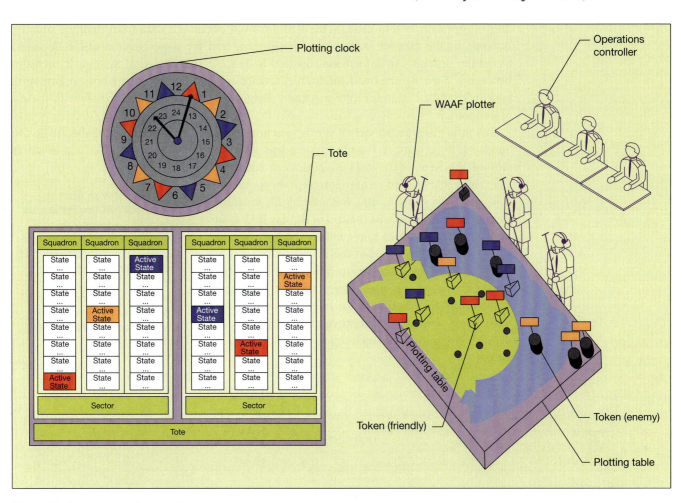

Figure 4.2 *Elements from the operations room*

The operations rooms at group and sector levels worked in the same way except that the maps used represented group and sector areas respectively. Group HQs received information from the Observer Posts and passed it on to command and sector HQs.

The sector room was set up with one unit duplicating the picture at command and group level. A second unit plotted on the map the exact location of their own planes from their radio transmissions. From here aircraft were assigned to a particular raid and their interception courses were continually plotted using compass, ruler, pencil and paper. The sector operations controller scrambled selected aircraft on command from the group HQ. Once in the air, command passed to the flight leader until combat was over. There were also links from the system to Anti-Aircraft command, the Observer Corps, the BBC and civil defence organisations, such as those sounding air-raid warnings.

As in any example of human organisation, we can interpret this case in terms of the three levels of infrastructure, as illustrated in Figure 4.3. Activity systems are social systems, they consist of people engaging in coordinated and collaborative action. In this example the activity system consisted of the command and control of fighter aircraft flown by the RAF.

Information and communications technology is any collection of artefacts used to support aspects of an information system. The ICT described in the example was subtly different from modern information and communications technology. ICT during the Second World War involved elements like RADAR, telephone communications and the use of maps, plotting tables and tote devices. The use of such technology constituted the data system of the time.

Information systems are systems of communication in which people send and receive messages (in this case, assertions about the current position of friendly and enemy aircraft) or directives (such as orders to fighter squadrons to intercept incoming enemy aircraft).

This information system used by the RAF involved organising data from multiple sources, interpreting the data for military decision-making and the dissemination of the decisions to fighter airfields. An information system is hence a sociotechnical system. It mediates between ICT on the one hand and human activity on the other. In other words, information systems constitute communication systems designed to support human activity with the aid of technology.

This infrastructure proved its worth in action from July to the end of October 1940. On Sunday 15th September 1940 the system was severely tested. A hundred German bombers crossed the Kent coast at 11:30, seventeen squadrons from three RAF groups went to intercept them. At 14:00 a second wave came in and was met by 31 squadrons (over 300 planes in all). At the end of the day RAF losses were 27 aircraft with 13 pilots killed. The Luftwaffe lost 57 aircraft. But the success of this infrastructure was not due to the technology, communication or the activity in isolation. The success of fighter command during the Battle of Britain was due to the effective way in which technology was used to improve communication and decision-making and through this to support purposeful action.

> **DID YOU KNOW?** Many of the principles of operation of the warning network are reproduced in the infrastructure of modern, commercial air traffic control. With, of course, the important difference that air traffic control systems are designed to keep aircraft apart whereas the systems in the case described were designed for one group of aircraft to intercept another.

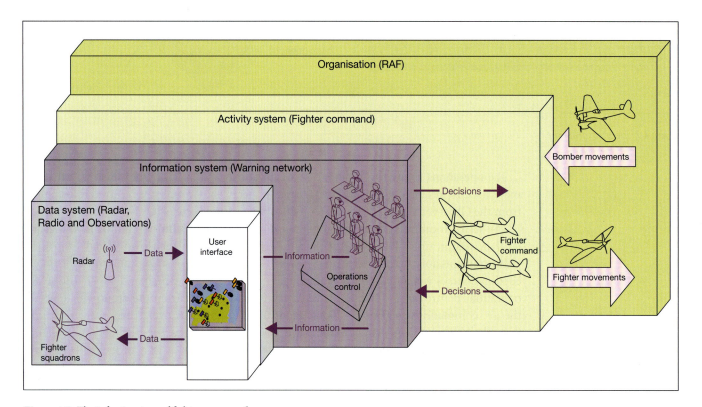

Figure 4.3 *The infrastructure of fighter command*

4.2.2   Modelling infrastructure

The case of the warning network demonstrates the importance of infrastructure as enabling. The data systems, information systems and activity systems in interaction not only produce the value of an organisation, they can also be used to leverage new forms of value-creation. For example, Singapore is very reliant on foreign trade, and by implication shipping. The republic therefore attempted to gain advantage over other ports in the Far East by developing an infrastructure that would significantly reduce the time required for shippers to clear customs. It did this by developing Tradenet, an ICT system that leveraged existing governmental ICT systems by linking traders in to them.

Legacy ICT system: An aging ICT system that is important for the organisation but which constrains infrastructure change

In contrast, **legacy ICT systems** (large and ageing corporate ICT systems) generally constrain an organisation, in the sense that they determine the way in which much corporate data must be collected, manipulated and distributed. Often they have been so heavily maintained that they become difficult to change and interface to other systems.

We mentioned previously that organisations must know a number of things if they are to perform effectively: they must know what they do; they must know what they communicate about what they do; and they must know what they represent about what they do and communicate. Another way of phrasing this is that organisations should ideally have explicit infrastructure, and they should have documented models of this infrastructure.

However, many organisations, both large and small, have much implicit infrastructure. They have never taken the trouble to document the activities they perform, how they communicate with each other or what records they make to help them do their work. Therefore, it is probably true to say that most organisations have a mix of explicit and implicit infrastructure. This often happens because there has not been any systematic analysis of activities, information and data requirements within the business.

There are clearly a number of advantages to having a more explicit business infrastructure. As we shall see, effective business analysis is a necessary pre-condition for effective business design. Making things more explicit through models makes it more feasible to integrate activity, information and ICT systems and make them interoperable, in turn making their management and development more straightforward.

RECAP: Business infrastructure consists of activity systems, information systems and data systems infrastructure. Infrastructure can be implicit or explicit, and is both an enabling and a constraining force in organisations.

The analysis of historical information systems is an extremely useful exercise for highlighting the essential features of information systems. Information systems are communication systems and are distinct from ICT. ICT supports communication within the information system. Good information systems are critical to efficient and effective action.

4.3   Activity systems infrastructure

Clearly each business is different. This may be due partly to different environments, in the sense that different business organisations operate in different sectors of the economy, such as retail, manufacturing or education. However, even organisations in the same economic sector will operate differently. Part of the reason for this may be to achieve an advantage over their competitors in the marketplace. Such competitive advantage may be achieved in a number of ways: through differentiation in human activity, efficiency of human activity and/ or effectiveness in activity.

Activity systems infrastructure: The entire set of activity systems performed by an organisation

Figure 4.4 provides a schematic of an **activity systems infrastructure** for a typical manufacturing company. Such an activity systems infrastructure can be expressed in terms of activity system models, which effectively serve to represent what we called performa in Chapter 3. In the typical business organisation, activity infrastructure consists of a number of activity subsystems such as sales, after-sales, marketing, purchasing, receiving, warehousing, production, human resources, packing and shipping. Such activity subsystems relate together in flows of physical items (broad arrows) as well as data (narrow arrows).

The flow of data in support of activity defines the information systems infrastructure of relevance to the business. On the one side, sales orders from customers act as the major input into the organisation. Sales orders trigger packaging and shipment of goods from customer-side inventory back to the customer. This part of information systems infrastructure therefore supports activities within what we shall refer to in Chapter 7 as the customer chain. Marketing and after-sales service also engage in an attempt to build a long-term relationship with the customer. On

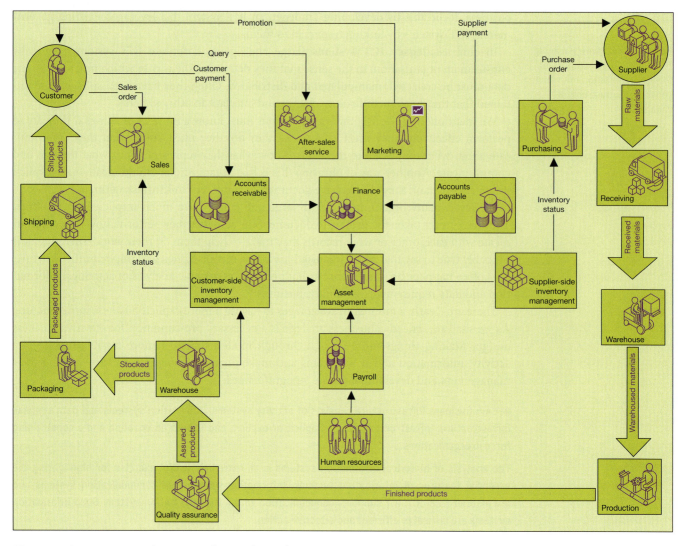

Figure 4.4 *Activity systems infrastructure of a typical manufacturing organisation*

the other side, purchase orders from the company trigger the shipment of raw materials by suppliers. Hence, these information systems support the activities of what we shall call in Chapter 7 the supply chain. This material is received into supply-side inventory management, which drives production, which replenishes customer-side inventory with finished products. Finally, payments from customers are recorded in a central finance system as well as payments to suppliers and employees. These information systems are critical to supporting the activities of the internal value-chain of companies.

> **REFLECT:** What business infrastructure is important to a retail operation such as a supermarket chain? How do supermarkets maintain sufficient stock on their shelves? What activities are needed to ensure this? How are these activities reliant upon communication? What data needs to be recorded and transmitted to achieve full shelves?

4.4   Information systems infrastructure

Information systems infrastructure: The entire set of information systems supporting activity in an organisation

The consequence of differing activity systems infrastructures is that each company's collection of information systems will necessarily be different. Hence, organisations may implement different operational procedures or may parcel up the basic elements of communication in different units. We refer to the entire makeup of an organisation's information systems as its **information systems infrastructure**. Such an information systems infrastructure can be expressed in information system models, which effectively represent a major aspect of what we referred to in Chapter 3 as business informa.

There are a number of core information systems that most businesses have in common at a high level (Figure 4.5). Financial data is the life-blood of most business organisations and is subject to a vast range of external regulation, in the sense that companies must prepare their financial reports in well-established ways. Therefore it is no surprise to find that, in most business organisations, ICT was first applied within the accounting or finance department and that financial information systems form the core around which a number of other information systems are located.

Most companies, of whatever size, will need an information system for recording orders for products/services from customers, orders made to suppliers for products/services and the amounts paid or due to employees. Many businesses that sell products are therefore founded around a number of key information systems, such as:

- Sales order processing is an information system that records details of sales orders from customers.
- Inventory management is the information system that maintains an inventory of raw material from suppliers and finished goods stored in warehouses ready to be shipped to customers.
- Purchase order processing is the information system that records details of purchase orders to suppliers.
- Finance is the system that records amounts owed and paid by customers, amounts owed to and paid to suppliers and amounts paid to and owed to employees.
- Payroll is the information system that records details of wages and payments made to employees.

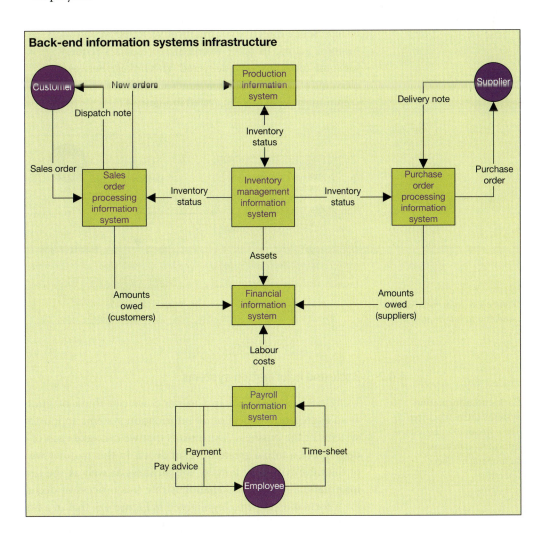

Figure 4.5 *Core information systems infrastructure*

Businesses which sell services will operate differently in the sense of having different activity systems. Hence, although they will have core information systems in similar areas these will operate differently from that described in this chapter.

Core information systems constitute the so-called *back-end* (sometimes referred to as the back-office) systems of a company. They are critical to the performance of core activity systems within business, such as sales and production. Around this core a number of *front-end* information systems will exist. These systems face the major stakeholders of the business: managers, employees, customers and suppliers. Hence, we refer to such information systems in terms of four groups: management information systems, employee-facing information systems, customer-facing information systems and supplier-facing information systems.

4.4.1   Informative acts

It must be remembered that an activity system diagram is an abstraction of a number of performative patterns evident in an organisational situation. Likewise, an information system diagram, such as the one in Figure 4.5, is an abstraction of a number of informative or communicative patterns supporting performative patterns. Hence, the arrow labelled *delivery note* in Figure 4.5 which flows between the actor *supplier* and the process *purchase order processing* can be seen to effectively represent an abstraction of an assertion that a particular order has been delivered between a business actor in the supplier organisation (such as a supplier clerk) and a business actor in the manufacturing organisation (such as a purchasing clerk). Likewise, the arrow labelled *purchase order* that flows between the same process and the supplier can be seen to represent a directive communicative act between two business actors. In other words, it represents a request for some materials to be delivered. This linkage between elements of an information systems diagram and specific communicative acts is illustrated in Figure 4.6.

DID YOU KNOW? One of the earliest forms of writing, Sumerian cuneiscript, which was used from the sixth to the third millennium BC, appears to have been invented not to convey narrative but to support early forms of financial administration. Because of cases such as this, some have even argued that without the need to record assets, written language might never have emerged. *Examine the Inka Khipu case and reflect on this.*

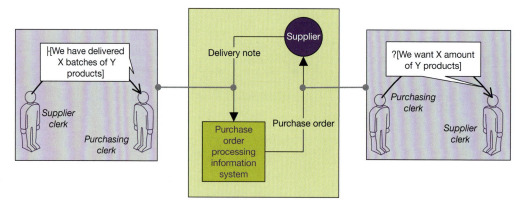

Figure 4.6 *Information systems models and informative acts*

4.4.2   Back-end information systems

Back-end information systems infrastructure: The core set of inter-related information systems supporting business operations

Using an idea discussed in Chapter 3 we can think of information systems infrastructure as an aggregate; a collection of information systems supporting the core, back-office activity systems of the business. This means that we can take each of these information systems and decompose it into a greater level of detail. In this manner we can assemble a detailed model of the information systems of the business as well as the inter-relationships between these information systems. We shall illustrate this process of decomposition in relation to one of the information systems highlighted in Figure 4.5, that of a financial information system.

Figure 4.7 outlines how a standard financial information system, or accounting information system, works within the typical organisation. Normally, this information system is divided into three major subsystems: accounts receivable, accounts payable and general ledger. The names of these three subsystems are actually taken from earlier types of forma employed within offices for many hundreds of years. Each consisted of the maintenance of a large book or ledger consisting of written records of the monetary transactions of a business, posted in the form of debits and credits.

Therefore, we introduce an additional symbol on Figure 4.7, known as a data store, which acts as a repository for data – a place where data collects and is retrieved from. In a manual information system this might be a filing cabinet or card index or ledger. In an information system making use of digital computers and communications, it is generally a database (see Chapter 9). We represent a data store by a labelled open box.

The data store used by the accounts receivable system is generally called a sales ledger, because it records details of the amounts owed by customers. The data store used by the accounts payable system is sometimes called the purchase ledger, because it details monies owed to suppliers.

The general ledger system is used to record details of all the financial transactions relevant to an organisation: income, expenditure and assets. Thus it receives data from accounts payable, accounts receivable and inventory management systems.

The accounts receivable system is essential for managing cash flow. When goods are shipped to customers, the system invoices them and updates their account with details of the amount owed. When customers send payments, their credit balance is reduced by the appropriate amount. The data about customer credit and amounts paid is regularly used to update the general ledger system.

The accounts payable system is also essential for managing cash flow. When goods are ordered from suppliers the system receives a record of the amount owed, and the supplier's account is updated. When payments are made against invoices received, the balance owed is reduced accordingly. This data too is regularly used to update the general ledger system.

The third key input into a general ledger system is a payroll information system, which regularly updates the general ledger with the costs incurred in paying staff. There will also be an input into the general ledger from the inventory management information system, so that a record is kept of the financial value of assets held.

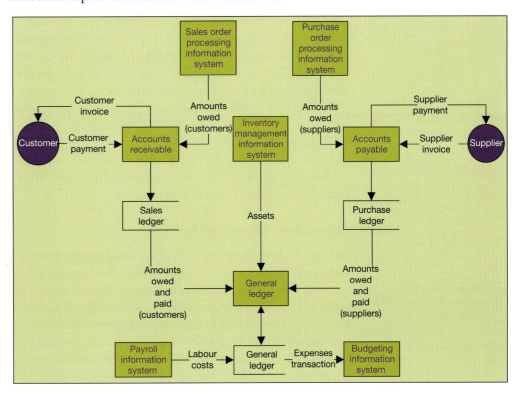

Figure 4.7 *Model of a financial information system*

CASE CHECK
LEO

LEO stands for the Lyons Electronic Office, a business-oriented computer system created by J. Lyons & Co. Ltd., one of the UK's leading catering and food manufacturing companies in the first half of the twentieth century (Mason, 2004). The LEO I (Lyons Electronic Office I) was the first computer used for commercial business applications. Modelled closely on the Cambridge EDSAC, LEO I ran its first business application in 1951. In 1954 Lyons formed LEO Computers Ltd to market LEO I and its successors LEO II and LEO III to other companies. LEO Computers eventually became part of English Electric Company (EELM), then International Computers Limited (ICL) and ultimately Fujitsu. LEO series computers were still in use up until 1981.

RECAP: The dynamics of an existing information system or a designed information system can be represented as an information system model. Back-end information systems include finance, sales order processing, purchase order processing, inventory management and payroll. Most companies, of whatever size, need an information system for recording orders for products or services from customers, orders made to suppliers for products or services, and the amounts paid or due to employees. Sales order processing is an information system that records details of sales orders from customers. Inventory management is the information system that maintains an inventory of raw material and finished goods. Purchase order processing records details of purchase orders to suppliers. Finance systems record amounts owed and paid by customers, amounts owed to and paid to suppliers and amounts paid to and owed to employees. Finally, payroll is the information system that records details of wages and payments made to employees.

DID YOU KNOW? The term *back office* comes from the building layout of early companies. The front office (which typically faced onto the street and had a public entrance) was where staff such as salespeople were visible to customers. The back office, which did not have a public entrance, was where staff worked on developing products or administration, without being seen by customers.

4.5   Front-end information systems

Front-end information systems infrastructure: The set of related information systems that interact with the major stakeholders of the organisation

In the previous section we described the typical back-end information systems infrastructure of the business. A large number of other information systems are normally built on this foundation. Such systems are front-end in the sense that they directly interface with the major stakeholders of the business: managers, employees, suppliers and customers.

Various information systems may feed off the information provided by core information systems in the back-end infrastructure and summarise such information for effective management and planning. In effect, this is a vertical extension to the back-end information systems infrastructure. These are the management-facing information systems of the business.

Extensions may also be made horizontally from the core information systems of the business. Connections may be made from the core information systems infrastructure to other information systems that interface with a company's customers, suppliers or employees. These are the customer-facing, supplier-facing and employee-facing information systems of the business. Figure 4.8 illustrates some of the relationships between back-end and front-end information systems in the typical business.

4.5.1   Management information systems

Management information system: A type of information system supporting management activities, particularly tactical decision-making

In terms of the control processes of organisations we may distinguish between three major types of information systems: transaction processing systems (TPS), **management information systems** (MIS), and decision support systems (DSS) or executive information systems (EIS).

Transaction processing systems are the operational information systems of the organisation. In a business organisation examples include order entry, accounts

DID YOU KNOW? The discipline of information systems, or as we have called it organisational informatics, was originally referred to in many quarters as Management Information Systems, or MIS for short. You may still find courses and modules with this label taught around the world.

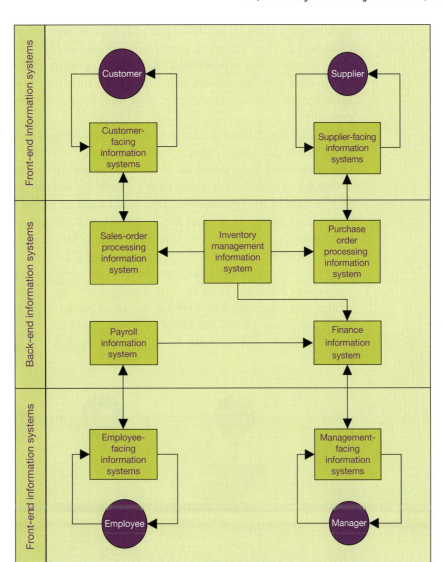

Figure 4.8 Front-end and back-end information systems infrastructure

payable and inventory management information systems, as described above. Such information systems process the detailed information generated in the day-to-day operations of the business. This detailed information is normally referred to as transactions and include customer orders, purchase orders, invoices etc. Such information is essential to supporting operations that help a company add value to its products and/or services. Hence, transaction processing systems are sometimes referred to as the life-blood of the organisation because they are so critical to effective everyday activity within organisations.

In Chapter 2 we described management as a key control process for organisations. As a system of human activity, management needs information systems to perform effectively. Management information systems (MIS) are used particularly by an operational layer of management to monitor the state of the organisation at any one time. From an MIS, managers would be expected to retrieve information about current production levels, number of orders achieved, level of inventory, current labour costs and other relevant managerial information.

Whereas MIS are generally used to enable effective short-term, tactical decisions about the operation of the organisation, DSS and EIS are generally expected to support longer-term, strategic decision-making. DSS/EIS will utilise the management information generated by MIS to model short-term and long-term scenarios of company performance. These scenarios are used to ask 'what-if' questions within business planning and to generate policy decisions in the area of business strategy. DSS and EIS are therefore critical to effective performance at the strategic level of management and will probably need information from key environmental sensors (such as a range of other front-end information systems) to function effectively.

For example, in a supermarket chain a management information system will be used to monitor stock in warehouses and cash flow through the company. In a local authority, a management information system may be used to monitor revenues from local taxes against expenditure.

Major things of interest such as employees, customers, orders, finance and inventory are important to the information systems infrastructure of our model organisation and data shared about such things are likely to form the key inputs into a management information system for an organisation. Using such a system, operational managers can continually monitor the state of the organisation. This is indicated in Figure 4.9 as one large management information system. In practice it may form a number of integrated MIS, perhaps for particular business areas. One of the key outputs from the MIS will be summary reports on major trends affecting the company, such as labour costs, current levels of assets and current levels of spending. This reporting may be written to a planning data store for use by an executive information system. The EIS is likely to be used to formulate high-level strategic decisions affecting the company.

> **REFLECT:** Could management in the modern organisation be performed effectively without management information systems? In what way do these information systems provide models of the organisation?

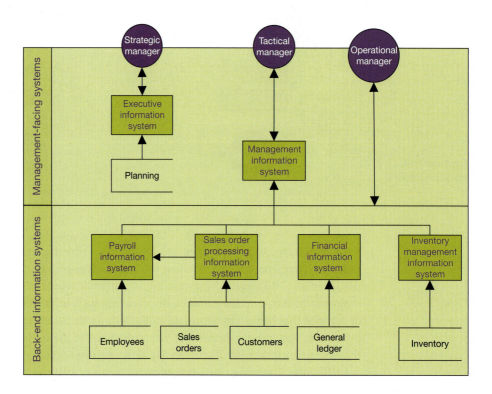

Figure 4.9 *Management information systems*

4.5.2   Customer-facing information systems

Customer-facing information system: A type of information system supporting interaction with the customer of the organisation

Customer-facing information systems support demand-chain activities and typically interface between back-end information systems such as sales order processing, inventory management and the customer. Traditional customer-facing information systems include sales, marketing, outbound logistics and after-sales systems. Recently, there has been increased emphasis on integrating such systems together to form a customer relationship management, or customer chain management, information system.

In terms of sales, particularly those associated with high-value products such as automobile sales or industrial equipment, some company customers would not normally fill out orders themselves, but are more likely to interface with the sales-force in relation to making orders. Hence, a sales information system is a common component of the information systems infrastructure of such organisations. This system will record the activities of the sales-force in terms of what sales have been made, to whom, by whom and when. This information will frequently be used to calculate commission owed to sales people on products sold.

Marketing is the organisational process devoted to promoting the products and/or services of an organisation. Good marketing is reliant on good customer information. Marketing is likely to utilise the information held about its existing customers to prepare and manage advertising campaigns for company products and services. A marketing information system is also likely to store details of various promotions, which customers have been contacted and the results of contacts made.

The distribution of goods to customers is sometimes referred to as outbound logistics. Orders processed by a sales orders processing information system will typically be passed to an outbound logistics or distribution system. This is a particularly important information system for medium to large companies with lots of customers, minimal stock and many points of distribution. Delivering products to customers efficiently and effectively is critical to customer retention. Hence, aspects of this logistics system will be concerned with optimising the use of delivery channels to customers. Such channels may involve the management of intermediaries, such as parcel post distributors.

An after-sales information system will be involved in tracking customer support and product-maintenance activities following a sale, possibly on a continuous basis for a number of years. The complexity of this system will probably vary with the type of product or service sold by the company. For low-value goods such as books or CDs after-sales may merely track customer complaints and product replacements. For high-value goods such as automobiles after-sales it is likely to involve the recording of maintenance or service schedules. For example, the lift manufacturer OTIS uses an after-sales system which pro-actively schedules maintenance of lifts by their engineers.

Each of the four systems of sales, marketing, outbound logistics and after-sales interacts with the customer in different ways and records different information associated with each interaction. Customer relationship management (CRM) has become a popular philosophy in the recent management literature. Winning new customers and keeping existing customers happy is seen as critical to organisational success. But effective CRM demands a unified view of the customer. This is provided by a CRM information system.

A CRM system would ideally track all customer interactions with a company from initial enquiries, through making orders, to the whole range of after-sales services that might be offered to and consumed by the customer. Typically then, CRM systems integrate the range of front-end and back-end information systems that have a bearing on the customer. Some of the relationships between the key customer-facing information systems are illustrated in Figure 4.10.

> **REFLECT:** Is it true that the introduction of a CRM system will necessarily and automatically contribute to increased customer service?

4.5.3   Supplier-facing information systems

Supplier-facing information system: A type of information system supporting interaction with the suppliers of the organisation

Supplier-facing information systems support supply chain activities. Traditional supplier-facing systems include inbound logistics and procurement and typically interface with back-end information systems such as purchase order processing, finance and inventory management. Not surprisingly, given the symmetric nature of buy-side and sell-side activities there has been increased emphasis on integrating supplier-facing information systems to form an integrated supply chain management, or supplier relationship management, system.

Inbound logistics is that process devoted to managing the material resources entering an organisation from its suppliers and partners. In the retail sector, for instance, large food retailers are likely to have fleets of vehicles involved in the delivery of goods to stores. These

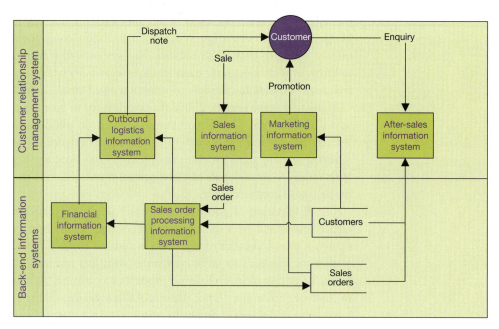

Figure 4.10 *Customer relationship management system*

vehicles may have to make up to 100 deliveries in any given working week. Clearly, effective and efficient systems are needed to plan and schedule routes for vehicles to deliver foodstuffs to stores using the lowest mileage possible.

Procurement is that process devoted to the purchasing of goods and services from suppliers at acceptable levels of cost and quality. It can be considered as the sister process of sales. A procurement system will be concerned with managing this process of procuring goods, services and raw materials needed by the company to operate effectively. It is likely to interact with both the purchase ordering information system and the inventory management information system.

Supplier relationship management is the sister system to the customer relationship management system. It keeps track of all supplier interactions with the company and integrates the information used by supplier-facing information systems such as procurement and inbound logistics.

Some of the relationships between the key supplier-facing information systems are illustrated in Figure 4.11.

Electronic procurement is the trend which involves using ICT to integrate many supply chain processes. Procurement information systems and supplier relationship management information systems in general are important parts of electronic procurement.

4.5.4   Employee-facing information systems

Employee-facing information system: A type of information system supporting interaction with employees of the organisation

Employee-facing information systems support the internal value-chain within organisations. Typical employee-facing information systems include human resource management and production control systems and they are likely to interact with key back-end information systems such as payroll.

A company is likely to need to build systems to record, process and maintain large amounts of information about its employees. Payroll information is only one facet of this information. Companies will also want to maintain detailed histories of the employment of their employees. Collectively, this would be referred to as a human resource information system.

A production information system will be involved in scheduling future production and monitoring current production. It will also interface with the inventory management information system in terms of requisitioning raw material for production and replenishing supplies of finished goods.

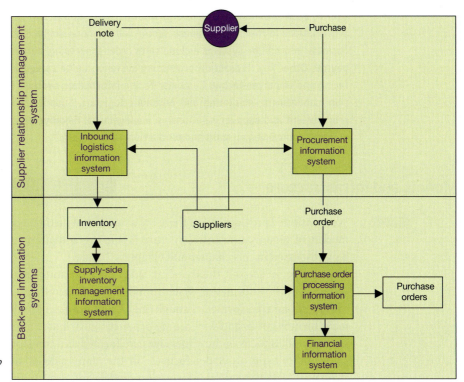

Figure 4.11 *Supplier relationship management system*

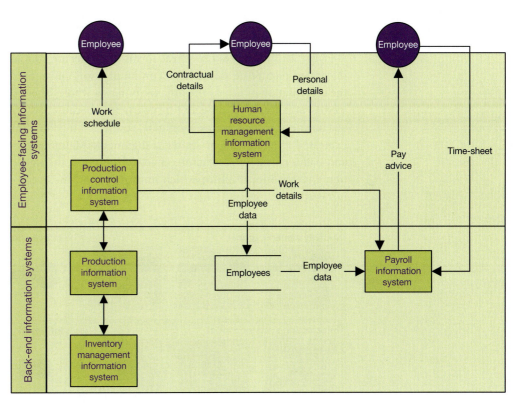

Figure 4.12 *Employee relationship management system*

Some of the relationships between the key employee-facing information systems are illustrated in Figure 4.12.

Human resource management systems and production or manufacturing systems are likely to integrate around activity information. Hence, detailed work patterns of employees may be integrated with production scheduling.

RECAP: Each business organisation's information systems will necessarily be different, although organisations in the same business sector will be more similar than those in different sectors. Key business information systems include sales order processing, purchase order processing, finance and payroll. Other key transaction processing systems can be categorised as supplier-facing, customer-facing and employee-facing. Customer-facing information systems include sales, customer relationship management, marketing and outbound logistics. Supplier-facing information systems include procurement and supplier relationship management. Employee-facing information systems include human resource management and production management.

4.6   Models and infrastructure

Designing and managing enterprise architecture **IS**2010

 key skill

We mentioned previously that there are a number of distinct advantages to developing explicit models of organisation infrastructure. There are actually two types among the models we have discussed in this chapter and Chapters 2 and 3.

One type focuses on the dynamic side of organisation infrastructure: on action. Activity system models, information system models and data system models all focus on how things move and are transformed through the organisation. Activity system models, for instance, focus on how goods and services are produced, distributed and consumed, while information system models focus on how messages are formed and transformed in support of activity.

The other type of model focuses on the static side of organisation infrastructure: on structure. Activity models, information models and data models all focus on what things are of interest to the organisation and how these things are related to each other. Information models, for example, focus on the classes important to messages and how classes are associated, whereas data models focus on the way in which data is organised in data structures.

Figure 4.13 illustrates how these forms of model are coupled and can be used to build an integrated picture of the activity, communication and representation either in one part of the organisation or across the organisation as a whole. There is a particular value in building a cross-organisational model of infrastructure because it starts us thinking about how various business systems are, or should be, connected together. In the literature this is frequently expressed as alignment or strategic alignment. Alignment is the goal of ensuring that data and data systems infrastructure effectively support the needs of information and information systems infrastructure, which in turn support the needs of activity and activity systems infrastructure.

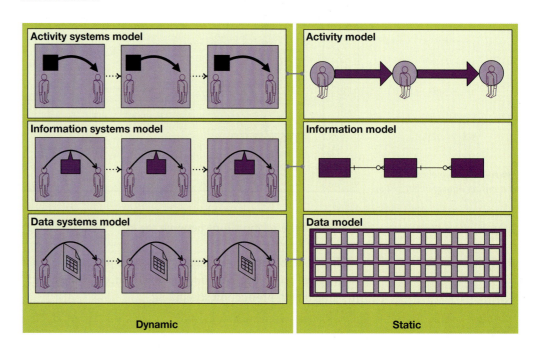

Figure 4.13 Dynamic and static model of organisation infrastructure

Models of infrastructure are therefore important in a number of ways within organisational informatics. They emphasise that an understanding of current organisation relies on the effective analysis of existing systems. Existing models of infrastructure act as the platform for any decisions as to organisational change. They are critical for understanding how existing systems can help leverage new systems. They are also important in deciding what is feasible in terms of designing new systems of organisation. Understanding of infrastructure is therefore important to the planning and management of informatics, particularly the formulation of both business and informatics strategy (Chapter 10). Understanding infrastructure is also important for conceiving new business systems, such as information systems, as well as designing and constructing their architecture (Chapter 12).

4.6.1   Information infrastructure

Information infrastructure:
The set of inter-related information models describing the information needs of the organisation

To refresh, as well as expressing the flow of communication between activities we also need to express the relationship between the objects of interest to an organisation; that is to say, the things about which communication takes place. As should be evident from the information system models presented in previous sections, most business organisations need to know and communicate about their customers, products, suppliers, stock and sales, among many other things. To document such information classes and the relationships between them we need an information model. An information model indicates the structure of information required by activities and processed within an information system for the purposes of business communication.

An information model can be developed not just in support of a single information system, but it is also often useful to make explicit what information classes are important across a range of information systems. This then forms a corporate, or organisation, information model.

Consider the case of a typical manufacturing company engaged in many of the activity systems we discussed as part of the activity infrastructure described in a previous section. Figure 4.14 represents a likely organisation information model supporting the key activity

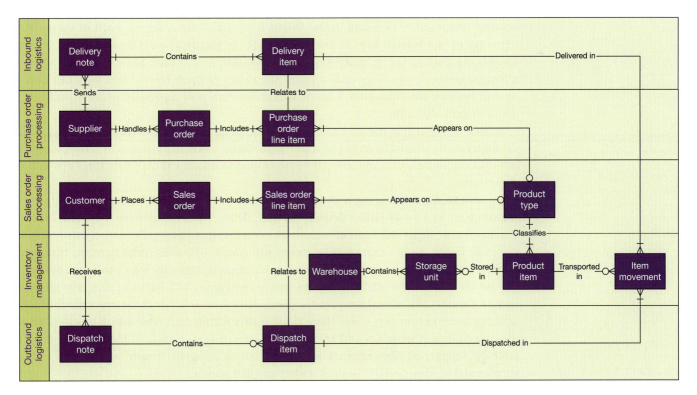

Figure 4.14 *Organisation information model*

systems of inbound and outbound logistics, sales and purchase order processing and inventory management. Note how key information classes are related across certain of these activity systems, such as a delivery item and dispatch item being linked through an item movement. Such cross-over relationships indicate important areas of communication between business systems and critical areas where data sharing is important.

> **REFLECT:** One difficulty many businesses face is that their information infrastructure is organised around transactions, products or services rather than customers. For instance, an insurance company might have an information system established for each financial product it sells, such as life insurance and car insurance. What difficulties do you think this form of information infrastructure might create for customer service?

4.6.2   Data infrastructure

Data infrastructure: The set of inter-related data models that define the data needs of the organisation

As we discussed in Chapter 3, the most common data model employed for representation of data, or persistent forma, is what we might call the file-based data model which uses the inter-related constructs of fields, records and files. This has much similarity with a data model employed in most contemporary business ICT systems known as the relational data model, which uses the data structures of tables, consisting of multiple data elements or rows, which in turn consist of a series of data items or columns.

So, to represent data relating to the dispatch advice notes of Goronwy Galvanising as described in Chapter 1, the table named *Dispatch notes* in Figure 4.15 consists of four data items (Dispatch no., Dispatch date, Customer code and Instructions) and three data elements corresponding to three rows in the table, one for each dispatch note.

Each row in a table is identified by values in one or more columns of the table, called the table's primary key. The values of a primary key must be unique and not null. In other words, we must have a value for each element of the primary key and each value must be unique in terms of other values of the primary key. For instance, in the *Dispatch notes* table the *Dispatch no.* data item is the only item having both these properties. It is therefore the most suitable candidate for a primary key for this table.

Values in columns may also act as links to data contained in other tables. Such columns are called foreign keys. A value for a foreign key must either be the value of some primary key elsewhere in the database or be null. The primary key of the Dispatch items table is actually composed of two data items: *Dispatch no.* and *Sales order no.* Each of these data items are in fact foreign keys in two other tables in the database: Dispatch no. acts as a foreign key back to the primary key of the Dispatch notes table; Sales order no. acts as a foreign key back to a Sales orders table. The values of these two foreign keys can never be null because we must always know which dispatch note and sales order a particular dispatch item relates to.

Related tables such as the ones in Figure 4.15 aggregate to form a database. Typically such databases are developed to serve particular information systems. However, as is the case with information models, data models can be developed to document data structures across the organisation.

Figure 4.16, for instance, expresses part of the data infrastructure for a typical manufacturing company as a set of tables: delivery advices, delivery items, suppliers, purchase orders, purchase order items etc. Each of these tables is represented as a collection of attributes or columns. Hence, a sales order row or record will consist of a sales order number, customer number and a sales order date. Each table has one or more attributes which form the primary key for the table. These attributes, as underlined in Figure 4.15, serve to uniquely identify each of the rows of a table. Hence, in the purchase orders table, purchase order number acts as the primary key for this table. There are also keys within each table which cross-relate to the data held in other tables and are known as foreign keys. Hence, in the purchase orders table the supplier number attribute serves to relate to a supplier record or row held in the suppliers table, identified by the primary key supplier number.

Dispatch notes	Dispatch no.	Dispatch date	Customer code	Instructions
	101	22/01/2012	BLW	
	102	25/02/2012	TCO	
	103	10/03/2012	BLW	

Dispatch items	Dispatch no.	Sales order no.	Customer product code	Dispatch quantity
	101	13/1193G	UL150	20
	101	44/2404G	UL1500	20
	101	70/2517P	UL135	20
	101	23/2474P	UL120	14

Figure 4.15 *Two relational tables*

Delivery notes	Delivery no.	Delivery date	Supplier no.	Instructions		
Delivery items	Delivery no.	Delivery item no.	Supplier product code	Delivery quantity	Delivery item price	Purchase item no.
Suppliers	Supplier no.	Supplier name	Supplier address	Supplier tel. no.	Supplier email	
Purchase orders	Purchase order no.	Supplier no.	Purchase order date			
Purchase order items	Purchase order no.	Purchase item no.	Supplier product code	Purchase item quantity	Purchase item price	
Product types	Product type code	Product description	Product length	Product weight		
Product items	Product item code	Product type code	Item qty			
Item movement	Product item code	Movement type	Movement date	Movement time	Delivery no.	Dispatch no.
Warehouses	Warehouse code	Warehouse location	No. storage units			
Storage unit	Storage unit code	Warehouse code	Product item code			
Sales orders	Sales order no.	Customer no.	Sales order date			
Sales order items	Sales order no.	Sales item no.	Customer product code	Sales item quantity	Sales item price	Sales item no.
Customers	Customer no.	Customer name	Customer address	Customer tel. no.	Customer email	
Dispatch notes	Dispatch no.	Dispatch date	Customer no.	Instructions		
Dispatch items	Dispatch no.	Sales order no.	Customer product code	Dispatch quantity		

Figure 4.16 *A corporate data model*

4.6.3   ICT and infrastructure

ICT as data infrastructure typically takes a supporting role within business infrastructure, assisting human communication and activity through efficient data storage and data processing (Heeks, 1999). However, ICT is also a catalyst for organisational change. The focus on infrastructure highlights the fact that ICT has the potential to change organisations either by supplanting aspects of informative and performative action or by innovating new forms of informative and performative action.

Information systems, as we have seen, are forms of communication system. But communication within information systems is no longer just between people, it is also between humans and machines – ICT systems. ICT can be used to automate major parts of information systems and in so doing supplant the role of human actors. As we have seen, ICT systems can engage in algorithmic decision-making and, on the basis of decisions made, communicate with human actors, such as customers or employees. ICT systems are therefore significant actors in the modern business.

ICT can also be used to innovate, that is to stimulate the design and implementation of new information and associated activity systems. Not just business but also public sector organisations can benefit from ICT innovation. For instance, ICT has been used to automate clerical processes, such as making benefit payments. It has also been used to improve government decision-making, communication and implementation. Finally, its use is fundamental to new forms of public service delivery. However, some have argued that until now, ICT has done little to transform the fundamental nature of government agencies (Fountain, 2001), nor has it been used substantially, as yet, to innovate. We consider the use of ICT within public sector information systems at a number of points in later chapters.

> **DID YOU KNOW?** One of the first uses of computers in business was the Lyons Electronic Office (LEO). This system was designed for the British company J. Lyons and Co. Ltd (Mason, 2004). Lyons invested in the latest technology for the same reason that organisations do so today, it hoped to improve its performance and gain an advantage over its competitors.

FOCUS ON VALUE

The key value of information systems lies in their role in support of activity systems in organisations. For the purposes of managerial control, single and isolated information systems in organisations have less value than integrated systems, so there is key value in having an explicit information systems infrastructure. However, the impact of information systems and their embedded technology depends on the organisational context.

Information systems, like systems in general and sociotechnical systems in particular, are not value neutral. Values are necessarily embedded in the application of technology for particular purposes. It is valuable to examine historical information systems, not only to gain a perspective on what an information system is in essence, but to see how information systems are necessarily ethical as well as communication issues. For instance, in 1890 the first automated census was conducted in the US following the innovation introduced by Herman Hollerith, the electronic tabulating machine.

Black (2002) documents the way in which early computing machines based on Hollerith's design were used by Hitler's Nazi administration to compile two censuses of the German population in 1933 and 1939. These censuses effectively could not have taken place without the technology first invented by Herman Hollerith (Biles et al., 1989), originally for use in computing the US national census. These tabulating machines allowed the Nazi regime to identify Jews, and other nominated groups in the population, for eventual transmission to the death camps. Tabulating machines were even used in the death camps themselves to process data about the 'performance' of the extermination effort (see Hollerith electronic tabulating machine case study)

4.7   Conclusion and key themes

This chapter has defined two of the book's final foundation concepts: business infrastructure and information system. An information system is a sociotechnical system, a communication system in which humans use ICT in support of coordinated and collaborative decision-making and action (that is, an activity system).

Information systems, like the human activity reliant on them, have been in existence for many thousands of years. Modern digital computers were invented over 50 years ago and stimulated enormous growth in technologies associated with data capture, processing and communication. They rapidly came to be used in business organisations and this stimulated rapid growth in the application of information and communication, both within and more recently between organisations.

Three layers of infrastructure are critical to the modern business: activity systems, information systems and data systems or ICT infrastructure. Each level supports the others. Every business organisation's information systems are necessarily different, but there are similarities, especially across organisations in the same business sector, so it is possible to develop generic descriptions or models of both back-end and front-end information systems infrastructure.

Key business back-end information systems include sales order processing, purchase order processing, inventory management, finance and payroll. The sales order processing information system records details of customer orders, and supports activity systems such as sales and after-sales service. The inventory management information system maintains an inventory of raw material and finished goods. It is important for providing sales staff with accurate information on quantities and pricing of products. It also supports procurement activity. The purchase order processing information system records details of purchase orders and supports the procurement process. The financial information system records amounts owed by and to, and paid by and to, customers, suppliers and employees. It supports other infrastructure activities such as management and planning. The payroll information system records details of wages and payments made to employees, and is a critical element of human resource management activity.

Front-end information systems interface directly with major stakeholder types: managers, employees, suppliers and customers. Management-facing information systems are built on the foundation of back-end information systems. Management information systems are used by operational management to monitor the state of the organisation. Decision support systems and executive information systems generally support longer-term, strategic and tactical decision-making. Typical customer-facing information systems include sales, customer relationship management, marketing and outbound logistics. Typical supplier-facing information systems include procurement, inbound logistics and supplier relationship management systems. Typical employee-facing information systems include human resource management and production control systems.

Chapter 2 considered systems of activity, and Chapter 3 the way in which information supports business activity. This chapter set the context for business infrastructure and considered systems of communication that provide information to the business. The next couple of chapters switch attention to systems of technology. Part III of the book provides a high-level overview of the typical ICT infrastructure that supports current forms of business and offers significant potential for the design of new organisational forms. This is the growing area of electronic business, considered in Chapter 8.

4.8   Review test

1   Information systems are distinct from _____. Fill in the blank.

2   Information systems are the same as activity systems. True or false?
☐ True
☐ False

3   Place the layers of infrastructure in order. In other words, which layer supports which other layer? Indicate the order using 1 to 3.
☐ Data systems infrastructure
☐ Activity systems infrastructure
☐ Information systems infrastructure

4   MIS stands for? Choose the most appropriate term.
☐ Manufacturing information system
☐ Management information system
☐ Modern information system

5   Core business information systems include? Select all that apply.
☐ Finance
☐ Inbound logistics
☐ Purchase order processing
☐ Payroll

6   A _____ is a repository for data, a place where data collects and is retrieved from. Fill in the blank.

7   An _____ model indicates the structure of information required by activities and processed within an information system for the purposes of business communication. Fill in the blank.

8   Sales order processing is the information system that records details of purchase orders to suppliers. It is likely to support major elements of the procurement process. True or false?
☐ True
☐ False

9   Typical management-facing information systems include sales, customer relationship management, marketing and distribution. True or false?
☐ True
☐ False

10   Customer-facing information systems include: Select all that are relevant.
☐ Sales
☐ Supplier relationship management
☐ Outbound logistics
☐ Procurement
☐ Marketing

11   Supplier-facing information systems include: Select all that are relevant.
☐ Sales
☐ Procurement
☐ Sales order processing
☐ Inventory management
☐ Supplier relationship management

12   Employee-facing information systems include: Select all that are relevant.
☐ Human resource management
☐ Sales order processing
☐ Production management
☐ Marketing
☐ Customer relationship management

4.9   Exercises

‣ Take a company known to you, and determine what its core information systems are. Determine the degree to which these systems are integrated.

‣ Try to provide more detail on one chosen process from a system in the core information systems infrastructure. Draw an information systems model for this process.

‣ Draw a model of another information system associated with a process known to you, such as student admissions at a university.

‣ Take an area of activity known to you, and determine what form of information system supports it.

‣ Take an organisation known to you, and determine the ways in which ICT has been used to supplant, support or innovate activity.

‣ Identify a management information system in an organisation known to you and try to determine how it works.

‣ Take a public sector organisation such as a local authority. Try to identify the key front-end information systems relevant to it.

‣ Try to identify the types of activity data that might be generated from an information system used to control manufacturing production. In what way might this information system update a human resource information system? What other information systems are likely to feed off a production system?

‣ Try to identify some of the purposes that the data collected by a customer relationship management system might be used for.

‣ Consider the management-facing information systems of an organisation known to you. Is it possible to identify distinct EIS and MIS? Develop a high-level information model of the information held in the EIS or MIS.

‣ Investigate the distinction between EIS, DSS and MIS in more detail. Investigate the role of data warehousing and data mining within such systems.

‣ Find a company close to you. Take along one or more of the generic models discussed in this chapter. Compare the operations of the company to those described on the model. How closely do they match? In what ways are they different?

‣ Consider a future situation in which corporations become involved in mining asteroids within the solar system. Would the information systems infrastructure of such corporations be different from the one discussed in this chapter?

‣ Produce a brief description of the functionality of one or more of the customer-facing, supplier-facing or employee-facing information systems of a company in the services, rather than the manufacturing, sector.

4.10   Projects

‣ Choose a historical information system and build a case description of its use along the lines of Herman Hollerith's invention and use of his tabulating machine for running the US national census and the management of railway ticketing in the nineteenth century (see ticketing). Some possible cases include the operation of Lloyd's of London's insurance activities and the production of the Domesday book. Distinguish between the activity system, information system and the ICT used in each historical case.

‣ Construct a high-level map of an organisation's information systems, perhaps using the modelling notation for information systems discussed in this chapter. Include both computerised (ICT) and non-computerised information systems, by using document symbols to indicate manual information systems. Consider the scope for extending ICT systems within the organisation.

‣ Choose an organisation and investigate the degree of integration between its information systems. Recommend ways in which the systems can be better integrated in the future. Use information systems models for this purpose.

‣ Choose an organisation and investigate the relevance of the distinction between management information systems and transaction processing systems for it. In other words, is it possible to identify systems specifically used by management and those used by other workers? Identify clearly the current users of such systems. Try to determine whether they deliver the information required by the users.

‣ Draw a detailed map of the information systems used in a business organisation known to you, using a hierarchical series of information systems models. Determine the extent to which they diverge from the systems described in this chapter. To what extent do they map onto the systems described in this chapter?

‣ Choose an organisation and attempt to develop a case study of the way in which its ICT systems have been built up over the last 20 years. On the lines of the Goronwy Galvanising case in Chapter 1, try to determine how these systems were planned for and designed. Does it have explicit or implicit informatics infrastructure? Do people in the organisation describe such infrastructure as enabling or constraining?

‣ Extend the information infrastructure model detailed in this chapter to include information of relevance to all the back-end and front-end information systems discussed.

4.11   Critical reflection

Infrastructure is both enabling and constraining. For instance, data systems infrastructure enables the coordination of organisational activities. But consider how current data systems infrastructure might constrain the development of new ways of doing things.

 If core information systems tend to have common features across organisations, what potential is there for gaining competitive advantage through information systems? In what sense are these core information systems critical for regulating the business organisation? What role do management information systems play in the regulation of organisations? How important is it that the information systems in this back-end infrastructure transfer data between systems easily? What potential business problems might arise from poor data transfer between systems? What part do front-end information systems play in organisational performance?

4.12 Further reading

A good general background reference for work in the discipline of information systems is *The Oxford Handbook of information systems* (Galliers and Currie, 2011). The concept of an information system is considered from a soft systems perspective in Holwell and Checkland (1998b), which also provides one of the earliest descriptions of the warning network case. Front-end and back-end information systems in business are also covered in Beynon-Davies (2012). Hay (1996) provides coverage of a range of 'patterns' or generic information models making up the information infrastructure of a typical company, on which the discussion of information infrastructure in this chapter is based.

4.13 References

Beynon-Davies, P. (2012). *eBusiness*. Palgrave Macmillan, Basingstoke.

Biles, G., A. A. Bolton and B. M. DiRe. (1989). Herman Hollerith: Inventor, Manager, Entrepreneur – A Centennial Remembrance. *Journal of Management* 15 (4): 603–615.

Black, E. (2002). *IBM and the Holocaust*. Time Warner, London.

Fountain, J. E. (2001). *Building the Virtual State: Information Technology and Institutional Change*. The Brookings Institution, New York.

Galliers, R. D. and W. L. Currie (eds) (2011). *The Oxford Handbook of Information Systems: Critical Perspectives and New Directions*. Oxford University Press, Oxford.

Hay, D. C. (1996). *Data Model Patterns: Conventions of Thought*. Dorset House, New York.

Heeks, R. (1999). *Reinventing Government in the Information Age: International Practice in IT-enabled Public Sector Reform*. Routledge, London.

Holwell, S. and P. Checkland. (1998a). An Information System Won the War. *IEE Proceedings Software* 145 (4): 95–99.

Holwell, S. and P. Checkland. (1998b). *Information, Systems and Information Systems*. John Wiley, Chichester, UK.

Mason, R. O. (2004). The Legacy of LEO: Lessons Learned from an English Tea and Cake Company's Pioneering Efforts in Information Systems. *Journal of the Association for Information Systems* 5 (5): 183–219.

See companion website **www.palgrave.com/business/beynon-daviesbis2e**

Understanding ICT

The use of informatics within modern business requires both technical and social infrastructures. Technical infrastructure is made up of interdependent information and communication technologies. Social infrastructure is made up of good practices in planning, management and operations. This part of the book examines issues relating to technology, while Part IV considers issues relating to social infrastructure.

Chapter 5 first examines the way in which technical infrastructure is designed to support **electronic delivery** of goods and services. This leads to consideration of the possible range of **access devices** and **communication channels** for modern organisations to connect remotely. Communication technology tends to be equated in contemporary business with the distinct but related concepts of the **Internet** and the **World Wide Web,** so both of these issues are considered in some depth. Organisational communication is also particularly concerned with the transmission of transactions as data, so the chapter outlines a number of standards for managing the flow of **transactional data** between organisations.

Chapter 6 focuses on the concept of the **ICT system** in more detail. It describes a layered model of the typical ICT system and the ways in which both processing and data tend to be distributed over communication networks. The chapter considers the concept of front-end ICT and the place of **websites** within the technical infrastructure. It also considers back-end ICT issues and the critical importance of **database** technology to corporate systems. The chapter concludes with coverage of **data security** issues, as they concern both ICT systems and communication networks.

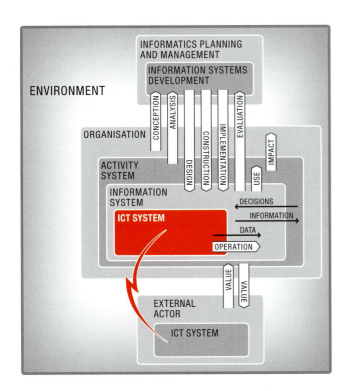

Overview

The chapters in this part cover the following key areas:

- Access devices and communication channels
- Communication networks
- The architecture of the Internet
- The key elements of the World Wide Web
- Standards for the transmission of transactional data
- Layered architecture of an ICT system
- Front-end technologies such as Websites
- Back-end technologies such as databases
- Cloud computing
- Data security

Communication infrastructure

'Man did not weave the web of life, he is merely a strand in it. Whatever he does to the web, he does to himself.'

Chief Seattle
(1786–1866)

Learning outcomes	Principles
Describe the concept of ICT infrastructure and explain its effects on modern business.	Modern business relies on ICT infrastructure consisting of access devices, communication channels, front-end ICT, back-end ICT and core data management. Such infrastructure supports connectivity to data on the part of information systems used by both internal and external stakeholders.
Distinguish between the Internet and the World Wide Web, identify some of the critical components of the Internet and explain some of the technologies underlying the Web and their relevance for business.	Modern communication infrastructure relies on two critical technologies: the Internet and the Web. The Internet consists of a set of technologies which facilitate the inter-connection between data communication networks globally. The Web is an application which runs on the Internet and consists of standards for the transmission of hypermedia documents.
Discuss the importance of transactional data to business to business interaction and describe some approaches to handling this issue.	Data communication infrastructure connects business organisations in flows of transactions. Since these transactions are typically in various forms of documentation the standards for electronic transmission of such documentation are critically important for commerce.

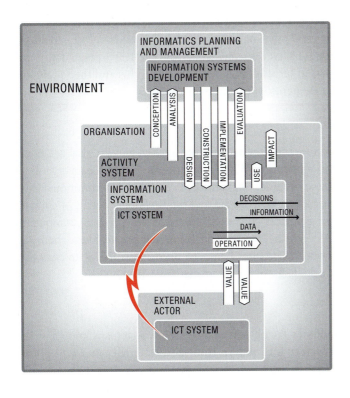

Chapter outline

AACSB learning objectives:
Use of IT

5.1   Introduction

Vannevar Bush was an American engineer and scientific administrator known for his work on the early analogue computer and his role as chief organiser of the Manhattan Project, the large-scale scientific effort which developed the first atomic bomb. Bush is also cited for a thought experiment he conducted in the 1940s. Bush imagined a '*device which is a sort of mechanized private file and library … in which an individual stores all his books, records, and communications, and which is mechanized so that it may be consulted with exceeding speed and flexibility. It is an enlarged intimate supplement to his memory.*' This device Bush named the memex – short for memory extender. The memex is normally seen as the forerunner of a technology known as hypertext or hypermedia, which in turn underlies the World Wide Web.

The modern digital computer developed shortly after the events which formed background to the warning network described in Section 4.2.1. Modern information and communication technology is therefore based in a number of advances in electronics with no more than fifty to sixty years of history. But such technological change has stimulated many changes in the ways in which we now do business, and also in the ways in which individuals interact with business.

Many texts on business information systems tend to skirt the issue of ICT, or provide a list of disjointed topics of interest. This book aims to provide a more holistic account, and it treats ICT as an important and integrated part of any modern business.

Chapter 4 discussed how modern business, by its very nature, relies on infrastructure. Activity systems form one layer of infrastructure within organisations, but rely upon two other layers. Information systems infrastructure consists of the information systems needed to facilitate communication between business actors. ICT infrastructure consists of the hardware, software, data and communication facilities needed to support information systems. This chapter and Chapter 6 look at this last aspect of infrastructure.

5.2   Electronic delivery of goods and services

The economic value of ICT lies in its ability to support communication and activity both internally within the business and externally with other business actors. Chapter 7 discusses how ICT is particularly promoted as a means of improving the delivery of services and goods to internal and external actors. The activity of redesigning activity systems and corresponding information systems to meet the challenges of electronic delivery relies on the creation of effective ICT infrastructure. Figure 5.1 illustrates elements from the ICT infrastructure of atypical organisation we discussed first in terms of business impact. In this and the following chapter we explain how each of these elements work and inter-relate.

5.2.1   Access channels and stakeholders

ICT infrastructure supports remote communication between the internal and external actors of the business and the ICT systems of the organisation. When people inside and outside an organisation connect to its ICT systems, they do so using access channels. Two of the most common channels, particularly for customer use, are face-to-face contact and the telephone. Today, of course, there are also electronic channels, using devices such as Internet-enabled personal computers (PCs), interactive digital television (iDTV) or the Internet-enabled mobile phone. These channels enable people to order services and products 24 hours a day, 365 days a year. This is an essential part of the eBusiness and eCommerce agenda for many companies (see Chapter 8).

5.2.2   Front-end ICT

As explained in Chapter 4, the stakeholder-facing part of a business's systems is known as its front end. The technological infrastructure for modern front-end ICT relies on two critical technologies, the Internet and the Web.

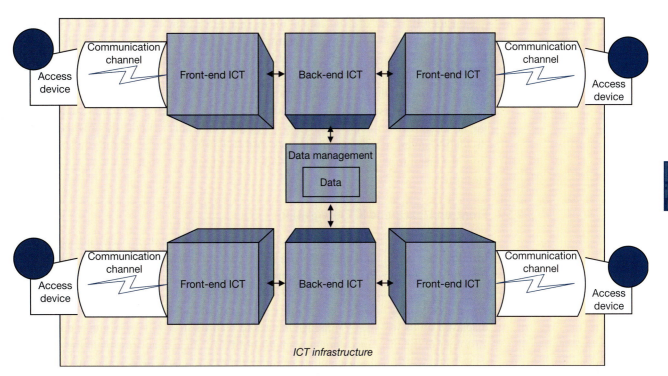

Figure 5.1 *Technical infrastructure*

The Internet is a set of inter-connected computer networks distributed around the world. We can think of it on a number of levels. Its base infrastructure consists of packet-switched networks and a series of communication protocols. On this layer run a series of applications such as electronic mail (email) and, more recently, the World Wide Web (or just the Web).

The Web is effectively a set of standards for displaying and distributing hypermedia documents over the Internet. Organisations set up their front-end ICT on the Web by creating websites. Many companies are investing heavily to make their websites more interactive so that a substantial proportion of customer interaction can be done online (See the Tesco case study as an example). This chapter examines these important technological foundations for the electronic delivery of goods and services.

5.2.3 Delivery of intangible goods and services

Certain goods and services are information-based or intangible in nature. Examples include music, software, movies and books. As such they are prime candidates for electronic delivery. A large proportion of intangible goods and services are now typically described as content and made available for access over the Internet and the Web.

Tangible goods and services in contrast cannot be delivered electronically, but customers can order and pay for them electronically. Examples include foodstuffs, electronic goods, automobiles and medical surgery.

5.2.4 Back-end ICT

A key focus within the electronic business agenda (Chapter 8) over the last decade or so has involved re-engineering service delivery around the customer. Hence, when a customer enters personal details, such as their name and address, into one system this information should ideally be available to all other systems that need that data. Such customer-focused strategy demands the integration and interoperability of ICT systems. Typically such integration is reliant on effective data management and data sharing. Chapter 6 focuses on database systems as critical back-end technology.

Consider the case of a customer of an insurance company. This customer holds three distinct policies with the same company: life insurance, house insurance and car insurance. In the past the insurance company would have run three separate ICT systems for each type of insurance, meaning that the same customer would appear in all three systems. This meant that it was quite difficult to identify those critical customers that conducted multiple lines of business with the company. It also made it difficult to develop strategies such as discounting arrangements to help retain such customers. Not surprisingly, this insurance company decided to invest in redesigning its back-end ICT infrastructure around the customer rather than the insurance policy. This has made it much easier to identify and retain important customers.

5.2.5   Front-end/back-end ICT integration

But integration is not just about establishing linkages between back-end systems; it also involves establishing linkages between front-end and back-end ICT. For instance, to enable fully transactional websites, the data presented needs to be updated dynamically from back-end databases. Also, the data entered by customers need to update company information systems effectively. Hence, an insurance company will need to refresh its financial products displayed on its website by making changes to records stored in its products database; or the customer of the insurance company might notify a change of address by filling out a form on its website, which will cause updates to an appropriate record held in the customer database. This is also discussed in Chapter 6.

5.2.6   Securing data

For effective eCommerce (see Chapter 8) people must trust electronic delivery. One important aspect of this is securing the privacy of electronic transactions, particularly payments. Chapter 6 examines the issues of securing data in ICT systems and ensuring secure electronic transactions along communication channels.

This chapter focuses on the first aspects of ICT infrastructure mentioned above. It looks at the concept of an **access channel**, and explains the critical role that the Internet and the Web now play in supporting remote access to organisations. It examines standards for the electronic handling of transactional data, and concludes with an examination of electronic payment systems.

Chapter 6 covers the last three aspects of ICT infrastructure. First it looks at the component elements of ICT systems and how they are both distributed and integrated across communication networks, in their processing and data storage. This leads to a discussion of the centrality of data and content management systems, and the importance of enterprise-wide integration. The chapter concludes with an examination of the critical issue of data security.

Access channel: A means of accessing the goods and services provided by an organisation

5.3   Access channels

Designing enterprise architecture   **IS**2010

In Chapter 3 we made the case for considering information in terms of communication or, more particularly, in terms of acts of communication. One of the most familiar forms of human communication is face-to-face communication; this is still a primary form of communication within business organisations. However, over the last hundred years or so many forms of technology have been used to enable *remote* communication within and between organisations. Such remote communication is sometimes called *tele*communication because it is performed by actors at a distance, actors not in the same location. To enable such telecommunication various forms of communication device must be used, each device forming a node in a communication network.

Consider the communication necessary for a consumer to access the products and services provided by any organisation. An organisation's services or products may be accessed in a number of different ways and each might be described as an *access channel*. Traditionally, such services or products would be accessed through face-to-face communication or postal channels. Nowadays, much communication between individuals and organisations is mediated communication, as in the case of telephone communication. In this example we would refer to the telephone as an access device. More recently technology is not only used to mediate communication, it becomes an independent actor in organisational communication. Hence, when an individual orders a product using a company website they are not generally communicating directly with a fellow human but with an ICT system.

ICT systems generally utilise a subset of telecommunications known as data communications. Data communication refers to the electronic collection, processing and distribution of data over telecommunication networks. The basic model of communication described in Chapter 3 can be modified for data communication in the following terms. A *sender unit* formulates a message and transmits it as a signal to a *telecommunication device*. This is a piece of hardware that performs a number of functions on the signal, and then transmits the signal along a *communication channel* to another *telecommunication device*. At this end the device reverses the process performed by the sending telecommunications device and passes the signal on to a *receiving unit* which decodes the signal as a message.

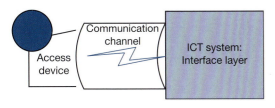

Figure 5.2 Data communication

It is convenient to combine the idea of a sender unit and telecommunication device into the concept of an *access device*. We shall refer to the receiving unit at the organisation end of the communication as the interface layer of an ICT system (Figure 5.2). This phenomenon, involving different mediated channels for the remote and interactive electronic access to products and services, is frequently referred to as *electronic delivery*. Certain products and services, such as digitised music or travel insurance, will be accessible directly via remote access channels. For other more physical products, such as bicycles, organisations are likely to provide data and ordering services but distribute the products to customers through conventional physical channels like the postal service.

5.3.1 Access devices

Access device: A device that enables access to organisation ICT systems

In modern electronic business various remote access channels can be used. Generally, there is an interdependence between certain **access devices** and channels. Access channels are conduits for the delivery of suitable goods and services and the recording of transactions. They are not mutually exclusive, and some electronic access devices and channels can be used together with traditional face-to-face access. Some organisations keep open traditional access channels because some customers prefer to use them (or will not use electronic channels), and it adds to overall effectiveness. However, it is usually cheaper for organisations to reduce the number of traditional channels and increase the number of remote channels.

For instance, when someone pays money into or withdraws money from a bank account over the counter, this costs the bank a few pence or cents. If they do it online, it costs a fraction of a penny or cent.

eBusiness and eCommerce (see Chapter 8) rely on individuals, groups and organisations being able to access electronic networks and systems. This applies particularly to customers, suppliers, partners and employees. Each of these types of stakeholder will have the option of using a variety of access devices and communication channels, and each type interacts with different front-end and back-end ICT systems.

This section considers these various devices and channels, which include telephones, television, personal computers, multimedia kiosks and mobile devices (see Figure 5.3).

5.3.2 Telephony

Telephony: A category of access device which includes fixed and mobile telephones

Telephony includes conventional audio telephones, modern video telephones and the now fading technologies of fax/telex for data transmission. Telephones have been used for a number of years as a form of retail access device. In more recent times a number of trends

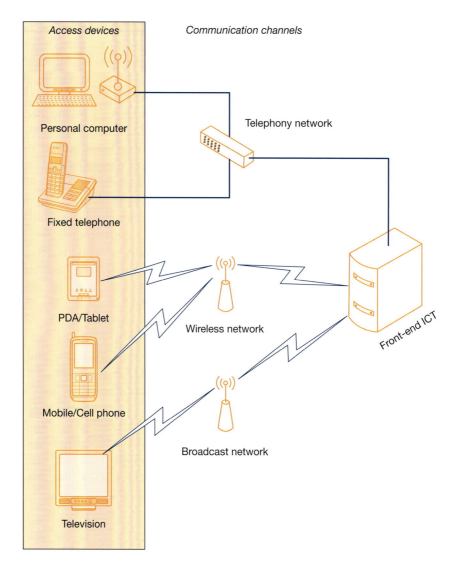

Figure 5.3 Access devices and channels

have enabled growth in the use of such devices for the ordering of products and services. Of these, the most significant are the development of touch-tone services, intelligent networks and the

growth of call centres. Telephony can be effectively combined with other access devices, such as interactive television (see below), to provide a more complete electronic retail experience. Of recent interest is the increasing availability of voice communication over the Internet through, so-called, Voice Over Internet Protocol (VOIP).

5.3.3   Television

In many parts of Europe television has converted from an analogue to a digital terrestrial channel. Television is already used as a form of electronic retail channel through terrestrial broadcasting in the sense that commercial advertising is piped into the home using this medium. With the emergence of satellite and, more recently, digital broadcasting a number of pay-per-view channels have emerged. Retailing already occurs via the medium of pay-per-view television through specialist shopping channels.

Because service providers in the area of pay-per-view need a mechanism for extracting payments from their customers the broadcasting signal is usually encrypted. This means that service providers normally have to provide some form of decryption equipment or set-top box for each customer. Such a device can easily be converted to offer a backward channel to the service provider through conventional telephony services (using modems) to enable interaction. More recently, digital televisions have been enabled with wireless devices that allow connection to the Internet directly though a home wireless network via conventional telephony.

Conventional television, both terrestrial and satellite, suffers from lack of personalisation and interactivity. This has changed with the possibilities offered by digital television. In a sense, the only thing that changes with the advent of digital television is the way in which the television signal is encoded. However, with digital television it becomes possible to deliver not only traditional television channels but also Web content (see below). This opens up the added possibility of **interactive digital television** (iDTV) in which hand-held, or other, input devices allow the customer to navigate through Web material and to input data such as orders and payments.

iDTV offers a similar electronic retail capability to the Internet-enabled PC (see below). However, perhaps it offers a lower level of actual content, reflecting the lower bandwidth of this access mechanism and inherent difficulties experienced with using current handsets for controlling access. The high start-up costs for companies also mean that there tend to be fewer service providers than in the area of Internet Service Provision.

Interactive digital television:
A combination of digital television and an up-channel using telephony

5.3.4 Personal computers

Personal computers are currently the preferred mode of access to the Internet. The vast majority of domestic users and small businesses connect to the Internet via standard analogue or digital telephone lines. Since these lines were originally designed to handle analogue speech transmission, a device known as a modem is typically needed to connect to analogue telephony channels. This converts the digital data transmitted by a computer into a series of analogue tones of various pitches and amplitudes that can be transmitted over the analogue telephone network.

To date, telephone lines have been the key technology supporting access to electronic organisations from personal computers in the home. Currently, a key constraint is the bandwidth that can be delivered into the home using a conventional modem. However, broadband technologies have impacted upon this market through technologies such as ADSL (see below).

A key problem with this access channel is the variable penetration of the technology across regions, within countries and between different social classes. Generally speaking, for instance, penetration varies between 20–70% of households in the UK compared to 100% penetration of television.

A significant degree of standardisation of the home personal computer has been achieved to date. This has encouraged a degree of domestication in its use. However, a key problem still remains. The average home user has to upgrade their hardware and software on a frequent basis, thus increasing the general cost of ownership above that involved in the maintenance of other access technologies, for example, television.

5.3.5 Multimedia kiosks/Public Internet Access Points

Public Internet access point:
Specialist access points to services provided on the Internet

Personal computers are designed for use from the home or office. Multimedia kiosks (sometimes referred to as **Public Internet Access Points**, PIAPs) are specialist access points to services provided on the Internet. Generally, these kiosks are specifically designed for certain forms of access and normally placed in public places. So a kiosk situated in a shopping mall is likely to permit access to a range of shopping services, while that sited in a hotel lobby is likely to offer access to tourist information. As the penetration of mobile access and electronic commerce increases it is likely that the need for PIAPs will decrease.

5.3.6   Mobile devices

Mobile device: Any access device that can be used for access on the move

Mobile devices include mobile phones, palm tops (sometimes referred to as personal digital assistants, PDAs), laptop computers and the latest tablet devices. Here, the mobile computer appears either in its general-purpose or 'fat' form (the laptop) or in more dedicated or 'thin' devices such as PDAs or wireless application protocol (WAP)-enabled mobile phones. The main difference between mobile access and that available through the conventional fixed PC is that the access channel is likely to be the cellular phone network. WAP servers have enabled access to the Internet from mobile devices such as mobile phones and tablet devices.

The idea of a tablet computer has been around for a number of years and in its early forms overlapped with the idea of a PDA. The PDA consists of a general-purpose computer contained in a single panel. Its distinguishing characteristic is the use of a touch screen as the input device. Modern tablets are operated primarily by the fingers, although a stylus is an option.

CASE CHECK
Apple p 426

In April 2010 Apple released the first iPad and sold 3 million in 80 days. In contrast to earlier tablet devices the iPad used a touch screen display and a virtual onscreen keyboard for input. Tablets such as the iPad can use both WiFi and cellular phone networks to access the Internet.

The mobility characteristic of devices such as smart mobile phones and tablet computers has encouraged a whole new range of ICT applications. For instance, various mobile access devices are central to supporting the work of utility companies such as gas and electricity suppliers. Workers in many gas supply companies, for instance, now use mobile devices to access corporate systems. Generally, such devices are used to enter data (for example, meter readings) and to update customer billing services while in the field.

5.3.7   RFID tags

RFID tag: Radio Frequency Identification tag, an access device that can be incorporated into an object

Radio frequency identification (RFID) is an automatic identification method, relying on storing and remotely retrieving data using devices called RFID tags. An **RFID tag** is an object that can be attached to, or incorporated into, a product, animal, or person for the purpose of identification. Data from the RFID tag is transmitted using radio waves. Some varieties of tag can be read over a distance of several metres.

Most RFID tags contain at least two parts. One is an integrated circuit for storing and processing data, modulating and demodulating a signal, and other specialised functions. The second is an antenna for receiving and transmitting the signal. A technology called chip-less RFID allows for identification of tags without an integrated circuit. This enables tags to be printed directly onto things such as clothing at a lower cost than traditional tags.

RFID tags are penetrating business more and more. For instance, such tags are now typically used within the supply chain to improve the efficiency of inventory tracking and management. Hence, a distributor might use RFID tags on large deliveries or shipments. These are automatically read at a number of points in transit and update an order-tracking system maintained by the company for its customers.

5.3.8   Multi-channel access centres

Multi-channel access centre: A centre that integrates various access channels into the organisation

One should not assume that traditional organisations, whether in the private or public sectors, can entirely switch over to one or more remote access channels; this may prove a risky strategy by excluding particular types of customers. Therefore, it is more than likely that such organisations will wish to maintain traditional access channels, such as face-to-face contact and telephone access, alongside some of the access channels discussed above. Even those companies that began as entirely Internet-based businesses have established a physical presence in an attempt to differentiate the quality of their service. Many organisations are also attempting to integrate various access channels within **multi-channel access centres**. Here, the organisation establishes a common entry point for all customer interaction of whatever form.

Cardiff City Council, for instance, like many local authorities in the UK, has created a multi-channel access centre it calls Connect to Cardiff. This consists of a large call-centre capable of handling telephone and Web-based enquiries. However, it has also established a number of 'one-stop shops' around the Capital to handle customer queries face-to-face.

> **REFLECT:** The sociologist H. L. Dreyfus (2001) has questioned whether it is possible to provide a sufficiently rich experience for consumers of private and public services using remote access channels. He believes some face-to-face contact will always be required. Consider this in light of the increasing use of electronic delivery in the public and private sector.

5.4   Communication networks

> Designing enterprise architecture   **IS**2010

Communication network: A set of devices connected with communication channels

LAN: A local area network – a type of communication network in which nodes are located relatively close together

WAN: A wide area network – a type of communication network in which nodes are geographically remote

Access devices and channels are generally organised into data communication networks, a term used for any set of devices joined by a communication technology that enables the transfer of data. There are several different kinds, defined by their coverage.

■ In a local area network (**LAN**), the devices are situated near each other: in one building, or a few buildings that are close together. These are often used to link a group of PCs and related devices such as printers, using either dedicated communication cables or wireless communication.

■ In a wide area network (**WAN**), the nodes are geographically remote. WANs may consist of a mix of dedicated and non-dedicated communication lines, as well as microwave and satellite communications.

■ A value added network (VAN) is a network that a third-party organisation sets up and maintains, selling the right to use it.

Figure 5.4 shows the components of a typical LAN. The PCs and the printer are linked to the cable via interface cards. These are pieces of firmware (a combination of hardware and software) which specify the data transmission rate, the size of message packets, the addressing information attached to each packet (see below) and the network topology. The cabling is likely to be coaxial or fibre optic. The server is likely to be a powerful PC which acts as a resource for programs and data used by other PCs in the network. The server will also run the network operating system, which operates the server facilities and manages communication on the network. A gateway device connects the LAN to other networks, and consists of a processor that translates between different communication protocols.

There are a number of major current alternatives for connecting access devices, such as the home or office PC or the mobile phone, to a front-end ICT system.

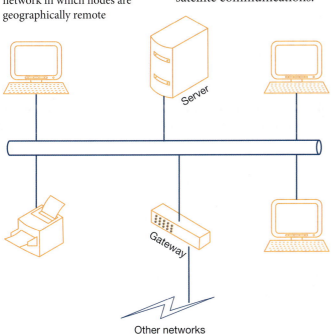

Figure 5.4 *A local area network*

5.4.1   Telephone network

The telephone network in most countries is a wide area telecommunication network. Its topology is a tapered star, with a relatively small number of main exchanges connected by long-distance trunk cables. Main exchanges are connected to a much larger number of local exchanges, which in turn connect directly to customers in the home or the office (see Figure 5.5).

The connections between main and local exchanges use cables that are designed for high-performance data transmission, typically of optical fibre and able to transmit many Mb/Sec (see Chapter 3). These can be upgraded much more easily than the cabling between customers

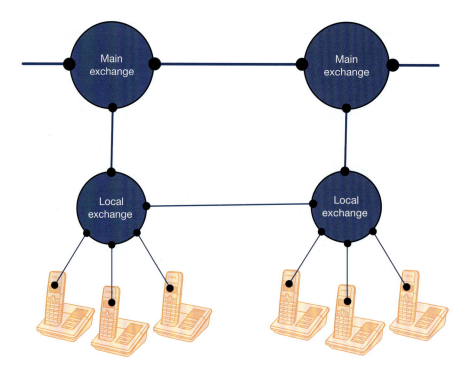

Figure 5.5 *The conventional telephone network*

and the local exchange. But the network's data transmission performance is heavily reliant on the **local loop**, that is, the communication medium between local exchanges and customers, which typically consists of copper cabling. At the time of writing, companies have started to replace such cabling with optical fibre for selected premises within major cities in the UK, such as London, Birmingham and Cardiff.

Local loop: The communication channel between the local telephone exchange and customer premises

> **REFLECT:** How important is an efficient telecommunication network to international trade? Try to think of ways in which telecommunication networks facilitate trade between countries and regions.

5.4.2   Digital transmission

Telephone companies are clearly interested in increasing the speed of data transmission (the bandwidth) over the telephony local loop. Digital services have been developed that allow the simultaneous transmission of multiple voice circuits into business premises. This allows the business to treat their local telephone network as subsumed under the integrated services digital network (**ISDN**). The data rates available can be as large as the business requires.

However, ISDN has now been almost subsumed by the technology of the digital subscriber loop or digital subscriber line (DSL). DSL or xDSL, is a family of technologies that provide digital data transmission over the wires of a local telephone network. DSL was originally developed as a means of providing video-on-demand services over the conventional copper telephony infrastructure within the local loop. It is now used as an effective means of providing fast, very high quality, access to the Internet. Some of the main advantages of DSL are a lower cost than ISDN and permanent connection to the Internet.

ISDN: Integrated Service Digital Network, a broadband communication channel for the local loop

However, DSL technology relies on short transmission distances between a local exchange and a domestic customer or business (typically 10 Km). Typically, the download speed of consumer DSL services ranges from 512 Kbit/sec to 80 Mbit/sec, depending on DSL technology used, line conditions and service level implemented. Typically, upload speed is lower than download speed for Asymmetric Digital Subscriber Line (**ADSL**) and equal to download speed for Symmetric Digital Subscriber Line (SDSL).

ADSL: Asynchronous Digital Subscriber Line, a broadband communication channel for the local loop

> **REFLECT:** Many businesses choose to pay extra for symmetric bandwidth via SDSL. Why is symmetric as opposed to lower-cost asymmetric bandwidth important to many businesses, particularly those involved in information work?

5.4.3 Cellular networks

Cellular network: A wireless network supporting mobile phones

Currently, radio networks are dominated by the use of cellular mobile phones. Such phones were originally devices capable of transmitting only voice traffic as analogue signals. However, the development of digital standards has enabled the development of integrated voice/data communications.

So-called third generation (3G) technologies enable **cellular network** operators to offer users a wider range of more advanced services, while achieving greater network capacity by improving the efficiency of method by which the digital signal is carried. Services include wide area, wireless voice telephony and broadband wireless data, all in a mobile environment. Typically, they provide services at 5–10 Mb/Sec. Certain countries, such as in Scandinavia, have already upgraded their cellular networks with a fourth generation (4G) infrastructure. 4G cellular networks can provide bandwidth of many hundreds of mega-bits per second.

5.4.4 WiFi and WiMax

WiFi: A series of standards supporting short range, high bandwidth communication networks

3G and 4G networks are wide area cellular telephone networks that evolved to incorporate high-speed Internet access and video telephony. In contrast, **WiFi** networks based on the IEEE 802.11 standard are short range, high bandwidth networks primarily developed for data transfer. Typical bandwidth for WiFi varies between 10 and 54 MB/Sec.

A WiFi enabled device such as a PC, mobile phone or tablet can connect to the Internet when within range of a wireless network connected to the Internet. The coverage of one or more inter-connected access points, referred to as *hotspots*, can comprise an area as small as a single room or as large as many square miles covered by overlapping access points. Some connections are provided free of charge, for example airports, hotels and restaurants often provide these as a customer service. Those who want to control their access point (either charge for it, or prevent others from using it) can make it secure through identifiers and passwords.

WiMax: A related technology to WiFi but designed to provide communication over longer distances

WiMax, the Worldwide Interoperability for Microwave Access, is a telecommunications technology based on the IEEE 802.16 standard that is aimed at providing wireless data over long distances in a variety of ways, from point-to-point links to full mobile cellular type access. The bandwidth and reach of WiMax makes it suitable for a range of potential applications including: connecting WiFi hotspots with each other and to other parts of the Internet; providing a wireless substitute for broadband access within the last few kilometres of cable

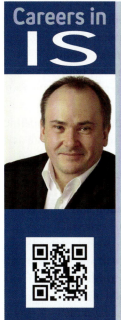

Careers in IS

John Linwood

John Linwood is the Chief Technology Officer for the BBC, managing the Technology, Distribution and Archive Division which sits within the Operations Group.

He took up the position in 2009, and is responsible for delivering the BBC's technology strategy. His role encompasses the delivery and management of the broadcast and enterprise technology infrastructure behind all BBC output and overseeing the Corporation's ICT requirements.

John joined the BBC from Yahoo!, where he was Senior Vice President of International Engineering. He covered the development of some of Yahoo!'s most successful consumer products including social networking, social media and user-generated content through to more traditional Web properties such as media, eCommerce and search.

Prior to Yahoo!, John spent eleven years at Microsoft, beginning as an Architectural Consultant in 1993 then progressing to a variety of senior positions within its MSN business. During his final post at Microsoft John managed all of MSN's international engineering, driving its global quality

of service initiatives, formulating its international hosting strategy as well as international product development.

Scan the QR code under John's picture or visit **www.palgrave. com/business/beynon-daviesbis2e/** to watch John talking about Information Systems and careers as an IS professional, and then think about the questions below:

- [ ] How significant was the 2012 Olympics to the content strategy at the BBC?

- [ ] Through what channels, and what devices, are the services provided by the BBC accessible? How are such channels integrated?

- [ ] How are apps being used in content delivery from the BBC?

- [ ] In what ways are mobile devices changing the way in which BBC employees work?

- [ ] How significant is cloud computing to managing the ICT infrastructure of the BBC and how is it used?

- [ ] How does the BBC manage the sustainability challenge?

and DSL; it has also been proposed as a technology for providing mobile connectivity. The actual bandwidth achievable through this technology depends on a range of factors but typically offers 2MB/Sec rates over a few kilometres between transmitters and receivers.

RECAP: Organisations provide access to their services or products through access channels, consisting of an access device and associated communication channel. The access device is used to formulate, transmit, receive and display messages. The communication channel is used to carry the message between customers, suppliers, partners and employees and the organisation's ICT systems. Stakeholder access devices include telephones, interactive digital television, PCs and mobile devices. Major ways of connecting access devices to front-end ICT systems include telephone networks, digital transmission and radio networks. Communication networks tend to be organised as local area networks, wide area networks or value added networks.

5.5   The Internet

Internet: A term used to denote the set of inter-connected communication networks that adopt the TCP/IP standard

When people speak of communication technology, as we have above, they generally speak of the Internet in the same breath. The **Internet** – short for inter-network –began as a Wide Area Network in the United States, funded by its Department of Defence, to link scientists and researchers around the world. It was designed primarily as a medium to exchange research data but has now become an essential part of the communication infrastructure of modern organisations in both the public and private sectors. Some have even claimed it to be the fundamental basis of a global information society.

Currently, the Internet is a set of inter-connected computer networks distributed around the globe. The Internet can be considered on a number of levels. Its base infrastructure is composed of packet-switched networks and a series of communication protocols. On this layer run a series of applications such as electronic mail (email) and more recently the World Wide Web, or the Web for short.

5.5.1   History

In August 1962 J. C. R. Licklider (the first head of the computer research programme at DARPA, the Defence Advanced Research Projects Agency in the United States) wrote a series of memos discussing his concept of a Galactic Network. This constituted a global, inter-connected set of computers through which any person, from any site in the network, could quickly access data and programs.

Lawrence G. Roberts at ARPA (DARPA changed its name to ARPA and back again a number of times) took up the idea and published his initial plan for the ARPANET in 1967. This exploited the development of appropriate routing hardware using the proposed theory of packet-switching networks (see below). In 1969 the ARPANET was created by linking four US university computers.

In October 1972 Bob Kahn gave the first demonstration of it to the public at an academic conference. In 1972 the idea of electronic mail (email) was introduced for the first time as a viable application running on this network.

The original ARPANET grew into the Internet, based around the idea that multiple independent networks of differing architectures could be made to work together through an open network architecture. Critical to this idea was the formulation of a high level, Internet working architecture, which specified the interfaces required between networks. Also critical to the development of the Internet was Bob Kahn's development of a protocol that enabled end-to-end network communication in the face of environmental problems causing transmission error. The robustness and survivability of the network were critical to its design, including the capability to withstand losses of large portions of the underlying networks. The eventual protocol, which became known as TCP/IP (see below), enabled effective error control across an open network architecture.

Four principles were central to Kahn's thinking:

- Each distinct network must remain autonomous and no internal changes should be required to enable a network to connect to the Internet.
- Communications should be on a best effort basis. If a data packet does not make it to the final destination, it should be retransmitted from the source.
- Black boxes (later called gateways and routers) were to be used to connect networks. They did not retain any information about the individual flows of packets, which kept them simple and avoided complicated adaptation and recovery from various failure modes.
- There would be no global control of the Internet at the operational level.

Part of the motivation for the development of ARPANET and TCP/IP was to enable the sharing of computer resources across a network. These were referred to as time-sharing computers. When desktop computers first appeared, it was thought by some that TCP was too big and complex to run on a PC. A research group at MIT set out to show that a compact and simple implementation of TCP was possible. They produced an implementation, first for the Xerox Alto (the early personal workstation developed at Xerox PARC) and then for the IBM PC.

Widespread development of LANs, PCs and workstations in the 1980s allowed the Internet to flourish. Ethernet technology, developed by Bob Metcalfe at Xerox PARC in 1973, is now probably the dominant network architecture underlying the Internet. PCs are also the dominant forms of computing device on the Internet.

A major shift occurred as a result of the increase in scale of the Internet and its associated management issues. To make it easy for people to use the network, host computers were assigned names, so that it was not necessary to remember the numeric or, so-called, IP addresses. Originally, there were a fairly limited number of hosts, so it was feasible to maintain a single table of all of them and their associated names and addresses. With the invention of LANs the shift to having a large number of independently managed networks meant that a single table of hosts was no longer feasible. Hence, the Domain Name System (DNS) was invented by Paul Mockapetris. The DNS provided a scalable, distributed mechanism for resolving hierarchical host names (such as www.acm.org) into an Internet address (see below).

Thus, by 1985, the Internet was already well established as a technology supporting a broad community of researchers and developers, and was beginning to be used by other communities for daily computer communications. Electronic mail was being used broadly across several communities, often with different systems, but inter-connection between different mail systems was demonstrating the utility of broad-based electronic communications. In 1984 the British JANET and, in the following year, the US NSFNET programmes explicitly announced their intention to serve the entire higher education community, regardless of discipline. This was a major stimulus to the idea of inter-networking.

On 24 October 1995, the Federal Networking Council (FNC) unanimously passed a resolution defining the term Internet. This definition was developed in consultation with members of the Internet and intellectual property rights communities:

RESOLUTION: The Federal Networking Council (FNC) agrees that the following language reflects our definition of the term 'Internet'. 'Internet' refers to the global information system that – (i) is logically linked together by a globally unique address space based on the Internet Protocol (IP) or its subsequent extensions/follow-ons; (ii) is able to support communications using the Transmission Control Protocol/Internet Protocol (TCP/IP) suite or its subsequent extensions/follow-ons, and/or other IP-compatible protocols; and (iii) provides, uses or makes accessible, either publicly or privately, high level services layered on the communications and related infrastructure described herein.

From initially connecting a handful of nodes on the ARPANET the Internet has grown astronomically. Some estimates for the number of users worldwide are:

- 1997: 100 million
- 1998: 200 million

- 2001: 390 million
- 2003: 640 million
- 2005: 1 billion
- 2008: 1.5 billion
- 2010: 1.9 billion

Let us now look in more detail at a number of the technical concepts that were mentioned in the history above and which make up this communication infrastructure.

5.5.2   Packet-switching networks

The early computer networks were modelled on the local and long-distance telephone networks which dated back to the early 1950s. Computer networks during the period tended to be composed of leased telephone lines. A connection between a caller and the receiver was established through telephone switching equipment (both mechanical and computerised) selecting specific electrical circuits to form a single path. Once the connection was established, data travelled along the path. This is known as a circuit-switching network.

Circuit-switching works well for voice communication but proves expensive for data communication because of the need to establish a point-to-point connection for each pair of senders and receivers. Most modern computer networks therefore use a form of network technology known as **packet-switching**. Here, the data in a message or file is broken up into chunks known as packets. Each packet is electronically labelled with codes that indicate its sender (origin) and receiver (destination). Data travel along the network from computer to computer until they reach their destination. Each computer in the network determines the best route forward for the packets it receives and must transmit. Computers that make these decisions are known as **routers**. The destination computer reassembles the packets into the original message.

There are a number of advantages to packet-switching networks for data communication. Long streams of data can be broken up into small, manageable chunks. This means that the packets can be distributed efficiently to balance the traffic across a wide range of possible transmission paths in a data communication network.

Packet-switching: The process of breaking up message data into packets that are disseminated over a communication network by routers

Router: Hardware and software that direct packets to their indicated destination along a communication network

5.5.3   TCP/IP

One of the key objectives of most computer networks is to achieve high levels of connectivity, that is the ability of computer systems to communicate with each other and share data. This means that standards must be defined, to enable communication between sender and receiver, and embodied in communication software.

One approach to developing higher connectivity uses open systems, built on public domain operating systems, user interfaces, application standards and networking standards. One of the oldest examples of an open systems model for data communication is the Transmission Control Protocol/Internet Protocol (**TCP/IP**). A protocol is a statement that explains how a specific networking task, such as the transmission of data, should be performed. TCP/IP divides the communication process into five layers of networking tasks:

TCP/IP: Transmission Control Protocol/Internet Protocol, the communications protocol underlying the Internet

- Application: the closest layer to the network user, which provides data entry and presentation functionality to the end-user.
- Transport/TCP: this layer breaks application data up into TCP packets known as datagrams. Each packet consists of a header comprising the address of the sending computer, data for reassembling the message and error-checking data.
- Internet Protocol: This layer receives datagrams from the TCP layer and breaks the packets down further. An IP packet contains a header with an address, and carries TCP information and data in the body of the packet. The IP layer routes the individual packets from the sender to the receiver.

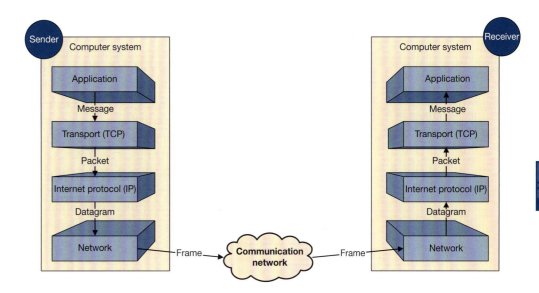

Figure 5.6 *TCP/IP layers*

- Network: this handles addressing issues within the operating system as well as providing an interface between the computer and the network. Each device on a network will normally have a unique identifier (an IP number) assigned to it, represented in the network interface of each device.
- Physical: this layer defines the basic characteristics of signal transmission along communication networks.

The advantage of this approach is that two different computer systems using TCP/IP are able to communicate with each other even if they are based on different hardware and software standards. Data sent from one computer passes down through the five layers of the protocol. Once the data reaches the receiving computer it travels up through the layers. If the receiving computer finds a damaged data packet it requests the sending computer to send again. This process is illustrated in Figure 5.6.

5.5.4   Email protocols, FTP and HTTP

Email protocol: A communication protocol designed for the transfer of electronic mail

FTP: File Transfer Protocol, a communication protocol designed for the transfer of electronic files

In addition to the TCP/IP protocol, other communication protocols are used to provide file transfer, email and Web applications on the Internet. File Transfer Protocol (**FTP**) enables the transfer of files between computers. Simple Mail Transfer Protocol (SMTP) enables mail transfer between computers. Multi-purpose Internet Mail Extensions (MIME) enable mail transfer in complex organisations. This is used by the Web to specify the media type contained in a message such as text, images or video. Hypertext Transfer Protocol (HTTP) is a protocol that defines how information can be transmitted between web clients and web servers in a network (see below).

5.5.5   IP addresses

IP address: Internet Protocol address ,a unique identifier for computers on a communication network using TCP/IP

An **IP address** is the fundamental way of uniquely identifying a computer system on the Internet. It is constructed as a series of up to four numbers each delimited by a period, so it can be described as a dotted quad. In a 32-bit IP address each of the four numbers can range from 0 to 255. Generally the first four numbers identify a computer network. The remaining numbers usually identify a node on this network. For example, 126.203.97.54 might be an IP address for a computer on the local area network at my university.

DID YOU KNOW? Because of the explosion in Internet usage more computers are being added to the global network. Hence, the 32-bit IP system will eventually run out of unique addresses. To offset this, a 128-bit IP address is being introduced globally.

5.5.6 Universal resource locators

Internet users generally find IP addresses difficult to remember, so more memorable identifiers have been introduced. These map to IP addresses (that is, each one refers to one IP address).

HTML documents resident on computers attached to the Internet (see below) are identified by universal resource locators (**URL**s), so URLs can be used to provide a unique address for each document on the Web. Links between documents are activated by hotspots in the document where a word, phrase or image is used to reference a link to another document.

URL: Universal resource locator, a unique identifier assigned to documents placed on the Web

The structure of a URL consists of at least two, and as many as four, parts. A simple two-part URL consists of the protocol used for the connection (such as HTTP) and the address at which a resource is located on the host. In the URL below, the protocol HTTP is placed before the symbols ://. The address after these symbols identifies a specific web page on the host computer, in this case the home page of my personal website.

http://www.peebeedee.org.uk

5.5.7 Domain names

The 'peebeedee' in this URL is the name I assigned to my website, the 'org' for organisation and the 'uk' for United Kingdom. Together these make up a **domain name**, an agreed string of characters that is used to provide greater meaning to a URL. In practice, a domain name identifies and locates a host computer or service on the Internet, it is therefore a specialist form of identifier. It often relates to the name of a business, organisation or service, and must be registered in a similar way to a company name.

Domain name: A hierarchical naming convention for identifying host computers on the Internet

A domain name is typically made up of three or more parts, referred to as domain levels. Levels therefore provide structure to the domain name and are read from right to left.

- Top-level domains consist of either generic names (such as .com) or country codes (such as .uk). Generic domain names are also referred to as first-level domain names.
- Second-level domains further refine the top-level domain name by typically suggesting the type of provider. For instance, .ac indicates an academic institution based in the United Kingdom.
- Domains below the second level are referred to as sub-domains and are typically used to refer to a specific content provider, such as *peebeedee* in the example.

5.5.8 The regulation of domain names

Internet protocol addresses are mapped to domain names by domain name servers. These are computer systems in the inter-network that perform this transformation. For such domain servers to work effectively standardisation is needed in domain names.

Such standardisation has traditionally been in the hands of the US government. During the late 1980s and early 1990s, the responsibility for allocating domain names was given to the Internet Assignment Number Authority (IANA). Then the company Network Solutions Inc. (NSI) was set up and started charging customers for the registration of domain names. In 1997, IANA and a number of other organisations advocated self-governance in the domain name service, and a year later the Internet Corporation for Assigned Names and Numbers (ICANN) was created. Its main role is to oversee the allocation of domain names and the distribution of addresses by domain name registrars. Domain name registrars are public and private organisations in different countries, tasked with maintaining registries (databases of domain names and addresses).

ICANN has responsibility for a number of naming conventions, including generic top-level domain names such as .com and .org, country codes such as .uk and .fr, sponsored domain names such as .coop and .museum and unsponsored domain names such as .biz.

Generic top-level domains consist of strings of three letters, which were originally:

- .com, signifying a commercial organisation
- .org, although it can be any type, typically a public sector or voluntary sector organisation

- .gov, initially used to signify government establishments generally, but now restricted to refer to US government establishments
- .edu, used generally to signify an educational institution internationally
- .mil, initially used to signify military establishments generally but now restricted to refer to US Armed Forces establishments
- .int, initially conceived to denote international entities
- .net, initially used to signify 'networks' and therefore to denote a generic free usage domain.

In 2011 ICANN decided to end most restrictions on the names of generic top-level domains. This means that organisations are now able to bid for any top-level Internet domain name and pay an annual fee for its registration. However, it is likely that the process of changing over to these new TLDs by organisations will take some time as many organisations decide upon the most appropriate names for their business and attempt to persuade users of the Web to adopt them.

CASE CHECK

dotCYMRU p 432

The dotCYM campaign is a not-for-profit pressure group that, for a number of years, has attempted to promote a distinct internet domain for the welsh linguistic and cultural community. The campaign believes that the welsh language and culture connotes a community that should be identified and enhanced by having its own top-level domain on the internet (see dotCYMRU case study).

5.5.9 Connecting to the Internet

Long-range data communications are rapidly moving off conventional telephony-based architectures to those based on the architecture of the Internet.

Layer 3 of the TCP/IP communications model described above – the transport layer – uses the Internet protocol (IP) to is split up data into autonomous packets, each carrying the address of the sender and receiver. The packets find their way across a range of inter-connected sub-networks. These might be either LANs or WANs connected to other networks by routers. The routers manage naming conventions for the sending and receiving units. This is illustrated in Figure 5.7.

ISP: Internet service provider, a company supplying connections to the Internet for customers

Domestic users and small businesses generally do not have LANs, so they are connected via a modem and a conventional telephone line to an Internet Service Provider (**ISP**). The customer achieves connection as a standard telephone call to a bank of modems held at the ISP. For the duration of the call the ISP provides a unique but temporary IP address to the customer's computer. It informs the computer of this address, which is used by the customer's browser in any communication with the Internet during the duration of the connection. This temporary binding of IP address to computer is typically achieved through a point-to-point protocol (PPP). This situation is illustrated in Figure 5.8.

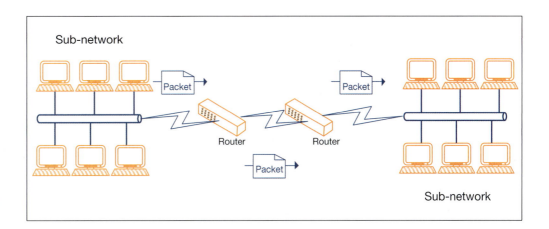

Figure 5.7 *Sub-networks and routers*

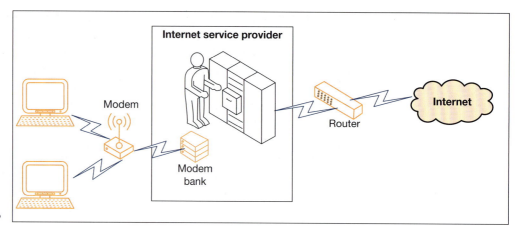

Figure 5.8 *Connection to an ISP*

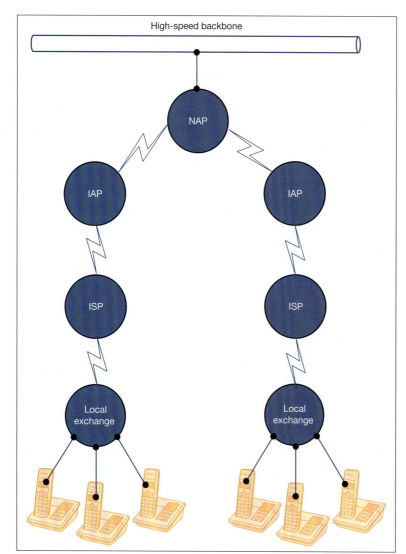

Figure 5.9 *Primary architecture of the Internet*

WWW: The World Wide Web, an application that runs over the Internet supporting the use and transmission of hypermedia documentation

Figure 5.9 displays graphically the primary architecture of the Internet. The Internet is supported by a high-speed communications backbone. Users access the Internet by connecting to an ISP via the local telephone loop. The ISP is connected to an Internet access provider (IAP), which has permanent access to a network access point (NAP). This is an inter-connection point that exchanges data traffic from a number of IAPs at high speed. Smaller ISPs may connect to the backbone via larger ISPs.

5.5.10 Applications that run on the Internet

The Internet is an inter-network on which a number of applications currently run, including **WWW**, email, newsgroups and chat.

- The World Wide Web (WWW) is effectively an application that allows the use and transmission of hypermedia documentation (see below) over the Internet.
- Electronic mail (email) was one of the first applications to run on the Internet. It uses email servers and email software to enable people to communicate primarily through the asynchronous one-to-one transmission of messages. It requires email addresses to be assigned to users.
- A mail list is a collection of email addresses. Using this technology the same message can be distributed precisely to the persons that need the information. Mail lists are therefore important for enabling one-to-many asynchronous communication. List servers permit the easy maintenance of mail lists.
- Newsgroups consist of threaded discussions and enable many-to-many asynchronous communication. Participants can post messages onto the newsgroup using email. Other participants can then thread comments or replies to each message. Bulletin boards and online fora are variants of the newsgroup idea.
- Chat enables people to engage in synchronous many-to-many communication in approximate real-time using messaging over the Internet.

RECAP: The most prevalent current example of the application of communication technology is the Internet, short for inter-network. The technical infrastructure of the Internet includes packet-switched networks, TCP/IP, HTTP, email protocols and FTP, IP addresses, universal resource locators (URLs) and domain names. Packet-switching networks employ protocols in which data in a message or file are broken up into chunks known as packets and distributed around the network. TCP/IP is an open systems model for data communication that employs a number of layers. In addition to the TCP/IP protocol, other protocols are used to provide file and email applications on the Internet, including FTP, SMTP, MIME and HTTP. Computers attached to the Internet, and the HTML documents resident on them, are identified by universal resource locators (URLs). A domain name provides more meaning to a URL, and identifies and locates a host computer or service on the Internet. Internet protocol addresses are mapped to domain names by domain name servers. A variety of applications run on the Internet, including the WWW, email, mail lists, newsgroups and chat.

5.6   The World Wide Web

Designing enterprise architecture   **IS**2010

The Web dominates any discussion concerning the communication infrastructure for modern business. People often confuse the Internet with the Web. The Internet is the backbone communication infrastructure as described above. The Web is effectively an application that runs on the Internet, and forms a set of core standards for most contemporary front-end ICT systems. This section considers the history of the Web and its basis in the technology of hypertext and hypermedia. It then describes hypermedia, HTML, websites and web portals.

5.6.1   History

Tim Berners-Lee (1999), the creator of the concept of the Web, has claimed that one major motivation was the inability of computers to store random associations, in the way the human brain does. A number of researchers in the academic community had proposed setting up networks of loosely connected nodes of textual material – referred to as hypertext (see below) – in a way that copied the brain's associative capacity. In 1989, while working at the European Particle Physics Laboratory, Berners-Lee proposed that a global hypertext space might be created in which any information on the network could be accessed by a single universal document identifier (UDI). His employers gave him the opportunity to write a program in 1990 called WorlDwidEweb. This constituted a point and click hypertext editor which ran on the NeXT machine, a hardware platform of the time. This hypertext editor and an associated specification for a web server were released to the high-energy physics community at first. In the summer of 1991 this technology, together with an early browser (see below) written by a student, was released to the hypertext and NeXT communities. The specifications of UDIs (now URLs), Hypertext Markup Language (HTML) and HTTP (see below) were also published on the first server in order to promote widespread adoption.

Between the summers of 1991 and 1994, the load on the first web server (info.cern.ch) rose steadily by a factor of 10 every year. The first three years of the development of the Web were devoted to attempts to get the technology adopted first by academia and then by industry. For this to prove successful Web clients were needed for other hardware platforms (as the NeXT computer was not commonplace), and eventually an array of browsers – Erwise, Viola, Cello and Mosaic – emerged.

Berners-Lee was under pressure to define the future evolution of the Web. After much discussion he decided to form the World Wide Web Consortium (W3C) in September 1994, based at MIT in the United States, INRIA in France, and now also at Keio University in Japan. Since then W3C has assumed responsibility for evolving the various protocols and standards associated with the Web.

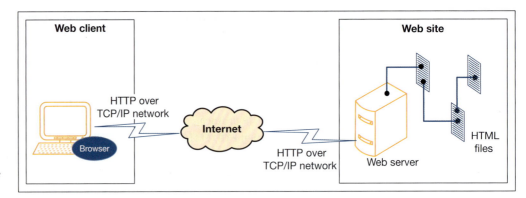

Figure 5.10 *Components of the Web*

5.6.2   Components of the Web

Figure 5.10 illustrates the primary components of the Web: hypertext/hypermedia, HTTP, HTML web browsers, websites and web portals.

The Web is effectively a client–server application (see Chapter 6) running over the Internet. Web clients run pieces of software known as browsers. This enables connection to web servers using two communication protocols, HTTP and TCP/IP. Web servers deliver hypermedia documents in HTML format over the Internet to Web clients.

5.6.3   Hypertext/hypermedia

Hypertext: A subset of hypermedia focusing on the construction of network text

Hypermedia: The technology supporting the construction of documents of multiple media associated together with links

Vannevar Bush (1945) envisaged **hypertext/hypermedia** systems in the 1940s. In a ground-breaking paper he discussed the concept of a memex (memory extender), a device capable of storing and retrieving information on the basis of content. In 1968, Douglas Englebart demonstrated the Augment system, which was an online working environment designed to augment the human intellect. It could be used to store and retrieve memos, research notes and other forms of documentation. Ted Nelson extended Bush's original idea in his Xanadu environment. Xanadu was designed to be an ever-expanding workspace that could be used to create and inter-connect documents containing text, video, audio and graphics. Nelson actually coined the term hypertext, and described it as being '*non-linear reading or writing*'. A number of prominent hypermedia prototypes were developed during the 1980s. However, a software tool bundled with the Apple Macintosh computer did most to popularise the concept. In recent times hypertext and hypermedia form the bedrock for the Web.

Text can normally be organised in three major ways. The first is linear text, as in a conventional novel. The reader is expected to start at the beginning and progress steadily to the end. Most textbooks and reports are organised as hierarchical text: they are divided into chapters, sections, subsections and so on. The reader can use the hierarchy to find the text that interests them. Dictionaries and encyclopaedias are examples of network text. Such documents do not have a hierarchical structure: each entry has an independent existence but is linked to a number of other entries via cross-references.

Hypertext is an electronic or online version of network text. A hypertext document is made up of a number of textual chunks connected with associative links called hyperlinks. Hypermedia is a superset of hypertext, including text, graphics, audio and video.

5.6.4   Hypertext transfer protocol (HTTP)

HTTP: Hypertext Transfer Protocol, a communication protocol designed for the transfer of hypertext documents

HTTP is a protocol that defines how information can be transmitted between Web clients and web servers, typically over a TCP/IP network. In an HTTP transaction, the client establishes a connection with a web server; the client sends a request message to a web server; the web server sends a response to the client; and the connection is closed by the web server.

HTTP is said to be a stateless protocol. This means that when a server provides a response and the connection is closed, the server has no memory of any previous transactions. This has the advantage of simplicity, in that clients and servers can run with simple logic and there is little need for extra memory.

5.6.5 Hypertext markup language (HTML)

The Web can be thought of as a collection of hypermedia documents residing on thousands of servers or websites situated on computers around the world. Electronic documents of any form are made up of two types of data: data that represents content, such as text and graphics, and data that describes to ICT applications how the content is to be processed. Typical processing involves formatting the document on media such as the printed page and the PC screen. The process information normally consists of a set of embedded tags that indicate how the content is to be presented. This process of tagging text with extra information is known as marking up, and the set of tags for doing this comprise a markup language. In the 1960s work began on developing a generalised markup language for describing the formatting of electronic documents. This work became established in a standard known as the standard generalised markup Language (SGML).

SGML is in fact a meta-language, a language for defining other languages, so it can be used to define a large set of markup languages. Tim Berners-Lee used SGML to define a specific language for hypertext documents known as **HTML**. HTML is a standard for marking up or tagging documents that can be published on the Web, and can be made up of text, graphics, images, audio clips and video clips. Documents can also include links to other documents stored on either the local HTML server or remote HTML servers.

HTML has undergone a number of versions since it was first introduced in 1991. A major part of the work of W3C has been to produce standard versions of HTML with increased functionality.

As suggested above, an HTML document contains both content and tags. The document content consists of what is displayed on the computer screen. The tags constitute codes that tell the browser how to format and present the content on the screen. The general form of this relationship between tags and content is expressed as:

<tagname properties> content </tagname>

The tagname is taken from a set of keywords established in the particular version of HTML. Tags are embedded in angled brackets. Certain tagnames and the grammar with which they are used convey specific meanings to Web browsers. For instance, in the tag <p align="right">, p is the tagname and acts as an abbreviation for the word paragraph, so this tag is designed to be placed at the start of a chunk or paragraph of text. The word *align* is a property which can be assigned a number of values from a limited list. One of these is *right*, which specifies that the paragraph in question should be right-justified on screen. An endtag </p> is placed at the end of the chunk of text.

Table 6.1 describes a number of the most common tags used within HTML.

As you probably know, to access the Web you need a web browser, a program that lets you read web documents, view any inbuilt images or activate other media and hotspots. After the invention of the concept of the Web the idea became established quickly in the scientific community. However, few people outside this community had software capable of reading HTML documents. In 1993 the first program that could read HTML documents and display them on a graphical user interface was written at the University of Illinois. It was called Mosaic.

It soon became apparent that there was an opportunity to sell a good browser, and members of the Illinois team formed the company Netscape Communications. Their key product, Netscape Navigator, became an immediate success. Microsoft entered the market with its Internet Explorer soon afterwards, and Navigator soon lost support. More recently, the open source browser, Mozilla Firefox, and the Google product Chrome offer a competitive alternative to Internet Explorer.

HTML: Hypertext Markup Language, a standard for marking up documents for publishing on the Web

Table 5.1 Some common HTML tags

Tag name	Functionality
<html>	Start of a html document
<head>	Establishes the header of web page
<body>	Establishes the body of a web page
<h1> <h2>...	Used to establish various levels of heading
<p>	Start of a paragraph
<b>	Embolden enclosed text
<i>	Italicise enclosed text
<u>	Underline enclosed text
<li>	Establish an item in a list
<center>	Centre text
<font>	Used to establish the font type, size and colour of some text
<img>	Short for image – used to refer to an image file for insertion within the text
<a href>	A tag for linking to parts in or outside a document
<ul>	Start of an unordered list
<ol>	Start of an ordered list

5.6.6   Websites, pages and portals

Website: A collection of HTML documents stored on a web server

A **website** is a logical collection of HTML documents normally stored on a web server. As mentioned in previous sections, we can distinguish between the content and presentation of a web page. The content consists of the text and other media bundled as HTML documents. The presentation concerns the way the content is displayed on the user's access device. As explained above, this is controlled by HTML tags. The term web page really describes how an HTML document is presented on a website.

Web pages can be used not only to display information but also as sophisticated data entry and query interfaces to ICT systems, so in many ways web page design is a hybrid activity. From one perspective, it is not dissimilar to designing newspaper or magazine pages when good graphic design capability is desirable. From another perspective, since web pages can interface with both front-end and back-end ICT systems, it is important for the designer to understand the principles of good user interface design (see Chapter 9).

In the Oxford English Dictionary, a portal is defined as a door, gate or entrance, especially one of imposing appearance. Web portals are specialised websites designed to act as an entry point into the Web. They can be seen as a form of electronic re-intermediation (see Chapter 8). A portal tries to attract users through a range of value-added services such as information, news, eShopping, directories and searching, making it an anchor site for them. There are two major types of portal. Horizontal portals attempt to serve the entire Internet community, typically by offering search functions and classification for all content on the Web. Vertical portals normally provide the same functionality but for a specific market sector, so they target a niche audience.

Typical examples of horizontal portals are Lycos.com and Yahoo!.com. Examples of vertical portals are the ones supplied by Dell (dell.com) and Cisco (cisco.com) (see Chapter 8).

A number of other software applications are heavily associated with the Web and its use, and enhance its functionality, although they are independent of it. For example, because of the information explosion on the Web, one major problem is knowing how to find the exact information you want. A search engine lets users specify a combination of keywords using logical operators such as AND, NOT and OR. It then looks up the keyword combinations in what is effectively a large index linking keywords to URLs, and displays a set of results. Search engines are typically offered by information intermediaries or infomediaries, normally organisations maintaining horizontal portals. One of the most used at present is google.com (Vise, 2005).

Bulletin board: Web facilities that permit users to post items to a central access area

Bulletin boards are virtual versions of physical bulletin boards since you can post news of events, products or services on them. Discussion fora are pages typically attached to a website that allow users to add comments to a long thread of discussion about a specific topic.

CASE CHECK
Google   CS p 440

Google Inc. is perhaps the best known of the recent American companies specialising in internet search and online advertising. When they were first introduced, search engines matched a series of search terms entered by the user against the terms found in web pages. They provided a list of web addresses, ordered according to how often the search terms appeared in them.

The founders of Google produced an algorithm called PageRank which improved on this, by analysing the links emanating from and pointing to web documents. It then assigns a numerical weighting to each element of a set of documents, with the purpose of measuring each document's relative importance in the set. In this sense, the PageRank algorithm treats links in much the same way that academics treat citations. Generally, the larger the number of citations an academic paper receives, the more important it is considered to be. Similarly, the more links made to a HTML document, the higher its rank in a Google search.

5.6.7   Web 2.0

Web 2.0: A collection of Web-based communities and hosted services which facilitate collaboration

The phrase **Web 2.0** tends to suggest a new version of the Web. The second generation it refers to is not a new set of technical specifications though, it is a second generation of Web-based communities and hosted services which facilitate collaboration and sharing. These include RSS feeds, social bookmarking, weblogs, folksonomies and wikis.

- RSS stands for 'Really Simple Syndication' and consists of a family of web feed formats used to publish frequently updated content, such as blog entries, news headlines or podcasts to subscribers.
- Social bookmarking technology enables users to store lists of Internet resources that they find useful. These lists are then made accessible to the public by users of a specific network or website. Other users with similar interests can view links by topic, category, tags, or even randomly.
- A weblog (or blog) is a website where entries are written in chronological order and commonly displayed in reverse chronological order. Blogs typically provide commentary or news on a particular subject such as food, politics or local news. Some blogs operate as personal online diaries. A typical blog combines text, images, and links to other blogs, web pages and other media related to its topic. The ability for readers to leave comments in an interactive format is an important part of many blogs.
- A wiki is a shared web page or site that can be updated using easy-to-use tools through a browser. This means they can be directly edited by anyone with access to them, so their main use is in collaborative content production such as creating articles about subjects or combining information from many different sources.
- Folksonomies are sets of tags developed and used collaboratively by a community of users to classify and retrieve content such as web pages, photographs and web links. Folksonomic tagging is intended to make a body of information increasingly easy to search, discover, and navigate over time.

CASE CHECK
Wikipedia   CS p 464

Wikipedia is a multilingual project which offers a free encyclopaedia on the Web. The name is a combination of the words wiki and encyclopaedia. Wikipedia uses wikis as tools for its members to collaboratively produce content.

Registered users of Wikipedia are able to create new articles, then once an article is on the site anyone with access to it can change its content. Changes made to pages are instantly displayed. The consequence of this is that Wikipedia does not declare any of its articles to be complete or finished.

This process of, so-called, collaborative content production is built upon the premise that collaboration among users will improve articles over time, in much the same way that opensource software develops (see Chapter 12). Some of Wikipedia's editors have compared this process to Darwinian evolutionary processes, where the 'fitness' of content improves over time.

5.6.8   The semantic Web

Semantic Web: An attempt to build semantics into the links used in associating Web content

The **semantic Web** is seen by many to be a natural extension to Web 2.0. The traditional Web, as we have seen, consists of content connected via a multitude of hyperlinks. The essential property of the Web is its universality, achieved through the power of links that can relate any content to any other content. The key limitation imposed by this universality is that links do not contain any meaning or semantics (see Chapter 3) over and above their ability to associate content items.

The semantic Web (Berners-Lee et al., 2001) is, by definition, an attempt to build semantics or meaning into the essence of Web architecture. It is proposed to do this using XML, a *resource description framework* (RDF) and the notion of an ontology described in Chapter 3. RDF will code the semantics of links in sets of triples (similar to the discussion of knowledge representation in Chapter 3). These triples will relate URLs using typed links that convey their relationship. Ontologies will consist of taxonomies of objects and relations plus sets of inference rules. Software agents will then traverse the Web and will need to share ontologies to enable them to perform tasks such as searching databases in multiple formats.

Suppose you have two web pages stored on two separate web servers. Currently you can associate these two pages by placing a hyperlink on one page which refers to the URL of the other web page. However, the only meaning currently represented in this link is one of 'see also'. When a user clicks on this link and is taken to the associated page she must work out herself why the two pages have been associated. Now, assume that you can create a link with an RDF triple of the form <web page 1><example of concept><web page 2>. Here, the reason why two pieces of content have been linked is much more easily established, not only by humans but also by machines.

RECAP: The (World Wide) Web is an application that runs on the Internet. Its primary elements are the concept of hypertext/hypermedia, its implementation in HTML and the use of web browsers. Hypertext is an electronic, or online, version of network text. A hypertext document is made up of a number of textual chunks connected using associative links called hyperlinks. Hypermedia is a superset of hypertext which allows the distribution of multimedia content. HTTP is a protocol that defines how information can be transmitted between nodes in a network. HTML is a standard for marking up or tagging documents that can be published on the Web, and can be made up of text, graphics, images, audio clips and video clips. People accessing the Web need a browser and a program that lets them read documents, view inbuilt images and activate other media and hotspots. The nodes of the Web are generally made up of websites and web portals. A website is a logical collection of HTML documents normally stored on a web server. Web portals are specialised websites designed to act as an entry point for users. Software applications that enhance use of the Web include search engines, bulletin boards and discussion fora.

5.7   Transactional data

To enable the effective flow of transactions, there need to be defined standards for the format and the transmission of electronic messages. Electronic messages are forms of data transmission. For any transactional flow along electronic communication channels three conditions must be satisfied:

- The electronic message comprising the transaction must have a defined format.
- The receiver and sender of the message must agree on its format.
- The message must be able to be sent and read by electronic devices.

Historically, a standard for transactional flow was based on electronic data interchange (EDI). More recently, standards have been defined using a Web-based technology known as extensible markup language (XML). Both EDI and XML are attempts to define standard data formats for the transmission of electronic messages between organisations.

5.7.1   EDI

Electronic Data Interchange (**EDI**) provides a collection of standard message formats and an element dictionary for businesses to exchange data through an electronic messaging

EDI: Electronic data interchange, a set of standards for the transfer of electronic documentation

service (Norris and West, 2001). It mainly supports the execution and settlement phases of commercial transactions (see Chapter 7).

Documentation such as sales orders, delivery notes, invoices and payment advices, which would once have been on paper, can instead be coded up as EDI messages. Each message consists of a number of data segments, each made up of a tag and a number of data elements. The tag identifies the data segment and the data elements include the codes and values required in the message. For example, in a purchase order a data element might detail shipment dates and times, and be given the code DTM (short for Date/Time).

The main benefits of EDI arise from its ability to streamline key business processes, particularly those associated with managing external stakeholders. For instance, if it is introduced for purchase orders, it should mean they are placed more rapidly, with fewer errors in data entry and transmission, reducing the staff time needed and improving inventory management and delivery times.

The main problems with EDI are that standardisation has never been sufficiently broad and technical implementation has proved expensive. For this reason organisations are looking to the next generation of business documentation standards based on Internet and Web technology. Standards are developing in Internet EDI that enables EDI to be implemented at a lower cost through virtual private networks or over the public Internet. However, most contemporary interest is in the use of an extension of the Web known as XML for document specification and transmission.

5.7.2   XML

One of the main advantages of HTML (see above) is its simplicity. This enables it to be used effectively by a wide user community. However, this is also one of its disadvantages. Sophisticated users want to define their own tags, particularly for functionality involved with the exchange of data. The World Wide Web Consortium developed **XML** in 1998 (W3C, 2000) to meet these needs. The term extensible means that new markup tags can be created by users.

XML: Extensible markup language, a meta-language for the definition of document standards

Like HTML, XML is a restricted descendant of SGML. Whereas HTML is used to define how the data in a document is to be displayed, XML can be used to define the syntax and some of the semantics of a document. So it can be used to specify standard templates for business documents such as invoices, shipping notes and fund transfers. XML is seen as a major way in which EDI could be replaced for electronic document transmission between organisations.

An XML document consists of a set of elements and attributes. Elements, or tags, are the most common form of markup. The first element in an XML document must be a root element. The document must have only one root element but this element may contain a number of other elements.

Suppose your company is a coffee wholesaler. You might wish to create XML documents for the exchange of shipping information to your customers. An appropriate root element might therefore be the tag <PRODUCTDETAILSLIST>.

An element begins with a starttag and ends with an endtag. The start tag in our document for the root element would be <ProductDetailsList>. The corresponding endtag would be </ProductDetailsList>. Note that tags are case-sensitive in XML. Hence <PRODUCTDETAILSLIST> is a different tag from <ProductDetailsList>.

Elements can be empty, in which case they can be abbreviated to <EmptyElement/>. Elements must also be properly nested as sub-elements within a superior element. So this XML element might be used to define a particular coffee product:

```
<ProductDetails ID='1234'>
<ItemName>Kenya Special</ItemName>
<CountryOfOrigin>Kenya</CountryOfOrigin>
<WholeSaleCost>20.00</WholeSaleCost>
<Stock>4000</Stock>
</ProductDetails>
```

Here we have a ProductDetails element with a number of sub-elements. Definitions for these sub-elements such as ItemName, CountryOfOrigin, WholeSaleCost and Stock are properly nested within ProductDetails.

In traditional database terms this would constitute a row in a products table (see Chapter 6). This row is made up of a number of columns, including an identifier for the product, the name of the item, the country of origin of the product, the cost of the product and the number of product items in stock.

Attributes are name-value pairs that contain descriptive information about an element. The attribute is placed inside the starttag for the element and consists of an attribute name, an equality ('=') sign and the value for the attribute placed within quotes. In the coffee producer example the tag <ProductDetails ID='1234'> contains the attribute ID and the value '1234'.

Traditionally, the structure or syntax of an XML document has been defined in terms of a document type definition or DTD. More recently, the trend has been to use XML Schema to define the structure of an XML document. It lists the names of all elements, which elements can appear in combination and what attributes are available for each type of element. It can also be used to specify certain rules on data elements, such as whether an element is a piece of text or a number, and whether an element has a default value or not.

5.7.3   Electronic payment systems

Payments are a special form of transactional data. Any payment system is effectively a mechanism for recording exchanges of monetary value.

In earlier times goods and services were exchanged using barter: swapping one good or service for another. A major characteristic of this form of economic exchange is that the value of an item or a service varies with the negotiated basis of the exchange.

A leap forward occurred with the invention of tokens that held their own intrinsic value, what we call money. This meant that tokens could be exchanged in place of goods and services. Money performs four functions: it is a medium of exchange, a means of accounting for amounts owed by actors in an economic exchange, it provides a standard of deferred payment and it is a defined store of value.

Traditionally, money has taken a tangible physical form, as first coinage, then banknotes. However, in the electronic world money assumes an intangible form (see Chapter 7). It is essentially data held in the information systems of financial institutions. Money is transferred between these systems electronically and accompanies the exchange of goods and services.

CASE CHECK
PayPal
(eBay)   CS p 435

PayPal is a global eCommerce business and acts as an electronic financial intermediary between individuals and organisations conducting economic exchanges over the Internet. PayPal performs payment processing for online vendors and charges a fee for this process. It sometimes charges a fee for purchasers using its facility. The company achieved significant growth as the preferred financial intermediary of users of eBay. Not surprisingly, in 2002 PayPal was bought out by eBay (see the case study) and is now a subsidiary of eBay.

eMarket: A market in which economic exchanges are conducted using ICT

Forms of eCommerce such as B2C eCommerce (see Chapter 8) rely on the concept of an electronic market (**eMarket**) (Bakos, 1997). An eMarket is one in which economic exchanges are conducted between businesses using ICT. In an eMarket, electronic transactions enable the efficient and effective flow of goods and services along the value network (see Chapter 7) (Malone et al., 1987).

The essential features of an eMarket are illustrated in Figure 5.11. The eMarket is the domain in which buying companies and selling companies meet. The exchange of goods and

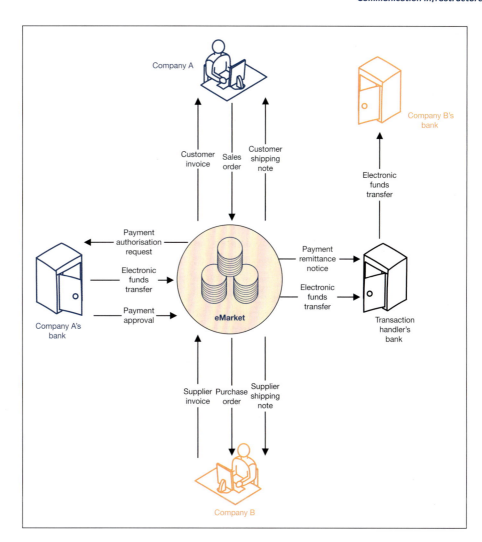

Figure 5.11 *Elements of an electronic market*

EFT: Electronic funds transfer is a means for transferring money electronically between financial repositories

EFTPOS: Electronic funds transfer at point of sale is a form of EFT in which the purchaser is at the point of sale

services is enabled through electronic transactions between buyer, seller and the financial institutions of each. The market handles all the transactions between companies, including the transfer of money between banks. Banks are effectively intermediaries in any trading relationship in the eMarket.

Electronic funds transfer (**EFT**) and electronic funds transfer at the point of sale (**EFTPOS**) are electronic mechanisms for the monetary flows accompanying the exchange of goods and services. EFT uses ICT to supply and transfer money between financial repositories (such as banks or bank accounts). EFTPOS is a form of EFT where the purchaser is physically at the point of sale, for example, at a supermarket checkout.

FOCUS ON VALUE

ICT as a technology has no inherent value in and of itself to organisations. The value of ICT arises in its application to organisational problems. One key way in which ICT is applied is in facilitating communication, not only within the organisation, but more recently between it and its external stakeholders. The value of communication infrastructure for customers is that it gives them remote access to goods and services. The technologies of the Internet and the Web open up a larger variety of access channels to the organisation, on a global scale. Communication infrastructure is also particularly important in managing transactions as records of value between two organisations, and between organisations and stakeholders such as customers and suppliers.

5.8   Conclusion and key themes

The ways in which people access services or products are known as channels of access. The access channel is used to carry messages between stakeholders such as customers, suppliers, partners and employees and the organisation's ICT systems. Any access channel consists of an access device and associated communication channel. The access device is used to formulate, transmit, receive and display messages.

Stakeholder access devices come in many forms including telephones, interactive digital television, personal computers and mobile devices. Major ways of connecting access devices to front-end ICT systems include telephone networks, digital transmission and radio networks.

The Internet – short for inter-network – dominates contemporary communication technology. It began as a wide area network funded by the US Department of Defence to link scientists and researchers around the world. Its technical infrastructure includes packet-switched networks, TCP/IP, HTTP, email protocols and FTP, IP addresses, universal resource locators (URLs) and domain names.

Packet-switching networks employ protocols in which data in a message or file is broken up into chunks known as packets and distributed around the network using TCP/IP: an open systems model for data communication that employs a number of layers. In addition to the TCP/IP protocol, other protocols used to provide file and email applications on the Internet include FTP, SMTP, MIME and HTTP.

Computers attached to the Internet, and the HTML documents resident on them, are identified by URLs. A domain name provides more meaning to a URL and identifies and locates a host computer or service on the Internet. Internet protocol addresses are mapped to domain names by domain name servers. A variety of applications run on the Internet, including the WWW, email, mail lists, newsgroups and chat.

The (World Wide) Web is an application that runs on the Internet. Its primary elements are the concept of hypertext/hypermedia, its implementation in HTML and the use of web browsers.

Hypertext is an electronic or online version of network text. A hypertext document is made up of a number of textual chunks connected by associative links called hyperlinks. Hypermedia is a superset of hypertext. HTTP is a protocol that defines how hypermedia documents can be transmitted between nodes in a communication network. HTML is a standard for marking up or tagging documents that can be published on the Web, and can be made up of text, graphics, images, audio clips and video clips.

Web users need browsers, programs that let them read web documents, view inbuilt images and activate other media and hotspots. The nodes of the Web are websites and web portals. A website is a logical collection of HTML documents normally stored on a web server. Web portals are specialised websites designed to act as an entry point for users. A number of software applications enhance use of the Web, including search engines, bulletin boards and discussion fora.

To enable the effective flow of transactions, standards have to be defined for the format and transmission of electronic messages. Electronic data interchange (EDI) is well established, but more recently standards have been defined using a Web-based technology known as XML. Both EDI and XML are attempts to define standard ways of specifying data formats for the transmission of electronic messages. The related technologies of electronic payment systems support monetary exchange in electronic markets. Technologies in this area include electronic funds transfer and electronic cash.

The next chapter shifts attention from the connective tissue that links individuals and organisations to the technologies underlying the internal ICT infrastructure of the typical business organisation. It defines the concept of an ICT system in more detail, and considers ways in which its functionality is distributed across communication networks.

5.9   Review test

1   The four primary components of the technical infrastructure supporting eBusiness are? Select all that apply.
- [ ] Access devices
- [ ] Communication channels
- [ ] Front-end ICT systems
- [ ] Messages
- [ ] Back-end ICT systems

2   An access channel consists of an access device and what else? Select the most appropriate term.
- [ ] Communication channel
- [ ] Telecommunications device
- [ ] Receiver
- [ ] Message
- [ ] Cable

3   An _____ is used to formulate, transmit, receive and display messages. Fill in the blank.

4   Remote access devices include? Select all that apply.
- [ ] Personal computer
- [ ] Satellite communications
- [ ] Mobile phone
- [ ] Public Internet Access Points
- [ ] Interactive digital television

5   Communication channels include? Select all that apply.
- [ ] Telephone network
- [ ] ADSL
- [ ] Cellular network
- [ ] Satellite communications
- [ ] Modems

6   How would you distinguish between a wide area network (WAN) and a local area network (LAN)? Write two sentences.

7   The Web is different from the Internet. True or false?

- [ ] True
- [ ] False

8   What is meant by packet-switching in the context of the Internet? Write two sentences

9   An ___ address is the fundamental way of uniquely identifying a computer system on the Internet. Fill in the blank

10   Internet Protocol addresses are mapped to domain names by _____ servers. Fill in the blank.

11   A Web browser is? Choose the most appropriate description.
- [ ] A piece of security software.
- [ ] A piece of software used for accessing hypermedia documents stored on the Web.
- [ ] A form of search engine.

12   HTML stands for. Choose the most appropriate description.
- [ ] Hypertext Markup Language
- [ ] Hypermedia Translation Language
- [ ] Hotspot Tracking Language

13   What is a universal resource locator and why is it important to the Web? Write two sentences.

14   XML stands for. Choose the most appropriate description.
- [ ] Extra Manipulation Language
- [ ] Extensible Markup Language
- [ ] Extensible Manipulation Language

15   Is Web 2.0 different to Web 1.0 and if so how? Write two sentences.

16   EFT stands for: Choose the most appropriate description.
- [ ] Electronic Funds Transfer
- [ ] Extensible Funds Transfer
- [ ] Extra Funds Transfer

5.10   Exercises

- In face-to-face communication, what are the access device and channel?

- Does a company known to you use any mobile devices to access ICT systems? What types of system are accessed through them?

- Consider a computer network known to you. Identify the types of communication media used to connect it.

- Investigate the communication networks used by an organisation known to you. Are there elements of LANs and WANs in their communication infrastructure?

- Determine the topology and coverage of a computer network known to you.
- If you use a computer on a network try to determine the IP address of the computer.
- Investigate some of the other common tags used in an HTML document.
- Classify a website known to you according to whether it solely provides information content, allows querying or enables transactions.
- Choose an organisation and determine its use of the Internet.
- Find an example of the use of EDI in a key industrial sector.

- Find an example of the use of XML in a key industrial sector.
- Try to determine the volume of monetary transactions occurring within a nation, such as the United Kingdom, in any one day.
- Investigate the degree to which 'content' such as television programmes are being delivered over the Internet into the home.
- Investigate the uptake of non-credit-based payment systems in an area of interest to you.
- Investigate how academic material such as a textbook may be presented via the Web.
- Determine how many distinct browsers there are in existence and how they differ in their functionality.

5.11   Projects

- HTTP is a stateless protocol. Determine more precisely what 'stateless' means in this context. Also determine some of the problems of this stateless nature in relation to building information systems on the foundation of such a protocol.
- Bandwidth was defined in Chapter 3 as a key property of a communication channel. Concerns have been raised over the level of bandwidth required not only in the workplace but also in the home over the next decade. Investigate the limitations of bandwidth in supporting individual and organisational activity in the near future.
- Choose an organisation and a remote access channel that it uses, and investigate the key costs of maintaining the channel. For instance, what access devices are supported? How much does the communication channel cost to run and maintain?
- Attempt to determine the current penetration of a chosen access device such as 3G mobile phones or tablet computers. Also investigate the degree to which such access channels are being used to conduct interaction with businesses.
- Search engines such as Google are beginning to act as a user's main portal to the Internet and the Web. Investigate some of the consequences of this for traditional web portals. Does it mean that they are no longer required, or what is their likely future role?
- The Internet and the Web have created what is sometimes called a global marketplace. Define precisely what globalisation means in relation to

communication technology. What consequences does communication technology play in globalisation? Would globalisation happen without communication technology?
- Technology does not stand still. Investigate likely changes to the technology of the Internet over the next decade. What are the likely trends and what effect will such trends have on global business?
- Investigate the effect of Web 2.0 on business organisations. For instance, business organisations are grappling with both the potential and the pitfalls associated with, so-called, social networking sites. Some businesses are using them as means of enhancing collaboration among organisational members. Other businesses see social networking as a high security risk.
- Investigate the use of blogs for business purposes. Do they offer a distinctive new channel of communication with customers? How are blogs managed within the overall communication strategy of a company? Are blogs considered part of the content management process or are they managed separately?
- Investigate the idea of mobile computing and its relevance for organisational informatics. What proportion of the workforce now works on the move, and how many workers are likely to do so over the next decade? What practical problems will organisations face in managing a mobile workforce, and what are the consequences for informatics infrastructure?

5.12 Critical reflection

Do you think we would have the Internet today without defence spending? In what respect do you feel the Internet is creating a global information society? One of the most important factors for business is the reach of the Internet into their potential customer population. Is it likely that we will ever achieve 100% penetration of the Internet into people's homes? What do you feel is the most important application of the Web within business?

5.13 Further reading

A vast range of material, both offline and online, has been published on the technologies of the Internet and the Web. Berners-Lee (Berners-Lee, 1999) provides the definitive account of the creation of the Web and also published on the continued progression of the idea in areas such as the semantic Web (Berners-Lee et al., 2001).

5.14 References

Bakos, J. Y. (1997). Reducing Buyer Search Costs – Implications for Electronic Marketplaces. *Management Science* 43 (12), 1676–1692.

Bush, V. (1945). *As We May Think*. Atlantic Monthly, New York.

Berners-Lee, T. (1999). *Weaving the Web: The Past, Present and Future of the World Wide Web by Its Inventor*. Orion Business Publishing, London.

Berners-Lee, T., J. Hendler and O. Lassilo. (2001). The Semantic Web. *Scientific American* 284 (5).

Dreyfus, H. L. (2001). *On the Internet*. Routledge, London.

Malone, T. W., Yates, J., Benjamin, R. I. (1987). Electronic Markets and Electronic Hierarchies. *Communications of the ACM* 30 (6), 484–497.

Norris, M. and West, N. (2001). *eBusiness Essentials*. John Wiley, Chichester, UK.

Vise, D. A. (2005). *The Google Story*. New York, Random House.

W3C. (2000). *XML 1.0*. 2nd edition. World-Wide-Web Consortium.

See companion website www.palgrave.com/business/beynon-daviesbis2e

chapter 6

ICT systems infrastructure

'All programmers are playwrights and all computers are lousy actors.'

Anonymous

Learning outcomes	Principles
Define the concept of an ICT system both in terms of its technological components and in terms of a number of interacting functional layers.	An ICT system may be defined in one of two ways: hardware, software, communication and data technology; or in terms of three interdependent functional layers.
Explain the ways in which both processing and data associated with ICT systems are typically distributed across communication networks and describe the importance of process and data integration to the ICT infrastructure of business.	With the rise of data communication networks functional parts of the ICT system, such as interface, business rules and data, are distributed around the communication network. However, an effective ICT infrastructure depends upon the integration of processing and data.
Distinguish between various types of Web application in the interface layer of an ICT system.	Web standards dominate contemporary approaches to the interface layer of an ICT system. Websites typically play a part within the use of the Internet by corporations, or in the establishment of corporate intranets and extranets.
Explain the idea of update functions, business rules and transactions and their relevance to the business tier of an ICT system.	Much of the logic of an ICT system is situated in its business layer, which consists of inter-related units of update functions, business rules and transactions.
Explain the importance of database systems to the data management layer of an ICT system and describe related technologies.	The data management layer relies on technologies related to database systems. A database system consists of a database and associated database management system, both of which are defined by a specific data model.
Identify the place of data security within ICT infrastructure and explain some of the major ways in which data security is achieved, both in terms of ICT systems and communication networks.	As more business moves online the issue of data security is increasingly significant. Security technologies and approaches apply not only to securing the data stored within ICT systems but also to the data transmitted along communication networks.

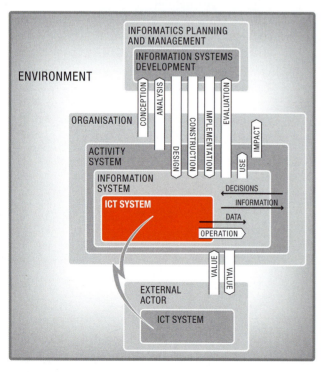

Chapter outline

AACSB learning objectives:
Use of IT

6.1   Introduction

The idea of a data system as described in Chapters 2 and 3 is similar to an abstract machine known as a Turing machine, so-called because it was proposed by Alan Turing in the 1930s (Copeland, 2004). Turing, a mathematician by trade, is generally seen as one of the founding fathers of modern Computer Science. In a famous paper published while he was a Cambridge don, Turing discusses a thought experiment in which he describes the properties of this abstract machine which supplies the core principles of modern computation.

In his ground-breaking paper he conjectured that his Turing machine possessed the power to solve any problem solvable by computational means. Hence, the Turing machine is generally described as a 'universal' machine, and the principles behind it helped drive the invention of the modern digital computer. The Turing machine defines the key properties of modern digital computers because it proposed the automation of certain of the manipulations exercised upon persistent forma and the storage of these sequences of operations as 'programs'.

Chapter 5 focused on the communication aspects of the information and communication technology (ICT) infrastructure, particularly the architecture of the Internet and the (World Wide) Web. The media, and much popular literature, sometimes imply that these two elements are all we need to know to understand the modern business relevance of ICT. For instance, many assume that Web developers are ICT professionals. This is a big mistake. Web development forms only a small, albeit an important, part of a modern business's ICT infrastructure.

The organising theme of this chapter is the central position data play in ICT. It focuses on the ways in which data are processed and stored. It reviews the concept of an ICT system and considers the modern trend to distribute both processing and data storage around the network. This brings us back to the distinction between front-end and back-end ICT systems. Websites, intranets and extranets are critical front-end concerns. Databases, data warehousing and content management are critical aspects of back-end ICT infrastructure. This leads to a consideration of securing data that is stored and communicated.

Chapter 4 defined ICT as any technology used to support data gathering, processing, distribution and use. This makes it possible to define an ICT system in one of two ways: as technological components (what it consists of), or as functionality (what it does).

6.2   Architecture of an ICT system

> Designing and managing enterprise architecture   **IS**2010

Hardware: the physical aspects of ICT consisting of processors, input devices and output devices

Software: programs of instructions for controlling hardware

Modern ICT consists of **hardware**, **software**, data management technology and data communication technology. Hardware comprises the physical (hard) aspects of ICT: processors, input devices such as keyboards and output devices such as monitors. Software comprises the non-physical (soft) aspects of ICT, essentially programs: sets of instructions for controlling computer hardware, which come in various forms such as operating systems, programming languages and office productivity packages. Data management technology consists of hardware artefacts for storing data on peripheral devices such as hard disks, managed by software technologies such as database management systems. The data are manipulated by programs and transmitted via data communication technology. Communication technology is the inter-connective tissue of ICT, and includes such components as cabling, transmitters and routers used to build communication networks between computing devices, as well as software that codes communication protocols (see Chapter 5).

Communication technology has been considered in Chapter 5. Data management technology is considered later in this chapter, as part of the coverage of back-end ICT systems. This section concentrates on hardware and software.

6.2.1   Hardware

A modern computer can be considered a technological system with five main subsystems: input, processing, storage, output and communications (see Figure 6.1).

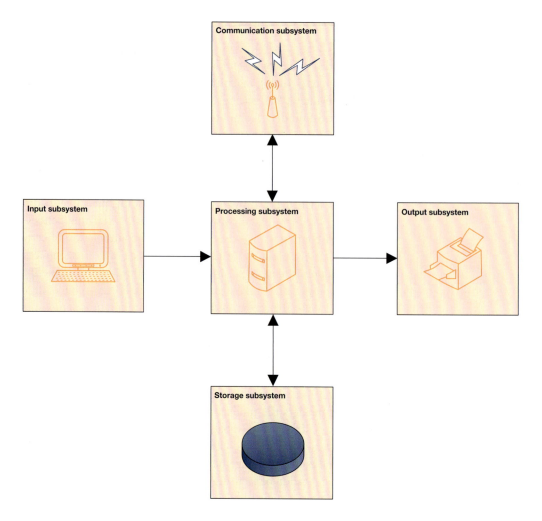

Figure 6.1 *Subsystems of a computer system*

Input to a computer is achieved through a variety of input devices, which make up the input subsystem of the computer system. Different input devices are designed to capture different types of data: character-based data, sound, images, graphics and movement.

Character-based input devices include keyboards and point of sale (POS) devices. Image-based input devices include digital cameras and scanners. Sound-based input devices include microphones and voice-recognition devices. Movement-based input devices include computer mice, touch sensitive screens and joysticks. Finally, graphics-based input devices include graphics tablets.

The processing subsystem is known as the central processing unit (CPU), and is the workhorse of a computing system. It can be subdivided (see Figure 6.2) into a control unit, logic unit, primary storage unit, registers and communication buses.

The control unit directs and coordinates the rest of the system in carrying out program instructions. The logic unit calculates and compares data, based on instructions from the control unit. The primary storage unit holds data for processing, instructions for processing and processed data waiting to be output. Registers are high-speed storage areas used to hold small units of program instructions and data temporarily, immediately before, after and during execution of the processing unit. These components communicate via physical connections known as buses.

Computers are controlled by programs, which consist of sequences of instructions. A computer operates by taking each instruction in turn and executing it.

The storage subsystem is a repository for data used by the processing subsystem. Data are stored there for both short- and long-term use. Data for short-term use are stored in primary storage, and those for long-term use in secondary storage.

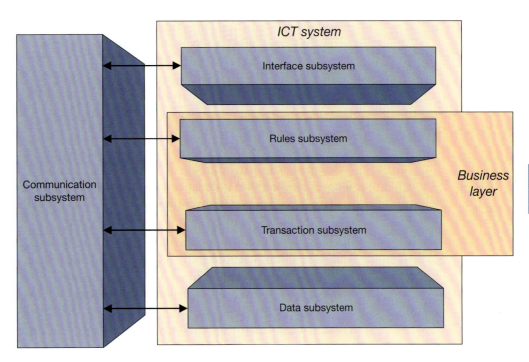

Figure 6.2 *Layers of an ICT system*

Primary storage includes media that can be directly acted upon by the CPU, such as main memory or cache memory. Primary storage usually provides fast access to relatively low volumes of data. Main memory is referred to as volatile memory because the data are lost when the power supply is switched off.

Secondary storage cannot be processed directly by the CPU, so it provides slower access than primary storage, but it can handle much larger volumes of data. It is referred to as non-volatile storage because it persists after power loss.

Among the hardware devices for secondary storage are magnetic tape, magnetic disks and optical disks. Magnetic tape is similar to that traditionally used in audio cassettes. Magnetic disks include both 'hard' and 'floppy' disk drives, so named because the magnetic media were originally made of hard and soft materials respectively. Optical disks include CD-ROM(compact disk read only memory disks) and DVDs (digital versatile disks).

A variety of output devices make up the output subsystem, depending on the type of data to be output. They include sound-based devices such as speakers, movement-based devices such as robotic devices or other forms of moving machinery, and character-based, image-based and graphics-based devices such as monitors and printers.

> **DID YOU KNOW?** Douglas Englebart called his new, innovative input device a mouse, 'because the tail came out the end'.

6.2.2 Software

Software is a generic term for computer programs, that is, a series of instructions for hardware. They transform the universal machine embodied in computer hardware into a machine specialised for some task. Programs are written using a formal language. Suites of programs designed for specialised tasks form the software architecture of an ICT system.

There are three major types of software in ICT systems:

- Application software, discussed below.
- System software to manage the computer system's resources. It includes operating systems, programming language compilers and utility programs such as virus protection software.
- Communication software to enable communication between different computing devices in a network.

A software application, or application system, is another term for an ICT system. It is a system, normally written using a programming language or tool-set (see Chapter 12), designed to perform a particular set of tasks.

Application software is software designed to perform a particular business function, and can be categorised according to the number of people who use it:

- Personal productivity software, such as word-processing packages, is designed for individual use.
- Workgroup software (sometimes known as groupware), such as electronic mail systems, is designed to be used by groups of users working together.
- Enterprise software is designed to be used across all, or a major part, of an organisation. Classic accounting systems are examples. Enterprise resource planning software (see below) is an integrated suite of enterprise software.

There is also a distinction between software that has been produced for the mass market, known as shrink-wrapped software, and software that has been produced specifically for an organisation, or bespoke software. Falling between these two poles is package software. This is software written to handle a generic organisational function such as sales order processing, but capable of being tailored to an organisation's specific needs. In a later section we shall consider a particularly important type of package software employed in business known as enterprise resource planning software.

Businesses are understandably interested in how software is distributed and priced. There are a number of different models. Direct purchase software is packaged and sold as a unit with a fixed price. This form of pricing is normally used for shrink-wrapped software. Leased software is paid for as it is used. The software remains the property of the producer but is hired for use. This is normally appropriate for enterprise software with a substantial cost. In application service provision (ASP), a software service is provided as an application. The application service provider runs the application for the customer. This is normally used for standard software services such as payroll. Finally, some software is available free from suppliers and is known as shareware. Programmers develop this software purely out of interest, and usually distribute it via the Internet. The open source software movement (see Chapter 12) is a pressure group challenging cost models of software distribution.

> **REFLECT:** In what way is software data? Can software also be regarded as information? Is it appropriate to think of a program as turning data into information?

6.2.3 The functionality of an ICT system

Functionality : what an ICT system is designed to be able to do

In contrast to considering an ICT system as a set of components, it is also useful to consider an ICT system as being made up of a number of subsystems or functional layers (see Figure 6.2):

- The interface subsystem is responsible for managing interaction with users, and is generally referred to as the user interface, or sometimes the human–computer interface (see Chapter 9).
- The rules subsystem manages the logic associated with an application, using a defined set of update functions and business rules (see below).
- A transaction subsystem acts as the link between the data subsystem and the rules and interface subsystems. Querying, insertion and update activity is triggered at the interface, validated by the rules subsystem and packaged as units (transactions) that will initiate formative actions in the data subsystem.
- A data subsystem is responsible for managing the underlying data needed by the ICT system in terms of inter-related data structures.

Take the example of an ICT system for storing details of research publications in a university. One part of the interface will be a data entry form to enter details of a publication. One of the rules or constraints used to validate data might be that the date entered for the publication must be less than or equal to that of today's date. A key transaction will involve insertion of new publication data into the system. Part of the data management layer will have data structures for the storage of both publication data and data about publication authors.

6.2.4   Distribution of processing

In a contemporary ICT infrastructure each of these parts of an application might be on a different machine, perhaps at a different site. This means that the parts need to be stitched together via a communication backbone. For consistency, in this book this backbone is called the communication subsystem.

Figure 6.3 illustrates a number of different distribution patterns for processing or functionality amongst ICT systems using the communication subsystem as a backbone. The figure is divided vertically into client computers and server computers. **Clients** request services from **server** computers across the communication subsystem.

Client: the computer that requests services from servers

Server: the computer that supplies services to clients.

Time-sharing

In the first phase of the development of ICT systems, all the component layers were on one machine (hence, all the functional blocks are placed closest to the server in Figure 6.3). Large mainframe systems would run an application's data management, transaction management, rules management and much of its interface management functions. Users connected to them via 'dumb' terminals, so called because they contained very little functionality and primarily enabled operators to control systems via command-based interfaces (see Chapter 9). Most of the processing on this type of system was conducted in batch mode, which consisted of carrying out a vast amount of transactions in sequence with very little direct user input. Specialist staff carried out data entry, and the output was usually in the form of paper reports.

Fat clients

Over time, more and more functionality has been placed on client machines. Technological developments enabled the user interface layer and some of the rules management layer to be located on 'intelligent' terminals, so called because they were able to take some of the processing off large centralised computers known as mainframes and minicomputers. This advance enabled the development of online systems, which made it possible for users to enter data directly into the ICT system, and to some extent to query the data in the system. The rise of online systems enabled the development of management information system (MIS) and decision support system (DSS) applications (see Chapter 4).

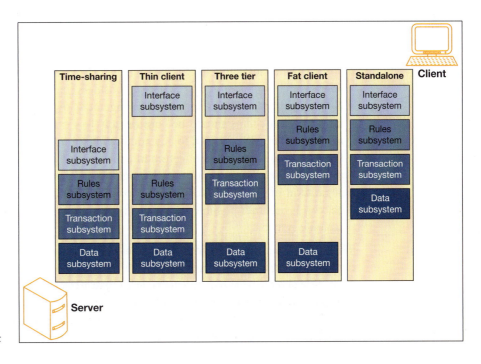

Figure 6.3 *Distributing functionality across the network*

With the rise of personal computers much more of the functionality of the ICT system began to be placed on desktop machines (called a standalone architecture on Figure 6.3). The growing sophistication of graphical user interfaces (see Chapter 9) meant that more power needed to be available on the desktop to run them effectively. With the rise of software for the personal computer, slices from the total functionality of an ICT system could be built using application development tools available for the desktop.

Three-tier

Many current applications run on three-tier client–server architectures, which correspond closely to the layered model of an ICT system described above. The first tier runs the user-interface layer, the second tier runs the application logic (business rules and transaction management in Figure 6.3) and the third layer runs data management functions. In a Web-based approach the client runs a browser, and the middle tier is a web server that interacts with a database server. Modern systems may extend this three-tier architecture to an n-tier architecture, in which more than three layers are involved. For instance, there could be a separation of business rules, web server and transaction management.

Thin clients

In recent years, Internet technology is causing a change from 'fat' clients to 'thin' clients. The corporate PC is currently a fat client. It requests information from a server and then processes and presents it at the client end using its own software. The thin client in its extreme form stores only a minimum of software (usually a web browser). The software which makes up the computer application resides on and is accessed from the server. This means that each user has a desktop system that looks like a PC or laptop but has no secondary storage. As we shall see, many of the features of, so-called, cloud computing can be seen to support a thin client model of ICT systems.

> **REFLECT:** Reflect on the degree to which many mobile access devices such as smartphones could be considered as thin clients. With the increase in cloud computing applications will the 'fat' personal computer eventually become a technological dinosaur, or not?

6.2.5   Advantages of an n-tier architecture

N-tier client–server architecture: a layered model of an ICT system in which N layers of the system interact

To summarise, a contemporary organisation's ICT infrastructure is typically built as a three-tier or **n-tier client–server architecture** with either thin or fat clients. The three tiers typically consist of the client or interface layer, the business or application layer and the data layer.

There are a number of advantages to constructing ICT systems in separate but interdependent layers:

- It makes for easier maintenance (see Chapter 12). Changes can be made to the interface separately from business rules, and changes to business rules can be made separately from data.
- N-tier architectures make for easier management and administration of ICT systems. For instance, thin clients should be considerably less expensive than PCs. Also, the network administrator will only need to buy and maintain one copy of each software application on the server. So an n-tier architecture in principle can reduce the costs of operating an ICT infrastructure and contribute to reducing the total cost of ownership (see Chapter 11).
- Separation of critical aspects of functionality permits easier integration of systems (see below). It becomes possible to share data structures and business rules across a range of separate systems.

RECAP: ICT systems can be defined using either key components or key functionality. In terms of key components, modern ICT consists of hardware, software, data management technology and data communication technology. In terms of functionality, an ICT system comprises a number of interacting subsystems: an interface subsystem, business rules subsystem, transaction subsystem and data management subsystem. Processing is likely to be distributed using an n-tier client–server architecture, which separates out the layers of the ICT system and distributes them at various points around the communication network.

6.3   The interface layer

Interface layer: that part of an ICT system concerned with managing the user interface

Most contemporary ICT systems within organisations have been designed to be accessed through various access devices running a Web browser. The *user interface* is therefore typically accessed through such a web browser and access channels may be over a LAN or over a WAN. This is the client or **interface layer**.

6.3.1   The user interface

In previous chapters we made the case for considering machines such as ICT systems as significant actors within modern organisations. Just like any other form of actor, ICT systems have to be communicated with. This communication is normally defined in terms of an interface. Each ICT system has an interface or, actually, a series of interfaces. Collectively, they are referred to as the user interface, or sometimes the human–computer interface. Such a user interface defines how human actors can interact with and control the ICT system. It also includes the ways in which the ICT system communicates with humans.

User interface: that part of an ICT system that allows users to control the functionality of the system

In this sense, the **user interface** can be seen as a collection of dialogues, each dialogue made up of a series of messages between the human user and the ICT system. Business actors use the interface to input data into the system and to receive data output from the system. Decisions are made on the basis of information interpreted from the data supplied and action is taken within the encompassing activity system. This is illustrated in Figure 6.4.

For example, a customer phones through an order for a certain quantity of an organisation's products to an order clerk working within a call centre. The order clerk inputs details of the order into the order processing ICT system through an order entry screen. In the act of doing this the ICT system may be able to automatically output details of an existing customer; on the basis of previous orders made by this customer the clerk may be able to make the decision to offer a discount to the customer. At a later point in time, the customer rings the call centre again to check progress against her order. This time a different order clerk accesses the ICT system and confirms the order by examining the results of a database query. This also enables him to confirm dispatch of the product to the customer.

Figure 6.4 *The user interface*

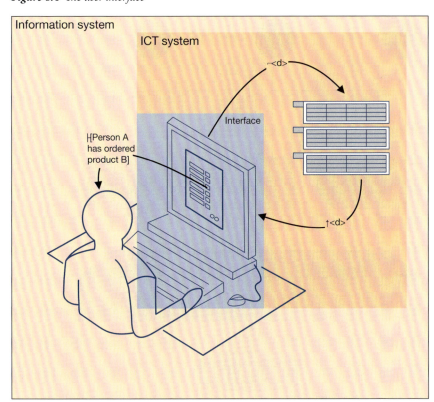

6.3.2 Stakeholders and access

The data entry and retrieval screen described in the previous example is more than likely to consist of a web page extracted from a series of web servers. Such web servers are likely to provide electronic services to the major stakeholders of the organisation: customers, suppliers, managers and employees.

Consider an ICT system run by a particular high-street bank which operates online banking for its customers. The client end comprises the web browser run on the customer's PC or some other access device. The client requests access to a web server run by the bank and interacts with a number of data entry screens with associated dialogue that undertakes authentication of the customer, that is, establishing that the customer is who she says she is. The web server will interact with a series of large banking databases storing data about customers and accounts. The mediating business or application layer is likely to consist of business rules, for example, a customer should not be able to go overdrawn to a degree greater than his or her overdraft limit. It will also contain update functions with embedded transaction types, for instance: *check an entered customer identifier against a recorded identifier for the customer in the customer database,* and *update the account balance of a customer by crediting or debiting a given account.*

Although Internet and Web technologies are being used to produce standard interfaces to ICT systems in organisations, such interfaces and communication channels will vary with the type of stakeholder and access devices used. Customers are likely to access services through an Internet-enabled device to a general website on the Internet. Internal stakeholders, such as employees and managers, are likely to access ICT systems through some form of corporate intranet: a corporate LAN or WAN that uses Internet technology and is secured behind firewalls. The intranet links clients, servers, databases and applications together. While using the same technology as the Internet, an Intranet is run as a private network. Only authorised users from within the organisation are allowed to use it.

In contrast, external stakeholders, such as suppliers and partners, are likely to access ICT systems through some form of extranet (Figure 6.5). Whereas an intranet is only accessible to the members of an organisation, an extranet provides a certain level of access to an organisation's Web-based information to outsiders. An extranet is an extended intranet. It uses Internet technology to connect together a series of intranets and, in the process, it secures communications over the extranet by creating 'tunnels' of secured data flows. The organisation will also utilise firewalls to ensure that outside access is secure.

Websites are now regarded as the most important mechanism for presenting content. The term ***content*** was originally used for what we described in Chapter 5 as hypertext (networked text implemented through HTML). The term then expanded to include a growing range of media incorporated on websites (images, graphics, audio, video); hypertext became hypermedia. However, the term content really came into its own with the rise of so-called content management and content management systems, introduced because of problems experienced in maintaining websites. Consider, for instance the process of simply changing one of the web

Content: a term now used to refer to any media stored in digital form

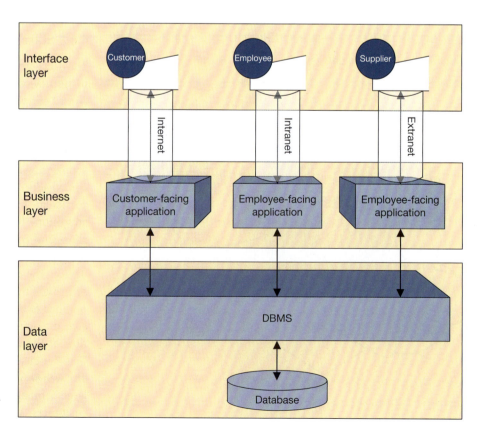

Figure 6.5 *Access via the three-tier architecture*

pages on a website. Changing the page not only involves putting the page up on the web server, it also involves making sure that all links that pointed to the old page now point to the new page. Not only that, the web developer must make sure that the new page points appropriately to other parts of the website.

Content as a term is now also used to refer to websites that display dynamic content, refreshed at query time from back-end databases (see below). The term has even, over the last few years, started to be used to include traditional media, everything from magazines, television programmes and music to movies. This is because the channels of delivery for this media have become subsumed by the Internet and the Web.

Typically, a commercial website will be organised hierarchically. The user enters at the site's *Home Page*. In terms of a commercial site, this usually establishes the range of products and services available from a particular company. From the home page the user may select a particular product or service by clicking on a hotspot or hyperlink, typically causing navigation to another page on the website. From here the user may be able to access further detail, or order from the website using a form, probably consisting of a series of sub-forms (Figure 6.6).

Major investment is currently being undertaken by organisations to increase levels of interactivity on their websites. Therefore, a typical assessment of the functionality of websites is made in terms of three major forms of content and assessments of the 'quality' of websites are frequently conducted in these terms. *Publish* content is one-way content, which allows the user to retrieve general information placed on the website or webpage. In contrast, *interactive* content is two-way content that allows users both to retrieve information as well as to communicate with internal organisational stakeholders and/or systems. *Transact* content is also two-way, but it allows users to transfer data to the organisation, or receive personalised data from the organisation, such as making bookings or payments.

Suppose a company sells toy soldiers. A *publish* site will provide simple details of the company and perhaps indicate how an order should be made. A *query* site would allow the user to search an online catalogue of toy soldiers for sale. A *transaction* website would allow the user to place an order online; perhaps even to pay online for the order.

Websites that primarily offer information content typically use static web pages. A static web page is produced as a standalone HTML document. Any changes made to the page demands that a new version of the page be posted to the website. In contrast, a dynamic web page consists of both HTML code and calls to back-end ICT systems such as database systems. A certain amount of the content may be retrieved from such back-end systems and displayed to the user. Hence, two tables from the back-end database are shown in Figure 6.6 being queried by web pages, while the two forms are shown creating rows within the tables of this database.

For both static and dynamic web pages the process of content management and associated content management systems are critical to the effective maintenance of websites (see below).

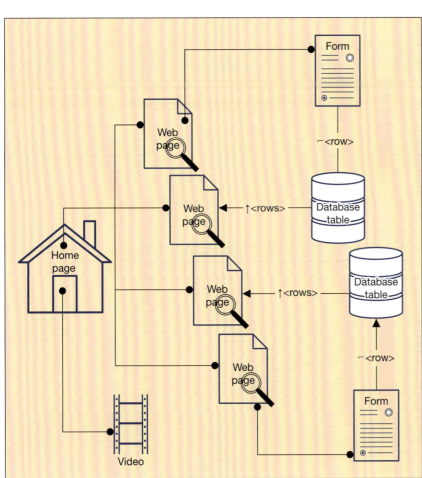

Figure 6.6 *Structure of a typical website*

6.3.3   Intranets

Firewall: a collection of hardware and software placed between and organisation's internal network and an external network such as the Internet

Intranet: the use of Internet and Web technology within the confines of a single organisation

As we indicated previously, an intranet is a corporate LAN or WAN that uses Internet technology and is secured behind **firewalls**. The **intranet** links clients, servers, databases and applications. It uses the same technology as the Internet, but is run as a private network; only authorised users from within the organisation are allowed to use it. At its most basic it involves setting up a web service for internal communications and coordination. At its most sophisticated, it involves using web interfaces to core corporate applications that rely on corporate-wide database systems.

Hence, an intranet can be considered as a special type of ICT system, and can be seen as comprising either horizontal or vertical components. Horizontally, just like any ICT system, an intranet is made up of hardware, software, communication technology and data (see Figure 6.7). Computers acting as both clients and servers are required, as well as communication 'lines' between them. Web browser software will be required on client machines and web server software on server machines. The role of the web server software includes processing requests from the client browser software and returning documents to clients.

An intranet may also have a domain server. This system translates between the numeric addresses assigned to each machine in the network under TCP/IP (Chapter 5) and more

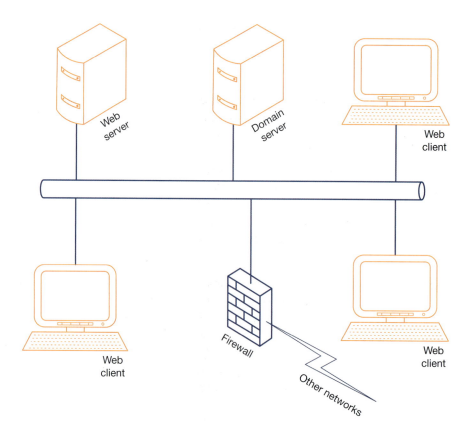

Figure 6.7 Horizontal components of an intranet

meaningful names, so the intranet relies on a corporate communication infrastructure. This may be a LAN, WAN or a combination of both. Hardware and software will be required to run the TCP/IP communication protocol. Data will primarily be held in the form of HTML documents on servers in the network. Some data may be held in database systems accessible from web pages.

Vertically, we can consider an intranet as a series of typical applications (see Chapter 5). Most intranets use both email servers and email software to enable users to communicate. They also use Internet technology such as browsers, HTML and TCP/IP to produce and disseminate information. They might also make available facilities such as mail lists, chat, FTP and online fora.

Typically an intranet is connected to the wider Internet through a firewall, which consists of hardware and software placed between the internal network and external networks. The firewall is programmed to intercept each message packet passing between the external and internal networks, examine its properties and reject any unauthorised messages, so it constrains the types of information that can be passed into and out from the organisation.

6.3.4   Extranets

Extranet: a network established such that external users can gain access to specified parts of the internal network of an organisation

Whereas an intranet is only accessible to the members of an organisation, an **extranet** provides a certain level of access to outsiders. An extranet is an extended intranet, and it too uses Internet technology to connect a series of intranets. It secures its communications by creating 'tunnels' of secured data flows, using encryption and authorisation algorithms (see below). The organisation will also use firewalls to protect its internal systems (see Figure 6.8).

The Internet with tunnelling technology is known as a virtual private network (VPN). Data on the extranet are shared with external stakeholders such as suppliers and other partners, so this enables collaboration between stakeholders. Access to it is restricted by agreements.

RECAP: Organisations use various front-end ICT systems to interface with their internal and external stakeholders. These typically involve some form of website accessible via the Internet, or on an intranet or extranet. An intranet involves using Internet technology in the context of a single organisation. An extranet is an extended intranet that uses Internet technology to connect a series of intranets, providing secure communications.

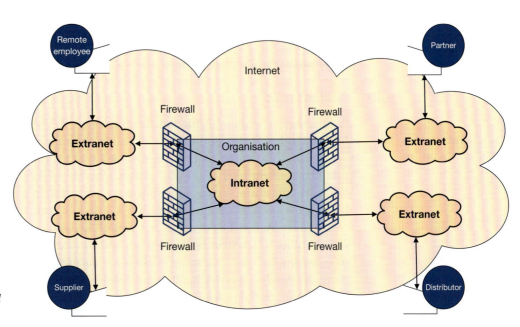

Figure 6.8 *Internet, intranet and extranet*

6.4   The business layer

Business layer: that part of an ICT application which deals with update functions, business rules and transactions

The *business layer* of a typical business ICT application consists of three inter-related elements: transactions, business rules and update functions.

6.4.1   Transactions

Transaction: a logical unit of work which transforms a database, or more generally a data structure, from one state to another

On one level, as we have seen in a previous chapter, a **transaction** represents the recording of some event, such as an economic exchange between two or more business actors. On another level a transaction represents a collection of formative acts which change a data structure, or a set of data structures, from one state to another.

As we have seen, a data system effectively records aspects of acts of communication, which in turn serve to support coordinated activity in an activity system. Hence, one key use of data systems is to assert institutional facts that become true in the wider information and activity system, or alternatively to deny facts that cease to be true about these business systems. Hence, in a university activity system we might enrol the student *Peter Jones* in the module *business information systems*. A registry assistant communicates this as an assertion by using the student ICT system to write a new enrolment record to the enrolments table. This is an example of a transaction which changes the state of the enrolments table in the database.

A transaction therefore consists of one or more formative acts that operate upon data structures. Transactions consisting of *create* formative acts bring into existence new data elements within the data structures of a database; retrieval or *read* transactions access data contained within the data structures of a database. In contrast, *update* transactions cause changes to values held within particular data items of particular data elements and data structures in a database; *delete* transactions erase particular data elements within the data structures of a database.

In a previous chapter we represented a create formative act using the symbol $\ulcorner$, the opposite of the mathematical symbol for 'not' ($\neg$) which is used to represent a delete formative act. Hence, $\ulcorner$<d> represents the bringing into existence of the named data representor *d* enclosed in angled brackets, while $\neg$<d> represents the removal from existence of a named data representor. Likewise, we represent an update formative act as ($\downarrow$<d>) and a retrieval or read formative act as ($\uparrow$<d>).

Hence, in a banking ICT system a *create* transaction might be used to enter a new credit or debit record against a particular bank account ($\ulcorner$<Credit: amount>). In contrast, a *read* transaction might be used to assemble a statement for a particular bank account for a particular period ($\uparrow$<Statement: period>). An *update* transaction might be used to change the contact details of a particular customer ($\downarrow$<Address: '12, the Avenue, Cardiff'>). Finally, a *delete* transaction might be used to remove a particular standing order or direct debit placed by a customer $\neg$<Direct debit: reference>.

6.4.2   Business rules

Business rule : a rule which specifies how a particular part of an ICT system should behave

A considerable amount of the functionality of an ICT system is taken up with, so-called, **business rules**. Such rules reside both within the rules management subsystem of an ICT system as well as in the data management subsystem. They ensure that the data held in the data management layer of the ICT system remains an accurate reflection of its universe of discourse (the business or activity system it represents). In other words, the data held in any ICT system should display integrity; that is, it should accurately reflect the institutional state of its activity system. For example, in terms of the universe of discourse relevant to a typical university, an ICT system established for student records should provide accurate responses to questions such as: *how many students are currently enrolled on a particular module*? In terms of an online banking application, customers should be able to obtain accurate current balances for their bank accounts.

Data integrity: ensuring that the data stored in an ICT system remains an accurate reflection of the state of the activity system it describes

Data integrity is ensured through integrity constraints. An integrity constraint is a business rule which establishes how a database is to remain an accurate reflection of its institutional domain. Integrity constraints may be divided into two major types: static integrity constraints and transition integrity constraints.

A static constraint is used to check that a transaction will not change a database into an invalid state, so it is a restriction defined on states of the database. For example, a static constraint relevant to a university domain might be: *students can only take currently offered modules*. So if Strategic Management was not a currently offered module, it would not be possible to enter the data, *John Davies takes Strategic Management*.

In contrast, a transition constraint is a rule that relates given states of a database. A transition is a state transformation and can therefore be denoted by a pair of states. A transition constraint is a restriction defined on a transition. An example is: *the number of modules taken by a student must not drop to zero during a semester*. If a user tried to remove the data that John Davies was taking a module, the system would first check that this would not leave him with any modules registered, and so cause an invalid transition. In banking, an example is that a customer should not be able to go overdrawn beyond an agreed limit, so before debiting an account the application would check that there were sufficient funds in it for this not to happen.

6.4.3   Update functions

Update function: individual components of functionality that are triggered by events in the interface and change the state of data structures

Sitting behind particular parts of the user interface are a number of update functions. ***Update functions*** represent individual elements of functionality associated with a particular business application. As such they encapsulate both business rules and transaction types. Update functions are triggered by events usually activated from the interface or client management layer, or sometimes from other update functions. The end-result of the activation of a particular update function is that transactions are fired at the data management layer of the ICT system.

Consider the interface of a typical automatic teller machine (ATM). Once the user has put in his debit card and typed in his personal identification number (PIN) the system will trigger a function that sends data extracted about the customer to a back-end ICT system. This system will probably do two things: it will decide whether the user should be able to access further aspects of the interface; it will probably write some data to a record which logs the precise location of the ATM, details of the customer requesting access and the date and time of access. This data structure will be used to help prevent fraudulent access.

An update function, such as the one described, will usually have a series of conditions associated with it. Such conditions typically represent integrity constraints. There will also be a series of actions associated with the update function. These will specify what should happen if the conditions are true and typically constitute transaction types.

For instance, we might specify an update function appropriate for a University application as follows:

ON Transfer Student X from module 1 to module 2

IF

($\uparrow$<Student: X takes module: 1>).AND
NOT ($\uparrow$<Student: X takes module: 2>)
($\uparrow$<Module: 2>)

THEN

($\downarrow$<Student: X takes module: 2>)).

This reads: If student X takes module 1 and Student X does not take module 2 and module 2 is offered then update student X takes module 2. Here, X, module 1, and module 2 are place holders for values. Hence, we might initiate a transaction using this update function by assigning the value *John Davies* to X, *Business Information Systems* to module 1 and *eBusiness* to module 2. This would record the institutional fact that student *John Davies* has transferred from the module *Business Information Systems* to the module *eBusiness* and would occur only if there are data which indicate that *John Davies* currently takes *Business Information Systems*, that he does not currently take *eBusiness* and that *eBusiness* is a currently offered module.

Traditionally, update functions and business rules within the business layer would have been coded using a programming language as part of the wider application system. Such a business layer is now frequently constructed using a business rules engine which allows the developer to enter and maintain update functions and associated rules separately from interface and data management layers.

6.5   The data layer

Data layer : that part of an ICT system concerned with managing the data required by the application

As discussed in Chapter 5, front-end ICT is likely to work in the modern business using Internet and Web technologies. Hence, the effective integration of front-office and back-office systems is critical to organisational effectiveness. For instance, to enable fully transactional websites, the information presented needs to be updated dynamically from back-end databases. Also, the information entered by customers needs to update company database systems effectively. For this reason we focus on a discussion of the technology of data management within this section, some of these ideas have already been introduced in Chapter 5.

Traditionally, data management in ICT systems has been part of the file system managed by the operating system. During the 1970s a class of software started being used for the higher-level management of data, the database management system (DBMS). DBMS are software systems for managing databases and constitute the fundamental technology in the data management layer of most contemporary ICT systems. A database system is therefore composed of a database and a DBMS; both the database and DBMS must conform to a given data model (Chapter 3). In this section we define these three terms in greater detail.

6.5.1   Database

Database: an organised repository for data

The data stored in a **database** is usually an attempt to represent the properties of objects in the activity system it is meant to model. Such properties represent institutional facts about the business domain.

A database is an organised repository for data having a number of critical properties. A database can be viewed as a model of its activity system. A database is normally accessible by more than one person, perhaps at the same time. One major responsibility of database usage is to ensure that the data are integrated. This implies that a database should be a collection of data that has no unnecessarily duplicated or redundant data. Another responsibility arising as a consequence of shared data is that a database should display integrity. In other words, the database should accurately reflect the universe of discourse that it is attempting to model. Besides the integrity constraints discussed above, one of the major ways of ensuring the integrity of a database is by restricting access; in other words, securing the database. The main way this is done in contemporary database systems is by defining in some detail a set of authorised users of the whole, or more usually parts of the database.

Consider a database held by an insurance company. The data structures in the database emulate information classes of interest to the activities of this company. Hence, the database maintains records about insurance policies, policy-holders and insurance claims. This data is typically accessed by a number of different users in the organisation for the purposes of opening new insurance policies for customers and handling claims against particular insurance policies. This data must be consistent and accurate; meaning that if a policy-holder has a record in the database then this record should accurately reflect properties of this particular customer. One way of ensuring that data has integrity is by restricting access to data to particular types of users. Hence, only those employees working in the claims department should be able to create and update a claims record.

6.5.2   Database management system (DBMS)

DBMS: an organised set of facilities for accessing and maintaining one or more databases

A database management system (DBMS) is an organised set of facilities for accessing and maintaining one or more databases. A **DBMS** is a shell which surrounds a database and through which all interactions with the database take place. The interactions catered for by most existing DBMS fall into four main groups.

- Structural maintenance consists of adding new data structures to the database, removing data structures from the database and modifying the format of existing data structures.
- Transaction processing typically involves inserting new data into existing data structures, updating data in existing data structures and deleting data from existing data structures.
- Information retrieval involves extracting data from existing data structures and presenting this data for use by both end-users and application systems.
- Database administration consists of creating and monitoring users of the database, restricting access to data structures in the database and monitoring the performance of databases.

6.5.3   Data model

Data model: an architecture for data or a blueprint of the data requirements for an application

In Chapter 5 we used the term **data model** to refer to a model of the data required for some institutional domain. The term is also used to denote the architecture for a particular database and DBMS in that it describes the general structure of how data are organised, stored and accessed within a database application. A data model in these terms is generally held to be made up of three components: data definition, data manipulation and data integrity.

- Data definition describes the way in which data can be represented in terms of the data structures, data elements and data items relevant to the data model.
- Data manipulation comprises a set of data operators for the insertion, removal, retrieval and amendment of data in data structures. These are the fundamental formative acts we considered in previous sections.
- Data integrity consists of a set of integrity constraints or rules that must form part of the database. Integrity is enforced in a database through the application of these integrity constraints.

One of the most popular forms of data model used in contemporary data management is the relational data model, which we introduced in Chapter 5. Here, we consider what data definition, data manipulation and data integrity means within this particular data model.

Data definition consists of only one data structure in a relational database, the table. Each table is made up of a number of data elements called rows and each row is made of a number of data items known as columns. The table in Figure 6.9 uses a university example. It consists

Module name	Level	Course code	Staff no.
Business information systems	1	BIS	244
Database systems	1	BIS	244
Business analysis	3	BIS	445
Informatics management	3	BIS	Null
Project management	2	BIS	247

Figure 6.9 *Tables as data structures*

Entity integrity: that each table must have a primary key

Referential integrity: that a foreign key must refer to a primary key value or be null

Domain integrity: that the values in a column of a table are defined on a pool known as a domain

of four data items (Module name, Level, Course code and Staff no.) and five data elements corresponding to five rows in the table, one for each module.

Data integrity in the relational data model corresponds to three types of integrity rule: **entity integrity**, **referential integrity** and **domain integrity**.

Entity integrity establishes that each row in a table is identified by values in one or more columns of the table, called the table's primary key. The values of a primary key must be unique and not null. In other words, we must have a value for each element of the primary key; each value must be unique in terms of other values of the primary key. Consider the relational database consisting of two tables in Figure 6.10. This represents data relating to the dispatch advice notes of Goronwy Galvanising as described in Chapter 2. The table named Dispatch notes in the figure consists of four data items (Dispatch no., Dispatch date, Customer code and Instructions) and three data elements corresponding to three rows in the table, one for each dispatch note. Within the *Dispatch notes* table the *Dispatch no.* data item is the only item having both properties of uniqueness and being not null. It is therefore the most suitable candidate for a primary key for this table.

Referential integrity establishes that values in columns may also act as links to data contained in other tables. Such columns are called foreign keys. A value for a foreign key must either be the value of a primary key elsewhere in the database or be null. The primary key of the Dispatch items table is actually composed of two data items: *Dispatch no.* and *Sales order no.* Both these data items individually are in fact foreign keys to two other tables in the database. Dispatch no. acts as a foreign key back to the primary key of the Dispatch notes table. Sales order no. acts as a foreign key back to a Sales orders table. The values of these two foreign keys can never be null because we must always know which dispatch note and sales order a particular dispatch item relates to.

Domain integrity ensures that values entered into data items or columns are of the right type or from the same domain. Domains are therefore pools of values from which actual values appearing in the columns of a table are drawn. The idea of a domain in the relational data model is therefore similar to the concept of a data type defined in Chapter 3.

Data manipulation involves functions for entering new rows into tables, deleting rows from tables and editing data held in the rows of a table. It also concerns ways of retrieving data from tables. Hence, in terms of the rows within tables, new records or rows are created or inserted into such tables. Once records exist they may be updated or deleted from the tables. Existing records or rows may also be retrieved and read.

Dispatch notes	Dispatch no.	Dispatch date	Customer code	Instructions
	101	22/01/2012	BLW	
	102	25/02/2012	TCO	
	103	10/03/2012	BLW	

Dispatch items	Dispatch no.	Sales order no.	Customer product code	Dispatch quantity
	101	13/1193G	UL150	20
	101	44/2404G	UL1500	20
	101	70/2517P	UL135	20
	101	23/2474P	UL120	14

Figure 6.10 A simple relational database

Suppose we wish to represent the data from a particular Goronwy delivery advice issued by a supplier within the data structures of the database created for the company. We would undertake the following create formative acts upon such data structures:

⌐<Delivery note (123456, 12/12/2012, 654321, 'Deliver to bay 4')>
⌐<Delivery items (123456, 01, AAB321, 20, 200, P234561)>
⌐<Delivery items (123456, 02, ABC221, 40, 600, P234562)>
⌐<Delivery items (123456, 03, BBB111, 60, 100, P234563)>

The first creates a new delivery note row. The remaining three acts or transactions create a new row in the delivery items table.

<aside>
DID YOU KNOW? The theory underlying relational databases was invented way back in the 1970s by mathematician and computer scientist Ted Codd. Codd had the key insight of mapping aspects of mathematical set theory – particularly the idea of tuples, organised sets – onto a data structure that had been around for many thousands of years, that of the file.
</aside>

6.5.4   SQL

SQL: a database programming language designed for use with relational databases

SQL is a database programming language standard which is used in most DBMS that follow the relational data model. As such, SQL contains commands for data definition, data manipulation and data integrity. It also contains some commands for administering or controlling data (see Chapter 11).

For example, the Modules table would be declared in SQL using the following statement:

```
CREATE TABLE Modules
 (moduleName CHARACTER(15),
level INTEGER,
courseCode CHARACTER(3),
staffNo INTEGER)
```

Note how each data item or column is given a data type (see Chapter 3). The *moduleName* column and *course Code* are declared to be character data types meaning that any alphabetic or numeric character can be entered in these columns. In contrast, the *level* and *staffNo* columns are declared to have an integer data type, meaning that only whole numbers can be entered in these columns. In some instances a column is also given a maximum length, meaning that no more than 15 characters can be used as a *moduleName* or three characters to form a *courseCode*. Such definitions restrict the type of data entered into each column and act as part of the definition of a domain.

To define primary and foreign keys on this table we add appropriate clauses to the table definition, like this:

```
CREATE TABLE Modules
 (moduleName CHARACTER(15),
level INTEGER,
courseCode CHARACTER(3),
staffNo NUMBER(5) NOT NULL,
PRIMARY KEY (moduleName)
FOREIGN KEY (staffNo REFERENCES Lecturers))
```

To insert a new row into the modules table we would use an INSERT INTO command such as:

```
INSERT INTO Modules VALUES ('Information systems development', 2, 'BIS', 247)
```

To retrieve all the rows in the modules table we would use the command:

```
SELECT * FROM Modules
```

where the asterisk stands for 'all data items (columns) and all data elements (rows)' from the table.

CASE CHECK

Open source software: MySQL

CS p 454

First released in 1995, MySQL is a multi-user relational DBMS which has millions of installations worldwide. This applications software is considered one of the most prominent examples of open source software. MySQL is popular for supporting web applications and acts as the DBMS component of the LAMP stack for application development (see Chapter 12). The DBMS has been used to as part of the ICT infrastructure of organisations such as Wikipedia.

6.5.5   Business intelligence

Business intelligence, sometimes referred to as business analytics, more broadly refers to a number of techniques for identifying and analysing patterns in business data. The aim is to use such intelligence for better business decision-making, particularly strategic decision-making. A number of critical technologies support business intelligence. These include data warehousing, OLAP and data mining.

Conventional database applications have been designed to handle high transaction through-put; because of this, they are frequently called online transaction processing (OLTP) applications. The data available in them is important for running day-to-day operations, and is manipulated in the core transaction-processing information systems, such as those described in Chapter 4. The data are also likely to be managed by a relational DBMS as described above.

Data warehouse: a type of contemporary database system designed to fulfil decision-support needs

Contemporary organisations also need access to historical, summary data and to data from sources other than the DBMS. This is where a **data warehouse** enters the picture. It requires extensions to conventional database technology, and a range of application tools for online analytical processing (OLAP) and data mining. Together these two technologies are critical in support of modern MIS, DSS and EIS. Collectively with database systems, they are important to an area known as business intelligence.

A data warehouse is a type of contemporary database system designed to fulfil decision-support needs, and forms a major part of contemporary MIS and DSS (see Chapter 4). It differs from a conventional decision-support database in a number of ways. First, it is likely to hold far more data than a decision-support database. Second, the data stored are likely to have been extracted from a diverse range of application systems, only some of which may be database systems. These systems are described as data sources. Third, it is designed to fulfil a number of distinct ways (dimensions) in which users may wish to retrieve data. This is sometimes referred to as the need to facilitate ad-hoc query.

DID YOU KNOW? Current estimates of the capacity of the human brain range from 1 to 1000 tera-bytes. This is equivalent to many of the data warehouses used by large companies.

Modern database applications, such as market analysis and financial forecasting, require access to large databases for the support of queries which can rapidly produce aggregate data. These applications are frequently called **OLAP** (online analytical processing).

OLAP: supports complex analytical operations such as consolidation, drilling down and pivoting

OLAP technology supports complex analytical operations such as consolidation, drilling down and pivoting. For instance, in a university, consolidation could mean that modules data is aggregated into courses data, and courses data is aggregated into schools data. Drilling down is the opposite, and involves revealing the detail or disaggregating data, such as breaking down or decomposing school-based data into data on particular courses or modules. Pivoting, sometimes referred to as 'slicing and dicing', is the ability to analyse the same data from different viewpoints, frequently along a time axis. For example in the university, one slice might be the average degree grade per course in a school. Another slice might be the average degree grade per student age-band in a school.

Data mining: the process of extracting previously unknown data from large databases

Data mining is the process of extracting previously unknown data from large databases and using it to make organisational decisions. It is concerned with the discovery of hidden, unexpected patterns within data, and usually works on the large volumes of data held in a data warehouse. As the size of a data warehouse grows, it becomes more difficult to find patterns using the conventional means of query and analysis. Also, large volumes are frequently needed to produce reliable conclusions. Data mining is useful in making strategic organisational decisions. For instance, in retail chains it has been used to identify the purchasing patterns of customers, and associate these with demographic characteristics such as their age and class profile. This is useful for deciding what products to sell in which stores and when. In the insurance industry data mining has been used to analyse the claims made against insurance policies, and feed into actuarial decisions, such as the pricing of policies.

A consequence of the trend for moving business communication online has been that much of this communication has become accessible to intelligence gathering and analysis purposes. Much of this is now referred to as Web analytics, which can be seen to be a subset of business analytics. Broadly, web analytics refers to a battery of techniques employed to measure website traffic. Techniques include measuring the number of visitors to a website, the number of page views and how users navigate around a website through clicks. Web analysis such as this is typically performed in association with advertising campaigns and is used as one means of assessing the success of promotions.

> **REFLECT:** What level of management is likely to get most value from the use of data warehousing, OLAP and data mining: operational, tactical or strategic management?

6.5.6   Content management

Content management: the process of ensuring that content is accurate, relevant and timely

The face of a modern organisation is presented through its website, so it is very important for the content to be well managed. **Content management** is the organisational process for the maintenance of Web-based material. Two dimensions are critical to establishing the case for content management: the volatility of content and its visibility.

Let's take a website designed for the electronic delivery of services and products. It is likely to be highly volatile, its content will be updated continually, and will include products, prices and promotions. Business to consumer or B2C sites like this are also highly visible, since their prime purpose is to attract and keep customers.

Now consider a website that is part of an extranet, designed for use by subcontractors. Its information is likely to be less volatile, as the content will be less subject to change. The content will be updated less frequently, and is likely to be less visible than a customer site.

The more volatile and visible the website, the more important it is to establish a content management process to ensure the content is accurate, relevant and timely. A content management process includes these activities:

- A team of content producers, including technical staff and representatives of business units, create the initial content and decide on its presentation.
- The proposed content is reviewed by stakeholders (e.g. the web manager, marketing manager and legal department), to ensure that it complies with company standards and does not infringe any laws.
- The content is tested on a site which is not live. Ideally, no content should be released until it has been thoroughly tested.
- The approved and tested content is published to a live site. This should only occur after full review and testing. The release might be planned to coincide with other organisational activities.
- Timescales are established for the content management process. They will vary depending on the type of content.

> **REFLECT:** Reflect on the damage inaccurate content on a company website can have for the business.

A range of ICT tools are now available to support the content management process. These are often integrated to form a complete content management system. For example, tools such as Dreamweaver enable content and its presentation to be produced and updated rapidly. Workflow tools such as Lotus Notes automate to some extent the flow of producing, distributing and checking content. These tools help to establish a clear audit trail for the authorisation of content. Many volatile and visible websites are now also integrated with back-end database systems. When product descriptions and pricing are updated in the database, this is automatically reflected on the website.

RECAP: The business tier of a typical business ICT application consists of three inter-related elements: update functions, business rules and transactions. Update functions are elements of functionality associated with a particular business application, and consist of business rules and transaction types. They are triggered by events which are typically initiated at the interface, and activate a set of business rules. Once these business rules have operated, transactions are fired at the data management layer of the ICT system. Back-end ICT systems include the core systems in the business, and tend to be located around databases storing important corporate data. Contemporary data management involves databases, DBMS and data warehouses.

6.6   Integrating ICT systems

We can look at the integration and distribution of ICT systems both vertically and horizontally. Vertically (as described above) means cooperative and distributed processing. Horizontally, the aim of many ICT strategies, is to integrate ICT systems across the organisation. This is generally focused around issues of integrated and distributed data.

Piecemeal ICT systems: ICT systems that lack integration

We can see how important this is by thinking about **piecemeal ICT systems**. When organisations first began to use computers they adopted a piecemeal approach to information systems development (see Chapter 12). One manual information system at a time was analysed, redesigned and transferred onto the computer, with little thought to its position in the organisation as a whole. This was largely unavoidable because of the difficulties in using a new and more powerful organisational tool.

However, a set of self-contained ICT systems, each with its own program suite, files and inputs and outputs, does not represent the way in which organisations work. An organisation normally consists of a complex set of interacting and interdependent activity, information and ICT systems. When systems have been built up piecemeal, it is often necessary to use non-automated forms of communication to interface between them. For instance, one system might produce a report which has to be transcribed to make it suitable for another system. These 'workarounds' proliferate inputs and outputs, and create delays.

Information obtained from a series of separate files is also less valuable to business actors because it does not provide a complete picture of activity. For example, a sales manager reviewing outstanding sales orders might not get all the information they need from the sales system, but have to manually add in information about stock from the inventory management system.

This also leads to data duplication, for example, the human resources department and the payroll section might both maintain the same types of data about employees. This creates unnecessary maintenance overheads and increases the risk of inconsistency.

Although this is what happened historically, rather than the way in which new systems are designed today, many 'legacy' ICT systems, designed some time ago but still in essential use, suffer from these problems. It is also common for these systems not to have been explicitly documented (see Chapter 4). This makes them difficult to maintain (see Chapter 12).

In contrast, an integrated ICT system is designed as a whole, to avoid duplication and incompatibilities. Take, for example, a chain of supermarkets, such as Tesco. In each supermarket there are checkouts operating electronic point of sale (EPOS) equipment, which allows checkout staff to record sales by scanning barcodes, and transmits details of each sale electronically to a database.

The sales data automatically update data on shelf levels, which are compared against periodic stock checks by staff, and the system generates a report prompting staff to replenish the shelves from the supermarket's own storeroom. The same thing happens in the storeroom: when stock falls to a fixed level, purchase orders are generated and sent electronically to the central supplies division. Data on sales, shelf and stock levels are also used by management to decide on marketing strategies: which goods to promote, how to site products on shelves and so on. In this example at least three effective uses are being made of the same integrated collection of data: the collection of customer transaction data, the management of stock and the marketing of goods.

6.6.1   Alignment

One intended benefit of an explicit informatics infrastructure (see Chapter 4) is a closer fit, or alignment, between an organisation's activities and its information systems. How is this fit or alignment measured? Four aspects of the informatics infrastructure can be measured and used to determine elements of fit: the levels of fragmentation, redundancy, inconsistency and interoperability.

Poor fit is evident when data are fragmented across information systems. This usually happens because information systems emulate structural divisions within the organisation and organisational units put up barriers of ownership around key data sets. Fragmentation can also be evident in processing, where separate ICT systems communicate through manual interfaces.

Another example of lack of fit is when large amounts of data are unnecessarily replicated. This usually happens because there are no interfaces between systems, so the same data is entered many times over. Redundancy also occurs when separate systems perform the same effective processing on data.

Poor fit is evident when the same data is held differently in different systems or processed differently by different systems, leading to inconsistencies in the ways in which information is produced, stored and disseminated.

The property of interoperability is related to the other three fitness criteria. Generally speaking systems that are fragmented, redundant and inconsistent are likely to suffer from poor levels of interoperability. This refers to the level at which systems communicate and cooperate within the ICT infrastructure.

Situations subject to fragmentation, redundancy and inconsistency create a series of information 'islands'; these make it difficult to model the organisation's information. Operational managers then find it difficult to plan effectively on a day-to-day basis, and strategic managers find it difficult to plan for the medium- and long-term future of the organisation.

6.6.2   Enterprise systems

Enterprise system: a system that integrates data and processes across the organisation

The layered model of an ICT system can be considered as the vertical integration, interoperability and distribution of ICT systems. This is described as cooperative and distributed processing. Integration, interoperability and distribution can also be considered in a horizontal sense. The aim of many strategies is to integrate ICT systems across the organisation. Generally speaking such integration is focused around issues of integrated and distributed data.

Traditionally integration has been achieved by effective planning and management of internally built ICT systems. More recently, many organisations have chosen to buy in large suites of ICT systems with in-built integration. This is an enterprise resource planning (ERP) package or mega-package. The strategy of buying these systems can be seen as an attempt to buy in a complete ICT infrastructure.

ERP system: a package that implements an enterprise architecture for an organisation

ERP systems typically have the following characteristics:

- They constitute a suite of software modules that support a common range of different organisational functions.
- Such modules can be implemented in an integrated manner across the organisation.
- Each of these modules runs upon a common database.
- Data can be updated and accessed in real-time (meaning near to instantaneously).
- The module interfaces have a consistent look and feel.

The term ERP was first applied by the consulting organisation Gartner Group in 1990. They used the term to describe developments built upon material requirements planning and

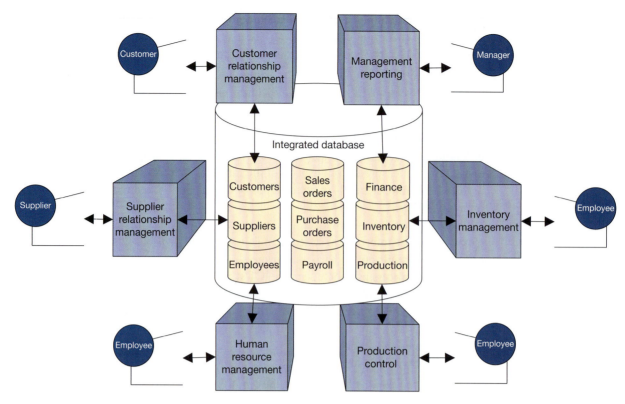

Figure 6.11 *A typical ERP package*

manufacturing resource planning (MRP) systems. Such systems experienced widespread adoption up to 2000 as many large- and medium-size companies sought to replace their aging ICT infrastructure.

Initially, ERP systems focused on automating back-office functions. More recently, modules in front office functions, such as customer relationship management (CRM), have been offered by vendors. Also, in recent times, many such systems have been re-written to run using Web-based standards, such as those in Web services discussed in the next section.

Figure 6.11 illustrates the typical suite available in a mega-package. These systems promise the seamless flow of information through an organisation: financial and accounting information, human resource information, supply-chain information and customer-chain information.

| **CASE CHECK** p 455 | SAP AG is the largest european software company. Its main product is the SAP ERP package, an integrated suite of ERP software targeted at supporting medium- to large-scale organisations in a number of industries and sectors. SAP ERP includes four individual modules that support key back-end functional areas: SAP ERP Financials, SAP ERP Human Capital Management, SAP ERP Operations and SAP ERP Corporate Services. |
| **SAP** | |

6.6.3   Web services

Web service: a component piece of an ICT system that implements a limited piece of functionality which can be distributed over the Web

Web standards are starting to support interoperable systems across computer networks, particularly through the idea of service oriented architecture (SOA) and the related idea of a **web service**. SOA represents a model in which ICT system functionality is decomposed into small, distinct units known as services, which can be distributed over a network and can be combined and reused to create business applications. These services communicate by passing data from one service to another, or by coordinating an activity between one or more services.

Web services typically implement software functionality that most humans would recognise as a service, such as filling out an online application for a bank account, viewing an online bank statement, or placing an order for an airline ticket online. Instead of web services communicating by making calls to each other, protocols are defined which describe how one or more services talk to each other. This architecture then relies on a business process expert linking services in a process known as orchestration, to meet a new or existing business system requirement.

Each element of a service oriented architecture can play one or more of three roles: service provider, service broker and service requestor. The service provider creates a web service and possibly publishes its interface and access information to a service registry or broker. The service broker is responsible for making the web service interface and implementation access information available to any potential service requestor. The service requestor or web service client locates entries in the broker registry using various find operations, then 'binds' to the service provider in order to invoke one of its web services.

The World Wide Web Consortium (W3C) defines a web service as a:

> software system designed to support interoperable machine-to-machine interaction on a network. It has an interface defined in a machine-processable format (specifically WSDL). Other systems interact with the Web service in a manner prescribed by its description using SOAP messages, typically conveyed using HTTP with an XML serialisation in conjunction with other Web-related standards.

In this jargon, WSDL stands for web service description language and is effectively a means to define the functionality of a web service in terms of XML grammar (see Chapter 5). SOAP stands for simple object access protocol, and consists of a framework for XML format messages sent between distributed ICT systems.

6.7   Cloud computing

Cloud computing: a term used to refer to a number of technologies that support remote computing such as SOA, data centres and virtualisation

In the 1960s the computer scientist John McCarthy made the prediction that '*computation may someday be organised as a public utility*'. This is the aim of the Cloud, or **cloud computing**, in which computing power is delivered to the user in much the same way as electricity or water is delivered as a utility over the Internet. The user of a cloud application does not require knowledge of the location or configuration of the application to use it, she merely connects to it over the Internet. Therefore, the term derives from the common representation of the Internet in diagrams, such as the ones used in this book, as a cloud. But cloud computing is not one technology but a series of technologies including: client-server computing, software as a service, data centres and virtualisation.

As we discussed in an earlier section, ICT systems as applications are typically divided up into layers such as interface, application, transaction and data. Each of these layers may be distributed on different machines, perhaps at different sites, connected through communication across a network. The most extreme version of this technical architecture is when a client machine runs little more than the user interface, probably through a browser. Most other parts of the application are run on remote data servers. Clients communicate with these servers through open software standards such as the Internet protocol and application programming interfaces.

Web standards are starting to support interoperable systems across computer networks, particularly through the idea of a service oriented architecture (SOA), discussed in the previous section. In this architecture, computing resources are typically owned and operated by a third-party provider located in one or more data centres. A data centre is a purpose-built facility which runs multiple computing servers, usually with associated infrastructure such as telecommunications, backup power supply and security. However, consumers of the resources provided by the data centre are not concerned with the underlying infrastructure as services such as Web applications or data storage are available on demand to the consumer.

Hence, the architecture associated with cloud computing assumes a massive network of 'cloud servers' interconnected as if in a grid. The servers run applications in parallel and sometimes use a technique known as data virtualisation to maximise computing power per server. This involves making multiple physical resources, such as storage devices or servers, appear to the user as a single virtual resource.

One of the most publicised cloud applications is Salesforce.com's customer relationship management system. This ICT system is broken down into several broad applications, such as Sales Cloud and Service Cloud, so that business actors, such as sales persons, can access them through an Internet-enabled mobile device or a connected computer. The Sales Cloud enables access to customer profiles and account histories, and allows sales persons to control data associated with the sales process (e.g. contact data and marketing campaigns). The Service Cloud enables companies to track customer transactions coming in from a number of access channels, and automatically route these for handling by appropriate persons.

Some of the claimed benefits of cloud computing include device and location independence, improved scalability, improved reliability and reduced cost. Cloud applications can be accessed on different access devices from any Internet-enabled location. The dynamic provisioning of computing resources means that a user's needs for computing power can scale upwards without significant new investment. The application itself, in terms of software and data, can be separated from physical resources such as hardware. Hence, if more computing power is required to handle peak loads additional cloud servers can be applied to the task on an as-needed basis. Well-designed cloud applications can ensure business continuity and reliability of ICT use. Finally, it is claimed that the pricing structure of cloud computing, typically offered as a subscriber or metred service, offers a more cost-effective means of operating ICT infrastructure than in-house computing.

However, there are a number of concerns expressed in relation to cloud computing. Cloud computing is a form of informatics outsourcing (see Chapter 11) and, just like any form of outsourcing, has to be closely controlled by the client company to ensure that the service provided meets changing needs. Particular attention needs to be paid to the security of business data held on remote data servers and that records of personal data held on such servers meet data protection standards.

DID YOU KNOW? Google is said to operate a global network of approximately 36 data centres to run its search engine. Microsoft's data centre in Chicago is reputed to need three electrical substations with a capacity of 198 megawatts to run effectively. The Environmental Protection Agency in the United States estimates that its 7,000 data centres use 1.5% of the country's electricity consumption..

6.8   Data security

Securing data and infrastructure   **IS**2010

Data security: The process of ensuring the security of stored and transmitted data.

Data security is a critical issue in modern societies and economies because of the increasing use of remote communication. Among the problems this creates are the need to authenticate users and the risks of unauthorised access to systems. Electronic commerce (see Chapter 9) cannot occur without the transfer of transactional data and the storage of data in ICT systems.

Data form the life-blood of much modern business and commerce. The level of computer-related crimes is growing creating an increasing number of measures, many of them technological, that organisations take in response. Data security is becoming a critical issue for most businesses and involves a vast range of technical and non-technical solutions.

This section considers three major technological dimensions to the issue of data security:

- ensuring effective personal identity management
- securing stored data
- securing transactional data.

Personal identity management consists of three inter-related processes – authentication, identification and enrolment – that serve to connect people, identifiers and identity in the information society. The data in an organisation's ICT systems are a valuable resource and must be protected. We consider both computer-based and non-computer-based ways of achieving this. Data privacy needs to be maintained too, keeping sensitive data from both internal and external unauthorised users. We also consider some technologies for achieving this.

6.8.1 The dimensions of data security

To provide a secure environment for the conduct of eBusiness and eCommerce three conditions must be satisfied:

- Privacy of data should be ensured. In other words, only authorised people should have access to stored data. In data transmission only the parties to an electronic transaction should have access to the data about it.
- Users of ICT systems need to be authenticated, as do parties to an electronic transaction. In general, messages should only be exchanged between parties whose identity has been confirmed in some way.
- Users of an ICT system should not be able to deny that they have used it, and the sender of a message cannot deny that they have sent it. This is known as non-repudiability.

Some of the major components of the technical infrastructure for ensuring data security are illustrated in Figure 6.12.

Consider someone who wants to move money from one bank account to another. Let's say they use a PC to access their bank's online banking facility. They will be asked to authenticate themselves to the system by entering data such as a username and password, which are checked against an access control list. If the authentication is successful, they are given a secure connection to the bank's web server. Depending on the activity, messages from the access device will then be encrypted and bundled with a form of identification known as a digital signature. The message will be sent over the Internet using its inherent communication protocols, decrypted and unbundled at the organisation end, and examined by a firewall. This validates the message in various ways and only allows access to particular web servers once security rules are satisfied. The personal bank account details are likely to be held in a database managed by a DBMS server.

CASE CHECK

UK National Identity Card

In the United Kingdom, the issue of personal identity management came to the fore in 2002 when the then Home Secretary David Blunkett resurrected the idea of introducing a national identity card, as had been done during the first and second World Wars. There was consultation for two years on draft legislation to create a national identity management infrastructure for the United Kingdom, consisting of a large central registry of personal identity data, and the issuing of biometric tokens to all UK citizens by 2013. Controversy surrounding this issue led to the scrapping of the idea in 2010.

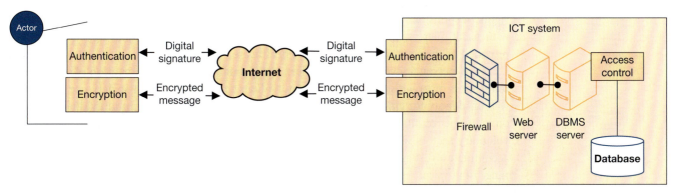

Figure 6.12 *The components of data security*

6.8.2   Personal identity management

Personal identity management : a term used to encompass all those issues involved with authenticating, identifying and enrolling individuals

In face-to-face communication between business actors personal identity is signified through natural signs such as appearance (how a person looks), behaviour (for instance, how a person speaks), or names (for example, personal names and nicknames). Within forms of mediated communication, such as when a person emails a company, these forms of natural identifier are not available. Mediated communication tends to use surrogate or artificial identifiers as a substitute. Examples of surrogate identifiers are codes (such as customer numbers), tokens (such as credit cards) or knowledge (such as PINs and passwords). More recently, there has been increasing interest in biometric identifiers. A biometric is a machine-readable measurement or a series of measurements of some bodily characteristic or behaviour, such as an iris scan, a fingerprint or a DNA pattern. These measurements can be used to build a unique profile of an individual; this profile can serve as a strong identifier in situations of remote communication.

Hence, when using an online banking website a customer is likely to be required to enter a range of identifiers to access the services of the website such as a customer number, a password and possibly even aspects of personal knowledge such as a father's name. Certain banks have now started to issue card readers to their online customers. This requires the customer to swipe an identity token, such as a debit or credit card, through the reader to gain access to the services provided by the website. It is possible for such readers and tokens to eventually store and manipulate biometric data held about the individual.

The banking customer in our example is actually engaged in a process of authentication. Authentication involves validating the association between an identifier and the person it stands for. An identifier, as we have seen, is a symbol or set of symbols that can be used to authenticate an object such as a person. Authentication is a process that involves answering the question, *Am I who I claim to be?* It involves validating the association between the identifier and the person and is a critical aspect of data systems that handle personal data.

Authentication is a prior activity to identification. Identification is the process of using an identifier to connect to a stream of data constituting a person's identity. Personal identification in the main involves answering the question, *Who am I?* This question is normally answered in terms of personal attributes, such as age, gender or occupation, as well as events in which the person has participated, such as having gained a qualification, made an order with a company or submitted a tax return. In this manner, personal identifiers are used to assign organisational identities to individuals within given information systems. For example, a country's public sector agencies frequently have to legitimate somebody as a legal resident or a taxpayer. Within the private sector, financial institutions have to validate the creditworthiness of a customer before offering a loan.

Organisations authenticate and identify people because this determines which persons are entitled to participate in some activity system provided by the organisation. Therefore, a validated identity serves to enrol the individual in a defined activity system. Enrolment in this sense involves answering the question, *What am I expected to do and to receive?* Hence, a validated identity such as that of a taxpayer will enrol the individual in a whole range of rights, responsibilities and expected actions in the government activity systems associated with fiscal matters. In some countries it will also entitle the individual to access services provided by the state authorities, such as healthcare.

Hence, personal identity in the modern age is entangled with the operation of a multitude of business or organisational systems. Individuals in the information society use a complex web of identity for existence and action. In our information society an individual may take on a number of different identities; one for each electronic service in the public, private and voluntary sectors with which the individual engages. As a consequence, an individual may accumulate a vast array of personal identifiers for such 'services' and is also likely to accrue a range of physical representations, or tokens, of such multiple identification: credit card, debit card, driving licence, passport, library card, parking permit etc.

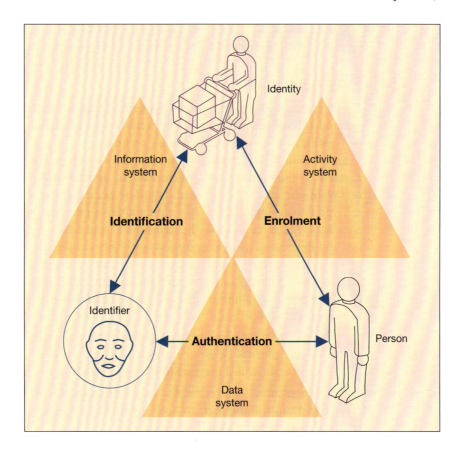

Figure 6.13 *Personal identity management*

6.8.3 Securing stored data

Effective electronic service delivery demands the storage of much personal data, so it is very important to protect this stored data from external threats (for example, hacking of customer databases). But most organisational data (for instance, financial details of company performance) is also sensitive and must be protected.

The threats include:

- Electronic theft and fraud: for example, someone falsely updating corporate data with the aim of defrauding their employer, or a hacker making an illegal entry into a database system and extracting corporate data without permission.
- Loss of confidentiality: such as an unauthorised person viewing information on confidential corporate policies and disclosing it to outside agencies.
- Loss of availability: for instance, a database system becoming unavailable because of a natural disaster such as fire and flood, or a human-generated disaster such as a bomb attack.
- Loss of personal privacy: when an unauthorised person views personal data someone wishes to be kept private.
- Loss of integrity: when data is corrupted, by a software virus, or a software or hardware failure.

Any organisation needs to take both computer-based and non-computer-based measures to counter these threats.

Computer-based measures include an authorisation strategy for operating systems, ICT systems and database systems. This normally involves system administrators assigning user names and passwords to individuals and groups. As mentioned above, it can also include physical tokens such as a card with an electro-magnetic strip, or a smart card with an embedded chip, which is read by a specialised input device, or a biometrics reader.

Non-computer-based measures include establishing a security policy and plan and enforcing it; establishing a policy on access to data (which can involve rethinking people's roles);

positioning computer hardware in secure environments through physical access controls; and securing copies of data and software in off-site, fireproof storage (see Chapter 11).

6.8.4 Securing transactions

Chapter 5 outlined how the increasing use of electronic data transfer leads to a need for security and privacy, and introduced key technologies, including encryption, digital signatures and certificates, firewalls and tunnelling technology.

Encryption and decryption have been carried out for thousands of years (Singh, 2000). Figure 6.14 shows the essential elements. An unencrypted message is normally referred to as a plain text message because of its historical association with the written word. It is first encrypted using a particular algorithm and an appropriate key which provides data for the algorithm. At the receiver end the algorithm is applied as a decryption method using another key, and this reveals the plaintext message to the receiver.

A very simple form of encryption consists of taking the letters of the alphabet and replacing each one with a letter from a cipher alphabet. The cipher alphabet is the key. The encryption and decryption algorithms detail the method of substitution. For instance, if this key is used to encrypt 'et tu brute?':

> Plain: a b c d e f g h I j k l m n o p q r s t u v w x y z
> Cipher: j l p a w I q b c t r z y d s k e g f x h u o n v m
> the coded message would read 'wx xh lghxw?'

Encryption ensures some privacy if only authorised people have access to the key, but a cryptologist can still use logic to decipher this kind of simply encrypted message, so more complex algorithms are used in practice.

Two types of algorithm employed in commercial data transmission are symmetric and asymmetric key encryption.

In symmetric key encryption, sometimes known as private key encryption, the same key is applied at both ends of the encryption process. The key is agreed in advance between the sender and receiver. The main problem is that messages can only be transmitted between parties known to each other and trusted to hold the private key.

Asymmetric key encryption, sometimes known as public key encryption, uses a pair of keys, one private and one public. A user with a private key can give a corresponding public key to anyone they wish. This then allows the user to send a message encrypted with the private key, safe in the knowledge that only users with the corresponding public key can decrypt it. There is no requirement for the sender to agree the keys in advance of sending a message since the user can place the public key in a register of selected users via encrypted messages.

Public key encryption provides the foundation for digital signatures. These are important in authenticating the senders of messages and for ensuring a degree of non-repudiability. The sender transmits a message using a private key. If the receiver of the message is able to decrypt the message successfully using the public key, this automatically acts as a way of authenticating the sender.

Encryption: the process of securing data through the application of a security algorithm

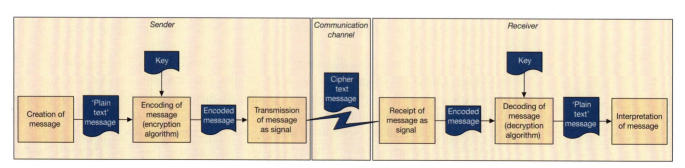

Figure 6.14 *Coding of messages*

The management of encryption and digital signatures requires an infrastructure that includes ensuring that keys are used only by legitimate holders, and contains procedures for managing the assignment and storage of keys. This is referred to as the public key infrastructure (PKI), and is provided by a trusted certification authority (CA). All legitimate users are required to register with the CA to use public key encryption. The CA issues a digital certificate, sometimes called a digital passport, to users. This consists of an electronic document that keeps a record of users and their public keys.

Public key encryption is also important to securing data transmission over the Internet. Secure socket layer (SSL) is an attempt to offer a secure channel of communication. It is a framework for transmitting sensitive information such as credit card details. It involves using a sophisticated protocol between client and server systems that is transparent to the user and provides a secure connection. It exchanges a digital signature between a client (such as an individual using an Internet-enabled PC) and a server (an organisation's front-end ICT system).

Leading vendors of Internet browsers such as Microsoft use standards for digital certificates to implement SSL. The customer first has to request a digital certificate from the certification authority. They provide details of themselves plus evidence of their identity to the certification authority. They also send their public key to the certification authority (that is, the key provided to them by the organisation they are trying to access). The certification authority produces a digital certificate and includes the public key within it. When the user later wants to engage in eCommerce, they use their digital certificate to prove their authenticity to the participating organisation.

A firewall is a system that attempts to protect a private network from hackers, software viruses, data corruption or unauthorised access. Effectively it restricts access to the private network by external users, and may also be used to prohibit internal users from accessing selected parts of the private network. For example, it is used to prevent public Internet users from accessing an organisation's private intranet.

Firewalls can be implemented in both, or either, hardware and software. They typically comprise a proxy server, which examines all messages entering or leaving the private network, and blocks those that do not match particular security criteria. In a Web environment a proxy server sits between a web browser and a web server. It runs routers, other communications software and special programs known as proxies. One proxy is normally assigned for each Internet service such as HTTP and FTP. When data packets from the external environment reach the firewall it checks the packets for details of their source and destination. It then makes a decision to accept or reject the packet depending on an inspection of an access control list and a set of associated security controls.

Tunnelling technology involves the transmission of data over the Internet using leased lines to the local ISP. With the use of encryption, authentication and other security technologies, this can be used to produce a virtual private network (VPN) over a wide area network (see Chapter 5). Data packets are encrypted and encapsulated into IP packets, then transmitted over the Internet using routers. At the receiver end the packet is decrypted and authenticity checks are made. This creates secure data tunnels between an organisation's systems and key external stakeholders such as suppliers and partners. This approach offers an inexpensive way for an organisation to extend the reach of its information systems, and is the key technology underlying extranets.

FOCUS ON VALUE

The value of an ICT system lies in its role as a producer of data. However, value also arises in the ability of the modern ICT infrastructure to integrate processing and data across the organisation, particularly for multinational and global organisations. Modern technology allows the distribution of processing and data around data communication networks, and the separation of the functionality of the typical ICT system into manageable layers. Organisations tend to rely increasingly on their data resources, and this means an increasing value for technologies that ensure the security of both stored and transmitted data.

6.9   Conclusion and key themes

This chapter has defined at a high-level the important component elements of business ICT systems. Practitioners need this in order to understand the ways in which ICT systems encode organisational practice in technologies such as interfaces, business rule engines and databases.

ICT systems can be defined in terms of key components or key functionality. In terms of key components, modern ICT consists of hardware, software, data management technology and data communication technology. In terms of functionality, an ICT system can be seen as being made up of a number of interacting subsystems: the interface subsystem, business rules subsystem, transaction subsystem and data management subsystem.

Processing in contemporary ICT infrastructure is likely to be distributed in an *n*-tier client–server architecture. This separates out the layers of the ICT system and distributes them at various points around an organisation's communication network. Recently, the idea of cloud computing proposes running major parts of the functionality of an application from large data centres accessed as a service run over the Internet.

Various front-end ICT systems interface with internal and external stakeholders. They typically involve a website accessible via the Internet or on an intranet or extranet. An intranet involves using Internet technology in a single organisation. An extranet is an extended intranet which uses Internet technology to connect a series of intranets.

The business tier of a typical business ICT application consists of three inter-related elements: update functions, business rules and transactions. Update functions are elements of functionality associated with a particular business application, and consist of business rules and transaction types. They are triggered by events that are typically initiated at the interface and activate a set of business rules. Transactions are then fired at the data management layer.

Back-end ICT systems include the core systems of the business, and tend to be located around databases storing important corporate data. Contemporary data management involves databases, DBMS and data warehouses. The integration of back-end ICT infrastructure is now frequently achieved through ERP systems.

To provide a secure environment for the conduct of business activity over the Internet three conditions must be satisfied: authentication, privacy and non-repudiability. Security is needed for both stored data and transactions. Key approaches to ensuring the security of stored data include authorisation schemes such as user names and passwords. Key technologies for ensuring privacy and authentication of transactional data include encryption, digital signatures and certificates, firewalls and tunnelling technology.

This chapter concludes our look at the ICT infrastructure of modern business. The next three chapters examine the application of business systems and their impact on the internal operations of the business, and also on relationships and activities with external stakeholders. First we need to consider in more detail the idea of the business as a value-creating system that exists within, and adapts to, a wider value network.

6.10   Review test

1 Types of input devices include? Select all that apply.
   - ☐ Character-based devices
   - ☐ Image-based devices
   - ☐ Sound-based devices
   - ☐ Access-based devices
   - ☐ Movement-based devices
   - ☐ Graphics-based devices

2 A _____ is a series of instructions for hardware. Fill in the blank.

3 Types of software include? Select all that apply.
   - ☐ System software   Software that is designed to perform a particular business function
   - ☐ Applications software   Designed to be used across the entire enterprise
   - ☐ Enterprise software   Software that manages the computer's resources

4 Front-end systems are information systems in an organisation which interact with the stakeholder

through specified electronic services. True or false?
- ☐ True
- ☐ False

5 Back-end ICT systems are information systems in the organisation which interact with front-end ICT systems and provide key data services to them. True or false?
- ☐ True
- ☐ False

6 An ICT system can be considered to have five major layers or subsystems. Place in order, with the layer closest to the user first.
- ☐ Rules subsystem
- ☐ Interface subsystem
- ☐ Data management subsystem
- ☐ Transaction subsystem
- ☐ Communication subsystem

7 Name the two types of integration of ICT systems. Select the most appropriate two.
- ☐ Data
- ☐ Transaction
- ☐ Process
- ☐ Physical
- ☐ Communication subsystem

8 An _____ is a corporate LAN or WAN that uses Internet technology and is secured behind firewalls. Fill in the blank.

9 Match the type of system to the most appropriate stakeholder type. Pair each lettered entry with the corresponding numbered entry.

a. Internet	1. Customer
b. Intranet	2. Supplier
c. Extranet	3. Employee

10 DBMS stands for? Select the most appropriate description.
- ☐ Data biometric migration system
- ☐ Database management system
- ☐ Database mission system

11 A database is the same as a DBMS. True or false?
- ☐ True
- ☐ False

12 An _____ constraint is a rule which establishes how a database is to remain an accurate reflection of its universe of discourse. Fill in the blank

13 Securing data in the ICT infrastructure involves? Select all that apply.
- ☐ Securing data in ICT systems
- ☐ Securing transactions
- ☐ Securing personnel

14 VPN stands for? Select the most appropriate description.
- ☐ Virtual private network
- ☐ Virtual positioning network
- ☐ Virtuous practical network

15 ERP systems integrate a number of different organisational functions under the umbrella of one system. True or false?
- ☐ True
- ☐ False

6.11 Exercises

▸ Find an ICT system, and analyse it in terms of the four-layer model described in this chapter. Is the ICT system distributed in any way? Which model of distribution best approximates its architecture?

▸ Consider an organisation's ICT infrastructure. How closely integrated are the systems? How much distributed processing and/or data are present in the infrastructure?

▸ Classify a website known to you in terms of whether it solely provides information content, allows querying or enables transactions.

▸ Try to find an organisation that maintains both an Internet and intranet website and determine how they differ.

▸ Determine whether an organisation known to you uses an extranet. Attempt to determine its functionality.

▸ If you have made any payments online, determine how sites inform you that they are secure. Determine the confidence you place in the security of such sites.

▸ Identify core database systems in an organisation known to you.

▸ Determine whether an application known to you uses an n-tier client–server architecture.

▸ Determine how privacy is handled in a system known to you.

▸ Determine how authenticity is handled in a system known to you.

- Determine the sort of access controls used in an ICT system known to you.
- Investigate what software is available under the open software movement.
- Consider an ICT system known to you. Attempt to estimate the volume of data stored in the system.
- Investigate the range of contemporary DBMS used in a specific organisation.
- Find an organisation that has adopted a mega-package. Why did the organisation decide to implement the package? What experience have they had of using it for their infrastructure?

6.12   Projects

- Conduct an assessment of the hardware used by a particular organisation in terms of the typical desktop. Develop policy guidelines for a standard hardware profile for the organisation. What advantages arise from an organisation maintaining a standard hardware profile?
- Conduct an inventory of the software used in an organisation known to you. Categorise the inventory in terms of the distinctions made in this chapter, such as operating systems and office productivity software. Use this inventory to determine the degree of standardisation of software in the organisation. Produce a brief for the organisation, highlighting the importance of standardisation to a successful ICT infrastructure.
- Thin client technology has been proposed as a solution to managing ICT infrastructure for a number of decades. Define more precisely what thin client technology means for modern organisations, and investigate its penetration.
- Open source software is now used by major organisations as part of their ICT infrastructure. Determine more precisely what open source actually means for these organisations. What benefits does open source software provide? Infer from this the likely success of the open software movement in the longer term.
- Most modern information systems projects utilise database technology. Investigate why this is the case and to what purposes such database systems are put. What DBMS are used in association with corporate databases and what facilities do such systems provide?

- Genetic sequences can now be determined and represented as data. Determine the precise characteristics of such data and the features of databases needed to handle such complex data. How important are such applications in bio-informatics to the developing biotech industries?
- Investigate the prevalence of data warehousing as an organisational technology. To what purposes are data warehouses put? How critical is the effective use of data warehousing to modern management decision-making?
- Gather data on a limited range of ICT systems within a specific organisation. Analyse their functionality in terms of the layered model discussed in this chapter. How easy is it to assign aspects of their functionality to a three-tiered model? Is an n-tiered model more appropriate?
- Build a high-level description of the functionality of a mega-package such as SAP. How much of a core information systems infrastructure, as described in Chapter 4, does it provide for organisations? Investigate the penetration of ERP systems, such as the one chosen, into a particular industrial sector, such as manufacturing and retail.
- ERP systems are frequently introduced into organisations in an attempt to import integration of data and processes. However, many organisations have experienced problems in implementing such large-scale package solutions. Investigate the problems and pitfalls of ERP implementation.

6.13   Critical reflection

Can the performance of an organisation be determined by the degree to which its information systems infrastructure is enabled with ICT? How significant is the degree of integration in this infrastructure to organisational performance? Does the adoption of mega-packages such as SAP reduce the degree to which companies can strategically use ICT to improve performance?

Databases have been seen as perhaps the central technology for modern business. Why do you think this might be the case? To what extent do you think common data formats influence the degree to which ICT systems can be integrated? How important is personal identity data to the operation of the average company?

6.14   Further reading

No one text covers all the material discussed in this chapter. Shneiderman et al. (2009) cover the interface layer. Graham (2006) covers the business layer in terms of service oriented architecture. Beynon-Davies (2004) covers the data management layer. Monk and Wagner (2012) cover ERP systems and their implementation.

6.16   References

Beynon-Davies, P. (2004). *Database Systems*. 3rd edition. Palgrave Macmillan, Basingstoke.

Copeland, J. B. (2004). *The Essential Turing*. Oxford University Press, Oxford.

Graham, I. (2006). *Business Rules Management and Service Oriented Architecture: A Pattern Language*. John Wiley, London.

Monk, E. and B. Wagner. (2012). *Concepts in Enterprise Resource Planning*. South-Western College Publishing, Andover.

Shneiderman, B., C. Plaisant, M. Cohen and S. Jacobs. (2009). *Designing the User Interface: Strategies for Effective Human-Computer Interaction*. Pearson, New York.

Singh, S. (2000). *The Science of Secrecy*. Fourth estate, London.

See companion website   **www.palgrave.com/business/beynon-daviesbis2e**

part III

Applying information systems to business

What distinguishes the field of information systems, or organisational informatics, from computer science is its interest in the application of technology. This part of the book examines issues relating to the introduction of information systems into organisations and the effect of this application in a number of different areas.

Chapter 7 examines the external **environment** within which an organisation operates and considers the organisation as a value-creating system that operates in a wider **value network.** This makes it possible to define what we mean by commerce in some detail, and consider the crucial relationships between flows of value, the control of commerce and the place of information.

Chapter 8 considers the rise of **electronic business** and **electronic commerce.** The term eBusiness is used to refer to all activity relating to the application of ICT within business; eCommerce is used to refer to the use of ICT to support and enhance relationships and activities that an organisation has with external stakeholders. Distinctions are made between forms of eBusiness that relate to different areas of the value network defined in Chapter 7.

Chapter 9 addresses directly the question of the value of ICT, which is considered through the related issues of use, impact and evaluation. As ICT impacts on more and more aspects of organisational life issues of **use** assume significance, not only for internal stakeholders such as managers and employees but also for external stakeholders such as customers and suppliers. The use of information systems is a necessary pre-condition for the **impact** on individuals, groups and the organisation as a whole. Although the impact is usually designed to be positive, it can be negative for individuals and groups. To assess it effectively we need to **evaluate** and determine the degree to which stakeholders regard information systems as successes or **failures.**

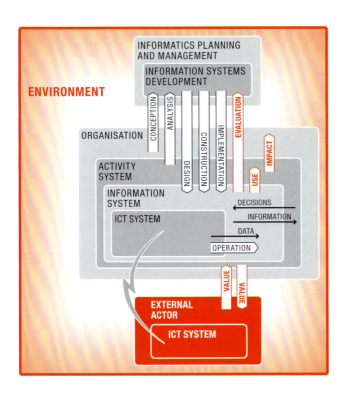

Overview

The chapter in this part cover the following key areas:

- The value-chain and the value network
- The place of organisations in the value network
- The interaction of the political, social and physical environment with information systems
- Electronic business
- Electronic commerce
- Electronic government
- The use of information systems
- The impact of information systems on individuals, groups and organisations
- Evaluating the success or failure of information systems
- Strategies for avoiding information systems failure

The business environment

'There can be no economy where there is no efficiency.'

Benjamin Disraeli
(1804–1881)

Learning outcomes	Principles
Define the key elements of the economic environment of the organisation and describe organisations as value-creating systems existing within a wider value network.	An organisation as an open system exists within a wider economic environment. Such an environment is considered in terms of a value network. An organisation maintains relationships with various actors in the value network. Flows of value and transactions occur across the value network.
Distinguish between critical parts of the value network and describe their relationship to forms of commerce.	Porter describes the organisation in terms of an internal value-chain. This can be extended to a consideration of the supply chain and the customer chain. We also argue for the modern relevance of what we call the community chain.
Identify the key forms of value travelling along the value network and distinguish between the different forms of control evident within the value network.	Value comes in three forms: goods, services and social capital. In terms of goods and services the distinction between tangible and intangible is important to understanding some of the recent changes to the value network of organisations. Social capital emerging in communities situated around the organisation is also important to modern commerce.
Explain the relationship between the concept of a business model and the value network and conduct a simple analysis of a value network in some organisation.	The concept of a business model is useful because it highlights the important relationship between strategy, business processes and enabling technologies. Designing a business model implies analysing the most appropriate application of these three things within a wider value network.

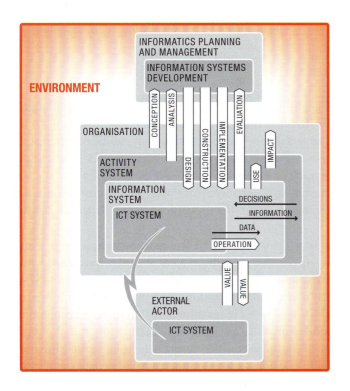

Chapter outline

AACSB learning objectives:
Analytical thinking, reflective thinking and ethical issues

7.1   Introduction

For well over a century people have been arguing about what has more effect on children's development: their environment or their genetic inheritance. The notable British geneticist and evolutionary biologist J. B. S. Haldane commented, '*We do not know, in most cases, how far social failure and success are due to heredity, and how far to environment. But environment is the easier of the two to improve.*' In a sense the same is true for organisations. Organisational success cannot be guaranteed solely by improving internal operations, their prior history and 'inherited' competitive position have a great influence too. In the long-term organisational sustainability definitely relies on effective interaction with the wider environment.

This book takes a primarily process or systems view of the organisation. In this sense, organisations are viewed as a number of interdependent activity systems. Information systems and information and communication technology (ICT) support activity in these systems. This entire complex system is affected by forces in its environment. Organisations are not isolated entities, they are open systems. The success (that is, both current viability and future sustainability) of any organisation will depend on how well it integrates with, and reacts to, aspects of its environment. In other words, we can view an organisation as a system that builds and uses information systems to cope with environmental forces. The form of its information systems will also be shaped by environmental constraints.

This chapter focuses on the wider environment. It first considers it as four major environmental systems: an economic system (economy), political system (polity), societal system (society) and physical system (ecosystem). Because of its critical importance for business organisations we focus particularly on the wider economic environment.

The chapter describes how organisations can be considered as systems creating value that travels within and between organisations. Activity systems provide the supportive mechanisms for customer, supply and internal value-chains. It outlines key elements of these value-chains, and describes them as conduits within a wider value network for the flow of goods, services and transactions. It also introduces the concept of the community chain as a social network, and discusses how the value it produces (social capital) is increasingly important for business.

The concept of the value network is critical to understanding the place of eBusiness and eCommerce (discussed in Chapter 8) and the forms these contemporary trends take. The material in this chapter is also important for understanding the worth of ICT, and information systems more generally, to organisations (considered in Chapter 9).

7.2   The external environment of the organisation

Environment: anything outside of the organisation, with which the organisation interacts and which influences the behaviour of the organisation

Environment is the general term for anything outside of the organisation with which it interacts (Worthington and Britton, 2009). The environment of most organisations can be seen as four major interdependent systems: an economic system, social system, political system and physical system (Figure 7.1). In this sense, it is made up of a complex network of activities and relationships between the organisation and other agencies.

Each of these systems has an impact on informatics activities, and the organisation's informatics activities in turn are likely to impact on the social, economic, political and even physical spheres.

Economic environment: that part of the environment concerned with material provisioning

An economic system is concerned with the way in which groups of humans arrange their material provisioning, and essentially involves the coordination of activities concerned with this. An organisation's **economic environment** is defined by its activities and relationships with economic actors. It is particularly concerned with national and international commerce and trade, and is influenced by such factors as levels of taxation, inflation rates and economic growth. Information systems are critical to organisational performance in economic markets. Recently, there has been a lot of growth in the specialised markets focused around the use of electronic networks. Not surprisingly, eBusiness and eCommerce have become significant strategies for modern organisations to improve their performance (see Chapter 8).

Figure 7.1 drawn diagram of overlapping circles:

- Economic environment (top)
- Political environment (left)
- Social environment (right)
- Physical environment (bottom)
- Organisation (centre)

Figure 7.1 *The external environment of organisations*

The social environment of an organisation concerns its position in the cultural life of a grouping such as a nation-state. We can think of it as a series of social networks consisting of activities and relationships that serve to bind various social groupings together. This chapter is particularly interested in the ways in which people relate to organisational activity through communities of consumption.

The political environment or system concerns issues of power. Political systems consist of sets of activities and relationships concerned with exercising power. This chapter deals especially with government and legal frameworks, which are a major constraining force on organisational behaviour. Among the issues we can consider here, are the influence of ICT on electronic government and electronic democracy.

The physical environment is the ecosphere surrounding organisational activity. In recent years there has been growing concern about organisations' impact on the physical environment, such as the effect of carbon dioxide emissions on the atmosphere and the resultant process of global warming. Businesses are increasingly expected to act to reduce their ecological footprint. Information systems have a part to play here. For instance, ICT makes it possible for many people to work from home, which means they commute to work less often and do not need to use so much energy for travel.

The relation of all four environmental systems to informatics is a huge subject, so the rest of this chapter focuses on the system of most interest to business organisations, the economic system. It also covers some aspects of the social environment – social networks, communities and social capital – to establish a basis for some of the discussion of virtual communities in Chapter 8.

7.3   Value and value-creating systems

Value: a general term used to describe the worth of something such as the output from some organisation or ICT system.

We organise our discussion of the business around the concept of **value**, which is a common thread tying together a range of topics considered in this book. The Oxford English dictionary defines value as *the importance or usefulness of something*. The management guru Michael Porter (Porter and Millar, 1985) uses the term value to describe, at a high level, the key output of a business organisation. This enables him to focus on the processes or activity systems which produce such value, collectively referred to as the internal value-chain. In such terms, organisations are considered as value-creating systems.

But economies are systems not only of value production but also of value distribution and value consumption. An organisation's value is hence determined by its position within a wider value network. Typically, the value associated with an organisation equates with the services and/or products provided by the organisation. However, value also emerges from dispersed forms of organisation evident in wider social networks. Such forms of value relate to social capital; the resources for mutual support available in forms of community. Social capital is the key value that members gain from participation in such social networks.

In a sense, this chapter is about axiology: the study of what people value or find to be of worth. In a purely materialist sense we could equate value with the satisfaction of human needs, such as the need for food, water and shelter. For the psychologist Abraham Maslow (1954) these constitute basic human needs that must be satisfied before other human needs are achievable, such as the need for safety, love and belonging, esteem and self-actualisation. In this manner, a hierarchy of needs is specified that translate into forms of value. Some of this value is material in nature, such as food, while other forms of value are non-material in nature, such as a sense of esteem or personal status.

The upshot of this is that value is a complex issue and one which is particularly associated with the different activity, communication and representation systems within which people engage. Hence, people have valued different things at different times and in different places. In this sense the concept of value is a significant concept in that value is arbitrary, it depends on what is considered of worth by that particular community of people.

In his famous book *Argonauts of the Western Pacific* (Malinowski, 1922) the eminent anthropologist Bronislaw Malinowski described a curious case of axiology. This involved the Kula exchange, sometimes known as the Kula ring, a system of goods exchange conducted amongst 18 island communities, including the Trobriand Islands, in the South Pacific. Participants in this exchange system travel hundreds of miles by canoe in order to exchange Kula, which consists of two types of goods: disc necklaces formed from a red seashell and armbands formed from a white seashell. Kula goods have no value as useful objects, but are traded purely for the purposes of raising social status. The act of giving a necklace or armband is used as a sign of the greatness of the giver. This exchange network is known as a ring because Kula necklaces are traded to the north in a clockwise direction and Kula armbands are traded to the south in an anti-clockwise direction. In this way, Kula valuables never remain in the hands of recipients for long. Instead, they must be passed on to other partners in the Kula exchange system within a certain amount of time and thus are constantly circling around the exchange network. However, even temporary possession of Kula by a participant brings prestige and status for the temporary owner.

A similar system was conducted on the Pacific Northwest Coast of North America in what was known as Potlatch. Potlatch is a festival ceremony practiced by the indigenous peoples, the word coming from the Chinook meaning 'to give away' or 'a gift'. At Potlatch gatherings, a family or hereditary leader hosted a feast for guests. The main purpose of the Potlatch was the redistribution of wealth. Hierarchical relations within and between clans, villages and nations, were observed and reinforced through the distribution, or sometimes destruction, of wealth. The status of any given family was raised, not by who had the most resources but by who distributed the most resources.

Figure 7.2 represents the Kula ring as a network, or more precisely as an exchange network. In very abstract terms, a network is a set of nodes connected by links. In communication networks,

DID YOU KNOW? The management gurus Peter Drucker and Michael Porter believe that all non-monetary expressions of value have eventually to be expressed in monetary terms. Drucker writes that *'customers pay only for what is of use to them and gives them value'* (Drucker, 1994). Porter believes that: *'... value is the amount buyers are willing to pay for what a firm provides them. Value is measured by total revenue, a reflection of the prices a firm's product commands and the units it can sell. A firm is profitable if the value it commands exceeds the costs involved in creating the product'* (Porter, 1985).

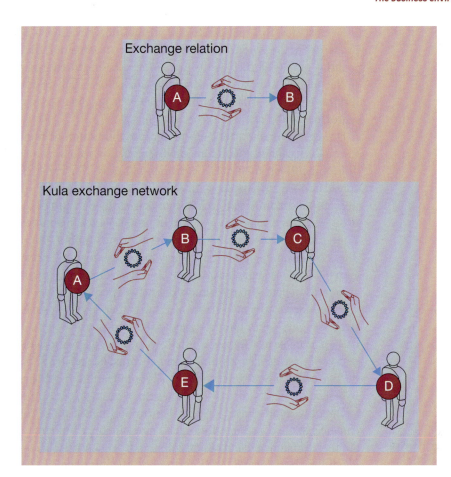

Figure 7.2 *An exchange network*

which we discussed in Chapter 6, the nodes are usually types of computing device and the links are data communication lines. In contrast, within social networks, the nodes are people and the links or relations are forms of social interaction and/or social bonds. The actual type of link, relationship, or more formally relation, represented in Figure 7.2 is that of an exchange relation. Within an exchange network, people exchange things they regard to be of worth, they exchange value.

7.3.1 Goods and services

Good: any product or commodity which is valued and exchanged

Service: some form of valued activity that is exchanged between actors

Even within systems or networks of gift exchange such as the Kula or Potlatch, the value exchanged traditionally comes in two forms: **goods** and **services**. It is no surprise that in English the word good is used to refer not only to something of worth but also to denote a type of value. A good is normally some physical thing which is valued and exchanged between one actor and another (for example, food or a Kula necklace). In contrast, a service is usually some valued activity which is performed for one actor by another actor, such as tilling a field, providing a potlatch festival or operating upon a malignant tumour. Later in the chapter we shall argue for consideration of a third type of value which we refer to as social capital. Social capital is a non-material form of value which is also exchanged between actors and bears a close relationship with the status derived from Potlatch and Kula described above.

As we have indicated in previous chapters, business actors can consist of organisations as well as human groups, individuals and even machines. In the modern world a good is normally considered to be some form of product produced by an organisation and distributed to customers of that organisation. Similarly, a service is typically some form of activity performed by an organisation for its customers. As such, goods and services can be considered the end-points of business processes, or activity systems, performed within business organisations (Chapter 2). They are outputs from such value-creating systems delivered to the customer of the organisation.

For instance, in a manufacturing organisation key aspects of value will be associated with properties of the products manufactured. Hence, an automobile manufacturer will be judged in terms of criteria such as the price of its manufactured cars and their reliability and safety. In the public sector, an organisation's value will typically be associated with properties of the services it delivers. Hence, a university may be judged in terms of the quality of the education it provides or the research it conducts.

However, it is important not to confuse the notion of money with that of value. Within the modern capitalist world, money is frequently seen as comprising the sole source of value. This is incorrect, money is a conventional proxy for value. Treated literally money can be considered a sign (Chapter 3) that serves to stand for, or refer to, value in other forms. Money in most of its manifestations has no intrinsic value in and of itself. It merely serves as a measure of exchange value. Hence, within modern exchange networks if an individual sells you some good, such as a book, you impart a certain amount of money in exchange for this book. That person can then use that money to engage in another relationship of exchange, perhaps exchanging it for some foodstuffs. This is why it becomes possible to represent money as data; as records in data systems supporting networks of exchange.

We alluded to the materiality of value earlier. This helps us distinguish between two types of goods: physical or tangible goods; and non-physical or intangible goods. This distinction has a particular bearing, as we shall see, on the degree to which such forms of value can be delivered over data communication networks; hence, it will be important in considering the degree to which electronic commerce is both feasible and desirable for a company or industry (Chapter 8).

Tangible goods have a physical form and hence must be distributed through physical channels to the consumer. **Intangible goods** may be fundamentally represented as data. They are therefore amenable to digitisation and as such may become digital goods. Clearly such goods may be delivered to the customer electronically over communication networks.

Tangible good: goods that have a physical form and which have to be distributed through physical channels

Intangible good: a good that can essentially be represented as data and hence can be delivered over data communication channels

Examples of tangible goods are mechanical goods such as automobiles, electrical goods such as televisions and perishable goods such as foodstuffs. Examples of intangible goods are text (as in books, magazines and academic papers), images (as in prints or photographs), audio (such as music) and video (as in movies). Many recent forms of intangible good, as we have seen, are frequently denoted with the label content.

> **REFLECT:** Is software a good or a service? Many countries have followed the United States in counting the acquisition of software not as a business expense but as an investment. This means that software contributes to the Gross Domestic Product of a country in the sense that it is considered an intangible good (Floridi, 2007). In what sense is it an intangible good?

Tangible service: a service that has to be performed physically by one actor for another

Intangible service: a service that effectively can be represented as data and hence delivered over data communication channels

Similarly services can be classed as either tangible or intangible. The inspection, ordering and delivery of such goods are data-based services that support the sale of both tangible and intangible products. However, certain services are tangible in nature and hence not amenable to electronic service delivery. Other services are intangible by nature and thus primarily constitute communication services. They are hence open to delivery through electronic channels. **Tangible services** include health treatments such as operations and beauty treatments such as hairdressing. **Intangible services** include legal advice, news reports and monetary transfers. Table 7.1 illustrates these distinctions.

Table 7.1 Types of goods and services

	Goods	Services
Tangible	Automobiles Foodstuffs	Health care Waste disposal
Intangible	Music Movies	Legal advice Monetary transfers

Goods and services are, of course, not mutually exclusive; indeed, in many businesses the sale of a particular tangible good will normally be associated with a range of services, some tangible, some intangible. For instance, when purchasing a tangible good such as an automobile the customer may be able to inspect images of the product, order the product and pay for the product using forms of electronic delivery. The customer may also, of course, inspect, order and pay for intangible goods such as music electronically. After purchase it is likely that the car will need regular servicing and inspection, which are tangible services.

CASE CHECK **The movie industry**	The movie industry is a particularly good example of an industry that has continuously been affected by the changing nature of value and the impact of technological change on its value proposition. A movie or motion picture was originally a story conveyed with moving images and the first true movies emerged during the 1880s with the invention of the motion picture camera and projector. In the 1920s new technology enabled a soundtrack to be added and synchronised with the moving image. In the mid-1930s the first colour movies were produced. Originally invented in the 1990s, digital cinematography started to be used seriously in the 2000s. Over the last couple of years major movies, such as Avatar, have been shot entirely in digital format. This opens up a number of new access channels to movies. Not surprisingly, over the next decade, the movie industry is likely to undergo fundamental change because of the way in which ICT transforms fundamental business models within the sector.
	Hence, movies are modern examples of digital content. The term content, as we have seen, used to be restricted to Web-based documents. Nowadays, the term is used to refer to all forms of goods that can be represented in digital form as data. Many forms of goods that can now be delivered as digital content, such as books, music and movies, have been tangible in nature for most of their history. Hence, you can still buy a physical book, or music on CD, or a movie on DVD. However, there has been a gradual movement by the, so-called, content industries to produce such goods in a form that can distributed and consumed over data communication networks. This enables a number of different business models for such industries which exploit the potential of digital access channels and associated devices.

7.3.2   Social networks and social capital

According to the poet John Donne, '*no man is an island entire of itself*'. Similarly, organisations are not isolated entities. Organisations exist within a wider community of actors. Such communities generate a distinct form of value that is not so easily measured in monetary terms. This form of intangible value is known as social capital. For instance, managers spend a considerable amount of time networking. This is because a manager's **social network** is a particularly valuable resource for the individual. For instance, studies of personal careers shows that the higher one moves up the managerial hierarchy the more important are social networks to promotional prospects.

Social network: a network of people joined together by social relations

For centuries people have argued over the term community and its key features. It is fruitful to consider the issue of community from the point of view of social networks. Consider Figure 7.3, which bears a resemblance to images produced by social networking sites such as Facebook. In a similar manner to the exchange network illustrated earlier, in this figure we have represented individuals as circles and links as double-arrowed lines. Suppose each line in this network is taken to represent a relationship of friendship. Hence, in network 1 the line between individual A and individual B indicates that A is a friend of B, and vice versa. This is because, unlike an exchange relation, that is asymmetric, a friendship relation is symmetric. When you exchange something with somebody else you pass on value from yourself to that someone. When you are a friend of someone however, that someone is also your friend.

In examining the two networks in Figure 7.3 the individuals considered remain the same, but a transformation occurs between networks 1 and 2. More people are connected together through friendship in network 2 than in network 1. Suppose we also overlay relationships of trust, collaboration and cooperation on these networks. In a community we would expect the

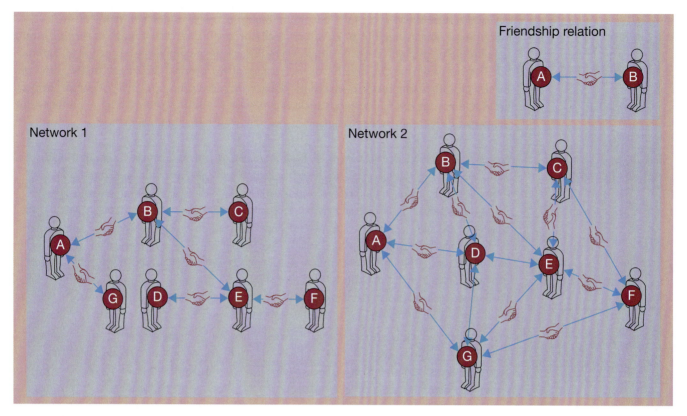

Figure 7.3 *Social networks*

connectivity – a measure of the inter-connectedness of the nodes in a network – in all four types of social network to be high. Hence, in Figure 7.3 network 2 is closer to most definitions of a community than network 1.

In recent literature, authors have argued that communities generate value just like organisations and hence it becomes possible to consider a chain of value that a community generates. However, the value of a community lies not in its physical or financial capital but in its social capital. The American sociologist Robert Putnam (2000) defines social capital as being '*features of social organisation such as networks, norms and trust that facilitate coordination and cooperation for mutual benefit*'.

Capital is traditionally defined as the financial assets available to a company. It is hence a key resource for production. In contrast, **social capital** is the productive value of people engaged in a dense network of social relations. Social capital consists of those features of social organisation, such as networks of secondary associations and high levels of interpersonal trust and reciprocity, which act as resources for individuals and facilitate collective action. Therefore, it is argued, a community rich in social capital is more likely to possess effective civic institutions and more likely to be effective at maintaining law and order.

This is similar in conception to, so-called, Metcalfe's law in relation to the value of a communication network. Metcalfe's law (proposed by the communication engineer Robert Metcalfe) states that the value of a communication network to a particular user of that network is proportional to the square of the number of users of the system (n^2). In Chapter 2 we used this notion to define the variety of a system as a network. The concept of variety in this sense and the density or inter-connectedness of a social network is related as a maximum to the number of unique connections in the network ($n*(n-1)/2$). Hence, in the networks in Figure 7.3 there are 6 actors. If every actor was related to every other actor through a relationship of friendship there would be ($6*(5)/2$) links which equals 15 links. Network 1 has 6 links while network 2 has 13 links. So network 2 is 2 links short of the variety of this network.

Social capital: a feature of social networks that facilitates coordination and cooperation amongst actors

Hence Metcalfe, and to a certain extent Putnam, propose that the variety of a social network is linked to the amount of social capital generated. The value of a communication network to the user is a function of its variety. For example, a single mobile phone is useless. The value of a mobile phone increases with the total number of mobile phones in the network because the total number of people with whom each user may send and receive messages increases. Likewise, in a social network the value of the social network to the individual is a function of the variety of the network. The more connected a person is to others in a community the more resources she is able to draw upon in collective action.

A scene from the classic movie *Witness* demonstrates the power of social capital. The Amish community, who are the backdrop to the story, come together to build a large wooden barn in one day. People contribute their labour for free in the expectation that this will be returned or reciprocated when they need to call upon the collective resources of the community at some future point.

However, the value of a social network does not directly correspond with its density or connectedness. Of equal importance is the quality of links in the network. A common theme in the literature on social capital and community is that changes towards the mass globalisation and urbanisation of society have led to a decline in community and hence a consequent decline in social capital. This supposes that not only are social networks in the modern age less dense or more widely dispersed, but that the links in such networks are in some sense less binding.

For example, trust between human beings is normally developed over time as individuals (actors) gain confidence in the reliability of the performance of other actors through interaction. Social capital rests on the transitivity of trust as a human relationship: A trusts C because B trusts C and A trusts B (Figure 7.4). This allows large social networks to exhibit trust without there necessarily being close contact between particular individuals.

DID YOU KNOW? The idea of mapping social networks has been popular in disciplines like sociology for decades. It is only recently with the rise of, so-called, social media that such research methods have been employed in understanding the role communication technology plays within generating social capital.

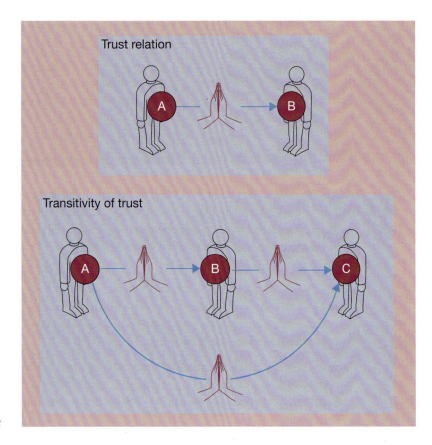

Figure 7.4 *Transitivity of trust*

Strong link: a relationship between two actors in regular contact with each other

Weak link: a relationship between two actors in irregular contact

The sociologist Mark Granovetter (1973) distinguishes between two forms of tie or link in a social network: **strong links** and **weak links**. Strong links exist between people who are regularly in contact and who share much in common. Hence, strong links typically exist between close friends, work colleagues or family members. Weak links exist between people in irregular contact, such as between acquaintances, business contacts and distant friends. Strong links are particularly important in support networks, particularly in the early and later stages of life. Weak links deliver new social and economic opportunities.

More recently it has been proposed that technology, particularly ICT, can be important to maintaining social networks of both strong and weak links. In the Information Society a large proportion of interaction between individuals is conducted remotely using forms of ICT. It is therefore proposed that this remote interaction may become more and more critical to the maintenance of strong links in social networks. Because of the location-independence of remote communication, the size and scope of weak links within social networks may also grow.

So why are businesses interested in social networks? The main reason is that the social capital embedded in social networks and its emergent effects, such as increased trust amongst the members of such networks, may become increasingly important to company activity, particularly sales. This is because there is an inherent association between networks of friendship and networks of trust. Generally speaking, you are more likely to trust your friends than acquaintances. For instance, you are more likely to trust a recommendation received for a particular product or service from a friend than a stranger. Businesses have known for some time of the part social networks play in the positive reporting of goods and services and the relationship this has to growth in sales. Many organisations have therefore attempted to foster what we shall refer to as adjunct communities, online social networks associated with a particular business activity. Organisations have also attempted to exploit the connections in such social networks to conduct, so-called, viral marketing. This is based upon the idea that word-of-mouth recommendations can travel through a social network in much the same way as viruses travel through epidemics (see Chapter 8).

CASE CHECK
The movie industry

The digital nature of movie content opens up its potential for marketing using social networks. For instance, movie companies now release snippets of movie content on social networking sites such as YouTube. This is seen as a means of stimulating interest, in the hope that recommendations to view such content will travel along the links in trusted social networks. Some movie producers have even experimented with the use of such sites to allow possible consumers to engage in the design of the eventual content, for example, in gaining feedback on the attractiveness of particular plot-lines. It is therefore no surprise to find big players in the movie industry investing in these new marketing channels.

RECAP: The primary environment of any commercial organisation is the economy. Economies are systems or networks for the exchange of value. Economies consist of systems not only of value production but also of value distribution and value consumption. An organisation's value is hence determined by its position within a wider value network.

Typically, the value associated with an organisation equates with the services and/or products provided by the organisation. However, value also emerges from dispersed forms of organisation evident in wider social networks. Such forms of value relate to social capital; the resources for mutual support available in forms of community. Social capital is the key value that members gain from participation in such social networks.

Goods and services can be distinguished in a number of ways. We have been particularly interested in the materiality of such goods and services. Tangible goods and services have a physical form. Intangible goods and services have a non-physical form and hence are amenable to representation as data.

7.4   Value-chain and value network

Value-chain: a defined set of activities that deliver value to the customer

Porter offers a template for considering an organisation's key activity systems in terms of the concept of value. This is a generic model of an organisation known as the **value-chain**. In this view organisations are seen as social institutions that produce and deliver value to customers through defined activities. The activities or processes in Porter's value-chain are modelled on an ideal manufacturing organisation, for instance, Goronwy Galvanising which we considered in previous chapters. However, these key activity systems can be adapted to service organisations.

An organisation's value-chain is therefore a series of interdependent activity systems that, in combination, deliver products and/or services to a customer. According to Michael Porter, such activities are of two types: primary and secondary activities. Primary activities constitute the core competencies of the organisation. Secondary activities are important to the successful operation of primary activities.

Primary activities: activities that constitute the core competencies of some organisation

In Porter's ideal type of organisation **primary activities** in the value-chain consist of the following:

- Inbound logistics: this process involves the receiving and storage of raw material needed by a company to produce its products. It also involves the associated activity of distributing relevant raw material to manufacturing premises.
- Operations: this would traditionally be called production or manufacturing. It involves transforming inputs (raw materials) into finished products.
- Outbound logistics: this involves the storage of finished products in warehouses and the distribution of finished products to the customer.
- Marketing and sales: marketing is the process of planning and executing the conception, pricing, promotion and distribution of ideas, goods and services to create exchanges that satisfy individual and organisational goals. Sales as a function is the associated activity involved in the management of customer purchasing activities.
- After-sales service: these are services that maintain or enhance product value by attempting to promote a continuing relationship with the customer. After-sales may involve such activities as the installation, testing, maintenance and repair of products.

Secondary activities: activities that are critical to supporting primary activities

Secondary activities consist of the following:

- Infrastructure activities: these are support activities for the entire value-chain, such as general management, finance, accounting, legal services and quality management.
- Human resource management: this involves the recruiting, hiring, training and development of employees of a company.
- Technology development: this involves the activities of designing and improving the product and its associated manufacturing process. Traditionally, it would be called the research and development function.
- Procurement: is the process of purchasing goods and services from suppliers at an acceptable quality and price and with reliable delivery.

REFLECT: Does the value-chain model cover all the activity systems discussed in Chapter 4 for the typical business?

7.4.1   Value network

Value network: the network of actors within which an organisation sits and with which the organisation exchanges value

Porter's notion of the value-chain focuses on the internal processes or activity systems of an organisation. However, the organisation as a system exists within a wider environment of both cooperation and competition. For the business organisation this primarily consists of the economic environment. An economic system consists of the way in which groups of humans arrange their material provisioning; it essentially involves the coordination of activities concerned with such provisioning amongst multiple business actors.

Three major forms of activity are relevant to all economic systems: production, distribution and consumption. *Production* is that set of activities concerned with the creation of goods and services for human existence. *Distribution* is the associated process of collecting, storing and moving goods into the hands of consumers and providing services for consumers. *Consumption* is the process by which consumers receive and use goods and services.

Production, distribution and consumption are activities that deliver value. Hence, economies can be seen as consisting of a multitude of chains of value both within and between economic actors. This means that economic actors inter-relate and interact in complex networks of value production, distribution and consumption. A particular economic actor will take on roles within a number of different chains of value within such networks. This means that organisations may be both buyers of goods and services and sellers of goods and services. Organisations may both compete with other organisations in the sale of particular goods and services as well as cooperate in the delivery of goods and services to particular customers.

Take Goronwy Galvanising. This company is a producer of galvanised goods which it sells to its customers. Blackwalls is its major customer, which means that Goronwy is a supplier for Blackwalls. But Goronwy also has its own suppliers such as those companies which supply it with zinc. For such companies Goronwy is a major customer.

CASE CHECK
The movie industry

Consider the movie industry in this manner. The movement of movies onto digital formats has affected the production, distribution and consumption of movies. In terms of distribution, traditional channels involve the use of cinemas and broadcast television channels to provide controlled access to movie content. The movement of movies onto digital format opened up new avenues for distribution of this content, particularly via DVD. It is a short step from the DVD to offering access to such content via electronic delivery channels over the Internet. There is every reason to expect that consumers will want increasing access to movie content online just as they currently access music, newspapers, television and radio.

7.4.2　Customer chain and supply chain

Supply chain: the set of activities between an organisation takes in relation to its suppliers

Customer chain: the set of activities that are involved in the delivery of value to the customer of the organisation

Two other chains of value flow are critical to the competitive environment and assume some significance for most commercial organisations: the **supply chain** and the **customer chain**. They are both chains of value flow in the sense that both customers and suppliers will typically be other organisations, who in turn will have relationships and engage in activities with further organisations. Hence, an economic system will be composed of a complex network of such chains and we refer to this as the wider value network.

The *supply chain* for a typical business is illustrated in Figure 7.5. The broad arrows on the diagram indicate the flow of goods and services between organisations. On the diagram we distinguish between direct suppliers one step removed in the supply chain and indirect suppliers two or more steps removed in the supply chain. Indirect suppliers are sometimes referred to as channel organisations or *intermediaries*. Typical intermediaries include warehousing companies, independent wholesalers, retailers and distributors.

The *customer chain* is the demand chain of the business. Figure 7.6 illustrates the customer chain of a typical organisation. Within these chains we can distinguish between local customers in an organisation's immediate marketplace and export customers in some form of global marketplace. For both forms of customers, but particularly in the global marketplace, forms of channel organisation or intermediary (such as distributors and retailers) may mediate between an organisation and its customers.

Clearly the shape of the value network, including the supply and customer chains, will vary depending upon the type of industry an organisation is in. In Figure 7.7 we illustrate three value-chains from different industrial sectors. In automobile manufacturing components are produced both by subsidiaries of the major car manufacturers and by external component suppliers. Such components are used to assemble cars, which are passed on to the dealer network, which sells cars to consumers. In food retail foodstuffs are supplied to supermarkets

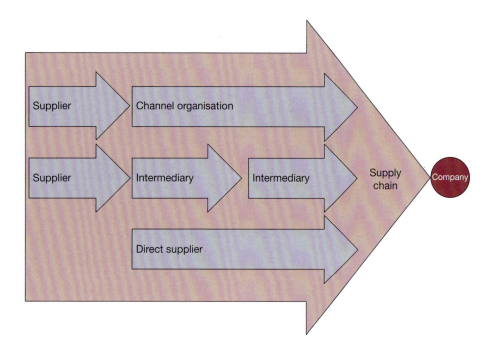

Figure 7.5 *The supply chain*

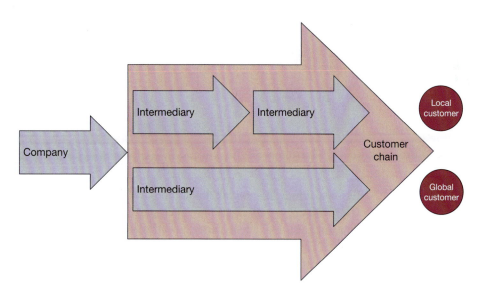

Figure 7.6 *The customer chain*

from warehouses and foodstuff suppliers and are sold on to the consumer. Within insurance there is little in the way of a supply chain. Insurance products are sold on to consumers via agents and brokers.

7.4.3 Community chain and partnership chain

The supply and customer chains define the immediate external environment for organisations and help define commerce or trade. However, one might argue that such chains overlap with two other frequently ignored chains of value of increasing significance to most organisations: the **community chain** and the **partnership chain**.

The *community chain*, as we have argued previously, is founded on social networks of individuals. The value of the community chain lies in its ability to generate social capital: the productive value of people engaged in a dense network of social relations. One indicator of high social capital is a high level of interpersonal trust in a social network. This is an increasingly important prerequisite for many forms of business and commerce.

Community chain: the chain of social networks within which the organisation sits

Partnership chain: the chain of activities conducted with partners in delivering value to a common customer

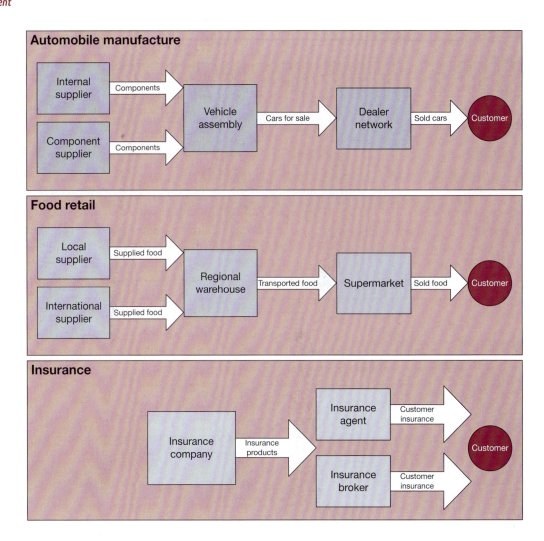

Figure 7.7 *Value networks*

Many modern companies also conduct trade or commerce in networks of partnerships. This is because participation in such partnership networks reduces costs and risks of operation for business. For instance, an airline might partner with both a car hire company and a hotel chain. Each member of the partnership network agrees to promote the goods and services of the other organisations in the network and may also share customer data to facilitate this. The key advantage of participation for the organisation in the partnership network is the ability to provide increased value to the customer. This in turn is likely to improve both customer acquisition and customer retention for the companies involved in the partnership.

7.4.4   Intermediation, disintermediation and re-intermediation

Intermediation: the process by which intermediate actors establish themselves within the value network

Disintermediation: the process by which intermediaries are removed from parts of the value network

Aspects of the external value-chains of organisations have been critically affected by the creation of electronic markets. As we have seen, the traditional retail value network is one of wholesalers, distributors and retailers. However, by using the Internet and applications built using the World Wide Web, producers can now sell directly to their customers. This process is known as **disintermediation** in the sense that intermediaries are removed from the customer chain. But the Internet and Web suffer from being large and complex mediums for supporting a market. Potential customers for particular products and services frequently find it difficult to find the precise company meeting their needs. Hence, in recent times a new breed of intermediaries, electronic, has emerged. Such organisations reimpose middlemen between the producers of products and services and their consumers. They supply a service to the consumer in locating companies fulfilling their needs and they supply a service to the producer in identifying potential customers. This process is known as re-intermediation.

CASE CHECK

The movie industry

Changes are taking place in many content industries, such as the movie industry, all founded on the process of digital convergence. Digital convergence is the process, occurring on a global scale, of media converging around representation in a restricted range of digital formats. This allows interoperability of a number of technologies, particularly what we referred to in Chapter 5 as access devices. The increasing availability of technologies for managing movie content in digital form is leading to profound changes in the value network for this industry: the production, distribution and consumption of movies.

The value network for the current movie industry is illustrated in Figure 7.8. A movie production company creates a movie, either under the umbrella of a film studio or as an independent. This movie then has to be taken up and distributed by a number of different types of distributor. These are intermediaries in the movie value network. Traditionally, the movie would be played for a set period in selected cinemas, perhaps owned by major cinema chains. A short time after this the movie would be released on DVD for distribution by video rental companies. More recently, the movie will be offered for digital download or for watching via a videostreaming service.

The conventional method of making a movie involves a sequence of three processes: pre-production, shooting and post-production. Pre-production involves performative activities such as establishing production schedules, establishing budgets, obtaining permits, hiring staff and purchasing equipment. Shooting involves the actual capture of pictures onto storage media using capture technology on and off set. Post-production involves the editing of movie content, including adding effects, music and other audio.

For movie companies, the whole process of production is a costly exercise because production staff, and particularly actors, are expensive. Studio space and the traditional equipment used to shoot and edit movies are also expensive. Filming certain scenes, such as action and stunt scenes, can prove particularly costly. With digital format, in terms of production, the cost of producing movies potentially decreases. For instance, the equipment required to produce high quality movie content in terms of capture and editing has decreased substantially. The use of computer generated imagery (CGI) has reduced the costs of producing action and stunt scenes. This means that potential barriers to entry are lowered, meaning that new producers could enter the industry.

Distribution involves traditionally 'printing' the movie onto a storage medium, as well as shipping and marketing the movie. These processes used to cost distribution companies many millions of US dollars. For this reason, the release of movie content was tightly controlled in a windowing sequence of cinemas first, then DVD for rental and release to pay-per-view television channels, then DVD for purchase and finally release to broadcast television.

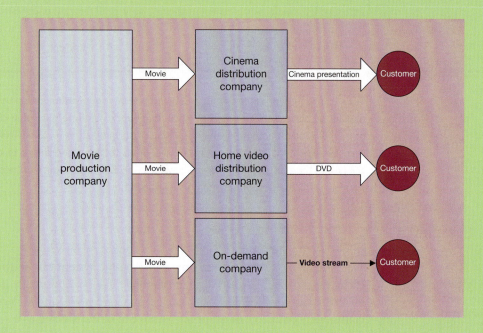

Figure 7.8 *Movie value networks*

CASE CHECK
The movie industry
(continued)

The introduction of digital projection equipment into cinemas has been undertaken not only to improve the quality of the projection itself but also to reduce distribution costs. Digital content can be transmitted electronically to cinemas around the world for a fraction of physical distribution costs. Potential supply-chain savings of billions of US dollars have been estimated in digital content submission to cinemas. The cost of storage of film content is also much reduced. For such reasons, the movie companies themselves have made a heavy investment in digital projection equipment in cinemas. However, this has meant that the movie producers wish to recoup their investment from the conventional delivery channels of cinema release before any new access channels such as movie streaming are considered. Successful films clearly allow the film industry to recoup their investment quickly. However, the film industry point to a vast number of other films making a considerable loss.

We mentioned above that the movement of movies onto digital format also opens up new avenues for distribution and consumption, such as video download and video streaming. As digital content, movies are normally considered as a form of data known as video. The term video is used to refer to a number of commonly used storage formats for moving pictures. As data, video can be delivered in one of two ways. The consumer can request the whole of the video file which is delivered over a communication network to an access device, such as a personal computer. The film is then stored on the access device and can be played at some later date. Alternatively, the video may be delivered as a continuous stream of data to the access device over the communication network. The video is not stored on the access device but is played at the point of access.

A number of websites now offer access to movie content, either as video downloads or as video streams. However, film producers and distributors have been slow to adopt these new business models both because of the risk they takes in film production and because, until quite recently, there was little incentive to move from a lucrative DVD market. Many now believe that DVD sales may have reached their peak and that the movie industry will need to investigate new ways of making revenue.

There are a number of key advantages to the online distribution of movie content. One key advantage is that movie producers and distributors can release their whole back-catalogue of content for the consumer to access. They can also distribute such content through a variety of what we shall refer to as access channels: direct to home movies on demand, via conventional satellite/cable into the home, via P2P sharing or IP television. Promoters of online distribution also point to the potential that digital movie content has for providing an added-value service to the consumer, such as increased interactivity with, and personalisation of, the content. Some have argued that once people are able to easily buy or rent films on demand over data communication networks, the chances are that they will pay for and watch more movie content.

Others have raised the difficulties posed to the distribution of movie content over the Internet, particularly the increasing potential for digital piracy. Until recently, online piracy cost the movie industry less than physical copying of DVDs. However, the gap seems to be diminishing and some see this trend undermining key revenue models for movie producers. It is even seen by some as possibly contributing to the demise of the movie industry as we know it.

RECAP: The flow of value within and between the organisation and external stakeholders defines a number of distinctive elements of a value network. The internal value-chain is made up of a series of interdependent activity systems. Linking the organisation to its environment are the supply chain, through which goods and services are delivered to the organisation to enable it to function effectively, and the customer chain, through which its value is distributed. The community chain consists of networks of individuals surrounding an organisation.

7.5   Commerce

Commerce: that process which deals with the exchange of goods and services between actors

We outlined in earlier sections how an economic system can be considered a system for the exchange of value between diverse economic actors. **Commerce** is the term normally used for that process which deals with the exchange of goods and services from producer to final consumer. Commerce of whatever nature can be considered as a system or process with the following generic phases of activity: pre-sale, sale execution, sale settlement and after-sale. *Pre-sale* involves activities occurring before a sale. *Sale execution* consists of the activities involved in the actual sale of a product or service between economic actors. *Sale settlement* involves those activities that complete the sale of product or service. Finally, *after-sale* involves those activities that take place after the buyer has received the product or service.

Consider the process of buying a book from a bookseller. Pre-sale activity might include the marketing of particular books though inclusion in various online and printed catalogues. Sale execution clearly involves the purchase of the book by a customer. The customer may be an organisation, in which case, it is likely that sale settlement will occur through a process in which the bookseller invoices the organisation and the purchaser makes payment at some later date. After-sale service may include site visits by sales personnel to particular educational institutions and perhaps initiatives such as discounting particular book lines.

The precise form of this generic process of commerce will vary depending on the economic actors involved, the nature of the goods or services being exchanged and the frequency of commerce between the economic actors.

Generally speaking we may distinguish between organisational actors and individual actors. In terms of organisational actors we may distinguish between private sector or commercial organisations, public sector organisations and other not-for-profit organisations, such as voluntary organisations.

The most important feature of a product or service is typically its price. We may distinguish between low-price items, low- to medium-price items, medium- to high-price items and high-price items. As considered in previous sections, another important distinction of relevance to eBusiness is whether the goods are tangible or intangible: tangible goods being those that have a physical existence; intangible goods those that are fundamentally information-based.

So commerce may involve different types of goods and services. There are also three major patterns of the frequency of commerce. **Repeat commerce** is the pattern in which regular, repeat transactions occur between trading partners. **Credit commerce** is where irregular transactions occur between trading partners and the processes of settlement and execution are separated. **Cash commerce** occurs when irregular transactions of a one-off nature are conducted between economic actors. In cash commerce the processes of execution and settlement are typically combined.

Cash commerce for low- and standard-price goods typically follows the four stages of the generic commerce model quite closely. For medium- to high-price items some form of credit commerce will operate. In other words, organisations will search for a product, negotiate a price, order a product, receive delivery of the product, be invoiced for the product, pay for the product and receive some form of after-sales service. For high-price and customised goods traded between organisations some form of repeat commerce model operates. The same processes occur as for credit commerce but the processes cycle around indefinitely in a trusted relationship between producer and consumer. These three forms of commerce are illustrated in Figure 7.9.

Most purchases of small items over the Internet occur in cash commerce mode. For example, the purchase of foodstuffs from an

Repeat commerce: the pattern in which regular, repeat transactions occur between trading partners

Credit commerce: where irregular transactions occur between trading partners and the processes of settlement and execution are separated.

Cash commerce: the exchange of low-price goods in irregular exchange between actors

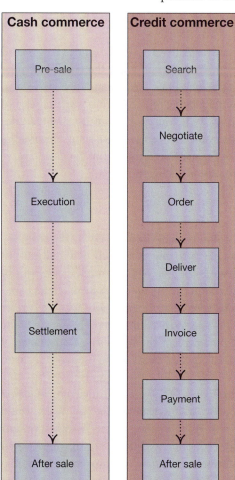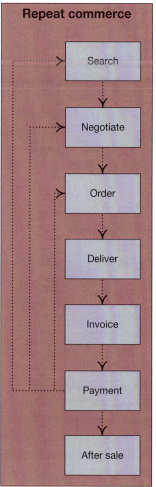

Figure 7.9 Forms of commerce

online supermarket chain by members of the general public commonly occurs as a form of cash commerce. In contrast, companies in established relationships tend to work with either a credit or repeat commerce model. Hence, a major supermarket chain will normally place a repeat order with a processed food supplier and will pay this supplier on a regular basis after invoicing by the supplier.

7.6   Transactions and coordination costs

Associated with the flow of any goods and services between business actors, in relation to exchange, is a corresponding flow of transactional data. As we have already seen, a transaction is fundamentally a set of formative acts (Chapter 2), operating upon one or more data structures, which serves to record some coherent unit of activity, typically an event within or between activity systems.

Data is needed to support not only the internal communicative and performative activity of organisations but also the exchanges between organisations and individuals in various forms of commerce. Transactions are hence critical to the recording of organisational activity past, current and future. Transactions typically write data to the data structures of a data system; such data is then used within information systems for the measurement of organisational performance.

A customer sales order is a crucial transaction for most commercial organisations. A customer sales order effectively amounts to the representation of what we called a directive communicative act in Chapter 2. It amounts to an instruction from the customer to the organisation, which details the good or service desired for a nominated price. For instance, when you order a book from Amazon you are effectively directing Amazon to deliver a copy of this good to you in return for a payment.

In practice, this sales transaction will trigger a create formative act, which writes a new record to a sales order file. This record acts as a collective memory of who made the order, when the order was made, for what goods or services and in what quantities. Such records are also critical for triggering other performative activities, such as the picking of goods from warehouses and the distribution of goods to customers. It is also likely to be important to measuring the sales performance of the company. Hence, each exchange event between business actors generates a transaction. As well as records which keep details of the order and transfer of goods and services, one of the most prominent types of transaction type is that of payments.

7.6.1   Coordination costs

One of the key questions that has concerned economics for many decades is why the economy is populated by a number of business firms, instead of consisting exclusively of a multitude of independent, self-employed people who contract with one another in complex networks of exchange, which is what classical economics would predict as the natural state of affairs based upon models of supply and demand. Transaction costs, or what we shall more accurately refer to as **coordination costs**, are critical to providing answers to this question of the nature of the firm. Coordination costs also, as we shall see, help to explain the increasing importance of ICT to commerce and the ways in which such technology can and is being used to transform economic systems.

Coordination cost: a cost incurred in making an economic exchange

The economist Ronald Coase, back in the 1930s (Coase, 1937), used the idea of *transaction costs*, or coordination costs, to develop a theory as to when certain economic tasks would be performed by firms and when they would be performed by the market. A transaction or coordination cost is a cost incurred in making an economic exchange. For example, when buying or selling a financial security a commission is normally paid to a broker; the commission is a coordination cost of undertaking a deal on the stock market. Or consider purchasing a textbook. The costs of such a purchase not only include the price of the book itself but also the energy and effort expended in finding the most appropriate textbook, for the most appropriate price, from the most convenient bookselling outfit.

Hence, Coase noted that there are a number of coordination costs to using any exchange network for the trading of goods and services. Firms attempt to balance production costs against coordination costs. Production costs include the processes necessary to create and distribute goods and services. Coordination, or transaction, costs include the costs of information and data processing (communication and representation) necessary to coordinate the work of people and machines.

This idea he used to suggest that firms will occur when they can arrange to produce what they need internally and thus reduce their coordination costs. This theory has also been used to attempt to explain why firms engage in relationships with other firms and what form such relationships take. This is fundamentally an issue of how the organisation controls its activities: does it perform them in-house or does it farm them out to other organisations in the wider value network?

> **DID YOU KNOW?** It has been estimated that as much as 25% of the healthcare budget in a country like the United Kingdom goes on transaction or coordination costs.

CASE CHECK

The movie industry

The movie industry can be considered to consist of a complex assemblage of business actors (not restricted to dramatic actors) including: film production companies, suppliers of cinematography equipment, specialist pre-production and post-production personnel, film directors, dramatic actors and other film personnel. This list does not include a vast range of potential movie distributors. During the 1940s and 1950s the Hollywood movie industry was dominated by a number of large studios. These studios pulled as many of the activities of the movie industry as they could in-house. This enabled them to better control their activities, both in terms of the costs of production and the coordination of the numerous people and activities involved. However, the modern movie industry, partly in response to technological change, consists of a much more diverse network of actors. A number of Hollywood studios still exist but large centres of film-making also exist in India, Hong Kong and Nigeria. The value network in the movie industry is now much more diverse and globally distributed.

RECAP: All kinds of commerce can be considered as a system or process with the phases of pre-sale, sale execution, sale settlement and after sale. The precise format varies depending on the nature of the economic actors involved, the frequency of their commerce and the nature of the goods or services.

Associated with the flow of both tangible and intangible goods and services is a corresponding flow of transactions. A transaction is a data structure that records some coherent unit of activity, typically an event within or between activity systems. Organisations incur transaction or coordination costs, costs incurred in making an economic exchange.

7.7   Control in the value network

The upshot of conceiving of organisations as value-creating systems raises the critical question of what activities the organisation itself needs to perform in-house and what activities it can outsource to other organisations. If the organisation decides to outsource activities it also needs to decide how it will manage or govern the interaction with other organisations. These questions therefore revolve around the issue of how to control parts of the value network.

This means that it is possible to see the design of the value network of a particular organisation as a response to the issue of control which we considered in Chapter 2. As we have argued in previous sections, a wider economy can be considered as a system, or network, of exchange. Within such networks of exchange, ways have to be found of controlling the flow of value (goods and services) amongst a multitude of business actors. It is useful to define two polar types of such control which are referred to in the literature as managerial hierarchies and markets. These forms are actually two poles of a dimension which help define a range of intermediate forms of control evident in actual value networks. These types of economic control process are important for understanding why various parts of the value network, such as supply chains, develop as they do. They also help us understand how both existing forms of eBusiness are formed in particular ways as well as the value of emerging forms of eBusiness (Chapter 8).

7.7.1   Hierarchies

Managerial hierarchy: organisations coordinate the flow of value by controlling and directing it at a higher level in management structures

Hierarchies, or more accurately **managerial hierarchies**, are a logical extension of the firm itself (Figure 7.10). Hierarchies coordinate the flow of value by controlling and directing it at a higher level in management structures. In hierarchies, order is designed and consciously organised to achieve outcomes. This is the traditional form of control exercised within and between public sector organisations. In government this typically constitutes bureaucratic control since behaviour is very much governed by rules and procedures. In hierarchies, the mechanisms of operation involve bureaucratic monitoring and interventions and, as such, hierarchies demonstrate overt, planned, purposeful governance.

Simplistically, hierarchies can be seen as typical systems of cooperation. A managerial hierarchy is a medium for exchanges between a limited number of buyers and sellers and the buyers and sellers exchange goods and services within established patterns of trade. For example, a car manufacturer is likely to establish a managerial hierarchy for control of relationships with its major component suppliers. Hence, hierarchies form the cooperative environment of organisations and, typically because of the established nature of relationships between economic actors, they rely on smaller volumes of communication and associated data flow than is the case in terms of markets (see below).

Most companies have established trading relationships with a limited number of suppliers; as such these relationships are traditionally managed in terms of managerial hierarchies. Hence, an automobile manufacturer is likely to build established trading relationships with a limited range of component suppliers. It is also likely to distribute its products through a specialised network of dealerships. Hence, both the supply chain and the customer chain within traditional automobile manufacture will be organised as a series of hierarchies. Within the movie industry a production company will normally interact with a limited range of suppliers such as equipment suppliers and agents of actors.

7.7.2   Markets

Market: a medium for exchanges between buyers and sellers

Markets coordinate the flow of value through forces of supply and demand and external transactions between actors in some exchange relationship (Figure 7.11). In markets, order is

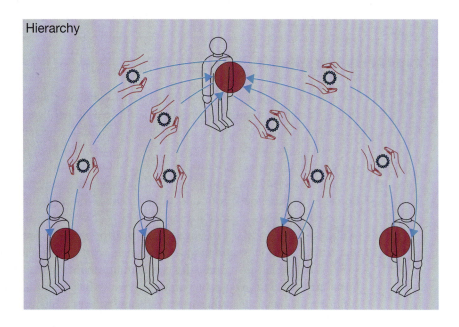

Hierarchy

Figure 7.10 *A managerial hierarchy*

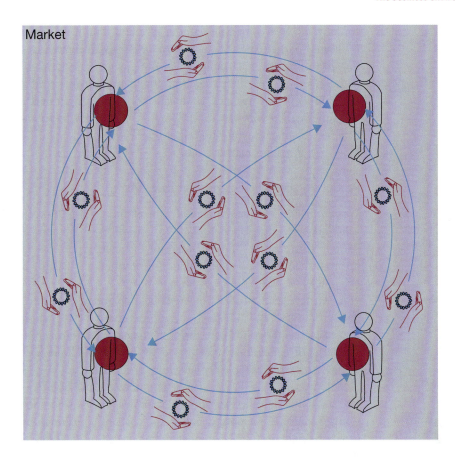

Figure 7.11 *A market*

not pre-defined; it develops or emerges from spontaneously generated outcomes. This is the form of control seen as typical in the private sector since, in markets, behaviour arises from private competitive decisions. Within markets operations are governed by price, competition and self-interest. Hence, markets do not display any overt form of governance. Instead, governance is implicit and emergent rather than planned.

Put simply, markets are typically systems of competition. A market is a medium for exchanges between many potential buyers and many potential sellers and, at least for larger companies, a series of markets forms the immediate competitive environment of the organisation. However, because of its many-to-many nature a market is heavily reliant on large volumes of data and communication flow. Participation in markets traditionally generates a large amount of, what we referred to above as, transaction costs for a company.

One of the crucial markets for financial companies is the stock market. The stock market is a market for the exchange of shares and other forms of securities. Companies trade shares through financial intermediaries to a vast range of financial consumers, many of whom will be other companies. The price of a particular company share is determined by the forces of supply and demand. In other words, the more demand for a particular security, the higher its price. The movie industry also partakes in a number of markets. For instance, it sells its movies to cinema chains, distributors of DVDs and, more recently, to online video on-demand operations.

7.7.3   Value networks

We have deliberately used the word network in terms such as social network, the value network and exchange network because such networks can be seen as a model of control that accommodates both market structures and managerial hierarchies. The value network of a particular company, for instance, is likely to involve both cooperation and competition with other business actors.

Many modern companies conduct trade or commerce in networks of partnerships. This is because participation in such partnership networks reduces the costs and risks of operation to businesses. Each member of the partnership network agrees to promote the goods and services of the other organisations in the network and may also share customer data in the process. For instance, a supermarket chain might partner with a financial institution. The supermarket will offer incentives to its customers to purchase nominated financial products. The financial institution might offer retail vouchers or discounts to its customers to be redeemed in a supermarket store.

7.7.4   Production costs and coordination costs

We can bring together the idea of control and transaction costs to help us understand how value networks develop as they do for a particular company and what influence technology plays in this process. Malone et al., for instance, argue that markets and hierarchies can be distinguished in terms of the balance of production costs to coordination (transaction) costs (Malone et al., 1987).

Production cost: the cost of producing something

As we have seen, **production costs** include the processes necessary to create and distribute goods and services. Coordination, or transaction, costs include the costs of the communication necessary to coordinate the work of people and machines. As we have argued above, markets are generally characterised by low production and high coordination costs. In contrast, hierarchies typically have high production and low coordination costs.

Malone et al. argued in the 1980s that increased use of ICT would stimulate a trend towards electronic markets and electronic hierarchies. They also argued for the dominance of market forms because ICT would decrease the costs of coordination and would enable companies to increasingly personalise goods and services; thus enabling them to better handle issues of product complexity and asset specificity.

More recently, Don Tapscott and Anthony Williams (2006) have proposed that the Internet and the Web is critically changing the logic of the firm. The presence of such technological infrastructure is forcing a decline not only in transaction costs but also in the costs of production. They attribute the latter to the growth in collaborative production facilitated by technologies built upon the global communication infrastructure.

So-called open source software production is a case in point. Open source software is produced by a large network of collaborating software developers. They infer from this that network forms of governance and control in economic systems will begin to overtake traditional hierarchy and market forms over the first quarter of the twenty-first century.

DID YOU KNOW? The ways in which public sector organisations control their services has changed in many countries. Traditionally, public sector organisations managed the provision of services through hierarchical control of their own activities. In recent years private sector organisations have been introduced to areas of service provision such as buildings maintenance and education. This means that aspects of competitive behaviour have been introduced into what had traditionally been a system based upon cooperation and collaboration.

RECAP: An economy is a system that controls the flow of goods and services along chains of value in three possible ways: hierarchies, markets and networks. Hierarchies are a logical extension of the firm itself, and coordinate the flow of value by controlling and directing it at a higher level in management structures. Markets coordinate the flow of value through forces of supply and demand, and external transactions between actors in an exchange relationship. Networks are a mediating form of coordination and governance between hierarchies and markets.

7.8   Business models

Business model: an organisation's core logic for creating value

The concept of a **business model** has become popular in recent times as a way of thinking about business change; particularly as such change incorporates some form of technological innovation. We would argue that the business model concept implicitly uses a model of the organisation based on the idea of an open, value-creating system. This means that the patterns of organisation that produce particular forms of value are not fixed. Open systems can be designed and it is in this light that the concept of business models is frequently discussed.

Therefore, we would argue that there are clear similarities between the concept of a business model and that of a value-creating system. To refresh, according to this view, organisations are conceived of as chains of activity systems associated with the production and dissemination of value which, in their entirety, can be portrayed as value-creating systems. Such value-creating systems have to manage not only their internal operations but also their relationships with other business actors within the wider value network.

As such, a business model can be considered the organisation's core logic for creating value. The business model idea, as we shall see, is useful in relating business strategy to activity systems, to information systems, to ICT systems. The pre-supposition of design implies that a given business has a number of different options in terms of the particular business model it may choose to adopt. With the rise of eBusiness and eCommerce such options multiply. Traditionally, business strategies specify how a particular business model can be applied to a particular industrial sector to improve competitive position. More recently, such strategies must specify relationships with customers, partners and suppliers.

Osterwalder and Pigneur (2010) argue that any business model is built from nine basic building blocks:

- value propositions
- customer segments
- channels
- customer relationships
- revenue streams
- key resources
- key activities
- key partnerships
- cost structure

These building blocks form a canvas for specifying or designing a particular business model. We adapt these building blocks in terms of the theory we have established in this and preceding chapters:

- A business model establishes the value proposition of the organisation. In other words, what does an organisation create, produce or provide?
- Value is created for particular customer segments. In other words, for whom are we creating value?
- Value is distributed to customer segments through access channels. This includes not only the physical delivery of a product or service but also the associated communication with the customer, such as allowing customers to purchase specific products and services as well as providing after-sales support.
- To be successful a business model must propose ways of building and sustaining customer relationships. This implies that it must suggest ways of managing what we shall call processes of customer acquisition and customer retention.
- A particular business model specifies the structure of activity, information and data systems appropriate for a particular business in terms of its environment. A key part of the argument used for adaptive systems is that the model of the business must fit environmental circumstances, it must be founded in its key value-chains and be viable in this environment. Its activities must also be sustainable long term.
- A business model should specify not only the value delivered to customers within the wider value network but also the value it gains from suppliers and partners. To create value for its customers an organisation needs resources from suppliers. It also needs to establish relationships with partnering organisations.
- A business model should specify the major streams of revenue and how the costs of producing value for customers are outweighed sufficiently by such revenue to make the business both viable and sustainable.

CASE CHECK

The movie industry

Let us consider the movie industry in this light. This case demonstrates the way in which ICT is starting to re-structure a major industry. The changes taking place in the movie industry are illustrative of the fact that any technology has opportunities as well as threats for industries. In particular, technology adoption is likely to change business models because of the ways in which it affects the wider value network.

As we have seen above, the traditional value network in the movie industry consists of major film producers, major global distributors and mass consumers. The content (value) along such a network has typically been heavily controlled in a sequence of release to cinema chains, then onto DVD to the rental network and finally for DVD sale to the general public.

For over twenty years the conventional business model for renting movies has been through a physical video, and more lately, DVD rental outlet. These are effectively intermediaries in the distribution of movie content to customers. However, over the last couple of years there has been a significant decline in the amount of exchange activity conducted with such physical rental outlets, partly due to the rise of online DVD rentals, as exemplified by Netflix and LoveFilm. These companies have built new business models for the distribution of DVDs and are progressively establishing yet another business model for the distribution of such content via on-demand video streaming.

LoveFilm, for instance, is a British subsidiary of Amazon.com. It provides a number of services through its website including online DVD rental, DVD direct sales and, more recently, video streaming of movies over the Internet. It provides an online delivery structure for an array of services in a series of partnerships with other companies. In 2011 it claimed to offer over 67,000 movie titles for 1.5 million customers and handled over 4 million rentals per month to customers located in five countries. LoveFilm charges a flat monthly rate for online DVD rental to its customers. Depending on the amount paid, customers receive through the post a number of DVDs which they can keep for as long as they wish. DVDs are returned in pre-paid envelopes to the company. Some members can stream a selected range of movies to their home PCs or to their interactive digital televisions free of charge. Other movies can be streamed on a pay-per-view basis. Netflix is an American company operating a similar business model within the USA and Canada. This company, which was established in 1997, offers over 100,000 titles on DVD to over 10 million subscribers.

RECAP: The concept of a business model can be related to the idea of the organisation as a value-creating system within the wider value network. A business model specifies the design for the organisation, and is a foundation for implementing business processes and information systems. It effectively specifies how the value-chain of the company should operate and fit into its wider value network.

7.9   The analysis of value

`Exploiting opportunities created by technology innovations   IS2010`

Although Porter's original value-chain model has been applied in many different settings, it has also received plenty of criticism. For instance, it is seen as more applicable to physical products than to services; it under-emphasises the role of informatics infrastructure in the delivery of value; it focuses on the internal value-chain to the detriment of the value network.

There is a clear relationship between what we referred to in Chapter 2 as business analysis, the idea of a business model and the concept of the value network. Business analysis can be seen to be that activity devoted to the building of business models, both current and future. Business models need to consist of not only an understanding of the internal value-chain of organisations, but also the current and future position of the organisation within its wider value network.

The idea of the value network is that organisations inter-relate and interact in complex networks of value production, distribution and consumption. A particular organisation will take on roles in a number of different chains of value. ICT can make it possible to deliver value along them more efficiently and effectively. Porter now acknowledges that with the rise of eBusiness certain secondary activities, such as ICT, offer far more than a support role (Porter, 2001). They have become critically embedded within primary activities. To deliver more efficiently and effectively requires organisational change. So the task is to analyse the existing value-chain and see how aspects of it can be redesigned to improve performance. In the wider value network, similarly, the task is to analyse activities and relationships with external stakeholders as preparation for redesigning those aspects of that network that are under the control of a particular organisation.

Conventional value-chain analysis distinguishes between primary activities that relate directly to getting goods and/or services to the customer, and secondary or support activities. Value-chain analysis involves analysing each activity in the value-chain, such as procurement, manufacture, sales and distribution, and identifying ways in which redesign will lead to performance improvement (adding value to customers). Performance can also be improved by redesigning interfaces between the elements: for instance, between sales and outbound logistics.

As we have discussed in this and previous chapters, within modern business there exists a virtual value-chain which parallels the physical value-chain. Here too, we conceive of the value-chain as a series of both physical and non-physical flows. The virtual value-chain consists of information flows, and involves the use of ICT to mediate traditional value-chain activities such as market research, new product development, marketing, procurement, production, and managing selling and fulfilment. Many of these have already been automated to some extent and, with the introduction of newer forms of ICT, many of them could become fully virtual or automated in the near future.

Value-network analysis is an extension of value-chain analysis which focuses on the activities and relationships of the business with external stakeholders. It looks for ways of disaggregating or deconstructing the value network, as well as ways of re-aggregating or reconstructing it. Disaggregation involves segmenting out elements of the value-chain and perhaps outsourcing them to partners. Re-aggregation involves integrating elements of the value-chain to streamline key processes.

Within such analysis there is also the importance of managing the value network of partners, which might result from a reconstruction of the value network. It might include supply side partners, primary activity partners, sell side partners and value-chain integrators. On the supply side, partners are likely to include traditional suppliers (perhaps managed through hierarchies), business-to-business exchanges (managed in market terms) and wholesalers/distributors (perhaps managed in networks). On the sell side, business-to-business exchanges, wholesalers and distributors will also exist alongside traditional customers. Partners may also fulfil certain primary value-chain activities such as inbound logistics. Value-chain integrators are organisations that integrate aspects of the internal and external value-chain for companies. An example is maintaining the informatics infrastructure (see Chapter 11).

A combination of the modelling approaches we have discussed in previous chapters can be used to conduct both value-chain and value-network analyses. Collectively this is called value-stream analysis, and its objective is to improve the efficiency of both internal and external processes, frequently through the application of ICT.

Some stages for value-stream analysis are:

- Identifying in close detail the nature of the value produced by the organisation. Distinctions between tangible and intangible products and services can help highlight potential areas for change.
- Drawing a map of the current value stream. Techniques such as activity systems modelling, process modelling and information systems modelling come in here.
- Conducting an assessment of the existing value stream. This uses criteria such as the three Es of performance (efficacy, efficiency and effectiveness). It should consider ways of improving the performance of activities and the flow of physical goods as well as the flow of information. From modelling it may become possible to identify problems with the value stream such as wastage in activities or delays in information handling.

Value-network analysis: the analysis of the value network appropriate to that organisation

III

- Considering ways of redesigning elements of the value stream to eliminate problems. This may involve looking at the role of intermediaries in supply and customer chains, and deciding whether to disaggregate or re-aggregate. The role of ICT in improving the flow of information and integrating activities needs to be part of this process.
- Defining new value streams, using a model or a series of models.
- Implementing anew value stream. This needs to take into account the scale of change that is both required and feasible. It may involve considerable organisational and technological change, and so the disciplines of project management (see Chapter 11) and change management (see Chapter 12) are likely to be critical to success.

CASE CHECK

Tesco

CS p 455

Let's go back to Tesco. It has relationships with customers and suppliers. Revenue flows into its value-chain from its customers and on to its suppliers. Customers are mainly attracted to supermarkets by a combination of low prices and a large variety of goods on offer. The stores sell large volumes, so the company's business strategy is typically based on low-cost/high-volume operations with low profit margins on each product. Costs are minimised by, for instance, buying in bulk from suppliers and letting customers bear the costs of picking products from shelves, packing them and taking them home. Above all, a supermarket needs to attract plenty of customers to its stores, so their location is critical; they need a good catchment area.

An eCommerce site such as Tesco.com (see Chapter 8) changes the business model. Relationships with customers and suppliers change, as do costs and revenue. For example, it will cost the store if a member of staff takes the order list, walks around the store picking goods, packs them and hands them to a delivery driver who takes them to the customer's home. Many supermarkets, including Tesco, pass on this cost as a delivery charge.

However, with eCommerce it becomes an option to do away with stores entirely. Instead, the goods can be stored in and delivered from low-cost warehouses. So the additional order fulfilment costs can be balanced by lower operational costs (larger range, reduced inventory, larger volume, lower margins). In a slightly different market, this is the business model adopted by Amazon.com.

FOCUS ON VALUE

Michael Porter uses the term value to describe, at a high level, the key output of the business organisation. It also enables him to focus on the processes that produce value, collectively referred to as the internal value-chain. But economies are systems not only of value production but also of value distribution and value consumption. An organisation's value is determined by its position in a wider value network. Typically, the value associated with organisations equates with the services and/or products they provide. However, value also emerges from dispersed forms of organisation evident in social networks. This is related to social capital, the resource for mutual support available in some communities. Social capital is the key value that members gain from participation in social networks.

Our emphasis on design focuses on the options an organisation has to do things differently, not only within its internal value-chain but also in positioning itself in the wider value network. There is key value in the concept of a business model in that it relates issues of strategy, activities and technology.

7.10   Conclusion and key themes

This chapter introduced the concept of value, and its production and distribution. It considered organisations as value-creating systems that interact with a wider value network. They have the option to design their internal activity systems and their relationships and activities with the wider value network to optimise their performance. Information is important for the support of both internal activity and activity with external stakeholders. The concepts considered in this chapter therefore provide a context for considering the place of ICT and information systems in organisations.

The primary environment of any commercial organisation is the economy. Economies can be considered as systems for coordinating the production, distribution and consumption of value. Value traditionally comes in two forms, goods and services (that is, products produced or activities performed by organisations). Goods and services can be seen as the end-points of activity systems performed in business organisations.

Goods and services can be categorised in a number of ways. Tangible goods and services have a physical form. Intangible goods and services have a non-physical form and are amenable to representation as data. The flow of both tangible and intangible goods and services has a corresponding flow of data or transactions. A transaction is a data structure that records a coherent unit of activity, typically an event in an activity system or between activity systems.

Activity between economic actors is typically organised in one of three ways: hierarchies, markets or networks. Markets are systems of competition. They are a medium for exchange between buyers and sellers. Managerial hierarchies are systems of cooperation. Exchange within hierarchies is conducted on the basis of established trading arrangements. More recently, a third form of economic control has been proposed. Networks are intermediate forms of economic control in which both cooperation and competition are evident.

Porter has proposed a template for the activity systems of the typical business, known as the internal value-chain and consisting of a defined set of primary and secondary activities. Two other chains of value are also seen as critical to the competitive environment: the supply chain and the customer chain. These three value-chains overlap with another, frequently ignored, chain of value of increasing significance to organisations: the community chain, founded on social networks of individuals. Its value lies in its ability to generate social capital, one indicator of which is a high level of interpersonal trust, an essential prerequisite for many forms of business and commerce.

The concepts of the internal value-chain and the wider value network provide the business analyst with ways of considering potential changes to business systems. These involve not only competitive performance, but also improvements in managing networks of cooperative relationships with other organisations and the global network of potential customers. The effective management of information is critical to ways in which the organisation continually adapts itself to its environment.

The next chapter uses the material in this one as a platform for considering the rise of eBusiness and eCommerce. These are defined in terms of the value-chain and the value network, and we consider the place of technological innovation in this mix. The role of ICT in reducing transaction costs is one crucial aspect. This is considered in Chapter 9. The concept of the value network also recurs in considering business strategy in Chapter 10.

7.11   Review test

1   A _____ is some form of product produced by an organisation. A _____ is some form of activity performed by an organisation. Fill in the blanks.

2   Intangible goods are those that do not have a physical existence and are fundamentally information-based. True or false?
☐ True
☐ False

3   _____ capital is the productive value of people engaged in a dense network of social relations. Fill in the blank.

4   A data structure that records a coherent unit of activity, typically an event in a human activity system. Choose the most appropriate terms for this definition.
☐ Database
☐ Transaction
☐ Value

5   Strong links exist between people who are regularly in contact and who share much in common. True or false?
☐ True
☐ False

6   Inbound logistics is a primary activity in Porter's value-chain. True or false?
   ☐ True
   ☐ False

7   Human resource management is a primary activity in Porter's value-chain. True or false?
   ☐ True
   ☐ False

8   Match the chain of value to the appropriate definition. Pair each lettered entry with the corresponding numbered entry.
   a. Customer chain
   b. Supply chain
   c. Community chain

   1. The flow of goods and services from suppliers
   2. The flow of social capital between individuals
   3. The flow of goods and services to customers

9   Commerce is the exchange of goods and services between businesses, groups and individuals. True or false?
   ☐ True
   ☐ False

10   The precise form of the process of commerce will vary depending on? Choose all that are relevant.
   ☐ The economic actors involved
   ☐ The type of technology
   ☐ The frequency of commerce
   ☐ The nature of the goods or services being exchanged

11   A _____ cost is a cost incurred in making an economic exchange. Fill in the blank.

12   Match the term for a type of commerce to the appropriate definition. Pair each lettered entry with the corresponding numbered entry.
   a. Repeat commerce
   b. Credit commerce
   c. Cash commerce

   1. Irregular transactions between trading partners and the processes of settlement and execution are separated
   2. Regular, repeat transactions occur between trading partners
   3. Irregular one-off transactions between economic actors with the processes of execution and settlement typically combined

13   Match the type of economic control to the appropriate definition. Pair each lettered entry with the corresponding numbered entry.
   a. Market
   b. Hierarchy
   c. Network

   1. System of collaboration
   2. System of competition
   3. System of competition and collaboration

14   Define disintermediation. Write a sentence.

15   A _____ specifies the structure of activity systems appropriate for a particular business in terms of its market. Fill in the blank.

16   How does the value-chain differ from the value network?   Write two sentences.

7.12   Exercises

- Service industries have been the largest growing sectors of western economies. Identify some such industries and the services they supply.
- Identify the production and distribution processes in an industry known to you.
- Identify the internal and external value-chains relevant to a company or organisation known to you.
- Provide one example of an economic market and describe what is exchanged in it.
- Provide one example of an economic hierarchy and determine what established trading relationships exist in it.
- Describe the actors, relationships, information and transactions in a segment of a market or hierarchy known to you.

- Identify the competitors, customers and suppliers of an organisation known to you.
- Describe some of the relationships between competitors, suppliers, customers and regulators in an industrial sector known to you. Determine the basis of competition and the state of technological deployment. Identify whether the industry is growing, shrinking or stable.
- In relation to the commercial activities associated with a product or service known to you, try to jot down what the four phases of commerce represent.
- eMedicine is a developing area of medical practice, and involves the remote treatment of patients using ICT. Experiments have even been undertaken in performing surgical operations using robotic

devices controlled across communication networks. How would you class this form of service, tangible or intangible?

- Choose an example of a commercial activity known to you. List the economic actors involved, the frequency of the activity and the type of product or service offered.

- Try to model a public sector organisation in terms of activities of the internal value-chain.

- Identify the elements of the customer chain and the supply chain of an organisation known to you.

- When you purchase a product through mail order, attempt to identify the flow of data transactions that accompanies the purchase.

- If you live in what you would class as a community, investigate how much social capital exists in it. Determine the evidence for this.

- List a number of the social networks in which you participate. How are you linked to other members? Would you describe the ties as strong or weak?

7.13   Projects

- Take a specific company and develop a case study of the effects of the economic environment on its information systems. For instance, who are the major economic actors in its environment? How much bargaining power do customers have?

- Develop a case study of the way in which a particular company has used information systems to improve its competitive position. How did the information system improve its profitability?

- Investigate ways of measuring social capital in a community. For instance, develop some ways in which you might map the social network underlying a virtual community. What types of bonds or links exist in this network? Are they strong or weak links, and what level of mutual support is provided to members of the social network through such links?

- Investigate the relationship between transaction costs and consumer behaviour. For instance, what transaction costs are involved in consumers changing their utility (gas, electricity, water, broadband) suppliers? Has the Web reduced these switching costs?

- Investigate the degree to which music constitutes an information commodity (intangible good) and the consequences this has for the music industry. Try to treat the problem as one demanding a form of value-network analysis.

- Investigate the degree to which movies constitute an information commodity (intangible good) and the consequences this has for the film industry. Try to treat the problem as one demanding a form of value-network analysis.

7.14   Critical reflection

Consider an industry known to you, such as banking, insurance or the publishing industry. Consider how the industry has changed over the last twenty years. Attempt to use the concepts of the value-chain, value network and business model to help describe what has been happening. Is it possible to consider the effect of ICT upon such industrial change purely in relation to coordination costs as compared to production costs?

How relevant is the idea of a value-chain for understanding the dynamics of public or voluntary sector organisations? What would constitute the supply and demand chains of a higher education institution such as a university? Would you say there is any disintermediation in the higher education sector?

7.15   Further reading

Porter's original conceptions of the value-chain and his model of the competitive environment of the organisation are reconsidered for the Internet age in Porter (2001). Sawhney and Parikh (2001) consider the issue of value and ways in which value changes in a connected world. Paolini (1999) introduces the idea of the organisation as a value-creating system. Coase's (1937) work on transaction costs forms the basis for Malone et al.'s (1987) treatment of electronic markets and hierarchies, and the more recent popular discussion of this in Tapscott and Williams' consideration of new collaborative forms of working supported through ICT (Tapscott and Williams, 2006). Value-stream analysis is a part of lean thinking, covered in the text by Womack and Jones

(2003). The theory of social networks has been around for some time, particularly in the work of Granovetter and others. The book by Christakis and Fowler (2010) has recently popularised the issue. Osterwalder and Pigneur (2010) provide a highly graphic account of the generation of business models, with many examples from eBusiness.

7.16   References

Christakis, N. and J. Fowler. (2010). *Connected: The Amazing Power of Social Networks and How They Shape Our Lives*. Harper Press, New York.

Coase, R. H. (1937). The Nature of the Firm. *Economica* 4 (16): 386–405.

Drucker, P. F. (1994). The Theory of the Business. *Harvard Business Review* 72 (5): 95–104.

Floridi, L. (2007). A Look into the Future Impact of ICT on Our Lives. *The Information Society* 23 (1): 59–64.

Granovetter, M. (1973). The Strength of Weak Ties. *American Journal of Sociology* 78 (6): 1360–1380.

Malinowski, B. (1922). *Argonauts of the Western Pacific: An Account of Native Enterprise and Adventure in the Archipelagoes of Western New Guinea*. Routledge Kegan Paul, London.

Malone, T. W., J. Yates and R. I. Benjamin. (1987). Electronic Markets and Electronic Hierarchies. *Communications of the ACM* 30 (6): 484–497.

Maslow, A. (1954). *Motivation and Personality*. Harper and Row, Cambridge, Mass.

Osterwalder, A. and Y. Pigneur. (2010). *Business Model Generation*. John Wiley, Hoboken, New Jersey.

Paolini, C. (1999). *The Value Net: A Tool for Competitive Strategy*. John Wiley, Chichester.

Porter, M. E. (1985). *Competitive Advantage: Creating and Sustaining Superior Performance*. Free Press, New York.

Porter, M. E. (2001). Strategy and the Internet. *Harvard Business Review* 79 (3): 63–78.

Porter, M. E. and V. E. Millar. (1985). How Information Gives you Competitive Advantage. *Harvard Business Review* 63 (4): 149–160.

Putnam, R. D. (2000). *Bowling Alone: The Collapse and Revival of American Community*. Simon and Schuster, New York.

Sawhney, M. and D. Parikh. (2001). Where Value Lies in a Networked World. *Harvard Business Review* 79 (1): 79–86.

Tapscott, D. and A. D. Williams. (2006). *Wikinomics: How Mass Collaboration Changes Everything*. Atlantic Books, London.

Womack, J. P. and D. T. Jones. (2003). *Lean Thinking : Banish Waste and Create Wealth in Your Corporation*. Free Press Business, London.

Worthington, I. and C. Britton. (2009). *The Business Environment*. 6th edition. Prentice Hall, Englewood Cliffs, NJ.

See companion website   **www.palgrave.com/business/beynon-daviesbis2e**

Electronic business, electronic commerce and electronic government

'Half the money
I spend on
advertising is
wasted, and the
trouble is I don't
know which half.'

Lord Leverhulme
(1851–1925)

Learning outcomes	Principles
Define the concept of electronic business and distinguish between electronic commerce and electronic business.	ICT has been used in organisations for a number of decades to support the internal value-chain. More recently it has been used to enable activities within the wider value network. Electronic business is a term we use to refer to any application of ICT within business. Electronic commerce is a term we reserve for ICT enablement of activities and relationships with external stakeholders.
Describe the major forms of electronic business and distinguish between these forms in terms of the features defined in Chapter 7.	Five major forms of electronic business are discussed which link to distinct parts of the value network discussed in Chapter 7. Internal eBusiness focuses on the internal value-chain. B2C eCommerce focuses on the customer chain, B2B eCommerce on the supply chain. C2C eCommerce on the community chain and P2P eCommerce on the partnership chain.
Identify the importance of electronic marketing to B2C eCommerce and describe key elements of eMarketing.	Electronic marketing is considered an important sub-process of B2C eCommerce. As more businesses move operations online the significance of managing electronic communications with customers assumes greater significance.
Discuss the importance of electronic procurement to B2B eCommerce and describe the key elements of eProcurement.	Electronic procurement is considered an important sub-process of B2B eCommerce. Managing procurement of supplies through electronic channels is a major way in which organisations improve their efficiency.
Identify the ways in which the principles of eBusiness have been applied in the public sector.	Over the last couple of decades considerable progress has been made in redesigning public sector systems with the aid of ICT. This is particularly important in the area of service provision from government agencies.

Chapter outline

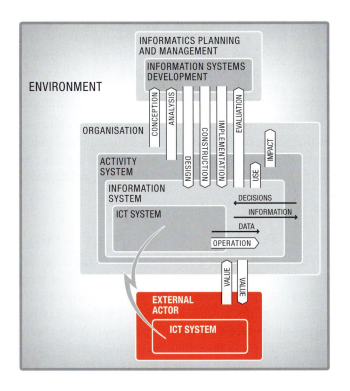

8.1 Introduction

The eminent British scientist Michael Faraday once gave a tour of his laboratory to the then Prime Minister. He was asked what use the discovery of electricity could possibly have. '*I cannot say*', Faraday replied, '*but one day Her Majesty's government will tax it*'.

Prediction of the impact of technology is an inherently tricky business. Over the years many predictions have been made as to the revolutionary potential of ICT in relation to business. Many predictions have missed the mark but others have hit the target. ICT has been applied over the last sixty years as a catalyst for change of internal business practices. More recently innovation within this area has shifted its attention externally and is now focused upon the application of such technology to external activities and in support of relationships with external stakeholders.

Within this chapter we make a clear distinction between these two application areas for ICT. As we have seen in Chapter 2, business can either be considered as an entity or as that set of activities undertaken by a commercial organisation. Electronic Business or eBusiness can be defined as the application of information and communication technologies in support of all activities undertaken by the business. In contrast, and as we saw in the last chapter, the term commerce is normally taken to describe the exchange of products and services between the business and external business actors: other businesses, groups and individuals. Therefore, electronic commerce, or eCommerce, focuses on the use of ICT to enable the external activities and relationships of the business with such external actors.

These distinctions allow us to distinguish the use of ICT to enable communication and coordination between the internal stakeholders of the business (intra-business eBusiness) from the use of ICT to enable communication and coordination with external actors (eCommerce). By definition intra-business eBusiness has been around as long as ICT has been applied within business. Many aspects of eCommerce also have a history of 20 years or so in terms of business application. However, we should not assume that we are at the end of innovation in this area. Both the technical (Chapter 6) and activity infrastructure (Chapter 10) of eBusiness is continually evolving to meet the challenges of an increasingly volatile and global environment within which the modern business must remain currently viable as well as sustainable in the longer-term.

Because of the central role ICT plays in supporting communication and activity within organisations, various innovative forms of eBusiness continue to multiply. In this chapter we consider a number of such further forms of eBusiness. First, eBusiness principles have achieved a certain success among public sector organisations, particularly government and its agencies. Second, we consider an important part of B2C eCommerce, that of electronic marketing. As more and more interaction with organisations occurs online, more and more potential exists for using electronic channels for marketing purposes. Third, we consider a critical part of B2B eCommerce, that of electronic procurement. This form of eBusiness innovation is seen as a means of reducing major supply chain costs to companies and public sector organisations. Finally, we consider the growth in mobile eCommerce and explain how this trend is a natural development of the ICT infrastructure model considered in Chapter 5.

8.2 eBusiness

eBusiness: the conduct of business using information and communication technology. A superset of eCommerce

Traditional businesses have been referred to as bricks and mortar businesses in the sense that they have a physical presence, usually in terms of being located in offices, factories or retail outlets. In contrast, traditional businesses that have moved into the world of **eBusiness** are referred to as clicks and mortar, or clicks and bricks, businesses. They still maintain a physical presence but also offer services and products accessible via ICT, particularly via websites (Chapter 6). Businesses that have emerged entirely in the online environment are known as clicks-only businesses. This chapter focuses on these last two business types. Decisions as to

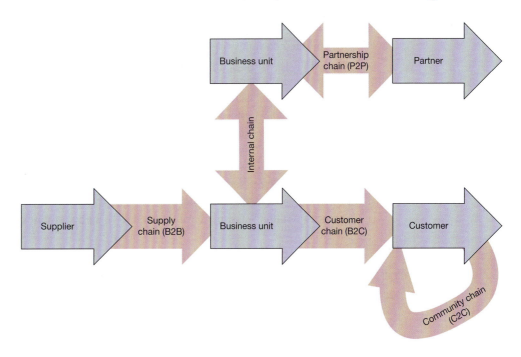

Figure 8.1 *Forms of eBusiness*

the strategy (Chapter 10) taken in relation to the particular type of eBusiness adopted by a company relies upon an understanding of the ways in which ICT can be used by businesses to innovate within their wider value network (see Chapter 10).

Figure 8.1 provides a framework for understanding the current makeup of electronic businesses based upon the idea of the organisation as a value-creating system working within a wider value network (Chapter 4). To refresh, the original value-chain model has proven useful as a generic business model for understanding the place of ICT in the business. More recently, the value-chain idea has been extended into the idea of the value network, which is particularly useful as a means of distinguishing between distinct forms of eBusiness. This figure also allows us to place some of the newer application areas for eBusiness (such as social networking sites) in relation to some of the more established areas of eBusiness, such as supply chain management systems.

eCommerce: the conduct of business to business commerce using information technology such as that supporting the Internet

The traditional view of **eCommerce** mapped onto the value network represents the use of ICT to support the external activities/relationships of business with two major stakeholder groups: suppliers and customers. Business to consumer (B2C) eCommerce is sometimes called sell-side eCommerce and concerns the enablement of the customer chain with ICT. Business to business (B2B) eCommerce is sometimes called buy-side eCommerce and involves supporting the supply chain with ICT. C2C or Consumer to Consumer eCommerce also has a place within this model and is a developing form of eCommerce recently linked to new media services. This is potentially the most radical form of eCommerce since it overlaps with non-commercial activity in the area of community (Chapter 4). C2C eCommerce is therefore built upon the community chain; a new range of business opportunities emerge within virtual networking as a phenomenon driving new levels of content and services.

But the massive levels of interest in eCommerce over the last decade have tended to devalue the importance of ICT to internal operations. This is a mistake. The model in Figure 8.1 emphasises that eBusiness is as much about internal operations as it is about external operations. It also highlights the increasing importance of integration between the internal and external foci across the value network. Therefore, Figure 8.1 also includes two areas that extend both the internal and external forms of electronic business.

First, any contemporary definition of eBusiness must include the growing range of issues associated with providing effective infrastructure for multi-part businesses located across the globe. The modern eBusiness is likely to be made up of numerous dispersed business units, some physically co-located, some mobile. Modern ICT infrastructure acts as a critical backbone for such complex organisations. For example, as we have seen in the case of Goronwy Galvanising, this organisation is actually one sub-unit of a larger conglomerate of companies, Rito Metals. To manage the global operation of these companies, Rito Metals needs an inter-organisational ICT infrastructure.

Second, any accurate conception of eBusiness must extend the notion of business cooperation and collaboration beyond that of the supply chain. This means that contemporary eBusiness is likely to be evident in a network of business partnerships of varying complexity. Hence, eBusiness involves the application of ICT in both cooperative as well as competitive activity. As we have seen in Chapter 4, a particular business may actually fulfil a number of different roles in the value network at the same time, such as being both a partner and a competitor. Therefore, some have referred to this phenomenon as co-option.

8.3   eCommerce

Exploiting opportunities created by technology innovations   IS2010

Electronic Commerce (eCommerce) is the use of ICT to enable the external activities and relationships of the business with individuals, groups and other businesses. eCommerce supports supply chains, customer chains and community chains of business (Chapter 4). eCommerce has traditionally been conducted in terms of eMarkets or eHierarchies. More recently, we have seen the rise of the network as a control mechanism for electronic activity and hence electronic social networks have become important for business activity.

Much hype has always been associated with eCommerce; particularly that experienced during the, so-called, Dot Com boom. This refers to the investment bubble that became associated with Internet start-up companies during the late 1990s. Many (Cassidy, 2002) have made the analogy between the irrational investment behaviour associated with Dot Com companies at this time and other financial boom and bust periods, such as the South Sea Bubble that occurred in the eighteenth century. Much of the Dot Com phenomenon was directed at B2C eCommerce, probably because it has always been the most visible form of eCommerce. However, a substantial amount of the business conducted electronically over the last couple of decades has been B2B eCommerce. Recent interest in the business opportunities afforded by social networking sites has provided renewed vigour to the phenomenon of C2C eCommerce.

On the basis of much of the material covered in previous chapters, we may distinguish between the major forms of eCommerce in a number of ways: in terms of the value-chain supported; the economic actors involved; the direction of transactional flow between economic actors; the form of commerce transacted; the nature of goods or services exchanged; and the typical model of economic exchange utilised. These distinctions, which build upon our discussion in previous chapters, are summarised in Table 8.1. We examine each of these forms in more detail in the following sections.

8.3.1   Business to consumer (B2C) eCommerce

B2C eCommerce: the use of eCommerce in the customer chain

These forms of eCommerce concern the use of ICT to enable modes of cash and credit commerce between a company and its customers/consumers. Hence, **B2C eCommerce** generally supports activities within the customer chain in that it focuses on sell-side activities. The primary difference between B2C and C2B eCommerce is in terms of transactional flow. In B2C eCommerce the primary direction of the flow is from business to consumer. In C2B eCommerce the primary direction of the flow is from consumer to business. To avoid confusion, we use the term B2C eCommerce to refer to both directions of flow in this text.

Customers, or consumers, will typically be individuals, sometimes other organisations. Cash commerce for low- and standard-price goods typically follows quite closely the four

Table 8.1 *Forms of eCommerce*

	B2C	B2B	C2C	P2P
Value-chain	Customer chain	Supply chain	Community chain	Partnership chain
Economic actors	Company/ consumers	Company/ suppliers	Consumers/ Consumers	Company/Partners
Direction of transactions	Consumer– company	Company–supplier	Consumer– consumer	Company–partner
Nature of goods/ services	Standard-price items	Customised/High-price items	Negotiated/ Low-price items	Shared goods and services
Form of commerce	Cash/Credit	Credit/Repeat	Cash	Credit/Repeat
Form of economic control	Markets	Hierarchies	Networks	Networks

stages of the generic commerce model discussed in Chapter 7. For medium- to high-price items some form of credit commerce will operate. Typically, B2C eCommerce will utilise a market model of economic exchange in which economic actors freely exchange goods and services in many-to-many interactions.

8.3.2 Business to business (B2B) eCommerce

B2B eCommerce: the use of eCommerce in the supply chain

B2B eCommerce supports the supply chain of organisations since it focuses on buy-side activities. B2B commerce clearly occurs between organisational actors (public and/or private sector organisations). Hence, this form of eCommerce invariably involves the use of ICT to enable forms of credit and repeat commerce between a company and its suppliers or other partners.

For high-price and customised goods traded between organisations a form of repeat commerce model operates. Typically, some form of managerial hierarchy is employed to control the operation of the commercial relationship. In particular, the use of inter-organisational information systems, such as extranets (Chapter 6), have become popular as a technological vehicle for supporting B2B eCommerce.

8.3.3 Consumer to consumer (C2C) eCommerce

C2C eCommerce: ICT enablement of aspects of the community chain

C2C eCommerce supports the community chain surrounding the organisation and can be seen as a commercial extension of community activities. It typically occurs between individuals and, where monetary exchange is involved, uses forms of cash commerce, generally for low-cost services or goods. eBay is a classic example of such C2C eCommerce, which tends to follow a market model for economic exchange. However, as we have seen, other forms of value may be generated in the communities or social networks that engage with C2C eCommerce. Of particular interest is the degree of social capital (Chapter 7) that may emerge in such social networks. Hence, the idea of network forms of economic control is particularly applicable to C2C eCommerce.

8.3.4 Partner to partner (P2P) eCommerce

P2P eCommerce: ICT enablement of aspects of the partnership chain

Organisations are likely to engage in partnerships with other companies in the delivery of goods and services to the customer. We referred to this as the partnership chain within the value network. **P2P eCommerce** supports this partnership chain through the sharing of

DID YOU KNOW? One of the most important forms of P2P eBusiness involves the partnership between a company and another that supports the whole or part of its informatics services.

data between company ICT systems. Such electronic commerce will be done on a continuing or repeat basis and managed through the dispersed control of an exchange network.

CASE CHECK **Amazon** p 424	To help illustrate how the different forms of eCommerce described play out within one organisation, consider the case of Amazon.com, an eCommerce company based in Seattle in the United States of America but which has global reach. The company was one of the first to sell goods over the Internet; it was launched on the Web in June 1995 by Jeff Bezos who had obtained the backing of venture capitalists in Silicon Valley to start the operation. Bezos chose to name his site after the world's longest river because he believed it was set to become the world's largest bookstore. At the time of Amazon's entry into the market it had no significant rivals and within one year of starting the company was recognised as the Web's largest bookstore. However, Amazon was also one of the most prominently traded securities within the late 1990s Dot Com bubble described above. When this bubble burst at the millennium, many claimed that Amazon's business model was unsustainable in the longer term. It took until 2003 before the company registered its first annual profit but since then the company has proceeded from strength to strength. The domain *amazon.com* attracts over 600 million visitors annually and, consequently, Amazon. com is probably the most cited example of a company that has succeeded at eCommerce. We examine why in the sections which follow.

8.3.5   Benefits of eCommerce

Many benefits have been claimed from the adoption of eCommerce, generally related to improving activities and/or relationships in the value network:

■ Reduced transaction or coordination costs. For instance, when sales and after-sales service operations replace paper-based communications with electronic communication, it should make the processes more efficient.

■ More efficient external-facing activity systems, such as outbound logistics; for example, enabling a company to manage its inventory better, and capture and process orders more quickly.

■ Closer integration of suppliers into inventory systems, enabling just-in-time manufacturing.

■ Innovative ways of marketing new products and services, leading to a general improvement in customer relations. This might allow companies that traditionally traded on a local scale to do business on a global scale.

> **REFLECT:** For a company such as Tesco, which type of eCommerce do you think provides most benefit, and why?

8.3.6   Problems with eCommerce

There are also a number of problems associated with eCommerce, such as:

■ Many people still do not trust eCommerce enough to use the Web to buy high-value goods or services. They are worried about the security of electronic transactions and are reluctant to release personal information over the Internet (see Chapter 6). The first is an issue of information security, the second an issue of information privacy.

■ Technological standards are developing rapidly in support of electronic trade, and sometimes they are not particularly secure, or not easily integrated with standards in other areas. Much work is being undertaken worldwide to create effective security standards for the transmission of electronic transactions.

■ It can be difficult to find specific suppliers of goods and services on the Internet. eBrokers (or information brokerages) try to satisfy this need as intermediaries in the electronic value network (see Chapter 7).

■ Some people worry about the digital divide; the fact that older and more economically disadvantaged people are less likely to have a home Internet connection so they are excluded from eCommerce.

■ Mistakes are very visible with online systems. For instance, the initial introduction of the cross-company loyalty card Nectar experienced problems because people were unable to register their details on a website established for this purpose. This appeared to have been because of the volume of traffic on the website in the first week of its launch. When Barclays Bank first introduced online banking, customers found they were able to access other customers' financial details, and the company had to apologise.

RECAP: eBusiness is a superset of eCommerce. Forms of eBusiness can be mapped onto the value network. Two forms are focused on internal relationships (internal eBusiness) and relationships with partners. There are three major forms of eCommerce: B2C, B2B and C2C. The benefits of eCommerce include cost savings and time savings. Its problems include issues of security and technological standards.

8.4   B2C eCommerce

Traditional business activity systems involving relationships between businesses and customers include sales, marketing and after-sales. All such activity systems have been amenable to ICT innovation for a number of years. However, two trends explain the current renewed explosion of interest in ICT-enablement of the customer chain. First, there has been increasing infiltration of ICT infrastructure into the home and public spaces stimulated by the on-going penetration of the Internet and the Web as key communication technologies (Chapter 6). This technological innovation has increased the variety of access channels to business products and services open to the potential consumer. Second, postal and telephone services have enabled customers to access services and products remotely for a number of years. Changes to worldwide ICT infrastructure have opened up increased opportunities for organisations to extend the realms of remote access by implementing efficient and effective electronic delivery systems. It is only comparatively recently, with the rise of such technology as the Internet and Web, that direct (disintermediated) and remote connections between customers and businesses have been made possible.

In this section we describe some of the major ways in which the customer chain is being supported and restructured using ICT. On one level, B2C eCommerce can be seen as an extension of the customer-facing information systems discussed in Chapter 4. It involves the integration of such customer-facing systems with an increasing range of access devices and channels used by consumers.

To get a handle on this phenomenon, we may think of an organisation's experience of B2C eCommerce as moving through a number of distinct stages of increasing ICT infrastructure complexity, which support the various activities of B2C eCommerce. These stages include: engaging in information seeking and communication; establishing an online marketing presence; creating an online catalogue; conducting online ordering; handling online payment; offering online delivery; and performing customer profiling and preferencing.

For example, small and medium-size enterprises (SMEs, those with less than 250 employees) will probably first use a computer and an Internet connection to seek out information about potential competitors. They will also probably use this facility to email suppliers. The more sophisticated it gets, and depending upon its business strategy, the SME may eventually reach the stage at which most of its business with customers is conducted electronically.

Each of these stages supports part of the model of commerce described in Chapter 7. Pre-sale activities include information seeking and communication, creating a marketing presence and establishing an online catalogue. Sale execution activities are online

DID YOU KNOW? Estimates of the number of websites worldwide vary, but many reckon there are over 100 million distinct ones, and between 15 billion and 30 billion Web pages.

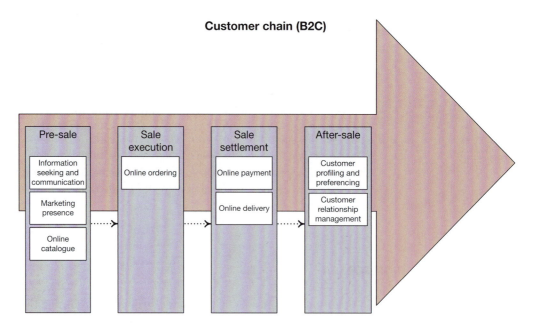

Figure 8.2 *Stages of B2C eCommerce*

ordering and, potentially, online delivery. Sale settlement activities equate to online payment. After-sales activities equate to customer profiling and preferencing (see Figure 8.2).

8.4.1   Pre-sale B2C eCommerce infrastructure

In the first stage, a company begins to engage with the Internet, probably using it primarily for information seeking and communication via email. The Internet and the Web have provided a much more effective and efficient way to look for information than existed previously, and there are many software tools(such as search engines) to help with this (see Chapter 5).

Email is a significant technology for business because it allows asynchronous communication between stakeholders (unlike a phone call, say, both parties do not need to be communicating at the same time). It also enables the easy transfer of electronic files. If a company has an email address this makes it easy for customers to make enquiries and place orders.

The next step is to establish a marketing presence on the Internet by setting up a corporate website. It will provide a company profile, most likely including a description of the main activities, the location and contact details. A simple website allows potential customers to communicate with the company through email.

Finally, the company provides an online catalogue of its products or services, which could consist of a series of static web pages, or may be dynamic in the sense that it is updated from a database. More sophisticated sites allow dynamic pricing of product information, so that different types of market segment (such as irregular and regular customers) can be given different information. Customers still have to place orders through traditional channels such as over the telephone, through the post or, potentially, through email.

Suppose, for instance, a music publisher produces an online catalogue of its limited range of specialist publications. The catalogue contains a cover image, a short synopsis of the contents of each publication, details the cost of each publication and delivery charges. To order publications customers still have to ring a telephone line or send an order form through the post with appropriate payment.

8.4.2   Online ordering and payment

The next logical step is to enable customers to place orders online. This is a key transition point for most businesses since it involves the integration of websites with back-end

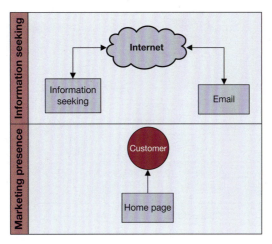 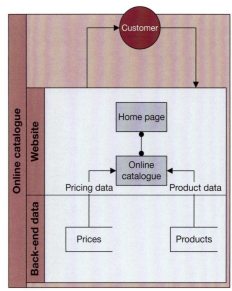

Figure 8.3 *Pre-sale B2C eCommerce infrastructure*

information systems. In forms of credit commerce the company invoices the customer for payment after delivery. This calls for integration between the website and the sales order processing information system. The sales order information system will trigger the outbound logistics information system that manages deliveries. Ideally, payment details will also be passed to the organisation's finance system, which sends an invoice and receives payment.

For example, a bulk supplier of specialist stationery to the trade might provide an online catalogue of its range of products. This material can be ordered via the Internet for established customers. The traditional outbound logistics, invoicing and finance systems of the supplier are used to support the B2C process.

The next scenario is where the customer both orders and pays for goods using the website. This is more usual for cash commerce in which the customer is an individual and the goods are standardised and relatively low-price, such as CDs or books. This form of B2C eCommerce demands a close integration between an organisation's front-end and back-end information systems.

Figure 8.4 outlines the typical functionality of many sites offering online ordering and payment. (Obviously, individual sites vary and might not exactly fit this template.) The customer first orders goods using an electronic shopping facility in the sales system. The shopping facility calculates the total cost of the order and includes the delivery charge. The customer enters credit or debit card details, and completes the purchase via a secure payment system.

Payment details are checked with a financial intermediary such as the customer's bank. Provided sufficient funds are available the intermediary makes an electronic funds transfer to the company's bank account, and details of the transfer are recorded in the company's finance system (Figure 8.4).

For a company supplying high-quality art prints, customers can search for prints by theme, period, artist and price. They can look at images of selected prints at various degrees of resolution, and order them in various sizes. They add their selected prints to an online shopping trolley and pay online by credit or debit card. The site automatically confirms orders via email.

8.4.3 Online delivery

As we have seen, there are established digital standards now not just for textual and numeric data, but for audio and video as well, so an increasing range of intangible goods can be

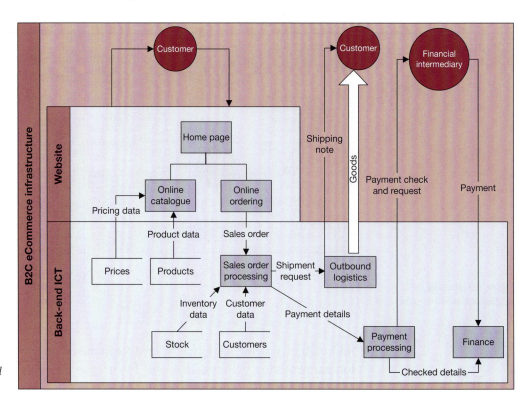

Figure 8.4 *Online ordering and payment*

delivered electronically in digital format. This means that the outbound logistics system in Figure 8.4 is replaced by an online delivery system. There is also less likely to be a need for separate inventory and product databases, since one database can hold both product descriptions and the data that comprise the products themselves.

Sometimes intangible goods and services are paid for per item, but in other business models there is a subscription system, perhaps with monthly payments. For instance, suppliers of virus protection software sometimes work on a subscription basis, in return for which they provide frequent updates. Music files are sometimes provided on a subscription basis (either a set limit of downloads per month, or as many as the user requires), others use a cash-based model with a payment for each individual download.

8.4.4   Customer relationship management

In the modern business world, where globalisation means that companies face increasing competition, the customer is a key focus. Winning new customers and keeping existing ones satisfied is seen as critical to organisational success, and electronic systems can help provide the efficient service that contributes to this.

Customer relationship management: the set of activities devoted to managing the customer chain

Customer relationship management (CRM, sometimes known as customer chain management) comprises a set of activities that support the entire customer chain. In an electronic CRM system (see Figure 8.5), an organisation's information systems track all customer interactions, from initial enquiries, through orders, to after-sales services. Often, for larger companies, the customer-facing systems are integrated with a customer profiling and preferencing system. This information system dynamically builds a profile of each customer, and adjusts it on the basis of new transactions. This profile is then used to offer the customer a targeted range of goods and/or services.

CRM is an attempt to establish long-term relationships with customers. It consists of three inter-related processes: customer acquisition, customer retention and customer extension.

Customer acquisition is the set of activities and techniques used to gain new customers. For eBusiness this clearly involves attracting customers to websites, so eMarketing is a critical part of this aspect (see below). It also involves attempts to persuade the customer to engage in a dialogue with the company, through which its systems can construct a profile of them: the products or services they have shown an interest in their demographic profile and general purchasing behaviour.

For a high-street bank, for instance, customer acquisition means persuading people to open an account or perhaps take up another financial product, such as insurance or a loan. Online banking has become an expected part of the services offered, so it plays an important part in attracting new customers.

Customer retention is the set of activities and techniques designed to maintain relationships with existing customers. For eCommerce it has the related goals of retaining customers (repeat customers) and persuading them to keep communicating online (repeat visits). Two factors are critical to retention: customer satisfaction and customer loyalty.

One technique used in customer retention is the personalisation of email content. Customers receive alerts about products or services that their profile has suggested they will find particularly interesting, for instance, a new album by a musician whose previous work they have bought. These alerts may also offer discounts or other added-value services in a bid to persuade customers to return to a B2C website.

For the bank, customer retention activities might include offering multi-channel access to accounts and aggregated products such as combined bank accounts, insurance and mortgages. Because online transactions are cheaper for the company, online customers may be provided with inducements to keep on using electronic communications, such as higher interest on balances in savings accounts.

Customer extension activities and techniques encourage existing customers to increase their level of involvement with a company. This is made easier in the online environment as more targeted promotions can be offered to customers.

All these activities depend heavily on good information: knowing who the customers are, what they are purchasing, how satisfied they are with the company and what future services and products they want. Hence, there has been an increasing emphasis on information systems to support the CRM process.

It might be argued that B2C eCommerce in general, and CRM in particular, are a natural consequence of increasing customer focus. Porter and Miller (1985) has argued that the value delivered to the customer is the key feature of contemporary business (see Chapter 7), so it is not surprising to find companies attempting to reorient their processes and systems around customers, instead of around business events, such as orders and sales.

Take, for example, the insurance company we previously mentioned whose products include life insurance, car insurance and home insurance. If this company structured its information systems around policy types (as most such companies used to do), it would find it hard to work out which customers were purchasing more than one type of insurance. It would also not be able to integrate its communications; for instance, if a customer's household insurance was renewed on the same day as their car insurance they would get separate communications about each one. With its systems restructured around customers, the company can tell who its most valuable customers are, and which customers for one type of policy have not, as yet, chosen the company for their other insurance needs. It can then initiate schemes aimed at retaining and extending its business, such as discount packages.

> **REFLECT:** Take an organisation known to you. At what stage would you describe it as being at in its B2C eCommerce?

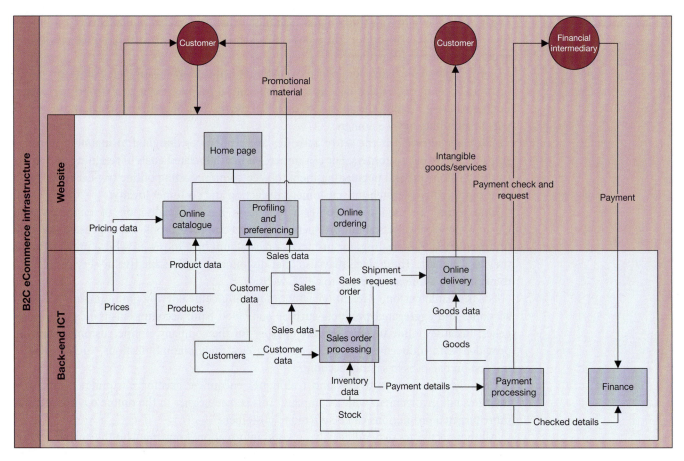

Figure 8.5　*Customer relationship management system*

CASE CHECK

Amazon

CS ▷ p 424

Amazon primarily engages in B2C eCommerce and provides a number of levels of functionality through its website, such as search features, additional content and personalisation. The site also provides searchable catalogues of books, CDs, DVDs, computer games etc. Customers can search for these products using keywords, title, subject, author, artist, musical instrument, label, actor, director, publication date or ISBN.

Therefore, the primary value-stream for Amazon is tangible products such as books and CDs. In recent times, it has attempted to broaden the range of this value by offering other products including computer software, video games, electronics, clothing, furniture, food and toys. It also provides added-value and intangible services such as a personalised notification service. More recently, it has started to offer delivery of intangible products such as electronic books, or eBooks.

In terms of added-value, the company offers a vast range of additional content over and above its products, through its website. For example, cover art, synopses, annotations, reviews by editorial staff and other customers, and interviews by authors and artists. The website attempts to personalise the customer experience by greeting customers by name, making instant and personalised recommendations, offering bestseller listings, personal notification services and purchase pattern filtering.

To order from Amazon customers have to register their details, including payment details. Amazon is able to combine this data with data gathered about customers' browsing and ordering behaviour to progressively update a profile held about each customer. Such customer profiling is used to drive targeted advertisements at the customer, such as suggestions about suitable reading matter or music to buy.

CASE CHECK

Amazon
(continued)

Currently, the company is claimed to be the Internet's number one retailer. However, although Amazon is a retailer, its key business strategy is based on differentiation in terms of technical infrastructure. For Amazon to keep this competitive differentiation it must be continually at the forefront of Internet technology. Jeff Bezos has indicated that he considers Amazon to be a technology company first and a retailer second. Hence, the key differentiating factor for Amazon over the conventional retailer is the Internet and Web. Not surprisingly, the company has to ceaselessly innovate in terms of such technology.

Amazon offers only one access channel to its goods, the Amazon.com website. Hence, Amazon is a clicks-only company, meaning that all its retail operation is conducted online and that the key access device used by its customers is the Internet-enabled PC. In recent times Amazon has been promoting the idea of electronic books and its associated eReader, the Kindle, as an additional access channel for its customers. After purchasing an eBook reader from the company book material in digital format can be downloaded onto this access device for a charge. Clearly, this form of access enables Amazon to substantially reduce its distribution costs for this type of product.

To maintain its B2C operation, significant investment in front-end and back-end ICT is required by Amazon. For instance, Amazon's service to customers relies on a close integration of its website to back-end information and activity systems. For instance, the company uses a streamlined ordering process reliant on previous billing and shipment details captured from the customer. Amazon also utilises secure server software that encrypts payment information throughout its integrated fulfilment process. Most of the company's products are available for shipping within 24 hours. The Amazon website run within each geographical region updates a large sales information system. This sales information system is also integrated with inventory management systems run at each distribution centre.

From this description it is possible to describe briefly some of the gains that Amazon experiences from its engagement with B2C eCommerce and, in particular, through its close integration of ICT infrastructure with its activity infrastructure. First, in terms of efficacy, Amazon has been able to diversify into a vast range of products for retail. Since Amazon is primarily a B2C company it is able to run without any physical retail outlets and can pass on efficiency gains in lower costs to its customers. Finally, in terms of effectiveness, Amazon is able to sell its products across the world, meaning that its potential customer base is huge, and is able to relate to a large range of suppliers to fulfil orders from customers.

Careers in IS

Stuart McMillan

Stuart McMillan is the Deputy Head of eCommerce for the footwear retailer Schuh.

Stuart started his working life in a supermarket, supervising the fruit and veg department, after leaving University where he studied Chemistry. He then went on to manage a small outdoor retail operation, where he helped start their eCommerce website as well as writing a back-office system to integrate the stock and sales information of four other branches.

After a brief period working for a biotech firm writing an intranet system, Stuart joined a digital agency as a senior developer, where he worked on the websites of several prominent fashion brands. One of these brands, AllSaints, hired him to help set up and run their own web development team.

While he had a proven technical background, Stuart always aspired to be a leader within business, helping to shape the direction of busy eCommerce websites. He joined the team at Schuh as a fantastic opportunity to do just that.

Stuart is also a keen participant in eCommerce conferences and writes a regular blog on the subject.

Scan the QR code under Stuart's picture or visit **www.palgrave.com/business/beynon-daviesbis2e/** to watch Stuart talking about Information Systems and careers as an IS professional, then think about the questions below:

- What sort of benefits does a company such as Schuh experience from both B2C and B2B eCommerce?
- How is it possible for a company selling physical goods to differentiate its eCommerce business from its competitors?
- In what way are mobile access devices important to the eCommerce strategy at Schuh?
- What are the advantages of providing customer service electronically?
- How does Schuh manage its ICT infrastructure to facilitate eCommerce innovation?
- How important is data security to successful eCommerce?
- Is successful eCommerce more of a business than a purely ICT issue?
- How has eCommerce changed consumer behaviour?

RECAP: B2C eCommerce focuses on ICT enablement of key processes in the customer chain. Customer chain processes include product identification, catalogue search, product comparison and purchase. An organisation's experience of B2C eCommerce moves through a number of stages of increasing complexity, including information seeking and communication, marketing presence, online catalogue, online ordering, online payment and customer relationship management.

8.5   B2B eCommerce

Until quite recently it was always argued that B2B eCommerce is even more critical to business activity than B2C eCommerce and that, potentially, ICT innovation in the area of business-to-business activity has enormous value for organisations. B2B eCommerce involves the use of ICT within the supply chain activity of organisations. Much discussion of B2B eCommerce is directed at supporting the repeat commerce model, discussed in Chapter 7. In Figure 8.6 a company sets up an arrangement with a trusted supplier to deliver goods of a certain specification at regular intervals. Each of the phases of this repeat commerce model may be impacted upon by B2B eCommerce.

In terms of *search*, buyers within organisations will be required to detail features of the product or service required from suppliers by completing online forms. Such forms may then be submitted via Web interfaces on the corporate intranet for requisition approval. After requisition approval the purchasing department will issue a request for a quote, electronically, to potential suppliers. This may be conducted through an online bulletin board or B2B hub that connects businesses online as buyers and sellers.

In terms of *negotiate*, after all bids have been received, a vendor is selected, probably using software that ranks bids on the basis of chosen key features. *Order* involves the supplier being notified of a successful bid and a purchase order being electronically transmitted to the chosen supplier. After *delivery* of goods the inventory management system is automatically updated and following receipt of the invoice from the supplier the company arranges an electronic funds transfer (*payment*) with the supplying company.

Finally, in terms of *after-sale*, supplier relationship management systems monitor all interactions with suppliers and can be used to check on their performance.

This approach to B2B eCommerce is primarily modelled on the economic model of an electronic hierarchy (Chapter 7) and can be considered as an extension to the supplier-facing information systems described in Chapter 4. In other words, the supply chain is considered an extension of the firm itself and the informatics infrastructure of the company is extended to manage supplier relationships. More recently, forms of market-based trading are infiltrating the B2B sector, leading to an overlap of both B2B and B2C business models and ICT infrastructure.

8.5.1   B2B eCommerce infrastructure

B2B eCommerce is a natural extension of a major part of the internal informatics infrastructure of commercial organisations. In Chapter 4 we referred to front-end information

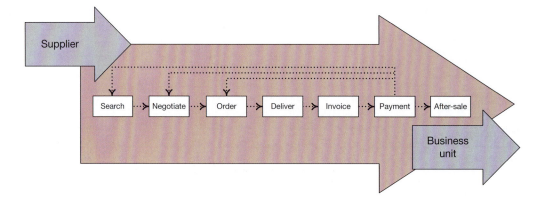

Figure 8.6 *Supply chain*

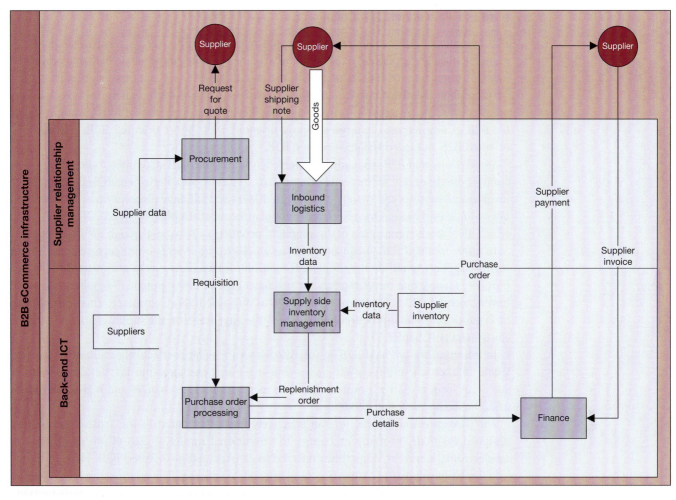

Figure 8.7 *B2B eCommerce infrastructure*

systems infrastructure as supplier-facing information systems. Purchase order processing and payment processing systems normally handle the settlement and execution stages of the commerce cycle. Such information systems are an established part of the information systems infrastructure of most medium to large organisations. The pre-sale and after-sale stages of the commerce cycle have been the most open to innovation in B2B eCommerce. Requisitioning, request for quote and vendor selection are part of what we previously called a supplier relationship management information system (Chapter 4). It is in this area that most of the discussion of B2B eCommerce occurs.

Figure 8.7 illustrates the relationships between the supplier-facing systems of supplier relationship management, procurement and purchase order processing and other infrastructure systems such as finance and inventory management. This serves to emphasise that successful B2B eCommerce relies upon integration with back-end information systems.

8.5.2   Supplier relationship management

Supplier relationship management: the management of supply chain activities. Sometimes referred to as supply chain management.

Supplier relationship management (SRM) is sometimes referred to as supply chain management and involves the coordination of all the supply chain activities of the company. Supply chain management encapsulates inbound logistics (Chapter 4), the management of material resources supplied to the organisation. It is also sometimes used to encompass outbound logistics, the management of resources supplied by the organisation to its customers. Just as customer relationship management can be seen to include electronic marketing, supplier relationship management can be seen to include electronic procurement (see below).

8.5.3　Business models for B2B eCommerce

B2B commerce traditionally relies on trusted relationships between a company and one or more established suppliers. Traditionally, management of the supply chain has been organised in terms of managerial hierarchies. With the rise of the Internet and the Web there has been an increasing trend for supply chain management to move more closely towards market-oriented models. In terms of pre-sale activity the Internet has enabled four distinct models for B2B eCommerce to emerge: supplier-oriented B2B, buyer-oriented B2B, partnership-oriented B2B and intermediary-oriented B2B.

Supplier-oriented B2B is sometimes referred to as sell-side B2B eCommerce and effectively is a mirror-image of B2C or buy-side eCommerce. Typically, supplier-oriented B2B eCommerce involves one supplier and many potential purchasers and will take place for low-cost items and low-volume purchases. One of the most popular forms of supplier-oriented B2B is the eShop which involves the promotion of the suppliers' products or services through the Internet.

In *buyer-oriented B2B*, a consumer opens an electronic market on its own servers. It then invites suppliers to bid on the supply information displayed on a website constructed for this purpose. Hence, one buyer tenders for products among many potential suppliers. As such, buyer-oriented B2B is sometimes referred to as buy-side B2B eCommerce. This scenario can be expanded into full eProcurement in which the later stages in the supply chain are handled electronically (Chapter 10).

In *intermediary-oriented B2B* an intermediary runs what is effectively a subset of an electronic market where buyers and sellers can meet and exchange products and services. As such, this form of B2B eCommerce involves many-to-many exchanges and is also referred to as B2B eMarket places or B2B hubs.

The three previous models are all effectively market-oriented in the sense that they are designed for many-to-many exchange. The traditional model of B2B eCommerce runs as an electronic hierarchy, sometimes referred to as partnership-oriented B2B. Here an established relationship exists between a company and its supplier. The relationship is likely to be supported by some form of integration of information systems within the business partnership using technologies such as extranets (Chapter 6).

Intermediary-oriented B2B is a key form of re-intermediation in the supply chain and can be conducted in a number of ways. Vertical portals aggregate buyers and sellers around a particular market segment. They produce revenue through subscription, advertising, commission and transaction fees. B2B auction sites enable buyers and sellers to negotiate the price and terms of sales. The seller holds inventory but the auction site handles fulfilment of goods and the exchange of payment. eMalls or eStores are general portals run by third parties offering a range of products/services from suppliers for customers; an eMall is effectively a collection of eShops.

> **REFLECT:** Take an organisation known to you. Does it engage in B2B eCommerce? If so, what type of B2B eCommerce best describes its activity in this area?

CASE CHECK

Amazon　　p 424

Although Amazon is frequently seen as just a B2C eCommerce company, much of its success as a company is based upon the efficiency and reach of its B2B eCommerce operations. Two of Amazon's core competencies are clearly to retail books effectively and deliver them efficiently to its customers. The latter competency relies upon efficient logistics. Amazon maintains a network of large warehouses or distribution centres which rely on ICT integration to perform effectively. Within these warehouses staff use handheld devices connected to an inventory management system to fulfil customer orders. Inbound logistics involves the management of the purchasing of books and the distribution of books to these distribution centres. The process of operations involves unpacking and storing these shipments as well as picking books to fulfil customer orders. Outbound logistics involves the distribution of books to the customer. Amazon actually operates separate B2C websites in Canada, the United Kingdom, Germany, France, Italy, China and Japan. Although it ships selected products globally it also runs a number of fulfilment centres in North America, Europe and Asia. This enables it to meet customer demand quickly.

RECAP: Most discussion of B2B eCommerce is directed at supporting the repeat commerce model. In this model a company sets up an arrangement with a trusted supplier to deliver goods of a certain specification at regular intervals. Changes to this business model tend to focus on pre-sales activity. Pre-sale activity can now be conducted using vertical portals, Internet auctions or eMalls.

8.6   C2C eCommerce

The Internet is not just a domain for business-to-business or business-to-consumer eCommerce, it is also a domain for consumer-to-consumer (C2C) eCommerce. We may define *C2C eCommerce* as ICT enablement of aspects of the community chain. In a way it is the most radical form of eCommerce since it overlaps with non-commercial activity in the area of community. Commercial and non-commercial organisations are attempting to incorporate aspects of their community chain into their operations or are attempting to formulate new business models embedded in various social networks external to the organisation.

As a type of exchange, many forms of C2C eCommerce revert to earlier models of markets and trade in which products and services are exchanged between individuals, where the fixed price model of products and services breaks down and where, in some instances, trade reverts to earlier forms of economic exchange such as barter. In these terms, C2C commerce is a many-to-many commerce model. It typically involves the exchange of low-cost items and monetary transactions. With C2C eCommerce a form of trade that typically survives in local marketplaces is opened up to global access.

In this section we reconsider our definition of a community from Chapter 7 and use this definition to introduce the idea of an electronic community.

8.6.1   Electronic community

Electronic community:
a community supported through ICT

The two concepts of a social network and social capital, as defined in Chapter 4, help us understand some of the different forms of **electronic community** (eCommunity). On the one hand, ICT is seen as an enabler or as a disabler of traditional forms of community, an eNabled community. On the other hand, ICT is seen as offering potential for newer forms of community based on communication networks, the virtual community. Virtual communities may exist separately from the organisation concerned or be built upon infrastructure provided by the organisation. The latter is the concept of an adjunct community. It is to adjunct communities that many businesses are turning to increase levels of value associated with their products and services.

An *eNabled community* is a traditional community enhanced with the use of ICT. Community is normally established on the basis of frequent and prolonged interaction between individuals resident in a clearly defined geographical area. This form of community chain addresses the rise of communication networks and considers whether they are vehicles for recreating community and social capital in local areas. Some argue that communication networks are a threat to existing forms of community; others that they provide a new basis for enhancing social capital.

The Internet and the Web were initially established for free information exchange between dispersed actors around the globe. Some have begun to consider such dispersed networks of individuals and organisations as examples of electronic communities. In these *virtual communities* social networks are constructed through electronic rather than face-to-face communication. Social networks based upon communication infrastructure may not only be dispersed geographically, they may also have a much more specific area of focus than traditional communities.

As a generalisation, public sector organisations have been particularly interested in making connections between their informatics activities and initiatives in the area of eNabled community. Such forms of eCommunity are seen as offering the potential for the stimulation of local economies, particularly in disadvantaged areas.

In contrast, private sector organisations have been particularly interested in connecting to the second form of eCommunity, that of a virtual community. The idea is that various forms of value produced by the community chain may support and encourage commerce of various forms. It is only comparatively recently that the Internet and Web have been used as vehicles for commerce and trade/business purposes. C2C eCommerce mediates between pure forms of trade and pure forms of communication exchange.

8.6.2   Virtual communities

Virtual community: a community consisting of a network of actors on a communication network.

Rheingold (1995) defines **virtual communities** as: '*social aggregations that emerge from the Net when enough people carry on those public discussions long enough, with sufficient human feeling, to form webs of personal relationships in cyberspace.*'

For example, it could be argued that one of the first virtual communities was the community of academics that started to use the Internet in the early 1970s to share data, exchange messages and collaborate together on various research programmes. As we have seen, Tim Berners-Lee originally produced the Web as a tool for networks of scientists to share documentation easily.

In more recent times the idea of virtual communities has become inherently associated with a range of websites collectively known as social networking sites. A social networking site is a website that provides a number of facilities for constructing and maintaining online relationships between members. Prominent examples of such social networking sites are Facebook, LinkedIn and MySpace. Globally, hundreds of millions of people have become members of these sites.

Virtual communities are founded in social networks and produce social capital just like traditional communities. However, there is still some question as to whether the bonds in the social network of a virtual community are as strong, and the social capital produced as great, as that produced in traditional communities. This is because there are a number of differences between virtual and traditional communities including issues of space, the form of communication used and the general focus of the community.

In terms of space, traditional communities are normally established on the basis of long residence by individuals in a prescribed geographical region. In contrast, virtual communities break geographical boundaries and individuals are effectively nodes in a wide area communication network. In traditional communities the dominant form of communication between community members will be face-to-face conversation. In virtual communities various forms of remote communication may be employed such as email, chat, telephone conversation or video-conferencing. Finally, the focus of a traditional community will be diverse. The focus of virtual communities is likely to be much more specific in nature.

It is possible to define various types of virtual communities. For instance, they can be based around different types of content provided on websites, such as transactions, area of interest, industry or expertise. Many sites are established to facilitate the buying and selling of products and services and to delivering data that is related to the completion of transactions. Many community websites focus on areas such as theatre, sports, science fiction or fantasy. Community websites frequently locate around key industrial functions such as accounting or manufacturing. Also, occupational groups may focus around key areas of expertise such as waste management and software engineering.

CASE CHECK

Arab Spring and social media

CS p 427

The establishment of virtual communities appears to have played a significant part in the Arab Spring – a term used to describe the wave of protests that began within a number of Arab countries in 2011, and which led to the overthrow of a number of regimes. Such communities formed initially around particular grievances but eventually became vehicles for actively organising political protest.

Virtual communities are now being used to enhance conventional eCommerce activity, which we shall call adjunct communities. Virtual communities also underlie forms of many-to-many eCommerce, which we shall refer to as C2C exchanges.

III

8.6.3   Social networking sites

Social networking site: a website that facilitates social networking

Recently, there has been much interest in the growth of **social networking sites**; sometimes referred to as *social networking media*, *social media* or *digital media*. All of these are somewhat bad names for this phenomenon because most social networks, as we have explained in Chapter 4, are not virtual. This phenomenon is really about using ICT, particularly Web 2.0 technologies (Chapter 6), to facilitate networking among dispersed individuals and therefore constitutes a variant on the virtual communities discussed above.

A key question is what impact this is having on business, or what potential it holds for business. Besides the obvious fact that these sites are in fact businesses themselves, there is interest from business more generally in utilising the technologies involved for internal and external use. For example, the Web 2.0 technologies (Chapter 6) on which social networking sites rely may have an internal impact, as in the case of fostering and supporting collaborative working and communication in distributed organisations. In an external sense, virtual communities of this form could be used to improve customer relationship management. For example, many companies are exploring the use of blogs and tweets as tools for marketing or customer relationship management.

Certain social networking sites, such as Facebook, are attempting to establish themselves as a third application layer on top of the Web and the Internet. In this sense these sites wish to encourage their members to engage in most of their online communication through the social networking site, rather than through the more open environment of the World Wide Web. For the user of the social networking site this offers a more convenient way of communicating with other members of the social network than through more open standards of communication, such as email. This enables the social networking site to gather masses of data about the attributes and activities of its users, which is of great value for business purposes such as marketing. Some commentators worry however about the possible infringements of data privacy that might arise from this and caution of a potential backlash against social media by its users.

REFLECT: Companies are using social networking applications for internal collaboration between organisational members. Consider some ways in which these technologies might be used in this manner.

CASE CHECK

Facebook

CS p 436

Facebook was launched in February 2004 as a social networking website by Mark Zuckerberg along with his fellow computer science students Eduardo Saverin, Dustin Moskovitz and Chris Hughes (Kirkpatrick, 2011). The name of the company is taken from the name applied to a book commonly given to university students within the United States at the start of the academic year.

On Facebook users may create a personal profile consisting of photos, lists of personal interests, contact information, and other personal data. To this profile other users may be added as friends. Friends may then exchange public or private messages, or use a chat feature. They may also receive automatic notifications when one of the friends in their network updates their profile. In addition, users may join user groups formed around common interests. Some of these, so-called *like* pages are maintained by organisations as a form of advertising.

8.6.4   Adjunct communities

Adjunct community: forms of virtual community that focus around the development of relationships between customers and the business

Certain electronic businesses are attempting to foster and support virtual communities as a means of adding value to their products and/or services. **Adjunct communities** are forms of virtual community that focus around the development of relationships between customers and the business. The key benefits to business are that, by creating and supporting such virtual communities, they will be better able to build membership audiences for their products and services. For instance, the motorcycle manufacturer Harley-Davidson has built an adjunct community to help support communication between fans about its products.

Certain features of social capital, such as increased mutual support among members of a virtual community, can be particularly beneficial to companies. Enhanced levels of trust between members of a virtual community may support increased levels of trade with a company. These forms of added value may increase customer loyalty and trust.

Timmers (1998) argues that there are two business models appropriate for adjunct communities. A *communication exchange* is a business model which attempts to add value to products and services through communications between a network of members. The company provides an environment in which members can partake in unedited communication exchange. Revenue is generated through membership fees, advertising revenue and cross-selling of products and services. In contrast, *collaboration platforms* tend to be much more focused on enabling collaboration between individuals and organisations and typically provide a set of tools and an environment for collaboration with a company.

8.6.5   C2C exchanges

C2C exchange: an ICT enabled facility that involves trade between complex networks of individual actors

Other business models for C2C focus more precisely on facilitating customer-to-customer relationships of exchange. **C2C exchange** involves trade of typically low-cost items between complex networks of individual actors. Revenues from C2C communities may be generated through advertising, transaction fees and/or membership fees.

Timmers (1998) argues that there are two main business models appropriate for C2C exchange. *Electronic auctions* constitute the prominent business model underlying C2C eCommerce and are discussed in more detail below. *Information brokerages* are companies specialising in the provision of information to consumers and to businesses. They help such individuals and organisations make buying decisions for business operations. Revenue models in this area include membership fees, advertising fees and cross-selling.

C2C exchanges involve trade between complex networks of individual actors. Although the typical monetary value of each exchange may be low, added together billions of dollars are traded annually in such forms of C2C commerce. However, C2C exchange is not a new phenomenon. A range of traditional business models have been created for this purpose which include newspaper classified advertisements, flea markets and auction houses.

Users of newspapers typically list items for sale, normally in newspapers distributed on a local basis. Buyers inspect items before purchase and may collect and pay for the item in person. In a flea market, sellers stock and display items for sale either at their own homes or at organised markets. Buyers browse for artefacts and will negotiate prices and collect and transport items themselves. Within auction houses, sellers take items to specialist organisations for sale. Buyers are able to inspect items before an auction, they will have to pay a registration fee to bid and are required to be at an auction or to nominate a proxy bidder. The highest bidder wins the auction and pays the auction house. The auction house in turn takes a percentage of the sale and pays the balance to the seller.

The value and take-up of a C2C exchange, such as that provided by eBay (see case study) is likely to be affected by Metcalfe's law (Chapter 4), where the community value of a network grows as the square of the number of users increase. It is likely that the variety in a C2C network will strongly influence the take-up and use of such applications. In other words, the more people available to communicate with and share goods and information the more likely it is that people will participate.

CASE CHECK
Amazon

 p 424

From the start Amazon offered a range of value-added services to its customers. A popular feature of the website is the ability for users to submit reviews for each product. As part of their review, users must rate the product on a scale from one to five stars. Such rating scales provide a basic measure of the popularity of a product. This reviewing facility has been seen by some as critical to the explosive growth of the company. Other added-value services include a personal notification service for customers requesting particular titles, a recommendations section where customers can recommend titles in various categories to other customers, an awards section which lists books that have won prizes, and an associate program where other sites can link to Amazon to sell their own selections.

At the start Jeff Bezos warned investors that they were unlikely to make a profit in the first five years of operation. However, Amazon has engaged in an aggressive expansion strategy and acquired a number of additional retail outlets, such as toys and CDs, and has provided a facility for online auctions of small goods. It introduced zShops in 1999, which is a facility that allows any individual or business to sell through Amazon.com – a form of C2C trading. Amazon has created an online community known as Mechanical Turk. This is an open marketplace in which workers perform tasks for requesters. Amazon receives a percentage of the fee charged for work by a worker.

RECAP: C2C eCommerce is ICT enablement of the community chain. The community chain is founded in social networks, and the value it produces is social capital. ICT has been used to enable community in local areas. ICT is also the infrastructure underlying the rise in virtual communities and social networking. Forms of electronic community include virtual communities and C2C exchanges.

8.7 Intra-business eBusiness and P2P eCommerce

Intra-business eBusiness: the use of ICT to enable the internal business processes of the firm

Figure 8.1 details two other forms of eBusiness beyond the forms of eCommerce discussed in previous sections: intra-business eBusiness and Partner to Partner (P2P) eBusiness. **Intra-business eBusiness** involves enablement of the internal value-chain with ICT, sometimes across separate business units. *P2P eBusiness* comprises the use of ICT to support the partnership chain, networks of organisations collaborating in the delivery of value to customers.

In a sense, all the material covered in previous chapters of this book is relevant to successful intra-business eBusiness. However, a number of issues are of particular relevance. First, intra-business eBusiness is very much about the importance of redesigning activity systems within organisations with the support of ICT to achieve improvements in efficacy, efficiency and effectiveness. Second, this redesign is based on the central importance of information and data as organisational resources for coordinated action. Third, to achieve performance gain organisations need to develop integrated and interoperable ICT infrastructure in support of improvements in organisational performance.

The traditional structure of organisations is founded in a functional model. In this view, organisations are structured in terms of functions such as marketing, finance and manufacturing. As a consequence, information systems have been designed to emulate this organisational structure; each functional unit tends to have its own information system to service its needs. , James Martin (1996) refers to this type of organisational model as a series of functional silos and the information systems infrastructure associated with it as one of stovepipe systems. Stovepipe systems frequently use incompatible data, making it difficult for communication across functional silos. They are also systems that are likely to suffer from redundancy and fragmentation.

Fragmentation is the situation in which data are fragmented across information systems because organisational units put up barriers of ownership around key data sets. Fragmentation may also be evident in processing where separate ICT systems communicate through manual interfaces, causing delay and other inefficiencies. Redundancy is the situation where large amounts of data are unnecessarily replicated across information systems, usually because interfaces do not exist between systems causing the same data to be entered many times. Redundancy may also be present when separate systems perform effectively the same processing on data.

Value-chain models of organisations stress the importance of cross-organisational processes or activity systems. The emphasis is on designing efficient and effective cross-organisational processes that deliver value to the customer. This model of the organisation encourages the design of integrated information systems to support key organisational processes. Martin argues that this form of information systems infrastructure not only provides more utility for organisations, it also enables the organisation to adapt more easily to changes in the environment.

As we have seen, electronic markets are founded on competition since a market is a network of interactions and relationships by which products and services are negotiated and exchanged. However, business can also be founded on cooperation and collaboration. A key way in which information systems may participate in business cooperation is through the concept of an *inter-organisational information system* (IOS) (Barrette and Konsynski, 1982). An IOS is an information system developed and maintained by a consortium of companies for the mutual benefit of member companies. Generally such systems provide infrastructure for the sharing of an application. IOS can prove a particularly effective way of sharing the costs of developing and maintaining large and complex information systems. Therefore an IOS is a type of information system directed at collaboration.

The automatic teller machine (ATM) networks run by major building societies and banks in the UK are key examples of IOS. These networks are constructed and maintained by consortia of financial institutions. This enables them to distribute the large costs of running such networks among the participating members. Another example is BACS, the clearing system of the major high-street banks in the UK that handles the debit and credit transactions to bank accounts.

An inter-organisational informatics infrastructure based upon developments in service-oriented software architecture has been proposed as a backbone for fostering what some have referred to as *digital business ecosystems*. The ideal is that businesses may flexibly utilise this backbone to develop new business models based on cooperation with other businesses.

REFLECT: Airlines run major inter-organisational information systems. For what purpose?

CASE CHECK
Amazon

CS ▷ p 424
Amazon engages in P2P eCommerce. For instance, the websites of Virgin Megastores (virginmega.com), and HMV (hmv.com) are hosted by Amazon. The company also runs multi-channel access for a number of companies such as Marks & Spencer and Mothercare. Such sites allow the customer to interchangeably interact with the retail website, standalone in-store terminals, and phone-based customer service agents.

8.8   eMarketing

Marketing can be defined as the process of planning and executing the conception, pricing, promotion and distribution of ideas, goods and services to create exchanges that satisfy individual and organisational goals. This definition emphasises that marketing is not just an activity that occurs after a product has been produced or after a service has been formulated. In modern business practice, marketing input is important in the design of a product and in the after-sales process; it is important to the design of the, so-called, value proposition of a company's business model. The Internet and ICT generally offer innovative ways of engaging in pre-sale activity with the customer. One of the most significant of such activities is the

eMarketing: the process of planning and executing the conception, pricing, promotion and distribution of ideas, goods and services using electronic channels

electronic marketing (eMarketing) of goods and services. In terms of customer relationship management, **eMarketing** is particularly directed at customer acquisition but it is also relevant to customer retention and extension. Not surprisingly, marketing strategy is typically an important part of organisational strategy and eMarketing strategy is likely to be a critical component of any eBusiness strategy.

8.8.1   Marketing channels

Marketing channel: a channel for the communication of marketing messages

The advertising of products and services is a substantial part of marketing. In our terms, it can be seen as a form of communication or information system between organisational actors and customers. Advertising involves attempting to transmit certain messages to particular customer segments in the hope of persuading people to buy products and/or services. Messages frequently take the form of assertions about particular properties of organisational value, such as quality or price. But many other messages consist of what we call expressives, communications which express people's feelings about particular forms of value. The intention is to attempt to build some form of emotional attachment to particular products or services.

Traditionally, marketing has focused on the transmission of messages to potential customers through channels such as television, radio, newspapers, magazines and, more recently, through direct-selling approaches using the telephone. Such approaches to marketing are normally described as being *push*, *passive*, *linear*, *event-driven* and *information-weak*. A company disseminates (*pushes*) the material to a perceived market of potential customers. Traditional modes of advertising require potential customers to find an advert either through browsing or through some more directed search. They are hence *passive*. The marketing material is scripted and is expected to be delivered in some *linear* sequence as a package. The material is *event-driven* in that it tends to be delivered at a specific point in time and the material is typically broadcast from one source to many potential customers. Because of such characteristics, it is typically difficult to gather direct data on the impact the distribution of a traditional marketing product has on a given population (*information-weak*).

Take an advertisement placed in relevant newspapers and magazines to promote a new type of car produced by an automobile company. The company pays to have the advertisement produced by a graphics company (scripting) and is likely to make a key decision on the types of newspapers and magazines to place the advertisement in on the basis of the intended customer-base for the car (push). For a multinational automobile manufacturer it will probably decide to run separate marketing campaigns in each of the countries it sends to (location-dependent). These decisions will be based on the assumption that potential customers will come across the advertisement while reading their newspaper or magazine (passive). The company will pay print companies to place the advertisement for a particular day; perhaps timed to coincide with some launch event for the car (event-driven). Since it appears in all copies of the particular newspapers and magazines it is effectively a broadcast of the advertisement. Advertising agencies have to engage in a number of post-hoc techniques to attempt to capture evidence of the impact of particular advertisements, such as interviewing a sample of customers (information-weak).

In contrast, electronic marketing uses electronic delivery and thus tends to be described as *pull*, *aggressive*, *interactive*, *time-independent* and *information-rich*. Potential customers themselves access the material using channels such as websites (*pull*). Such advertising also involves actively seeking out customers through technologies such as email and initiating some form of contact with them (*aggressive*). The potential customer can communicate with the company about its products and services using channels such as email and there is also potential for customising the material for particular customers (*interactive*). The marketing material can be accessed 24 hours a day, 365 days a year (*time-independent*). The material can also be accessed in different contexts, in a one-to-one or one-to-many relationship between the potential customer and the business or in a many-to-many way between the customer audiences themselves. Because of the transaction-based nature of B2C eCommerce sites a vast amount of data can be captured which relates customer searching with eventual purchase (*information-rich*). Finally, marketing via the Internet can be achieved on an international scale from one location.

However, a website will not prove effective as a marketing tool without sufficient numbers of people accessing it. Hence, eMarketing cannot be divorced from traditional promotional activities. Such promotional activities have to be undertaken over and above the creation of a website to achieve sufficient levels of traffic to the site. Once a sufficient level of traffic has been produced then a number of eMarketing techniques may be applied.

8.8.2   eMarketing strategy

Good marketing is reliant on good planning and planning for eMarketing will be an important part of general eBusiness planning (Chapter 10). Such planning will include an analysis of the environment for eMarketing, an assessment of current internal infrastructure available to the company for eMarketing, establishing a vision for eMarketing, specifying an eMarketing strategy, implementing such a strategy and evaluating the contribution eMarketing makes to the business.

Market analysis is the process of determining the demand for eCommerce in particular segments of the market. It will also involve close attention to the behaviour of competitors and partners such as intermediaries in this area. Market or customer segmentation is the process of identifying the characteristics of different segments of the population to which a company sells or wishes to sell its products or services. Customer segmentation is a concept frequently used within marketing strategy. The assumption is that a customer population can be distinguished in terms of a number of key dimensions. Different customer segments are likely to have different behaviour patterns with an organisation and, potentially, have different expectations of eCommerce.

Some key dimensions as far as segmentation is concerned are socioeconomic group, age, sex and ethnicity. Customer segmentation may be an important part of a channel strategy for organisations. Different customer segments will have different profiles of interaction with an organisation. Different access channels may also need to be maintained for different customer segments. It is also likely that different customer segments will need different content on websites.

On the basis of an analysis of customer segments it becomes possible to determine particular marketing requirements for each segment. There are five key questions companies should ask themselves in relation to customer segmentation: who are our customers? how are their needs changing? which do we target? how can we add value? how do we become first choice for the customer?

Assessment will involve evaluating the performance of the current infrastructure and determining the feasible options available to a company in terms of extending its eMarketing infrastructure.

Establishing a vision will involve setting clear objectives for the use of eMarketing in terms of online contribution to company performance and the marketing mix of product, price, place and promotion. As a *product*, companies will be looking to offer added-value associated with using electronic channels. Value could be added to products within electronic delivery channels by improving search facilities to online catalogues or providing more personalised products.

Pricing strategies for products and services should reflect the capabilities of electronic channels. In terms of pricing, companies may offer discounts for using online ordering or differentiate pricing more dynamically in terms of time of purchase or customer segment. For instance, EasyJet.com, like most low-cost airlines, operate a dynamic pricing policy for its ticketing based on advanced booking on its flights and on customer demand.

Due consideration should be given to the most appropriate *place* to promote goods and services through electronic channels. Placing decisions will involve consideration of whether to disintermediate or re-intermediate in particular markets. It will also involve decisions as to the degree of integration between a company's promotional strategies and that of its partners.

Finally, *promotion* will involve consideration of the integration of electronic promotional channels with conventional promotional channels. It will also concern decisions about the appropriate mix of online and conventional promotion. Promotional decisions will critically concern the amount of investment to be made in eMarketing as opposed to traditional marketing. Low-cost airlines, such as RyanAir, have used newspapers to offer discounts for advanced booking. Potential customers collect tokens from the newspaper and then contact the company via telephone or the Web.

Specifying an eMarketing strategy will involve detailing the part that eMarketing plays in general eBusiness strategy. *Implementing an eMarketing strategy* will involve building a technical infrastructure for eMarketing and putting the associated activity systems in place. *Evaluating eMarketing contribution* will involve monitoring the performance of eMarketing in terms of defined objectives such as online contribution.

REFLECT: How important would you say eMarketing is to an organisation such as a university? How successful do you think universities are at eMarketing?

8.8.3 The techniques of web-based eMarketing

key skill

Banner advertisement: adverts typically displayed across the top of a Web-page

Target advertisement: one-to-many active advertisements

Websites are now the primary approach for eMarketing. The main techniques of Web-based eMarketing include among others: banner adverts, target adverts, the use of domain names and email, and more recently the use of viral marketing.

Banner advertisement are so-called because they are usually displayed across the top of a Web page. These are one-to-many passive advertisements that are encountered by the user merely be accessing a Web page. **Target advertisements** are one-to-many active advertisements in the sense that the user must click on something in order to be taken to the particular advertisement page. Certain banner advertisements may also be click-through. *Email,* or other forms of remote communication such as SMS texting and instant messaging, can also be used to contact existing customers directly with offers or promotions. Use of direct email is a one-to-one aggressive promotion strategy. Email can also be used to contact potential customers from purchased customer databases.

Banner advertisement campaigns may involve placing such adverts on many different forms of website such as portals, generalised news services and special interest sites. Certain large online companies may utilise a large-scale network of affiliates. Affiliates will place small target advertisements on their websites encouraging users to re-direct to the home page of the major company for certain products and services.

Companies are likely to make charges for advertisements on their websites and this may form an important revenue stream for a Web-based intermediary such as a Web portal or affiliate. Generally there are four main ways of charging for online advertising: flat fee, CPM, Click through and CPA. *Flat fee* is a traditional model for advertising revenue. Here a set fee is charged for placing the advertisement for a set time-period. Cost per thousand Presentation Model, or *CPM,* is a method of billing based on the number of advertisements viewed. *Click through* is relevant to target advertisements and involves billing on the basis of the number of consumers who click through to the particular advertisement. Many companies offering advertisements on the Web, such as Google, are now using a Cost Per Action/Acquisition (*CPA*) revenue model. Cost per action is when an advertiser pays for each specified action, such as a purchase or a form submission, achieved through an online advert. **Cost per acquisition** is a related type in which the advertiser pays for new acquisitions such as new customers, prospects or leads achieved through online adverts.

Cost per acquisition: a form of revenue generation in which the advertiser pays for new acquisitions such as new customers, prospects or leads achieved through online adverts

Search engines provide an increasingly important gateway into products and services for consumers. Since Google is the most prominent example of such a gateway into the Web it is not surprising to find that most of its multi-billion dollar revenue is generated from banner and targeted advertisements on its website. Such revenue is generated in two major ways under its Adwords programme. First, advertisers bid for a series of keywords that they think should trigger an advertisement from their company on the Google Web page. If they are successful in their bid such keywords, when typed into the search engine, generate a sponsored link placed in a list displayed on the right hand side of the Google Web page. Where the link is placed in the list depends on an algorithm based upon factors such as the level of bid paid by the advertiser and a historical analysis of the rate of previous click-throughs for particular advertisements.

One other important tool in the eMarketing armoury is the use of branding in *domain names*. Brands are classic examples of signs. The logo or brand name of a company is an example of a symbol. Generally speaking such symbols signify certain referents such as particular products or the overall company activity. However, particular logos or brand names are also associated with a range of other connotations or concepts, such as perceived company values and behaviour. In the online world it is particularly important to ensure that a brand is used to maximum effect. This may involve copyrighting the brand, registering an existing and well-recognised brand name as a domain name, registering the domain name with the most well-used search engines, ensuring that the domain name returns high in the lists of returned results to users of search engines and monitoring access from search engines and adjusting strategies to maintain a presence.

One of the much discussed marketing techniques in recent times is that of **viral marketing**. This is the idea of using pre-existing social networks to produce an increase in brand awareness or to achieve other marketing objectives, such as increases in product sales. In traditional social networks these marketing objectives would be achieved through normal face-to-face communication between actors. The idea is to get ideas, such as product referrals, to spread throughout a social network in a similar manner to the way in which a virus might spread through a population – hence the name, viral marketing. As we argued in Chapter 4 this is fundamentally reliant on the level of social capital generated in a social network. In more recent times viral marketing relies particularly upon the growth in social media and the transmission of various forms of content such as video clips, images or text messages through such technologically enabled social networks.

Three other technologies are also mentioned as relevant to marketing through social media: blogs, **podcasts** and **tweets**:

A Weblog or *blog* for short was covered in Chapter 6 and is a website where entries are written in chronological order and commonly displayed in reverse chronological order.

A podcast or webcast is a series of digital media files, such as audio or video files, that are released episodically to users. The word podcast has replaced the more accurate term webcast in common usage following the success of the Apple iPod. The mode of delivery differentiates podcasting from other means of accessing media files over the Internet, such as direct download, or streaming. Normally, a list of all the audio or video files currently associated with a given series is maintained centrally on the distributor's server as a web feed. The listener or viewer then employs special client application software that can access this web feed, check it for updates, and download any new files in the series. This process can be automated so that new files are downloaded automatically. Web or podcasting is normally achieved with *RSS* (Really Simple Syndication) and consists of a family of Web feed formats used to publish frequently updated content, such as blog entries, news headlines or podcasts to subscribers.

Twitter is social networking site which enables its users to send and read text-based posts of up to 140 characters, informally known as tweets. Many business organisations are now using tweets as an advertising channel.

Viral marketing: the idea of spreading product referrals through a social network in a similar manner to the way in which a virus might spread through a population

Podcast: a series of digital media files such as audio or video files that are released episodically to users

Tweet: a text-based post of up to 140 characters

RECAP: Marketing can be defined as the process of planning and executing the conception, pricing, promotion and distribution of ideas, goods and services to create exchanges that satisfy individual and organisational goals. eMarketing is the use of electronic channels for the delivery of promotional material. Techniques for Web-based eMarketing include banner advertisements on websites and email to contact potential customers. Electronic marketing revenue can be achieved through flat fee, CPM, CPA or click-through. Branding domain names is a significant component of successful eMarketing.

8.9   eProcurement

eProcurement: a term used to refer to ICT enablement of key supply chain activities

The pre-sale activity of search, negotiate and order in the supply chain is frequently referred to under the umbrella term of procurement. Sometimes the term procurement is used to refer to all the activities involved in the supply chain. Hence, *procurement* is an important business activity system in the value-chain and involves purchasing goods and services from suppliers at an acceptable quality and price and with reliable delivery.

Electronic procurement (**eProcurement**) refers to the use of ICT to enable the whole of the procurement process. EProcurement is a specific and important feature of B2B eCommerce. In this section we consider some of the key differences between conventional procurement and eProcurement. In terms of this distinction we examine some of the key areas of performance improvement possible with this form of eCommerce. This leads us to examine various forms of eProcurement and suitable technologies for supporting this form of process strategy (Chapter 10) for eBusiness.

8.9.1   The conventional procurement process

It is possible to distinguish between two types of procurement performed by companies: production-related and operating procurement.

Production-related procurement: procurement designed to support manufacturing operations

Production-related procurement is designed to support manufacturing operations. As such, procurement must be geared to the fulfilment of long-term needs, it generally involves the procurement of customised items and is frequently undertaken through established and regular relationships with suppliers. As such, procurement for production-related activities tends to be organised as managerial hierarchies. Hence, a motorcycle manufacturer will engage in production-related procurement to source its components.

Operating procurement: procurement conducted to support all the operations of the business

Non-production or **operating procurement** is conducted to support all the operations of the business. Such procurement is designed to fulfil immediate needs, typically for commoditised items. As such, relationships with suppliers tend to be irregular and temporary. Hence, operating procurement is frequently organised in terms of a market-based model of economic exchange. For example, while a motorcycle manufacturer needs components to build its motorcycles it also needs office equipment and stationery, ICT equipment and various other commodities to run its business. These items are likely to be purchased through the market.

Historically, procurement has been a human-intensive process involving activities such as requesting quotations, submitting purchase orders, approving and confirming orders, shipping, invoicing and payment. Traditionally, procurement has been performed by a specialist-purchasing department typically employing many people using paper documentation, the telephone and fax to communicate with suppliers. An activity systems model of this traditional procurement process is illustrated in Figure 8.8.

Employees first search for a product matching a particular need. Details of the product are then entered on a requisition form, which is sent for authorisation to the purchasing department. This department receives the requisition, authorises production of a purchase order and then produces the purchase order which is sent to an established supplier. The supplier despatches goods to the company with an attached shipping note. When the goods have been checked a payment authorisation is issued to the accounting department who pay the supplier. The goods are then despatched internally to the originating department.

It is possible to analyse the performance of this activity system in a number of ways. One approach is to analyse the average time taken to conduct each of the activities in this process. These are indicated on the diagram as annotations and Table 8.2 provides us with a total lead time for the procurement process.

It is important to recognise that this estimate of the average duration of the procurement process is large because of inherent delays, lags or waiting times embedded within the current

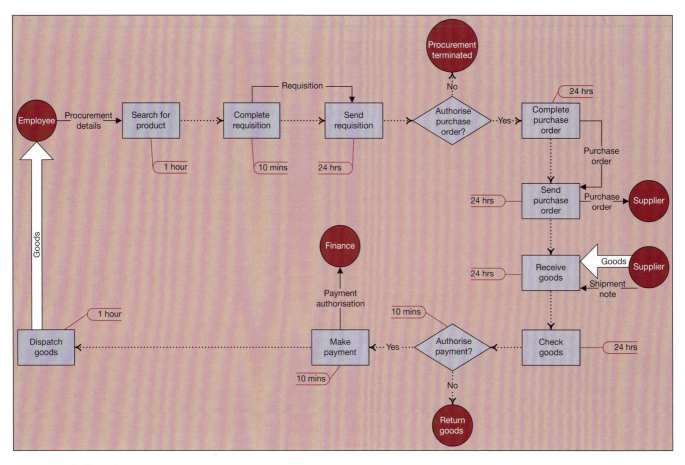

Figure 8.8 *Traditional procurement process*

Table 8.2 *Activities and timings for a traditional procurement process*

Activity	Average time
Search for product and product identified	1 hour
Complete requisition	10 minutes
Send requisition	24 hours
Receive requisition	12 hours
Authorise and complete order	24 hours
Send order	24 hours
Delivery from supplier	24 hours
Receive goods	24 hours
Check goods	24 hours
Authorise payment	10 minutes
Dispatch goods	1 hour
Total	6 days 2 hours and 20 minutes

activity system. Key delays are evident in the receipt of paper work and goods. For instance, items of documentation such as requisitions may sit in a person's in-tray for up to 12 hours before receiving attention.

Figure 8.9 illustrates an activity system that has been redesigned with the use of ICT. We are assuming here that employees are able to order directly from supplier websites. It therefore represents a model of a typical eProcurement process.

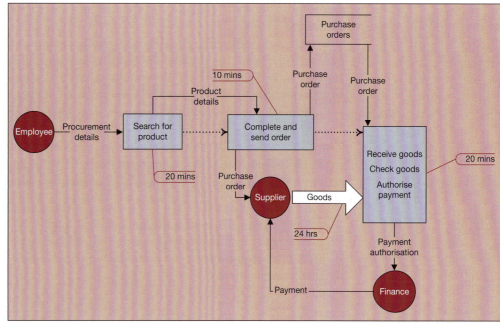

Figure 8.9 An eProcurement process

Table 8.3 Activities and timings associated with a re-engineered procurement process

Activity	Average time
Search for product and product identified	20 minutes
Complete order	10 minutes
Delivery from supplier	24 hours
Receive goods, check goods and authorise payment	20 minutes
Total	1 day 50 minutes

The same sort of analysis may be conducted for this electronic procurement process. The analysis is presented in Table 8.3.

It is evident that the speed of procurement is significantly increased using this activity system. This is because there is more automation of activities and more electronic transmission and storage of data. Consequently, certain activities are no longer required and there is less waiting time in the process.

> **REFLECT:** Besides obvious efficiency gains such as cost savings, what other benefits might eProcurement provide, particularly for public sector organisations?

8.9.2   Forms of eProcurement

It is possible to distinguish between three broad categories of eProcurement, roughly corresponding to the interdependent activities found in all procurement processes: electronic sourcing, purchasing and payment.

Electronic sourcing typically involves the use of electronic tendering systems that enable organisational agents to create requests for quotation (RFQ). Electronic RFQs can then be issued to suppliers. Forms of electronic auction may then be utilised to source best-price contracts with suppliers.

Once a contract with a given supplier is awarded then a number of tools may be used to search catalogues, select desired goods or services, place them in an electronic shopping basket and automatically raise a requisition or purchase order. This is *electronic purchasing*.

Invoices may be issued in XML-format from a supplier once goods have been dispatched. Also, once the buyer has received the goods an invoice can be automatically matched to the purchase order for price and to the goods received for quantity. Various electronic payment systems may then be used to transfer payment to the supplier.

To facilitate standardisation of data and hence effective analysis for management information, many forms of eProcurement will use standard commodity classification coding. Such standard coding schemes may also enable faster searching for a particular item among a range of possible suppliers. Commodity coding is the assignment of standard codes to item records (at the part number level) and to purchase orders (at the purchase order line item level).

RECAP: The pre-sale activities of search, negotiate and order in the supply chain are jointly known as procurement, also a term sometimes used for all the activities in the supply chain. eProcurement is the use of ICT to enable the whole of the procurement process. Forms of eProcurement include eSourcing, ePurchasing and ePayment.

8.10   Mobile commerce

Many see mobile eCommerce, or mobile commerce, as a significant new avenue for eBusiness. We shall argue that this area is really a logical extension of the model of eBusiness discussed in earlier sections. The ICT infrastructure model discussed in Chapter 5 and the value network model discussed in Chapter 7 are particularly useful as a way of understanding the position of mobile commerce within the wider context of eBusiness and eCommerce. Mobile commerce relies upon the use of a growing range of access devices, particularly mobile phones, laptops and tablets, by a range of different business actors to access and interact with the informatics infrastructure of organisations. This may be accessing the B2C and B2B eCommerce websites of organisations while on the move or at a location remote from the organisation. Hence, mobile commerce may involve online delivery of content to such access devices and includes the issue of remote working using access devices.

8.10.1   Remote/mobile working

As we mentioned previously, it is possible to identify four major places that remote access devices may be used: from the home, within public spaces, while on the move (mobile) or while in the workplace. Particular access channels will be associated with particular places of access and use. Hence, as a means of improving access to electronic services, governments have been putting more access devices into public places such as schools, libraries, community centres and museums. Also, an increasing range of WiFi hotspots are being offered in private sector cafés and other public spaces.

This technological change supports changes in work and leisure activity. Within countries such as the UK a growing number of people are working outside traditional organisational settings such as offices. Some of these workers are nomadic, in the sense that they move around or between countries in conducting their work. Some of these workers still work from a fixed location such as home, either on a full-time or a part-time basis, and some are working for themselves (their own businesses) or for a larger organisation.

All such workers rely on critical elements of our model of technical infrastructure discussed in Chapter 6. First, they need to have regular access to an access device such as a personal computer, laptop and/or mobile phone. Second, they need to connect such access devices easily to a ubiquitous broadband infrastructure, whether this is to the conventional telephony network, the mobile cellular network or a growing range of WiFi and WiMax facilities. Third, such mobile actors are likely to need to access organisational services, either in terms of dedicated services run as part of an organisation's informatics infrastructure, or more widely in terms of software as services run on cloud servers.

Let us just look at one facet of remote working to emphasise some of the costs and benefits associated with this change in working practices. In terms of remote working from home there are a number of proposed benefits for the individual. Remote working might provide improved access to work for persons who might find it difficult to travel regularly to a place of work, such as carers or the disabled. For certain persons, such as parents with young children, working from home might provide the opportunity for an improved work-life balance. For many, remote working reduces the need for commuting to work; freeing up more work time and reducing the stress of regular travel.

There are also a number of held benefits for the organisation employing remote workers. For instance, it has been found that remote working generally increases worker productivity while also reducing absenteeism. Remote working means that organisations can easily tap into a supply of personnel willing to work outside normal office hours and providing quality customer service. Remote working can also reduce an organisation's overheads, particularly the costs of maintaining expensive office space and associated services. Generally, remote working has also been found to improve staff loyalty and retention. It encourages valuable staff with particular skills but with other commitments to stay within the workforce.

Lastly, there are a number of benefits for the physical environment arising from increased remote working. Less people commuting as a result of increased remote working, means that there is reduced congestion on the road network. Reduced road traffic means less CO_2 emission and lower expenditure on maintaining road infrastructure.

However, remote working does raise a number of challenges. First, this style of work does not suit all individuals. Many workers prefer a structured working day; they appreciate contact with other workers and the group support familiar within traditional forms of work. Second, some have raised the reduced visibility of remote workers, which places them at a disadvantage in terms of work assignments and promotions. From the point of view of the organisation, remote working demands significant investment in and management of ICT infrastructure. Also, increased home working demands a certain degree of culture change. For instance, managers are no longer able to directly observe and control workers. This means that more trust has to be invested in the manager–employee relationship and that clearer performance management practices need to be established.

8.10.2 Virtual organisation

A key theme of this book is that ICT is an effective tool which supports the design of new activity systems or the redesign of existing activity systems. One of the most radical forms of such redesign is the virtual or network organisation. A virtual organisation has one or more of the following characteristics:

- Physical structures such as offices are reduced in number; or perhaps removed entirely.
- Workers are provided with electronic work-spaces rather than physical work-spaces. Where office space is required workers are encouraged to 'hot desk' – to share office facilities on a booking basis.
- Physical documentation is discouraged; electronic documentation is promoted.
- Work is organised in terms of loose projects which workers join and leave in a flexible way.
- The members of the organisation communicate and collaborate using ICT.

In these senses, the informatics infrastructure, including the communications network, becomes the organisation.

Virtual organisations such as this have been proposed as viable business models, particularly for knowledge-intensive industries and corresponding sets of knowledge workers. Hence, for instance, the production of content such as magazines or software can be managed by loose sets of project workers, collaborating remotely or in a nomadic manner.

8.10.3 Mobile B2C eCommerce

The term mobile eCommerce is better expressed as mobile B2C eCommerce. This term is now particularly used to refer to a growing range of applications available to the consumer or to a range of mobile access devices, such as tablets and mobile phones. As we have seen in Chapter 6 it is possible for consumers to access the Web via a mobile device. However, the access to such content is typically much slower than through a fixed device connected to the Internet through a conventional wide area network. The interface of certain access devices such as the mobile phone is also not ideal in that it does not permit easy navigation of Web content. Some organisations specifically produce websites with reduced functionality for mobile access. The growing range of tablet devices offers a more convenient interface to web content through larger, touch sensitive screens.

The key growth in the mobile B2C eCommerce sector in recent years has been in so-called apps. Apps, short for mobile applications, are small pieces of software developed specifically for the operating systems of handheld devices such as mobile phones, PDAs and tablet computers. Mobile apps can come preloaded on handheld devices or can be downloaded by users from app stores over the Internet. The most popular operating platforms that support mobile apps are Windows Mobile, Android, Symbian, Java ME and Palm. There was something like 17 billion downloads of mobile apps in 2011. However, the technological standards supporting such apps are frequently closed or proprietary leading many to question the long-term viability of this business model.

Mobile access devices, such as the mobile phone, often contain global positioning technology. This opens up a whole range of location-based services through the use of apps. For example, a retail organisation might supply a free app which allows users to locate their nearest store. A city tourist office might supply an app which helps the tourist locate sights of importance within a city centre and the app might supply background information which changes as the tourist moves through space.

8.11 eGovernment

As a term, eBusiness is normally used to refer to the ICT-enablement of activity systems within private sector organisations. But the redesign of activity systems is also of importance to the public sector, particularly within government and its agencies. Government typically fulfils three major functions: enabling and supporting democracy, developing and implementing policy, delivering services. To date, electronic government (**eGovernment**) in most countries around the World has traditionally focused on the last of these functions, perhaps because of the ease with which a model of service delivery has been adapted from the commercial sector.

eGovernment: the application of ICT within government organisations

We may view government in systems terms as the major control process in a political system; this provides meaning to the concept of governance. In the modern Western world it has been argued that governance is now undertaken by a network of stakeholders not all of whom are traditional political organisations or even public sector organisations. In this view, the disaggregation of the government value network which this implies demands an increasingly sophisticated technology infrastructure to support communication and coordination between a diverse network of actors.

It is possible to identify at least five major forms of eGovernment in terms of the value network idea. These forms are located around the major value-chains within the network and hence typically involve different stakeholders.

Internal eGovernment refers to the enablement of internal processes within the government body itself with ICT. The major stakeholder involved is the employee of the government body and the value-chain supported is the internal value-chain. In this area the significant innovation is the integration of back-office systems and processes within government. For example, many back-office activities in government agencies such as the UK Passport and Identity service rely heavily upon ICT infrastructure.

G2C (government to citizen) eGovernment is a form of external eGovernment since it is particularly involved in supporting the customer chain of the government body. Since the major stakeholder involved is the citizen, many of the so-called customer chain issues in eBusiness travel over into G2C eGovernment. However, many distinct issues arise located in the public sector nature of service provision such as diffuse, sometimes conflicting, goals characteristic of government bodies and the difficulties inherent in the customer/citizen distinction. The key promise of eGovernment in this area is particularly seen as the process of disintermediation, providing direct contact between citizen and government. For instance, much of the effort made by the Inland Revenue (now Inland Revenue and Customs) over the last decade, has been devoted to re-engineering key aspects of its customer chain by providing G2C services via its website.

III

CASE CHECK
Citizens Advice Bureau   CS p 430

The Citizens Advice Bureau, now named Citizens Advice in the UK, is one of the foremost independent charities in the country and delivers advice free of charge. Advice ranges from personal finances, housing matters, legal matters or consumer issues. Citizens Advice also run a website accessible to the general public known as Adviceguide. This website had almost 14.2 million visits to its home page in 2009/10.

G2B (government to business) eGovernment concerns electronic enablement of the relationships between government bodies and the private sector. One of the major forms of such relationships involves management of the supply chain. Hence, many of such supply chain issues are held to be similar in nature to eBusiness issues in this area. However, many features of the context of public sector procurement shape the relevance of technological solutions in this area. For example, a number of G2B portals have been built around Europe in an attempt not only to improve the efficiency of government procurement but also to enable the private sector greater access to public sector contracts.

Much of eGovernment success is based on delivering what has been referred to as joined-up government. This is the key issue for *G2G eGovernment*, the use of eGovernment to support intra-government cooperation and collaboration. This can be seen to be an internal value-chain issue for the super-system of government. Significant issues in this area include the interoperability of systems and data sharing between government agencies. For instance, many of the held benefits claimed for the introduction of a national identity card in the UK revolved around improving public service delivery through better data sharing between government agencies.

C2C eGovernment concerns enablement of the community chain of government bodies with ICT. C2C interaction is not traditionally seen to be a part of government. However, it is likely to be an important part of future governance, particularly in the way it links with two of the other functions of government, democratic accountability and policy-making. As an example, the UK government has set up a petitioning system on its central Web portal. Using this system any UK citizen can establish an online petition and collect signatories. If a petition collects 100,000 signatures, the issue may be debated in the House of Commons.

Lenk and Traunmuller (2002) argue that it is important to include all these forms within an extensive definition of eGovernment. Definitions of eGovernment should also include conceptions of **eDemocracy** like the use of ICT to support informed deliberation among citizens and help them to participate in decision-making. Hence, eDemocracy can be seen as a component part of eGovernment along with eAdministration. Forms of eDemocracy can also be seen to mirror forms of eAdministration as described above.

In narrow terms, eDemocracy can be used to refer solely to the enablement of democratic processes between members of some political grouping and their governmental representatives.

eDemocracy: the application of ICT to support democratic processes and systems

This is clearly a form of *external* eDemocracy and mirrors external forms of eAdministration such as G2C. For instance, government representatives may establish their own websites and communicate with citizens by electronic means such as email or tweets.

On the other hand eDemocracy can serve to refer to the way in which ICT can be used to improve internal democratic processes within government. This is a form of *internal* eDemocracy which closely mirrors both forms of internal eGovernment and G2G. For example, the Welsh Assembly Senedd (debating chamber) is set up in a radically different arrangement from most government debating chambers. Each assembly member is given a permanent kiosk within the chamber, where they can not only listen to the on-going live debate but also access internal ICT systems and the wider Internet.

There is also the notion of *local* eDemocracy. Local eDemocracy occurs where local groups use ICT to create democratic forms, forums and processes to facilitate political interaction within the community itself. It hence has a close relationship to C2C eGovernment. One key example here is the way in which social media were used in support of a number of uprisings such as those in Libya and Egypt.

Careers in IS

David Thomas

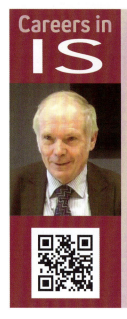

David Thomas is the Director of Technology and Chief Technology Officer at the National Archives, UK. David is a senior archivist and records specialist at The National Archives; the main focus of his career has been on improving access to archives and information in both government and the archive sector.

David is responsible for information technology services at The National Archives. In this role, he is leading on the major cross-government project to develop a shared service for preserving digital records.

Scan the QR code underneath David's picture or visit **www.palgrave.com/business/beynon-daviesbis2e/** to watch David talking about Information Systems and careers as an IS professional, and then think about the questions below:

- What advantages do digital records offer over paper records?
- What is the biggest challenge for the National Archives in relation to digital records?
- What does Digital by Default mean and how does the National Archives achieve this aim?
- Do you think that some of the services provided by the National Archives might be described as a form of G2C eGovernment? Why?
- From the citizen perspective, in what ways could digital access to the government documents stored in the National Archives promote forms of eDemocracy?

FOCUS ON VALUE

The idea of a transaction cost helps explain the value of information to business. Some would argue that it explains the existence of business itself. Businesses continually have to balance and control the costs of production with the costs of coordination. The value of ICT lies in its ability to lower costs of coordination in business hierarchies, markets and networks. Hence, electronic business and electronic commerce are seen as being of value in a general business strategy. ICT has value in enabling internal coordination of activities within the business. More recently, ICT has been used to facilitate new forms of collaboration and coordination with external stakeholders, so in general, ICT has key value in both supporting and innovating organisational behaviour in value networks.

8.12   Conclusion and key themes

This chapter introduced the term electronic business or eBusiness, to encompass the entire range of ICT application in businesses, both to improve internal operations and to extend systems into the environment. Electronic commerce (eCommerce) is the term used for the use of ICT in the external activities and relationships of the business with individuals, groups and other businesses.

Different forms of eBusiness can be identified, related to the features of the value network discussed in Chapter 7. There are also three major forms of eCommerce: B2C, B2B and C2C.

B2C eCommerce concerns the attempt to support the organisation's customer chain with ICT, and involves the ICT-enablement of key processes in the customer chain: pre-sale, sale execution, sale settlement and after-sale. It moves through a number of distinct stages of increasing complexity. A company is likely to first use the Internet for information seeking and communication, then establish a marketing presence on the Internet, and subsequently put an online catalogue of its products and/or services on a website. Online ordering and online payment are two additional levels of functionality likely to be provided on a company B2C site. At the highest level of sophistication forms of customer relationship management enable a company to better track its interactions with its customers.

B2B eCommerce represents the attempt by organisations to use ICT to improve elements of their supply chains. A typical supply chain includes activities such as search, negotiate, order, delivery, invoice, payment and after-sale. B2B eCommerce systems are likely to be built on a bedrock of sound back-end information systems infrastructure. Supply chain management has arisen as a distinct philosophy which helps frame the objective of B2B eCommerce.

C2C eCommerce is the ICT enablement of the community chain, or social networks surrounding the organisation. Public sector initiatives have been interested in enhancing traditional communities with increased ICT use. Private sector initiatives have been particularly interested in the community chain as a new revenue source or as a means of adding value to traditional commercial activities.

eMarketing is the use of electronic channels for delivery of promotional material. Traditional marketing channels are characterised as push, passive, linear, event-driven, one-to-many, and information-weak. In contrast, electronic marketing channels are characterised as pull, aggressive, interactive, time-independent, one-to-many and many-to-many, and information-strong. Techniques for Web-based eMarketing include banner advertisements on websites and email to contact potential customers. Revenue is achieved through schemes such as flat fee, CPM, CPA or click-through.

The pre-sale activities of search, negotiate and order in the supply chain are given the umbrella term procurement, which sometimes also refers to all the activities involved in the supply chain. Electronic procurement (eProcurement) is the use of ICT to enable the whole of the procurement process. Significant performance improvement is possible through forms of eProcurement such as eSourcing, ePurchasing and ePayment.

Whereas recent interest has been directed at the ways in which networks of consumers generate value, there has also been interest in the ways in which networks of businesses can use ICT to collaborate as well as compete. Internally, organisations are beginning to manage collaboration across internal units and divisions globally. Externally, digital ecosystems of businesses are emerging. This is known as P2P eBusiness.

Just as for eBusiness, it is possible for eGovernment to be thought of in terms of the value network idea. For instance, a government body's delivery of a service can be considered as a process of producing value for a number of different stakeholders. Each stakeholder will participate at different points in the value network and therefore will interact with different government systems. It is possible to identify at least five major forms of eGovernment in terms of the value network idea. Internal eGovernment refers to the enablement of internal processes within the government body itself with ICT. G2C or government to citizen eGovernment is involved in supporting the customer chain of the government body. G2B eGovernment concerns electronic enablement of the relationships between government bodies and the private sector. G2G eGovernment is the use of eGovernment to support intra-government cooperation and collaboration. Finally, C2C eGovernment concerns enablement of the community chain of government bodies with ICT.

At a number of points this chapter touched on the benefits of eBusiness and eCommerce. Chapter 9 looks at benefit or worth in more detail. It considers the related issues of the use of information systems in organisations and the impact they have. It also considers approaches to evaluating this impact.

8.13 Review test

1. eCommerce is a superset of eBusiness. True or false?
   - [ ] True
   - [ ] False

2. There are three main forms of eCommerce. Select all that apply.
   - [ ] B2C eCommerce
   - [ ] B2B eCommerce
   - [ ] G2G eCommerce
   - [ ] C2C eCommerce
   - [ ] G2C eCommerce

3. Some of the benefits of eCommerce are? Select all that apply.
   - [ ] Cost savings
   - [ ] Time savings
   - [ ] Increased security
   - [ ] Connection improvements

4. B2C eCommerce is an extension of customer-facing information systems. True or false?
   - [ ] True
   - [ ] False

5. Place the stages of B2C eCommerce growth in increasing order of complexity. Use 1 for the lowest level of complexity.
   - [ ] Marketing presence
   - [ ] Information seeking and communication
   - [ ] Online catalogue
   - [ ] Online payment
   - [ ] Online ordering
   - [ ] Customer relationship management

6. Customer relationship management is composed of which three main processes? Select all that apply.
   - [ ] Customer search
   - [ ] Customer acquisition
   - [ ] Customer satisfaction
   - [ ] Customer retention
   - [ ] Customer extension

7. B2B eCommerce is an extension of supplier-facing information systems. True or false?
   - [ ] True
   - [ ] False

8. Match the type of B2B eCommerce to the appropriate definition. Pair each lettered entry with the corresponding numbered entry.

   a. Buyer-oriented B2B

   1. In this approach a consumer opens an electronic market on its own server.

   b. Supplier-oriented B2B

   2. In this model, producers and consumers use the same marketplace.

   c. Intermediary-oriented B2B

   3. In this model an intermediary runs effectively a subset of an electronic market where buyers and sellers can meet and exchange products and services.

9. ____ eCommerce supports the partnership chain through the sharing of data between the ICT systems of companies. Fill in the blanks.

10. C2C eCommerce is: Select the most appropriate definition.
    - [ ] ICT enablement of the community chain
    - [ ] Connect to Cardiff
    - [ ] Competitive eCommerce

11. Match the type of community to the appropriate definition. Pair each lettered entry with the corresponding numbered entry.

    a. eNabled community

    1. A traditional community in which most interaction is conducted offline and some interaction is supported by communication networks.

    b. Virtual community

    2. A community in which all interaction between members is conducted via communication networks.

    c. Social networking site

    3. Using ICTs, particularly Web 2.0 technologies, to facilitate networking among dispersed individuals.

12 Marketing can be defined as the process of planning and executing the conception, pricing, promotion and distribution of ideas, goods and services to create exchanges that satisfy individual and organisational goals. True or false?
- ☐ True
- ☐ False

13 Techniques for Web-based eMarketing include? Select all that apply.
- ☐ Use of banner advertisements on websites
- ☐ Use of email to contact potential customers
- ☐ Use of cookies
- ☐ Use of pop-ups

14 _____ refers to the use of ICT to enable the whole of the procurement process.   Fill in the blank.

15 Forms of eProcurement include: Select all that apply.
- ☐ eSourcing
- ☐ ePurchasing
- ☐ ePayment
- ☐ eShopping

16 Match the type of procurement to the appropriate definition. Pair each lettered entry with the corresponding numbered entry.

a. Production-related procurement	**1.** Procurement designed to support manufacturing needs, typically for customised goods and consequently organised as a hierarchy.
b. Operating procurement	**2.** Procurement designed to fulfil immediate business needs for commoditised items and hence typically organised as a market.

17 Electronic government refers to the ICT-enablement of activity systems within private sector organisations. True or false?
- ☐ True
- ☐ False

18 Match the type of eGovernment to the appropriate definition. Pair each lettered entry with the corresponding numbered entry.

a. Internal eGovernment	**1.** Involved in supporting the customer chain of the government body.
b. G2C eGovernment	**2.** The use of eGovernment to support intra-government cooperation and collaboration.
c. G2G eGovernment	**3.** Concerns electronic enablement of the relationships between government bodies and the private sector.
d. C2C eGovernment	**4.** Concerns enablement of the community chain of government bodies with ICT.

8.14 Exercises

- Determine whether an organisation known to you has adopted eCommerce. If so, attempt to determine the benefits it derives from it. If not, determine what benefits it might derive.
- Access a B2C site and attempt to assign the features you find to the phases of the customer chain.
- Consider a company known to you. Determine at what stage it is in as far as B2C eCommerce is concerned.
- Take a company known to you, and determine what information is searched for using the Internet.
- Find a website for an SME in your local area. Determine how successfully it markets itself through the Internet.
- Find a website with an online catalogue. Describe the features of the online catalogue.
- Make a list of the types of goods you can order over the Internet and what you cannot. Reflect on the types of products characteristic of markets and hierarchies.
- Visit the Amazon.com site and attempt to determine what forms of customer profiling it employs.

- Investigate the range of CRM systems offered by vendors.

- Try to find an example of a community website and determine what content is provided on it.

- Produce a brief statement of the characteristics of a traditional promotional channel such as a television advert. Produce a brief statement of the characteristics of an eMarketing promotional channel such as a banner advertisement.

- Generate a list of the efficiency and effectiveness improvements relevant to a particular organisation's use of eMarketing.

- Access a particular web portal and determine what eMarketing techniques are used.

- Select a particular eMarketing technique and try to determine the revenue model used.

- Examine and analyse the whole of or part of a procurement process known to you in terms of the time taken to complete activities.

- Determine what forms of eProcurement are suitable for operational as opposed to production-related procurement.

- Find one example of an eMarket and describe its key stakeholders and features.

- Find one example each of a vertical and horizontal Internet portal and describe their key features.

- Find one example of an inter-organisational information system and analyse some of the reasons for its creation.

- Consider whether the costs and benefits associated with eCommerce differ with the size of company.

- Try to identify the sort of services provided electronically by a particular government agency, such as a local authority.

- See if you can identify two practical examples of G2G eGovernment.

8.15 Projects

- Investigate the take-up of eBusiness and eCommerce by companies in your local area. Attempt to determine the importance of eBusiness to their operations.

- Choose an industrial or commercial sector. Investigate the degree to which B2B and B2C eCommerce has penetrated the sector. As a consequence how have the value networks in your chosen sector been transformed?

- Determine the levels of disintermediation and re-intermediation among eCommerce conducted in a particular market sector, such as travel agencies or high-street banking. In other words, what sort of structural change has been caused to the market through ICT?

- Inter-organisational information systems are important to collaboration between business partners such as high-street banks or major airlines. Determine the benefits associated with them for a particular partnership network. Also determine the costs associated with building and operating them.

- Choose a market sector and determine the most appropriate organisational form for eBusiness. Can the business be run entirely online or is it important to maintain a physical presence?

- Study the take-up of B2C eCommerce among a limited range of companies. Discover the degree to which the evolution of eCommerce in these companies corresponds to the growth model discussed.

- The rise of online trading has caused a parallel increase in online theft and fraud. Investigate the impact this growth has on the issue of consumer trust. Will trust be a major brake on continued growth in B2C eCommerce?

- Customer relationship management is now a major philosophy for companies. Determine the degree to which it relies on customer relationship information systems. How do these information systems help improve organisational performance, and how can this be measured?

- Consider the most effective ways of evaluating B2C systems. How can companies determine the value that B2C eCommerce provides for them? Does conducting B2C eCommerce inevitably make such measurement easier, and if so, why?

- Among the various forms of B2B eCommerce described in this chapter, determine the most prevalent. For instance, determine the level of usage of intermediary-oriented B2B in a market sector known to you, such as retail.

- Those companies that survive in the eEconomy will be those that effectively integrate their front-end information systems, such as their B2B systems, with their existing core information systems infrastructure. Investigate the degree to which such integration is critical to the success of eBusiness.

- Choose two nation-states. Determine what stage they are at in terms of eGovernment. Use the forms of eGovernment discussed in this chapter to help compare the two nations.

8.16   Critical reflection

Will the traffic to websites ever reach a position where it will become possible to replace conventional channels of marketing solely with electronic channels? In what ways is the marketing mix likely to be different for intangible as opposed to tangible products and services? What type of business is likely to have a high online revenue contribution? Cyber-squatting occurs when a person or organisation purchases a domain name in the hope of selling it on to another company who might wish to use it to market their brand online. Does cyber-squatting damage the potential for eMarketing?

Besides the time it takes to complete tasks in the process, what other measures of the efficiency of the procurement process might be employed? Is it possible to identify the most important efficiency or effectiveness improvement produced through eProcurement? What forms of market models are most appropriate for electronic sourcing?

Attempt to access one of the many government websites. What did you think of the content? Do you regard it as useful? How might it be improved? To what degree is the modern welfare state dependent on information systems? Could the modern welfare state operate effectively without ICT? Can you provide examples?

8.17   Further reading

My new edition of *eBusiness* provides expanded coverage of most the material covered in this chapter (Beynon-Davies, 2012). Barrette and Konsynski (1982) provide the original formulation of an inter-organisational information system. Chaffey et al. (2009) provide a thorough coverage of eMarketing approaches. Farrington and Lysons (2012) cover forms of electronic procurement within the general context of supply chain management. The various models for eGovernment are discussed in my paper (Beynon-Davies, 2007). Cordella and Iannacci (2010) provide an alternative viewpoint on eGovernment infrastructure.

8.18   References

Barrette, S. and B. R. Konsynski. (1982). Inter-Organisational Information Sharing Systems. *MIS Quarterly* 6 (4): 93–105.

Beynon-Davies, P. (2007). Models for eGovernment. *Transforming Government: People, Process and Policy* 1 (1).

Beynon-Davies, P. (2012). *eBusiness*. Palgrave Macmillan, Basingstoke.

Cassidy, J. (2002). *Dot.Con*. Allen Lane/Penguin Press, London.

Chaffey, D., R. Mayer, K. Johnston and F. Ellis-Chadwicj. (2009). *Internet Marketing*. 3rd edition. Pearson, Harlow.

Cordella, A. and F. Iannacci. (2010). Information Systems in the Public Sector: The e-Government Enactment Framework. *Journal of Strategic Information Systems* 19 (1): 52–66.

Farrington, B. and K. Lysons. (2012*). Purchasing and Supply Chain Management. Financial times*. Prentice Hall, London.

Kirkpatrick, D. (2011). *The Facebook Effect: The Real Inside Story of Mark Zuckerberg and the World's Fastest Growing Company: The Inside Story of the Company That is Connecting the World*. Virgin Books, London.

Lenk, K. and R. Traunmuller. (2002). Preface to the Focus Theme on e-Government. *Electronic Markets* 12 (3): 147–148.

Martin, J. (1996). *Cybercorp*. American Management Association, New York.

Porter, M. E. and V. E. Millar (1985). How Information Gives you Competitive Advantage. *Harvard Business Review* 63(4): 149–160.

Rheingold, H. (1995). *The Virtual Community: Finding Connection in a Computerised World*. Minerva, London.

Timmers, P. (1998). Business Models for Electronic Marketplaces. *Electronic Markets* 8 (1): 3–8.

See companion website   www.palgrave.com/business/beynon-daviesbis2e

Assessing the use and impact of information systems

Learning outcomes	Principles
Understand the relationship between the value of ICT and questions of its use and impact.	The value of ICT lies in the interaction of technology with the activity systems of an organisation. Successful information systems rely upon successful use and such use is a pre-condition of successful impact.
Describe elements making up the use context of an information system and distinguish between the impact of information systems upon the organisation at large and upon groups and individuals within organisations.	The use context consists of stakeholders of various types engaging with the interfaces to an ICT system. The usability of this interface, as well as user satisfaction with the overall information system, establishes a good base for successful impact. The impact of information systems will be felt in terms of the jobs and work of particular individuals and groups. Impact also needs to be assessed in terms of performance improvement within activity systems in organisations.
Relate the importance of understanding the causes of information systems failure to achieving success in this area.	The failure of information systems is commonplace. Definitions of failure are relative to the expectations that particular stakeholder groups have of that information system. Avoiding failure and achieving success relies on understanding and managing the complex relationship ICT and information systems have with organisations.
Understand the importance of the evaluation of information systems and explain the distinction between strategic, formative and summative evaluation.	Evaluation is an assessment of worth. Such assessments are important at a number of points in the life of an information system: before it is conceived (strategic evaluation); during its development (formative evaluation); and after it is delivered into its context of use (summative evaluation).

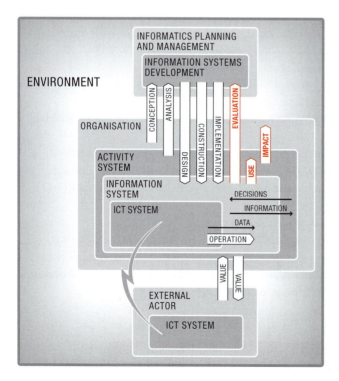

Chapter outline

9.1   Introduction

Davenport (Davenport and Prusak, 2000) makes an interesting analogy between ICT and plumbing. Imagine a world, he says, obsessed with the technology of plumbing. Only two things are missing in this strange world. The first is an interest in the qualities of the material handled by this technology, namely water. The second is an interest in the uses to which water is put: drinking, washing, cleaning and so on. Substitute ICT for plumbing and data for water, and you get an appreciation of the way in which technology, information and action are inevitably intertwined in considerations of the worth of ICT.

In other words, the value or the worth of ICT cannot be divorced from the question of what it delivers, that is, data for use in information systems. The worth of ICT is also directly related to the degree to which ICT systems are used and the impact they have on organisations. Judgements of worth ultimately relate to assessments of success and failure, so they rely on critical processes of evaluation.

After an information system is introduced into an organisation, it begins to have effects on that organisation. These come in two forms, first-order effects and second-order effects. First-order effects concern issues of use. This chapter considers them in the use context, and looks at how this helps determine stakeholder commitment to and satisfaction with information systems.

Second-order effects concern the impact of the information system on activity systems in organisations: on individuals, groups and the organisation as a whole. To help explain the issue of organisational impact more clearly, we use the distinction between efficacy, efficiency and effectiveness measures of performance that were introduced in Chapter 2.

Both use and impact are critical inputs into any assessment of the success or failure of an information system. This chapter therefore considers information systems failure in some detail. This helps to show the systemic relationship between elements that affect the success of information systems.

The question of the worth of ICT and information systems raises the important issue of evaluation. The chapter concludes with a discussion of a number of forms of evaluation appropriate to organisational informatics. These forms link directly to the processes needed to ensure effective informatics planning, management and development activities.

9.2   The worth of an information system

Some years ago DeLone and McLean (1992) systematically reviewed the literature on the success of information systems in organisations, and produced a model of the factors influencing it (see Figure 9.1). This model has been much debated but it is still useful for highlighting some of the key variables, and has been used to organise some of the discussion here.

To the left of the figure are two issues of technical quality: the quality of the information system itself and the quality of the information it produces. Both are likely to influence the use of the system and perceptions of user satisfaction. The use of the system will have an

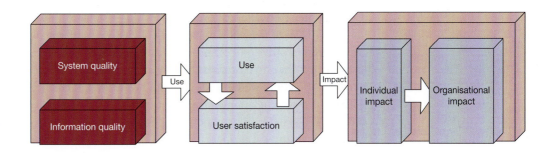

Figure 9.1 *The DeLone and McLean model*

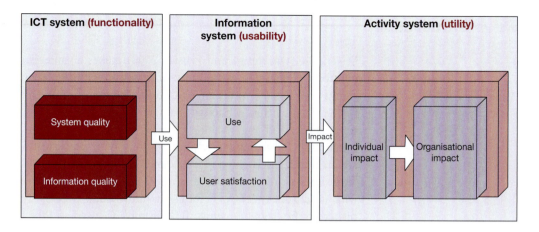

Figure 9.2 *The domains of functionality, usability and utility*

impact on individuals in the organisation, which in turn will have an impact on the organisation as a whole.

In a later paper (DeLone and McLean, 2003), the authors suggested two amendments to the model. The concept of service quality was added alongside system and information quality. Service quality is meant to extend the focus from the products of the informatics function (see Chapter 11) to the service this function provides. The issues of individual impact and organisational impact were also brought together in the notion of net benefits achieved from information systems. This is meant to encompass the fact that multiple stakeholders, both inside the organisation (such as differing work groups) and outside it (such as customers and partners) are likely to benefit from the introduction of an information system.

Elements from the DeLone and McLean model can be overlaid onto a far simpler scheme of functionality, usability and utility (see Figure 9.2).

Information systems have to be designed, in the sense that their key features need to be determined before they are constructed and implemented. These key features, or properties, provide core ways of assessing the system's worth or success. Since an information system mediates between technology and activity, we can consider it in terms of three properties: functionality, **usability** and **utility**.

The *functionality* of an information system is normally determined by a close examination of organisational requirements. It is what the system does, or should do. Specifying the core functionality is a critical aspect of information systems development (see Chapter 12). For instance, to describe a system as an order processing system indicates that it, in some way, captures, stores and manipulates data associated with the processing of orders.

Usability is evident in the way in which an information system embeds itself in activity. It is a measure of how easy it is to use for the purpose for which it has been constructed. Usability is evident at the human–computer interface (see below), the point at which the user interacts with the ICT system. An order processing system's usability will be determined by how easy it is for users, such as order clerks or customer service representatives, to input and extract data about orders.

Whereas functionality defines what an information system does and usability defines how it is used, *utility* defines how acceptable the information system is in terms of doing what is needed. It judges the system by the contribution it makes to its activity system and the organisation as a whole. An order processing system's utility might be defined as the contribution it makes to the efficient handling of customer orders. It might contribute to significant cost savings in order processing, and/or to improvements in organisational effectiveness. For instance, if it leads to customers getting an improved service, that should be apparent in their level of satisfaction, which feeds through to the level of customer retention.

There is a clear relationship between functionality, usability and utility on the one hand, and an ICT system, information system and activity system on the other. Functionality is typically seen to be a property of the ICT system, whereas utility emerges as a property of

Usability: an information system's usability is how easy a system is to use for the purpose for which it has been constructed

the activity system. Usability is a mediating feature between the technical system (the ICT system) and the social system (the activity system), and is evident at the user interface (see below).

In the Delone and McLean model, system quality, information quality and to a certain extent service quality are primarily issues of functionality. Functionality is established in the context of the informatics service (see Chapter 11), and in particular the process of information systems development (see Chapter 12). As a result these issues lie mostly in the domain of the ICT system (Chapter 6). Use and user satisfaction are primarily issues of usability, which is established in the context of use, and lies in the domain of the information system (see Chapter 4). Impact at a number of levels is primarily an issue of the utility of the information system within an activity system. Utility is established in the context of the consequences or impact of the information system on aspects of the activity system.

Put these together, and we have a way of judging the worth of an information system. It might be judged to lack functionality and so to have failed; it might be regarded as adequately functioning but unusable, and hence to have failed; or it could be judged that it is adequate in both functionality and usability, but has not delivered any key organisational benefit, so it has failed in terms of utility. So judgements of the success or otherwise of an information system depend upon which aspect you are focusing on: the technology, the communication or the activity. We shall consider this issue of information systems failure in more detail later in the chapter.

9.3   The context of use

The context of use of an information system is defined by a number of key issues including:

- usability
- the user interface
- the use setting
- stakeholder involvement
- stakeholder satisfaction.

Conventional conceptions of use see it in terms of the usability of ICT systems, that is, how easy the system is to use for the purpose for which it was constructed. So the definition of usability hinges on the activity system it is meant to serve.

Evidence suggests that, for successful use, activity systems must be designed in parallel with the design of ICT systems. The identification and involvement of key system stakeholders is therefore essential for the successful development and use of ICT systems (see Chapter 12).

One of the key reasons for involving stakeholders in the development of information systems is that this involvement appears to increase levels of user satisfaction with the systems. Systems that are not accepted and do not have the commitment of system stakeholders are likely to be subject to stakeholder resistance.

These issues are neatly summarised in a series of propositions concerning ICT systems design expressed nearly two decades ago by Eason (1988):

> IT technical design is not enough because benefit can only come if these systems are effectively harnessed and exploited by their users. The achievement of this involves the creation of compatible social and technical systems to serve some important organisational purpose. This in turn means the design of a social system to serve this purpose and the creation of a technical system which will support the users in the social system. The design process by which this is achieved requires a process of planned change which not only creates the appropriate system but creates in the users a motivational and knowledge state where they are able and willing to exploit the technical capabilities. This involves the participation of the stakeholders in the design process and individual and collective learning processes.

9.3.1   The user interface

In Chapter 6 we considered the interface layer as an important part of the modern ICT system. As we discussed there, a user interface can be seen as a collection of dialogues, each made up of a series of messages between the user and the ICT system. As such, the user interface is the technology supporting human–machine communication. There are three major aspects to this human–machine communication:

- the content of messages between the user and the ICT system
- control, which refers to the way the user moves between aspects of one dialogue, or from one dialogue to another
- the layout or format of messages and data on input and output devices.

Take the interface to the Goronwy Galvanising ICT system first described in Chapter 1. Control will involve aspects such as the navigation between the main menu and a jobs data entry screen, through use of pointing and clicking using a mouse. Format refers to the structure of menus and data entry screens. Content refers to the actual data entered and retrieved via these screens (Figure 9.3).

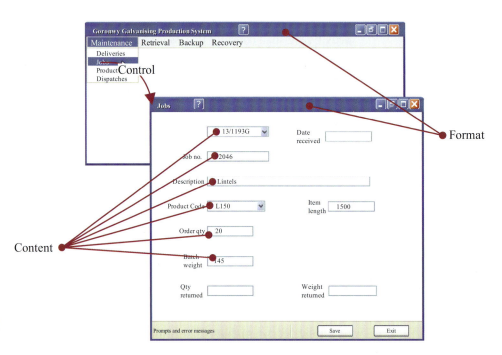

Figure 9.3 *Format, content and control*

9.3.2   Types of interface

There are a number of broad categories of interface format: menus, forms, command language, natural language, direct manipulation, multimedia, virtual reality and gestural interfaces. They can be used in combination, for instance, the interface to an order processing system might be made up of menus, data entry forms and elements of direct manipulation.

Menus are interfaces consisting of a displayed list of choices. The user selects an item from the list by pressing a key combination, moving a cursor to the choice and clicking the mouse, or typing in a value and pressing 'enter'.

Forms effectively emulate the idea of a paper form on the computer screen and are used for data entry and retrieval. A form is simply a set of fields laid out on a screen, or more readily these days in a window on the screen. The data entry fields are normally labelled, and there is also usually a header and an area for the display of error messages or prompts.

Command language interface: an interface in which the user enters statements in a formal language

In a **command language interface**, the user enters statements in a formal language. Historically, command level interfaces were the first type of online interface. Typically, operating systems have command language interfaces, and many database management systems also offer command level interfaces to the database sub-language SQL (see Chapter 6).

Natural language interface: an interface in which the user enters statements in a natural language, such as English

Natural language interfaces are slightly misnamed because they will not generally accept everyday English input as character strings. They are more accurately described as being restricted language interfaces. The system is programmed to decipher a range of statements and commands, but it is limited in the grammar and vocabulary that is accepted. So the statement, '*give me all the salaries of my employees*' might be acceptable, but '*list my employees' salaries*' might not. Natural language statements can be either typed via the keyboard or spoken through a microphone with associated voice recognition software. These interfaces have achieved some success as ways of querying database systems (see Chapter 6).

Direct manipulation interfaces are generally associated with icon-based, windows environments, and are referred to as direct manipulation because the user causes events to happen by manipulating graphic objects using a mouse or similar input device. They are now dominant in most areas of ICT systems.

Multimedia interfaces are a direct extension of the direct manipulation interface, in that they employ the same mechanisms for controlling input, but rather than having menus and data entry forms, a full range of media types is used to build the interface. The prevalence of the Web has caused an explosion in the types of media used in interfaces, which often include animation, video and audio. However, adding multimedia to interfaces does not always improve their usability.

In some applications, such as simulations, it is important for the user to experience feedback through an interface that closely resembles the real-world situation being simulated. For instance, aircraft simulators are used to train commercial and military pilots, and their controls are copies of actual aircraft control panels. Aspects of this form of virtual reality interface have now become feasible on the desktop, and organisations have experimented with the use of such immersive interfaces in the domain of information systems.

Gestural interface: an interface controlled by forms of bodily gesture such as hand gestures

In recent years **gestural interfaces** have become popular, particularly in association with hand-held devices such as tablet computers. Gestural interfaces are extensions of direct manipulation and multimedia interfaces which accept input from parts of the human body such as the hand. Such input, in the form of movements of the hand, can be used to control aspects of the graphical interface.

9.3.3   Use setting

It is important to recognise that, increasingly, interfaces to systems will differ depending on the access channel used by stakeholders (see Chapter 5). For example, both a customer service employee and a customer might have access to a CRM system, but their interfaces are likely to be significantly different in both functionality and usability. Interfaces are also likely to differ depending on the access device used and the place of use.

There are four major types of location for remote access devices: at home, in public spaces, while on the move (mobile), or in the workplace. Particular access channels are associated with particular places of access and use. For example, as a means of improving access to electronic services, many governments have put more access devices in public places such as schools, libraries, community centres and museums. An increasing range of WiFi hotspots are also being offered in cafés and other public spaces.

Use setting: the setting within which a particular interface is used

These three issues of stakeholder type, access device used and place of use together make up a **use setting**, a concept which also includes the information-handling behaviours and practices established in a context, particularly in the workplace. For instance, Marchand, Kettinger and Rollings (2000) make the important point that what they call the information orientation of people in organisations has a bearing on the success of information and ICT systems. This means a set of positive practices and behaviours established in relation to information handling, and is a facet of organisational culture (see Chapter 2).

In some organisations the information orientation is focused on individuals rather than groups. The organisational culture encourages people to build and maintain their own data repositories. There is little incentive for people to share data, which might even be thought of as bringing a potential loss of power. In other organisations people are encouraged to collect data about customers but not given any incentive to enter it in the core information system. This makes coherent customer resource management difficult.

9.3.4 Usability

Usability normally considers both a defined user group and a defined set of tasks. The design of a user interface must consider the roles of its users, and what tasks they will need to carry out. For the interface in Figure 9.3, for example, the defined user group is likely to be production controllers at Goronwy. The tasks to be performed are the entry of new job sheets, the retrieval of existing job sheets and the amendment of data on existing job sheets.

The usability of an ICT system is how easy it is to use for the purpose for which it has been constructed, the task that can be undertaken through the interface. Nielsen (1993) suggests that it can be evaluated on five dimensions:

- Learnability, or how easy it is to learn to use the interface.
- Rememberability, or how easy it is for the user to be able to remember learned operations.
- How efficient it is to use, for instance, users should not face delays when they try to input data.
- The interface should promote reliable human performance in the sense that it should lead users to make fewer errors.
- The interface should satisfy the users in the sense that it leaves them subjectively pleased with using it. This is known as user satisfaction (see below).

Since the interface is now an increasingly large part of the structure of most ICT systems, its design has become an established part of information systems design (Chapter 12). There is also an increasing emphasis on assessing, evaluating and testing the usability of systems. The discipline devoted to these activities is now frequently known as usability engineering.

9.3.5 The quality of the user interface

Whichever combination of formats is chosen for the user interface, a number of design guidelines have been shown to improve usability:

- It is important to use consistent and meaningful terminology. This fundamentally means applying a consistent and relevant set of signs within the interface constructed for a particular domain. For instance, if menus are used, it is important to provide a consistent way for the user to select options, to title every menu, to align options and to have no more than seven options per menu. Menus also need a consistent way of displaying error messages, and it is useful to organise menus in a hierarchy that emulates the division of tasks in the system.
- A different user interface should be designed for each distinct user group. The terms used should be familiar to the proposed group of users. Naive users will need different interfaces to experienced users. For instance, naive users might prefer menu selection because of ease of use, whereas sophisticated users might prefer a command-line interface because of speed of use.
- Feedback should be provided for users: when they do something right, they need to see a result; when they do something wrong, help should be provided.

- Dialogues should be designed with a well-defined start, middle and end. This and feedback are sometimes discussed under the concept of closure, because they both concern the importance of showing users whether or not they have successfully completed an operation.
- Simple, meaningful error messages should make it easy to correct a mistake. It is also useful to allow users to backtrack to a previous state.
- Information overload should be avoided. Interfaces should not be cluttered with too much information. Also, images and other media should be used only when they contribute to usability.

9.3.6 Stakeholders

Use implies a user, a term often used to refer to everybody in an organisation except the ICT developers. So it might include, for instance, top-level managers, middle managers and operational staff.

As in Chapter 2, this book prefers the term stakeholder group or stakeholder rather than user, to help distinguish between different groups inside and outside an organisation who might have an effect on the system's use and impact. A number of major types of stakeholder relevant to this context can be distinguished at a high level.

First, there are the stakeholders that form the development context for an information system (Chapter 12): producers, clients and end-users. Producers are the people tasked with developing the information system. Clients sponsor and provide resources for the project, they are normally managers. Users, or more accurately end-users, are the people involved in using the information system, and are only rarely managers; most information systems are designed to support other workers, as was described in Chapter 4.

Second, since information systems are increasingly being used to support external relationships and activities, stakeholder groups such as customers, suppliers, regulators and partners are increasingly important. Some of these groups, such as customers and suppliers, may even overlap with end-users for certain classes of front-end information systems. Partners and regulators are likely to have a key influence on the design of an information system.

Within Goronwy Galvanising, for instance, the clients are the managers in the company's headquarters. Producers are the developers brought in to construct the ICT system for the company. The end-users are workers at Goronwy, including inbound and outbound logistics staff, production controllers and shift foremen. As the system developed into an extranet, customers such as Blackwalls were involved in the design of aspects of it.

Third, a stakeholder is a political concept in that it is related to issues of power and its exercise (see Chapter 2). Stakeholder groups are social groups that have a stake in, and potentially a degree of influence over, the development of an information system. An organisational group can also be defined in terms of a set of shared meanings, in other words a subculture. Each stakeholder group might form a distinct subculture (see Chapter 2) in an organisation. In this chapter, the main interest is in the set of assumptions, expectations and knowledge a group might use to frame technological change.

9.3.7 Technological frames

Technological frame: a collection of underlying assumptions, expectations and knowledge that people have about technology and its use

Orlikowski and Gash (1994) suggest that people approach technology on the basis of their **technological frame**: a collection of underlying assumptions, expectations and knowledge about technology and its use. Managers, technologists, users and other stakeholders have significantly different technological frames, which influence how they understand the development, use and change of technology.

Orlikowski and Gash use the example of a project which attempted to introduce the ICT package Lotus Notes into a consulting organisation to help illustrate differences in such frames:

- Nature of technology: the technologists saw Notes as an information sharing and group-work tool, but users framed it more as an individual productivity tool.

- Technology strategy: technologists expected the package to leverage the work of the firm. Users tended to see Notes merely as a substitute for existing ICT, such as fax and telephone.
- Technology in use: technologists assumed that Notes was an end-user tool which needed little support from the informatics service (see Chapter 11). But users did not really know how they were expected to use it or what it could do for them, and felt they should have been given demonstrations by the technologists.

9.3.8   Stakeholder involvement and satisfaction

A number of critical principles affecting use arise from the concept of a stakeholder group. First, it is important to identify stakeholder groups that are likely to influence the development process as part of the planning for an information system (see Chapter 10). Second, it is important to involve representatives of various stakeholder groups in the development process (see Chapter 12). Third, it is important to identify differences in meanings assigned to technology by different stakeholders.

Stakeholder involvement in the development of information systems is seen to improve system acceptance and satisfaction with systems. **Stakeholder satisfaction** refers to a subjective assessment of the success of an information system, so determining its level is an important part of assessing the worth of a system. It can be assessed at a number of levels. Satisfaction with the interface may serve as a measure of usability. Satisfaction with the ICT system itself may serve as a measure of functionality. Finally, satisfaction with the information system may serve as a measure of utility.

This section on usage issues concentrates on user interface satisfaction, although this is difficult to separate from issues of functionality. User satisfaction criteria with systems include: output assessments such as accuracy, quality, completeness and relevance of output: process assessments such as availability of service, mean time between failure, down-time and number of security breaches; and input assessments such as ease of use and response time.

Satisfaction is often measured using questionnaires with a series of attitude questions. One popular approach is **QUIS** – Questionnaire for User Interface Satisfaction – consisting of 27 items using a nine point Likert scale. Figure 9.4 provides an example of the questions that are asked within this questionnaire.

By placing a cross at some point along each scale the respondent to the questionnaire forms an informative act (Chapter 3). She expresses her feelings towards a user interface by relating

Stakeholder involvement: Involvement of stakeholder representatives in the development of an ICT system

Stakeholder satisfaction: The state of satisfaction expressed by a stakeholder group in an information system

QUIS: questionnaire for user interface satisfaction, a means of assessing user satisfaction with an interface

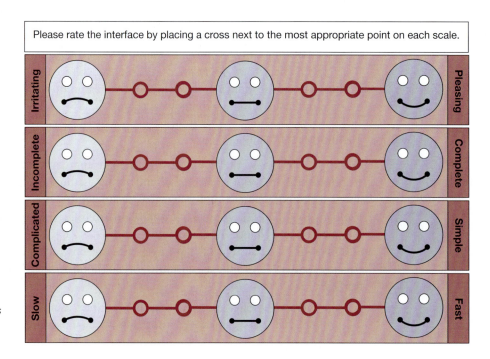

Figure 9.4 Example questions from a user satisfaction questionnaire

them to the appropriate emoticon (happy, neutral and sad). The entire collection of such formative acts, expressed by a cross-section of users, can be aggregated to form a measure of the satisfaction with a particular interface, as well as suggesting areas for improvement.

9.3.9   Stakeholder resistance

Stakeholder resistance: the resistance of stakeholder groups to the introduction of an information system

After delivery, an information system is subject to use and maintenance (Chapter 12). The further development and maintenance of a system is known as its post-implementation trajectory.

One of the key ways in which organisational politics may affect the post-implementation trajectory is through user or **stakeholder resistance**. Hirschheim and Newman (1988), for instance, provide a case study that illustrates how user resistance depended on the amount of stakeholder involvement in implementation. Keen (1981) details a number of counter-implementation strategies that users may take to impede the development of an information system. One of these strategies is to lay low or to be too busy to be involved. In other words, if a stakeholder does not wish a system to succeed, then keeping out of the way and not giving help and encouragement can help make it a failure. Another strategy is to exploit the development team's lack of inside knowledge. The technical staff in particular will probably know very little about the detailed nature of the work involved in a particular business area and, if users do not help by telling them what goes on, the system they design will probably prove to be inadequate.

RECAP: After information systems are introduced in an organisation, the context of use begins to affect the activity system. Information systems may be closely aligned with their activity system, through design or by accident, generating both intended and unintended positive effects. If they are misaligned they can have a negative effect on organisational activity. They are more likely to be well aligned if the developers identify the stakeholders, understand the differences in their technological frames, and involve representatives of stakeholder groups in the development process.

9.4   Impact

Once introduced, information systems have immediate effects within their context of use, which is largely determined by the activity system into which they are placed. The effects can be positive or negative depending on how well the system is aligned with its context.

Impact: the effect of information systems on individuals, groups and organisations

Second-order effects, or **impact**, can be separated into impact on individuals, on groups and on the organisation as a whole. All these can be either positive or negative. At the level of groups and individuals, perceptions of the positive or negative nature of impact will relate to people's organisational position: for instance, the system might bring about shifts in power and influence. Of the impacts on the organisation as a whole, the relationship between

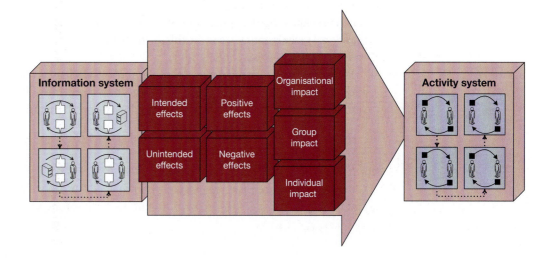

Figure 9.5 *Dimensions of impact*

information systems and productivity has been hotly debated (see Figure 9.5). Some impact will have been predicted and designed for, but much of the impact of information systems can be unintended.

CASE CHECK	CS ▶ p 438	The UK Child Support Agency's information system, CS2, is a good example of a system which had an unintended negative impact upon its organisation. It failed so disastrously that it contributed to the closure of the Agency, and cost the UK taxpayer over £1 billion.
Failure in government ICT systems (UK Child Support Agency)		

Orlikowski (1996) made a second study of the introduction of Lotus Notes in a company selling marketing software, and noted how it changed planned ways of working. Initially, the technology was intended to help manage a large increase in phone calls to software support staff at local offices. The idea was that the individual call-handlers would use the package to document calls electronically, so they could track and respond to them more effectively. What actually happened, Orlikowski noticed, was that people started to use the system to proactively respond to other people's calls for which they had a ready solution during downtime periods in their work. This change was so successful that managers began to assess support specialists in terms of their ability to collaborate proactively with their colleagues. Eventually the system began to be used as a way of training new support staff in appropriate ways of performing support work.

Less successful is the example Button and Harper (1993) give of the introduction of a computerised order processing system in a foam manufacturing company. It upset existing work practices to such a degree that it interfered with effective fulfilment of orders: '*It slowed things down.*' Likewise, Sachs (1995) demonstrated how the introduction of a centralised work scheduling system in a telephone engineering organisation disrupted the effective troubleshooting work of maintenance engineers.

Landauer (1995) compiled an impressive list of evidence against the usefulness and usability of many computer systems, providing examples of misalignment at organisational, individual and group levels. He maintains that there was little evidence that computer systems actually contributed to organisational effectiveness, and particularly to increases in productivity. There were examples of the effective use of computer technology to improve business performance, such as computer-aided telephony, but he believed they were in the minority.

To help explain this, Landauer made a distinction between phase one and phase two computer applications. In phase one applications, computers are used to automate functions that had either previously been performed by humans, or that no human would be capable of. These applications exploit the computer's calculating power, examples are missile control and accounting systems. Because of their inherent deterministic and limited context, phase one applications proved relatively successful. Landauer argued, however, that there were fewer and fewer areas left for them to penetrate. Phase two applications are about augmentation, encompassing that range of tasks that people do that cannot be taken over entirely by numerical calculations. It was in this field that it was hard to be clear whether the systems were making a positive contribution.

However, Landauer did believe that computer systems can be used to improve performance; much of his argument was that they had been introduced with little formative or summative evaluation of their usability and usefulness. This issue of evaluation is discussed in a later section.

9.4.1   Impact on the organisation

Chapter 2 introduced the idea of control, the need for a system to be able to regulate itself and to adapt to changes in its environment. Control can be seen as a monitoring subsystem that controls the behaviour of other subsystems by comparing their behaviour against defined levels of performance and acting appropriately.

What systems analysts see as control, business theoreticians tend to see as performance management, the process of measuring past action. The assumption is that past action determines current performance. In a systems context, as we have seen, performance can be measured in terms of efficacy, efficiency and effectiveness. The level of performance an organisation attains is a function of the efficacy, efficiency and effectiveness of the actions it has undertaken. The difference between these performance measures is illustrated in Figure 9.6.

Efficacy is a measure of the extent to which a system achieves its intended transformation. Porter would argue that for any company this transformation involves delivering greater value to customers (see Chapter 7). So efficacy is primarily focused on the outputs from the organisation, or producing the appropriate value. Efficacy gains are typically measured as improvements in the volume or quality of a service or product.

Efficiency tends to correspond, at least for commercial organisations, to an economic model of the firm. It is a measure of the extent to which the system achieves its intended transformation with the minimum use of resources. Efficiency gains can be achieved in an activity system through doing more with the same resources, or the same with less resource, so they can be measured by comparing inputs against outputs using a systems model of the organisation. If inputs and outputs can be expressed in numeric terms, efficiency can be expressed as the ratio of inputs to outputs: Efficiency = Inputs/Outputs.

In the traditional open systems model of organisations, capital and labour are the two inputs that the organisation takes from its environment. A microeconomic model of the firm permits capital to be freely substituted for labour to produce similar levels of output or production. Such models predict that ICT can be freely substituted for labour through the automation of processes, thereby introducing cost savings.

Another type of economic model of the firm, as we saw in Chapter 7, is based around the idea of transaction costs. These are the costs incurred by the organisation when it buys in the marketplace. Firms seek to reduce transaction costs particularly by reducing the costs associated with using markets, such as locating and communicating with suppliers, maintaining contracts and obtaining information on products. ICT can help in these ways.

For commercial organisations, improving efficacy and efficiency are strategies to make more money, that is, to increase profitability. Efficacy and efficiency gains will lead to more customers and improve the competitive position of the company.

Efficacy, efficiency and consequently profitability all have to be measured and monitored. Successful companies institute both single- and double-loop learning (Chapter 2) through single- and double-loop feedback mechanisms. These rely on data collected, stored and disseminated through information systems, so information systems and their associated ICT systems are critical to modern organisational performance. The key question is how to measure the effectiveness of the information and ICT systems in organisations?

Effectiveness is a measure of the extent to which the system contributes to the purposes of a higher-level system of which it may be a subsystem. For example, a company that was a member of a larger business group would be judged on the contribution it made to group profitability. An autonomous company's effectiveness might be assessed through competitive benchmarking to discover its competitive position in its key markets. In terms of the relationship between the information system and the activity system it supports, effectiveness involves measuring the impact of the information system on the purpose of the activity system. Much of the discussion of the effectiveness of information systems is directed at attempting to determine the strategic advantage they offer to businesses (see Chapter 10).

Efficacy: a measure of the extent to which a system achieves its intended transformation. See also Utility

Efficiency: a measure of the extent to which a system achieves its intended transformation with the minimum use of resources

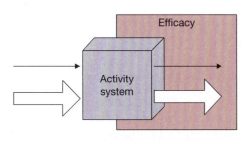

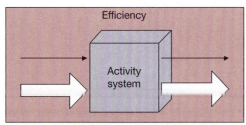

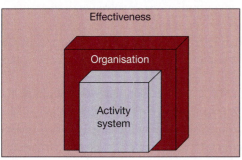

Figure 9.6 Efficacy, efficiency and effectiveness

Effectiveness: a measure of the extent to which the system contributes to the purposes of some higher-level system

III

CASE CHECK
Tesco CS p 455

Consider some of the benefits of Tesco maintaining its online arm, Tesco.com. The site offers a different access channel for its primary value flow, the sale of foodstuffs. This is a gain in efficacy. The online channel also offers the company the possibility of reaching a larger base of customers and selling a wider range of products for little additional resource. This is a gain in efficiency. Finally, the online channel offers improvements in market position for the company. It is able to use the site as a means of gaining greater market share. These are primarily gains in effectiveness.

Traditionally, performance measurement systems tried to use financial criteria to measure tangible efficiency gains. More recently, companies have attempted to build more holistic performance measurement systems that encompass the broad range of efficacy, efficiency and effectiveness. One of the most famous is the **balanced scorecard** invented by Robert Kaplan and David Norton (1992). This has been much used in business consulting. It maintains that if an organisation has a good, well-balanced measurement system, it should have the data needed to answer four main questions:

Balanced scorecard: a popular performance measurement system for organisations

- The financial perspective. How do we look to our shareholders?
- The customer perspective. How do our customers see us?
- The internal perspective. What must we exceed at?
- The innovation and learning perspective. How do we continue to innovate and create value?

It is argued that these questions should be approached sequentially, and a few key performance indicators should be used for each. The balanced scorecard has been proposed as a useful instrument for the assessment of eBusiness concerns. For example, to assess CRM systems from the customer perspective key performance indicators might be customer acquisition rate, customer retention rate and customer satisfaction measures.

9.4.2   The productivity paradox

But does the introduction of an information system always have a positive impact? Evidence suggests that there are some inherent paradoxes, or contradictions, involved with their introduction. One of the most significant is the **productivity paradox**.

Organisations expect new information systems to raise the productivity of their workforce but, over a number of years, this link between information system usage and productivity has been questioned by Brynjolfson (1993).

Brynjolfson's early paper examined the literature on the relationship between productivity and the application of ICT for office-based (white collar) organisations in the United States. The evidence suggested that whereas delivered computing power increased by two orders of magnitude between the 1970s and 1990s, productivity, particularly in the service sector (the heaviest users of ICT), had stagnated. Spending on computers reached its peak in the mid-1980s, but although productivity (measured in terms of service transactions handled per worker) increased rapidly during the early 1960s, it remained relatively stable up to 1990.

Brynjolfson considered four main explanations for the productivity paradox:

Productivity paradox: the paradox that those organisations that have invested significantly in ICT do not appear to have experienced significant improvements in productivity

- Mis-measurement of inputs and outputs. A proper indicator of ICT impact has yet to be formulated and analysed. Measures such as the number of service transactions multiplied by their unit value tend to ignore sources of value such as increased quality and speed of customer service.
- Lags due to learning and adjustment. The long-term lag between cost and benefit may be the result of the extensive learning required for individuals, groups and organisations to fully exploit ICT.
- Redistribution and dissipation of profits. This explanation proposes that those investing in technology benefit at the expense of others in a particular industry, Hence, there is no aggregate benefit to an industrial sector such as financial services.

- Mismanagement of ICT. This is the basic informatics argument, which is given greater credence in subsequent work by Brynjolfson (Brynjolfson and Hitt, 1998). It proposes that companies have systematically mismanaged and have not planned systematically for the introduction of ICT, so they have not reaped benefits in terms of productivity.

9.4.3   Impact on groups and individuals in the organisation

At a more micro level, as well as having an impact on organisations as a whole, information systems have an impact on the work of groups and individuals. Again, the impact may be positive or negative. The assessment of the value of such impact depends on the position of the stakeholder group within the organisation. Some potential consequences for groups and individuals are discussed below.

The introduction of ICT systems may increase levels of work monitoring and permit greater control of work by managerial groups. ICT systems may enable large amounts of transactional data to be captured about the day-to-day activities of the workforce. This could be used, for instance, to decide on promotion and redundancy strategies.

In contrast, ICT systems can be used to enrich jobs and provide greater degrees of worker empowerment. They could be used to remove many burdensome administrative activities, freeing workers to devote more time to issues such as customer service. One key way in which customer service can be improved is by letting front-line personnel make instantaneous decisions (for example, on how to handle customer complaints) with the aid of ICT systems.

The introduction of ICT systems typically causes changes in forms of collaboration and coordination between groups. For instance, email is now extensively used in organisations as a means of scheduling activity such as meetings, and this could mean there is less face-to-face contact.

ICT systems may change the patterns of power and influence in and between groups. For example, when office software was first introduced it began to replace typical secretarial skills such as typing. This had a major impact on the work of both secretaries and their bosses.

Zuboff (1988) has argued that ICT makes work more visible. There is the potential for workers to establish more clearly what is happening in their organisation, identify problems with work processes and suggest alternative ways of doing things. Hence, ICT systems have significant potential as vehicles for learning in organisations.

All this should make it clear that the design of information systems (see Chapter 12) is not a value-neutral activity. Decisions made, particularly about the shape of an activity system to be used in association with an information system, can affect a number of dimensions of work in a positive or negative way, including the level of skills required and the variety of the tasks undertaken. Information systems can increase (upskill) or decrease (deskill) the levels of skill required in a particular work setting. They can increase or decrease the variety of tasks required of workers. They can increase or reduce the size of a task relative to the overall purpose of the organisation. They can be designed to increase the autonomy of workers, in the sense that they are given responsibility for planning and controlling their own work, or to control their work, sometimes in minute detail. Finally, information systems can be designed to encourage or discourage levels of social interaction between workers.

9.4.4   Impact on groups and individuals outside the organisation

Information systems and the ICT embedded in them do not only affect internal stakeholders, they also affect external stakeholders. Two particular issues are considered here: the relationship between the use of systems and data protection, and unequal access to electronic delivery of goods and services.

The definition of the information society considered in Chapter 3 relies on a critical mass of the populace using electronic delivery as their preferred method of accessing services and products from public and private sector organisations. Many organisations are producing

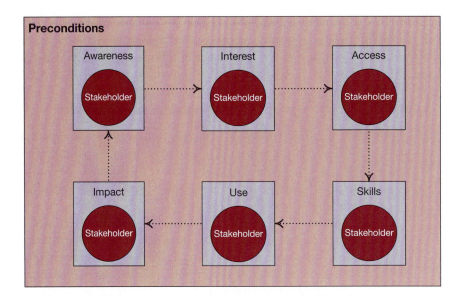

Figure 9.7 *Pre-conditions for electronic delivery of products and services*

strategies to encourage this, but there are a number of pre-conditions to the successful uptake of remote access channels. These represent the interaction of a range of social factors, including awareness, interest, access, skills, use and impact (see Figure 9.7).

The increasing penetration of electronic delivery into business strategies provides some evidence that modern Western societies are information societies. However, at its heart, the idea of an information society relies on a critical mass of the populace using electronic delivery as a preferred method of accessing the services and products of public and private sector organisations.

Although organisations are producing strategies to encourage their external stakeholders, such as customers, to use remote modes of access to their services and products, a number of pre-conditions exist for the successful uptake of such access channels. These pre-conditions represent the interaction of a range of social factors likely to affect take-up of remote access devices and channels and the use of such channels to interact with forms of electronic delivery.

Business actors or stakeholders must be aware of the benefits of using various remote access channels (awareness). Such benefits must also be seen to outweigh the costs of using electronic delivery in people's minds.

However, awareness in and of itself is no guarantee of effective take-up. Actors must also be interested in using various remote access channels for specific purposes (interest). For people to change their conventional way of interacting with organisations over to new access channels there is a substantial and immediate set of transaction costs which include: the costs of finding relevant information, the costs of learning new ways of conducting such interaction and the costs of correcting mistakes. These are all typically referred to as switching costs, because they refer to the costs incurred by individuals in switching from one mode of access to another. Evidence suggests that small, up-front transaction costs of this nature frequently discourage people from making a commitment to electronic delivery. To outweigh such transaction costs, interest from customers is likely to depend on substantial and perceived added value offered by using electronic access over traditional modes of access.

Assuming a suitable level of both awareness and interest, stakeholders must further have access to remote access devices from the home or other convenient location (access). Measures of such access are frequently expressed in terms of forms of connectivity to the Internet. Access can be determined by a whole number of factors, particularly income, since the money available to an individual or household will determine whether or not a computer and Internet access (as well as its associated costs) are affordable. There is no such thing as free access to the Internet. All those who enjoy free access do so because the university, organisation or other institution in which they work pay the costs. For those who cannot enjoy this luxury, Internet access can include the costs of the hardware and software, payments to the Internet Service Provider (ISP), as well as telephone bills for those using Internet access through fixed telephony. The cost of upgrading equipment and replacing obsolete software compounds the financial burden imposed on individuals with Internet access.

But even if a person has access they must also have the skills necessary to effectively use access devices such as the Internet-enabled PC (skills). This is frequently seen as the problem of eLiteracy, the low-level skills required to use ICT effectively. Such low-level skills include being able to use a keyboard and a computer mouse, to conduct basic operations with operating systems such as Microsoft Windows, to use productivity packages such as office software, and to use Internet and Web tools such as browsers. Clearly, there are a substantial number of transaction costs for the individual associated with learning such a range of new skills.

If a person is aware, interested, has access and is skilled enough, he or she must commit to using remote access channels on a regular basis in core areas of life (use). In other words, people accept technological innovations if such innovations become domesticated into personal, everyday routines, in a similar way that other technological devices such as telephones, televisions, fridges, washing machines and microwave ovens are domestic appliances.

Finally, use of various access channels must approach a threshold that encourages the provision of more content and services delivered electronically (impact). The hope for many organisations is that a virtuous cycle is established in which better content and services, perhaps directed at particular social, economic or political groups will encourage greater awareness of, interest in and use of remote access channels as the preferred method of interaction with organisations.

9.4.5 The digital divide

Given the nature of technological innovation and the way such innovations diffuse through society it is perhaps no surprise to find differential rates of awareness, interest, access, skills and use of ICT among different groups in society. However, as more and more areas of everyday activity rely upon the use of remote access channels and electronic delivery there is a concern that a **digital divide** continues to disadvantage many groups. For instance, there is substantial evidence to suggest that the older you are the less likely you are to be aware and interested in using ICT. Elderly groups also have the least access to ICT, the lowest levels of electronic literacy and use electronic services the least.

The digital divide is fundamentally related to issues of social exclusion, the processes by which certain social groups are excluded from participation in key activities of society. The potential for ICT to improve economic, social and political processes is limited by a number of major forces of such social exclusion present both within and between societies. Particular sectors in society may be excluded economically, socially and politically from effective communication and participation in the information society. On the economic front the cost of ICT equipment and maintaining a connection to the Internet may prove prohibitive for many disadvantaged groups. Socially, low levels of eLiteracy may exclude certain customer segments from participation. Finally, politically, government institutions may wish to impose levels of political/state control on the network infrastructure that prohibit or discourage certain opinions from being aired, or activities undertaken, through electronic channels. A key concern here is that information elites will be able to exploit economic, social and political advantages of the information society. For business a key concern is that major sectors of a potential customer-base will miss out on electronic delivery of services and products.

As well as the digital divide between social groups in Western societies, there is concern over the divide between developed and less developed countries. This forms the background to initiatives such as the one laptop per child non-profit organisation, which aims to '*create educational opportunities for the world's poorest children by providing each child with a rugged, low-cost, low-power, connected laptop with content and software designed for collaborative, joyful, self-empowered learning*' (www.laptop.org).

Digital divide: the phenomenon of differential rates of awareness, interest, access, skills and use of ICT among different groups in society

9.4.6   Data privacy and data protection

Data privacy: ensuring the privacy of personal data

There are also some major privacy concerns associated with people using the Internet for eCommerce. These include the collection and storage of personal data by companies, its disclosure to third parties, and its use by companies or other agencies in ways that people might feel invade their privacy.

For example, cookies are data files placed on Internet users' machines by Web browsers, which the browser uses to store data like passwords and when a site was last visited. This is particularly useful to companies because they can identify particular customers, monitor their surfing behaviour and use the data to tailor the user's interaction with their site. However, many people feel that the use of cookies is an invasion of privacy, because it is not apparent to them when they are created or what data is held in them and, of course, they might not choose for the company to have access to this kind of detailed record of their activities.

Spamming is sending unsolicited emails to large numbers of people whose data is held on address lists. This is seen by many to be both an inconvenience and an invasion of privacy. During the 1990s thousands of Usenet news groups were spammed by the US legal firm Canter and Siegel, offering to help potential US immigrants get green cards.

The UK Data Protection Act (1984) laid down a number of principles to enforce good practice in the management of personal data by organisations. In 2000 the UK government implemented new legislation to bring the Act in line with the EU Data Protection Directive.

Data protection: the activity of ensuring data privacy

Data protection in the European Union is based upon five main principles:

- Personal data should be collected for a specific and declared purpose.
- The collection and processing of personal data should be adequate, relevant and not excessive in relation to the declared purpose.
- Organisations should maintain accurate and current data on people; inaccurate or incomplete data should be erased or rectified.
- Personal data should be preserved in a form that permits identification of individuals for a period no longer than is required for the purposes for which the data is stored.
- Appropriate security measures, technical and organisational, should be taken to protect personal data from unintended or unauthorised disclosure, destruction or modification.

European countries have generally legislated on data protection and privacy. In the United States the strategy has been to rely more on self-regulation by organisations. This makes it difficult for many multinational companies to transfer data internationally, because actions that are permissible in one country might not be in others. In order to ease data transfer, the US Department of Commerce and the European Union have created the Safe Harbour Framework. Companies which sign up to this framework, such as Microsoft, are seen as having adequate data protection procedures for cross-border data transfer.

In the United Kingdom, all organisations that maintain personal data must register details of it with the Data Protection Registrar, and are obliged to ensure that their use of it conforms with data protection legislation. Many other countries, such as those in Scandinavia, have stronger data protection legislation in place.

> **REFLECT:** How much personal data do you hand over to organisations, both in the public and the private sector? How concerned are you over the privacy of data held about you by organisations? Would you be liable to change your consumption practices if it was found that certain companies were using data held about you in ways they never told you about?

RECAP: Information systems have an impact on individuals, groups and organisations as a whole. The impact of introducing them can be either positive or negative at each of these levels, and different stakeholders will have different views on which it is. Most common assessments of ICT focus on the effects ICT has on organisational efficiency and/or effectiveness, but ICT does not deliver performance gain in and of itself. Rather, it can contribute to changes in activity systems, which in turn can affect the performance of organisations.

9.5 Success and failure

The two issues of the use of information systems and their impact are tied up with assessments about their worth or value. In very broad terms, assessments of worth or value focus on considerations of their success or failure.

In many ways the success or failure (and so the value) of information systems is the key dependent variable for the discipline of organisational informatics. In other words, organisational informatics is particularly concerned with determining those practices (independent variables) that have an effect on the success of information systems (dependent variable).

This section concentrates on the issue of information systems failure, using the assumption that analysing failures can provide important lessons for formulating successful strategies for the planning, management, development and operation of information systems.

9.5.1 Dimensions of information systems failure

Information systems failure: the development or use failure of an information system

Information systems failure, as well as strategies for avoiding it, have both horizontal and vertical dimensions. Horizontally, there is a distinction between development failure and use failure. Vertically, failure can be explored at the level of ICT systems, information system projects, organisations or the external environment. These two axes are illustrated in Figure 9.8.

Vertically, we can address information systems failure on a number of levels: technical, project, organisational and environmental. In very general terms these form a hierarchy of problem complexity:

- Technical failure is the failure of hardware, software and communication networks, such as system crashes.
- Project failure involves failures in project management and control, such as cost or time overruns.
- Organisational failure is the failure of a system to deliver organisational benefits, such as an increase in efficiency or effectiveness.
- Environmental failure is caused by changes in environmental factors, such as regulations and labour relations.

There are two important phases in the way human beings approach problems, problem setting and problem solving. As we have seen in Chapter 2, in some areas of human activity it is relatively easy to set problems, but in other areas there is vast disagreement on how to define key problems.

Technical problems tend, by their very nature, to be relatively easy to define. At this level we can usually identify quite precisely what the problem is, which leads to a search for suitable solutions. These

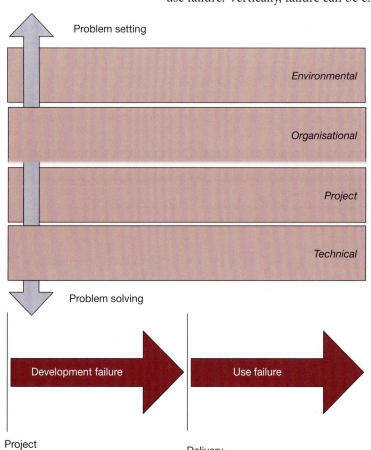

Figure 9.8 Dimensions of information systems failure

problems are described as *hard*. Problem setting is un-contentious, and most effort is devoted to problem solving.

At the opposite end of the scale lie organisational and environmental problems. These are frequently difficult to identify, not least because different stakeholder groups perceive the problems differently. These *soft* problems are sometimes also called ***wicked* problems**, and they are characterised by a focus on problem setting rather than problem solving.

Wicked problems: complex problems in which the problem itself is open to interpretation

III

Problems at the project level tend to lie between the poles of hard and soft. Some, such as forming project teams, are relatively tractable. Other aspects of project management are less clearly definable. A good example is the frequent difficulty in estimating the scale of an information system project and the resources needed to complete it (see Chapter 12).

There is also a distinction between failure during development and failure in use. Development failure occurs when the whole or part of a system is abandoned prior to implementation. Use failure occurs during the post-implementation trajectory. It is apparent when a system is abandoned after a period of use, or needs large amounts of adaptive maintenance (see Chapter 12).

9.5.2   Studies of information systems failure

Studies of information systems failure fall into four categories: anecdotal evidence, theory building, case studies and survey research.

For a number of years the Association for Computing Machinery (ACM) collected anecdotal descriptions of information system failures in its Software Engineering Notes. McKenzie (1994) analysed this material and found that, of the computer-related accidents (examples mainly of use failures) reported, 92% involved failures in what he called human–computer interaction. This means that more human accidents that are associated with computer system failure seem to be caused by interactions of technical and organisational factors than by technical factors alone.

Expectation failure: the inability of an information system to meet a stakeholder group's expectations

Lyytinen and Hirschheim (1987) also explored the literature on failures, and put them into four categories: correspondence failure, process failure, interaction failure and **expectation failure**.

- Correspondence failure is the most common, and typically reflects a management perspective on failure. It is based on the idea that design objectives are first specified in detail. When the system is evaluated against these objectives, if it does not match up, it is regarded as a failure.
- Process failure is caused by unsatisfactory development performance. Usually, this means either that the development process has failed to produce a workable system, or that it has overrun its cost or time budget.
- In interaction failure the emphasis shifts to system use. The argument is that if a system is heavily used it constitutes a success; if it is hardly ever used, or there are major use problems, it can be judged a failure.

Lyytinen and Hirschheim describe expectation failure as a superset of the three other types. It is a more encompassing, politically and pluralistically informed view of information systems failure than the other forms; in their model, correspondence, process and interaction failure are all based on a highly rational image of information system development, seeing an information system as mainly a neutral technical artefact. Expectation failure is seen, in contrast, as the inability of an information system to meet a stakeholder group's expectations. So, for particular stakeholders who see the system as a failure, there is a gap between the existing situation and their desired situation, although their judgement might not be entirely reasonable from the viewpoint of other stakeholders, such as developers.

Sauer (1993) criticises Lyytinen and Hirschheim's model for its plurality. He points out that this last category means that all information system projects would rate as failures to some extent. His model uses a more conservative definition of failure; that an information system should only be deemed a failure when development or operation ceases, leaving supporters dissatisfied with the extent to which the system has served their interests. This means that a system should not be considered a failure until all interest in progressing the project has ceased, leading to what he calls termination failure.

Sauer uses this concept to develop a model of information system failure based on exchange relations. In this, the development of an information system is seen as an innovation process based on three components: the project organisation, the information system and its supporters (see Figure 9.9). Project organisation in this sense means the producers or developers of the system; supporters mean various stakeholder groups, particularly clients and end-users.

The development of ICT systems is an innovation process based on three sets of actor or agent: producers, the ICT system, and its consumers. Each of these actors is arranged in a triangle of dependencies. The ICT system depends on the producers; the producers depend on consumers; and the consumers depend on the ICT system. The ICT system requires the efforts and expertise of the producers to sustain it; the producers are heavily dependent on the provision of support in the form of material resources and help in coping with contingencies from agencies of consumption; consumers require benefits from the ICT system (Figure 9.9).

The three exchange relations between these agents are fundamentally processes of production, consumption and investment. Organisations usually cycle around these relations in various degrees of rapidity depending on the scale of the system being developed. Sauer uses this model to understand and explain the ways in which development projects frequently terminate or fail. This occurs when the level of perceived flaws in a developing ICT system triggers a decision to remove levels of investment in a development project.

One key way in which Sauer distinguishes termination failure from expectation failure is through the concept of a flaw. The development process is open to flaws, and every information system is flawed in some way, but flaws are different from failures. They can be corrected at a cost, or accepted at a cost. So a flaw is what someone perceives as a problem to be solved, such as a program bug, a shortfall in hardware performance, or a need for organisational change. Unless flaws are dealt with they will reduce the capability of the system and could lead to further flaws in the innovation process. At some stage, the volume of flaws might trigger a decision to remove support and terminate a project, and that brings us back to failure.

The London Ambulance Service Computer Aided Dispatch System (LASCAD) project (see Chapter 13) is often quoted as an example of information systems failure. My study of this case (Beynon-Davies, 1995) argues that it gained this profile more because of its safety-critical nature and the claim that 20 to 30 people may have lost their lives as a result of its failings than because of the scale of the project or its failure. Indeed, LASCAD (which cost £1.1–£1.5 million) is dwarfed by other British information system failures such as Wessex Regional Health Authority's RISP project (£63 million) and the UK Stock Exchange's TAURUS

III

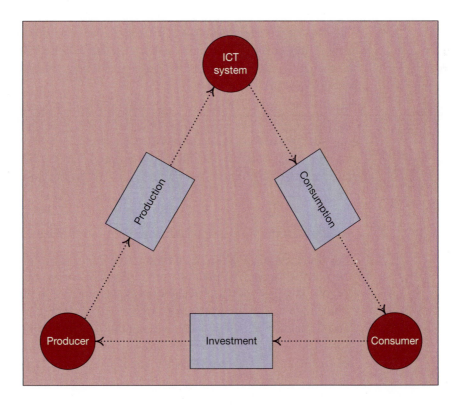

Figure 9.9 Sauer's model of information systems failure

settlement system (£75–£300 million) More recently, the attempt to build a national personal identity management infrastructure for the UK was abandoned in 2010 with an estimated wastage of billions of pounds sterling (see the *Failure in government ICT systems* case study for discussion of two other more recent failures of information systems in the public sector).

Information system failure is, of course, not specifically a British malaise. Accounts of failures elsewhere in the world are provided by Oz (1994), on the CONFIRM reservation system in the United States ($125 million), and by Sauer (1993), on a large Australian government information system project, Mandata (A$30 million), abandoned during the 1970s.

Lyytinen (1988) describes an exploratory study of systems analysts' perceptions of information systems failure. This major stakeholder group has a rather different view of information systems and their failure to that of users or management. He found they believed that only 20% of projects were likely to prove failures, and preferred to explain failures in highly procedural and rationalistic terms. The reasons they gave for failures included inexact development goals and specifications, inadequate understanding of users' work and inadequate understanding of system contingencies. He put this down to their professional expectations of the information system development process, which conceived of it as a rational task involving high technical and professional competence.

Ewusi-Mensah and Przasnyski (1994) make a slightly different distinction, between project abandonment and system failure. In their terms information system failure is the failure of usage and/or operations, whereas project abandonment is concerned with the system development process. This is similar to Lytinnen's distinction between development and use failure. Ewusi-Mensah and Przasnyski (1995)distinguish between three types of project abandonment, all of which take place prior to full implementation. Total abandonment involves complete termination of all activities on a project. Substantial abandonment involves major truncation, or simplification, of the project to make it radically different from the original specification, and partial abandonment involves reducing the original scope of the project but not significantly changing the original specification. They suggest, from their small survey, that total abandonment is the most common type of development failure in the United States. They also found that organisational factors, particularly the amount of senior management involvement and the degree of end-user participation in the project development, were the most widespread and dominant factors in success or failure.

CASE CHECK
Failure in government ICT systems (The UK Passport Agency)

CS ▷ p 438

In July 1996 the UK Passport Agency announced its planned introduction of digital passports, to minimise the risk of fraudulent use. This meant it needed to replace its existing ICT system. In October 1998 the new information system (ICT system and procedures, including those outsourced) was introduced in the Agency's Liverpool office.

In summer 1999 there were a number of problems. Over a half a million British citizens were less than happy to discover that they would not get their new passports in time for their holidays. In June passport applications were taking up to 50 working days to process. In July the Home Office introduced emergency measures including a free two-year extension to passports. It had to pay millions in compensation to citizens and in the staff overtime required for managing the backlog of applications.

9.5.3   Lessons from the evidence on information systems failure

■ Information system failure is commonplace. A survey conducted by the US Government Accounting Agency in 1979 (US, 1985) found that less than 3% of the software the US government paid for was actually used as delivered. More than half was never used at all. Gladden (1982) reported in a similar survey that 75% of all system development undertaken is either never completed or the resulting systems are not used. In an international survey conducted by Coopers and Lybrand, 60% of organisations internationally and 67% of organisations in the United Kingdom had suffered at least one systems project that had failed to deliver planned business benefits or had experienced cost and time overruns.

- Failure and success are inter-subjective, not objective concepts. Their definition depends on the position and perspective of the definer. Lyytinnen and Hirschheim's (1987) concept of expectation failure is useful here.
- It is important to identify stakeholders and judge what views and impact they will have on the project. It is their expectations and desires that define some types of failure.
- Understanding and monitoring project trajectory is important. This is defined as the historical shaping of an information system both before and after delivery. Often this is affected by the power play between different stakeholder groups. An information systems project and the resulting information system are significant power resources.
- Failure can occur prior to the delivery of an information system. This is the notion of project abandonment, or what Lyytinnen and Hirschheim (1987) call development failure. Sauer makes it clear that, as well as termination failure and total abandonment of a project, there are partial failures which lead to rethinks of the project scope. Failure can also occur after delivery; this is the idea of use failure, often because, although the system works after a fashion, it does not match stakeholders' needs or expectations.
- Information system projects are frequently the subject of escalation in decision-making. Drummond (1994) defines escalation as '*the predicament where decision-makers find themselves trapped in a losing course of action as a result of previous decisions. Costs are incurred; there is an opportunity to withdraw or persist; and the consequences of withdrawal or persistence are uncertain. Typically the response to such dilemmas is irrational persistence.*' This means that major stakeholders might continue to support a project, even in the face of major system flaws, because of the heavy investment in personnel and other resources.
- It is important to evaluate information systems and projects. Evaluation is the process of assessing the worth of something, which ties in with definitions of success or failure. There is a distinction between the worth of the product (the information system) and the worth of the process (the activities involved in producing the information system). In practice, it is clearly difficult to separate the two. The worth of the information system development process is normally evaluated by assessing the worth of the product

9.5.4   Avoidance strategies

Since the value of information systems is a key dependent variable for the discipline of organisational informatics, strategies for ensuring success or avoiding failure are important. This section briefly examines some conventional and extended strategies for preventing failure and ensuring success, and gives pointers to relevant material elsewhere in the book. It is obviously easiest to employ solutions or avoidance strategies in lower levels of the hierarchy of failures. This issue is revisited in Chapter 13.

First, at the level of ICT systems the appropriate selection and use of tools can significantly reduce the risk of failure. Appropriate use of information system development methods (Chapter 12) and analysis and design techniques also reduces the risk of failure.

Second, at the level of projects, good and effective management and control of informatics personnel (Chapter 11) and their activities can significantly reduce the occurrence of failure. Success is also more likely when stakeholders participate in development projects.

Third, at the organisational level, effective planning of the information system development portfolio and the structure and activities of the informatics service can affect the risk of failure (see Chapter 12). Proper management of the informatics services function (Chapter 11) is also crucial to the long-term health of organisations.

Fourth, at the environmental level, effective alignment of informatics strategy with business strategy is critical to the performance of the informatics services function and the information systems under their development and control. Effective organisational analysis (see Chapter 2) needs to be conducted to guide this alignment.

In summary, ideally an organisation wishing to avoid failure would do well to engage in many of the best practices described in this book: organisational analysis, informatics planning, informatics management, project management, information system development. Many years of experience have been accumulated in the development of information systems, and many lessons have been learned on how, for instance, to manage information system projects. Yet information system failures are still commonplace. Perhaps in part this is because although most medium- to large-scale organisations do a lot of information systems management, development, operation and maintenance, few seem to take organisational analysis, informatics planning and, particularly, the evaluation of information systems seriously.

RECAP: Perhaps the most extreme example of negative impact is the abandonment of an information system either during development or during use. This might be done because of technical reasons, problems with a development project, problems of an organisational nature or unintended effects of the business environment. Information systems failure appears commonplace. However, analyses of previous failures suggest a number of strategies for avoiding failure at the technical, project, organisational and environmental levels.

9.6   Evaluation

key skill

Information systems evaluation: assessing the worth of an information system

General managers often ask a number of questions about information systems and ICT, including:

- How much is currently spent on information systems and ICT?
- What value results from this spending?
- How should information system alternatives be justified/prioritised/financed?
- Why do information system projects continually experience cost and time overruns?
- Why do informatics budgets continue to rise while ICT unit costs continue to fall?
- How can we regain our belief in the return provided by information systems?

All these relate to the issue of evaluation. This section focuses on evaluation, and discusses its importance. It highlights the different forms of evaluation and indicates some of the problems in the way it is conducted. A model of **information systems evaluation** linked to the development process (see Chapter 12) is used to structure the discussion.

Figure 9.10 is a model of information systems evaluation fitted to the life-cycle of information systems development (Beynon-Davies et al., 2004). This illustrates the importance of evaluation to organisational learning. Organisations need to conduct evaluation for a number of reasons: to assess and prioritise investment in information systems and ICT; to control information system costs; to determine the value arising from information systems and ICT; to determine changes needed to the organisation's information systems portfolio; and to learn successful strategies for information systems management and development.

Information systems evaluation can be defined as the attempt to assess the success or failure of an information system and the associated process by which it is developed and implemented. Although evidence suggests that organisations do not conduct evaluation of their systems and projects very effectively, systematic evaluation is critical to improvements in both development and organisational success.

Figure 9.10 makes a distinction between four types of information systems evaluation activity: strategic evaluation, formative evaluation, summative evaluation and post-mortem evaluation. That is, during its conception, as it is being built, while it is being used, or when it has failed.

Large-scale ICT in government agencies in the United Kingdom is now procured from external vendors rather than being built in-house. To manage this process effectively, acquisition programmes and procurement projects in central civil government are subject to a process known as Office of Government Commerce (OGC) Gateway Reviews. The OGC Gateway Process examines a project at critical stages in its life-cycle to look for assurance that it can progress successfully to the next stage. Hence, there are similarities between this process and the model of information systems evaluation discussed in this section.

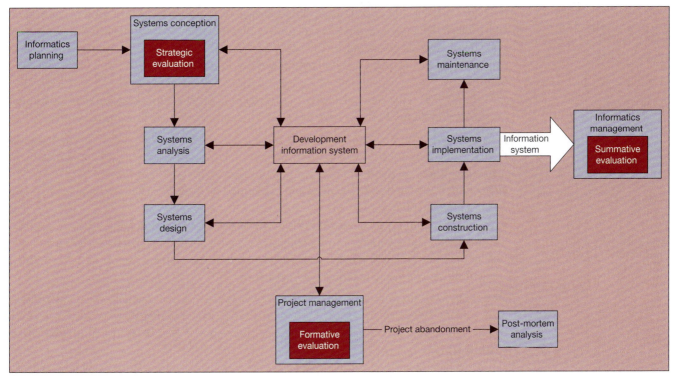

Figure 9.10 *Information systems evaluation and the development process*

9.6.1 Strategic evaluation

Most organisations conduct some form of strategic, or pre-implementation, evaluation of information system projects. This type of evaluation involves assessing or appraising an information system investment. This is usually achieved by assessing the balance of costs and benefits of an intended project, and leads to a go/no-go decision. It may also be used to prioritise potential investments.

Strategic evaluation is fundamentally part of the systems conception phase in the process of information system development (see Chapter 12). The most popular techniques are return on investment and payback period. These are effective ways of evaluating tangible costs against tangible benefits. One of the most popular frameworks, which includes an assessment of intangible costs and benefits, is Information Economics (Parker et al., 1988) (Chapter 11).

Strategic evaluation: the evaluation of the strategic benefit of an information system

9.6.2 Formative evaluation

Formative evaluation involves assessing the shape of an information system within the development process itself. It is an inherent part of the process of project management (see Chapter 12). In iterative approaches to development, it can be used to make crucial changes to the design of an information system. It is also critical to effective decisions on the degree of project abandonment.

Development projects should be assessed continually against objectives, and careful attention should be paid to this activity to avoid project escalation; that is, continued commitment to a project in the face of continual negative information from formative evaluation exercises. Major stakeholders might be reluctant to withdraw support when it would be reasonable to do so, if there has already been heavy investment in personnel and other resources.

Formative evaluation: assessing the shape of an information system within the development process itself

9.6.3 Summative evaluation

The model also contains an important organisational learning feedback loop. Even if a project reaches completion, it might fail in some sense when it is delivered. Therefore, at a suitable

Summative evaluation:
assessing a delivered
information system against its
strategic evaluation

time after delivery the organisation should engage in a **summative evaluation** of the system and project. This is sometimes called post-implementation evaluation. Ideally, summative evaluation involves returning to the costs and benefits established in strategic evaluation after a period of use. Hence, it is a critical activity in effective informatics management (see Chapter 10).

Kumar (1990) reports on a US empirical study of the prevalence and form of evaluation of information systems after they have been implemented. He found three major results:

- The major reason for performing post-implementation evaluation is the formalisation of the completion of the development project. Summative evaluation is thus a major tactic in a project disengagement strategy.
- Much of the evaluation is managed and performed by those who have designed the system being implemented.
- The most frequently evaluated criteria seem to be information quality criteria (accuracy, timeliness, adequacy and appropriateness) along with facilitating criteria such as user satisfaction and attitudes. Sociotechnical criteria, such as the system's impact on users and the organisation, are evaluated much less frequently.

One framework proposed for the summative evaluation of information systems is benefits management (Ward et al., 1996). Even at this point it is possible that the system may be wholly or partially abandoned, in which case there should also be a post-mortem analysis (see below).

It must be emphasised that no system is ever complete. A summative evaluation is likely to suggest a number of ways in which it could be modified or extended. These are normally both classed as systems maintenance (Chapter 12). The conclusion is that effective evaluation leads to effective management of system maintenance.

9.6.4   Post-mortem evaluation

If a system is abandoned prior to implementation or after a period of use, then a variant of summative evaluation needs to be performed on the project, not only to determine the reasons for failure but also to consider and suggest changes to organisational practice. This is known as **post-mortem evaluation**.

Post-mortem evaluation:
examining the reasons for an
information systems failure

The results are important for suggesting ways in which the organisation might improve its development practice; thus the report of the analysis needs to be disseminated to senior management, project management and members of the project team. It is important to assure all project participants that there will be no recriminations, or this cannot be done effectively. Ideally, the analysis should be conducted by a reputable senior executive not involved in any way with the project. Alternatively, it should be undertaken by an external body or consultant.

Wherever possible, post-mortem information should be made public outside the organisation. This is important in enabling the validation of information system development and management practice, and the effective progression of the profession of informatics.

FOCUS ON VALUE

Evaluation is the process by which assessments of worth or value are made. Informatics evaluation can focus on the relationships between the three distinct forms of business systems discussed in this book. Functionality is fundamentally an assessment of the value of an ICT system. Usability is an assessment of the use of an ICT system within its wider information system. Utility is an assessment of the impact of the system on its wider activity system. An alternative focus is based on the position of the assessment in the system life-cycle: during its conception, as it is being built, while it is being used, or when it has failed. The question of value is therefore embedded in judgements of the success and/or failure of information systems. These judgements are normally relative to stakeholder position.

9.7   Conclusion and key themes

Previous chapters touched on the issue of value in a number of ways, but this chapter considered the worth of information systems directly. When information systems are introduced into organisations they have immediate effects upon the activity system in which they are placed. Information systems may be closely aligned with their activity system, through design or by accident, and generate both intended and unintended positive effects. They might also be misaligned with their activity systems, which normally has a negative effect on organisational activity.

Close alignment is made more likely if the project team identify the stakeholders, understand the differences in their technological frames and involve representatives of stakeholder groups in the development process. Misaligned information systems are likely to be subject to user resistance, which can take numerous forms.

There can be an impact on individuals, groups and the organisation as a whole, which is either positive or negative at each of these levels. Judgements about the impact are frequently subjective. Most common assessments of ICT are concerned with its effects on organisational efficiency and/or effectiveness. However, ICT does not deliver performance gain in and of itself. It contributes to changes in activity systems, which in turn can affect performance.

At the most extreme, a system's negative impact is seen as its failure. Information systems failure can be analysed on the technical, project, organisational and environmental levels. Technical problems tend to be hard while environmental problems tend to be soft. There is also a distinction between failures during development and during use. Information systems failure appears commonplace, and has been much studied, producing anecdotal evidence, theory-building, case studies and survey work. This work offers lessons and suggests strategies for avoiding failure and ensuring success.

One key lesson is that it is important for organisations to evaluate their ICT systems and their impact on activity systems. Strategic evaluation involves assessing the system's potential for delivering benefit against estimated costs. Formative evaluation involves assessing the shape of an information system during the development process. Summative evaluation involves returning to the costs and benefits established in strategic evaluation after a period of use. A variant of this is post-mortem analysis, summative evaluation of a failed information system project to determine lessons for organisational practice.

The effective planning, management and operation of informatics have a critical bearing on the use, impact and success or failure of information systems. The next part of the book covers these topics.

9.8   Review test

1   The context of use is largely determined by the _____ into which the information system is placed. Fill in the blank.

2   The _____ of an ICT system is how easy an ICT system is to use for the purpose for which it has been constructed. Fill in the blank.

3   The identification and involvement of key system _____ is essential for the successful development and use of ICT systems. Fill in the blank.

4   Systems that are not accepted and do not have the commitment of system stakeholders are likely to be subject to stakeholder _____. Fill in the blank.

5   A user interface can be seen as a collection of dialogues between the user and the ICT system. Each dialogue is made up of a series of messages. It is useful to distinguish between three major aspects of such a dialogue: content, control and format. Match the appropriate definition to the term. Pair each lettered entry with the corresponding numbered entry.

a. Content   **1.** The way in which the user moves between aspects of one dialogue or from one dialogue to another.

b. Control   **2.** The layout of messages and data on input and output devices.

c. Format   **3.** The actual messages travelling between the user and the system.

6 The impact of introducing ICT systems may be either positive or _____. Fill in the blank.

7 How would you distinguish between efficiency gains and effectiveness gains in terms of the organisation? Write two sentences.

8 ICT does not deliver efficiency or effectiveness gains in and of itself. True or false?
☐ True
☐ False

9 The productivity paradox is? Select all that apply.
☐ The poor productivity of ICT workers.
☐ The mismatch between investment in ICT and improvements in productivity.
☐ The difficulty of building productive ICT systems.

10 Information systems failure can be analysed on four major levels. Identify them. Select all that apply.
☐ Technical
☐ Vertical
☐ Project
☐ Horizontal
☐ Environmental
☐ Organisational

11 Match the type of failure to the definition. Pair each lettered entry with the corresponding numbered entry.
a. Use failure
b. Development failure
1. Failure occurs when the whole or part of a system is abandoned prior to implementation.
2. Failure occurs during the post-implementation trajectory of an information system.

12 Distinguish between problem setting and problem solving. Write two sentences.

13 Evaluation involves assessing the _____ of something. Fill in the blank.

14 Identify three of the main types of information systems evaluation.
☐ Strategic evaluation
☐ Technical evaluation
☐ Formative evaluation
☐ Summative evaluation

15 _____ analysis involves the summative evaluation of a failed IS project. Fill in the blank.

16 What is meant by alignment in terms of information systems? Write two sentences.

9.9   Exercises

▸ Take an information system known to you and try to identify the major stakeholders that affected the project trajectory. Use the taxonomy of producers, clients, end-users, customers and regulators.

▸ Were representatives of any stakeholder groups involved in the project? In what ways were they involved? Is it possible to assess the effect this involvement had on the success of the project?

▸ For an organisation, or part of an organisation, known to you consider in what ways an information system has been used to improve either the efficiency or the effectiveness of a human activity system in that organisation. How might you measure the improvements in efficiency and effectiveness?

▸ In terms of strategic, summative and formative evaluation, what are we evaluating: usability, functionality or utility?

▸ Provide an example of strategic, formative and summative evaluation.

▸ Try to estimate the percentage of projects in an organisation known to you that are regarded as successes. What percentage are regarded as failures? What are seen as the major reasons for failure? What are seen to be the major features of success?

9.10   Projects

▸ Identify the stakeholders relevant to an information system known to you. From their viewpoints, generate an analysis of the negative and positive effects of the information system on each stakeholder group.

▸ The usability of an information system is critical to its success. Investigate in more detail the issue of usability as a property of an information system. Determine appropriate ways of assessing usability.

- Apply an established technique, such as QUIS, to the assessment of user satisfaction with the interface of an information system known to you. Try to evaluate not only the interface itself but also the technique used, such as in terms of the degree to which it is easy to administer.

- User resistance is a frequent contributor to information systems failure. Try to determine the levels and forms of user resistance to the introduction of information systems in a particular sector such as the health service.

- The impact of information systems on organisational performance can be measured in a number of ways. Decide on one simple and straightforward measurement of organisational performance, such as level of sales of products. Try to trace the effect of any information systems innovations on the chosen measurement.

- The productivity paradox was initially identified in the financial services sector in the United States. Investigate whether the productivity paradox holds in another sector, such as manufacturing or government, or in another nation-state.

- All information systems projects fail to some degree. Develop a natural history of one or more information systems development projects. Assess the degree to which they can be considered as a success or failure, using any published accounts from the organisations themselves. What measurements did they use to evaluate success and failure?

- Information systems failure is frequently a result of their not meeting expectations. Investigate why expectations are an important facet of the phenomenon of information systems failure. Consider appropriate ways of managing expectations and try to identify the likely effects of these approaches.

- Investigate a range of published case studies of failure, and classify them as development or use failure. In other words, how many were abandoned prior to use and how many were abandoned after implementation? How many projects engaged in effective information systems evaluation? Besides post-mortem evaluation, what sort of evaluation was conducted?

9.11 Critical reflection

Think about how many different forms of ICT system you actually use on a regular basis. How do the interfaces of these systems differ? How much of the functionality available in a typical ICT application, such as Microsoft Word, do you actually use?

In your opinion has the application of ICT within work made such work better? Is work more or less varied than fifty years ago? What impact has ICT had on the availability of jobs in the economy?

How often do you think organisations analyse the reasons for their information systems failures? Even if they analyse them effectively, are private sector organisations liable to release the results?

Many commentators would argue that organisations are not very good at evaluation. Why do you think this might be the case? What barriers must be overcome for successful evaluation? Many information systems have failed to return satisfactory levels of benefits to costs. Why should this be the case? Many commentators have argued that the benefits of ICT are frequently intangible in nature. What consequences does this have for the effective evaluation of ICT?

9.12 Further reading

The original Delone and McLean paper (1992) provides a good review of information systems use and impact. The user interface and principles of good design are covered in Schneiderman et al. (2009). Chan and Reich (2007) review the issue of alignment of information systems with organisations. Venkatesh et al. (2003) provide a comprehensive review of the user acceptance of information technology. The papers Brynjolfson (1993) and Brynjolfson and Hitt (1998) examine the productivity paradox and the reasons for it. Fortune and Peters (2005) provide one of the most recent accounts of information systems failure and strategies for avoiding it. Benbasat et al. (1987) provide the definitive paper on using case research within Information Systems. Beynon-Davies et al. (2004) provide more detail on the various forms of information systems evaluation.

9.13   References

Benbasat, I., D. K. Goldstein and M. Mead. (1987). The Case Research Strategy in Studies of Information Systems. *MIS Quarterly* 11 (3): 269–279.

Beynon-Davies, P. (1995). Information Systems 'Failure': The Case of the London Ambulance Service's Computer Aided Despatch System. *European Journal of Information Systems* 4 (1): 171–184.

Beynon-Davies, P., I. Owens and M. D. Williams. (2004). IS Failure, Evaluation and Organisational Learning. *Journal of Enterprise Information Management (formerly Logistics and Information Management)* 17 (4): 276–282.

Brynjolfson, E. (1993). The Productivity Paradox of Information Technology. *Communications of the ACM* 36 (12): 67–77.

Brynjolfson, E. and L. Hitt. (1998). Beyond the Productivity Paradox. *Communications of the ACM* 41 (8): 49–55.

Button, G. and R. H. R. Harper. (1993). Taking the Organisation into Accounts. In G. Button (ed.), *Technology in Working Order: Studies of Work, Interaction and Technology*. Routledge, London.

Chan, Y. E. and B. H. Reich. (2007). IT Alignment: What Have We Learned? *Journal of Information Technology* 22 (4): 297–315.

Davenport, T. H. and L. Prusak. (2000). *Working Knowledge: How Organisations Manage What they Know*. 2nd edition. Harvard Business School Press, Boston, MA.

DeLone, W. H. and E. R. McLean. (1992). Information Systems Success: The Quest for the Dependent Variable. *Information Systems Research* 3 (1): 60–95.

DeLone, W. H. and E. R. McLean. (2003). The DeLone and McLean Model of Information Systems Success: A Ten Year Update. *Journal of Management Information Systems* 19 (4): 9–30.

Drummond, H. (1994). Escalation in Organisational Decision-Making: A Case of Recruiting an Incompetent Employee. *Journal of Behavioural Decision-Making* 7: 43–55.

Eason, K. D. (1988). *Information Technology and Organisational Change*. Taylor and Francis, London.

Ewusi-Mensah, K. and Z. H. Przasnyski. (1994). Factors Contributing to the Abandonment of Information Systems Development Projects. *Journal of Information Technology* 9 (3): 185–201.

Ewusi-Mensah, K. and Z. H. Przasnyski. (1995). Learning from Abandoned Information System Development Projects. *Journal of Information Technology* 10 (1): 3–14.

Fortune, J. and G. Peters. (2005). *Information Systems: Achieving Success by Avoiding Failure*. John Wiley, Chichester.

Gladden, G. R. (1982). Stop the Lifecycle I Want to Get Off. *Software Engineering Notes* 7 (April) (2): 35–39.

Hirschheim, R. and M. Newman. (1988). Information Systems and User Resistance: Theory and practice. *Computer Journal* 31 (5): 398–408.

Kaplan, R. S. and D. P. Norton. (1992). The Balanced Scorecard: Measures That Drive Performance. *Harvard Business Review* January–February: 71–79.

Keen, P. (1981). Information Systems and Organisational Change. *Communications of the ACM* 24 (1): 24–33.

Kumar, K. (1990). Post Implementation Evaluation of Computer-Based Information Systems: Current Practices. *Communications of the ACM* 33 (2): 236–252.

Landauer, T. K. (1995). *The Trouble with Computers: Usefulness, Usability and Productivity*. MIT Press, Cambridge, Mass.

Lyytinen, K. (1988). The Expectation Failure Concept and Systems Analysts View of Information Systems Failures: Results of an Exploratory Study. *Information and Management* 14: 45–55.

Lyytinen, K. and R. Hirschheim. (1987). Information Systems Failures: A Survey and Classification of the Empirical Literature. *Oxford Surveys in Information Technology* 4: 257–309.

Marchand, D. A., W. J. Kettinger and J. D. Rollins. (2000). Company Performance and Information Management: The view from the Top. In D. A. Marchand, T. H. Davenport and T. Dickson (eds), *Mastering Information Management*. Pearson, Harlow, Essex.

McKenzie, D. (1994). Computer-Related Accidental Death: An Empirical Exploration. *Science and Public Policy* 21 (4): 233–248.

Nielsen, J. (1993). *Usability Engineering*. Academic Press, Boston.

Orlikowski, W. J. (1996). *Realising the Potential of New Technologies: An Improvisation Model of Change Management*. Business Information Technology, Manchester Metropolitan University.

Orlikowski, W. T. and T. C. Gash. (1994). Technological Frames: Making Sense of Information Technology in Organisations. *ACM Trans. on Information Systems* 12 (2): 17–207.

Oz, E. (1994). When Professional Standards are Lax: The Confirm Failure and Its Lessons. *Communications of the ACM* 37 (10): 29–36.

Parker, M., R. Benson and H. Trainor. (1988). *Information Economics: Linking Business Performance to Information Technology*. Prentice-Hall, New Jersey.

Sachs, P. (1995). Transforming Work: Collaboration, Learning and Design. *Comm. of ACM* 38 (9): 36–45.

Sauer, C. (1993). *Why Information Systems Fail: A Case Study Approach*. Alfred Waller, Henley-On-Thames.

Schneiderman, B., C. Plaisant, M. Cohen and J. Steven (2009). *Designing the User Interface: Strategies for Effective Human-Computer Interaction*. Pearson, New York.

US (1985). US Government Accounting Office Report . FGMSD-80–4. *ACM Sigsoft Software Engineering Notes* 10 (5).

Venkatesh, V., M. G. Morris, F. D. Davis and G. B. Davis. (2003). User Acceptance of Information Technology: Toward a Unified View. *MIS Quarterly* 27 (3): 425–478.

Ward, J., P. Taylor and P. Bond. (1996). Evaluation and Realisation of IS/IT Benefits: An Empirical Study of Current Practice. *European Journal of Information Systems* 4 (1): 214–225.

Zuboff, S. (1988). *In the Age of the Smart Machine: The Future of Work and Power*. Heinemann, London.

III

See companion website **www.palgrave.com/business/beynon-daviesbis2e**

Managing information systems in business

Because informatics infrastructure is so important to modern organisations, they need to invest in effective practices for planning, managing, developing and operating it. This part of the book introduces a number of best practices in these areas.

Chapter 10 considers the importance of planning to effective informatics infrastructure. **Planning** is particularly concerned with the development of **informatics strategy** and the alignment of informatics strategy with organisation strategy. **Management** involves putting plans into action.

Chapter 11 considers first the context set by the **informatics industry** in terms of major producers and consumers. The **informatics service** refers to that organisational function devoted to planning, management, development and operation of informatics infrastructures for an organisation. Parts of, or the whole of it, including operation, may be outsourced to vendors in the wider informatics industry. These operations tend to be considered today in terms of **ICT services management,** which includes important issues such as the provision of helpdesks, disaster recovery and managing the total cost of ownership of ICT infrastructure.

It is impossible to understand the processes of planning, management and operations without a high-level understanding of how organisations procure or build new information systems. **Chapter 12** considers approaches to this **development process.** Since information systems are sociotechnical systems, activity systems and ICT systems need to be looked at together. The chapter begins with a consideration of the development process and the supporting toolkit of methods, techniques and tools. Each of the phases of the development **life-cycle** is then considered in some detail: conception, analysis, design, construction, implementation and maintenance.

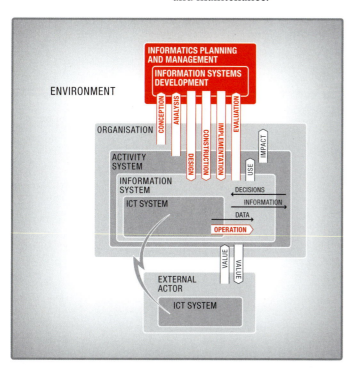

Overview

The chapters in this part cover the following key areas:

- Informatics planning
- Informatics strategy
- Informatics management
- Project management
- Informatics industry
- Informatics service
- Operating the ICT infrastructure
- The use of information systems
- The information systems development life-cycle
- Development methods, techniques and tools

Planning, strategy and management

'There is nothing more difficult to take in hand, more perilous to conduct, or more uncertain in its success than to take the lead in the introduction of a new order of things.'

Niccolo Machiavelli (1469–1527) *The Prince* (1513), chapter VI

Learning outcomes	Principles
Define and describe the critical organisational processes of planning and management of informatics infrastructure.	The planning and management of informatics infrastructure are two critical processes for the modern organisation. Planning is the process of producing informatics strategy. Management is the process of implementing informatics strategy.
Distinguish between organisational strategy and informatics strategy and discuss ways in which informatics strategy can be built.	Informatics strategy consists of the interdependent layers of information strategy, information systems strategy and ICT strategy. Informatics strategy exists in a mutually dependent relationship with organisational strategy. Organisational strategy typically drives informatics strategy but the implementation of informatics strategy is likely to cause changes to organisational strategy.
Define some of the critical activities of informatics management.	Informatics management not only involves managing the development of future informatics infrastructure, it also involves managing the operation and maintenance of current informatics infrastructure.

IV

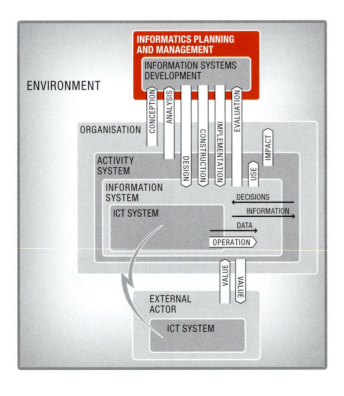

Chapter outline

AACSB learning objectives:
Analytical thinking and reflective thinking

10.1   Introduction

 key skill

The Austro-American economist Joseph Schumpeter coined the phrase *creative destruction*, originally to describe a process embedded within capitalism where one economic system is destroyed and another economic system is created from its ashes. Management theorists have adapted the term to refer to a process by which new ways of doing business effectively destroy pre-existing approaches. For example, as we have seen in previous chapters, many content industries are undergoing a process of creative destruction. Technological change is facilitating new ways of producing, distributing and consuming, music, books, movies and so on.

In the face of environmental turbulence organisations do two things: they plan strategy and they manage change. The current chapter considers these issues, particularly in relation to the idea of organisation as the complex adaptive system that we discussed in previous chapters. Managers have to steer their organisations through environmental turbulence by strategically considering the necessary interdependence between activity and technology.

A classic management theorist, Henri Fayol, described the process of management as being '*to forecast and plan, to organize, to command, to coordinate and to control*' (Gray, 1984). This chapter considers the activities of planning, commanding and control in relation to eBusiness infrastructure, that is, the interdependent activity systems infrastructure and informatics infrastructure of an organisation.

Figure 10.1 illustrates the relationships between the critical processes of planning, management and development. In systems terms, these can be seen as a hierarchy of control:

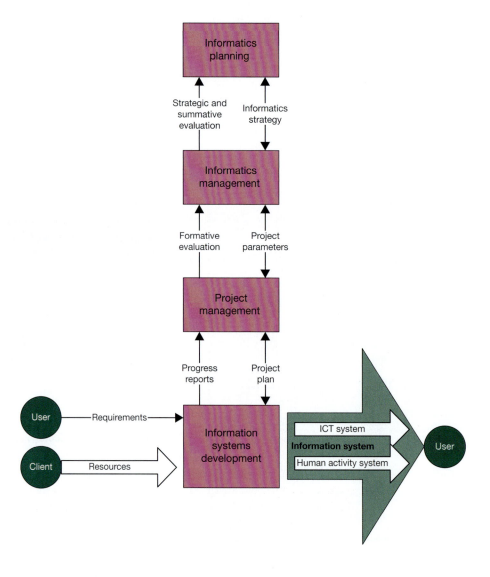

Figure 10.1 *The hierarchy of control*

informatics planning is a control system for informatics management, which in turn is a control system for project management; project management, in turn, is a control system for information systems development.

Here, planning is the processes of deciding on the optimal informatics infrastructure for an organisation, and engaging with the transformation of one informatics infrastructure into another. The key output from informatics planning is informatics strategy. The planning process also typically includes performance monitoring – information fed back from the management process – which is critical to an on-going evaluation of strategy.

Two forms of management are outlined on Figure 10.1: general informatics management and project management. Informatics management is the process of putting into action joint plans for organisational and technological change, and monitoring performance against plans. Management typically define, resource and implement a portfolio of projects. Individual projects need to be managed as autonomous fields of activity, and progress is reported to general management processes. General informatics management is covered in this chapter; project management is considered in Chapter 11.

Development is the process of implementing the plans documented in the strategy and resourced from management. As we have seen, information systems are sociotechnical systems which form a bridge between ICT systems and the activity systems they support. They are constructed by a development organisation, using detailed requirements provided by potential users and key resources supplied by clients of the development organisation, usually managerial groups. This process is the topic of Chapter 12.

Informatics strategy, project parameters and project plans are all control inputs in this hierarchy of control. Development progress, project reports (formative evaluation) and strategy evaluations (summative and strategic) are all forms of control signal in feedback processes. Figure 10.1 is meant to emphasise that planning, general informatics management, project management and development are continuous processes. As in any activity system, it is important that the feedback loops work effectively for the infrastructure of an eBusiness to be a viable system. Information systems are just as critical to these processes as they are to conventional business processes such as sales and manufacturing.

IV

10.2 Informatics planning

Informatics planning:
the process of developing
informatics strategy

Informatics planning needs to take place in the context of general business planning, since there are a number of advantages to doing this. It is important to ensure that there is a close match between the proposed direction of an organisation and its information services. Informatics planning can be used to ensure that information system projects correctly balance business objectives with technical objectives. Planning helps with effective resource allocation. It makes it easier to estimate the effect (and the risk) of proposed information system projects, in terms of their contribution to business objectives, and to evaluate the effectiveness of current systems. Planning should lead to greater integration of both current and future information systems. Good planning is a necessary part of good management of information systems, and is likely to improve the ability of an organisation to react to unforeseen circumstances.

10.2.1 The value of informatics planning

However, the value of informatics planning varies depending on the type of organisation. Cash, McFarlan and McKeney (1992) provide a useful way of assessing the importance of both existing and potential information systems to the strategy of organisations. If we consider importance along the two dimensions of existing and future systems, we come to the four organisational possibilities illustrated in Figure 10.2.

Strategic organisations are those in which the smooth functioning of existing informatics activity is critical to their daily operation. Applications under development are also critical to

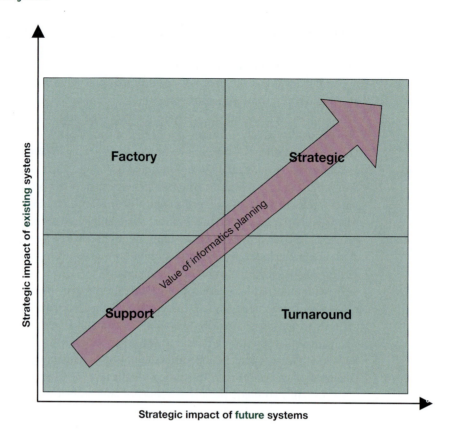

Figure 10.2 *Cash's taxonomy*

Cash's taxonomy: a taxonomy of organisations which indicates the value that informatics planning will have for the organisation

the organisation's future competitive success. Since strategic companies are so dependent on the smooth functioning of their informatics infrastructure, both now and in the future, they benefit from considerable amounts of well-considered informatics planning.

Many organisations in the financial industry are clearly in the strategic sector of **Cash's taxonomy**. ICT is at the heart of modern banking, for instance. Developments in the area of online banking have had a major effect on the industry and are likely to continue to be very important to its future.

Turnaround organisations require considerable amounts of informatics support, but their activities are not absolutely dependent on the uninterrupted, cost-effective functioning of informatics infrastructure to achieve their short- or long-term objectives. Applications under development however are absolutely vital to their long-term health. Turnaround companies also need a substantial informatics planning effort since, although current organisational effectiveness is not critically dependent on informatics, future performance is likely to be.

Many organisations in the retail industry come into this category. Food retail, for instance, used not to be a heavy user of ICT, but in the 2000s ICT innovation and the development of applications have become critical to competitive success, at least for the large supermarket chains.

A *factory* organisation is heavily dependent on a cost-effective, reliable informatics infrastructure for its smooth operation. However, its system development portfolio is likely to be heavily dominated by maintenance work, and the applications under development, though important, are not fundamental to its ability to compete. So, for organisations in this category, mass effort in informatics planning is probably not needed, although year-by-year operational planning is still essential.

The manufacturing sector has implemented many systems, such as just-in-time manufacturing systems, that are heavily reliant on good informatics infrastructure. However, it is currently unclear in many organisations how ICT will be able to stimulate further improvements in internal manufacturing processes.

Some organisations are not particularly dependent on the smooth functioning of ICT, nor are their applications portfolios critical to future effectiveness. In *support* organisations there is a tendency to assume that little if any informatics planning is needed. The danger, however, is that there might be opportunities opening up as a result of evolving technology that they will miss. For instance, organisations in the agricultural sector have historically not been heavy investors in ICT, and look relatively unlikely to be large investors in the future.

This taxonomy can be applied to parts of organisations as well as a whole organisation. Different divisions, departments or business units may be in different quadrants of the innovation matrix at different times. For instance, a company's manufacturing operations might be in the factory or support segment, whereas the marketing division is in the strategic or turnaround quadrant. Organisations can also move around the quadrants over time, starting in the support quadrant, then moving through turnaround and strategic quadrants into the factory quadrant.

> **REFLECT:** What sort of measurements might be used to place an organisation accurately in one of Cash's sectors? In other words, how would you assess which quadrant is most appropriate for all or a part of an organisation?

10.2.2 Sensing the environment

Planning is not a one-off process. Organisations must continually sense their environment and adapt to environmental change (see Chapter 2). Typically, three main types of sensing activity provide input to the informatics planning process (see Figure 10.3):

- Organisational analysis feeds in information concerning the shape of current organisational processes/activities and plans for change. Part of this activity will be an assessment of infrastructure (see below).
- Environmental analysis inputs information concerning current and future trends in the immediate environment of the organisation, the economic, social, political and ecological trends affecting the organisation. It particularly involves assessment of its current and potential place in its value network (see Chapter 7).
- Technology analysis provides information on trends in ICT that are likely to affect the organisation in the short- to medium-term, and that are likely to stimulate a need for change in its ICT infrastructure.

For example, in the financial services sector an organisational analysis might identify key problems with business processes, such as response time to customer enquiries (see

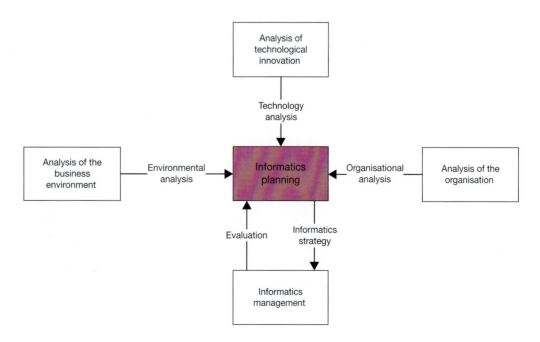

Figure 10.3 *Inputs into the informatics planning process*

Chapter 2). An environmental analysis might highlight opportunities and threats posed by the deregulation of key areas (see Chapter 5). A technology analysis might highlight the potential of critical technologies such as CRM systems (see Chapter 6) for customer acquisition and retention

The objective of informatics planning is to develop an effective informatics strategy. The practical output of informatics planning is a document, or set of documents, that describes strategy in this area. Informatics planning will also receive feedback from management activities, in the form of various types of evaluation of the performance of the organisation and its information systems (see Chapter 9).

10.2.3   Planning approaches

There are three major approaches to the planning of informatics strategy (Ward and Peppard, 2012) (see Figure 10.4):

- Target-driven is a top-down approach to the planning of strategy. Here strategy is directed through goals or targets set. Consideration is then given to ways of achieving targets and what resources are needed to conduct activities.
- Resource-driven planning is a bottom-up approach to strategy. Here strategy begins with available resources. Activities are specified in terms of these resources and goals achieved in relation to activities.
- Implementation-driven planning is a middle-out approach to strategy. Here means and ends are continually assessed and adjusted over time in the shaping of activities.

The top-down, or target-driven, approach to informatics planning is certainly the best documented, and it receives the most attention in this chapter. In target-driven planning the organisation establishes a mission, consisting of a series of measurable objectives such as to improve profitability by 5% in three years. A series of activities are then planned to achieve

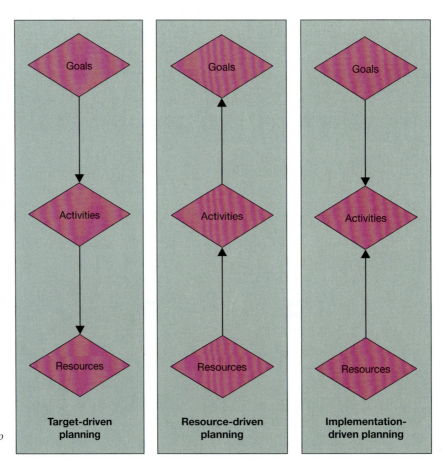

Figure 10.4 *Three approaches to planning of strategy*

these goals, for example, to decrease inventory levels through the introduction of an integrated inventory and production information system. Development and project management resources, such as programmers, hardware and software, then have to be provided to support the planned development activities.

Among the generic activities for the informatics planning process using a target-driven approach are:

- Setting up a planning unit and approach
- Assessment of the current informatics infrastructure
- Establishing a vision for informatics
- Specifying the informatics strategy
- Developing strategic plans for the informatics service
- Developing operational plans for the informatics service.

These phases can be adapted to resource-driven and implementation-driven approaches.

DID YOU KNOW? The American general and president Dwight D. Eisenhower once said that in preparing for battle he found plans useless but planning indispensable.

10.2.4 Setting up a planning unit and approach

Most organisations start to develop an informatics strategy by evaluating existing planning methods and choosing or customising one. The organisation then sets up an informatics planning unit. If it is using a proprietary planning method from an external organisation, its supplier is likely to provide training to help guide the planning study. Next, the unit carries out the multiple phases of the study, which generally last several months. Its staff first look to define current business processes, drawing on existing documentation and other techniques, such as interviewing other stakeholders (see Chapter 2). They will also study how the current information systems support these processes. Using its documented understanding, the unit then identifies and prioritises key information systems for the future infrastructure, and draws up an implementation schedule. It prepares a report that includes a plan with recommendations for hardware, software, data, communication technology and personnel support.

IV

10.2.5 Assessment of the current informatics infrastructure

Any planning process must begin with an assessment of the current situation. This means that current performance is compared with a set of objectives. For informatics planning these normally include both business and informatics objectives, because it is a sociotechnical exercise in which all four layers of organisational infrastructure need to be examined: activity, information, information systems and ICT. Once the team has established the current performance of these layers, it can start to define what future performance should be, and determine the shape of associated performance management systems (see Chapter 7).

The informatics planning process typically begins with an assessment of the use of information, information systems and ICT throughout the entire organisation, as well as an assessment of the work of the informatics service (see Chapter 11). This assessment might be conducted by a group of both informatics professionals and user-managers. Outsiders, particularly from informatics consultancies, are also frequently used to provide a cross-organisational view of the situation.

An informatics assessment will probably document current levels of information, information systems and ICT use, and compare them against a set of standards, perhaps produced as benchmarks of past performance or by analysing industry norms. A technical assessment of current information systems and technology infrastructure will also form part of the picture, as will an assessment of current attitudes to information systems and ICT in the organisation.

Another important part of the assessment is a review of the mission of the informatics service (see Chapter 11). This should address the important issue of the business rationale for having an informatics service, looking at the three issues of efficiency, effectiveness and competitiveness. In efficiency terms, a key question is whether the informatics service helps the organisation remain active with the minimum use of resources. In terms of effectiveness, the key question is whether the informatics service helps the organisation spend its time doing the right things. Finally, in terms of competitiveness, the key question is whether the informatics service is engaged in projects that will improve the position of the organisation in its environment.

Many organisations have clearly answered '*no*' to questions such as these, and considered alternatives to an internal informatics service, such as facilities management and outsourcing. Outsourcing means transferring the whole or part of the informatics service to outside suppliers. In facilities management the management of the informatics infrastructure is also transferred to outside contractors (see Chapter 11).

10.2.6   Establishing a vision for informatics

Establishing a vision for informatics normally involves assessing the competitive advantage that information systems can deliver. Among the frameworks that have been proposed for doing this are:

- Critical success factors
- The five forces model
- The customer resource life-cycle
- The value-chain.

The value-chain was discussed in Chapter 7, along with the idea of the value network and value-network analysis, so this section focuses on the other three approaches.

10.2.7   Critical success factors

Critical success factor: a factor which is deemed crucial to the success of a business

Any organisation needs to identify areas in which it has relative superiority, and to use that superiority both to create barriers to entry and to launch strategic offensives. The **critical success factor** (CSF) concept is a popular way of doing this. A CSF is a factor that is considered core to the success of a business, so it is an area that must be given special attention by management. CSFs are also critical points of leverage for achieving competitive advantage. Each organisation normally has only a few CSFs – perhaps between three and eight – so CSFs are said to follow a Pareto or 80/20 rule, where only a few issues really count in levering improvements in organisational effectiveness.

CSFs are usually contrasted with CFFs, or critical failure factors. The poor management of a CFF is likely to precipitate organisational failure. A CSF for a chain of high-street jewellers might be location of its outlets; for a health authority, it will be the quality of service it gives to patients. A CFF for the high-street jeweller chain could a high amount of shrinkage in consumer demand, while for the health authority it might be poor coordination of staff, particularly subcontractors.

CSFs and CFFs are useful ways of identifying areas for the maximal application of information systems and ICT. For instance, the jeweller chain would benefit from an information system that enabled managers to select optimal locations for stores based on factors such as population density and the state of local economy. A health authority would benefit from an information system that ensured the efficient work scheduling of nursing staff.

10.2.8   The five forces model

Five forces model: a strategic planning framework based on Porter and Millar

Another framework for assessing competitive advantage is based on the work of Porter and Millar (Porter, 1985) (see Chapter 5). They argue that a successful firm shapes the structure of competition by influencing five primary forces that define the relationship between an organisation and economic actors:

- Competitive structure of the industry. This really defines the relative power of competitors to determine things like pricing policy in the economic environment.

- Bargaining power of buyers. This highlights the degree to which customers have control over issues like pricing and quality of products and services.
- Bargaining power of suppliers. This highlights the important position that suppliers play in influencing organisational strategy.
- Threat of new entrants. This refers to the ease with which new competitors may establish themselves within a particular market sector. From an alternative point of view, strategists frequently refer to the barriers of entry to a particular market, meaning the factors that have to be taken into account when breaking into particular markets. For instance, the state of technological deployment in a particular market sector may make it difficult for new competitors to establish themselves.
- Likelihood of substitutes. This refers to the degree of availability of alternative products and services in a particular market.

Below we provide a brief analysis of the effects of informatics on each of these forces (Porter, 2001).

- Industrial rivalry, the competitive position of rival organisations. Bricks and mortar companies in certain sectors such as banking, travel and insurance have already experienced increasing competition with the rise of clicks-only organisations such as online banks. In many sectors there has also been increased disintermediation, in others significant amounts of re-intermediation through electronic delivery channels.
- Customer bargaining power. Electronic trading has increased the bargaining power of customers in the sense that they are able to search for and examine a wider array of goods and services. This appears to have a collective effect of driving down prices.
- Supplier bargaining power might decrease with the increasing adoption of B2B eCommerce. Companies might insist that their established suppliers use electronic communication to improve supply-chain efficiency. Also, the cost of switching to alternative suppliers might be reduced with the rise of B2B hubs.
- Barriers to entry and the threat of new entrants. Arguably there are lower start-up costs for entering digital rather than conventional markets, so the barriers to entry are lower and the threat of new entrants is higher. However, as the Dot Com crash demonstrated, it seems to be just as, if not more, difficult to maintain a sustainable online presence as to keep up a conventional physical market presence.
- Threat of substitutes. In the eBusiness arena the rise of digital products (such as digital music) and the increasing degree of digital convergence pose major threats to companies whose products are primarily intangible. For services, new business models for electronic service delivery threaten existing delivery channels.

Combinations of these factors, such as low industrial rivalry, high barriers to entry and low buyer bargaining power, can lead to sustainable, above-average, long-term profits. eBusiness can be used to achieve these goals by changing the basis of competition, strengthening customer relationships, overcoming supplier problems, building barriers against new entrants and generating new products or services.

For example, customer information systems for marketing and sales can have a strategic impact by winning customers from the competition. They could do this by using a large customer database, market research databases to target customer need, and eMarketing and direct mailing to improve sales. The cost of setting up and maintaining an accurate customer database is itself a considerable barrier to entry in certain sectors.

10.2.9 The customer resource life-cycle

Customer resource life-cycle: a strategic planning framework based on Ives and Learmonth. Also useful in defining elements of the customer chain

Ives and Learmonth (1984) define an information system as strategic if it changes a company's value-proposition (product or service created) or the way it competes in its industry. They use the idea of a **customer resource life-cycle** to identify potential strategic information systems. This model considers a firm's relationship with its customers (the customer chain) and how this relationship can be changed or enhanced by the strategic application of ICT.

The customer resource life-cycle is a sequence of 13 stages based around the customer's interaction with a resource. A resource in this sense is a product and/or service delivered by an organisation:

- The customer establishes requirements, in the sense of how much of a resource is required.
- The customer details the attributes of the required resource.
- An appropriate supplier for the resource is selected.
- A quantity of the resource is ordered from the supplier.
- The customer authorises and pays for the resource; authority for the expenditure must be obtained and payment made.
- The customer acquires or takes possession of the resource.
- The customer verifies the acceptability of the resource before putting it to use.
- The resource is added to an existing inventory.
- The customer monitors to ensure that the resource remains acceptable while in the inventory.
- If requirements change, it may be necessary to upgrade resources.
- It may prove necessary to maintain or repair a resource.
- The customer may transfer or dispose of a resource.
- The customer accounts for the resource in the sense of monitoring where and how money is spent on resources.

The idea of a customer resource life-cycle is relevant to both private sector and public sector organisations, such as the UK National Health Service (NHS). In this setting, the patient is the primary health service customer and can be considered as consuming a health service resource. The customer resource life-cycle might then be:

- Requirements specification. ICT can be used as a means to aid a general practitioner (GP) and the patient in establishing what health resource is required, in what quantity.
- Selection. A series of options are presented to the patient, for instance, which hospitals are able to offer the chosen treatment.
- Order. The GP queries a hospital's elective admission system to find out whether it can schedule the treatment. If what is available suits the patient, a provisional booking is made.
- Authorise and payment. Appropriate routines update the treatment accounts of the hospital and the budget of the general practice.
- Acquire. When the patient arrives for their stay in hospital, their details are transferred from the GP's system to its patient administration system.
- Test. The patient is given details of the proposed treatment and requested to sign an agreement.
- Integrate. The consumption of the health care resource is added to the patient's history record in a regional data register.
- Monitor and upgrade. Preliminary investigation might change the initial prognosis, leading to modification of the original health care plan. Any changes or additions to the plan are recorded by hospital systems.
- Maintain. The patient is given regular check-ups to make sure they are recovering from the treatment. Details are notified to patients by the GP system, and the results recorded by the system.
- Accountability. The patient receives a report of every treatment given, with the cost to the health service budget.

10.2.10 Strategic and operational plans for the informatics service

An informatics services strategic plan sets goals for this organisational function over an agreed timeframe. It normally includes:

- A statement on the organisation of the informatics services function. Prior planning processes should already have established the basis for financial control. There are two main options: an unallocated cost centre, in which the service is given a budget and user departments do not pay directly for informatics work; or an allocated cost centre and charge-out, in which user departments have informatics budgets and the service charges them when they use it (Chapter 11).

■ Details of how the informatics strategy is aligned with the business strategy. Cash and colleagues (1992) discuss one significant difficulty here, that business strategy is generally set within a one-year frame of reference, whereas informatics strategy, because of the speed with which technological change occurs, must consider a three- to five-year frame of reference. They suggest that one way of improving the coupling between business and informatics is for a chief information officer (CIO) to be established with responsibility for informatics infrastructure and for this person to be a member of the main board.

■ Portfolios of development plans for new information systems and maintenance plans for existing information systems.

■ A portfolio of operational and support plans for the informatics infrastructure, including training and helpdesks (see Chapter 11). Operational plans relate the activity of the informatics service to goals and budgets. They normally include descriptions of development projects, maintenance activity, operational effort and planning and management activity, all with associated resource implications and costing.

RECAP: Informatics planning is the process of deciding on the optimal informatics infrastructure for an organisation. It uses as input three major forms of strategic analysis: organisational analysis, environmental analysis and technological analysis. There are three major approaches to the planning of informatics strategy: target-driven, resource-driven and implementation-driven. In target-driven strategy, informatics planning involves setting up a planning unit and approach, assessing the current informatics infrastructure, establishing a vision and specifying an informatics strategy. Establishing a vision for informatics normally involves assessing the competitive advantage that information systems could deliver. Among the frameworks proposed for this purpose are critical success factors, the five forces model, the customer resource life-cycle and value-chain or value-network analysis.

10.3   Informatics strategy

Strategy: the art of a commander-in-chief; the art of projecting and directing the larger military movements and operations in a campaign

The term **strategy** has its historical roots in military operations. According to the Oxford English Dictionary, strategy is the art of a commander-in-chief; the art of projecting and directing larger military movements and operations in a campaign. It is not the same as tactics, which concern the mechanical movement of bodies set in motion by strategy. The terms strategy and tactics are now used in much the same sense in a business context.

Ansoff (1965) defines strategic decisions as primarily concerned with a firm's external rather than internal problems, and specifically with selection of the product mix (what the firm will produce) and the market to which it will sell. Given the discussion in previous chapters, we might generalise from this and say that strategy is about deciding on the nature of the value-proposition for an organisation and how such value will be both created and distributed within the wider value network. Strategic decisions are concerned with establishing an 'impedance match' between the firm and its environment. In other words, they focus on deciding what business the firm is in and what kinds of business it will seek to do. In systems terms, strategy involves defining critical issues concerned with the viability and sustainability of organisations (see Chapter 2).

10.3.1   Organisational strategy

Organisational strategy: the general direction or mission of some organisation

Over the last 20 to 30 years the trend has been for the high-ranking manager's job to be seen as developing an explicit **organisation strategy** and creating effective ways of planning and implementing it. In the informatics field, the manager's concern is with how strategies for information, information systems and ICT can be developed and aligned with organisation strategy. This is the notion of informatics strategy. More recently there has been a lot of interest in the strategic implications of closely linking changes to activity infrastructure and technological change. This is what is meant by eBusiness strategy.

Porter has argued that there are three major ways in which organisations can gain competitive advantage (Chapter 7): cost advantage, differentiation and location. These can be seen as particular types of organisational strategy:

- Cost advantage. A commercial organisation can gain competitive advantage or leadership by establishing itself as a low-cost leader in the market. Cost advantage is usually achieved by doing things more efficiently.
- Differentiation. It can gain competitive advantage by differentiating its product in the marketplace. This generally involves persuading consumers that it offers something special in the way of a product or service. There are two parts to this, of course: having a unique and desirable offering to sell, and persuading consumers that this is so.
- Location. Finally, a commercial organisation can gain competitive advantage by finding a niche in the marketplace for its value(its product or service). This can be achieved in a number of ways. For example, it might offer an entirely new product or service, or offer its product or service to a previously untapped group of customers, perhaps through an innovative access channel (see below).

> **DID YOU KNOW?** One of the earliest texts on strategy is thought to have been written by the Chinese general Sun Tzu (544–496 BC), *The Art of War*. Interestingly, he stated that it was always desirable to conquer the enemy without resorting to war, through the application of strategy. This text is often cited in modern treatises on business strategy.

10.3.2   Formulation of business strategy

According to Johnson et al. (2007), the formulation of business strategy involves three interdependent activities:

- Strategic analysis: of the environment, expectations, objectives, power and culture in the organisation and organisational resources. Strategic analysis involves determining the organisation's mission and goals, and answering the questions: what should we be doing and where are we going?
- Strategic choice: generating strategic options, evaluating them and selecting both an option and a suitable strategy to achieve it. Strategic choice involves answering the question: what routes have we selected?
- Strategic implementation: organising resources, restructuring elements of the organisation, and providing suitable people and systems. Strategic implementation comprises determining policies, making decisions and taking action. It aims to answer the questions: how do we guide our collective decisions to get there? What choices do we have? How shall we do it?

Strategic thinking is normally documented in an organisation's mission statement. This comprises a short list of statements of future intention, for each of which a number of goals may be formulated. In turn, for each goal a number of strategies or routes forward may be planned. Each strategy has to be made operational in a series of plans. Plans in their turn are collections of decisions which involve a series of actions, so strategic planning involves constructing a hierarchy of goals, strategies, policies, decisions and actions. For example:

- Mission: to be the industry cost leader.
- Goal: achieve staff productivity gain of 5% within three years.
- Strategy: reduce the time to process a customer transaction.
- Policy: improve customer-facing information systems and integration.
- Decision: introduce a corporate-wide CRM information system.
- Action: set up and resource an implementation project.

An organisation's mission statement at various levels of the hierarchy consists of a limited number of objectives, which act as a guide to future intention. These should be SMART objectives:

- Specific: each objective should be clear and focused.
- Measurable: it should be clear how achieving the objective can be measured.
- Achievable: the objective should be achievable with organisational resources.
- Realistic: the objective should be realistic in terms of organisational constraints.
- Timely: the objective should specify a duration by which it will be achieved.

10.3.3 eBusiness strategy

eBusiness strategy: the development of strategy for the electronic business

But how does general business strategy relate to **eBusiness strategy**? There are at least three different viewpoints on what eBusiness strategy is. None of them is the sole correct view, since the appropriate viewpoint is defined by organisational context. In other words, eBusiness strategy will depend on the business model we develop for eBusiness and whether this business model is the same as the business model for the entire business or whether it is subsumed within the general business model. Options therefore include a complete overlap between organisation and eBusiness strategy, eBusiness strategy as a business unit strategy, and eBusiness strategy as a process strategy.

In the most extreme form there is little or no distinction between organisation strategy and eBusiness strategy. This definition is appropriate if the eBusiness is effectively the entire corporation. In practice it may only be applicable if a traditional bricks and mortar company sets out to completely re-engineer its processes around ICT, or a new greenfield eBusiness is established: a clicks-only strategy.

In many companies the eBusiness strategy applies only to a particular part of the business: a division, department or unit. In one approach a firm segments its eBusiness activities as a separate organisation isolated from the parent firm. This organisation is expected to innovate with new products and services. At the other extreme, the eBusiness activity is fully integrated with the parent organisation but under the control of specific business units: a clicks and mortar strategy. In a middle path, companies run their eBusinesses as separate but parallel operations, implying a certain level of integration between the parent organisation and the eBusiness, but also a certain degree of autonomy for the eBusiness.

The company might choose a key organisational process or activity system, or perhaps an integrated set of processes, for radical redesign with ICT innovation. For example, it could concentrate on redesigning its supply chain or customer chain processes. This is probably the most common current form of eBusiness strategy.

So Amazon.com's eBusiness strategy will equate to its organisation strategy, because it is an eBusiness-oriented company. Other companies might develop supply chain management or customer relationship management as an eBusiness strategy, or pick an area of eCommerce such as B2C or B2B eCommerce (see Chapter 8). These might be either business unit or process strategies depending on the structure of the organisation.

> **REFLECT:** As more and more companies embrace eBusiness, which form of eBusiness strategy will become the most prevalent? Will the type of eBusiness strategy vary by industry? In other words, will companies in the financial services sector have a different profile of eBusiness strategies from those in retail or manufacturing?

10.3.4 Competitive advantage and information systems

Information systems can be used in two ways in organisations. First, they can be used to support current activity systems, which form part of the current informatics infrastructure. Second, they can be developed to support new activity systems. These information systems directly assist an organisation in achieving its strategy, and are designed to have a direct impact on its competitive advantage For this reason, they are sometimes referred to as **strategic information systems**.

Strategic information system: an information system that delivers competitive advantage

Strategic information systems contribute to one or more of the generic organisational strategies discussed above. For instance, banks worldwide have set up online banking facilities. There are a number of reasons that this can lead to performance improvements, not least the low cost of banking transactions online compared with traditional banking services, so online banking could at one time be seen as a form of strategic information system. Internet-based retailing is an obvious area for establishing new ways of delivering products and services. Amazon.com was one of the first to sell books and CDs online, and has established a relative dominance in this segment of online retail, sometimes called eTailing.

An analysis of cases like this produces a list of common characteristics of strategic information systems:

- Many strategic information systems are built from an established informatics infrastructure. Organisational leverage is frequently achieved simply by integrating systems and creating more effective information flows in support of business processes.
- Many strategic information systems link the organisation more efficiently or effectively with its customers and suppliers. To be of benefit, strategic information systems must offer real value to the customer or supplier.
- A strategic information system must not be too easy to copy by competitors. It must be able to offer a medium- to long-term impact on organisational performance to justify the investment in its development.
- A strategic information system must be capable of changing the marketplace's perception of the firm; for example, by enabling it to offer new products or services, or offer its existing ones in different ways.
- Many strategic information systems are strategic in the sense that they provide high-level management with better information about internal operations and/or the organisation environment, enabling them to plan strategically far more effectively.

An information system is only likely to remain strategic for a limited period of time. Usually the competitive advantage it provides will be eroded in time because of emulation by competitors, but the first entrant into an area frequently determines standards in terms of technology and its use. This often means that customers face a switching cost if they abandon it for a later rival. A strategic information system will therefore offer a strategic advantage to an organisation in intangible as well as tangible ways.

> **REFLECT:** Consider a university as an organisation to which ICT transformation might be applied. What would be an appropriate strategic information system in this context and why?

CASE CHECK

UK Revenue and Customs

 p 460

The Inland Revenue was, until recently, the UK government department responsible for collecting and administering taxation. It has attempted to be at the forefront of eGovernment in the United Kingdom by transforming its performance using ICT. The department set out its first eBusiness strategy in 2000. The key feature was the development of a number of electronic channels for different customer groups, with clear incentives to encourage their use.

10.3.5 Informatics strategy

Informatics strategy: a definition of the structure within which information, information systems and information technology is to be applied in an organisation

eBusiness strategy, as we have seen, is subtly different from, but interdependent with, informatics strategy. An **informatics strategy** defines the structure within which information, information systems and ICT are to be applied in an organisation over a future timeframe. It therefore has three major layers:

- An information strategy details the information needs of the organisation, and the processes necessary to communicate effectively.

- An information systems strategy consists of a specification of the information systems needed to support organisational activity.
- An ICT strategy is a specification of the hardware, software, data, communication facilities and ICT knowledge and skills needed by the organisation to support its information systems.

Classic models of informatics strategy formulation try to achieve the ideal of alignment between organisation strategy and informatics strategy. This issue of alignment was considered in both Chapters 4 and 6. Ideally, four layers of strategy support each other with a strategy for activity systems in the organisation (organisation strategy) supported by the three layers of informatics strategy. The information needed by the organisation will determine the information systems it requires. In turn, the information systems needed determine the ICT infrastructure required.

The notion of alignment suggests that business strategy formulation should ideally come before informatics strategy formulation, as is illustrated in Figure 10.5. Organisation planning is the process of formulating an organisation strategy. Informatics planning is the process of formulating an informatics strategy. An organisation strategy will critically affect the direction of an informatics strategy. However, in the modern business world organisational and informatics strategies are typically related in a mutual cycle of reinforcement. The formulation of an informatics strategy is likely to have a major influence on the formulation of future business strategy.

Figure 10.5 *The relationship between organisation and informatics planning*

REFLECT: How are mergers between companies or public sector organisations likely to affect informatics strategy, and why?

CASE CHECK   CS p 470

Peak experiences and strategic IT alignment at Vermont Teddy Bear

In 2010 the new CIO at Vermont Teddy Bear was of a mind to modernise the company's informatics infrastructure. He faced the considerable task of making explicit many implicit aspects of this infrastructure as a step towards developing future informatics strategy for the company. The CEO of the company also sought new sources of revenue, which would impact upon decisions made by the CIO. Should the CIO consider long-term investment in enterprise systems or should he take immediate steps to produce tangible results quickly? (Have a look at this case).

IV

The objective of informatics planning is to develop a strategy in each of the three areas outlined above. The practical output of informatics planning is a set of documents which describe strategy in these three areas. An informatics strategy can be described as the structure within which information, information systems and ICT are intended to be applied in the organisation. It should establish a long-term infrastructure that will allow information systems to be designed and implemented efficiently and effectively. An informatics strategy is particularly directed at avoiding fragmentation, redundancy and inconsistency among information systems (see Chapter 6), and increasing their interoperability.

An informatics strategy will be constrained by an existing informatics infrastructure (Chapter 4). Very few organisations are able to build a cleanslate, or greenfield, strategy in this area. Usually existing information needs, information systems and ICT have to be taken into account in formulating strategy.

10.3.6 Channel strategies

Channel strategy: a set of choices for the organisation about how, and through what means, services and goods will be delivered

The relationship between general business strategy and eBusiness strategy is easily demonstrated in **channel strategy**. As we have seen, an access channel is a means for an organisation to deliver goods and/or services to its customers (see Chapter 6). Traditional access channels include voice and face-to-face contact. There are also a range of remote access channels, of which the most familiar are telephone contact and, more recently, Internet access through devices such as the personal computer. Goods and services can either be delivered directly by an organisation or indirectly using intermediaries (Chapter 6).

A channel strategy is a set of choices for the organisation about how, and through what means, services and goods will be delivered. This typically means deciding which access channels will be made available to which customer segments (see Chapter 9). Different levels of interactivity and content may be required to meet the needs of differing customer segments. The capability of a particular access channel to cope with demand is a critical part of any channel strategy, and so is integration between different access channels.

For example, a local government authority's channel strategy will involve deciding what proportion of services (if any) it will deliver remotely to PCs or through digital TV. It will also involve deciding to what extent it will use contact centres to manage the delivery of its services, and ensuring that it can deliver them seamlessly across multiple access channels.

Channel strategies typically involve tiered access to products and services. Most large-scale private and public sector organisations offer at least three tiers, each of which has different cost and availability implications. The first tier is remote direct access through a subset of the access devices discussed in Chapter 6. The second tier is through a multi-channel access centre where contact centre staff manage delivery through computer integrated telephony. The third tier involves direct contact with employees through face-to-face communication or letter. This is illustrated in Figure 10.6.

The channel strategy chosen will have a major impact on informatics strategy. For instance, if an organisation provides tiered access, it needs to ensure that it can deal in a uniform way with customer data acquired through different access channels, which is likely to mean setting up a customer relationship management system (see Chapter 4). For this purpose it might either buy a packaged system or build one in-house, perhaps using existing ICT infrastructure (for example, customer databases) as a platform.

> **REFLECT:** Are call centres run by major companies the same as contact centres? How important is effective integration of information systems to the performance of contact centres?

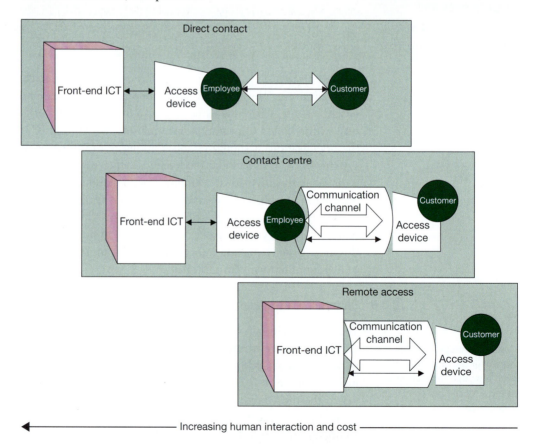

Figure 10.6 *Tiered access*

10.3.7 Developing information strategy

The top level of informatics strategy consists of an information strategy. An information strategy details the information needs of the organisation and the processes necessary to support effective communication. There is no rule about the form of one, but it usually has three core elements:

- An **organisation information model**, which details the structure of the major information classes used by the organisation and the relationships between them (see Chapter 3). For medium- to large-scale organisations this will be described at a high level of abstraction.
- An organisation process model, which details the key activities relevant to a particular organisation.
- A process/information matrix, which documents which information classes are used by which processes. This matrix allows managers and developers to identify key clusters of common applications and databases around which new information systems should be built. It is also of particular use for managers in considering issues of integration or fragmentation in the informatics infrastructure.

The diagram in Figure 10.7 is a simplified example of an organisation information model for a UK university. At the centre of the information model is the information class *academic staff*. On one side this class links to information classes relevant to supporting the administration of teaching such as *module*, *course* and *student*. On the other side *academic staff* links to information classes necessary for knowing about research (such as *publication* and *research grant*) as well as engagement with industry (such as *consultancy project* and *customer*).

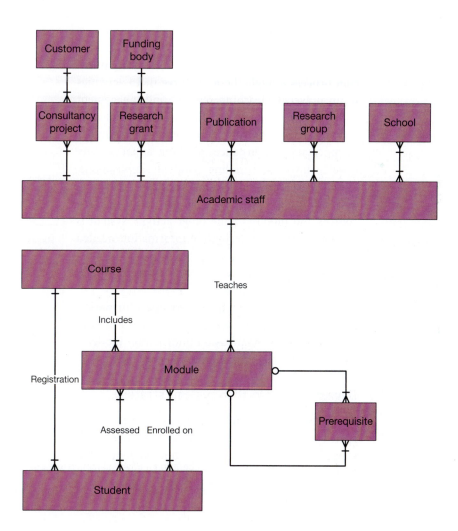

Figure 10.7 *University information model*

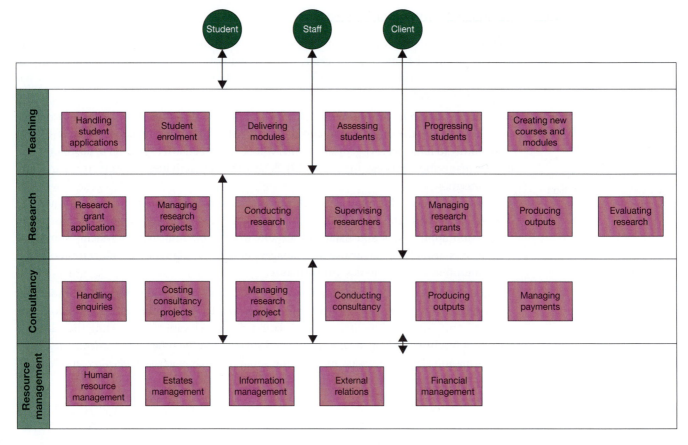

Figure 10.8 *University process model*

Organisation process model:
details the major processes of
an organisation

Figure 10.8 is an example of the related **organisation process model**. There are three main activities in any university: teaching, research and engagement with industry (sometimes in the form of consultancy activity). Each activity system consists of a number of processes. For instance, teaching as an activity system involves handling student applications, enrolling students, delivering modules, assessing students, progressing students and creating new courses and modules. One other activity system is included for administering the information needed to manage learning resources such as books, journals, and digital media, as well as other resources such as buildings and staff.

Figure 10.9 is a simplified **process/information matrix**. The shaded boxes indicate which information class on the organisation information model is used by which major organisational process.

Process/information matrix:
a matrix which indicates
which information class on
the organisation information
model is used by which
organisational process.

10.3.8 Developing information systems strategy

Information systems strategy: a specification of the
information systems needed
to support organisational
activity

An **information systems strategy** consists of a specification of the information systems needed to support organisational activity, not only now but in the planned future. Therefore, an information systems strategy should include details of the current and future information systems portfolio.

Process/Information Matrix

	Teaching	Research	Consultancy	Resource administration
Funding body		▨		
Consultancy project			▨	
Research grant		▨		
Staff	▨	▨	▨	▨
Course				▨
Publication		▨	▨	
Research group		▨		
Module	▨			▨
Student	▨	▨		
School	▨	▨	▨	

Figure 10.9 *A process/information matrix for a university*

This portfolio needs to be justified in terms of how information systems link to supporting current and future organisation processes. To achieve this, there needs to be an effective organisational analysis, and an awareness of the core competencies or key mission of the organisation.

Although a strategy normally looks to the future, most organisations need to build a detailed inventory of their current information systems and the links such systems have with organisation processes. This is a key element of the informatics infrastructure, and should include documentation of non-computerised as well as computerised information systems. High-level information system models as described in Chapter 4 are useful for this.

A future information systems portfolio should detail the planned information systems projects for the organisation over a time frame of perhaps three to five years. It will include projects such as corrections to existing information systems, enhancements to existing information systems, major new information systems development projects, major new infrastructure systems, technologies that attempt to integrate systems across the organisation, and research projects to investigate possible new information systems and technologies.

10.3.9 Developing ICT strategy

ICT strategy: a specification of the hardware, software, data, communication facilities and ICT knowledge and skills needed by the organisation to support its information systems

An **ICT strategy** consists of a specification of the hardware, software, data, communication facilities and ICT knowledge and skills needed by the organisation to support its information systems. The five major elements of an ICT strategy are:

- An ICT systems model: a detailed inventory of both current and future ICT systems.
- Hardware standards: a list of the standards to be adopted in connection with computers and peripheral devices.
- Software standards: a list of the standard system, communication and application software to be adopted throughout the organisation.
- Communication standards: details of the appropriate makeup of needed communication technology and networks.
- Data standards: documenting agreements about data representation and formats.

The major objectives of an ICT strategy are to reduce fragmentation, inconsistency and redundancy among ICT systems, and improve levels of interoperability. This might be achieved by buying new software packages (such as an ERP system as discussed in Chapter 6), or developing new bespoke information systems. Part of the ICT strategy must also consider the operational support (see Chapter 11) and maintenance needed for both current and planned ICT systems (see Chapter 12).

REFLECT: Consider an organisation such as Tesco. In running its supermarket network, what sort of concerns might feed into its ICT strategy?

RECAP: An informatics strategy defines the structure within which information, information systems and ICT are to be applied in an organisation. It should establish an organisation's long-term informatics infrastructure, which will allow information systems to be designed and implemented efficiently and effectively. It is particularly directed at avoiding fragmentation, redundancy and inconsistency between information systems. It is also a key vehicle in promoting the interoperability of systems. So an informatics strategy should be directed at ensuring an optimal fit between an organisation and its information systems. It typically comprises three levels, an information strategy, information systems strategy and ICT strategy. It can be specified using an organisation information model, an organisation process model and an associated information/process matrix. It should document the current information system portfolio and a future information system portfolio. It should include an ICT systems model and standards for hardware, software, communication technology and data management technology.

10.4   Informatics management

Because informatics is so embedded in the modern business, good management of informatics assumes critical significance for business. Take an example, in June of 2012 a software upgrade to an important part of the ICT infrastructure of the British banking group – RBS/Natwest/Ulster Bank – was undertaken. This upgrade to a batch processing module of its core back-end transaction processing systems failed. As a result, the overnight updates (credits and debits) to customer bank-accounts were not applied correctly, meaning that account balances were incorrect. This situation took days to resolve as the volume of transactional data needing to be handled backed up. The situation caused numerous problems for customers of these banks. For instance, wages were not paid into bank-accounts and payments were not made into business accounts. As a result, customers experienced difficulties in withdrawing cash from ATMs or paying for goods and services using their debit cards; businesses suffered major problems to their cash flow. Besides the obvious effect this had on customer attitudes this problem caused substantial additional spending by the banking group as they sought to address the problems caused by an ICT failure.

Informatics management:
the process of implementing plans produced by informatics planning and monitoring their results

Changes to informatics infrastructure are a critical part of informatics planning. **Informatics management** is the process of implementing plans produced by informatics planning and monitoring their results. It is a key control process for effective project management; in turn, informatics planning forms a control for informatics management. Therefore, informatics management is one of the important activities of the informatics service and is critically important to get right in the modern business (see Chapter 11).

10.4.1   Information, information systems and ICT management

Michael Earl (1989) distinguished some time ago between three forms of management relevant to informatics, on the criteria of their primary objective, the basis of management and their primary focus and responsibility:

Information management is concerned with the general planning, regulation and coordination of information policies in the organisation. It determines the overall strategic direction of the organisation in terms of its information. Earl suggests that it needs to be a role of senior management.

Information systems management is concerned with the management of information-handling applications in the organisation. It deals with the planning, execution and operation of information systems to support organisational activities. As such, Earl suggests that it is a role for managers of business units.

ICT management is concerned with the maintenance of the ICT infrastructure, developing new applications and maintaining existing ICT applications. It is the concern of technical specialists.

This framework is interesting in that it suggests that a range of competencies are required in the management of information, information systems and ICT, and that the forms of management should logically be sited at various levels within organisations. It also presumes that business managers are given informatics knowledge, experience and responsibilities through some form of training. As discussed in an earlier section, it suggests that organisations need to have three levels of planning in place, and three corresponding levels of informatics strategy.

10.4.2   Management, strategy and infrastructure

An informatics strategy is the major output of informatics planning. This acts as the major control input into the informatics management process. Informatics management is also constrained by the current informatics infrastructure. Hence, this is also a key control input into the management process. Each element of informatics management takes responsibility for different aspects of both strategy and infrastructure.

There are two major aspects to informatics management: controlling the informatics infrastructure and implementing the informatics strategy. Control essentially means managing the current information, information systems and ICT; this is a regulatory process. Implementation essentially consists of managing the development of future information, information systems and ICT; this is an adaptive process (Chapter 2).

Ideally, information management should drive information systems management, which in turn drives ICT management. An organisation needs to identify its information needs then decide on the information systems that will supply those needs, and finally decide on appropriate ICT for supporting its information systems.

10.4.3 Information management activities

Information management: that part of informatics management concerned with the management of information

In recent years many organisations have recognised the importance of information and of effective management of this critical resource. The rise of **information management** is a result of the recognition that information is critical to the effective operation of activity systems, and particularly to measuring their performance. It should be managed in a similar manner to other organisational resources, such as human resources (staff) and material resources (plant and machinery).

In essence, information management activities consist of the two major processes of managing the current information infrastructure and implementing the future information strategy.

Managing an information infrastructure involves a number of activities. Since any organisation is in a continuous state of flux it needs to continuously evaluate whether the information it generates is adequate for supporting its activities. It also needs to continuously identify opportunities for integrating information across business activities. To enable this, the organisation needs to refresh its organisation information model, process model and information/process matrix on a regular basis. It also needs to develop and maintain standards for the representation of information as data within records across the organisation.

Implementing an information strategy involves enforcing standards for the representation of information and checking the conformance of new information systems with the information infrastructure defined within the organisation information model and process model.

Knowledge management: consists of knowledge creation, knowledge codification and knowledge transfer

A number of terms are used to describe various approaches to what is here called information management. This section considers three: data management or administration (the administration of the data resource); **knowledge management** (the management of organisational memory); and records management. The related issue of content management (the management of Web-based material) was considered in Chapter 6. All four are fundamentally forms of information management, and all are concerned with the administration of various aspects of the information resource. This might be in traditional paper-based form, or stored in a range of ICT including databases, data warehouses and Web material.

Data administration: that function concerned with the management, planning and documentation of the data resource of an organisation.

It is easy to confuse data management as an organisational function (what used to be referred to as data administration) with data management as a technical role (particularly focused around issues of database administration). **Data administration** involves the planning, management, documentation and operation of an organisation's data resource (Gillenson, 1991). It is concerned with the management of an organisation's metadata, that is, data about data, and is a function that deals with the conceptual or business view of an organisation's data resource. In contrast, database administration involves the technical implementation of database systems, managing the database systems currently in use and setting and enforcing policies for their use (Chapter 7).

Consider the importance of data administration to an organisation such as a university. Without data on, for instance, what students are enrolled, what students are taking which modules and what grades students have been awarded, a university would be unable to operate effectively. Now imagine that the different university departments, or schools, maintain their own distinctive collections of data, with their own distinctive definitions for data structures,

IV

data elements and data items. As a consequence, data are frequently missing, incomplete, or out of date, and staff have incomplete knowledge on what data are collected, and where they are kept.

In the larger sense, data management encompasses all of the issues of data storage, integration, sharing and security discussed in Chapter 6, as well as others important for the effective management of the data resource, such as data definition, data integrity and data control. In this sense effective data administration inherently assumes an interest in both the physical and electronic records of organisations, so it includes records management (Earley, 2010). Records management is defined by the International Standards Organisation as '*the field of management responsible for the efficient and systematic control of the creation, receipt, maintenance, use and disposition of records, including the processes for capturing and maintaining evidence of and information about business activities and transactions in the form of records*'.

Data management is important not only for internal processes, but also for effective data sharing between organisations, so it is particularly important to effective B2B eCommerce (see Chapter 8). Key innovations, such as eProcurement in both the private and public sectors, could not occur without inter-organisational standards for data storage and transfer.

It has been argued that knowledge is a significant resource for organisations (Alavi and Leidner, 2001), because increased knowledge leads to an increased ability to perform effectively. Knowledge is also complex and usually difficult to imitate, so it has the potential to generate long-term and sustainable competitive advantage. When organisations lose personnel with significant amounts of knowledge (when they retire, quit, or are made redundant through downsizing) it is a significant loss. It is less so if their knowledge remains in the organisation, so there has been much emphasis on capturing, storing and sharing knowledge.

People clearly acquire knowledge that improves their performance in specific fields, but to what degree is it appropriate to speak of groups and organisations as having knowledge? One useful concept is organisational memory. This is what an organisation knows about its processes and its environment. The knowledge in an organisation's memory is a critical resource for organisations in that it enables them to act effectively in economic markets.

If knowledge is networked information (see Chapter 3), then information is clearly a prerequisite to effective knowledge. Knowledge management can be seen as the topmost layer of management processes in organisations that are reliant on effective information management. It consists of three key processes (Davenport and Prusak, 2000):

- Knowledge creation involves the acquisition of knowledge from organisational members and the creation of new organisational knowledge.
- Knowledge codification and storage consists of the representation of knowledge for ease of retrieval.
- Knowledge transfer involves the communication and sharing of knowledge between organisational members.

10.4.4   Information systems management activities

Information systems management: concerned with the management of information-handling applications, both computerised and non-computerised

Information systems management is concerned with the management of information-handling applications, both computerised and non-computerised. Its activities include management of the current information systems infrastructure, which involves maintaining an inventory of it, and ensuring its effective operation and maintenance. It also comprises managing the development of information systems planned in the information systems strategy. This involves monitoring and controlling the range of development projects both underway and planned. As a consequence, controlling budgets for information systems investment is important. Controlling budgets requires strategically monitoring planned against occurred expenditure. Finally, completed information systems need to be evaluated. Evaluation is based on conducting rigorous summative assessments to determine how successful they are. For abandoned projects it also involves conducting a post-mortem analysis to ensure that the organisation learns from its mistakes (see Chapter 9).

10.4.5 ICT management activities

ICT management: concerned with the maintenance of the ICT infrastructure, developing new applications and maintaining existing ICT applications

ICT management is concerned with the maintenance of the ICT infrastructure, developing new applications and maintaining existing ICT applications. Its activities are the two major processes of managing the current ICT architecture and implementing future ICT strategy.

Managing ICT infrastructure involves activities such as maintaining ICT system standards, hardware standards, software standards, data standards and communication standards. It also involves operational activity such as monitoring the total cost of ownership of the ICT infrastructure and providing helpdesk facilities. These issues are considered in Chapter 11.

Implementing the ICT strategy involves managing the development of bespoke and packaged ICT systems, the maintenance of existing ICT systems, the purchase of hardware, software, data and communication technology. It also concerns making sure ICT systems match with corporate objectives established in the organisation strategy.

> **REFLECT:** The role of chief information officer (CIO) has been proposed to oversee all of informatics management within an organisation. In what way do you think such a role might be important to effective informatics management?

10.5 ICT governance

 key skill

ICT governance: a subset of the discipline of corporate governance, focused on ICT systems and their performance

IT or ICT governance is a subset of the discipline of corporate governance, focused on ICT systems and their performance. Its primary goals are to ensure that ICT investments generate business value and to mitigate the risks associated with ICT (Weill and Ross, 2004). This is achieved by implementing organisational structures and processes with well-defined roles and clear lines of responsibility for, or decision rights over, various aspects of informatics infrastructure.

There are three reasons for the contemporary interest in **ICT governance**:

- A growing acknowledgement that ICT is critical to the modern organisation and that therefore key decision-making in this area must be a responsibility at board level.
- An acknowledgment that ICT system projects easily get out of control and this can profoundly affect the performance of an organisation (Chapter 9).
- The fact that certain organisations, particularly in the public sector, have to follow compliance rules such as the Sarbanes-Oxley Act in the United States and Basel II in Europe.

COBIT: Control Objectives for Information and related Technology, a method for ICT governance

There are a number of frameworks for ICT governance. One of the most prominent internationally is Control Objectives for Information and related Technology (**COBIT**). This is a framework of measures, indicators, processes and best practices for ICT management created by the Information Systems Audit and Control Association (ISACA), and the IT Governance Institute (ITGI). Originally created in 1992, COBIT assists managers, auditors and ICT users to achieve benefits through the use of ICT and to develop appropriate control of the ICT infrastructure.

COBIT 5, which was released in 2012, is the latest version of the framework. This has 34 high-level processes which cover 210 control objectives categorised in four domains: Planning and Organisation, Acquisition and Implementation, Delivery and Support, and Monitoring (see Figure 10.10) These domains overlap with both the planning and management processes considered in this chapter and the operational activities to be discussed in Chapter 11.

- Plan and organise focuses on the use of ICT to achieve business goals. High-level control objectives for this domain include defining an ICT strategy and ICT infrastructure, managing ICT human resources and managing ICT projects.

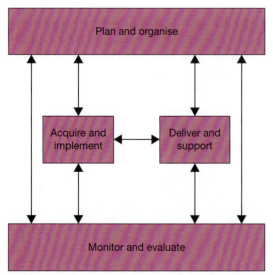

Figure 10.10 *COBIT domains*

- Acquire and implement focuses on identifying ICT requirements, acquiring technology and implementing ICT systems aligned with business processes. High-level control objectives for the domain include acquiring and maintaining application software, enabling operation and use, and managing change.

- Deliver and support focuses on ensuring the effective operation of ICT systems and support processes. High-level control objectives for the domain include defining and managing service levels, educating and training users, and managing operations.

- Monitor and evaluate focuses on continually assessing needs and whether ICT infrastructure meets them. High-level control objectives for the domain include monitoring and evaluating ICT processes and ensuring regulatory compliance.

> **REFLECT:** Will better ICT governance contribute to better governance of large corporations such as the financial institutions that played a major role in the financial crisis of 2008?
>
> Some people argue that the discipline of ICT governance and frameworks, such as COBIT, might constrain ICT innovation in organisations. Why do you think this might be the case?

FOCUS ON VALUE Most modern organisations could not perform effectively without information, information systems and ICT. Hence, there is key value for organisations in controlling their informatics infrastructure. The planning of informatics strategy should be aligned with general business strategy. Following from this there is key value in managing informatics infrastructure appropriately. This means controlling current informatics infrastructure as well as implementing new informatics infrastructure.

10.6 Conclusion and key themes

This chapter has considered the related issues of informatics planning and management. Because informatics is increasingly embedded in organisations, informatics planning and management are major control processes for them. Effective planning and implementation of informatics strategy is seen as critical to the successful development and use of information systems. In modern, information intensive, business practice, they are both determinants of organisational success (see Chapter 9).

Informatics planning is the process of deciding on the optimal informatics infrastructure. It uses as input three major forms of strategic analysis: organisational analysis, environmental analysis and technological analysis. There are three major approaches to planning an informatics strategy: target-driven, resource-driven and implementation-driven. In the target-driven form, informatics planning involves setting up a planning unit and approach, assessing the current informatics infrastructure, establishing a vision and specifying an informatics strategy.

Establishing a vision for informatics normally involves assessing the competitive advantage that information systems can deliver. Among the frameworks for this are critical success factors, the five forces model, the customer resource life-cycle, and value-chain or value-network analysis.

An informatics strategy defines the structure within which information, information systems and ICT is to be applied within an organisation. An informatics strategy should establish an organisation's long-term informatics infrastructure, which will allow information systems to be designed and implemented efficiently and effectively. It is particularly directed at avoiding fragmentation, redundancy and inconsistency, and is also a key vehicle in promoting the interoperability of systems. Hence, an informatics strategy should be directed at ensuring an optimal fit between an organisation and its information systems.

There are three levels to an informatics strategy: an information strategy, an information systems strategy and an ICT strategy. An information strategy is specified through an organisation information model, an organisation process model and an associated information/process matrix. An information systems strategy consists of documentation of the current and future information system portfolios. An ICT strategy includes an ICT systems model and standards for hardware, software, communication technology and data technology.

There are three forms of informatics management: information management, information systems management and ICT management, which correspond both to the three levels of informatics strategy and to the three levels of informatics infrastructure discussed in Chapter 3. One side of informatics management involves implementing strategy in each of these three areas: that is, implementing future information systems that deliver new forms of information to support new forms of activity The other side of informatics management involves managing the existing informatics infrastructure: ensuring that current information systems work efficiently and effectively in support of current activity.

Chapter 11 considers the management of existing infrastructure and operations in more detail. The operation of the current informatics infrastructure is a neglected but critical part of the provision of informatics, and is often run nowadays as a service partnership in organisations.

10.7   Review test

1 Put the classic phases for informatics planning into the correct order. Label the first phase 1 and so on.
- ☐ Developing the information systems architecture
- ☐ Assessing the informatics infrastructure
- ☐ Setting up a planning organisation
- ☐ Developing the informatics services strategic plan
- ☐ Developing information services operational plans and budgets
- ☐ Establishing a vision of how the organisation should use information systems

2 A CSF is a factor that is deemed crucial to the success of a business. True or false?
- ☐ True
- ☐ False

3 Identify Porter's five forces that influence the competitive position of a company. Select all that apply.
- ☐ Customer bargaining power
- ☐ Industrial rivalry, the competitive position of rival organisations
- ☐ Competitive advantage
- ☐ Supplier bargaining power
- ☐ Threat of substitutes
- ☐ Company size
- ☐ Barriers to entry, threat of new entrants

4 The _____ considers a firm's relationship with its customers (the customer chain) and how this relationship can be changed or enhanced by the strategic application of ICT. Fill in the blank.

5 Distinguish strategy from tactics. Write two sentences.

6 An informatics _____ is the major output of informatics planning. Fill in the blank.

7 An informatics strategy comprises three levels, what are they? Select all that apply.
- ☐ ICT strategy
- ☐ Information strategy
- ☐ Computing strategy
- ☐ Information systems strategy

8 How do strategic plans differ from operational plans? Write two sentences.

9 As a minimum there are three major elements of an information strategy, what are they? Select all that apply.
- ☐ Process/information matrix
- ☐ Organisation information model
- ☐ Organisation process model
- ☐ Object model

10 Information management is concerned with the maintenance of the ICT infrastructure, developing new applications and maintaining existing ICT applications. True or false?
- ☐ True
- ☐ False

11 Why is ICT governance important to informatics management? Write two sentences.

IV

10.8   Exercises

- Write a brief description of what you feel should be included in any organisational analysis. Do the same for an environmental and technology analysis.

- Determine how planning is best described in an organisation known to you; target, resource or implementation-driven.

- Determine whether there is a specific unit devoted to informatics planning in an organisation known to you. Determine the way it is organised.

- Attempt to apply one of the approaches to establishing an informatics vision to a public sector organisation, such as a university.

- Determine whether an organisation known to you has an organisation information model and a process model.

- Provide an example of each of the activities listed under managing the information, information systems or ICT architecture.

- Develop a small analysis of how information systems might be used to improve the strategic position of an organisation using one or more of the frameworks discussed in the chapter.

- List two critical success factors for an organisation known to you.

- Produce one example of how information systems might affect Porter's five forces model.

- From the planning frameworks discussed, choose what you feel to be the most effective framework and briefly justify your choice.

- Consider an information system known to you. In what respect would you define it as strategic, and why?

- Find one example of a modern strategic information system in the cost leadership, differentiation or niche strategy.

- Find one example of a system which can be regarded as strategic but which is built on existing informatics infrastructure.

10.9   Projects

- Informatics planning is important but do organisations engage in it? Investigate the degree to which a small sample of organisations conduct systematic informatics planning. Determine the forms of informatics planning undertaken.

- Find an organisation that conducts informatics planning. Determine the key benefits experienced by this organisation. Also, attempt to determine the costs associated with conducting informatics planning. In other words, what sort of business case does the organisation have for conducting continuous informatics planning?

- Assess the current state of the information systems in an organisation known to you. Attempt to measure the degree to which the information systems are integrated. How has the infrastructure been built over time?

- The customer resource life-cycle can be seen as a model of the customer chain. Determine its applicability for considering B2C eCommerce. In other words, assess how useful it is for considering ways in which an organisation may use B2C eCommerce to improve its performance.

- Analyse either B2B or B2C eCommerce in terms of Porter's five forces model. In other words, what effect does B2B eCommerce have on issues such as supplier bargaining power?

- Collect data on a given organisation's informatics strategy. Does it distinguish between an information, information systems and ICT strategy? How was the strategy formulated? How is it used and maintained?

- Develop a high-level organisation information model, organisation process model and information/process matrix for some organisation. How useful and practical are these models to help decide where information systems are important?

- Develop a high-level information systems strategy based on your information strategy.

- Use business motivation modelling to produce a specification of a new business plan for a particular company. How successful is such modelling for linking strategy, processes and technology?

- Consider outsourcing as part of an informatics strategy. Examine some of the literature on this topic, and determine the critical success factors for successful outsourcing of informatics.

- Develop a case study of a strategic information system in the area of eCommerce. What made the information system strategic? How long did the system remain strategic?

- The management of informatics is likely to be organised differently in different organisations. Try to investigate some differences in a small range of organisations. For instance, how closely do organisations distinguish between information, information systems and ICT management?

‣ ICT governance is an important part of corporate governance, and organisations are increasingly required to implement controls in these areas. Investigate the application of ICT governance in a range of organisations. Identify the approaches

used and the costs and benefits of applying ICT governance.

‣ Earl argues that informatics management demands different competencies. Take an organisation and try to examine the extent to which the management of informatics is distributed through the technical and business sides.

10.10 Critical reflection

What is the relationship between a business model and a business strategy? What potential problems exist in adopting a top-down, or target-driven, approach to strategy-making? In terms of low-level business strategies, what is the relationship between customer intimacy and customer relationship management? What is the relationship between supplier intimacy and supplier relationship management? Is it possible to develop measures of the fit between an organisation and its information systems? What sort of knowledge and skills does an eBusiness manager require as compared to a general business manager? Are three types of roles really required in organisations to manage information, information systems and ICT?

10.11 Further reading

Ward and Peppard (2012) provide one of the most cited texts on planning issues as it affects informatics. Applegate, Austin and McFarlan (2009) build on the classic work by Cash, McFarlan and McKeney (1992) on informatics management. Galliers and Leidner (2003) also provide a good overview of issues relating to the management of informatics. Galliers (2006) provides a critical review of discourse in relation to informatics strategy.

10.12 References

Alavi, M. and D. Leidner. (2001). Knowledge Management and Knowledge Management Systems. *Management Information Systems Quarterly* 25 (1): 107–136.

Ansoff, H. I. (1965). *Corporate Strategy*. McGraw-Hill., New York.

Applegate, L. M., R. D. Austin and F. W. McFarlan. (2009). *Corporate Information Strategy and Management: Text and Cases*. 8th edition. McGraw-Hill, New York.

Cash, J. I., F. W. McFarlan and J. L. McKeney. (1992). *Corporate Information Systems Management*. 3rd edition. Richard Irvin, Homewood, Ill.

Davenport, T. H. and L. Prusak. (2000). *Working Knowledge: How Organisations Manage What They Know*. 2nd edition. Harvard Business School Press, Boston, MA.

Earl, M. J. (1989). *Management Strategies for Information Technology*. Prentice Hall, Hemel Hempstead.

Earley, S. (2010). *DAMA-DMBOK Guide: The DAMA Guide to the Data Management Body of Knowledge*. Technics Publications, LLC.

Galliers, R. D. (2006). On Confronting Some of the Common Myths of Information Systems Strategy Discourse. In R. Mansell, D. Quah and R. Silverstone (eds), *The Oxford Handbook of Information and Communication Technology*. Oxford University Press, Oxford.

Galliers, R. D. and D. Leidner. (2003). *Strategic Information Management: Challenges and Strategies in Managing Information Systems*. Butterworth-Heinemann, New York.

Gillenson, M. L. (1991). Database Administration at the Crossroads: The Era of End-user-oriented, Decentralised Data Processing. *Journal of Database Administration* 2 (4): 1–11.

Gray, I. (1984). *General and Industrial Management*. IEEE Press, New York.

IV

Ives, B. and G. P. Learmonth. (1984). The Information System as a Competitive Weapon. *Communications of the ACM* 27 (12): 1193–1201.

Johnson, G., K. Scholes and R. Whittington. (2007). *Exploring Corporate Strategy: Text and Cases*. 8th edition. Prentice-Hall., Englewood-Cliffs.

Porter, M. E. (1985). *Competitive Advantage: Creating and Sustaining Superior Performance*. Free Press, New York.

Porter, M. E. (2001). Strategy and the Internet. *Harvard Business Review* 79 (3): 63–78.

Ward, J. and J. Peppard. (2012). *Strategic Planning for Information Systems*. 4th edition. John Wiley.

Weill, P. and J. Ross. (2004). *IT Governance: How Top Performers Manage IT Decision Rights for Superior Results*. Harvard Business School Press, Boston.

See companion website   www.palgrave.com/business/beynon-daviesbis2e

Services, projects and operations

'Civilisation advances
by extending the
number of important
operations we can
perform without
thinking about them.'

Alfred North
Whitehead (1867–
1947)

Learning outcomes	Principles
Explain the structure of the informatics industry in terms of the distinction between producers and consumers.	The informatics industry is a significant element of the service sector of the economy. Actors in this sector can be distinguished as either informatics producers or informatics consumers.
Describe what is meant by the informatics service and define various ways such a service can be organised, including the idea of informatics outsourcing.	Within consuming organisations with a significant informatics infrastructure it is important to establish the form and management of an important function: the informatics service. Many organisations have decided that the whole or part of this function should be outsourced to external vendors.
Distinguish between informatics management and project management, and explain the distinction between project planning, project control and project organisation.	Since much informatics work is organised in terms of projects, good project management practice assumes significance for organisations. Project management involves the inter-related processes of planning a project, establishing a project organisation and controlling a project.
Define what is meant by informatics operations in terms of the philosophy of ICT services management and outline some of the major processes involved in managing ICT services.	Ensuring the effective operation of informatics infrastructure is an important part of any informatics management. Operations is now generally considered as a set of inter-related service processes including service strategy, service delivery, service support and service improvement.
Identify the place of green ICT in the operational management of informatics.	Any activity has an impact upon the physical environment. An increasing focus has been given to the proper management of ICT to reduce an organisation's carbon footprint.

IV

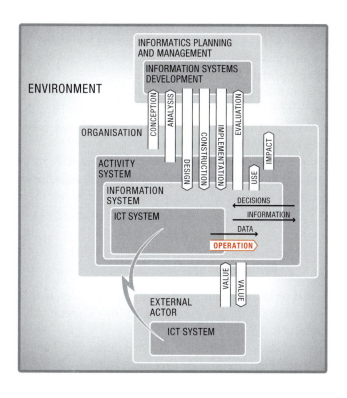

Chapter outline

AACSB learning objectives:
Analytical thinking and reflective thinking

11.1   Introduction

As we have established in previous chapters, in organisational terms a service is the non-material equivalent of a good. It typically involves an activity performed by an organisation for an external stakeholder (see Chapter 7). The vocabulary of servers and services is familiar in the informatics infrastructure of organisations. Service-oriented architecture, for instance, is seen as a means of improving the interoperability of systems (see Chapter 6). This chapter considers the term services in another light, as the way in which informatics as an organisational function is delivered as a service, or more accurately as a collection of services.

Since ICT is embedded in modern organisational life as well as in the wider environment, not surprisingly informatics is a vast industry of both producers and consumers, which forms an important part of the service sector in an economy.

In consuming organisations there is normally a function charged with developing, maintaining and operating the informatics infrastructure, which we shall refer to for convenience as the informatics service. Technology has enabled organisations to transform their informatics service as they have transformed other organisational functions. The outsourcing of various aspects of informatics infrastructure, and how to manage this effectively, are therefore critical issues for modern organisations.

Informatics operations: that process devoted to the successful operation of existing informatics infrastructure

Much informatics work is organised in projects, so the effective management of projects is critical not only to the successful development of information systems, but also to their maintenance and operation. The servicing of **informatics operations** is frequently taken for granted and unexplored in texts on business information systems. Because of its increasing importance to modern-day organisations, this chapter considers a number of issues of concern, including ensuring the availability and continuity of informatics infrastructure. To help organise this topic, recent approaches in the area of ICT services management are discussed.

11.2   The informatics industry

Informatics industry: a vast industry developed worldwide to service the informatics needs of organisations, groups and individuals

Information systems and their associated technologies are essential for the effective working of modern economies, societies and polities. Therefore, not surprisingly, a vast industry has developed worldwide to service the informatics needs of organisations, groups and individuals. Many people are now employed in information-rich industries, and these are heavily reliant on efficient and effective information systems.

Informatics is primarily part of the service sector of the economy. One of the notable facets of the change in employment patterns in many countries over the last 40 years has been the rise in the service sector. The most rapid growth in employment has been in office-based private services such as financial, business and professional services.

Informatics personnel work either for a producer of information systems and ICT, or for an established user of information systems and technology (what we might call informatics consumers). Providers produce elements of information systems, and consumers use them for organisational purposes.

11.2.1   Providers

Informatics provider: a producer of hardware, software or communication technology

Informatics providers can be divided into:

- Hardware providers, organisations that produce computing devices, input devices, output devices, storage devices and communication devices (see Chapter 6). Representative organisations are Dell, Intel and Apple.
- Software providers, organisations that produce software such as office software and enterprise software. Representative organisations are Oracle and Microsoft.

- Application providers, a special type of software provider offering integrated package solutions to informatics infrastructure problems. A representative company is SAP AG.
- Communication infrastructure providers, companies that build, maintain and support the physical telecommunication infrastructure of organisations, regions and countries. Representative companies are BT (British Telecom) and Deutsche Telefon.
- Internet service providers, companies that provide access to the Internet for individuals, groups and organisations. Representative companies are America Online (AOL) and BT Internet.
- While application providers provide software applications for purchase by companies, application service providers (see below) are companies that operate and maintain aspects of an organisation's informatics infrastructure through the provision of applications as services. They are similar to what used to be known as service bureaux. A representative company is Storagetek (Oracle).
- Informatics consultancies, companies that provide informatics services, particularly in the areas of planning, management and development. A representative company is PriceWaterhouseCoopers.
- Outsourcing vendors, companies that offer informatics outsourcing solutions either in whole or in part. Representative companies are HP Enterprise Services (previously EDS) and CapGemini.

> **REFLECT:** How much of a typical Western economy do you think the informatics industry makes up? How much does it contribute to the gross domestic product?

CASE CHECK

Microsoft   p 449

Microsoft was founded to develop and sell interpreters for the programming language BASIC, which ran on an early microcomputer, the Altair 8800. It rose to dominate the personal computer market with its sales of the operating system MS-DOS, produced in the mid-1980s.

Microsoft is organised as three core divisions: the Microsoft Platform Products and Services Division, the Microsoft Business Division and the Microsoft Entertainment and Devices Division.

The Platform Products and Services Division produces the Windows operating system, Microsoft Visual Studio (a set of development tools) and enterprise software such as Microsoft SQL Server (a relational DBMS).

The Microsoft Business Division produces Microsoft Office, which includes Word (a word processor), Access (a personal relational database application), Excel (a spreadsheet program), Outlook (Windows-only groupware), PowerPoint (presentation software), and Publisher (desktop publishing software).

The Entertainment and Devices Division produces software for mobile devices such as Windows CE for PDAs, gaming software for its own gaming console the Xbox, and computer games that run on Windows PCs, including titles such as *Age of Empires*, *Halo* and the Microsoft *Flight Simulator* series. It also produces a line of reference works which includes encyclopaedias and atlases, under the name Encarta.

11.2.2 Consumers

Informatics consumer: a consumer of aspects of informatics, such as hardware or software

There are **informatics consumers** in almost all industrial sectors, such as manufacturing, agriculture, process industries such as petrochemicals, transport, financial services, retail, and local and central government. Some sectors are much more advanced in ICT use than others. For instance, the financial services sector has invested heavily in ICT, but the agriculture sector continues to be a relatively poor investor.

Informatics consumers can also be divided into large, medium, small and micro enterprises. In recent years in the European Union there has been a particular focus on small- and medium-sized enterprises (SME), companies with less than 250 employees. They are seen as the major seedbed for innovation in industrial economies. There have been several major initiatives to stimulate their adoption of ICT and eBusiness.

11.3   Informatics careers

Informatics professionals work for either informatics providers or informatics consumers, and have become an increasing part of the workforce of developed countries. This is clearly an indicator of growth in the information society (Chapter 3).

Informatics is a relatively young area of industrial practice, and one that is subject to rapid change. Recruitment patterns tend to be driven by requirements for short-term technological skills, such as the ability to program in the Java language, rather than longer-term transferable skills such as the ability to design effective and efficient programs. This has made it difficult to establish coherent and consistent career patterns across the industry.

Professional bodies such as the British Computer Society (BCS) have attempted to address some of these difficulties. For instance, the BCS has developed an industry structure model which tries to specify career paths for informatics professionals. It classifies some 200 roles in the informatics domain into nine broad functional areas: (1) management, (2) policy, (3) planning and research, (4) systems development and maintenance, (5) service delivery, (6) technical advice and consultancy, (7) quality, (8) customer relations, education and training, (9) support and administration.

Ten levels of autonomy, accountability and responsibility are defined across these nine functional areas, ranging from unskilled entry, through experienced practitioner, to senior manager/director/consultant. Not all functions are performed across all levels of responsibility. Programming as a role, for instance, only involves the lower levels, whereas management involves the higher levels. For each role, the BCS has specified the ideal background for the person to fill it, as well as the range of activities they are likely to undertake. The emphasis is on generic skills, such as an ability to design and build databases, rather than specific vendor-related skills such as abilities in the Oracle tool-set.

Because informatics is now central to most organisations, the demand for skilled informatics staff has remained steady, and in some sectors has grown significantly over the last decade, fuelled by growth in eBusiness and eCommerce strategies in both the private and public sectors. Because there is a shortage of skilled informatics professionals in many countries, many economies have looked to other countries worldwide to supply workers. Many US companies, for instance, have outsourced informatics activities, such as development and maintenance, to the Indian subcontinent, particularly the Bangalore region. Countries such as the United Kingdom have included informatics workers in their list of preferred occupations, so that those who offer these skills get priority in immigration procedures.

Careers in IS

Katherine Coombs

Katherine Coombs is the global Chief Information Officer (CIO) for Proxima, a leading pure-play outsourcer and provider of procurement services. Coombs is a Board-level executive with dual responsibility for both client-facing ICT solutions and internal ICT operations, spanning Europe and the US.

Coombs holds a degree in computer science and numerous technical certifications.

Her ICT career spans more than 10 years and covers a diverse range of sectors, from finance and government to services and retail. An Australian national, Coombs worked internationally as an ICT consultant specialising in large-scale infrastructure programmes for clients such as Virgin Atlantic, HMRC, and Standard Chartered Bank.

Relocating to the UK in 2005, Coombs joined Lloyds TSB as senior manager of its ICT innovation and research team in 2007. Coombs delivered a £50M IT-led innovation pipeline exploiting new revenue streams or reducing costs before being appointed as CIO of the Savings division when Lloyds TSB acquired HBOS, forming the UK's largest bank, Lloyds Banking Group.

Scan the QR code underneath Katherine's picture or visit **www.palgrave.com/business/beynon-daviesbis2e/** to watch Katherine talking about Information Systems and careers as an IS professional, and then think about the questions below:

☐ There is a gender imbalance in people opting for a career in informatics. More male than female students take secondary, tertiary and higher-level courses with an ICT component. Why do you think this is, and how would you begin to address this imbalance?

☐ Do you think that it is important for a CIO to be a member of the executive board of the company? Why?

11.4 The informatics service

As consumers in the informatics industry, most medium- to large-scale organisations have people specifically employed in informatics work. This section considers a number of important issues relating to the organisation of business units that do this work. Some organisations call this the ICT or IS department, or the DP (data processing) department. This chapter refers to it generically as the **informatics service**, to emphasise that in most organisations information systems and technology are a critical strategic service supplied to the organisation in support of other activity.

11.4.1 Structure

Some organisations, particularly small ones, do not have a specific section or department specialising in informatics, but there is a specialist function in most medium- to large-scale organisations, in both the private and public sectors. It can be structured in several different ways. This section discusses its structuring by division of labour and location.

Division of labour refers to the way in which various jobs, or roles, are defined and structured in the informatics service (see Chapter 2). It used to involve rigid job specifications based around a hierarchy of control. Over the last 20 years or so a number of pressures for change have caused the gradual fragmentation of this structure and newer, more flexible structures for the informatics service have emerged.

Figure 11.1 shows the old structure, which derived from the day-to-day demands of building and running informatics on large, centralised mainframes. It had a hierarchy of clearly delineated jobs. At the bottom were operating staff, tasked with maintaining the operation of the centralised mainframe and the systems that ran on it. Next came programmers, organised

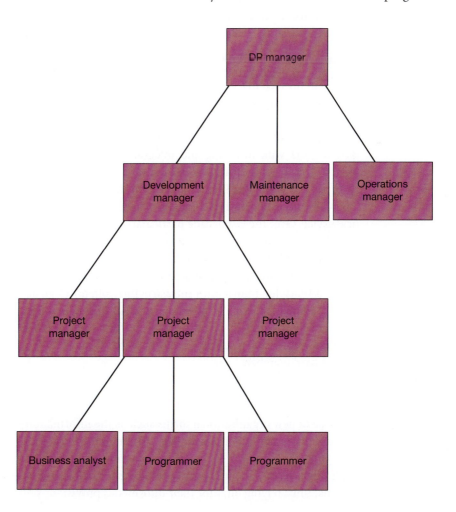

Figure 11.1 *Traditional structure of the informatics service*

typically into groups such as maintenance programmers and development programmers. Development programmers built new applications while maintenance programmers repaired and extended existing applications. Systems analysts were the next rung in the hierarchy. These were professionals primarily involved in the analysis and design of information systems, who made contact with business users. Many organisations segmented staff further into project teams of analysts, programmers and sometimes operators, each headed by a project manager. The head of department was often called the data processing (DP) manager. In a large organisation there were frequently a number of middle-level managers, such as operations managers, development managers and maintenance managers, each coordinating a particular aspect of informatics work.

Technical changes in the 1970s and 1980s, which led to changes in this structure, accelerated during the 1990s.

Desktop computers came to be used more and more, which meant that computing power could be sited wherever it was required. Desktop packages, such as word-processing software and spreadsheets, were specifically written for end-users rather than ICT professionals, so they gained much more experience of computing and became much more confident in expressing their requirements, sometimes even building applications themselves.

The developing use of databases and in particular the database approach meant that organisations began to plan for and manage data at the corporate level. Organisations saw key added value from integrating information systems across sectors.

More and cheaper processing power and storage capacity meant that these resources no longer needed to be centralised (see Chapter 6). Processing and storage could be distributed around the organisation on diverse sets of hardware platforms and diverse software-enabled applications to cooperate across local and wide area networks.

In response to these pressures and others, the informatics service recast itself in various different forms. One was the information centre, a body of informatics expertise whose role was to service other departments who handled a large proportion of their informatics work themselves. So, unlike the traditional ICT department, the information centre no longer had a monopoly over organisational informatics.

This in turn led to a greater diversification of informatics staff. Roles such as hybrid managers, analyst/programmers, database administrators, data analysts, business analysts and systems integrators took shape. One particularly notable trend was the growth in support or operations staff (see below) who were not directly tasked with developing new information systems, but with installing and integrating existing ICT, operating corporate information systems and helping end-users in the use of technology and systems.

In recent years the increasing importance of the ICT infrastructure to organisations, coupled with its increasing complexity, has led to changes in the conception of the informatics service. Over the last decade particularly, service management practices have been applied to ICT. In this philosophy the informatics service is seen as a strategic business partner rather than purely a technology function.

Wedded to this change, organisations started to create a senior management role with responsibility for informatics infrastructure, often designated the chief information officer (CIO), following the US terminology of chief executive officer (CEO). Because of the importance of informatics to organisational performance, and the need to integrate informatics strategy with business strategy (see Chapter 10), many have argued that the CIO should be a main board member.

11.4.2 Location

The rise of new organisational forms such as the information centre is partly the result of an increased number of options for the location of the informatics service.

A centralised service is the traditional model in which informatics provides one service with single access. The informatics service is located in one large office, with all other organisational units relying on it for their informatics provision.

In a decentralised model the informatics service is structured around a number of smaller units, each providing single access. Under this model the informatics service still forms a logical whole, but the various functions it provides, such as planning, management, development, maintenance and operations, are segmented off into separate organisational units.

Within a distributed model the informatics service is made up of a set of connected functions each providing multiple services. This is because in large-scale organisations, such as multinationals, it may prove impossible to provide any one function on a centralised basis. Each country might have its own informatics services function, providing all the activities to their national units.

A devolved model also has a distributed framework, but each informatics unit is not independent. Instead, the informatics service is made up of a matrix of units each sited close to the point of need and falling under direct business unit control.

Because many organisations were not satisfied with the informatics service provided in any of these ways, many have recently pursued an outsourcing strategy. Here, the informatics service is provided in whole or in part by external contractors. This issue is discussed in more detail in a later section.

Each of these forms of location has advantages and disadvantages, which can be illustrated by comparing a centralised and a decentralised service.

The advantages of a centralised informatics service revolve around the issue of control. Fundamentally, centralisation makes it possible to exercise greater control over the management and operation of informatics resources. For instance, recruiting and maintaining informatics skills becomes easier, and there can be economies of scale in procuring hardware and software. Duplication of effort is more easily avoided and greater standardisation and compatibility of systems can be achieved. Overall, speedier and more consistent strategic decision-making is possible, particularly for issues such as integration of systems and the development of large infrastructure projects.

Disadvantages tend to centre on the fact that a centralised informatics service is more likely to be divorced from the coal face of the business. It can prove less able to adapt quickly to changes in the business environment and technology. Business units sometimes become dissatisfied with the level of personal attention they are given and the speed of response to their needs. Some diseconomies may also be evident, such as high back-up costs.

IV

CASE CHECK	CS p 455	In 2008 Tesco announced its intention to overhaul its ICT infrastructure. It planned to replace a number of separate voice and data networks with a single communication network, which was eventually outsourced to Cable & Wireless. It intends to use this network to standardise its key ICT systems in areas such as finance, human resources, payroll, in-store management, distribution and sales.
Tesco		

The intention is to manage these ICT systems centrally across the entire network from its ICT services centre in Bangalore, India (see also Bangalore case study). Informatics professionals based in other countries of operation will supply only front-line support. This standardisation is built on an effort the company initiated in 2005, known as 'Tesco in a box'. It was a programme of standardisation, based on an Oracle ERP system, that was implemented in all countries of operation.

The rollout of these standard ICT systems is seen as a key enabler for standard business processes and standard management information across the Tesco group. This allows stores newly opened in Malaysia and Japan to operate and be managed in exactly the same way as a store in the United Kingdom.

11.4.3 Key processes

Depending on the size of the function, the informatics service may engage in a vast range of activities. Essentially however every informatics service has six major roles (see Figure 11.2):

- Informatics planning
- Informatics management
- Project management

- Development
- Maintenance
- Operations.

As discussed in Chapter 10, planning involves formulating strategy for information, information systems and ICT in an organisation. The strategy includes plans for changing aspects of the informatics infrastructure, so it produces a portfolio of system development work.

Management involves both implementing plans for future infrastructure and controlling existing informatics infrastructure. As such it involves continual evaluation of the investment in information systems, and monitoring the success of development, maintenance and operations projects as well as the service itself. Other management roles are recruiting and organising informatics personnel, and maintaining staff development programmes.

Concrete work in informatics is likely to be organised as projects of development, maintenance or operations activity, so effective project management is a critical aspect of the informatics service. Development is the activity of constructing and delivering new application systems: analysing, designing, producing, testing and implementing them. Maintenance is the activity devoted to fine-tuning aspects of the informatics infrastructure to make sure it works effectively. Operations is an area of the informatics service that runs and supports the use of information systems throughout the organisation (see below).

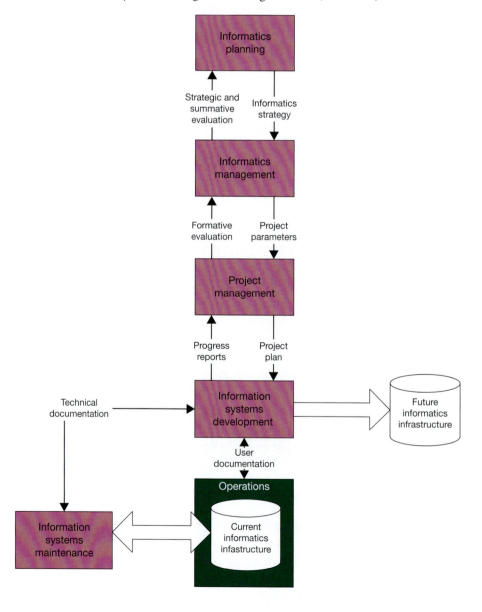

Figure 11.2 *Processes of the informatics service*

11.4.4 Strategy of the informatics service

An important part of any informatics strategy (Chapter 10) is a strategy for the informatics service itself. This will consider issues such as the size and location of the service and which informatics processes to outsource (see below) or maintain in-house.

Each of the different possibilities for the structure of the informatics service discussed in previous sections reflects historical features of the environment of commercial computing. In his global, historical study of the commercial information systems industry, Friedman (Friedman and Cornford, 1989) identified three phases in the history of commercial computing which the authors projected up to the late 1990s. Each phase is dominated by a different set of constraints determining a different strategy for the informatics service.

The period up to the mid-1960s was subject to hardware constraints, when high hardware costs and limitations in the capacity and reliability of equipment dominated commercial computing. Not surprisingly, the shape of the informatics service reflected the need to maintain large corporate data centres. Much of the strategy for the informatics service in this phase was dominated by a concern with controlling costs and maintaining effective allocation of the limited computing resource.

During the period between the mid-1960s and the mid-1980s hardware costs declined substantially. Therefore, this phase was dominated by software constraints such as the productivity of systems developers and the difficulties of delivering systems on time and within budget. The emphasis shifted from strategies focused around hardware to strategies focused around the need to manage the information systems development process more effectively.

Between the mid-1980s and early 1990s software concerns moved from centre stage with the increasing availability of packaged software. This phase became dominated by user relations constraints focused around system quality problems. It was argued that many informatics services had an inadequate perception of user demands and were inadequate in servicing user needs. In this phase the information centre was born as a way of attempting to satisfy concerns over the benefit that informatics services were providing to companies.

Since the early 1990s commercial computing has entered a fourth phase dominated by organisational and environmental constraints. The particular focus of this phase is the search for ways in which information systems and ICT can improve the position of the organisation in its environment. Some have argued that a continuing key emphasis of this phase is the need for close alignment of business with informatics strategy. As we argued in Chapter 10, in many organisations business strategy is being subsumed within eBusiness strategy.

11.4.5 Funding the informatics service

Since informatics is normally a service function, a crucial feature of any strategy for the informatics service is a clear specification of how it is funded. The options include free service, profit centre, separate company and outsourced arrangements.

Traditionally an internal informatics service was farmed out, free of charge, to other departments or functions. Each business unit had its budget top-sliced in some way to finance informatics work. In the profit centre model the informatics service bills other departments for its work using service level agreements (SLAs), which specify a fixed fee for a specified number of services for a given contract duration. An excess fee is usually negotiated for additional services. This is the philosophy underlying the move to ICT service management, described below.

One step removed from the profit centre is the concept of the informatics service run as a separate company, a subsidiary which contracts its services to the parent company and potentially to external customers as well. Finally, in outsourcing the service, informatics is given over, either in whole or in part, to an unrelated specialist company.

11.4.6   Outsourcing the informatics service

Although information systems and ICT are now seen to be central to the performance of most organisations, the informatics service has traditionally experienced great difficulty in quantifying its benefits to the organisation (see Chapter 9). For this reason many organisations have decided over the last decade to outsource their informatics service. Outsourcing is the use of external agents to perform one or more organisational activities. A contract is negotiated with an external supplier, normally in the form of a service level agreement.

There are a number of types of **informatics outsourcing**:

Informatics outsourcing: the use of external agents to perform some aspect of informatics

- Body shop outsourcing, where contract programmers are brought in to supplement in-house informatics personnel, particularly for development or maintenance work.
- Project outsourcing, where outside vendors are used to develop new systems.
- Support outsourcing, in which vendors are contracted to maintain and support a particular application system.
- Hardware outsourcing, where organisations outsource hardware operations, disaster recovery, and management of the communication network.
- Keys to the kingdom, the most radical form, outsourcing the entire informatics service including development, operation, management and control.

There are a number of claimed benefits for outsourcing. For instance, scale and specialisation enable vendors to deliver the same value for less money than in sourcing. More effective control of vendors is also claimed to lead to a better quality of service, and fixed-price contracts and service-level guarantees eliminate uncertainty for the business. Business growth can be accommodated without quantum changes in infrastructure, and scarce and costly informatics talent can be refocused on higher-value activity.

During the 1990s Lacity and Hirschheim (Lacity and Wilcocks, 2006) conducted a major research of outsourcing strategies in the United States. Their results questioned many of these benefits, and in particular three dominant assumptions:

- Organisations initiate outsourcing for reasons of efficiency. Lacity and Hirschheim argued that organisations may initiate outsourcing for a variety of other reasons, such as to acquire or justify additional resources, to react to positive media reports of outsourcing, to reduce personal risk to management associated with uncertainty, and to enhance the personal credibility of CIOs.
- An outsourcing vendor is inherently more efficient than an internal informatics service through economies of scale. They found that an internal informatics service can frequently supply a service as efficiently as an external vendor.
- Vendors are partners. If a company decides to outsource, the contract is the only mechanism to ensure that expectations are realised, so partnerships in this area need to be heavily controlled.

CASE CHECK

CS ▷ p 452

Offshoring in Bangalore

Offshoring stands for the relocation by an organisation of one or more of its business processes or activity systems from one country to another. Offshoring might involve an operational process, such as manufacturing, or a supporting process, such as some aspect of informatics infrastructure. In recent years much of informatics outsourcing has occurred through offshoring to geographical areas such as Bangalore on the Indian subcontinent.

11.5   Project management

key skill

A project is any concerted effort to achieve a set of objectives. All projects comprise teams of people engaged in the achievement of explicit objectives, usually with a set timescale. Most informatics work in organisations is structured as projects, so planning, management

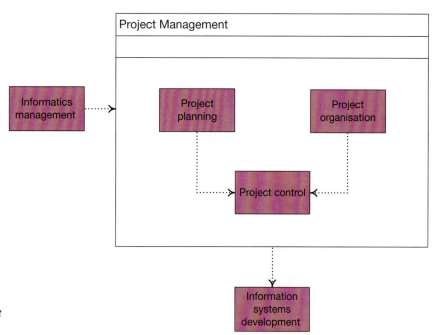

Figure 11.3 *The process of project management*

and even business analysis (Chapter 2) are conducted as projects. This section focuses on development projects as concerted efforts to develop an information system.

Consider a university that has identified an information system to support research administration as part of its informatics strategy. It sees such a system as important to its future organisation strategy because research is one of the key activity systems for the university. Whereas information systems are currently in place for support of teaching and consultancy there are no information systems in place to support research activity. The bringing into existence of this system will typically be organised as a project.

Initiating development projects is part of an organisation's informatics planning and informatics management process (see Chapter 10). Project management interacts with the development process (see Chapter 12) in the sense that it acts as the major control process for development. These connections are illustrated in Figure 11.3.

Project management: the process of planning for, organising and controlling projects

The process of **project management** can be divided into three inter-related activities (O'Connell, 2001):

- Project planning involves determining as clearly as possible the likely parameters associated with a particular project.
- Project organisation concerns how to structure staff activities to ensure maximum effectiveness.
- Project control involves ensuring that a project remains on schedule, within budget and produces the desired output.

In terms of the research information system, project planning will involve determining the necessary activities for achieving the goal of the project. Project organisation will involve creating the team of people to achieve the goals for the project. Finally, project control will involve ensuring that the project remains within budget and meets its deadline.

11.5.1 Project planning

The classic questions of **project planning** are what, who, when, how, and progress?

Project planning: determining as clearly as possible the likely parameters associated with a particular project

In terms of what, the product or output of the project must be defined and the project must be broken down into a series of activities or tasks. Keeping to a standard model of information systems development (see Chapter 12) clearly aids this process. It is important also to identify standards to be used in the project, such as, in the case of a development project, appropriate notations for specifying requirements.

In terms of who, staff must be assigned to the project and responsibilities identified. The most popular method of estimating the number of staff needed for a project is to use experienced people who have conducted similar projects in the past. Another approach is to estimate the size of the proposed product and derive a staff estimate from this figure by applying an appropriate formula.

Software metric: a number extracted from a software product

In this latter approach software metrics have a place. A **software metric** is a number extracted from a software product. Metrics are used in a number of ways: to provide feedback to staff on the quality of their work; to monitor the structural degradation of a system during systems maintenance (Chapter 12); and to aid in costing and estimating software projects.

The class of metrics used for project estimation is known as function-based metrics, and they are associated with an estimating technique known as function-point analysis. Project managers conduct this by counting the features of a functional specification (Chapter 12), such as the number of information classes or processes in a system. These numbers are then inserted into an algebraic expression that produces a function point count. Function point counts and actual costs of projects are stored in a historical database. These figures are used to produce a statistical estimate of resources required for the current project.

For example, we might examine information models produced in previous development projects and the costs associated with producing the data management layer for these systems. Through applying a function point count we can effectively compare the number of information classes on the current information model with previous models. This will then provide us with an estimate of how much time and effort we will need to produce the new database.

In terms of when, it is important for milestones to be identified and schedules established. Many experienced project managers recommend that a software project is divided into sequential phases, and a milestone or control point is established at the end of each phase.

In terms of how, a budget for the project must be constructed and resources must be allocated to it. The likely cost of the project must be calculated and a case made for a budget. This is a critical aspect of the systems conception (see Chapter 12) phase of a development project.

In terms of progress, an effective mechanism for monitoring the progress of projects must be established. Milestones can be used as points of audit to ensure that standards are being adhered to and that the project is on schedule.

Since a project is effectively an activity system, the conventional way of planning a project is to segment it into a number of activities, each of which can be managed independently. Each of these activities may be broken down further into a series of tasks.

One popular method of representation is to lay out a project in diagrammatic form as a network (see Figure 11.4). This can use a notation slightly modified from the one used for process modelling (see Chapter 2). Boxes are used to represent project activities and dotted lines to indicate their precedence. The planner then estimates the resources required to achieve each activity, usually expressed as a number of person-days. The sum of these person-days, plus a contingency factor for emergencies, is the estimated time required for each activity. Doing this calculation for each activity in a project will give the project manager an idea of the overall person-days required for the project. Since person-time is also the most significant cost factor, this gives an idea of total approximate cost.

For each activity the earliest possible start date is calculated on the basis of a schedule assigned to predecessor activities. A latest completion date is also calculated for each activity on the basis of the scheduled start dates for each of the activity's successors and the target completion date for the overall project. The difference between the calculated time available to complete an activity and the estimated time required to complete it is known as an activity's float. If the float is zero, the activity is said to be critical, since any delay in completing it will cause a delay in completing the final project.

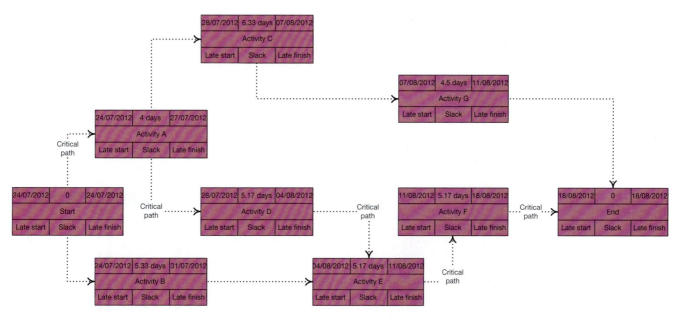

Figure 11.4 *An activity-based plan*

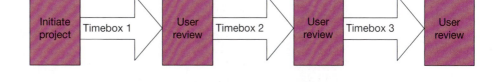

Figure 11.5 *Product-based planning*

Critical path: an activity within a project whose float is zero

A related concept is the **critical path**. This is the longest possible continuous path between the start activity for a project and the end or terminating activity. Since the critical path determines the total calendar time required for a project, any time delay along the critical path will delay the project as a whole by an equivalent amount.

This estimating approach is usually complicated by the fact that since no two information systems projects are ever the same, there is uncertainty about the time required for each activity. Brooks (1997) has also discussed how using person-days, person-weeks or person-months as the central unit of estimating and scheduling can be misleading. It is tempting to infer from this that the progress of a project improves with the number of people assigned to it, but Brooks argues that '*adding manpower to a late software project makes it later*'. There are many reasons: people take time to settle into a project, new personnel need to be trained, the amount of communication between team members increases the greater the size of the group, and so on.

Activity-based planning: a form of project management in which planning and control is conducted in terms of project activities

Product-based planning: a form of project management in which project planning and control is focused around information systems products

Timebox: an agreed period of time for the production of a deliverable

This process of project planning described above is focused around activities, so it is known as **activity-based planning**. More recently there has been an emphasis on a form of project planning based around products rather than activities. **Product-based planning** is particularly popular in agile approaches to development work (see Chapter 12).

Fundamentally, product-based planning works with two concepts: deliverables and **timeboxes**. A deliverable is a part of an information system that the development team agree to demonstrate to representatives of relevant stakeholder groups at a review session. A deliverable is normally expressed in terms of what the information system module will be able to do. A timebox is an agreed period of time for the production of a deliverable, and is normally expressed as a fixed deadline. The timebox is never changed once established. However, the functionality of a deliverable may be renegotiated to fit the timebox.

11.5.2   Project organisation

Project organisation concerns how to organise staff so that they produce the desired output. Essentially there are three alternatives in organising staff: around projects, roles or a combination of the two (see Figure 11.6).

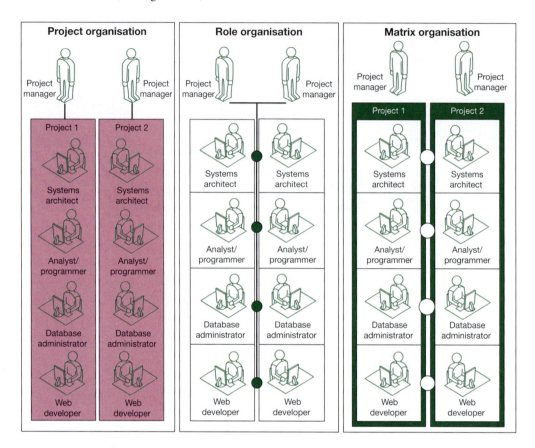

Figure 11.6 *Forms of project organisation*

In terms of projects, staff are organised within project boundaries. This form of organisation encourages quick decision-making, minimises interfaces between staff and generates high identification with projects among staff members. This is the style of project organisation promoted in agile approaches (see Chapter 12). The disadvantages are that it only works well for small projects, the economies of scale are low, and the sharing of expertise across projects is minimal.

In terms of roles, staff are organised according to development roles, each role supporting a number of different projects. This form of organisation generates economies of scale, promotes the growth of specialists, and reduces the effects of staff turnover. It is probably the most common type of project organisation in large development centres. The disadvantages are that it generates lots of communication across projects, decreases the number of people with a general feel for a project and reduces the cohesion of projects.

In a matrix organisation, staff are mixed across projects and roles. The basic organisation is based around development roles, but a project organisation is imposed under a series of project managers. The advantages of this approach are that short-term objectives (the success of a project) are maximised via the project organisation whereas long-term objectives (such as promoting specialism among developers) are maximised via division around roles. The major disadvantage is that the needs of a project and of the developer roles might conflict.

11.5.3   Project control

Project control is a type of formative evaluation (see Chapter 9). Its aim is to ensure that schedules are met, that the project stays within budget and appropriate standards are maintained. The most important objective of project control is to focus attention on problems in sufficient time for something to be done about them. This calls for continual monitoring of progress.

Figure 11.7 illustrates the need for two major forms of information system in support of the development process. The actual process of development needs documentary support to enable collaboration between the development team (Chapter 12). The process of managing a project also needs its associated information system. This will store both project plans and data concerning progress against plans.

In activity-based project management the primary document used for the evaluation of progress is a progress report (Figure 11.8). This contains information on time estimated for each activity plotted against actual time spent. Another useful measure is an estimate of the percentage of completeness.

Time actually spent on a project is usually collected via weekly timesheets, which indicate the tasks performed by development staff and their duration. They are also useful in highlighting time spent on unplanned work.

Progress reports can be used by either management reviews or project audits. Management reviews are scheduled opportunities for project managers to consider the accomplishments and problems associated with a project. Project audits are formal events scheduled into the life-cycle of a project, in which an independent audit team examines the documentation and interviews key team members. The process of activity-based project control is illustrated in Figure 11.8.

In product-based project management, project control is normally exercised through user review sessions. These are scheduled events at the end of each timebox at which versions of a developing information system are demonstrated to representatives of the user community.

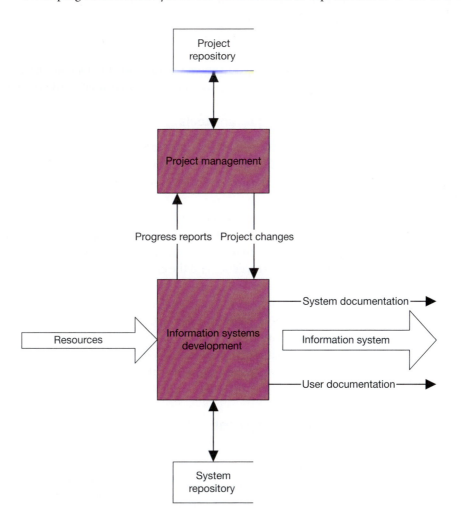

Figure 11.7 *System documentation and project documentation*

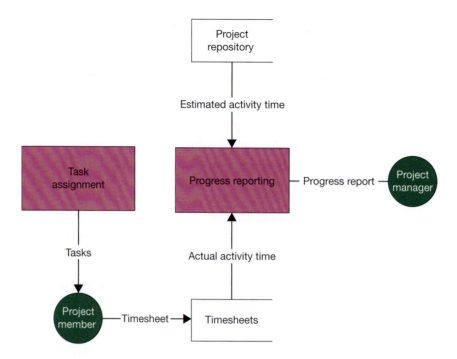

Figure 11.8 *Activity-based project control*

This might lead to the parameters of the system being renegotiated for the next timebox (Stapleton, 1997).

Information system projects may also use a change control mechanism. This involves setting up a systematic mechanism (sometimes known as configuration management: see Chapter 12) for handling all changes to a developing piece of software. Normally a change management committee is instituted for decision-making and a change management procedure is established. The essence of this procedure is to ensure that each version of a product associated with a project can be uniquely identified, and that time and money is not wasted on unimportant work such as searching for an appropriate version of software to work upon.

11.5.4   Methods, techniques and tools

There are a number of different methods, techniques and tools for project management. For instance, PRINCE (PRojects IN Controlled Environments) is a structured method for project management, originally developed from a UK government-sponsored initiative in the 1970s (see below).

PERT (Programme Evaluation Review Technique) was developed in the late 1950s and is also known as the critical path technique. It is frequently used as an aid to activity-based planning, and is similar to the approach discussed under project planning, in which activities are related through precedence and the critical path is determined.

Many automated tools, such as Microsoft Project, are now available to aid project managers. They use a graphical approach to show plans and estimates associated with each activity. Timesheet data can be fed into the system and progress reports automatically generated. Some software packages for project management even allow the manager to perform what-if reasoning on the project model.

REFLECT: How much of working life in an organisation known to you is taken up with project work of any form? In what way does organising work as projects fit with ideas of the virtual organisation?

11.5.5   Programme management

Programme management: the management of a suite of linked projects

Recently, organisations have started to distinguish between **programme management** and project management. Whereas a project is a coherent piece of, usually one-off, work of definite duration, a programme is an on-going or continuous piece of work implemented in a business to consistently achieve certain results. In this sense, informatics planning, management and operations are all examples of coherent programmes of work associated with informatics infrastructure.

Programme and project management are related in that a programme is frequently organised as a set of interdependent projects for the purposes of effective organisational control, so programme management can be seen as a higher-level layer above project management. This is the position taken in the PRINCE2 method.

11.6   PRINCE2

The acronym PRINCE stands for PRojects IN Controlled Environments. PRINCE is a structured method for project management, originally developed from a UK government-sponsored initiative in the 1970s which resulted in the method known as PROMPT. PRINCE2 was introduced in 1996, and the most recent version at the time of writing was released in 2005. PRINCE2 is now used in more than 50 countries (Bentley, 2009).

PRINCE2 assumes that a customer and supplier will work together to complete a project. These two groups will frequently come from separately managed areas and often from separate organisations. Customers specify the desired outcomes, make use of the final product and in most cases fund the project. Suppliers provide resources to create the intended outcome.

PRINCE2 includes a method for defining the organisation structure for a project as well as a definition of the host company. This ensures that both business interests and technical concerns are covered. It outlines the structure and content of project planning, and defines a set of controls and reports that can be used to monitor whether a project is proceeding to plan. It also defines procedures for dealing with exceptions to the plan. It actively encourages the monitoring of quality.

PRINCE2 considers a project as a system or process consisting of a number of generic subprocesses or activities: starting up a project, initiating a project, planning, directing a project, controlling a stage, managing product delivery, managing stage boundaries, and closing a project (see Figure 11.9). The arrows on Figure 11.9 indicate necessary data flows between sub-processes.

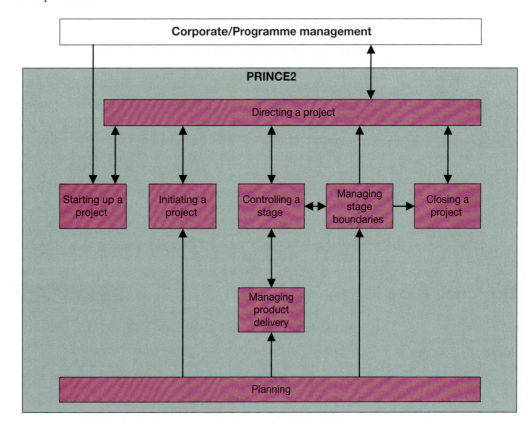

Figure 11.9 *The PRINCE2 process*

In starting a project, a project board and project management team are appointed. The project board is given overall responsibility for project governance. The project manager and project management team are given overall responsibility for implementing the project. The main objective of this sub-process is to produce a project brief. This describes, in outline, what the project is attempting to achieve and the business justification. In addition, the overall approach to be taken is decided and the next stage of the project is planned. A decision point is then reached when the project board is asked to authorise the next stage, initiating the project.

Planning is an overarching and repeatable sub-process which plays an important role in other processes. The application of PRINCE2 revolves around identifying the products that are to be created by a project, rather than the more usual concentration on the tasks to be completed. Identifying products leads to identifying the activities needed to produce them, as well as the dependencies between activities. Once the activities have been identified it is possible to estimate the effort required for each activity, and schedule activities into a plan. The risk associated with completion of activities is analysed. Finally, a process for completing a project is agreed.

Initiating a project follows start-up activity and involves shaping the brief for the project into a coherent business case. The approach taken to ensure quality on the project is agreed, together with the overall approach to controlling the project itself. Project files are also created, as is an overall plan for the project and a plan for the next stage of the project. This information can be put before the project board for them to authorise the project.

PRINCE2 suggests that projects should be broken down into stages. Controlling a stage is therefore a sub-process that dictates how each individual stage should be controlled. This includes the way in which work packages are authorised and received for each stage. It also specifies the way in which progress should be monitored and how summaries of progress should be reported to the project board. The method suggests means for capturing and assessing project issues, together with the way in which corrective action should be taken. It also lays down the approach by which project issues should be referred to the project board when necessary.

Managing project delivery specifies how a work package should be accepted, executed and delivered. Managing stage boundaries dictates what should be done towards the end of a stage. In particular, the next stage should be planned and the overall project plan, risk log and business case amended as necessary. The sub-process also details what should be done in the case of a stage that has gone outside its tolerance levels. Finally, the process dictates how the end of the stage should be reported.

Directing a project is an overarching sub-process which enables the project board to control the overall project. It runs from project start-up to project close-down. The project board uses reports generated from other sub-processes at a number of decision points. It authorises project initiation and close-down as well as the plans for each stage of a project. It can also authorise additional resource for a stage following slippage or other unforeseen circumstances.

The sub-process closing a project details activities that should be done at the end of a project. The project should be formally decommissioned and resources freed up for allocation to other activities. A series of follow-on actions should be identified and the project itself needs to be formally evaluated.

11.7   Operations

Informatics operations: that process devoted to the successful operation of existing informatics infrastructure

Of the various processes illustrated in Figure 11.2, informatics planning and informatics management are covered in Chapter 10. Project management has been covered in this chapter, and information systems development and maintenance are covered in Chapter 12.

This section devotes its attention to the process of **informatics operations**. This is an area of the informatics service that is frequently forgotten and left unexplored in many accounts of ICT and organisations. However, an increasing range of informatics professionals are now involved in operations work rather than planning, management, development and maintenance work. This is not surprising in that once an organisation has invested in informatics infrastructure it needs a continuing commitment to ensuring it operates properly.

We can frame operation of the ICT infrastructure using the philosophy of ICT service management. This means that the ICT infrastructure is considered as a set of defined services delivered to users in the organisation. Considering ICT infrastructure as a portfolio of services in this way encourages organisations to think of those services they need to provide internally and those that can be sourced externally.

Take email as a service provided by the ICT infrastructure. It is now a major communication medium, both inside and outside organisations, so its effective management has become a significant issue. Email management involves developing and operating procedures for ensuring that inbound and outbound email is stored and processed efficiently.

For emails from outside the organisation, procedures and technologies need to ensure they reach the appropriate person promptly, and responses are sent within a specified timeframe. Frequently, auto-responders or mail-bots are used to notify the sender that their email is being processed. Various workflow technologies are used to aid processing by back-office staff. Outbound email may be a significant aspect of eMarketing strategy (Chapter 8). For instance, outbound emails to customers might be sent as part of a marketing campaign, or on a more regular basis, such as an electronic newsletter.

Many organisations now impose constraints on employees' use of email, because of concerns with the volume of internal emails generated and the dangers of their inappropriate use. For example, in flaming attacks emails are used to abuse or bully fellow employees. Many companies have trained staff in email etiquette, and some have even barred use of email for certain corporate communications.

11.7.1 Approaches to ICT services management

ICT services management: the management of ICT as a service

A number of related approaches have been published for **ICT service management**, all based around an integrated process model. This section concentrates on an approach based on ITIL.

ITIL: Information Technology Infrastructure Library, a method for ICT services management

The Information Technology Infrastructure Library (**ITIL**) (OGC, 2009) was established in 1989 by the former UK Central Computer and Telecommunications Agency (CCTA), and is now managed by the UK Office of Government Commerce (OGC). In November 2000 the British Standards Institute published a new standard for IT service management, BS15000. This has been largely adopted as the ISO 20000 standard for IT service management. Both standards extend the original ITIL specification.

The description of ICT service management here is based on these standards but has been adapted in part to fit with the description of other key processes of the informatics service in this chapter and Chapters 10 and 12.

This type of approach generally sees ICT service management as a number of high-level processes such as service strategy, service support, service improvement and service delivery (see Figure 11.10).

11.7.2 Service strategy

In the philosophy of ICT services management, an organisation must first define services relevant to its ICT infrastructure. The definitions can be based on functional requirements, such as producing a service report or generating an invoice, or non-functional requirements (see Chapter 12), such as providing service availability and information security. Service definitions then need to be published in a service catalogue, preferably as one central catalogue available to all potential users of ICT services.

ICT service strategy: defining a strategy for the ICT service

Service strategy also involves specifying an end-user request model or subscription model for services. The request model enables the user to select services from the service catalogue.

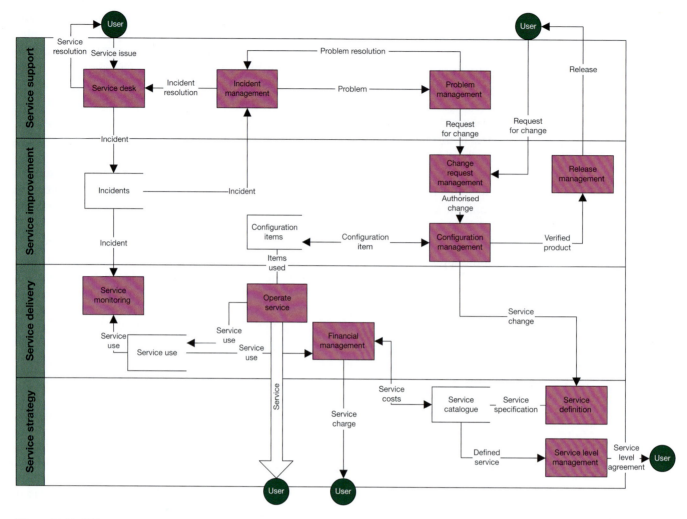

Figure 11.10 *ICT services management*

The subscription model automatically delivers a standard set of services according to a prearranged service level agreement. For example, one service might be create a new email account and automatically create a request to subscribe a particular user to the email service.

Effective planning for ICT services relies on an effective grip on the significant investment made in ICT infrastructure. This investment is not solely associated with the acquisition of hardware (such as computers, printers and storage) and software (such as operating systems and enterprise software). Other costs include installation costs, environmental costs (wiring, furniture, air conditioning and so on), running costs (electricity, communication costs and so on), maintenance costs (on hardware and software), security costs (risk management and disaster recovery mechanisms), networking costs (network hardware, software and maintenance), training costs and wider organisational costs (new salary structures, management and the like).

The cost of running the informatics infrastructure is also not a one-off cost; it is an on-going cost of ownership. Hardware, software and the skills of personnel, for instance, have to be upgraded regularly. Total cost of ownership (TCO) is a financial estimate designed to help informatics managers assess direct and indirect costs associated with operation of the informatics infrastructure. It is perhaps better called the total cost of operation. A TCO estimate ideally reflects not only the purchase costs of hardware, software, data and communication technology, but all costs involved in the use and maintenance of the equipment, devices or systems considered part of the infrastructure. This includes the costs of training support personnel and the users, costs associated with failure or outage, diminished performance, costs of security breaches, costs of disaster preparedness and recovery, floor space, electricity, development expenses, testing infrastructure and expenses, quality assurance, decommissioning equipment and eWaste handling.

Strategies for reducing TCO include the use of a thin client model of distributed computing (see Chapter 9), the adoption of open source software (see Chapter 12) and the outsourcing of informatics operations (considered above).

11.7.3   Service support

ICT service support: supporting users in the use of the ICT service

Service support can be considered as consisting of a number of inter-related sub-processes: running a service desk, incident management and problem management, change request management, configuration management and release management.

A service desk provides a single and first point of contact for the customer/user of defined services. It helps users with difficulties or queries, handles requests for changes and communicates with the user community, particularly releasing new versions of infrastructure to users.

End-users require support in the operation of their ICT environment. This environment will differ depending on the hardware, software and communication facilities the user has access to, as well as the degree of sophistication needed to use them. The help desk helps solve problems that end-users face with their ICT environment. This can range from replacing a printer cartridge to producing reports from a corporate database. Because of the high degree to which ICT is embedded in modern organisations, the help desk is now a significant organisational function. Satisfaction with the help-desk service frequently reflects on the overall satisfaction with the informatics service.

A key part of the help desk is ensuring that care is taken in managing user requests and solving them promptly. A common approach has a front-line interface to the help desk in which junior staff log problems and consult a stored knowledge base of common solutions. If they cannot solve the problem it is passed on to appropriate technical experts. Not surprisingly, the help desk in a large organisation frequently overlaps with a training facility, because metrics generated from problem logging are a useful means of identifying user training needs.

Service desk operation relies on effective incident and problem management. An incident is any deviation from the expected and defined operation of a service. Incident management is the process that restores normal service operation as quickly as possible, by whatever means possible. A problem is a condition that has been identified and defined from incidents exhibiting common characteristics that have no known cause. The objective of problem management is to ensure the stability of ICT services by identifying and resolving known errors in the ICT infrastructure.

11.7.4   Service improvement

ICT service improvement: managing the process of improving aspects of ICT infrastructure

Incidents and problems are resolved through the operation of three inter-related processes of service improvement: change request management, configuration management and release management. A configuration item is a component of the ICT infrastructure. Configuration management is the process involved in managing the ICT infrastructure by identifying, recording and controlling configuration items. A change is an action triggered by a request that results in a change of state for a configuration item. The objective of change request management is to effectively handle the recording, authorisation and control of all changes requested to ICT infrastructure. The objective of release management is to ensure that only authorised versions of ICT infrastructure, both software and hardware, are made available to users.

Suppose a company is using a software package to manage sales orders across the country and during continuous use of this package users experience a problem in retrieving customer details. These problems will be raised as incidents. Since this issue appears in a number of logged incidents a problem is identified and reported back to the software supplier. The software supplier eventually fixes the error and supplies a new version of the software module back to the company. This module will be a configuration item which will have a change request logged against it. Once this module has been tested effectively it will be authorised for release. An update to this software is then scheduled for release across the company, normally at an off-peak time to avoid disruption.

CASE CHECK

CS p 470

Finding the process edge: ITIL at Celanese

Celanese is a global leader in the chemical industry and spent years implementing an ERP solution and integrating its divisional IT functions into a shared services model. Around 2007, after years of growth in its ICT infrastructure, many within the informatics service at the company still believed that their internal operations would benefit from tighter coordination of business processes. They looked to ITIL to guide their effort at process integration. This case study describes the first three years of experience with ITIL by Celanese's informatics service.

11.7.5 Service delivery

ICT service delivery: delivering services, monitoring operations and costing services

The **service delivery** process consists of three sub-processes, service monitoring, service operation and financial management:

- Service monitoring ensures the continual review of agreed levels of service as required by the business.
- Service operation involves ensuring the effective delivery of services through capacity, availability and continuity management. Capacity management involves matching ICT resources to business demand. Availability management means ensuring ICT availability in order to support the business at a justifiable cost. Continuity management is concerned with the rapid restoration of ICT services in the event of disaster.
- Financial management involves costing the delivery of services and charging users for them.

Disaster recovery is a critical aspect of continuity management, restoring operations critical to the resumption of business after a disaster, either natural or human. For informatics this particularly involves regaining access to aspects of ICT infrastructure, particularly data and communication networks that support key business processes.

To achieve effective recovery a well-established and thoroughly tested data recovery plan needs to be developed. It should include procedures for coping with the unexpected or sudden loss of communications and/or key personnel, but the focus here is on the recovery of data. This typically involves backing up data to peripheral storage, such as tape, and sending it offsite at regular intervals (preferably daily). It also includes back-ups to disks onsite and automatically copied to offsite disks, or made directly to offsite disks.

A more sophisticated approach is replication of data at an offsite location. Organisations such as online banks, which demand high-availability systems, might replicate both data and processing offsite, enabling continuous access if there is an onsite disaster. Many organisations outsource disaster recovery, using an external provider of a standby site and systems rather than their own remote facilities.

In addition to making plans to recover systems, organisations need to take precautionary measures to reduce the likelihood of disasters occurring. These include: mirroring systems and data; surge protectors to minimise the effect of power surges on delicate electronic equipment; uninterruptible power supplies to keep systems going in the event of a power failure; and anti-virus software and other security measures such as firewalls (see Chapter 6) to prevent data corruption and loss.

11.7.6 Infrastructure provision and administration

One of the key objectives of informatics operations is to ensure the effective running of large, multi-user, back-end and front-end information systems (see Chapter 4). To do this it not only needs to operate and maintain the systems themselves, it also needs to provide and administer associated technology such as database systems.

Database administration: involves technical implementation of database systems, managing the systems currently in use and setting and enforcing policies

Chapter 10 distinguished between data administration and **database administration**. The database administrator (DBA) is responsible for the technical implementation of database systems, managing the systems currently in use and setting and enforcing policies. Whether a specialist database administration function is needed depends mostly on the size of the database system. The main user of a small desktop database system will probably perform administration tasks such as regularly backing up data themselves. However, when a database has many users and the volume of data is significant, there needs to be a designated person to do this. The database administrator's core responsibilities are administration of the database, administration of the DBMS and administration of the database environment.

Database administrators normally also get involved in the design and implementation of databases, so they are part of development teams (see Chapter 12). They also ensure that the data is documented in a standard way so that multiple applications and end-users can access it effectively. Database administration involves monitoring live running against a database and modifying the structure of the database system to increase its performance. Finally, the database administrator will establish a strategy for archiving 'dead' data and a procedure for backing up and recovering data in the event of hardware or software failure.

Administering a DBMS also involves a range of activities. For instance, it includes taking key responsibility for installing a DBMS or DBMS components, and enforcing policies and procedures for managing updates and changes to the software of the database system. It also involves monitoring live running of the DBMS and tailoring elements of the DBMS structure to ensure its effective performance.

Administering the database environment means monitoring and controlling access to the database and DBMS by users and application systems. Activities in this area include establishing user groups and assigning passwords to users and groups. Users are assigned various levels of access privileges both to DBMS facilities and to parts of databases. The database administrator will also ensure that strategies laid down by data administration for data integrity, security and privacy are adhered to at the technical level.

Increasing connectivity and performance of communication networks has enabled applications to be provided remotely. Application service provision (ASP) is the process by which a business provides informatics services to customers over a network. Software services offered using ASP are also known as on-demand software and software as a service. ASP has been proposed as part of a solution to the TCO problem, in the sense that an ASP might be able to provide the latest software at lower cost to customers over computer networks. ASP can also be considered as a type of informatics outsourcing in that a provider typically provides 24 x 7 technical support and physical and electronic security as well as the service itself.

There are several types of provider. A functional ASP delivers a single application, such as credit card payment processing or timesheet services. A vertical market ASP delivers a solution package for a specific customer type, such as a dental practice. An enterprise ASP is likely to deliver a broad spectrum of applications to organisations, while a local ASP will deliver services within a limited area.

ASP relies on a distributed processing model (see Chapter 6). The application software resides on the vendor system and is accessed by users through a Web browser using HTML or special-purpose client software provided by the vendor. Custom client software can also interface to such systems through XML (Chapter 5) and application programming interfaces. So the provider fully owns and operates the software application(s) and owns, operates and maintains the servers that support them, and makes information available to customers via the Internet or a thin client (see Chapter 6). The provider bills the customer either on a per-use basis or via a monthly/annual fee.

IV

11.8　Green ICT

Green ICT: considering and managing the impact ICT has upon sustainability

Any activity, whether it be performed by individual actors or groups of actors working for organisations, has an impact upon the physical environment. As ICT has become more and more embedded within the activity of the modern business, an increasing focus has been given to the proper management of ICT to mitigate its effects upon the ecological footprint of the business organisation (ONeill, 2010).

The idea of an ecological footprint is an attempt to measure the impact of human activity upon the physical environment. Any human activity on this planet consumes resources of natural capital such as land, sea and the atmosphere. As a by-product of such activity humans also produce waste, which has the potential to contaminate the physical environment, thereby degrading resources of natural capital. As a measure, an ecological footprint is the amount of natural capital (expressed as a planet Earth) that it takes to supply resources for current human activity. In 2006 this was calculated as 1.4 planet Earths. In other words, humanity is consuming physical resources 1.4 times faster than the Earth can renew them; clearly an unsustainable and potentially unviable system.

At the level of nation-states and business organisations another related measure is typically used as a measure of environmental impact, that of a carbon footprint. This is the total amount of greenhouse gas (GHG) emissions caused by some actor, such as an organisation, person, plant or machine. A greenhouse gas is a gas in the atmosphere that absorbs and emits radiation within the thermal infrared range. This property of such gases is the fundamental cause of the greenhouse effect which contributes to global warming. The primary greenhouse gases in the atmosphere are water vapour, carbon dioxide, methane, nitrous oxide and ozone. Greenhouse gases are emitted directly in various ways such as through transport, land clearance or industrial manufacture. Such gases are also an indirect consequence of the production and consumption of food, fuels, manufactured goods and services. For simplicity of reporting, a carbon footprint is typically expressed in terms of the amount of carbon dioxide, or its equivalent, emitted by some activity system.

The ICT infrastructure of an organisation can impact on an organisation's carbon footprint in a number of ways. Consider, for instance, the life-cycle of a typical piece of ICT hardware such as a personal computer. To produce a typical PC and its associated monitor over 27 different materials are likely to be used. The extraction and production of these materials causes considerable GHG emissions. These materials then have to be transported to the site of manufacture, frequently from diverse parts of the globe, generating up to 5% of the GHG emissions associated with the PC's entire life-cycle. In the manufacture of a PC, crucial processes such as semiconductor manufacture use more than 1,000 hazardous substances. Once a PC is put into use its lifetime of electricity consumption typically amounts to 50% of its original purchase cost. At some point the hardware is disposed of, meaning that processes have to be devised for recycling as much of the original material as possible, currently that is as much as 75%.

What has become known as green IT is a collection of IT- or ICT-related initiatives which aim to directly reduce the carbon footprint of an organisation. There are many such initiatives including: environmentally-friendly printing, energy-efficient computing, sustainable data storage and cloud computing.

11.8.1　Environmentally-friendly printing

Environmentally-friendly printing involves the replacement of standalone printers dedicated to one PC with network-enabled printers that are shared between a number of personal computers. Such printers should also be configured to print in duplex mode (on both sides of the page) and on recycled paper for most internal business uses. Finally, printers should never be left in standby mode for long periods of time, but turned off.

11.8.2 Energy-efficient computing

One of the most effective ways of improving the energy efficiency of computing infrastructure is through the replacement of desktop personal computers with laptops. Laptop computers are designed as a matter of course with energy efficiency in mind because of the need to prolong battery life. Normally, for instance, such machines can be configured to go into hibernation mode when unused, consuming little energy. In this manner, the typical laptop can, if properly configured, consume as much as 85% less energy than the comparable desktop personal computer.

11.8.3 Sustainable data storage

Data storage devices consume large amounts of energy. Organisations can minimise their use of such a resource by reducing the amount of redundancy in their data resource. This involves actively searching for unnecessary duplication among files backed-up to external storage and removing the duplication to reduce the amount of stored data and consequently the amount of storage needed.

11.8.4 Cloud computing

At first glance cloud computing does not appear a good idea in terms of impact upon the physical environment. For instance, Google is said to operate a global network of approximately 36 data centres needed to run its search engine. Microsoft's data centre in Chicago is reputed to need three electrical substations with a capacity of 198 megawatts to run effectively. The Environmental Protection Agency in the US estimates that the 7,000 or so data centres that exist in the country consume 1.5% of the country's electricity consumption.

However, there are a number of environmental advantages proposed for cloud computing. From the point of view of the producer the infrastructure, such as data centres, can be located in areas with lower property costs, close to water (for cooling purposes) and within easy access of electricity supplies. This centralisation of resources may make it easier to mitigate the environmental impact of ICT infrastructure. For example, from the point of view of the consumer cloud computing has the potential to make applications much more scalable. Hence, if a company expands its activities it does not need to purchase vast new communication and data resources, it merely extends its use of cloud services. Further, the application itself in terms of software and data can be separated from physical resources such as hardware. Hence, if more computing power is required to handle peak loads additional cloud servers can be applied to the task on an as-needed basis. This on-demand use of computing resources may be more energy-efficient than having vast communication and data resources managed by consuming organisations themselves.

FOCUS ON VALUE	An organisation with an informatics infrastructure must establish ways of operating and servicing it. A key decision is whether to do this internally or outsource it. Organisations need to make significant investments not only in planning and management work but also in providing the informatics service. Also, since much informatics work is project-based there is key value in good project management.

11.9 Conclusion and key themes

Chapter 10 established that informatics planning and management are critical activities for modern organisations. Organisations used to do these in-house, but more recently there has been a trend to outsource them.

Informatics is primarily part of the service sector and is an increasingly prominent part of many economies. The informatics industry can be divided into producers of informatics products and services, and their consumers. Informatics in both producing and consuming organisations suffers from a lack of defined career paths. Professional bodies are attempting to address this problem through the introduction of clear skills profiles for various forms of informatics work.

The informatics service is that part of the organisation tasked with supporting information, information systems and ICT. It can be structured in various ways, including outsourcing in whole or in part. Its four main processes are planning, management, development and operations. It delivers services in support of current informatics infrastructure, and project management and development services in support of future informatics infrastructure.

In the informatics service, planning, management, development and even operations activity are typically organised as projects. Project management can be divided into project planning, project organisation and project control. Project planning involves determining as clearly as possible the likely parameters associated with a particular project. Project organisation concerns how to structure staff activities to ensure maximum effectiveness. Project control involves ensuring that a project remains on schedule, within budget and produces the desired output.

Informatics operations are frequently forgotten in accounts of ICT and organisations, but an increasing range of informatics people work in operations, which is now typically packaged as ICT services management. There are a number of approaches and it can be seen to consist of four high-level processes: service strategy, service delivery, service support and service improvement.

Any activity has an impact upon the physical environment. As ICT has become more and more embedded within the activity of the modern business, an increasing focus has been given to the proper management of ICT to mitigate effects upon the physical environment. The ICT infrastructure of an organisation can impact on an organisation's carbon footprint in a number of ways. Green ICT is a collection of ICT-related initiatives which aim to directly reduce the carbon footprint of an organisation, such as: environmentally-friendly printing, energy-efficient computing, sustainable data storage, virtualisation, cloud computing and use of software as a service.

This chapter and Chapter 10 gradually travel down the hierarchy of control relevant to informatics, from informatics planning and management to operations and project management. Chapter 12 considers the last level in this hierarchy, the process of developing new information systems and maintaining existing ones.

11.10 Review test

1 How would you distinguish between informatics producers and consumers? Write two sentences.

2 A model in which informatics provides one single service with single access provision. Select the most appropriate type of location.
- [ ] Distributed
- [ ] Decentralised
- [ ] Centralised

3 The informatics service includes four main processes. What are they? Select all that apply.
- [ ] Planning
- [ ] Management
- [ ] Development
- [ ] Business Strategy
- [ ] Operations

4 CIO stands for: Select the most appropriate description.
- [ ] Central information officer
- [ ] Chief intelligence officer
- [ ] Chief information officer

5 PRINCE2 is a project management method. True or false?
- [ ] True
- [ ] False

6 _____ might be defined as the use of external agents to perform one or more organisational activities. Fill in the blank..

7 A _____ is any concerted effort to achieve a set of objectives. Fill in the blank.

8   Project management involves three high-level activities. What are they? Select all that apply.
☐ Project planning
☐ Project estimation
☐ Project organisation
☐ Project control

9   There are two major project planning approaches based on focus. Name them. Select all that apply.
☐ Product-based planning
☐ Technology-based planning
☐ Activity-based planning
☐ Information-based planning

10 Project control is a type of _____ evaluation. Fill in the blank.

11 PRINCE stands for? Select the most appropriate description.
☐ Project in Computer Environments
☐ Projects in Controlled Environments
☐ Projects in Controllable Environments

12 A _____ provides a single and first point of contact for the customer/user of defined services. Fill in the blank.

13 The operation of an organisation's ICT infrastructure is now framed in terms of the philosophy of ICT _____ management. Fill in the blank.

14 TCO stands for? Select the most appropriate description.
☐ Total control of ownership
☐ Total cost of ownership
☐ Total conception of ownership

11.11   Exercises

‣ Search the Internet for companies in each of the informatics producer areas identified in this chapter.

‣ Look through job advertisements in various informatics magazines and try to develop precise job descriptions for the roles described in this chapter.

‣ Discuss the importance of regulation to the development of clear career paths for informatics professionals.

‣ Develop a brief policy statement indicating possible strategies for addressing the skills crisis in informatics.

‣ Take an organisation known to you and find out whether it has an informatics service function. In what way is the informatics service organised? Use the distinctions made in this chapter to help describe it. Is the department seen purely as a service function or in a more strategic sense? Is the service centralised, devolved or distributed? How is the service funded?

‣ At what point do you think a critical mass is reached in project group size?

‣ Discuss three of the main problems arising in the management of large project groups.

‣ Which form of organisation do you think is most prevalent in the informatics service: project organisation, functional organisation or matrix organisation?

‣ What sort of timings, effort and resource information should be kept in an organisation's project experience base?

‣ Even the most carefully planned of projects fail. Suggest some reasons.

‣ Try to identify the costs of maintaining a small network of personal computers.

‣ Does an organisation known to you have a help-desk? Who staffs the help-desk? How would you rate satisfaction with it?

‣ How do your back up your own personal data? How regularly? Do you store it offsite?

11.12   Projects

‣ A number of different forms have been considered for the informatics service. Investigate two or more organisations. Consider differences in structure and function between their informatics services and why these differences have occurred.

‣ ICT, information systems and information are increasingly important to successful organisational performance. Does this mean that the informatics service has more power in organisations? Investigate the power that the informatics service has in modern organisations. For instance, how prevalent is the practice of placing CIOs on the board?

‣ Determine the precise makeup of informatics in a nation. For instance, try to determine whether it is possible to state the percentage in each producer area and the major consumers of informatics.

- How commonplace are professional development schemes for informatics in organisations and how seriously are they treated? Investigate the use of the professional development schemes in the area of informatics in an organisation known to you.

- Is there a skills shortage in the informatics area in your nation? If so, are there any attempts to address this shortage? If the shortage is not addressed, what effect is likely on the economy?

- Good project management practices have been around for many years but information systems projects still fail frequently. Investigate the limitations of project management with respect to this problem.

- Investigate the range of project planning techniques and how frequently they are applied in information system projects in one large organisation or across a small number of organisations. Would you describe their project management practices to planning as activity-based or product-based?

- Determine the prevalence of use of the PRINCE project management method in a specific area of the private sector. Is PRINCE used specifically for information systems projects or more generally?

- Investigate the benefit provided by project management tools such as Microsoft Project to effective project management. What facilities do these tools provide and how do they aid the project manager?

- How important is the successful operation of a help desk to the general rating of user satisfaction with informatics? Investigate the activities of the help desk in two or more organisations. Are there effective ways of measuring satisfaction with the help desk itself and more generally with the informatics service?

- Attempt to calculate the total cost of ownership associated with desktop computing in an organisation known to you. How does the organisation attempt to control such costs? For instance, does the use of open source software have any part to play?

11.13 Critical reflection

What sort of project planning is best for a project to build a B2C eCommerce website? Is outsourcing informatics infrastructure necessarily a good thing? What sort of problems do you think might emerge in outsourcing informatics in organisations? Will employing an approach such as ITIL necessarily improve the operations of the informatics service?

11.14 Further reading

Bott (2005) contains an overview of informatics as a profession. The edited book by Lacity and Wilcocks (2006) brings together much published material on informatics outsourcing. Lacity, Khan and Wilcocks (2009) provide a review of the outsourcing literature and its lessons for practice. Oshri, Kotlarsky and Wilcocks (2008) consider business process outsourcing as well as ICT outsourcing. Brooks (1997) provides the classic study of the dangers inherent in project planning and Bentley (2009) provides a classic account of the PRINCE2 project management method. The Information Technology Infrastructure Library is introduced in a text from the UK Office of Government Commerce (2005). The Journal of Strategic Information Systems ran a special issue on the greening of ICT in March 2011.

11.15 References

Bentley, G. (2009). *Practical PRINCE2*. 3rd edition. Stationery Office Books, London.

Bott, F. (2005). *Professional Issues in Information Technology*. 2nd edition. British Computer Society Publications, London.

Brooks, F. P. (1997). *The Mythical Man Month and Other Essays on Software Engineering*. 2nd edition. Addison-Wesley, Reading, Mass.

Friedman, A. L. and D. S. Cornford. (1989). *Computer Systems Development: History, Organisation and Implementation*. John Wiley, Chichester.

Lacity, M. C., S. A. Khan and L. P. Wilcocks. (2009). A Review of the IT Outsourcing Literature: Insights for Practice. *Journal of Strategic Information Systems* 18 (3): 130–146.

Lacity, M. C. and L. Wilcocks. (2006). *Information Systems and Outsourcing*. Palgrave Macmillan, Basingstoke.

O'Connell, F. (2001). *How to Run Successful Projects II: The Silver Bullet*. 3rd edition. Prentice Hall, Hemel Hempstead.

OGC. (2005). *Introduction to ITIL*. Stationery Office Books, London.

OGC. (2009). *ITIL V3 Foundation Handbook*. Stationery Office Books, UK, London.

O'Neill, M. G. (2010). *Green IT: For Sustainable Business Practice*. British Computer Society, Swindon.

Oshri, I., J. Kotlarsky and L. Wilcocks. (2008). *Outsourcing Global Services: Knowledge, Innovation and Social Capital*. Palgrave Macmillan, Basingstoke.

Stapleton, J. (1997). DSDM – *Dynamic Systems Development Method: The Method in Practice*. Addison-Wesley, Harlow, England.

See companion website   www.palgrave.com/business/beynon-daviesbis2e

IV

12

Information systems development

'I must create a
system, or be enslaved
by another man's. I
will not reason and
compare: my business
is to create.'

William Blake (1757–
1827) *Jerusalem* (1815),
chapter 1

Learning outcomes	Principles
Define the key stages of the information system development process and identify differences between major approaches to information system development.	The development of new information systems is a significant investment for organisations. Since information systems are sociotechnical systems, development involves the joint design of activity systems with ICT systems.
Describe the key front-end activities of the development process: conception, analysis and design.	The information systems development process consists of six major activities. The three front-end activities establish a business case for a development effort (conception), elicit and document the requirements for the information system (analysis) and express the shape of the proposed information system (design).
Describe the key back-end activities of the development process: construction, implementation and maintenance.	The back-end activities of the development process include the actual build of the information system (construction), the introduction of the information systems into its context of use (implementation) and the on-going repair and adaptation of the information system over time (maintenance).

Chapter outline

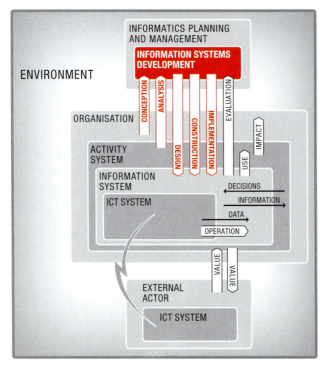

AACSB learning objectives:
Analytical thinking and use of IT

12.1   Introduction

In the practical world of organisational informatics many lament the death of the term programmer and its replacement with what is thought to be a poorer and vaguer term, developer. In a sense they are right. Developer is much less specific than programmer, and deliberately so. This is because modern development as an activity is much larger than simply programming. Indeed, as we shall see, much of the activity of modern information systems development in organisations does not produce any traditional program code whatsoever.

In Chapter 10 the case was made for the importance of informatics planning, management and strategy. Each of these areas is concerned with the issue of informatics infrastructure. The importance of these issues lies in the continuous need to adapt both informatics infrastructure and the infrastructure of activity in organisations to changing environmental circumstances.

This chapter considers the issue of development, a term which has traditionally been associated solely with the building of ICT systems. However, here information systems development is seen as one of the key organisational processes for modern-day organisations. This means that, following the definition of an information system as a sociotechnical system, this process must necessarily consider the joint development of both ICT systems and activity systems within and between organisations.

Since it is a process information system development can be considered as a system in itself. The key inputs to the development process are ICT resources and developer resources. A critical part of developer resources is the toolkit of methods, techniques and tools available to the developer. The key output is an ICT system designed to support an information system as well as an associated human activity system. A number of key activities are involved in the development process: conception, analysis, design, construction, implementation and maintenance.

The development process is normally organised in projects and is managed through these units of activity. It is also normally undertaken by a specialist organisation, which was referred to in Chapter 11 as the informatics service. This is typically either part of the organisation in question or a vendor organisation servicing its needs.

Consider the case of a research information system mentioned in Chapter 11. A university wishes to create a system to extend its informatics infrastructure. It decides to set up an information system development project to do this and resources this project with a team of developers and a budget to spend on necessary hardware and software. The key output from this project will be a new ICT system that will manage data on research outputs needed across the university. But the introduction of this new technological system will lead to necessary changes to the system of research administration in the university.

12.2   The development process

Information system development process: that activity system devoted to the creation of a new information system or the maintenance of an existing information system

Information system development is the sociotechnical system concerned with the design, construction, implementation and maintenance of key aspects of an organisation's informatics infrastructure. This critical activity system for modern business is represented in Figure 12.1. The key inputs into the system are ICT resources and developer resources. ICT resources can be hardware and communication technology as well as construction tools or software packages. Developer resources include not only people but also a toolkit of methods, techniques and tools available to the development team.

The key outputs from this process are an ICT system and its associated activity system. Information system is used here as the anchor term for both these constructs. Information systems in themselves are sociotechnical systems since they include both an ICT system and a system of use. Hence, the activity system and the ICT system should ideally be designed

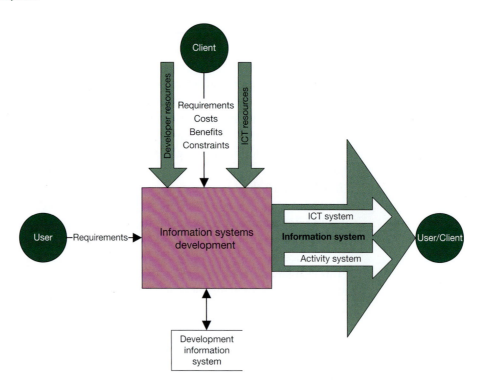

Figure 12.1 *The development process*

in parallel. The ICT system might be a bespoke system or a configured/tailored software package.

Three key types of organisational stakeholder are critical to the development process:

- **Clients** are typically managerial groups involved in setting the major parameters for an information system development project. This stakeholder group provides budgets for projects to use for funding ICT and developer resources. They also typically define expected benefits and set constraints on the degree of organisational change.
- The eventual users (**end-users**) of an information system are also likely to be involved in the development process. They will typically be involved in analysis and design work, and provide important detailed requirements for the functionality and usability of the intended system.
- **Developers** are the persons tasked with analysing, designing, constructing and implementing the information system. They may also have a key part to play in delivering the information system into its context of use.

The process of information systems development involves a number of activities arranged in what is frequently referred to as a life-cycle of development (see Figure 12.2). The activities in a typical information system development project provide project managers (see Chapter 11) with a blueprint for controlling the project.

12.2.1 Conception

Conception is the first phase in the development process and typically follows on from informatics planning and management. In this phase the development team produce the key business case for an information system, an evaluation of the system in strategic terms (see Chapter 7). The team also attempt to estimate the degree of risk associated with the project. Finally, they consider the feasibility of the information system project in terms of organisational resources. A project that passes the strategic evaluation, risk analysis and feasibility tests goes on to a process of systems analysis.

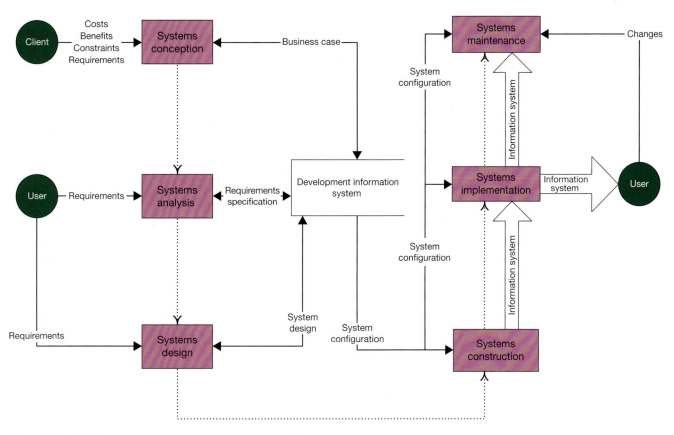

Figure 12.2 *Activities of information system development*

12.2.2 Analysis

Information systems analysis involves two inter-related activities:

- **Requirements elicitation** is the process of identifying requirements.
- **Requirements specification** is the process of representing them in various ways.

Generally, information systems analysis benefits from forms of stakeholder participation (see Chapter 7), especially in the process of elicitation.

12.2.3 Design

Systems analysis provides the major input into systems design. Design is the process of planning a technical artefact to meet requirements established by analysis as well as the use context into which it will be placed. It involves consideration of requirements and constraints, and selection from among design alternatives. The sociotechnical design of ICT systems and associated activity systems benefits from the participation of system stakeholders. A design or system specification acts as a blueprint for systems construction.

12.2.4 Construction

This phase involves building the information system to its specification. Traditionally, ICT system construction involves the three related processes of programming, testing and documentation. This is done either by an internal team or by an outside, or outsourced, contractor. Many information systems are now bought in as a package and tailored to organisational requirements. Construction also involves the introduction of new job specifications and procedures associated with the intended use of the ICT system.

12.2.5 Implementation

The process of systems implementation (sometimes called systems delivery) follows on from systems construction. Systems implementation involves delivering an information system into its context of use. Since an information system is a sociotechnical system, its implementation involves the parallel implementation of both an information system and an associated activity system. Once a system is delivered into its context of use it will be subject to the processes of operation and systems maintenance. Operation (see Chapter 11) is not included in the development life-cycle since it is an issue of use and management rather than a direct concern for the development team.

12.2.6 Maintenance

Systems maintenance follows on from systems implementation. Maintenance is the process of making necessary changes to the functionality and/or usability of an information system. Information systems rarely stand still. They may change for a number of reasons. In the process of use, errors might be found or changes proposed. At some point in time a system might be abandoned or need to be re-engineered to fit new organisational circumstances. Changes also occur over time in adjustments made to the way both the information system and its context of use work. Maintenance activity may also stimulate suggestions for new systems. Hence, it may act as a key input into the process of systems conception and thus provides a form of feedback (Chapter 2) within the process of information system development.

12.2.7 Developing an eCommerce website

Suppose a company wishes to set up an eCommerce website. We can map some of the actual activities in the plan for the development of this system against the phases of the development process described above:

- Conception is likely to involve building the business case for the new eCommerce site, registering the domain name, producing a tender document, issuing the tender, reviewing submissions and awarding the contract.
- Analysis involves eliciting key requirements for the site from clients and users and producing key content and presentational requirements for the website.
- Design is the phase of producing key prototypes of content and presentation, considering changes to work practices and reviewing them with users.
- Construction involves producing the final content (HTML pages and graphics), programming any integration with back-end systems such as databases, testing the pages individually and as an integrated set, and setting up new organisational structures and processes to ensure that content in the website remains current.
- Implementation consists of producing a marketing campaign to accompany release of the website, updating stationery and registering the site, as well as publishing the site on its appropriate server and putting new organisational processes into action.
- Maintenance involves measuring the performance of the site, managing the content on the site over time and reviewing organisational structures and processes where necessary.

12.3 Approaches to information systems development

There are a number of distinct approaches to information system development. This section considers two major dimensions, the type of information system product and the form of sequencing of activities (Figure 12.3).

12.3.1 Type of information systems product

The product dimension contains two main types of development activity, bespoke development and package development.

Bespoke development: the development style in which an organisation produces a new information system to directly match the organisation's requirements

Package development: in package development an organisation purchases a piece of software from a vendor organisation and tailors the package to a greater or lesser extent to the demands of a particular organisation

In **bespoke development** an organisation builds an information system to directly match its requirements. This might involve programming the entire system, or building a system out of pre-established components. Bespoke development normally offers the organisation the opportunity to match closely the design of the information system to organisational processes. The main disadvantage is that the organisation must make a considerable investment in developing the information system. In particular it has to maintain a suitably skilled internal informatics service (Chapter 11) or put the work out to tender and manage an external supplier.

In **package development** an organisation obtains an existing piece of software and tailors the package to a greater or lesser extent to meet its own demands. The packaged software might be purchased from a software vendor, run under application service provision (see Chapter 11), or obtained under some form of open source software licensing agreement.

A software package is a software application designed to provide the functionality needed to support activity in a generic business area. It might be customisable to a specific organisation's needs. In package development the usual relationship between system development and organisational processes is reversed. Traditionally, the ICT system is designed to meet the requirements of established or intended organisational processes. In package development, generally speaking, organisational processes have to be adapted to the package requirements.

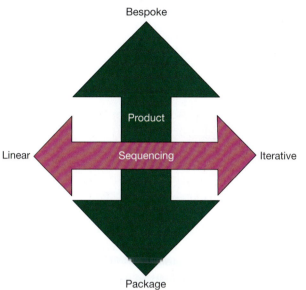

Figure 12.3 Approaches to information systems development

It is not normally feasible for small- to medium-sized organisations to develop bespoke systems because this is so expensive, so they normally obtain a package or hire an external contractor to produce a system. Even for these alternative approaches to development, the key phases above have to be followed. For instance, it is critical that organisations make a business case for the use of a package, just as they would if they were proposing to construct the system themselves.

Suppose we are the development team tasked with producing a new research information system for a university. The team has two major choices: it can develop the system itself or it can purchase a package from an external supplier. If it produces the entire information systems itself then it has the opportunity to build the system to match the needs of the university as closely as possible. However, this will take considerable effort and will tie up valuable informatics staff for a considerable period of time. If it purchases a package then it may be possible for the system to be up and running relatively quickly. However, it is likely that much time will be spent adapting the activities of the organisation to that demanded by the package.

REFLECT: Reflect on an organisation known to you. How many of the information systems do you think have been developed in a bespoke and how many in a package manner?

12.3.2 Form of sequencing

Linear development: the phases of development are strung out in a linear sequence with outputs from each phase triggering the start of the next phase

Sequencing is the way the various phases of the development process are organised. There are two broad forms, linear and iterative.

The **linear model of the development** process is shown in Figure 12.4. Here the phases are strung out in order, with outputs from each phase triggering the start of the next phase. In the first three phases the key outputs are forms of system documentation. In the last three phases the outputs are elements of an information system.

The linear model has been particularly popular as a framework for large-scale development projects. This is mainly because a clear linear sequence makes for easier project planning and control (see Chapter 11). The major disadvantages lie in the difficulties associated with changing early analysis and design decisions later on in a project.

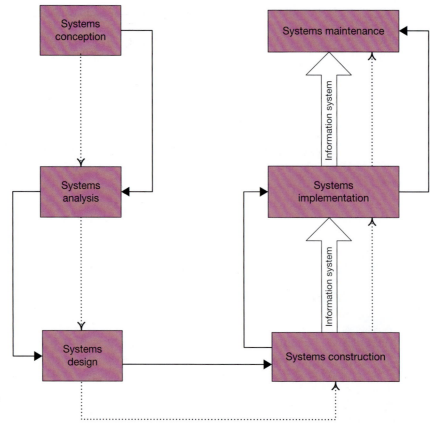

Figure 12.4 *The linear model of development*

Iterative development: in this model systems conception triggers an iterative cycle in which various versions of a system (prototypes) are analysed, designed, constructed and possibly implemented

The **iterative model of the development** process is illustrated in Figure 12.5. In this model systems conception triggers a cycle in which various versions of a system, known as prototypes, are analysed, designed, constructed and possibly implemented.

The iterative model has been particularly popular for small- to medium-scale projects. Iteration, the construction of prototypes (prototyping) and significant amounts of user involvement, seems to reduce the risk associated with ICT innovation and generates a stronger commitment from stakeholders. However, because it is frequently uncertain in an iterative approach how much resource will need to be devoted to the project, this approach can lead to more difficult project planning and management.

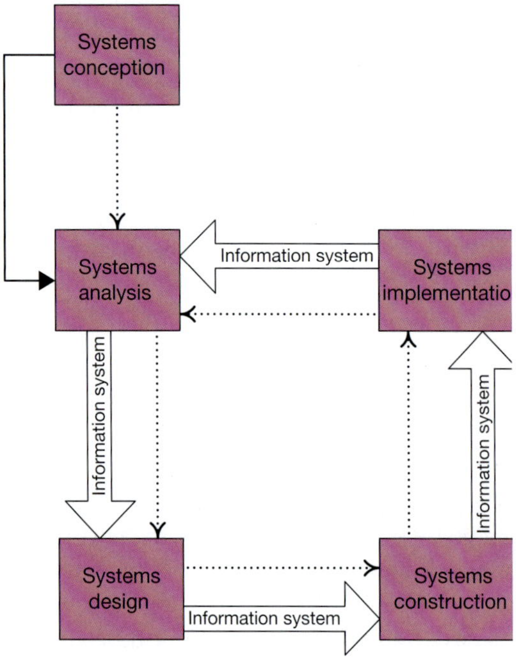

No one approach to development is applicable to all circumstances. Development projects are likely to use a range of approaches depending on development resources, the scale of the project and whether the system affects the front-end or back-end ICT infrastructure (see Chapter 6).

Generally speaking, large-scale, back-end information system projects, which often involve implementing a large corporate database system, are likely to use a linear, bespoke model of development. Major modules in an ERP system (see Chapter 6) are also likely to be tailored using a linear, package approach. In contrast, front-end ICT systems, particularly those that are Web-based, are likely to adopt iterative approaches because of the time pressures associated with them, and the high levels of interactivity and hence user involvement required.

Figure 12.5 *The iterative model of development*

REFLECT: Besides those mentioned, what other advantages do you think there might be to using a linear as opposed to an iterative approach to information systems development?

12.4   Development organisation, information system and toolkit

Development organisation:
the group of people involved in a particular development effort

Development is normally organised in projects. All projects comprise teams of people engaged in achieving explicit objectives (Chapter 2), usually with a set duration. Most informatics work in organisations is structured as a project; planning, management and development activities are all normally conducted on a project basis. This chapter focuses on development projects, concerted efforts to develop information systems.

Initiating development projects is normally part of an organisation's informatics planning and management processes (see Chapter 10). Project management (O'Connell, 2001) interacts with the development process in the sense that it acts as the major control process for development (see Figure 12.6).

Figure 12.6 illustrates the need for two major forms of information in support of development. The actual process of development needs documentary support to enable collaboration between the development team. The process of managing a project also needs an associated information system. This will store both the project plans and the data on progress against them.

Before the development process starts a development team is normally assembled. A number of development roles are critical to particular phases of the development process:

- A business analyst undertakes organisational analysis (see Chapter 2) and systems conception activities such as cost/benefit analyses and risk analysis.
- A systems analyst undertakes feasibility study, analysis and design activities.
- A project manager is concerned with managing the development process as a unit.
- A programmer undertakes construction and maintenance activities.
- A change manager is particularly concerned with the successful execution of implementation activities.

Representatives of other stakeholder groups, particularly clients and end-users, are also likely to form part of the development team, either throughout the development process or at key points in the development of the information system, such as in analysis and design.

A development information system is essential to ensure the effective operation of the activity system that is the development process. Any reasonably sized development project

IV

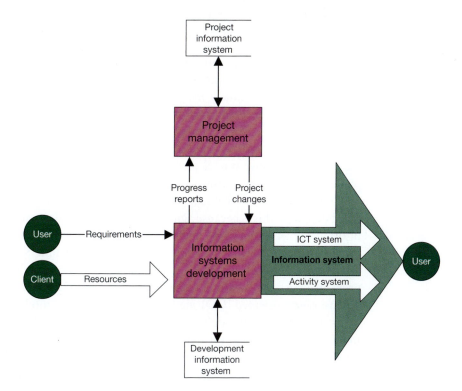

Figure 12.6 *The relationship between project management and information systems development*

will need an information system to support communication between teams of developers, feed into a project management and an informatics management process, and communicate with other stakeholder groups such as users and business managers.

12.5   Development toolkit

Development toolkit: The methods, techniques and tools available to the development organisation

The human species has been described as *Homo habilis*, man the toolmaker. We make tools to extend our physical and mental grasp and to help us to change our world. To undertake any development effort the information systems developer needs a toolkit. It consists of methods, techniques and tools that support the activities of the development process: conception, analysis, design, implementation and maintenance. Methods, techniques and tools are the supporting technology for information systems development. The term technology is used here in its broadest sense to refer to any form of device, conceptual or physical, that aids the work of a person or group of people.

DID YOU KNOW? The noted American psychologist Abraham Maslow once noted the effect that tools can have on both the problem-setting and problem-solving mind-set of the tool user. If the only tool you have is a hammer, he said, you tend to see every problem as a nail.

12.5.2   Information systems development methods

Information systems development method: a specified approach for producing information systems

Development methods are frameworks that prescribe how to go about development activity. An **information systems development method** has these main components:

- a model of the information systems development process
- a set of techniques
- a documentation method associated with these techniques
- some indication of how the techniques chosen, along with the documentation method, fit into the model of the development process.

There are three major types of development method: structured methods, agile development methods and object-oriented methods.

Structured methods emerged during the 1980s and initially used a linear model of the development process. Clear phases are identified, with clear inputs to and outputs from each phase. Techniques in areas such as information modelling (see Chapter 3) and information systems modelling (see Chapter 4) were initially developed within structured frameworks, so structured methods propose a standard notation for this kind of modelling. For example, Structured Systems Analysis and Design Method (SSADM) is a structured development method introduced initially in the early 1980s as a public domain standard development method. It has been used extensively in both the public and private sectors and has been substantially revised several times.

Agile methods, such as rapid application development (RAD) or extreme programming (XP), use an iterative model of the development process and generally specify high-level phases based around a form of prototyping. They are frequently referred to as lightweight methods in contrast to the heavyweight methods available in the structured and object-oriented domains. This is because agile methods are generally contingent, they do not prescribe in detail the techniques (see below) to be used. A variety of techniques can be adapted to the needs of a particular project. As an example, Dynamic Systems Development Method (DSDM) is a non-proprietary RAD method. It is produced by the DSDM consortium, a non-profit-making organisation of vendors, users and individual supporters of RAD.

Most object-oriented (OO) methods use a contingent model – sometimes linear , sometimes iterative – for the development process. OO methods tend to focus on objects and modelling, as discussed in Chapter 3. Unified modelling language (UML) and the rational development process is a popular OO development method. UML is a standard notation for object modelling developed as a hybrid of earlier OO specification methods. Rational development process is a method which specifies how UML can be used in a model of the development process based in OO development.

These three method types focus on the development of ICT systems. A number of other methods focus more on the development of human activity systems, such as those in the area of participatory design (see below).

12.5.3 Development techniques

Information systems development technique: development techniques are normally used to guide activity within one phase of the development process

Techniques guide activity within one phase of the development process. They are particular approaches to supporting the processes of systems analysis, systems design and systems construction. The modelling approaches discussed in previous chapters are all examples of techniques primarily for supporting the process of analysis. A technique consists of the three elements discussed in Chapter 2: a set of constructs, a notation for representing constructs, and principles of constructing models in the chosen technique.

A distinction can be made between developer-centric techniques and user-centric techniques. Developer-centric techniques are designed particularly for enabling developers to understand, document and communicate information system problems to other developers. Most of these techniques are primarily directed at specification, and they provide major input to the development information system. They include information modelling, information systems modelling and object modelling.

Information modelling techniques are typically directed at specifying the information classes relevant to an information system. A key example is entity–relationship–attribute diagramming, described in Chapter 3. Information systems modelling techniques are directed at specifying the behaviour of an information system. An example is the approach discussed in Chapter 4. Object analysis techniques are directed at specifying the object–space of an information system. They are in some ways similar to the ways of representing business knowledge as discussed in Chapter 3.

User-centric techniques are directed at supporting and developing an understanding of a work environment, and the potential ICT has in such settings. So they are primarily directed at elicitation and negotiation, and drift into the realm of activity systems. They include prototyping, scenarios and use cases. Prototyping involves building various representations, or early versions, of an information system, which are shown to clients and end-users in order to get feedback. Scenarios are informal descriptions of the use of ICT systems in a particular situation. Use cases are representations of the major actors and interactions with an information system.

12.5.4 Development tools

Information systems development tool: the hardware, software, data management and communication technology used to construct information systems

Development tools are the hardware, software, data management and communication technology used to construct information systems and to support the development process. They can be categorised using the layered model of an ICT system discussed in Chapter 6.

The four parts of a conventional ICT application used to be constructed using one tool, a high-level or third-generation programming language (3GL). A language such as COBOL was used to declare appropriate file structures (data subsystem), encode the necessary operations on files (transaction subsystem), validate data processed (rules subsystem) and manage the display screen for data entry and retrieval (interface subsystem). However, over the last couple of decades there has been a tendency to use specialised tools for one or more different layers. For instance, graphical user interface tools have developed as a means of constructing sophisticated user interfaces. Fourth-generation languages have developed as a means of coding business rules and application logic. Transaction processing systems have developed to enable high throughput of transactions. Database management systems have developed as sophisticated tools for managing multi-user access to stored data.

Communications are enabled by a vast range of software supporting local area and wide area communications.

An application server provides most of the functionality detailed in the definition of an ICT system in Chapter 6. Since application servers are a major part of the ICT infrastructure of organisations, interest has grown in the use of open source development tools to construct and maintain them (Fitzgerald, 2006). Open source software is software for which the source code is available under licence or some other arrangement whereby users are permitted to use, change, and improve the software, and redistribute it in modified or unmodified form. It is often developed in a public, collaborative manner. The main advantages of using open source software for development purposes are its low cost and the high degree of control it provides to the developer.

The acronym LAMP is used for a commonly available and much-used stack of open source software, which offers most of the functionality required to build and maintain application servers. It consists of:

- the operating system Linux
- the Web server software Apache
- the MySQL DBMS
- the PHP, Perl or Python programming languages.

Information systems development is an activity system. Most activity systems need information systems to support them, and the development process is no different. Also, ICT has been used to help automate aspects of the development process. This area is frequently known as computer-aided software engineering (CASE) or computer aided information systems engineering (CAISE). CAISE is a logical consequence of a recursive view of information systems development. It has stimulated the view that information systems development, considered as an activity system with its associated information system, should be subject to and benefit from the same sorts of automation as everyday information systems.

CAISE is therefore based on a particular model of the information systems development process. In this model, the development process is seen as a set of activities operating on objects to produce other objects. The objects manipulated by these activities can be documents, diagrams, file structures or even programs. Similarly, the activities involved may be relatively formal (for instance, compile a program) or informal (for example, obtain a user's requirements). It is not surprising therefore that the linear model of information systems development and the development methods associated with it are particularly suited to the application of CAISE. However, in recent times many CAISE tools have been adapted to handle object-oriented methods as well as agile development approaches.

A distinction is normally made between back-end CAISE tools, front-end CAISE tools and integrated CAISE tools. Front-end CAISE tools are generally directed at the analysis and design stages of information systems development. Back-end CAISE tools are directed at the construction, implementation, testing and maintenance stages of information systems development. Integrated CAISE tools, sometimes known as integrated development environments, offer assistance at all the stages of information systems development; they normally work in association with an integrated data repository which models the developing information system at various stages of development.

RECAP: The process of information systems development consists of the generic phases of conception, analysis, design, construction, implementation and maintenance. A development information system is essential to ensure the effective and efficient operation of the activity system that is the development process. Development is normally organised in projects. A development project is any concerted effort to develop an information system. To undertake any development effort the information systems developer needs a toolkit. This consists of methods, techniques and tools for supporting the activities of the development process.

REFLECT: What do you think are the advantages for developers of using open source development tools for development work? What are likely disadvantages?

12.6 Conception

Conception: That part of the development process devoted to assessing the investment potential and feasibility of systems

Conception is the first phase in the development process. It involves four major sets of activities: producing the key business case for an information system (strategic evaluation); estimating the degree of risk associated with an information systems project; considering the feasibility of the information system project in terms of organisational resources; and identifying stakeholders and their likely impact on the project. A project that passes the strategic evaluation, risk analysis, feasibility and stakeholder exercises moves on to the process of systems analysis. This is illustrated in Figure 12.7.

12.6.1 Developing a business case

 key skill

Developing a business case for a proposed information system is a part of strategic evaluation (see Chapter 9). This form of evaluation involves assessing or appraising an information system investment in terms of its potential for delivering benefit against estimated costs (see Table 12.1).

 IV

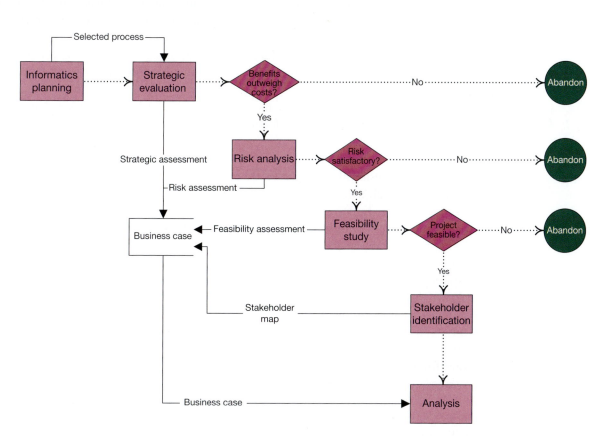

Figure 12.7 *The process of systems conception*

Table 12.1 *Types of costs and benefits associated with information systems*

	Costs	Benefits
Tangible	Hardware costs	Staff savings
Intangible	Wider organisational costs	Increased customer satisfaction

Business case: the case made for the utility of an information system

Information system projects that do not offer an appropriate level of benefit for the organisation are normally rejected. Those projects that have a reasonably substantial **business case** are subjected to some form of risk assessment and feasibility study.

There are two types of costs associated with information system projects: tangible or visible costs, and intangible or invisible costs. Tangible costs are frequently referred to as visible costs because they are reasonably straightforward to measure. Intangible costs are frequently referred to as invisible costs because most organisations experience difficulty in measuring them.

Information system projects normally incur the following costs: hardware, software, installation, environmental, running, maintenance, security, networking, training and wider organisational costs (see Chapter 11). These must be taken into account over the entire useful life of an information system, not just during its development. Organisations often forget that deciding to introduce an information system means a long-term commitment to paying for its operation and maintenance.

Information system benefits consist of the value that an organisation gains from having an information system. These too are both tangible and intangible. Often the project objective is to gain tangible benefits, such as reducing staff count or increasing productivity (see Chapter 9). Tangible benefits are generally associated with issues of organisational efficiency. More recently, people have started to argue that intangible benefits, such as increasing customer satisfaction or building better links with suppliers, are just as relevant in investment decisions. Intangible benefits are generally concerned with issues of organisational effectiveness.

The classic direct benefits associated with information systems include the ability to handle a greater volume of information, getting information more quickly, increased accuracy of information, better quality information, more useful information, more relevant information, more secure information, the ability to use more information and use it more flexibly (see Chapter 4). Indirectly or intangibly, information systems influence features of the activity system they serve, with benefits that can include increased levels of work and productivity, increased work satisfaction, more effective working and providing a more reliable service to customers (see Chapter 9).

Cost–benefit analysis is critical to assessing whether an information system is likely to be a worthwhile investment. The investment can be justified in terms of efficiency gains such as cost savings, effectiveness gains such as better customer relations, or obtaining strategic advantage such as business growth. Most of these benefits are concerned with the utility of the system, that is, its impact on organisational activity (see Chapter 9).

Most of the established techniques for evaluating information system investments focus on tangible costs and benefits, and are directed primarily at assessing efficiency gains. Two of the most popular are return on investment and payback period. Most practitioners still seem to rely mainly on one or the other of these hard evaluation techniques.

The return on investment (RoI) associated with a project is calculated using the equation RoI = average (annual net income/annual investment amount). So the calculation needs an estimate of the income (that is, the tangible benefit) likely to come from the introduction of the information system, and the costs associated with it, over a defined future period.

Table 12.2 shows an example. It assumes it will take two years to get the system up and running, that the development costs will be £300,000 and that the life of the project is ten years.

DID YOU KNOW? A typical investment in ICT costs from 5% to 10% of the yearly turnover of a company.

Information economics:
Information Economics
attempts to include the
evaluation of intangible as
well as tangible benefits into
the process of IS evaluation

Information economics (Parker et al., 1988) tries to improve on these standard methods by allowing for intangible as well as tangible benefits. It does this by assessing feasibility in the business domain and viability in the technological domain. It uses an extended form of RoI which includes both traditional cost–benefit analysis and a number of value assessments: value linking, value accelerating, value restructuring and innovation valuation.

Table 12.2 An example of a RoI calculation

Year	Income	Investment	Income/investment
1	£0	£200,000	0
2	£0	£100,000	0
3	£50,000	£10,000	5
4	£300,000	£10,000	30
5	£500,000	£10,000	50
6	£600,000	£11,000	55
7	£600,000	£11,000	55
8	£600,000	£12,000	50
9	£600,000	£12,000	50
10	£500,000	£13,000	38
11	£400,000	£13,000	31
12	£300,000	£14,000	21

RoI = Average (annual net income/annual investment amount) = 32

Value linking and value accelerating are attempts to estimate the ripple effect of technology change on the organisation. Value restructuring is an attempt to assess the increase in productivity that arises from the introduction of information systems. At a practical level, information economics involves completing a scorecard for each information system and computing the weighted score as an indication of the value of the system to the organisation. Table 12.3 shows an example.

On this scorecard, RoI is a traditional return on investment calculation. Strategic match is the degree to which the system matches the strategy of the organisation. Competitive advantage is the degree to which the system is expected to deliver advantage for the company. Management information support is the degree to which management receives the information it requires. Competitive response is the degree to which the system will enable the organisation to react quickly to its environment, and organisational risk is that associated with developing the information system. Strategic information systems architecture is an assessment of the degree to which the system matches the architecture (that is, the infrastructure) for information systems in the organisation. Domain, or definitional, uncertainty is the degree to which requirements for the information system remain uncertain, while technical uncertainty corresponds to the number of technical imponderables in the project. Finally, information systems infrastructure risk is the degree to which the system might adversely affect the information systems infrastructure.

Some columns are labelled as '+', these items positively contribute to value so their scores are positive. Other columns are labelled '-', representing items that will negatively contribute to value and which should be subtracted from the score. Note also that each of the factors on the scorecard can be weighted. This allows the evaluator to indicate the importance of each factor

IV

> **REFLECT:** Many organisations now use portfolio management in considering the business case for information systems development. In other words, a range of possible projects are considered together and evaluated for their overall impact on the information systems infrastructure. Why do you think this approach is important?

Table 12.3 An example of information economics

Evaluator	Business domain						Technology domain				
	Return on investment	Strategic match	Competitive advantage	Management information support	Competitive response	Organisational risk	Strategic information systems architecture	Domain uncertainty	Technical uncertainty	Information systems infrastructure risk	
	+	+	+	+	+	−	+	−	−	−	
Business domain											
Technology domain											Weighted score
Weighted value											

to a particular project. In one project, strategic match might be critically important and weighted as 10, but for another project, perhaps to produce a more operationally based or support information system, this factor may be judged to be of low importance and weighted as 4.

12.6.2 Risk analysis

Information economics includes specific reference to the concept of risk. Perhaps because information systems failure appears commonplace (see Chapter 9), risk and risk assessment play a large part in research and discussion on software engineering and information systems development.

Risk is clearly involved in all information system projects. It can be defined as a negative outcome that has a known or estimated probability of occurring, based on experience or theory. Most people think of information system failure as the big risk but, as we have seen, this is a relative and not an absolute concept. Emphasising the relationship between stakeholders and risk, Wilcocks and Margetts (1994) maintain that '*risk of a negative outcome only becomes a salient problem when the outcome is relevant to stakeholder concerns and interests. Different settings and stakeholders will see different outcomes as salient.*'

Risk analysis: the identification, estimation and assessment of risk

Risk analysis involves:

- identification: generating a checklist of risks for a particular project
- estimation: assessing the likelihood or probability of a risk occurring, and determining its likely impact
- assessment: prioritising risks and planning how to avoid or monitor them.

Researchers have developed several frameworks which can be used to analyse risks. For instance, Cash, McFarlan and McKeney (1992) suggest that at least three important dimensions influence the risk of a project: project size, experience with the technology, project structure. In general, the smaller the project, the more experienced staff are and the more structured a project is, the less the risk associated with it:

- Project size can be defined in a number of ways, such as the level of investment needed or, just as important, to assess how many stakeholders will be affected by a project (see below).
- In general, the more experience the organisation has with the proposed technology, the less risk there is. This clearly relates to the skill and experience of developers. It also applies to the prior experience of various stakeholder groups in using or being aware of particular technologies.
- Generally, the more highly structured the project, the less risk is likely to be associated with it. If the project has clearly established and uncontroversial goals, it is likely to succeed. If stakeholder groups have not agreed on its goals, it is likely to fail.

12.6.3 Feasibility study

Feasibility study: that part of systems conception concerned with assessing the feasibility of developing an information system

A **feasibility study** can be considered as part of systems conception, or the first activity in the systems analysis process. This is an attempt to determine whether an information system is achievable given organisational resources and constraints. In order to assess the feasibility of an information system project, the assessor needs an initial idea of its functionality, usability and utility. An initial scope for the information system is then compared with the existing informatics infrastructure, to see whether the available hardware, software, data storage and communication infrastructure could handle it. Another aspect of feasibility is the development demand, the assessor needs to consider what resources will be needed in development and whether they will be available. Ideally the feasibility study will assess a number of alternative solutions to the development problem, such as whether bespoke or package development is preferable.

12.6.4 Stakeholder identification

Stakeholder identification: identifying the group of people to which an information system is relevant

Chapter 2 defined a stakeholder as any group in or outside an organisation that has a vested interest in an organisational system. Stakeholder groups are likely to affect the trajectory and consequent success or failure of an information system (see Chapter 9). It is therefore important to identify them at the start of a project and make sure they are suitably involved.

One useful technique is to take the major types of stakeholder group defined in Chapter 9 and use a responsibility assignment (RACI) matrix. This considers the responsibilities of various roles or resources in delivering activities in a project, or operating a process. It is particularly useful when projects and/or processes cross functional or departmental boundaries. Usually between four and seven responsibilities are assessed. These are the ones normally important to an information system project:

- A role is responsible (R) for the performance of an activity if the role-holder has to engage in work to complete the activity.
- A role is accountable (A) if the person is ultimately answerable for the correct and thorough completion of an activity. Someone in this role is therefore normally expected to sign off the activity before it becomes effective.
- A role is consulted (C) if it is necessary to seek its opinion on the exercise of some activity. In other words, there needs to be two-way communication with people fulfilling this type of role.
- A role is informed (I) if it needs to be kept informed of the progress or performance of some activity. In other words, there needs to be one-way communication with people fulfilling this type of role.

Clearly, responsibilities will vary depending on the shape of a particular project. Generally however, producers tend to have responsibility for the various activities of development work, clients are accountable for such work and representatives of end-users should be consulted on the shape of an information system, as illustrated in Table 12.4.

Table 12.4 *A high-level template for stakeholder identification and involvement*

	Producer	Client	End-user	Partner	Customer	Supplier
Conception	Responsible	Accountable	Consulted	Informed	Informed	Informed
Analysis	Responsible	Accountable	Consulted	Informed	Informed	Informed
Design	Responsible	Accountable	Consulted	Informed	Informed	Informed
Construction	Responsible	Accountable	Consulted	Informed	Informed	Informed
Implementation	Responsible	Accountable	Consulted	Informed	Informed	Informed
Maintenance	Responsible	Accountable	Consulted	Informed	Informed	Informed

12.7 Analysis

> Understanding and managing IT risks **IS2010**

Any system can be analysed. Here the term systems analysis is used to apply to the analysis of two types of system, ICT and activity. They should ideally be analysed in parallel. Systems analysis in information systems development is a form of sociotechnical analysis, and is normally conducted by specialists known as systems analysts.

Analysis: that part of the development process devoted to eliciting and representing the requirements for systems

Analysis can start by documenting current ICT systems and current activity systems, and will probably also involve the analysis of new requirements for each system.

The analysis of activity systems will receive inputs from the process of business or organisational analysis (see Chapter 2), in the sense that a process suitable for redesign is likely to have been identified. The analysis of ICT systems will receive inputs from the process of systems conception. The entire process of analysis provides outputs to the process of systems design, and is illustrated in Figure 12.8.

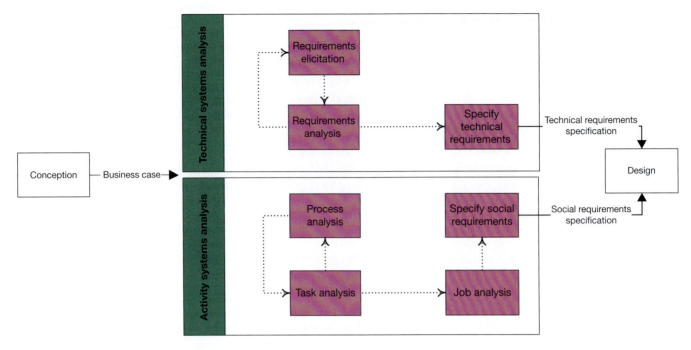

Figure 12.8 *The process of systems analysis*

12.7.1 ICT systems analysis

ICT systems analysis involves three primary and inter-related activities:

Requirements elicitation:
the process of identifying requirements for the system from stakeholder groups

- **Requirements elicitation** is the process of identifying requirements for the system from stakeholder groups.
- Requirements analysis involves negotiating and agreeing requirements with the various stakeholders.
- Requirements specification involves representing requirements using various modelling approaches.

One of the first things that must be done in any information systems project is to identify the relevant stakeholders (see above). For developing effective requirements, three types of stakeholder are important. First, clients normally set the key organisation objectives for the ICT system, particularly in terms of utility. Second, end-users are particularly important for setting the key functionality and usability requirements for an information system. Third, external stakeholders such as customers may be important in setting objectives for assessing the worth of the activity supported by the ICT system.

A requirement is any desired feature of an information system. It is sometimes thought that these are unproblematic, in the sense that it is not that difficult to find out from the stakeholder community what they want. However, as was argued in Chapter 9, requirements can vary depending on the stakeholder group. They are not objective, in the sense that they will be the same for everyone; they are relative to a particular stakeholder's perspective or worldview (see Chapter 2). Different stakeholders' requirements might conflict. Requirements analysis therefore involves attempting to achieve an inter-subjective agreement between stakeholder groups on their requirements. Requirements must be frozen at some point in order to construct an ICT system – an artefact – but they are likely to change over time. Part of the reason for the maintenance of systems is that requirements change, and organisations should plan for this.

A distinction between the functional and non-functional requirements of any ICT system is frequently made. Functional requirements are expected features of an information system. Non-functional requirements are constraints set on the systems development project. The set of functional and non-functional requirements establishes the scope of the information system.

Requirements elicitation is the process of identifying requirements. It is sometimes called requirements capture, but this term does not really reflect the issues just outlined. Requirements cannot be captured, since they are inter-subjective constructs; they have to be established via a process of negotiation.

The techniques for requirements elicitation include interviews, observation, documentary analysis, workshops, prototyping and ethnography.

- Interviews are the most commonly used technique. These are either formal or informal discussions with representatives of key stakeholder groups. Formal interviews are structured conversations in which questions are determined beforehand. Informal interviews are a form of discussion in which the questions are formulated within the flow of the interview itself.

- Interviews are often used together with other elicitation techniques such as observation. Observation usually involves being present in work settings and recording the detailed work behaviour of people.

- Documents are a valuable resource in most organisations. They are particularly important, for instance, in indicating data that needs to be stored in an information system and the type of reports that need to be generated from it. This suggests the importance of documentary analysis to requirements elicitation.

- Workshops are sessions in which developers and representatives of stakeholder groups get together in a structured situation. They provide controlled environments for the negotiation of requirements, so are often known as joint requirements planning workshops.

- Stakeholder groups might not be able to formulate what they require until they see a representation of what is planned. Prototyping involves building early versions of particular parts of a system to demonstrate to stakeholder representatives, in order to obtain their feedback.

Any one elicitation technique gives only a partial picture of the requirements space. Frequently, what people describe in interviews only partly reveals how they go about their everyday work. So it is important to triangulate, using a number of techniques in combination. The analyst might, for example, use interviews together with an elicitation technique such as observation, to check that what people say they do, they actually do in practice.

> **REFLECT:** Of the range of requirements elicitation techniques, which do you think is the most commonly used in practice, and why?

Requirements specification: representing the requirements established in the requirements elicitation process

Use case: a use case model provides a high-level description of major user interactions with some information system

Scenario: a narrative description of what people do and experience as they try to make use of computer systems and applications

Requirements specification is representing the requirements established in the requirements elicitation process. It conventionally involves a form of intermediate representation, notation for representing requirements that is frequently graphical, sometimes textual and occasionally mathematical.

Two user-centric requirements elicitation techniques, **use cases** and **scenarios**, are particularly relevant to specifying the high-level scope of the use context of an information system. Often these are used in a development workshop for negotiating requirements. The requirements are then specified in more detail using developer-centric techniques.

A use case model provides a high-level description of major user interactions with an information system. It uses two constructs, actors and use cases. An actor within this technique is any person, organisation or system that interacts with an information system. A use case is a delimited set of activities that collectively form an important element of the functionality of the system.

Figure 12.9 is a simple use case model for an automatic teller machine (ATM) system. There are three main actors: bank customers, ATM operators and back-end banking

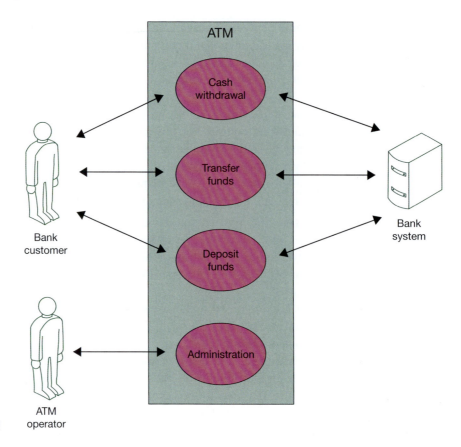

Figure 12.9 A use case model

systems. Four main use cases are defined: withdrawing cash from the ATM (cash withdrawal), transferring funds between bank accounts (transfer funds), depositing funds in bank accounts (deposit funds), and administering the ATM (administration). The first three use cases are generic interactions between customers and banking systems. The last use case is a specialised function provided for technicians given the task of maintaining the operation of the machine.

Each use case in a use case model can be specified in more detail as a scenario. Scenarios are described by Carroll (1995) as '*a narrative description of what people do and experience as they try to make use of computer systems and applications*'. Other definitions differ from this, but there are some common elements. Scenarios normally consist of key situations or episodes in the activity of people working with computers. The emphasis in a scenario is on concrete representation of use rather than abstraction of use. The focus is on specific instances of use in a work context. Scenarios are therefore a middle-level abstraction between the formality of an ICT system specification and the informality of everyday discussions between developers and users, so they tend to provide more of a user-centric than a developer-centric representation.

This is a short scenario describing the use of a company database for marketing purposes:

> An advert is placed in the local newspaper for short training courses. A person from a company phones up with an enquiry but is not in the company database. Operator needs to record their details while on the phone. Enter company details including interests as tags. Company details copied across to contact form. Enter contact details. Tag with interest in courses on personal computing. Place memo against contact – posting a letter. Back to to-do list. Removing items from to-do list.

This brings out the key elements of interaction with the data entry screens of this company's intended information system.

12.7.2 Activity systems analysis

In most information systems projects it is important to analyse the larger context of activity surrounding an ICT system. At the macro level this may involve some form of organisational analysis (see Chapter 2). At the micro level it focuses on issues such as process analysis, task analysis and job analysis.

An activity system or organisational process can be decomposed into a set of activities. Each activity, in turn, can be decomposed into a set of tasks and subtasks. So there is a hierarchy of processes, activities and tasks which can, in principle, be specified for a given activity system.

Consider the simple example of an ATM again. Using the ATM is a major element of the activity system of a high-street bank. The process of using an ATM can be considered as a set of activities or use cases, as in the scenario above. Each activity can in turn be decomposed into tasks, which in this example might be inserting a debit or credit card, entering a personal identifier number (PIN), selecting/entering an amount, selecting a withdrawal slip, receiving cash, receiving the returned card, and receiving the withdrawal slip.

A variant of task analysis, particularly relevant to collaboration among teams, is the analysis of work flow. This involves determining ways in which ICT can be used to support collaborative work and improve the effectiveness of collaboration. A key feature of this activity is mapping existing work flow. This has many similarities with the idea of process modelling as considered in Chapter 2.

Job analysis: involves the analysis of the content and relationships of current jobs in terms of both organisational and individual objectives

Job analysis involves analysing the content and relationships of current jobs in terms of both organisational and individual objectives. Organisations generally have objectives such as improving the efficiency and/or effectiveness of work. Individuals also generally have objectives, such as increasing their levels of fulfilment and job satisfaction.

Traditional approaches to analysing activity systems break them down into various levels of activities and tasks, which are then closely studied using tangible performance measures. Increasing specialisation and segmentation of tasks is seen as the primary way of achieving organisational objectives, but this often conflicts with individual objectives. Heavy specialisation can lead to substantial deskilling of the workforce, and people tend to find this unfulfilling and demotivating. It also leads to a decreasing level of flexibility.

Ideally, requirements are generated for new work systems as well as new technical systems. The aim is to achieve an optimal balance between social and technical objectives.

So information systems design has to be focused not only on issues of efficacy, efficiency and effectiveness, but also focus on the ethics of designing particular forms of activity for people. For instance, many researchers have looked at issues of job satisfaction, and it is fairly clear what features characterise jobs that give workers satisfaction. People like jobs that allow ample opportunity for them to exercise their skills and extend them through learning. They like it if it is easy to understand how their work fits into the organisation, and if their work is explicitly valued. Also, the more people can control their own work, the higher their levels of satisfaction. Jobs supply satisfaction if they include collaboration and communication with others, and include a mix of routine and new demands. People also appreciate control over which new demands to accept, and jobs that do not interfere with their ability to participate in family and community life.

DID YOU KNOW? Many ICTs are not appropriate for particular activity systems. For example, a few years ago a major investment bank planned to introduce voice recognition software on its trading floor. It reasoned that the activities of buying and selling stocks and shares on the trading floor seemed to consist primarily of verbal communication between traders, so a trading information system should be able to automatically track trades using voice recognition software. However, when the analysts probed deeper, they realised that traders tended to communicate in single words (such as yes or no) or even single syllables (such as uh!). These terse verbal communications were accompanied by non-verbal cues such as holding up a number of fingers to signal the volume of a trade. Not surprisingly, the analysts decided that the voice recognition system would not work in this situation.

12.8   Design

Design: that part of the development process devoted to designing the functionality of systems

Design can be conducted on any system, but systems design is used here to refer to the design of ICT systems and activity systems. As with analysis, such systems should ideally be designed in parallel, so information systems design is a form of sociotechnical design.

Design is planning the shape of something to meet requirements established by analysis. It involves a reflective conversation with the situation, considering requirements and constraints, and the selection from among design alternatives. Design benefits from the participation of system stakeholders (see Chapter 9).

Information systems design produces a system specification that is the major input into systems construction. This system specification acts as a blueprint for construction work. This is illustrated in Figure 12.10.

The design of information systems and the activity systems within which they exist is related in a cycle. Information systems are normally built as a reflection of organisational work, since designing an information system involves investigating and defining organisational work. Introducing and using an information system may cause changes to organisational work. The introduction of ICT is normally an attempt to improve organisational work in some way, but it can decrease organisational effectiveness if not handled carefully (see Chapter 9).

An example of nursing in general hospitals should help show the interdependence of activity and information systems. There are three basic models of activity system appropriate for organising nursing on a hospital ward:

- *Round nursing* is very much task oriented. Each nurse has responsibility for one task on the ward. For example, one nurse is responsible for giving all patients their prescribed medicines.

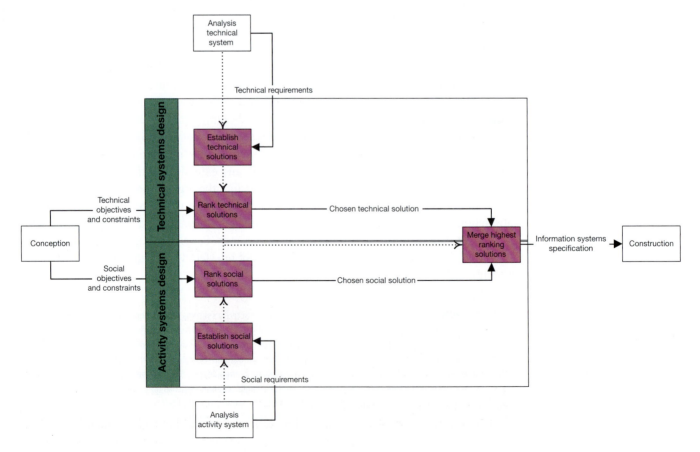

Figure 12.10 *The systems design process*

- *Primary care* is patient oriented. One nurse has the responsibility for carrying out all the tasks associated with one patient. Usually each nurse is responsible for a small group of patients. In primary care, for instance, one nurse is likely to be responsible for giving all medicines to their group of patients.
- *Group nursing* is a mixture of the above. A group of nurses have the responsibility for carrying out several tasks, but only for one group of patients. In group nursing, for instance, one nurse may be given the responsibility for distributing regular medicines while all nurses give out additional medicines according to patient need.

Each of these nursing activity systems demands a substantially different information system. Figure 12.11 helps show this by drawing three information models for the three different forms of activity system. In round nursing there is a need to communicate about medical care, such as which medicines have been given to which patients, but there is little need to communicate about the coordination of tasks between nurses. In contrast, within primary care there is very little need to communicate about medical care between nurses, but there is a need to know which nurses care for which patients. In group nursing there is need to exchange both medical data and the data necessary to the effective coordination of nursing tasks. This last form of activity system therefore demands the most complex information system to support its work.

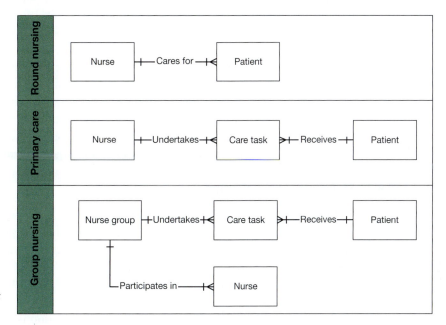

Figure 12.11 Information models corresponding to distinct activity systems for nursing

12.8.1 Sociotechnical design

Figure 12.10 is an attempt to represent the essence of sociotechnical design in the context of informatics work. It is based on three major approaches in this area.

Sociotechnical design: the parallel design of both technical and social systems

The work of the late Enid Mumford (1983) provides one of the most coherent accounts of how to do **sociotechnical design** in an informatics context. She developed a method from her decades of work on the effective design of sociotechnical systems called ETHICS (Effective Technical and Human Implementation of Computer Systems). The objective of ETHICS is to design a new form of work organisation with the dual objectives of improving job satisfaction (the social system) and work efficiency (the technical system) (Mumford, 2006). Other approaches in the same vein include the Multiview method (Avison et al., 1998) and soft systems methodology (Checkland, 1999).

Analysis involves establishing both technical requirements (the shape of the intended ICT system) and social requirements (the shape of the intended activity system). These requirements should make a number of design solutions feasible in both the technical and social areas. These can then be assessed and ranked using the objectives and constraints established in the systems conception process. The highest-ranking technical solution is merged with the highest-ranking social solution, and this is then developed into a full specification for the information system.

Mumford provides a case study of a customer orders and accounts system which was analysed by the ETHICS approach, leading to the introduction of a new social and technical system. Although this case was conducted in the 1980s, it still illustrates the essential principles of the sociotechnical approach.

The basic technical system involved orders clerks filling out order forms, accounts clerks updating customer ledgers and any problems being resolved by passing around lots of paper. In the social system there was a clear distinction between orders clerks and accounts clerks, with each accounts clerk working across a number of different customer accounts. Problems were resolved by two senior clerks.

The motivations for change were both technical and social. Examples of technical problems were orders incorrectly filled out, customer ledgers incorrectly updated and slow methods of resolving problems. Examples of social problems were high absenteeism, high staff turnover and some industrial vandalism.

Workers were asked to fill in a job satisfaction questionnaire, and this showed that they had low job satisfaction as a result of piecework, lack of seeing the overall picture, individual isolation, low status and poor prospects for advancement. What they wanted from the redesign was more responsibility, group working, more important work and better opportunities for advancement.

After the study was complete a new work and technical system was put in place. The technical system involved online input of orders, batch update of a central database and regular reports output from the ICT system. The social system was changed to small work groups of five clerks, with each work group handling orders and accounts for a group of customers. The group handled customer problems thrown up by printouts. When the new system was evaluated later, the assessors found increased rates of job satisfaction and increased productivity.

12.8.2   Stakeholder participation

As this example demonstrates, systems design benefits from forms of stakeholder participation. End-users are probably the most significant stakeholder group to involve in a development project. Some benefits of participation include a closer match between the information system and the requirements of stakeholders, a closer match between the information system and the activity system, and a greater commitment of stakeholders to the new sociotechnical system.

However, Hirschheim (1983) maintains that participation is not the same as involvement. All information system projects have some degree of stakeholder involvement, if only at the implementation phase, but only some are participatively developed. The major differences between user involvement and user participation relate to decision-making power. In user involvement the users are normally given a degree of power over decisions on the shape of the information system. In user participation that power is extended to decisions about social and job considerations.

The forms of participation can be categorised using the dimensions of level of participation and type of participation. Mumford distinguished between three different levels of user participation in systems design. In consultative participation, decision-making is still in the hands of systems analysts and systems designers, but staff at every level are consulted. With representative participation, a design group is formed made up of representatives of all grades of staff plus systems analysts. The representatives are selected by management. In consensus participation, a design group is formed as in representative participation, but representatives are elected by staff and given the responsibility to communicate group decisions back to staff.

REFLECT: It is probably true that most development projects in commercial organisations involve stakeholders but few allow participation as described above. Why do you think this is?

There is also a distinction between intensive and phased modes of participation. In intensive mode stakeholder representatives are assigned for the entire duration of the project, so they form a permanent part of the development team. In phased participation stakeholders are invited to review the development effort at regular intervals. Intensive participation tends to be used more frequently on iterative development projects, whereas phased participation is typically characteristic of linear development projects.

12.8.3 The components of design

Logical design: the attempt to specify the design of an ICT system independent of any implementation detail

Physical design: the design of the implementation of a system, a blueprint for its construction.

Another useful distinction is between two levels of ICT systems design. **Logical design** is the attempt to specify the design of an ICT system independent of any implementation detail. **Physical design** is the design of the implementation of a system, a blueprint for its construction.

Logical design involves activities such as input design, output design, processing design, the design of key data structures, the design of a communication framework and the design of disaster recovery and security management. Physical design involves activities such as detailing hardware devices needed, describing the shape of programs, detailing the forms of communication hardware and software, designing database systems and designing the user interface.

Activity systems consist of people and the activities or procedures they perform. Three inter-related activities are part of activity systems design. Job design has the aim of balancing the needs of job satisfaction with work efficiency. Team design has the aim of establishing teams with clear structures of authority and control. Procedure design involves detailing established patterns of work.

In most commercial organisations, managerial groups usually determine the shape of designed activity systems. McGregor (1960) identified two distinct worldviews (Chapter 2) that influence the way in which managers think about workers, and so influence the design of activity systems. He called them theory X and theory Y. According to theory X, the average person dislikes work and avoids it wherever possible, they avoid responsibility and have little ambition. According to theory Y, physical and mental effort are important and natural human functions. If humans are committed to objectives they will exercise self-direction and self-control. The capacity to exercise imagination, ingenuity and creativity is widely distributed in the population.

Using theory X, activity systems are designed with the clear intention of monitoring the workforce and controlling their behaviour through coercion. The objective is to provide sufficient information to management to enable them to exercise close control. Using theory Y, activity systems are designed to encourage ingenuity and creativity. Information systems are there to encourage cooperation and collaboration among the workforce in the achievement of objectives.

Adopting a theory Y perspective, a number of strategies can be used in the design of activity systems to increase levels of job satisfaction:

- Job rotation involves increasing variety and learning opportunities for the workforce. It also has substantial benefits in improving organisational flexibility.
- Job enlargement involves combining a number of tasks, and offers the potential of creating more complete, and hence more meaningful, jobs.
- Job enrichment involves increasing the scope of a job and giving workers more responsibility for making decisions about their own work. The key aim is to improve the motivational aspect of work.
- Group working acts as an important source of support, encouragement and security for individual workers.

IV

12.9   Construction

Construction: that part of the development process devoted to building information systems

Systems construction is the actual process of building the information system. It follows on from systems design and is followed by systems implementation. This sequence is illustrated in Figure 12.12. Since an information system is a sociotechnical system, two parallel **construction** activities must take place: constructing the ICT system and constructing the activity system.

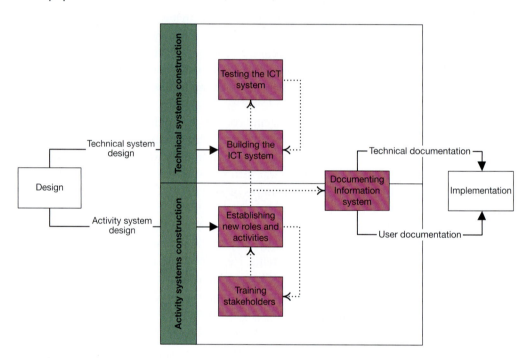

Figure 12.12 Systems construction

Testing: part of systems construction; ensuring that an information system is working effectively

Traditionally ICT system construction involves the three related processes of programming, **testing** and documentation. These activities differ depending on whether the development is based on bought packages or is bespoke.

12.9.1   ICT system construction

Building ICT systems normally involves constructing the four layers of the ICT systems model and its associated communication facilities. This means building the user interface (constructing data entry forms, menus and reports), building the business rules and application logic (specifying integrity constraints and elements of processing), building the transaction layer (specifying the major update functions for the system) and building the data management layer (creating the data structures for storing data).

Although historically the four parts of a conventional ICT application were built using one tool, a high-level or third-generation programming language (3GL), over the last couple of decades there has been a tendency to use a different, specialised tool for one or more layers.

There are variants to this tool-based approach to building ICT systems. Package development using software packages involves the inter-related activities of package selection and package tailoring (see below). Building with software components involves using pre-built software components to construct either the whole or part of an ICT system.

In the process of constructing the system various tests must be conducted to ensure that it is working effectively. Effectiveness is defined by specified functional requirements and non-functional requirements such as performance.

There are a number of distinct types of testing. Unit testing is testing individual programs or software modules. System testing tests an entire system as a unit. Volume testing involves testing the application with large amounts of data and use. At some point the system has to be assembled as a complete unit and testing conducted of all related systems together. This is known as integration testing. Finally, acceptance testing consists of conducting any tests required by the users, to ensure that the user community is satisfied with the system. Generally, these forms of testing are performed in sequence, and some of the testing may pass over into the implementation phase.

An ICT system needs to be documented to ensure that it can be used and that adequate information is provided to ensure effective maintenance of the system. Two major types of documentation are required. User documentation is a source of reference for users to turn to when puzzled about aspects of use. Systems or technical documentation describes the structure and behaviour of the ICT system for developers, particularly for use in maintenance (see below).

12.9.2 Package construction

Package construction involves a buy not build strategy, and blurs the traditional boundaries of systems construction and systems implementation. Typically, standard software modules for core business processes are combined with bespoke customisation to help the organisation differentiate itself and gain competitive advantage. Package implementation normally involves selecting software modules and then deciding on the profile of adoption throughout the company. At one end of the scale an organisation might choose to standardise modules across organisational functions; at the other end, it varies module adoption. Customisation normally involves programming configuration (tables) associated with each software module.

Enterprise package construction is subtly different from traditional package construction. In a traditional model, companies decide what they want in terms of functionality, usability and utility, choose a package to meet those needs closely and then rewrite large portions of the software to ensure that there is a close fit with organisational imperatives. The enterprise or mega-package model of development involves a change of emphasis. The organisation selects an enterprise resource planning (ERP) system, then adapts the enterprise to fit it. Some degree of customisation is possible, but the complexity of the system makes major modifications impractical. In this sense, mega-package procurement can be considered as another form of outsourcing information system development (see Chapter 10).

12.9.3 Activity system construction

Change management is the term for a structured approach to moving an organisation from a current state to a desired future state. How much change is involved will reflect the degree to which ICT is used to transform organisational processes. If the ICT system is to be used in an existing activity system, to support existing ways of doing things, change management will be restricted to training users thoroughly to use it. If it is used to supplant or automate existing human activities, or it transforms the activity system in a major way, the change management process will involve establishing new jobs and roles, organising teams and establishing new work procedures.

Take the example of the research information system mentioned previously. This system might be produced as a piece of bespoke development and designed to support existing ways of administering research outputs in the university. Change management in this case will involve training existing research administrators in the use of the new ICT system. But consider the case in which it is decided that the input of research outputs into the ICT system should no longer be the responsibility of administrators but instead should be done by academics themselves. This information system clearly involves automating certain administrative processes and supplanting the role of research administrators.

12.10 Implementation

Implementation: that part of the development process devoted to delivering the system into its context of use

The process of systems **implementation** (sometimes called systems delivery) follows on from systems construction. This involves delivering an information system into its context of use (see Chapter 9). Since an information system is a sociotechnical system, an ICT system and some form of activity system are implemented in parallel. Once a system is delivered into its context of use it will be subject to the processes of operation (see Chapter 11) and maintenance.

12.10.1 Types of systems implementation

Systems implementation involves both technical and social systems. Technical systems implementation means ensuring that the appropriate hardware, communications, software and data are in place. Social systems implementation involves ensuring that the appropriate users are identified, trained and supported in the use of the technology.

Systems implementation can take place in three major ways:

- *Direct conversion* is sometimes called Big Bang implementation. This is a confident approach in which the new system directly replaces the old system. There is no overlap between the implementation of the new system and the system it replaces.
- In *parallel implementation* two information systems, the old and the new, run in parallel for a while. This is a cautious approach in that, if there are problems with the new system, the organisation can revert to the old system until they are resolved. Eventually, the organisation should be happy enough with the new system for the old system to be terminated.
- *Hybrid implementation* introduces particular components in a phased manner as replacements, or pilots major modules of the system. It is an evolutionary approach in the sense that the impact of implementation is distributed more evenly over time than in direct conversion.

12.10.2 Technical systems implementation

Technical systems implementation involves the following activities, generally in some form of sequence:

- Software acquisition is the acquisition of operating systems, DBMS, and possibly packaged software.
- Hardware acquisition is the purchase of computers, peripheral devices and communication networks.
- If a new system replaces an old system, there needs to be a form of data transfer between the systems. Data may have to be prepared for the transfer. For greenfield systems certain data elements, such as reference data, will probably need to be prepared for entry into the system.
- Implementation involves the installation of hardware, software and entering data into the system.
- It also involves testing that the system works effectively as a complete configuration. Acceptance testing normally leads to a formal or informal sign-off of the system. This indicates some level of acceptance with the levels of performance the system provides.
- Finally there is introduction or delivery, and going live with the system in its context of use.

12.10.3 Activity systems implementation

As a minimum, social systems implementation involves activities such as team formation, training and user acceptance. User group formation involves forming the appropriate user groups for using the system. There will need to be user and operator training in work practices and procedures for use of the system. This can be done by the developers of the system or by a user representative who becomes expert in the use of the system then passes on this knowledge to other users. Finally, the system needs to be formally accepted by user groups. This involves some acceptance testing.

As part of any implementation a user document or manual is normally produced. This should act as a source of reference for the use of the system (see Chapter 9). Support is also usually provided in the form of a helpdesk or support service (see Chapter 11). This is a specialised service designed to answer any questions users may pose on the use of the system.

A system is not always unconditionally accepted by its user community. There is a lot of evidence of systems being resisted (see Chapter 9), so strategies for stakeholder management must be included, not just in the implementation process but across all phases of development.

REFLECT:
Implementation is probably one of the most critical stages at which an information system can fail. Why do you think this might be?

12.11 Maintenance

Maintenance: that part of the development process devoted to maintaining systems

Systems maintenance follows on from systems implementation. **Maintenance** is the process of making necessary changes to the structure of an information system. Maintenance activity can stimulate suggestions for new systems, so it can act as a key input into the process of systems conception and thus provide closure to the process of information systems development.

An organisation might decide to make changes to an information system for several reasons:

- Bugs may be present, errors which need to be corrected.
- Changes in processes. An organisation rarely stays still. It continually needs to make changes to its organisational processes to compete in its environment, so changes are likely to be required in the information systems supporting these processes.
- Requests for new functionality may come from organisational stakeholders. However closely they have been involved in the development process, when people start to use a system they will produce a whole range of requests for changes in the way it works.
- Technical problems may be experienced with current hardware and software. For instance, the hardware and software might be faulty, or fail to perform effectively on criteria such as response time. It will then need to be replaced or perhaps upgraded.
- Changes in the environment may be a cause of maintenance. An example is a change in government regulation, obliging the organisation to do something that the system design has not allowed for.

Maintenance activity is a core part of the work of most informatics departments. This is primarily because information systems are domain-dependent systems, in the sense that there is a necessary interdependence between the information system and the domain of activity within which it is placed. When an information system is introduced it might change the nature of the activity system and so the nature of the problem being solved. Just as the organisation adapts to it, the information system might need to adapt to changes in the organisation of activity.

There are four major types of maintenance activity:

- Perfective maintenance involves changes to the information system which improve it without affecting its functionality.

■ Adaptive maintenance consists of changes to the information system to provide a closer fit between it and its environment, the activity system.

■ Corrective maintenance involves corrections of previously unidentified system errors.

■ Preventive maintenance consists of changes aimed at improving a system's maintainability, such as documentation or improving flexibility.

Surveys of the cost of maintenance suggest that for old ICT systems (legacy systems), it can be as much as five times greater than the cost of development. Not surprisingly, maintenance costs are often a heavy component of the costs of supporting the informatics infrastructure, so an explicit plan and process for maintenance needs to be an inherent part of any informatics strategy (see Chapter 10).

> **DID YOU KNOW?** Over 50% of the activity of informatics departments can be involved with maintenance.

12.11.1 The process of systems maintenance

Systems maintenance is a stage of both the bespoke and package development life-cycle. It could be argued that tailoring a software package to the specific requirements of an organisation is a form of maintenance. Unfortunately, in many organisations systems maintenance is not seen as a valued activity by either developers or the organisation at large. Nor has it had much attention from academics and researchers (Burton Swanson, 1992).

Since maintenance is a significant activity for many organisations, it should be managed as a process. There are various ways in which this may be achieved. One strategy is to initiate specialist maintenance teams responsible for modifying, fixing and updating ICT systems. Reward structures can be created to reward good maintenance activity. Systems can be designed with maintenance in mind. Systems can also be designed to be as flexible as possible in terms of likely future changes. This is termed flexibility analysis (Fitzgerald, 2000). Organisations can plan for the upgrade of ageing systems onto new software, hardware and communication environments. This should be an essential part of any ICT strategy (see Chapter 10). Finally, effective configuration management is a necessary condition for effective maintenance; every ICT system **configuration** in the organisation must be documented as fully as possible.

> **REFLECT:** Why do you think maintenance activity is not typically seen as a desirable form of development work by developers?

Configuration: a version of some development product

12.11.2 Configuration management

Configuration management: the process of controlling the changes made to an information system over time

Configuration management is a key umbrella activity applied throughout the development process by the informatics service. It involves identifying changes to products of the development process, controlling the changes made to products, ensuring that the changes are properly made, and reporting the changes to others. The conception of configuration management in this section is thus a small part of the way in which configuration management is treated in ICT services management (see Chapter 11).

Products of the development process include programs, data structures and documentation. Each type of product may be subject to change at various points during the development process. For instance, changes might be made to requirements specifications during analysis or testing, and they need to be echoed in the development information system. This documentation forms the project repository, an organised collection of all output from the development process.

Configuration management overlaps with systems maintenance but is also distinct from it. Systems maintenance occurs after the system is delivered to the customer. Configuration management is a set of monitoring and control activities that begin with the start of a development project and terminate only when the system is taken out of operation. There is a clear overlap with the ICT services management discussed in Chapter 11.

Configuration management is an important element of quality assurance. This is a planned and systematic pattern of all the actions necessary to provide adequate confidence that a system conforms to established requirements. Quality assurance is a form of evaluation activity (see Chapter 9).

A configuration management process works with baselines established in the project repository. A baseline is a version of a development product that is formally reviewed and agreed upon. Any changes to a baseline involve formal change control procedures. A simplified configuration management process is illustrated in Figure 12.13. Any person wishing to make a change to a baseline accesses the product in the project repository. There should be controls in place to ensure that only authorised persons are allowed access to certain development products. Once changes have been made, the modified product is subject to a formal review. This considers such issues as the impact of the change on other aspects of the repository, and the suitability and validity of releasing the change into the project repository. If the change is sanctioned, the approved product is released into the project repository and forms the next baseline for development work.

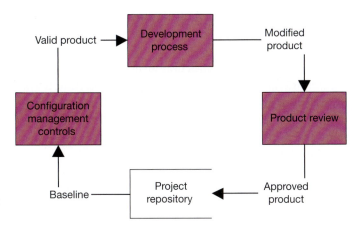

Figure 12.13 *The configuration management process*

FOCUS ON VALUE

Organisations continually need to adapt their informatics infrastructure in line with organisational change, so the development of new information systems is critical to organisational success. There needs to be an evaluation process before deciding which information systems to build. The business case for an information system is typically based on assessments of the weighting of tangible and intangible benefits against tangible and intangible costs. Deciding on what requirements to include in the design of an information system also needs a form of evaluation of options. Since information systems are sociotechnical systems they are not value-neutral. Values are embedded in the process of systems design.

12.12 Conclusion and key themes

As has been emphasised throughout this book, business organisations need to continually refresh their informatics infrastructure to remain competitive. They do this through the organisational process of information system development, whose activities include conception, analysis, design, construction, implementation and maintenance. A development information system is essential to ensure the effective and efficient operation of the activity system that is the development process.

Development is normally organised in projects. A development project is any concerted effort to develop an information system. The information systems developer needs a toolkit to carry out the development work, which consists of methods, techniques and tools for supporting the activities of the development process.

Conception follows on from informatics planning, and involves producing the key business case, analysing risk and assessing the feasibility of an information system project. Any business case, or strategic evaluation, of an information system considers information system costs and benefits, both tangible and intangible. Appraisal techniques such as payback period primarily assess tangible benefits. Risk analysis is the process of identifying risks, estimating their likelihood and planning for avoiding them. A feasibility study is an attempt to determine whether an information system is achievable given organisational resources and constraints.

Information system analysis involves two primary and inter-related activities: requirements elicitation and requirements representation. A requirement is any desired feature of an information system. Requirements are not objective phenomena since they may vary depending on the stakeholder group. Requirements elicitation is the process of identifying requirements, and requirements specification is concerned with their representation. Requirements elicitation involves working to find an inter-subjective agreement on stakeholder groups' requirements. Ideally, requirements are generated for new work systems as well as new technical systems. The aim is to achieve an optimal balance between social and technical objectives.

Information system design involves planning the shape of an ICT system to meet the requirements established in systems analysis. It also involves designing the activity system into which this technical artefact will be placed, so it is a form of sociotechnical systems design.

Information system construction involves the actual process of building the information system. Since an information system is a sociotechnical system, two parallel construction activities must take place: constructing the ICT system and constructing the activity system. Traditionally ICT system construction involves the three related processes of programming, testing and documentation. In contrast, package development involves customising a package to meet the requirements of an organisation.

Information system implementation involves delivering an information system into its context of use, and includes both technical and social systems implementation. Technical systems implementation covers software acquisition, hardware acquisition, data conversion, installation, testing and delivery. Social systems implementation involves user group formation, user training and user acceptance.

Information system maintenance is the process of making changes that are needed to an information system, it is a significant activity for organisations and should be planned for and managed by the informatics service. There are several types of maintenance: corrective, perfective, adaptive and preventative. Configuration management is an umbrella activity applied throughout the development process, and involves identifying changes to products of the development process, controlling the changes made to products, ensuring that the changes are made properly, and reporting the changes to others.

This chapter concludes the coverage of the substantive content of organisational informatics. Chapter 13 considers this content in terms of a body of knowledge relating to best practice. To help understand the relevance of this body of knowledge, a case study is used. This is one of the most widely discussed of all cases of information systems application, the London Ambulance Computer Aided Dispatch System.

12.13 Review test

1 The development process can be seen as a _____ system. Fill in the blank.

2 The development process relies on an _____ for effective performance. Fill in the blank.

3 Distinguish between the linear and iterative models of the development life-cycle. Write two sentences.

4 Place the phases of the information systems development life-cycle in the correct sequence. Mark the first phase with a 1 and so on.
   ☐ Maintenance
   ☐ Design
   ☐ Analysis
   ☐ Construction
   ☐ Conception
   ☐ Implementation

5 Information systems are built either as bespoke products or tailored from software _____. Fill in the blank.

6 A developer's toolkit consists of _____, techniques and tools. Fill in the blank.

7 _____ are particular approaches to supporting the processes of systems analysis, systems design and systems construction. Fill in the blank.

8 Conception is the phase in which the key business case is developed, risk analysed and the feasibility of an information system assessed. True or false?
☐ True
☐ False

9 Distinguish between information system costs and information system benefits. Write two sentences.

10 Intangible costs are frequently referred to as visible costs because they are reasonably straightforward to measure. True or false?
☐ True
☐ False

11 The return on investment (RoI) associated with an information systems project is calculated using which equation? Select the most appropriate one.
☐ average (annual gross income / annual investment amount)
☐ average (annual net income / annual investment amount)
☐ average (annual net income / annual expenditure)

12 Payback = investment − cumulative benefit (cash inflow). True or false?
☐ True
☐ False

13 Requirements _____ is that process devoted to the identification of requirements. Fill in the blank.

14 Requirements elicitation techniques include: Select all that are appropriate.
☐ Interviews
☐ Scenarios
☐ Observation
☐ Use cases
☐ Prototyping
☐ Workshops

15 Match the type of analysis technique with the appropriate definition. Pair each lettered entry with the corresponding numbered entry.

a. Developer-centric   **1.** Directed at supporting the development of understanding of a work environment and the potentialities of information technology in this setting.

b. User-centric   **2.** Designed particularly for enabling developers to understand, document and communicate IS problems to other developers.

16 A use case model provides a high-level description of major user interactions with an information system. True or false?
☐ True
☐ False

17 Distinguish between a theory X and theory Y perspective on human behaviour. Write two sentences.

18 What are the major benefits of stakeholder participation in analysis and design work? Write two sentences.

19 System construction involves the three related processes of programming, testing and documentation. True or false?
☐ True
☐ False

20 Match the type of testing to the correct definition. Pair each lettered entry with the corresponding numbered entry.

a. Unit testing   **1.** Testing an entire system as a unit.

b. System testing   **2.** Testing individual programs or software modules

c. Integration testing   **3.** Testing the acceptance of a system with users.

d. Acceptance testing   **4.** At some point the system has to be assembled as a complete unit and testing conducted of all related systems together.

21 Systems implementation can take place in three major ways, what are they? Select the three most appropriate.
☐ Hybrid implementation
☐ Direct conversion

☐ Parallel implementation

☐ Phased implementation

22 Maintenance is all about correcting bugs. True or false?

☐ True

☐ False

23 Project control is a type of _____ evaluation. Fill in the blank.

24 Why is configuration management important to effective maintenance? Write two sentences.

12.14 Exercises

- Produce a list of some other benefits and/or costs associated with some information system. Categorise the costs and benefits in terms of tangible costs/benefits and intangible costs/benefits.

- Choose an intended information system. Try to assess its utility using one of the standard techniques such as return on investment.

- Apply the three risk factors identified in this chapter to a project known to you.

- Identify actual clients, end-users and customers for a project known to you.

- What requirements elicitation techniques are most readily used in an organisation known to you and why?

- List two actual requirements from a development project.

- Perform a small use-case analysis of some information system known to you. Develop one scenario of use for the system.

- Consider an information system known to you. Assess the degree to which the surrounding human activity system encourages job satisfaction.

- Find one other example of the interdependence of information systems with human activity systems.

- Assess the degree of stakeholder participation in an information systems project known to you.

- Find one example of each of the forms of testing described in this chapter.

- Find some user documentation and describe its key elements.

- Consider a specific ICT system. How many tools were used in its construction and for what purpose?

- Consider a specific information systems project. What approach to implementation was taken and why?

- Determine a more complete analysis of the advantages and disadvantages of each form of implementation strategy.

- Assess the relative importance of data preparation and conversion to two ICT system projects known to you.

- How much of a specific organisation's informatics service activity is taken up in maintenance?

- What strategies has an organisation taken to manage maintenance activity more effectively?

- Develop a brief configuration management strategy for a small-scale development.

- Find a completed information systems development project and describe the elements contained in the information system supporting the project.

- Consider an organisation known to you. Investigate what percentage of development is bespoke and package.

- Investigate whether development primarily occurs in a sequential or iterative manner in an organisation known to you.

- Find a past information systems development project. Determine how closely the project undertook activities similar to the phases described in the life-cycle.

- Apply the information economics scorecard to the project to develop a specific information system.

- Identify actual clients, end-users and customers for a project known to you.

- Find one other example of the interdependence of information systems with human activity systems.

- Assess the degree of stakeholder participation in an information systems project known to you. Determine whether such participation is consultative, representative or consensus. Determine whether the participation is intensive or phased.

12.15 Projects

- A common information system for a project is considered important for enabling collaboration

among members of a project team. Investigate the shape of this project information system in a range of development projects. What sort of information is held in this repository and how is it used?

- There is no standard approach to organising a development team. Survey the structure of development teams across a range of information system development projects. For instance, determine the degree to which representatives of users are included within development teams.

- In a limited range of organisations investigate how many new systems have been developed in a bespoke manner and how many systems have been package development projects. Try to identify why organisational members chose bespoke or package development.

- Agile development is seen by many as a solution to development problems. Investigate the degree to which organisations use a linear or iterative development process. For what sorts of application are these different approaches used?

- Build a business case for a small-scale information system. Try to include an assessment of intangible costs and benefits as well as tangible costs and benefits. What risks are involved in the project? How feasible is it for the organisation to develop the information system?

- Establish empirically, by collecting data on a small number of projects, the breakdown of tangible and intangible costs on bespoke compared with package projects. In other words, is the profile of costs and benefits substantially different in these two types of project?

- Investigate the range of approaches that include ways of assessing intangible benefits, such as information economics. How often are they used in organisations? How successful have these applications proven?

- Many people have proposed that informatics professionals need to have a wider range of skills than the purely technical. For instance, if requirements elicitation is a process of inter-subjective negotiation, investigate the key skills needed by successful analysts.

- Determine which are the most commonly used requirements elicitation techniques in an organisation known to you. Build a detailed analysis of the strengths and weaknesses of particular requirements elicitation techniques.

- Gather some actual requirements specification documents. Investigate how long it took to produce them and how closely the resulting information systems matched them. Determine which are the most commonly used requirements specification approaches in the organisations chosen.

- Determine the degree to which some specific information systems projects truly are examples of sociotechnical design. For instance, do job considerations such as job satisfaction play a part in analysis activities? Does design include the design of activity systems as well as ICT systems?

- Documentation has tended to move from the printed page to being online and Web-based. Determine the degree to which user documentation is now offered online, and consider some of the disadvantages and advantages of this over the paper form.

- Investigate which type of system implementation is the most popular among a group of organisations and why. Construct an implementation plan for a small-scale information system and justify your proposals.

- Determine the relative occurrence of each of the reasons for maintenance described in this chapter in the maintenance portfolio of a specific organisation. In other words, for one operational information system, attempt to determine the levels of perfective, corrective adaptive and preventative maintenance that has been applied to it.

12.16 Critical reflection

How much does having a good business case contribute to the success of a development project? If companies use similar packages, what effect does this have on the role of ICT in business strategy? What happens if organisations do not treat job analysis and design seriously? How does the notion of configuration management relate to that of content management?

12.17 Further reading

We lack a good recent introduction to information systems development. The closest text is that of Avison and Fitzgerald (2006), which provides a comprehensive overview of most of the topics covered in this chapter. Vidgen and colleagues (2002) describe the application of the Multiview approach to modern information systems.

Multiview as a sociotechnical development approach has informed much of the discussion in this chapter. Mumford's (2006) paper on sociotechnical design provides a good overview of the history and background to this approach.

12.18 References

Avison, D. E. and B. Fitzgerald. (2006). *Information Systems Development: Methodologies, Techniques and Tools.* 4th edition. McGraw-Hill.

Avison, D. E., A. T. Wood-Harper, R. T. Vidgen and J. R. G. Wood. (1998). A Further Exploration into Information Systems Development: The Evolution of Multiview2. *Information Technology & People* 11 (2): 124–139.

Burton Swanson, E. (1992). *Maintaining Information Systems in Organisations.* John Wiley, Chichester.

Carroll, J. M. (ed.) (1995). *Scenario-Based Design: Envisioning Work and Technology in Systems Development.* John Wiley, New York.

Cash, J. I., F. W. McFarlan and J. L. McKeney. (1992). *Corporate Information Systems Management.* 3rd edition. Richard Irvin., Homewood, Ill.

Checkland, P. (1999). *Soft Systems Methodology: A Thirty Year Retrospective.* John Wiley, Chichester.

Fitzgerald, B. (2006). The Transformation of Open Source Software. *Management Information Systems Quarterly* 30 (3): 587–598.

Fitzgerald, G. (2000). Adaptability and Flexibility in IS Development. In R. Hackney and D. Dunn (eds), *Business Information Technology Management: Alternative and Adaptive Futures.* Macmillan, London:13–24.

Hirschheim, R. A. (1983). Assessing Participatory Systems Design: Some Conclusions from an Exploratory Study. *Information and Management* 6: 317–327.

Maslow, A. (1954). *Motivation and Personality.* Harper and Row. Cambridge, Mass.

McGregor, D. (1960). *The Human Side of the Enterprise.* McGraw-Hill, New York.

Mumford, E. (1983). *Designing Participatively.* Manchester Business School Press, Manchester.

Mumford, E. (2006). The Story of Socio-Technical Design: Reflections on its Successes, Failures and Potential. *Information Systems Journal* 16 (4): 317–342.

O'Connell, F. (2001). *How to Run Successful Projects II: The Silver Bullet.* Prentice Hall, Hemel Hempstead.

Parker, M., R. Benson and H. Trainor. (1988). *Information Economics: Linking Business Performance to Information Technology.* Prentice-Hall, New Jersey.

Vidgen, R. T., D. E. Avison, B. Wood and A. T. Wood-Harper. (2002). *Developing Web Information Systems: From Strategy to Implementation.* Butterworth-Heinemann, London.

Wilcocks, L. and H. Margetts. (1994). Risk Assessment and Information Systems. *European Journal of Information Systems* 3 (2): 127–138.

See companion website www.palgrave.com/business/beynon-daviesbis2e

Successful informatics practice

This chapter reviews the material covered in depth in the chapters of the book. It also considers some of the future for the domain of organisational informatics.

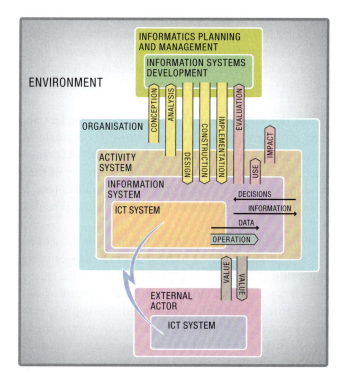

Chapter outline

13.1   Introduction

Chapter 1 explained that the domain of organisational informatics is necessarily interdisciplinary in nature because it bridges technical and social areas. Another way of thinking about the nature of organisational informatics is that it engages with three types of science. From one direction it is inherently a social science because it is interested in organisational behaviour. From another direction it is inherently a natural science because it is interested in the makeup of physical artefacts, such as electronic devices. From a third direction it is a design science in the sense that it is interested in the productive application of ICT to organisations and their management (Hevner et al., 2004). This last perspective on organisational informatics is the subject of this final chapter.

This chapter attempts to do three things. The first is to synthesise the material from the previous chapters in terms of the domain model introduced in Chapter 1. The second is to apply this model to one of the most prominent cases of information systems application. Third, it demonstrates some of the best practice in the design of business systems, using the model of the domain that has structured this book.

The model of information systems, and their interaction with organisations, introduced in Chapter 1 attempted to capture the systemic nature of organisational informatics. This model is used in this chapter to reflect on what constitutes the core body of knowledge (Hirscheim and Klein, 2003) on good practice in organisational informatics. This means the knowledge that is transferable from one organisation and one programme or project to another.

We use a well-known historical case to reflect on the nature of this body of knowledge. The case of the London Ambulance Services Computer Aided Dispatch (LASCAD) system is important for a number of reasons. As one of the most discussed cases of information systems failure it has been much used in academic and professional teaching. It is perhaps surprising that there are still very few well-documented cases of information systems failure (Chapter 7), and there are even fewer well-documented cases of information systems failures that were turned into successes.

This new edition has been written about 24 years after the original failure and 15 years or so after the successful turnaround. This provides a useful intellectual distance to reflect on the lessons for successful practice in organisational informatics. Obviously, the technology used in LASCAD is outdated now, and the functionality that was regarded as innovative in the 1992 system is now commonplace for command and control systems in ambulance services in the United Kingdom, as is described later in the chapter. However, the informatics planning, management and development issues highlighted in the case remain relevant today. The evidence from this case study supports some well-established lessons of good informatics practice, and shows that ways are needed to formulate these in a defined body of knowledge for organisational informatics.

This historical case makes it clear that this body of knowledge is time-independent and universal. In the United Kingdom and elsewhere, there have been numerous examples of public sector information systems failing to deliver both before and since LASCAD. These failures continue right up to the present day. There have been inquiries into many of these information system failures whose findings have been made public; these inquiries tend to identify the same reasons for failure, and recommend the same mechanisms and processes for avoiding it and achieving success.

The chapter concludes with a look at the likely near future environment for organisational informatics. Increased connectivity in ICT infrastructure is likely to lead to changes in the exploitation and use of this technology within and between organisations. Substantial change is also likely to occur in the ways in which consumers or citizens interact with organisations. Both these trends are likely to affect the general economic environment, leading to greater global penetration of eBusiness and eCommerce, and increased potential for new organisational forms. This increased activity is likely to reinforce the continuing need for business professionals who engage in good informatics practice.

13.2   The LASCAD failure and its turnaround

On 27 October 1992 an information system made the lead story on the BBC's Nine O'Clock News. It was reported that a new computerised system at the headquarters of the London Ambulance Service (LAS) (the LAS Computer Aided Dispatch system, or the LASCAD system) had failed, and that as a direct result of this failure the lives of 20 to 30 people might have been lost (Beynon-Davies, 1995).

The key value produced by the London Ambulance Service (LAS) was, and still is, the care it provides to patients. As is the case with any activity system, its performance can be judged in a number of ways. For many years the key performance indicator used by ambulance services in the United Kingdom has been the time taken between receiving an emergency call and the arrival of an ambulance at an incident.

In 1992 the LAS was under pressure from government and the wider National Health Service to make changes, to address a number of perceived failings in performance. The argument was that the LAS was clinging on to archaic practices and needed to update its activity systems if it was to perform effectively.

There had already been two attempts to introduce computerisation, but bad relations between stakeholder groups, a prior history of poor labour relations and a general distrust of management by the workforce made it difficult, and both projects had been abandoned as a result. So there was considerable pressure on the 1992 developers to introduce a system that would make major changes to bring the service up to date.

At the time LAS operated a largely un-automated activity system of ambulance dispatch, which consisted of three core processes: call-taking, resource identification and resource mobilisation.

Call-taking was the process of emergency calls being received by ambulance control. Control assistants wrote down details of incidents on pre-printed forms. They noted the location of each incident and recorded reference coordinates on the form. The forms were then placed on a conveyor belt which transported them to a central collection point.

The activity of resource identification involved other members of ambulance control collecting the forms, reviewing their details and, on the basis of the information provided, deciding which resource allocator should deal with each incident. Each resource allocator examined the forms passed to their sector, compared the details with information on each ambulance they controlled and its crew, and decided which ambulance should be sent where. The status information on the forms was updated regularly from information received via a radio operator. The resource allocated was recorded on the original form, which was passed on to a dispatcher.

In resource mobilisation, the dispatcher either telephoned the nearest ambulance station, or passed the mobilisation instructions to the radio operator if an ambulance was already out in the field. This triggered the dispatch of an ambulance to an incident. These activities are represented as a process model in Figure 13.1.

The essential functionality of the information system that was designed to replace this manual system is shown diagrammatically in Figure 13.2.

In the automated system, telephone operators routed all 999 calls concerning medical emergencies as a matter of routine to LAS headquarters (HQ) in Waterloo, central London. 18 HQ receivers were then expected to record on the system the name, telephone number and address of the caller, and the name, destination address and brief details of the patient. This information was then transmitted over a local area network to an allocator. The system pinpointed the patient's location on a map display of areas of London. The system was expected to continuously monitor the location of every ambulance via radio messages transmitted by each vehicle every 13 seconds. This would enable it to determine the nearest ambulances to the patient.

Experienced ambulance dispatchers were organised into teams based on three zones (south, north-east and north-west). The system was designed to provide the dispatchers with details of the three nearest ambulances and the estimated time each would need to reach the scene. The dispatcher then chose an ambulance and sent incident and patient details to a

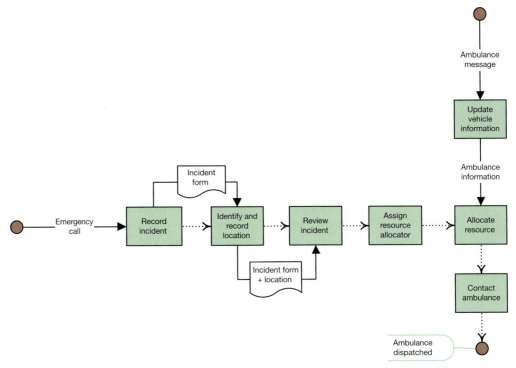

Figure 13.1 *The original activity system for ambulance dispatch*

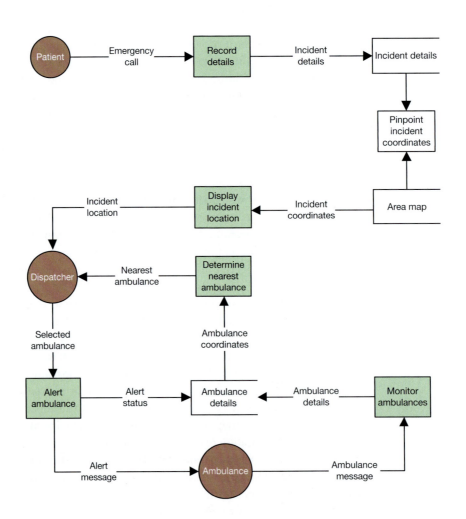

Figure 13.2 *The LASCAD information system*

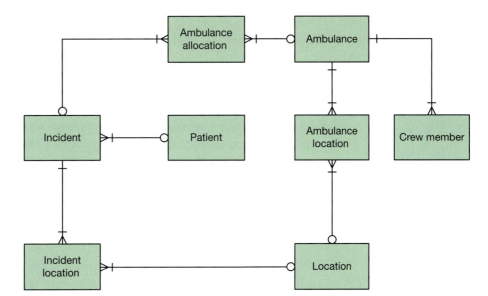

Figure 13.3 *An information model for the LASCAD system*

small terminal screen located on the dashboard of the ambulance. The ambulance crew were then expected to confirm to the system that they were on their way to the incident.

If the selected ambulance was in an ambulance station, the dispatch message was received on the station printer. The ambulance crew were always expected to acknowledge a message, and the system automatically alerted LAS HQ if no acknowledgement was made. A follow-up message was then sent from HQ. The system could also detect from each vehicle's location messages if any ambulance was heading in the wrong direction, and alert controllers. Further messages told HQ when the ambulance crew had arrived with the patient, when it was on its way to a hospital and when it was free again.

Figure 13.3 shows an information model which would support this information system. The information classes on the diagram such as ambulances, incidents and patients indicate objects about which records needed to be maintained in the system.

All this might appear perfectly reasonable, but unfortunately the system was a disaster when it went live. Instead of ambulances being dispatched more promptly to incidents, they were dispatched more slowly, or multiple ambulances turned up for the same patient. The chaos was headline news, as noted above, and the LAS chief executive resigned a couple of days after the launch. He was quoted as saying he had done so because of the evident lack of confidence in the LAS.

A new chief executive was appointed the next day. Under pressure from a number of sources, the health secretary announced a public inquiry into the system, which was headed by the South Yorkshire ambulance chief. The findings of the inquiry were eventually published in an 80-page report in February 1993, which immediately became news in the UK computing and national press.

According to the report, the reason for the system's, so-called, failure was not that the ICT system crashed. The hardware and software worked reasonably well, but that the communications and the sociotechnical system did not. Crews pressed the wrong buttons on their dashboard access device; no messages were received by HQ when ambulances were in radio black-spots. This led to a build-up in the amount of incorrect vehicle information. This had a knock-on effect because the ICT system then made incorrect allocations on the basis of the data it had. For example, multiple vehicles were sent to the same incident, or the closest vehicle was not chosen for dispatch. As a consequence, the ICT system was left with fewer ambulance resources to allocate.

The system also placed calls that had not gone through the appropriate protocol on a waiting list, and generated exception messages for incidents for which it had received incorrect status information. The number of exception messages appears to have increased to such an extent that staff were not able to clear the queue. It became increasingly difficult for staff to attend to messages that had scrolled off the screen. The increasing size of the queue slowed the system. All this meant that, with fewer resources to allocate, and the problems of dealing with the waiting and exception queues, it took longer to allocate resources to incidents. Eventually, a decision was made to switch off the system and return to a manual mode of operation.

Although the inquiry found evident problems with both the organisation and its ICT system, the report recommended that the LAS continue to seek to build an ICT system to support ambulance dispatch (Fitzgerald and Russo, 2005). However, it also recommended an extended timescale for development and implementation, and suggested that there should be effective stakeholder consultation, quality assurance, testing and training. As a result of this, the LASCAD project organisation was restructured and a new head of ICT appointed. This new head was reported at the time as having been given until August 1997, and a provisional budget of £13.5 million, to deliver an effective dispatch system for the LAS.

While the new system was being built the original manual system continued in operation but with greater staff resource. A series of warm-up projects, such as the construction of a new control room, the introduction of a digital phone system, and the upgrading of the ambulance fleet, were used to build a new level of trust between LAS management and the workforce.

In contrast to the earlier development project, it was decided to build the new system in-house using prototyping to help involve users in the development process. A slow and deliberate approach was adopted to provide time for the necessary user involvement and the iterative development required of prototyping. A new development platform was adopted, built around the Informix database management system running under the UNIX operating system. This allowed access from around 60 workstations. A mirror system was implemented, a backup to which operations could immediately switch over in the event of a failure in the main operational system.

The first stage of the work involved building a system with much reduced functionality from that originally intended. This included features for call-logging, call transfer and address-finding against a computerised gazetteer. This system went live on 17 January 1996, and after a week of successful operation was moved into the new control room. Enhancements to this basic system were introduced gradually. For instance, additional functionality allowing early viewing of emergency calls was introduced in September 1996, followed by the implementation of an automatic vehicle location system.

The introduction of the new system into the LAS control room was seen by the new LAS management to be a core factor in operational performance improvements. For example, in the period 1996/97 the service faced an increase of 16% in emergency calls. Nevertheless, the LAS managed to increase its proportion of ambulances dispatched within a three-minute activation period from 44% in 1995/96 to 80% in 1996/97. The number of complaints from users also fell from 100 per month to around 25 per month after the introduction of the new information system.

However, just like any organisation the London ambulance service continues to experience problems in managing its ICT infrastructure. For example, in 2012, it was reported that in an attempt to replace its call logging software with some more up-to-date software LAS lost a small number of emergency calls from its system. Fortunately, none of these incidents proved to be life-threatening and most only suffered from a slower response than normal.

13.3   The domain model

Let us go back to the domain model presented in Chapter 1. Figure 13.4 attempts to represent the complex, systemic interaction between an information system and the organisation in which it exists. In a sense, it represents some of the core or critical elements of the domain of organisational informatics.

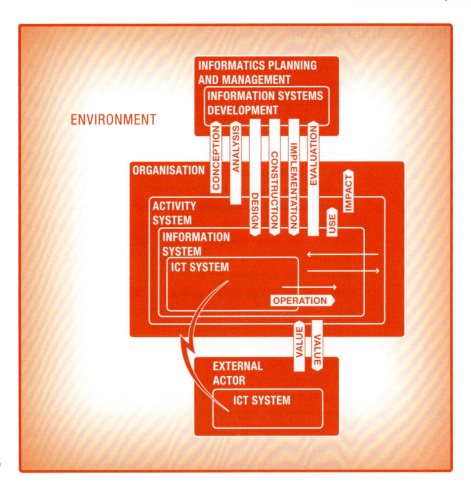

Figure 13.4 *The domain model*

Central to the model is the information system (Chapter 4), acting as a sociotechnical system utilising ICT (Chapters 8 and 9) in support of human activity. The operation of ICT systems and their use (Chapter 7) take place within the larger information system, and foreshadow the impact of the information systems on the organisation. The organisation itself (Chapter 2) is considered as a series of interdependent activity systems, directed by strategy (Chapter 10), which interact with a wider environment (Chapter 5). Informatics planning and management form the context for development projects (Chapter 10). These projects are typically enacted as a process (Chapter 12), consisting of the activities of conception, analysis, design, construction, implementation and maintenance.

This book has used the term informatics rather than information systems throughout in order to keep the terminology as clear and consistent as possible. Informatics is the term for both an academic field and a practical discipline devoted to trying to improve the fit between information systems and organisations. All the component elements of the model have an effect, both separately and in their interaction, on the fitness for purpose of an information system.

To recap, informatics is the study of information, information systems and ICT applied to various phenomena. The term has been used repeatedly by various branches of the European Union to refer to the application of ICT in support of the information society. In Germany the term *informatik* and in France the term *informatique* are much used. The term has also been much used in the health and biological sciences fields. For instance, health informatics, medical informatics and bioinformatics are now common terms.

This book has used the term in the sense implied by Kling and Allen (1996), who use organisational informatics as a label to denote the application of information, information systems and ICT in organisations. This is similar to Kling and Scaachi's (1982) interest in what they called the 'web of computing'.

13.4   The information system

This rather dry discussion about the use of the term informatics is important, because it demonstrates that one problem lies in the language used to describe elements of concern in this general field. In much of popular, academic and professional literature the term information system is used to refer to a system of technology. This tends to focus vision and practice on the successful construction of technology. But technology is only part of the sociotechnical systems that are used in organisations, as this book has worked to show. It has argued for a clear distinction between three interdependent systems of concern: activity systems, information systems and ICT systems.

Organisational informatics is a systemic discipline. This means that the concept of system is central. A system is a coherent set of interdependent components that exists for some purpose, has some stability, and can usefully be viewed as a whole. Systems are generally portrayed in terms of an input–process–output model which locates them in a specific environment. The environment is anything outside the system that has an effect on the way the system operates, and can be defined as the actors with which the system interacts. The inputs to the system are the resources it gains from actors in its environment. The outputs from the system are those things that it supplies back to actors in its environment. The process of the system is the set of activities that transform system inputs into system outputs. Systems can also be viewed hierarchically as a collection of subsystems and sub-subsystems.

A human activity system (or just activity system) is a social system, sometimes referred to as a *soft* system. It is a set of activities performed by a group of people in fulfilment of a defined purpose. Activity systems are designed systems in the sense that sets of activities, roles, procedures and business rules are typically used to specify their workings. The output of an activity system is action.

Technology amounts to a set of artefacts for doing things. ICT is any technology used to support data gathering, processing, distribution and use. ICT provides a means of constructing ICT systems. Modern ICT consists of hardware, software, data and communications technology (see Part III).

It is important to recognise that information systems existed in organisations long before the invention of modern ICT, so information systems do not depend on modern ICT. However, in the modern, global and consequently complex organisational world, most information systems rely on hardware, software, data and communication technology to a greater or lesser degree. This is because of the performance gains that are made possible through the use of this technology.

An ICT system is a technical system. Such systems are frequently referred to as *hard* systems in the sense that they consist of an assembly of designed artefacts. An ICT system is an organised collection of hardware, software, data and communication technology designed to support aspects of an information system. An ICT system takes data as input, manipulates such data as a process and outputs manipulated data for interpretation within an activity system.

Many systems in organisations are examples of sociotechnical systems. A sociotechnical system is a system of technology used within a system of activity. Information systems are primary examples of sociotechnical systems. Information systems consist of ICT used within an activity system. They therefore include both ICT and human activity. Part of the activity will involve the use of ICT systems. The input to an information system consists of data supplied from its associated ICT system. The output of an information system is information, and the information it provides drives decision-making, leading to further action within the organisation.

In much media coverage of public sector failures such as LASCAD, the blame is placed on the 'computer system' or 'ICT system', but that does not do much to show where the problem really lies. It particularly fails to separate out elements of technology from elements of communication and activity. And usually it is in the subtle interaction between activity systems, information systems and ICT systems that things work out in ways that lead to judgements of success or failure.

The functionality of the 1992 ICT system at LAS was undoubtedly complex. It was in many ways ground-breaking for its day, and tried to automate most of the functions involved in dispatching ambulances to incidents. The new ICT system was dependent on bringing in a substantially different information system and activity system for the LAS command and control operations. It also called for significant changes to the activity of ambulance crews, because they had to get used to communicating in new ways.

When a second new system was introduced in 1996, it was deliberately kept simple at first. Its functionality only covered call-taking. In a sense, this reduced functionality could be used to support most of the elements of the existing activity system. This clearly reduced risk, and enabled the project organisation to introduce both technical and organisational change in a much more controlled manner.

A number of lessons can be drawn from this. First, the use of clear terminology is important. A set of terms that make these differences apparent need to be adopted and used in practice. The term information system should be understood to mean a sociotechnical system which spans a social (activity) system and a technical (ICT) system. This is important because it implies that undertaking an information systems development project calls for the parallel design and implementation of technology systems and corresponding social (activity) systems. Developing an ICT system independently of any concern with its encompassing information system and activity system is likely to lead to failure.

It is interesting that since the period described in the case, both the ICT and activity systems for UK ambulance command and control have changed substantially, and the systems are now similar to the one introduced in 1992. In other words, this organisational sector has seen substantial process and activity systems change as well as technology change.

13.5   The use and impact of information systems

The distinction between an ICT system, an information system and an activity system is useful in locating three distinct ways in which the quality of a development effort can be assessed.

Traditionally the quality of an information system has been assessed in terms of its functionality. This is what an information system does, or should be able to do. Specifying the core functionality of a given information system is a critical aspect of the process of information systems development (see Chapter 12). Its functionality is normally determined by a close examination of organisational requirements. Assessments of functionality involve determining how closely an information system's constructed functionality matches the functionality that was specified in the early stages of the development project.

An ICT system is one major agent in the wider information system; the other major agent is human beings. The interaction between the two is typically judged in terms of the usability of the ICT system. Usability concerns how easy an ICT system is to use within its wider information system. Usability can also cover user satisfaction with the system. So usability is evident at the human–computer interface (see Chapter 9), the place where the user interacts with the ICT system.

While functionality defines what an information system does and usability defines how an information system is used, utility defines how acceptable the information system is in terms of doing what is needed. Utility assesses the worth of an information system by the contribution it makes to its activity system and to the organisation as a whole. This is essentially a judgement of issues of information quality in decision-making as a forerunner to action.

There is a clear relationship in the distinctions between functionality, usability and utility, and those between an ICT system, information system and activity system. Functionality is typically seen to be a property of the ICT system, whereas utility emerges as a property of the activity system. Usability is a mediating feature between the technical system (the ICT system) and the social system (the activity system), and is evident at the user interface.

As we move from the area of functionality into the areas of usability and utility, the issue of system stakeholders comes to the fore. This book has used the term stakeholder rather than user to emphasise that not just users, but many groups in organisations may have a stake in an information system. For example, managerial groups typically support the development of an ICT system by allocating resources to the project, so they have a real interest and stake in it, even if they do not use the live system in any way; and the output from the ICT system may have a major effect on the performance of the workforce the manager is responsible for.

Ultimately, judgements about the success or failure of ICT systems are made by stakeholder groups, so issues of stakeholder satisfaction and possible stakeholder resistance emerge as key. Power differentials between stakeholder groups also have an impact on the trajectory of information systems development projects.

There were at least three stakeholder groups in the initial LASCAD project: management, control room staff and ambulance crews. Each of these groups was affected in different ways by the introduction of the ICT system. Staff in the control room were typical end-users of the system, and bringing in the new technology led to radical changes in their activity system. The ambulance staff saw more minor changes in their work; they were required to use remote access devices (as we call them now, see Chapter 5) to input data to the central ICT system and receive instructions via it. The managers were clients of the development effort, and had a definite stake in that they wanted the system to improve performance in LAS's overall activity systems. This was the main objective behind the introduction of the new information system, to improve organisational performance, by, for instance, improving response times to incidents.

In 1992 some of the expected impacts of the new system were clearly not achieved. It actually caused a deterioration in the activity system performance; this was an especial problem because ambulances are such a time-critical service, and lives might well have been lost as a result.

Research has pointed to a number of ways in which stakeholder satisfaction with ICT systems can be improved and stakeholder resistance avoided. Stakeholder involvement in the design and development of ICT systems has a positive effect on satisfaction with them and commitment to their use. Comprehensive user training in the system prior to implementation is also critical to effective use, and so is continuous operational support post-implementation.

In 1992 control room staff and ambulance crews had little involvement in the development of the LASCAD system. The public inquiry also found that there had been poor and incomplete user training, and judged this to be a contributory factor in the project failure. There was also some evidence of stakeholder resistance; it was suggested that some ambulance crews were opposed to the new system, and rather than simply pressing the wrong buttons by mistake, they might have deliberately misused it.

In 1996, in contrast, the development team took great care to involve control room staff in the development of the new system. They were also given comprehensive user training and, not surprisingly, there was evidence of increased user satisfaction with, and commitment to, the system. The project organisation also deliberately built and introduced elements of the functionality of the system in a phased manner. This helped ensure that the system was introduced smoothly, and did much to help it meet its objective, that is, meeting the response time targets set by the ambulance services' external regulators.

The key lesson from this is that the impact of ICT must be assessed on a number of levels. An ICT system cannot be assessed solely as a collection of hardware and software. Organisations are generally interested in the contribution it makes to the wider information system and, in turn, the wider activity system. This also means that the impact of the ICT system should be assessed or evaluated at a number of points in its life, and particularly after a period in use.

13.6   The organisation

Generally speaking the discipline of informatics is interested in human activity within organised groupings of individuals, that is, organisations. Organisations are collections of people in which formal procedures are used for coordinating the activities of members in pursuit of joint objectives (see Chapter 2). We see an organisation as being something separate from the people who belong to it, but it needs to be borne in mind that, because the organisation is made up of the changing actions of a large group of people, it is not fixed and static, but is in a continual state of flux.

Business organisations in particular consist of complex chains of human activity concerned with the production and distribution of value. For commercial organisations this value resides in their goods or products, and for public sector organisations it is embodied in the services they provide. In the wider community, there is a form of value that is defined as social capital, networks of trust and reciprocity.

Control is the idea that any system, including a social system such as an organisation, needs to include a process that regulates it and enables it to adapt to changes in its environment. This is normally a feedback process, in which information is collected from a monitored process or subsystem and compared against defined levels of performance. The flow of information between a control process and its monitored process triggers actions designed to maintain the state of the system within given bounds. This is control as regulation. Control is also evident in the way in which a system monitors its environment and makes changes to its behaviour to adapt to this environment. From this perspective, information systems are essential for the effective strategic and operational management of modern organisations.

The immediate context for information systems is the activity systems infrastructure in an organisation. The key lesson here is that organisational features such as structure, culture and strategy have an influence on the success or otherwise of an information system; if only because organisational actors or stakeholders are the most important judges of success and failure.

Various stakeholder groups in organisations tend to frame the technology in different ways, so it is essential for informatics professionals to identify who the stakeholders are and assess what their impact on the development is likely to be. It is also important to manage stakeholder groups' expectations about the benefits they will derive from a system.

We have seen that, in spite of the pressure for change, the 1992 introduction of the LASCAD system was a disaster that had to be reversed. In 1996 there was still pressure to change. However, ironically, the previous highly public failure had reopened the agenda for change amongst all stakeholder groups. External agencies such as the government and NHS could not countenance another failure in what had become a highly publicised area of healthcare. The new chief executive of LAS therefore exploited this new situation to obtain additional resources, and to open up discussions with the workforce and reassure them of the importance of their participation in the intended change effort.

13.7   The external environment

An organisation is affected by its environment. Organisations are not isolated entities but are open systems that build information systems to cope with environmental pressures and constraints. The success of any organisation depends on how well it integrates with aspects of its environment. Any organisation contributes value to this environment and receives value from it, so it is not surprising that changes and forces in the environment influence the direction of organisational change, and by implication the direction of information systems change.

The NHS is one of the largest organisations in Western Europe. The organisation and delivery of health care has always been a politically sensitive issue in the United Kingdom because it is publicly funded. All political parties have tended to suggest that management, administration and administrative systems are generally a burden on the health service and, in many senses, a brake on the effective delivery of healthcare. Political fixes for the NHS have frequently been directed at improving the efficiency of its managerial and administrative systems and, as a consequence, its information systems. However, paradoxically, informatics management has never been given the prominence it deserves in the health service. Attempts to coordinate its informatics management have proven unsuccessful over a number of decades.

Over the period from 1992 to 1996 the environment of the UK health service did not change substantially. Although there were on-going reforms, which caused significant levels of structural change, little attempt was made to control ICT planning and strategy. Indeed, planning and strategy were increasingly devolved to regions and hospitals, making central coordination of information, information systems and ICT management extremely difficult.

Fitzgerald and Russo (2005) argue that because the environment did not change substantially over the period, it cannot be seen as a key influence on the failure and subsequent success of LASCAD. However, the prominence of the failure in itself changed the environment for the LAS. The LAS became a special case within the NHS, it had to be turned around to demonstrate that computerising command and control in ambulance services was both desirable and feasible. So the new project organisation was given an unusual amount of staffing and time following the initial failure. Improvements to the general work environment were used to increase levels of trust between management and workforce.

13.8   The development process

The successful development of information systems relies in the end on good development practice. Oscar Wilde once said that the problem with common sense is that it is not widely distributed, unfortunately much the same is true of good development practice. Although there are many good suggestions for development practice, they are ignored time and again in development projects.

For instance, it is important to use a systematic process for development. This book has outlined the process of information system development as a series of activities, and these provide a template for establishing good practice.

Conception is the phase in which an organisation develops a key business case for an information system. Before embarking on an investment, an organisation should evaluate an information system strategically and assess its feasibility. The organisation should also attempt to estimate the degree of risk associated. Only an information systems project that passes this strategic evaluation and feasibility assessment should pass on to a process of systems analysis.

Analysis consists of requirements elicitation, to identify the requirements for new information systems, and requirements specification, which is the process of documenting these identified requirements.

Design is the process of planning the shape of an information system to meet the requirements established by analysis. The design or system specification acts as a blueprint for systems construction.

The system can be constructed by either an internal team or an outside contractor. Many information systems are now also bought in as a package and tailored to organisational requirements.

Implementation involves the delivery of the system into its context of use. This can be done in a confident manner by immediately moving from the old to the new system. Alternatively, it can be approached in a cautious way, where the old and new systems are run in parallel for a period to ensure that there is a fall-back position.

Maintenance can be considered as a feedback process that involves changes to information systems and to elements of the organisation. Information systems may need to be changed for a number of reasons, including system error and user requirements. At some point a system may need to be substantially re-engineered to fit new organisational circumstances.

Many parts of the development process, as well as the management of development projects, are frequently highlighted as deficient in public sector information systems projects. Examples of particular areas of concern are poor requirements management, poor configuration control and testing, inadequate user training and inadequate planning for changeover.

In the 1992 LAS effort, aspects of both project management and systems development were poor. The project management method PRINCE was mandated but not used. There was poor management of stakeholder expectations because of low levels of involvement. A linear development approach was used consisting of the sequence of phases discussed in the last chapter. However, the approach was used in a domain subject to high degrees of uncertainty about requirements. There was also a direct changeover with little thought for a fall-back position in the event of problems. This was compounded by a lack of thorough testing of the software.

In the 1996 project much effort was devoted to addressing failings in previous project management and development practices. Incremental development and implementation were used to manage the uncertainty in the setting. There was a lot of stakeholder involvement to improve design work, increased levels of user commitment and reduced levels of user resistance. PRINCE was used for effective project management and the system was tested thoroughly. Changeover was managed closely, with the use of fall-back systems in the event of difficulty. As a result, development remained on time and within budget.

13.9   Informatics planning and management

The introduction of information systems can have a number of negative effects. Some people have argued, for instance, that information systems have largely been used not to enhance effectiveness but to increase job loss and deskilling, so workers do not view them positively and they lead to a rapid loss of morale. Information systems have also been used as a way of monitoring and controlling staff more closely. Not surprisingly perhaps, many large-scale information system projects have either been abandoned at great expense, or failed to deliver expected benefits in use.

So, information systems do not always have the intended benefits, and sometimes have unintended drawbacks. How can we ensure that failure and negative effects do not occur but that positive effects do?

The main point is that we cannot do this by directing attention and resources solely at the information system itself. We must consider information systems in the context of an organisation, and the organisation in the context of its environment. Perhaps a better way of putting this is that an information system in some way contributes to the success of an organisation within its environment. But what makes a successful organisation?

Peter Drucker's *Theory of the Business* (1994) attributes organisational success to three factors:

- businesses understanding their external environments
- businesses undertaking missions (developing strategies) consistent with their external environments
- businesses developing core competencies needed to accomplish their missions.

Because information is so central to modern organisations, their success depends in large part on the success of their information systems. Effective informatics planning and management are necessary conditions for ensuring information systems success. Planning and management are necessary to ensure that information systems are aligned with organisational strategy.

Informatics planning is the process of deciding on the optimal informatics strategy for an organisation. Its objective is to develop strategy in each of the areas of information, information systems and ICT. The practical output of the planning process is a set of documents that describe strategy in these three areas.

Planning is the process of determining what to do over a given time period. Managing is the process of executing, evaluating and adapting plans in the face of contingencies. There are three forms of management relevant to informatics, closely related to the three levels of informatics strategy and informatics infrastructure. Information management is concerned with the overall strategic direction of the organisation, and the planning, regulation and coordination of information in support of this direction. Information systems management is concerned with providing information handling to support organisational activities. ICT management is concerned with providing the necessary technical infrastructure for implementing this information handling.

The LASCAD case demonstrates the importance of a number of good practices in the area of planning and management:

- setting realistic budgets for development
- the importance of obtaining top-level management commitment to projects
- the need to avoid naïve notions of technological determinism, particularly the idea of using ICT as a driver for changes to work practices
- engaging in effective change management, such as parallel implementation of activity and technological change.

In 1992 unrealistic timescales were set for the project organisation, which also had a tight budget. There was clearly an attempt by the LAS management to introduce organisational change on the back of technological change. However, there was also poor change management in the attempt to achieve this.

In 1996 realistic timescales were set for the delivery of system elements and the project organisation was provided with a larger development budget. There was also evidence of good change management, in that ICT was carefully introduced in parallel with organisational change, albeit the change to organisational processes was not significant in the first instance.

13.10 Operations and service

Most medium- to large-scale organisations employ people specifically in informatics work. The informatics service is the specialist function devoted to activities such as informatics planning, management, development and operation.

This service plans the strategy for changing aspects of the informatics infrastructure, and is also concerned with supporting, maintaining and evaluating the existing informatics infrastructure. Its activities include constructing and delivering new information systems: analysing, designing, producing, testing and implementing them. It also operates large, multi-user systems and/or supports the use of information systems throughout the organisation.

Although informatics is now seen to be central to most organisations, the informatics service has traditionally experienced great difficulty in quantifying its benefits to the organisation. For this reason many organisations have decided to outsource their informatics service. Outsourcing is the use of external agents to perform one or more organisational activities. Since the mid-1990s there has been a trend, particularly in large-scale companies, to hand over either the whole or part of the informatics function to external agents.

The LAS case highlights some of the difficulties in outsourcing aspects of the informatics service. It particularly highlights the importance of domain knowledge to successful development, because of the sociotechnical nature of information systems. This implies that any development organisation does not only need technical knowledge for the construction of an ICT system, it also needs social knowledge of the activity system within which the ICT will be placed. This domain knowledge frequently proves problematic when organisations outsource information systems development, so the effective planning and management of informatics becomes even more critical when ICT infrastructure operation, development and maintenance are outsourced.

There is always a potential for project escalation, particularly in development projects seen as critical for organisational viability, so projects need to be evaluated at a number of levels: prior to development itself (strategic evaluation), during the development process (formative evaluation) and after the system is in use (summative evaluation).

In 1992 there was evidence of a lack of domain knowledge in the contracted development organisation. It was its first experience of command and control systems in a health environment. There were also clear difficulties with the management of the contracted development, as is evident in the lack of thorough training and testing of the system. Since this was the third in a series of computerisation projects at LAS, there is evidence of a lack of good evaluation practice and, not surprisingly, also evidence of project escalation (the continued investment in a project in the face of continued poor reports from formative evaluation).

In 1996 LAS deliberately decided to move development back in-house to provide more control. A new project organisation was established, with in-house developers recruited who had domain knowledge of command and control systems in the public sector (McGrath, 2002).

13.11 Modern ambulance command and control

In 1996 a review of ambulance service performance concluded that more clinically relevant performance measures were needed for the service. It suggested that the focus should be on the potential for saving lives, with shorter response times to patients suffering life-threatening conditions. From 1996 to 2006, demand for emergency ambulance services in the United Kingdom increased by over 50% while funding only increased by 17.5%. The review recommended a long-term performance target of 90% of life-threatening calls responded to within eight minutes. Subsequently, an interim target of 75% of life-threatening calls to be responded to within eight minutes was introduced, and ambulance services were required to achieve this target by 2001.

Until 1997 the ambulance service in the United Kingdom worked using a first-come, first-served basis for responses to emergency calls. However, to achieve targets set by the performance review, most ambulance services have now instituted a triage process to prioritise the response to incidents.

Most ambulance services in the United Kingdom have the freedom and responsibility to establish their own business processes and technology. This means that there is a variation between their activity systems, information systems and ICT systems. The description below is therefore based on a composite, and does not represent the system for any specific trust. The composite information system for ambulance command and control is shown in Figure 13.5.

In this system, telephone operators take an emergency call and identify the caller's area code or closest mobile phone cell. The call is then routed to the ambulance control call centre. A call-taker matches the number calling with an address using a computerised gazetteer, then asks a set series of questions prompted by a protocol embedded in the ICT system. On the basis of the answers, the system suggests appropriate action.

As soon as the location is identified, a dispatcher listens to the call. If it is rated as category A (life threatening) or category B (serious), a paramedic dispatcher might be asked to assist. Some ambulance services employ paramedics in the control room so they can be consulted if there is any doubt about the priority of the incident. The dispatcher manually assesses the nearest appropriate ambulance by using a number of screens: a screen indicating a plan designed to maximise the efficient use of resources (known as the system status management or SSM plan); a screen listing the status of all current resources; and a screen which plots the current location of ambulance resources against a computerised map and a touch-screen telephone. The SSM plan is an attempt to dynamically deploy vehicles around the area covered by the ambulance service, according to demand patterns established for day and time, geographical area and clinical urgency. As part of the ICT functionality the SSM

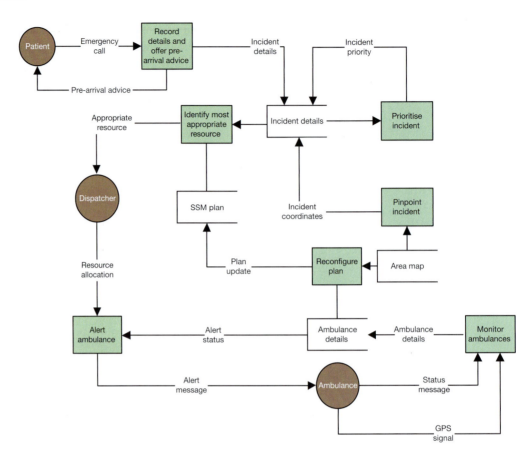

Figure 13.5 *An information system model for modern ambulance command and control*

plan is capable of prompting control room staff to shift resources, such as ambulances, on a continual basis to stay within plan.

Using this technology and their knowledge of the local area, the dispatcher assigns an ambulance to the incident. This means that the dispatcher does not always send the nearest ambulance; they can take known issues into account , such as the traffic flow in rush hour, to decide which ambulance is likely to get there soonest. Many ambulance services have a policy of recruiting control room staff from their pool of operational crews, because this kind of domain knowledge is so important to effective dispatch.

During this process the call-taker gives pre-arrival advice to the caller, relying on both the software and their own training. Meanwhile, the dispatcher typically uses a radio message to tell the chosen ambulance crew to attend the incident, and send them the location (including a grid reference) and details of the patient's condition. Some ambulance services have communication systems that enable control staff to page ambulance crews.

Ambulances are fitted with a communication set, and a member of the crew signals when they go mobile. They are also fitted with global positioning system equipment which updates the dispatch system every 13 seconds with their location. Crews are guided by satellite navigation to the incident location, supplemented by radio communication with the control room. When the crew arrive at the incident they press an *arrive* button on the communication set. They press a *leave scene* button when leaving the incident and an *at hospital* button when they arrived at a hospital. Finally, they press a *clear* button when they are available to be allocated as a resource again.

The general conclusion to be drawn from the description of this case is that the informatics infrastructure and activity infrastructure in organisations is a continually changing landscape. Many of the features introduced in the failed information system at the LAS have now become commonplace for ambulance command and control activity systems in the United Kingdom.

13.12   Improving practice

The key argument in this book is that the systemic interaction of all the elements described in the domain model contributes to information systems failure and success. Comparing the LAS situation in 1992 with that in 1996 suggests that improving any one aspect of the LASCAD project trajectory in isolation would not have led to success in and of itself. For instance, say the new in-house project organisation had decided to produce a new system to the original specification with little further consultation. Most likely, it would not have worked very well, because it would not have addressed problems such as the mistrust between management and workforce.

The domain model is useful for understanding the theory of business information systems, and their good practice, but it also has a practical use as a vehicle for guiding and controlling practice. Success in organisational informatics comes first from an awareness of as many model elements as possible. Contracted, outsourced and offshored information systems development has always proved difficult; arguably, this is because it is hard to acquire awareness of critical elements such as the prior history and culture of the organisation without intensive periods of immersion.

Moving from awareness to implementation, the project organisation and the wider organisation need to manage the interaction of the elements of the domain model as effectively as possible. Some aspects, such as subcultural differences between stakeholder groups, are likely to be outside the control of the project organisation. However, it needs to be aware of them and explicitly include them in risk assessments. Sometimes the imponderable nature of aspects such as these might cause an organisation to think twice about developing a new information system.

13.13   The future of informatics

Predicting the future is, by its very nature, prone to error and never more so than in the area of technology and its impact. Four historical predictions relating to the future of ICT and its application make this very clear:

- In 1946, the head of 20th Century Fox predicted that people would get bored with watching television after six months.
- In 1949 ENIAC, an early computer, was equipped with 18,000 vacuum tubes and weighed 30 tons. It was predicted at the time that computers in the future might have only 1,000 vacuum tubes and perhaps weigh 2 tons.
- In 1957 the late Arthur C. Clarke predicted that in 50 years satellites would be positioned in space to provide television and microwave coverage for the whole planet.
- In 1977, the president of Digital Equipment Corporation predicted that no one would ever want to have a computer in their home.

Three of these predictions from well-respected people proved spectacularly wrong. One was treated with much scepticism at the time but proved spectacularly correct.

However, if we extrapolate from trends that are already apparent there is more chance of success than with wild guesses. This enables us to provide a picture of some of the issues in the area of informatics that are likely to arise over the next ten years or so. They involve both individuals and organisations, and their use of the informatics infrastructure.

13.13.1   Communication infrastructure

At the time of writing there are an estimated 2.3 billion users of the Internet worldwide. This is almost a third of the world's population and this figure is growing at a rate between 8% and 10% per year. Broadband communication channels are already in common use and are likely to be used by an increasing range of the World's population in future. As a consequence of this, an increasing range of social, economic and political activity will rely on an efficient and effective ICT infrastructure. Commercial organisations will depend heavily on it, and so will individuals, particularly in their interactions with organisations, obtaining entertainment and using electronically delivered private, public and voluntary sector services.

13.13.2   Convergence

The convergence of technologies around standards will become critical, to make content accessible from a range of different devices and to create easy coordination between devices. This will also foster an increasing range and sophistication of content, applications and services. The greater demands on communication channels will create a need for more bandwidth.

13.13.3   Access devices

The range and functionality of access devices will undoubtedly increase, so people will be able to access a host of new applications, services and content in public, home and work settings through high-bandwidth data communication infrastructure. Convergence of devices such as mobile phones, personal computers and digital TV will be driven by an increasing adoption of common technical standards. The role of television itself is changing from a passive receiver to a significant platform for accessing and delivering electronic content.

However, some have become concerned over the increasing tethering of particular access devices to the digital ecosystems of specific companies. Major players such Apple, Google, Amazon and Microsoft already offer devices running their own proprietary software. This gives them control over devices and can constrain the uses to which these devices are put.

13.13.4   Consumer applications

Consumers will see a continued growth in conventional applications such as Web surfing, instant messaging and music downloading. Alongside this, an increasing range of applications will develop, supporting an increasing variety of content, much of it personalised. The key applications driving the increased provision of broadband to the home are likely to be voice over Internet protocol (VOIP), video download, IPTV (TV over the Internet) and HDTV (high-definition television). IPTV and HDTV are emerging as a major delivery platform for the delivery of broadcast content. As well as being used to deliver commercial content, this platform could be a significant channel for the introduction of public sector applications such as electronic medical monitoring and care.

13.13.5   Consumers and citizens

Floridi (2007) argues that the threshold between online and offline has already started to breakdown. As a result, we have all become *information organisms*. By this he means that the informatics infrastructure that penetrates everywhere causes a fading between face-to-face and remote or mediated communication. The transition between the offline and the online worlds becomes almost invisible to the average citizen and consumer.

13.13.6   Human–computer interfaces

As humans spend more and more of their time communicating remotely we should expect that the technologies we use for this communication will change significantly. One of the most important areas of development is in the user interfaces to the increasing range of access devices we use to communicate both with other people and with organisations. Currently, we are seeing the increasing use of gestural interfaces to hand-held devices such as tablet computers. In the relatively near future we should expect that machines such as ICT systems will not only be controlled through hand gestures but will be able to read other aspects of body language such as facial expression. This is expected to improve the levels of interaction available through the human–computer interface.

13.13.7 Content delivery

Much of the new generation of online content will be produced outside commercial and public sector organisations. Content delivery channels will multiply, leading to a continued increase in user-generated content. With this explosion new approaches to ensuring the quality control of content will develop. A new generation of content will be targeted at the person, not the place or the device. A mixed economy model of delivery of content is likely to develop in the future. Narrowcasting of content will become the norm, although a considerable proportion of content delivered will still be from broadcast organisations where the quality of content is assured.

13.13.8 Changes to work

The near future should bring an increasing demand for penetration of high-bandwidth broadband into the home to support multiple and sophisticated use by households for both leisure and work purposes. This is likely to be a critical driver for increased levels of home or remote working. There is predicted to be a growth in the number of people working from home at least one day per week. This will probably be accompanied by a greater rise in the number of people who work on the move or nomadically. As part of their contingency planning for the 2012 Olympics, for instance, many London-based companies and public sector organisations actively encouraged their staff to work from home using technology.

The growth in employee remote access channels and the convergence of access devices, coupled with the growth in nomadic working, will need to be supported by a reliable, efficient and widespread communication infrastructure (*Economist*, 2008). Much more communications traffic is likely to be loaded onto this network as traditional telephony moves onto the IP network. A growing range of collaborative applications supporting nomadic working will also rely on the increasing connectivity of different access devices, particularly mobile ones.

13.13.9 ICT infrastructure

The interoperability of components in the ICT infrastructure is likely to rely on the increased adoption of service-oriented architecture. The growing migration of infrastructure to Web services should enable a greater integration of ICT systems. This will act as a continuing impetus to the distribution of data and processing around wide area networks through technologies such as cloud computing.

There should also continue to be a movement to the application of Web 2.0 technologies. Web 1.0 was characterised by static Web content; Web 2.0 has been typified by a range of technologies that encourage interactive content. The most prominent consequence of this has been the rise of social networking sites and systems.

In the period to 2020 there are likely to be attempts from various quarters to provide greater control to aspects of both the Internet and the Web. For instance, what some people have called Web 3.0 will involve limits on the openness of the Web. Also, increasing fears over data privacy will lead to the greater embedding of privacy-enhancing technologies in the architecture of the Web. Media companies are also likely to introduce greater restrictions on the distribution of content.

But many see it as critical to maintain the openness of the Internet and the Web. The major challenges facing the planet, such as climate change, over-population, deforestation, and income inequality, demand new forms of organisation on a global scale. Such organisations will need free and open communication provided by an enhanced, not restricted Internet and Web.

13.13.10   Economic growth

Chapter 1 claimed that in these early years of the twenty-first century, societies are moving from an industrial to an information basis. The provision of informatics infrastructure will have a significant impact on economic growth worldwide. Many new industries will rely on it, and competitive advantage will depend heavily on effective and efficient data communication infrastructures, as business activity is increasingly designed to be location-independent.

13.13.11   Electronic delivery

In the near future an increasing range of services in the private, public and voluntary sectors should be delivered electronically in an increasing number of areas of life. In the home, the integration of communication between domestic devices such as fridges and cookers, and access devices such as the mobile phone is forecast to lead to remote operation of devices. The growth of the use of ICT in schools will continue, with an increased range of educational content online and an increased use of eLearning as a delivery mechanism. In the public sector, there will be an increased range and penetration of government services available online, and of eHealth applications.

The sophistication of electronic delivery will demand intra-organisational data sharing between back-end and front-end information systems. We should also expect increased inter-organisational sharing of data, particularly in the public sector. This is likely to occur not only between public sector organisations such as health bodies and social services, but also between a growing range of private and voluntary sector intermediaries. Data sharing in this context demands forms of inter-organisational records management.

13.13.12   Identity management

The key issue of identity management arises with intra-organisational data sharing and particularly with inter-organisational data sharing. The information economy is likely to see an increasing need for identity registers, not only of persons but also of land, buildings, products and, potentially, services.

As levels of remote interaction between individuals and organisations increase, situations in which the correct identification of people is important multiply. So the management of personal identity will assume increasing significance. This will act as an impetus to an increasing range of sociotechnical activity aimed at embedding personal identity management in and between organisations. Successful attempts at this are likely to further enable growth in levels of remote interaction between people using communications technology.

13.13.13   Data privacy

As more and more activity moves online, securing data and systems is becoming increasingly critical for organisations in both the public and private sectors. Deviant activity associated with remote electronic delivery, such as identity fraud and theft, is likely to continue to be a problem. Ensuring the privacy of personal data and transactions will become critical to the trust invested in both public and private sector organisations. Protecting their identity and data will also become an increasing area of concern for individuals in everyday activities.

13.13.14   Organisational forms

Networking effects created by increased connectivity to informatics infrastructure are likely to create space for new organisational forms. Channel applications may be key drivers of a network effect in the private, public and voluntary sectors. A key aspect of organisational strategies will be finding spaces for organisational innovation in the wider value network through the application of ICT.

Over the last few years interest has grown in virtual or network organisations. These are organisations built on an informatics infrastructure that enables collaborative, remote and nomadic working. They are also characterised by flat organisational hierarchies, and workers are typically organised in teams working on transitory projects. Virtual organisations do not use traditional physical infrastructure, such as office space. People work out of their homes or from wherever they can access communication infrastructure. This trend is likely to accelerate over the next few years as ICT innovation penetrates more aspects of organisational activity.

However, the inertia embedded within existing organisational structures and cultures will act as a brake on this kind of transformation through ICT. This means that traditional organisational forms will persist, and conventional support and supplant strategies for the application of ICT will continue to be evident into the near future.

13.13.15   eBusiness

Information systems and ICT will continue to be embedded in organisational life. This will involve continued attempts to 'informate' aspects of the value-chain distributed over internal communication networks. It will also increasingly include attempts to integrate the wider value network with the internal value-chain.

13.13.16   eCommerce

A tipping point in B2C eCommerce has already been reached, in that in countries such as the UK online shopping has become embedded in consumer behaviour. Once used solely for business-to-business purposes, today the majority of persons have made at least one purchase using an eCommerce platform. This means that there should be an increasing penetration of types of B2C eCommerce such as online retail, and also an increasing range of information-based corporations supplying content in various forms.

However, one should not expect the demise of the bricks and mortar organisation. Such organisations will merely change to meet the requirements created by new business models in different value networks. Some have predicted that the change in consumer behaviour caused by online shopping is reshaping the offline shopping experience. Within the next ten years we are likely to see many clicks and mortar businesses reshaping their offline operations to better match customer expectations. For many organisations the high-street store is likely to change into a B2C hub where customers can collect goods ordered online or obtain added-value services associated with online purchases. Such stores will also provide Internet access points where customers can browse products or provide free WiFi services to attract customers.

B2B eCommerce is also likely to merge with P2P eCommerce over the longer term. Some have referred to the development of a digital business ecosystem in which both competition and cooperation activity is supported through ICT. The Digital Business Ecosystem (DBE) is an Internet-based software environment in which business applications can be developed and used. The hope is that this will provide a common supporting infrastructure for the wider value network.

The community chain is likely to assume greater levels of significance. Companies are already interested in using Web 2.0 technologies to build communities of interest. The use of technologies such as wikis and blogs in the commercial context is therefore likely to increase.

13.13.17   Globalisation

The increasing penetration of informatics infrastructure worldwide is seen by many as contributing to the process of globalisation. This term is typically used to describe the process by which regional economies and societies become more closely integrated through greater inter-communication, transportation and trade. On the downside many see globalisation as a cultural process in which Western norms, values and ideas replace indigenous ideologies and value-systems. On the upside globalisation increases interdependencies between countries and as such may act to reduce international conflict.

The Internet and Web have helped form a global communications infrastructure. The downside of this technological globalisation may be that local industries find it increasingly more difficult to compete within a global market. On the upside, the existence of such a global communications infrastructure improves the capability of people around the world to organise political protest. Some have suggested that this capability may imbue the infrastructure with the status of a human right in the near future. Access to communication infrastructure will be a prerequisite for free speech and political influence. A clear recent example is that of Egypt where, in an attempt to subdue increasing political protest, the government of the day ordered the country's Internet Service Providers to stop providing a service. Within a few days, in the face of international outrage, connection was re-established.

13.13.18   Informatics practice

Informatics practice will have to adapt to technological change, but it is likely that most of the generic practices described in this book will continue to be relevant, at least until 2020. In a sense they will assume greater significance as societies, economies and polities rely more and more on the successful development and maintenance of informatics infrastructure. In development, collaborative production models for software are likely to grow in importance, and experiments are likely in distribution and pricing models for software. However, the informatics industry is still likely to be dominated by major software and hardware producers using traditional business models.

13.13.19   Informatics professionals

The increased penetration of informatics infrastructure will mean a continued demand for people with informatics knowledge and skills. Informatics planning, management, operations and evaluation skills will become as important as traditional development skills over the longer term. This will reflect the need for organisations to develop informatics as a critical and embedded part of organisational planning, management and strategy.

13.13.20   Value of informatics

Let us return at the close of the book to the issue of value. The trends discussed above suggest that the value of informatics is likely to increase over the next decade for organisations of various forms. Informatics infrastructure will become embedded and universally available. Organisational, group and individual activity will, as a consequence, become more dependent on its effective and efficient provision. Hence, there will be an increasing demand for individuals with an understanding of the multifaceted nature of informatics and its implications for organisations.

The first chapter raised three questions in relation to value and ICT:

■ What is the value of ICT to business?
■ How do we ensure the value of ICT to business?
■ How do we improve the value of ICT to business?

This is the point at which to suggest a response to each of these three questions:

■ The value of ICT to business emerges from the systemic relationship between three forms of business system: ICT systems, information systems and activity systems. ICT provides data which is interpreted as information in an information system; the information system provides information for deciding on appropriate action in an activity system.
■ The value of ICT to business must be controlled in a systemic way. ICT has to be planned for, managed, developed and operated effectively. Its use has to be continually monitored and the impact on the organisation evaluated.

■ Improvement in the value of ICT will arise from the adoption of the good practices in informatics described in the domain model. Adoption of the holistic approach implied in the model clearly demonstrates the value of organisational informatics as an important area of organisational practice.

13.14 Conclusion

In a book of classic science fiction the author Ursula Le Guin (1974) provides a quote which is very relevant to the issues considered in this book. A character says: '*The idea is like grass. It craves light, likes crowds, thrives on cross-breeding; grows better for being stepped upon.*'

Organisational informatics is a practical discipline. Its growth relies on continuous engagement with the application of information, information systems and ICT in and between organisations. Readers are encouraged to engage with the field-testing of the ideas described in this text, and contribute to the successful planning, management, development, operation and evaluation of information systems in organisations of many shades.

So give the ideas and approaches discussed in this book some light. Become part of the crowd engaged in good practice in organisational informatics. Don't be afraid of transporting new ideas into the mix and cross-breeding them with the ideas expressed here. Most importantly, don't be afraid of 'stepping on' the ideas. Please contact the author (beynon-daviesp@cardiff.ac.uk) and tell him when you have found the ideas useful, but more importantly, when you have not and why not.

13.15 References

Beynon-Davies, P. (1995). Information Systems 'Failure': The Case of the London Ambulance Service's Computer Aided Despatch System. *European Journal of Information Systems* 4 (1): 171–184.

Drucker, P. F. (1994). The Theory of the Business. *Harvard Business Review* 72 (5): 95–104.

Economist. (2008). Nomads at last: A special report on mobility, pp. 75–76.

Fitzgerald, G. and N. L. Russo. (2005). The turnaround of the London Ambulance Service Computer-Aided Despatch System (LASCAD). *European Journal of Information Systems* 14 (3): 244–257.

Floridi, L. (2007). A Look into the Future Impact of ICT on Our Lives. *The Information Society* 23 (1): 59–64.

Hevner, A. R., S. T. March, J. Park and S. Ram. (2004). Design Science in Information Systems Research. *Management Information Systems Quarterly* 28 (1): 75–105.

Hirscheim, R. and H. Klein. (2003). Crisis in the IS Field? A Critical Reflection on the State of the Discipline. *Journal of the Association for Information Systems* 4 (5): 237–293.

Kling, R. and J. P. Allen. (1996). Can Computer Science Solve Organisational Problems? The Case for Organisational Informatics. In R. Kling (ed.), *Computerisation and Controversy: Value Conflicts and Social Choices.* Academic Press, San Diego.

Kling, R. and W. Scaachi. (1982). The Web of Computing: Computer Technology as Social Organisation. *Advances in Computers* 21: 1–90.

Le Guin, U. (1974). *The Dispossessed.* Harper and Row, New York.

McGrath, K. (2002). The Golden Circle: A Way of Arguing and Acting About Technology in the London Ambulance Service. *European Journal of Information Systems* 11 (1): 251–256.

See companion website   **www.palgrave.com/business/beynon-daviesbis2e**

Case studies

Specially written cases featured in full in this section

		Learning goals of IS2010 curriculum											
		Organisations and systems	Data, information and knowledge	Infrastructure and information systems	Communication infrastructure	ICT systems infrastructure	Business environment	eBusiness, eCommerce and eGovernment	Use, impact and evaluation	Planning, strategy and management	Service, projects and operations	Information systems development	Page numbers in this section
1	Amazon	✓		✓	✓	✓	✓	✓		✓	✓		424
2	Apple	✓		✓	✓	✓	✓	✓		✓	✓		426
3	Arab Spring and social media		✓		✓	✓	✓	✓					427
4	Cisco	✓		✓	✓	✓	✓	✓	✓		✓		428
5	Citizens Advice Bureau	✓	✓	✓	✓	✓	✓	✓		✓	✓		430
6	Dell	✓		✓	✓	✓	✓	✓	✓		✓		430
7	dotCYMRU	✓		✓	✓	✓	✓	✓	✓		✓		432
8	eBay	✓		✓	✓	✓	✓	✓					435
9	Facebook		✓		✓		✓	✓		✓			430
10	Failure in government ICT systems	✓	✓	✓	✓	✓	✓	✓		✓		✓	438
11	Google		✓		✓	✓	✓	✓					440
12	Hollerith electronic tabulating machine	✓		✓			✓						442
13	Indian identity number		✓		✓	✓	✓	✓					444
14	Inka khipu	✓	✓	✓									445
15	Microsoft	✓			✓	✓	✓	✓			✓	✓	449
16	Music industry				✓	✓	✓	✓	✓				451
17	Offshoring in Bangalore						✓	✓		✓	✓	✓	452
18	Open source software				✓	✓						✓	453
19	SAP				✓	✓			✓	✓	✓	✓	455
20	Tesco	✓	✓	✓	✓	✓	✓	✓	✓	✓	✓	✓	455
21	Twitter		✓		✓	✓	✓	✓					459
22	UK Revenue and Customs	✓	✓	✓			✓	✓	✓	✓			460
23	Victorian railway clearing house	✓	✓	✓				✓					462
24	Wikipedia		✓		✓	✓	✓					✓	464

Please see also the Case Study overview on pp. xviii–xx of the book for details of the CASE CHECKS and online support where available.

1   Amazon

See pages: 240, 246, 250, 255, 256

Case description

Amazon.com is an American eCommerce company based in Seattle, Washington State, US. The company was one of the first major companies to sell goods over the Internet. It was also one of the most prominent traded securities of the late 1990s Dot Com bubble. When this bubble burst, many claimed that Amazon's business model was unsustainable. The company made its first annual profit in 2003. Consequently, Amazon.com is probably the most cited example of a company that has succeeded at B2C eCommerce. The domain amazon.com attracted over 4.4 million visitors per day in 2012.

Amazon.com was launched on the Web in June 1995 by Jeff Bezos. Bezos obtained backing from venture capitalists in Silicon Valley to start the operation. He chose to name his site after the world's longest river because Amazon, according to Bezos, was set to become the world's largest bookstore. At the time of Amazon's entry into the market it had no significant rivals. Within one year the company was recognised as the Web's largest bookstore.

At the start Bezos warned investors that they were unlikely to make a profit in the first five years of operation. However, Amazon has engaged in an aggressive expansion strategy since its inception. It has acquired a number of additional retail outlets, such as toys and CDs, and has provided a facility for online auctions of small goods. It introduced zShops in 1999, which is a facility that allows any individual or business to sell through Amazon.com – a form of C2C trading. It also has invested in a number of Dot Com companies such as Pets.com and Drugstore.com and has opened a number of distribution centres and operations around the world.

Amazon has separate websites in Canada, the United Kingdom, Germany, France, Italy, China, and Japan. However, it ships certain selected products globally. It also runs a number of fulfilment centres in North America, Europe and Asia. The company provides a number of levels of functionality through its website, such as search features, additional content and personalisation. The site also provides searchable catalogues of books, CDs, DVDs, computer games, etc. Customers can search for titles using keyword, title, subject, author, artist, musical instrument, label, actor, director, publication date or ISBN. In terms of added-value, the company offers a vast range of additional content over and above its products. For example, cover art, synopses, annotations, reviews by editorial staff and other customers and interviews by authors and artists. The website attempts to personalise the customer experience by greeting customers by name, instant and personalised recommendations, bestseller listings, personal notification services and purchase pattern filtering.

The primary value-stream for Amazon is tangible products such as books and CDs. As primarily a books retailer the major transformation of its value-creating system is distribution and sales. It offers a vast range of books for sale and then delivers them to customers. Over the last decade, it has attempted to broaden the range of this value by offering a more products, including computer software, video games, electronics, clothing, furniture, food and toys. It also provides added-value services such as a personalised notification service.

From the start Amazon offered a range of value-added services to its customers. A popular feature of the website is the ability for users to submit reviews for each product. As part of their review, users must rate the product on a scale from one to five stars. Such rating scales provide a basic measure of the popularity of a product. Such a reviewing facility has been seen by some as critical to the explosive growth of the company. Other added-value services include a personal notification service for customers requesting particular titles, a recommendations section where customers can recommend titles in various categories to other customers, an awards section that lists books that have won prizes and an associate program where other sites can link to Amazon to sell their own selections.

In 2007, Amazon launched its Kindle eReader. This has enabled the company to offer content as an intangible good in the form of an electronic book or eBook. Customers owning a Kindle can both download content from the Amazon website and pay for it. Some have predicted that this will grow to become the major revenue stream for Amazon over the next decade.

Amazon primarily engages in B2C eCommerce but has recently started a C2C operation in support of its B2C site. For instance, Amazon created an online community known as Mechanical Turk. This is an open marketplace in which workers perform tasks for requesters. Amazon receives a percentage of the fee charged for work by a worker.

Amazon's service to customers relies on a close integration of its website to back-end information and activity systems. For instance, the company uses a streamlined ordering process reliant on previous billing and shipment details captured from the customer. Amazon also utilises secure server software that encrypts payment information throughout its integrated fulfilment process. Most of the company's products are available for shipping within 24 hours.

Currently the company is claimed to be the Internet's number one retailer. However, although Amazon is a retailer, its key business strategy is based on differentiation in terms of technical infrastructure. For Amazon to keep this competitive differentiation it must continually be at the forefront of Internet technology. Bezos has indicated that he considers Amazon to be a technology company first and a retailer second. Hence, the key differentiating factor for Amazon over a conventional retailer is the Internet and Web. Not surprisingly, the company has to ceaselessly innovate in terms of technology. Amazon, in particular, must ensure that back-end systems managing its supply, sales and distribution processes work effectively. To be continuously able to upgrade its informatics infrastructure the company employs a vast range of software developers situated in a number of centres around the world. Amazon's main software development outfit is now based in Seattle, US.

Amazon requires a range of integrated back-end systems to be in place. Inbound logistics involves the management of the purchasing of books and the distribution of books to large warehouses. The process of operations involves unpacking and storing shipments, as well as picking books to fulfil customer orders. Outbound logistics involves the distribution of books to the customer. Marketing and sales involves the advertisement of books on its web catalogue and handling the purchasing of books through its website. After-sales service involves the handling of customer enquiries and complaints.

Since the mid-2000s Amazon has engaged in a strategy of attempting to build upon its core business model of online retail as a basis for engaging in two major forms of B2B eCommerce: providing order fulfilment and Web services for external business actors.

Fulfilment allows small and large companies to pay to use Amazon's order fulfilment infrastructure for their own purposes. Amazon stores the company's inventory in their own warehouses and provides product picking, packing and shipping to the customer once an order is received.

Amazon played a significant part in the development of cloud computing. An analysis of the performance of its data centres in the early 2000s found that they were utilising only 10% of their capacity at any one time. Introducing aspects of cloud architecture, such as data virtualisation, allowed it to operate its data centres far more efficiently. This led to the development of an effort to provide cloud computing to external customers. Amazon Web Service was launched in 2006. This developed from a major revision of its ICT infrastructure which separated its back-end from its front-end functions. This initially enabled the company to manage its websites more effectively. Eventually, it was realised that a new business offering could be built upon this technological change.

Now Amazon offers not only base utility functions, such as cheap online storage to external businesses, but also the ability to run complete applications for companies on Amazon servers.

This infrastructure has also enabled the company to engage in forms of P2P eCommerce. For instance, the websites of Borders (borders.com, borders.co.uk), Waldenbooks (waldenbooks.com), Virgin Megastores (virginmega.com), CDNOW (cdnow.com), and HMV (hmv.com) are all hosted by Amazon. The company also runs multi-channel access for a number of companies such as Marks & Spencer and Mothercare. Such sites allow the customer to interchangeably interact with the retail website, standalone in-store terminals, and phone-based customer service agents.

It is possible to describe briefly some of the gains that Amazon experiences from its engagement with B2C eCommerce and, in particular, the close integration of its ICT infrastructure with its activity infrastructure. First, in terms of efficacy, Amazon has been able to diversify into a vast range of products for retail. Since Amazon is primarily a B2C company it is able to run without any physical retail outlets and can pass on efficiency gains in lower costs to its customers. Finally, in terms of effectiveness, Amazon is able to sell its products across the world and is able to relate to a large range of suppliers.

Issues

- Amazon obtained dominance in online book retail by being the first into a niche market. This raises the question of the importance of niche strategies in the online world.
- It took a considerable while for Amazon to make a profit. Many Dot Com companies created in the same period as Amazon now no longer exist. What caused Amazon to survive and other companies to go under?
- Dot Com companies such as Amazon rely on a critical mass of people with access to the Internet and prepared to order and pay for goods and services online. What effect does the digital divide have on the customer base of companies like Amazon?
- Online retail of low-cost, packaged goods such as books, CDs and DVDs now outstrips physical retail of these items in many countries. How has online retail affected consumer behaviour generally?
- Amazon has comparatively recently opened up the online delivery of content to its Kindle eReader. How important will this business model be to Amazon in the near future?
- Amazon relies on effective management of a supply and distribution (customer) chain to make a profit. How effectively does Amazon engage in B2B eCommerce?

CS

- Amazon.com does not publish a customer service number on its own website. Customers are instead asked to submit written service requests (which are answered by email) or to use a click-to-call service to be connected by phone to an available service representative. Despite the perceived difficulty in reaching customer service by phone, Amazon.com remains high in customer satisfaction surveys. Why do you think this might be?
- Amazon has been an early adopter of cloud computing? How important will the provision of Web services be to Amazon's strategy in the near future?

2   Apple

See page: 144

Case description

Based in Cupertino, California, Apple is a multinational company that designs and markets a variety of products, including personal computers, software and consumer electronics. Apple, which was created in 1977, has established a unique reputation in the consumer electronics industry for the aesthetic principles exercised in its design work and its distinctive advertising campaigns.

The range of Apple hardware products has evolved over time, from the Macintosh line of personal computers to the iPod, the iPhone and, most recently, the iPad. The Mac OS X operating system, the iLife suite of multimedia and creativity software, the iTunes media browser, and the iWork suite of productivity software are well-known examples of Apple software.

The company operates a number of retail stores in a number of countries worldwide, as well as an online store. In mid-2010 Apple was reported to be one of the largest companies in the world. It was also reported as the most valuable technology company in the world, having surpassed Microsoft in this regard.

Part of the secret of the company's continued success is ceaseless innovation. In 2001, Apple introduced the iPod digital music player. This was not the first of the, so-called, MP3 players, but in 2003 the company introduced the iTunes music store, which was closely integrated with the iPod. This online store essentially connected music providers directly with a large market of music consumers and soon made Apple the world's largest online music retailer. It also made the iPod the market leader in portable music players.

In 2007 the company announced the iPhone, a product that integrated an Internet-enabled smartphone with an iPod. In 2008 the company launched its app store for the iPhone, which enabled iPhone users to directly download applications and install them on their iPhones. Apps are created in large part by external software producers, but Apple takes a 30% royalty on all apps sold through its app store.

In 2010 Apple announced their tablet computer, the iPad. As well as offering much of the functionality of the iPhone it allows access to a wider range of media content through a device controlled by a touch-sensitive screen interface. The iPad has resurrected interest in tablet devices and raised questions about whether such devices will be used within work settings as well as in leisure situations.

Apple develops software to support its increasing range of devices. It has always used its own operating system, Mac OS X, for its personal computers and laptops. The company also independently develops its own productivity software, which is normally installed on Apple computers. Software applications such as iDVD, iMovie, iPhoto, iTunes, GarageBand and iWeb, for example, are bundled together in the iLife software package. The Apple package for presentation, page layout and word processing is iWork. Sometimes Apple software can be downloaded for free; this is the case for the QuickTime media player or the Safari web browser, that can be used on both Mac OS X and Microsoft Windows.

Apple has sourced the production of much of its technology, such as the iPod, from Chinese manufacturers, for example, Foxconn and Inventec. In 2006, a number of media outlets reported that sweatshop conditions existed in some of these factories in China, with employees regularly working in overcrowded conditions for more than 60 hours per week and for little pay. Apple reacted to these allegations by launching an investigation and introducing yearly audits of all its suppliers regarding worker's rights. However, there is much debate over the success or otherwise of such initiatives. In 2010, it was revealed that the workers making iPads and iPhones in a Foxconn facility in China had to sign a legally binding document in which they pledged that they would not commit suicide; apparently, this was due to the high number of suicides among the company's employees . In 2011 Apple recognised that some of the factories of its major suppliers in China employed a growing number of child workers.

Issues

- Apple has a large and loyal customer base for its products. Reflect on how this loyalty is maintained.
- How does Apple compete in terms of software with other established suppliers, such as Microsoft?
- Apple has demonstrated the power of what some refer to as a digital ecosystem business model. It did this with the iPod and iTunes store and the app store and the iPhone. Reflect on the similarities and differences between the business model of Apple and Amazon in these terms.

- Many hardware suppliers, such as Apple, rely on production facilities based in the Far East. Reflect upon the pros and cons of this strategy.
- iPads are used extensively by people in leisure situations. How effective are they as access devices within work situations?

---

3   Arab spring and social media

See page: 253

Case description

In December 2010, a man in Tunisia burned himself to death in protest at his treatment by police. This event is generally accepted to mark the start of the Arab Spring, a term used to describe the revolutionary wave of demonstrations and protests which spread across the Arab world in early 2011. Across many countries in the region protest has mainly involved campaigns of civil resistance involving strikes, demonstrations, marches, and rallies. Such civil unrest has led to the overthrow of a number of ruling regimes, such as in Tunisia, Libya and Egypt. This case study focuses on the role that social media played in the organisation of such mass resistance. It also considers the way in which various states attempted to control the impact of technology by censoring content on the Web and limiting access to the Internet.

For the past couple of decades within the Arab world radical Islamists and jihadis such as Al Qaeda have made extensive use of the Internet, the Web and, more recently, social media for their ends. Evidence suggests, for instance, that Al Qaeda made extensive use of the Internet in planning the 9/11 attacks in New York. However, the Arab Spring demonstrated that these media can also be used to promote the principles of democracy within the region.

Political analysts put this down to a number of factors. Firstly, the fact that the Middle East population is disproportionately younger than in Western nations; in many Middle Eastern countries between 55% and 70% of the population are under the age of thirty. Secondly, it is the young who are likely to have the highest levels of eLiteracy. Thirdly, youth are more likely to seek their information on world events from the Web and international media rather than internal broadcast television channels and newspapers, which traditionally have been state-controlled or influenced.

Each of these factors served to establish a base for political activism which fuelled the Arab Spring. Within many Arab states the Internet, Web and social media have become a place for expressing ideas, concerns, complaints and frustrations that cannot be voiced through other channels. Within the virtual communities of the Web, social restrictions such as gender segregation can be subverted. Also, social media allow people not only to communicate and build common feeling, but also to organise themselves for political protest.

An example of how social media can encourage political activism is when someone establishes a page on Facebook debating some political issue. The page is then seen by various other Facebook members, who first comment on it and then begin to interact with one another. Once the group has achieved some solidity, members of this virtual community start to post photographs, video footage and links to YouTube. As this happens, further communication occurs through other social media such as Twitter. This expands the virtual community of people who are linked in to this debate. Since social media are not limited by geography, an issue which starts within one nation-state can quickly become global.

Take two specific examples of how this occurred and continues to occur: one from Egypt and one from Tunisia.

In January of 2011 the President of Tunisia, Zine el Abidine Ben Ali, was deposed in what many refer to as the Jasmine revolution. At the start of this revolution the rap artist Hamada Ben Amor recorded and distributed via Facebook and YouTube a song entitled Rais Lebled. This song raised awareness of the poverty and oppression experienced in the country. What made this song even more potent as a rallying cry for protest was the fact that rap as a musical form had been banned by Ben Ali's regime.

In February of 2011 President Hosni Mubarak of Egypt was overthrown. This wave of popular protest was encouraged by the activism of young bloggers such as the Egyptian student Kamel. Kamel began writing his blog to denounce his brutal treatment at the hands of the Egyptian police. It all started with a banal accident with Kamel falling off a train onto a platform. When policemen approached, he expected them to offer assistance, but instead received a beating. In response to his public humiliation Kamel created his blog which quickly gained a wide and sympathetic audience. Many such persons turned to Facebook as a medium to document their own degrading experiences at the hands of the regime.

The case of a young Egyptian businessman from Alexandria, Khaled Said, was much discussed in this manner. He was reportedly beaten to death by two police officers in 2010. Popular outrage resulted in the creation of a Facebook page entitled, 'We are all Khaled Said'. This page is seen as instrumental in forming a network of activists who planned the first day of protest on 25th January in Egypt.

The use of the Internet, the Web and social media was, of course not restricted within national boundaries. Such technology ultimately played an important part in

CS

distributing pictures, videos and reports about the civil unrest in these countries around the world. Not surprisingly, governments in the region did not stand still in the face of these tactics. One counter-tactic they employed was to attempt to control not only conventional media but also access to social media. Within Egypt in February of 2011 there were 13.5 million users of the Internet. 3.5 million of these were Facebook users and 12,000 Twitter users. On January 25th 2011 the Egyptian government attempted to block access to these two social media sites, both via the fixed telephony network and the mobile telephone network. On January 27th the government even switched off the national access provider for the Internet within the country for a short period. Internet services were not restored fully until February 2nd and SMS services were not re-established until February 6th.

However, this attempt at switching off the communication infrastructure in the country appears to have backfired. It seems to have alienated not only those persons with a grievance but also large apolitical segments of Egyptian society, such as the business community. Also, the blackout did not actually prevent access to social media by determined activists. Numerous activists were able to use circumvention software to enable them to access Facebook and Twitter during the blackout period.

We should emphasise that the Internet, the Web and social media should not be seen as the cause of the Arab Spring. The causes of this are clearly complex and to do with deep social, economic and political factors present within Arab states. What these technologies did was to help support the organisation of a political process, the coordination of political activity through convenient communication channels that were reliant on convenient ICT infrastructure.

Issues

- Social media appears to have been used in a number of different ways within the Arab uprising, such as to raise awareness and to organise political protest. Try to identify other areas of the world where social media has been used in a similar manner.
- Some commentators have recently raised concerns that governments worldwide may be tempted to switch off access to the Internet for their citizens at times of political instability, such as that experienced in Egypt. Assess the likelihood of this occurring and also the potential consequences.
- Facebook and Twitter are both private operations, subject to commercial pressures. Other commercial operations have bowed to government pressure to censor communications traffic. Consider whether the use of commercial media for purposes such as political protest is viable in the long-term.

4   Cisco

Case description

Cisco Systems was founded in 1984 at Stanford University by husband and wife team Leonard Bosack (who developed early router technology) and Sandra Lerner and three colleagues. Cisco is generally regarded as the leader in the market for inter-networking equipment. It is generally seen as the company which commercialised the router – a device which determines the optimal path along which packets of data should flow on a computer network. The growth of Cisco is also attributed to its setting of standards for networking equipment through its proprietary Internet Operating System (IOS). Both routers and IOS are key technologies supporting the Internet and enables customers of the company to build large-scale, integrated computer networks. Growth of the company has been driven by the surge in data traffic on the Internet. The company initially targeted universities, aerospace and government facilities relying on word-of-mouth and contacts for sales. The market for routers opened up in late 1980s and Cisco became the first company to offer reasonably-priced, high-performance routers. It went public in 1990 and soon after initiated an acquisitions strategy to broaden the range of products offered. Originally focusing on corporate data networking it began to target both Internet Service Providers and the home networking market.

The primary value-stream for Cisco is products, particularly routers. It has attempted to broaden the range of this value by offering a wider range of products. It also provides traditional added-value services such as its after-sales service. However, Cisco also provides value by managing its wider value network with a range of partners. These include resellers that sell and support Cisco products, service specialists providing network integration and operations and component manufacturers that provide most of the company's actual manufacturing capability.

In system's terms, Cisco's main transformation is the assembly of inter-networking equipment such as routers. The key inputs for Cisco consist of parts from a vast range of suppliers as well as a vast range of data associated with this supply. The key outputs from Cisco are completed products. The competitive environment for Cisco consists of companies producing comparable products in support of the infrastructure of the Internet. Control for Cisco means ensuring that it has sufficient information about its internal operations to ensure the efficient and effective delivery of goods to its customers (regulation). It also needs to ensure effective monitoring of its competitive environment to ensure that it develops new products for its marketplace (adaptation).

Cisco engages in B2C and B2B eCommerce. In terms of B2B eCommerce it has integrated its ERP systems with key suppliers through an extranet. In terms of B2C eCommerce it has built a Web portal which enables its customers to order and configure products online.

It is possible to describe briefly some of the gains that Cisco experiences from its engagement with eBusiness. In terms of efficacy, Cisco is able to relate to a large range of suppliers and assemble a vast range of parts to produce its technical products. In terms of efficiency, Cisco uses B2C and B2B eCommerce as well as intra-business eBusiness to lower its costs. In terms of effectiveness, Cisco maintains that eBusiness has allowed it to grow quickly and allows it to adapt more quickly to environmental changes. It is therefore better able to compete in its key markets.

Cisco has implemented an eBusiness strategy to enable fast integration of its supply chain with key business processes. The supply chain is critical to the business as Cisco's global manufacturing operation consists of 34 plants, only two of which are owned by the company. Suppliers make up to 90% of the subassembly of Cisco products and 55% of the final assembly. This means that suppliers regularly ship finished goods directly to Cisco customers.

A key component of Cisco's B2B eCommerce strategy is integration of its ERP systems with the information systems of its key suppliers. Suppliers use their ERP systems to run their Cisco production lines, allowing them to respond to demand from Cisco in real-time. This is enhanced by the introduction of Cisco Manufacturing Online, an extranet portal that allows partners to access real-time manufacturing information including data on demand forecasts, inventory and purchase orders.

Such a technical infrastructure means that changes in parts of the supply chain are communicated almost instantaneously to the company. For instance, if one supplier is low on a component then Cisco can analyse its supply chain for excess supplies elsewhere. Changes in forecasted demand are also communicated in real-time, enabling suppliers to respond immediately to requests for products or materials.

Payments to suppliers are triggered by a shop-floor transaction in the ERP system indicating that production is complete. The transaction initiates an analysis of inventory to determine the value of components sold by suppliers and triggers an electronic payment to suppliers. Annual benefits from the use of this ERP system integration are estimated to be in the realm of millions of dollars of savings per year.

Cisco has also engaged in B2C eCommerce innovation. It has introduced a Web portal known as Cisco Connection Online which consists of a dynamic online catalogue, a facility for ordering and configuring products online, a status agent that allows customers and retailers to track orders, a customer service section, a technical assistance section and a software library. The company currently estimates to earn 75% of its $20 billion sales through its portal. The portal is also indicated as contributing to a 20% reduction in overall operating costs.

Cisco created an internal online community within its emerging technologies group, called the Idea Zone or I-Zone. Within this space anyone can propose ideas for new products, processes or markets. Ideas are critiqued by others and filtered for further development.

In 2011 Cisco is reported as having revenues of $43 billion and employing over 71,000 people. This revenue was driven largely by its core business: sales of hardware devices such as routers and switches, software such as its network operating system and the provision of associated services such as network management. More recently however, Cisco has diversified into a large range of associated businesses such as optical networks, wireless equipment and Internet telephony. It is also developing technologies associated with supporting the increase in video traffic via the Internet. As part of this strategy, Cisco has produced a technology known as telepresence, which provides a high-quality videoconferencing facility.

Cisco has organised its structure around key functions rather than customer segments. To manage innovation in new markets it has introduced an elaborate system of committees made up of managers from different functions. These committees are supported by fluid working groups. This form of matrix organisation is supported by collaborative working using online tools provided by the company itself, such as Telepresence.

Issues

- Cisco does have a general Internet website. Could this be regarded as a form of B2C eCommerce? Who are the typical customers of Cisco?
- How much of Cisco business is P2P eBusiness? Does this company maintain partnership networks and what role does ICT play?
- Cisco uses an extranet to ensure integration of external relationships with suppliers. Consider the benefits as well as costs of extranets in managing the supply chain.
- Cisco is a heavy user of technology for collaborative working. How important are such online tools within companies worldwide?

CS

5   Citizens Advice Bureau
See page: 267

Case description

The Citizens Advice Bureau (CAB) is one of the foremost independent charities in the UK. It has two main goals: to provide the advice people need for the problems they face (with regard to debt, benefits, employment, housing or discrimination) and to improve the policies and practices that affect people's lives (for example, the CAB recently campaigned for improvements in council tax collection procedures). The organisation delivers advice free of charge largely through over 20,000 part-time volunteers working out of some 3,500 community locations in England and Wales, run by 382 individual charities. Advice ranges from personal finances and housing matters to legal matters and consumer issues. During 2010/11, the organisation in the UK helped 2.1 million people to solve 7.1 million problems. Citizens Advice Bureaux exist in a number of other countries such as Australia, New Zealand, Israel and the USA.

The first 200 CAB offices were opened in 1939, four days after the outbreak of the Second World War. In 1972 the CAB became independent of government, although the National Association of Citizens Advice Bureaux is still publicly subsidised. In 2003, this organisation changed its operating name to Citizens Advice (in England and Northern Ireland) and Cyngor ar Bopeth (Advice on Everything) in Wales. Each local bureau is a separate, autonomous charity with its own independent appointed trustees; some of the bureaux receive significant funding from local government authorities as well as central government. Each of these local bureaux are members of the Citizens Advice network.

During much of its history CAB advisors used a paper-based system to record data about casework. Comprehensive paper manuals of legislation and welfare information were provided to help advisors in their work. Staff communicated with other government agencies and private sector organisations primarily through letters. In recent years, to help support its dispersed activity infrastructure the CAB has created a shared ICT infrastructure.

As a member of Citizens Advice, each bureaux is provided with Internet access through a Virtual Private Network. This allows staff to access a national Web portal, known as AdviserNet. This portal provides access to a large and continuously maintained resource of content on matters ranging from employment law to benefits entitlement, housing regulation and debt management. Since 2008, advisors are required to enter data about clients and their problems into the central national database (CASE). The data on CASE is centrally stored and backed up by Citizens Advice. However, the database is designed such that data is owned and accessible only to the bureau that entered it. Aggregated data is available for use in generating statistics about the activities of the organisation and the needs of its clients. This is used not only to help tailor its day-to-day advice work but also to help inform its work as a pressure group.

Citizens Advice also runs a website accessible to the general public known as Adviceguide. This website had almost 14.2 million visits to its home page in 2009/10. The organisation has also developed the website *www.advice4me.org.uk* specifically aimed at young people. On these sites a number of advicepods (podcasts) are available that can be downloaded to mobile devices. The organisation also has a Twitter account tweeting advice tips and campaigning news. At the time of writing, the CAB account has more than 17,000 followers. Similarly, CAB has a Facebook account in which members post their questions on the wall to get advice.

Not surprisingly given its prominence, Citizens Advice has started to play a role within electronic government. For instance, in 2002 central government in the UK issued guidance to government bodies, encouraging them to develop channel strategies. These strategies were described as a set of choices about how, and through what means, services will be delivered to the citizen. A critical channel is through intermediaries such as Citizens Advice, organisations fulfilling a key role in tiered access to government services.

Issues

- Each local bureau is relatively autonomous in terms of its operations and management. In what ways does having a centralised ICT infrastructure help ensure consistency of operation across a large network of separate bureaux?
- Have a look at the *adviceguide* website . What advice and help can you get from this site? What are the advantages of such a site as compared to visiting a local bureau? What disadvantages are there as compared to face-to-face interaction with an advisor?

6   Dell

Case description

The US-based technology company Dell Inc. has its headquarters in Round Rock, Texas. It develops, manufactures, markets, sells, and supports personal computers, servers, data storage devices, network switches, software, televisions, computer peripherals, and other technology-related products. The company employs over 100,000 people worldwide.

Michael Dell, the founder of Dell Computer Corporation, is often credited with creating a revolution in the personal computer industry. Dell's business model built around direct selling to the customer and, by managing its inventory and distribution processes effectively, is credited with a rapid growth in the business.

The idea for the company originated in a business run from Michael Dell's parents' home when he was a teenager. From here he originally sold memory chips and disk drives for IBM PCs. Michael Dell was able to sell his products through newspapers/magazines at 10%-15% below retail prices. He dropped out of college in 1984 and started assembling his own IBM clones selling direct to customers at 40% below retail price. In 1988 his company went public. Having experienced some problems in 1990 the company re-established its position by selling its PCs via mail order through the Soft Warehouse/ CompUSA superstores. In 1994 the company abandoned superstores to return to its mail-order/direct retail roots. Dell is now a worldwide business based around integrated manufacturing and supply of hardware.

The primary value-stream for Dell is tangible products such as computers and peripheral equipment. A certain degree of other intangible items such as software are also provided to customers. It attempts to provide added-value services such as customisable configuration and online help and support. Dell originally started its Internet initiative in the late 1980s to attempt to increase its level of customer support. The company traditionally provided the customer support using a call-centre. At the call-centre Dell customer care representatives normally advised customers to obtain software updates either sent on disks or as software downloads from a site run by Compuserve. By 1989 Dell began online distribution of software updates.

In system's terms, Dell's main transformation is the assembly of computing equipment. The key inputs for Dell consist of parts from a vast range of suppliers as well as a vast range of data associated with this supply. The key outputs from Dell are completed products. The competitive environment for Dell consists of hardware companies producing comparable products. Control for Dell means ensuring that it has sufficient information about its internal operations to ensure the efficient and effective delivery of goods to its customers (regulation). It also needs to carry out effective monitoring of its competitive environment to ensure that it develops new products for its marketplace (adaptation).

Dell engages in both B2C and B2B eCommerce. It also has integrated its internal information systems to become an effective intra-business eBusiness, through strategies such as just-in-time inventory management. In terms of efficacy, Dell has been able to diversify into a vast range of hardware products for retail. In terms of efficiency, Dell has been successful at lowering its internal costs and is able to pass on lower costs to its customers. In terms of effectiveness, Dell is able to sell its products across the world and is able to relate to a large range of suppliers.

In 1996 the company launched *www.dell.com* to provide technical support online. Initially, the website was used to provide technical information to customers. Later, customers were able to order through a website that provided an online catalogue of products. Customers can now also enter details of specific configurations of hardware they require and hence configure systems online. Dell routes technical support queries according to component-type and to the level of support purchased. For instance, there are five levels of support offered for business customers. For individual consumers the company offers 24 x 7 telephone and online troubleshooting.

Dell engages in supply chain innovation including customisation of hardware and direct retailing to customers. Customers may order a personal computer through a website that provides an online catalogue of products. Customers can also enter details of specific configurations of hardware they require through this website. Such build-to-order retail requires assembly plants around the world (Austin, Texas; Limerick, Eire; Penang, Malaysia) close to suppliers such as Intel (chips), Maxtor (hard drives) and Selectron (motherboards). Order forms follow each PC across the factory floor. As well as online customer support the Dell site provides order and courier-tracking and pages of technical support related to the tagging of machines. Dell associates a service tag, a unique alpha-numeric identifier, with most of its products.

Traditionally, Dell has sold all its products, whether to individual consumers or to business customers, using a direct-sales model via online and telephone channels. The company receives payments for products before it has to pay for the materials and practices just-in-time (JIT) inventory management. This means that Dell builds computers only after customers place orders and by requesting materials from suppliers as needed. Dell advertisements have used several channels including television, the Web, magazines, catalogues and newspapers. Marketing strategies include lowering prices at all times of the year, offering free bonus products (such as Dell printers), and offering free shipping. Dell also runs its own online community site in which members can access and contribute to fora and blogs on the use of latest technology. Dell introduced a customer community known as IdeaStorm. The aim was to allow users of Dell products to help each other with problems such as software installation. One aim of IdeaStorm was to take pressure off the company's helpdesk. IdeaStorm also enabled the

CS

company to gather information about use of their products and what their customers thought.

Issues

- Would you describe Dell as engaging in customer relationship management through its website?
- Dell uses just-in-time inventory management and manufacturing. How important is ICT to this business philosophy?
- How important is tracking of products to the Dell business; not only in terms of the supply chain but also in terms of its customer chain?
- IdeaStorm could be considered a type of adjunct electronic community. Is it appropriate to describe it as such?

---

7   dotCYMRU

See page: 153

Case description

Domain names are a significant part of the pragmatics of the World Wide Web in particular and the Internet more widely. They form an important element of Internet governance and act as supporting infrastructure for critical aspects of the global information society, such as electronic business and electronic government. In this case study, first, we provide a description of the context for domain names on the Internet and the World Wide Web (Web) and particularly focus upon, so-called, top-level domain names or TLDs. The Internet Corporation for Assigned Names and Numbers (ICANN) control the assignment of domain names internationally. Second, we help ground issues relating to the promotion, assignment, administration and use of TLDs by describing an interesting case in progress from a distinctive geographical region of the UK, Wales. The dotCYM campaign is a not-for-profit pressure group that, for a number of years, has attempted to promote a distinct Internet domain for the Welsh linguistic and cultural community. The campaign believes that the Welsh language and culture connotes a community that should be identified and enhanced by having its own Top Level Domain on the Internet.

International control of domain names

Domain names arose as an attempt to provide meaningful conventions enabling connections to be made between computer systems across the Internet. Any domain name is typically made up of three or more parts referred to as domain levels. Levels therefore provide structure to the domain name. In a particular URL, domain levels read from right to left: sub-domain, 2nd level domain, top-level domain. Top-level domains (TLDs), consist of either, so-called, generic top-level domain names (such as .com) referred to as gTLDs, or country codes (such as .uk), referred to as ccTLDs. gTLDs are also referred to as 1st level domain names. 2nd level domains serve to further refine the top-level domain name by typically suggesting the type of provider. For instance, .ac indicates an academic institution based in the UK. Sub-domains refer to those domains below the 2nd level and are typically used to refer to a specific content provider. In our example, cardiff signifies the website of Cardiff University.

Internet Protocol addresses are mapped to domain names by domain name servers. These are computer systems in the inter-network that perform such transformation. For such domain servers to work effectively standardisation is needed in domain names. ICANN have responsibility for a number of naming conventions including gTLDs such as .com and .org and ccTLDs such as .uk and .fr. They also have responsibility for sponsored top-level domain names (sTLDs) such as .coop and .museum and un-sponsored TLDs such as .biz.

IANA, the precursor organisation to ICANN, originally created seven Generic Top Level Domains (gTLDs), consisting of strings of three letters taken from the following list: .com. (signifying some form of commercial organisation), .org (signifying any type of organisation but typically used to signify public sector or voluntary sector organisations), .gov (initially used to signify government establishments generally but now restricted to refer to US government establishments), .edu (used generally to signify an educational institution internationally), .mil (initially used to signify military establishments generally but now restricted to refer to US Armed Forces establishments), .int. (initially conceived for international entities), .net (initially used to signify networks and therefore a generic free usage domain).

However, in 'an uncharacteristic lapse of consistency on the part of early Internet designers' IANA established a parallel list of ccTLDs. Part of the reason ccTLDs were introduced and began to be used was because gTLDs gradually began to be perceived internationally as US TLDs. For instance, the original intention was that any educational institution in the world could register itself under the .edu gTLD. In practice, it turned out that, with a few exceptions, only US-based institutions registered under .edu.

Country code top level domains (ccTLDs) consist of strings of two letters, for example .uk, .fr, .es. ICANN clearly states that it does not decide on the status of a country. The verification of countries is therefore delegated to the International Standards Organisation (ISO) and more specifically to inclusion in its ISO 3166 list of country codes. However, there are considerable anomalies in the ccTLD naming conventions arising both from inconsistencies in the ISO list and from the presence of early naming agreements established before the creation of ICANN. The ISO list is derived primarily from a list of country names published by the United Nations, which also assigns unique codes to a number of inhabited overseas territories. Thus, in 2002 there were 189 countries which had seats in the UN General Assembly but 239 countries on the ISO 3166–1 list. Some countries have also established country codes that conflict with the ISO 3166–1 list. The .uk country code is a notable example in that the specified country code for Britain in the ISO 3166–1 list is .gb. Some regions within this country also have codes established in ISO 3166–1 list. Examples here are .gg (Guernsey), .im (Isle of Man) and .je (Jersey). The current ICANN namespace contains 255 registered ccTLDs.

Therefore, over time the domain system has been gradually extended, sometimes in an apparently piecemeal manner. For instance, the current ICANN namespace contains 21 registered gTLDs all of which are open for use as supporting infrastructure for the Internet. Adding to its complexity, since 2000 a number of sponsored top-level domain names (sTLDs) have been created, typically backed by some defined community. The named sponsor of an sTLD is delegated the responsibility of administering the domain in the sense that it decides if a person or legal entity can register for use of the domain. Such sponsored domain names include, .aero (signifying the aeronautical industry), .coop signifying cooperative organisations, .museum (signifying museums), and .cat (signifying the Catalan language and cultural community, discussed below).

Also since 2000 a number of un-sponsored domain names have been created. These are generic top-level domain names, not backed by a community but which operate under the policies established by the global Internet community, directly through ICANN. Such un-sponsored domain names include: .biz. (signifying businesses), .info (signifying information resources – an extension of .net), .pro (signifying independent professionals – lawyers, doctors, etc.), .name (signifying individuals or legal entities that wish to register their names as domains).

Applications for the approval of a new TLD are made to ICANN using a defined process. Decision-making on applications within ICANN is conducted via a series of meetings held by ICANN's board of governors, and within a variety of committees such as the GNSO (Generic Names Supporting Organisation), the ALAC (At-Large Advisory Committee), the GAC (Governmental Advisory Committee) and other constituencies. Representation from various interest groups is included at committee level. After approving a new TLD domain, ICANN delegates the administration of issuing it to IANA. Domain names frequently launch with a defined sunrise period, which refers to the period of time at the launch of a new top level domain during which owners of trademarks may register a domain name containing the owned mark.

dotCYM campaign

The dotCYM campaign is a not-for-profit organisation which has been seeking for a number of years to establish a TLD for the Welsh linguistic and cultural community. It believes that the Welsh language and culture is a community that should be identified and would be enhanced by having its own TLD on the Internet.

However, in terms of the international process described in the previous section, the options available to establish a Welsh Identity on the Internet through a TLD are limited. In terms of assigning a two-letter country code for Wales, ISO maintains that it cannot include Wales in the ISO 3166–1 list as Wales does not meet the criteria established by the UN for assuming the status of an independent country. However, given that regions such as Guernsey (.gg) are included in the list, as well as territorial possessions such as the Faroe Islands (.fo) and the Falkland Islands (.fk), it was suggested that a campaign sponsored by the Welsh Assembly Government might increase the chances of a further exception to the rule being made in favour of Wales. However, in the case of this becoming a possibility the two-letter string .cy had already been taken by Cyprus. Available alternatives include .wa, .wl and .cw.

In terms of assigning a three-letter sponsored TLD for Wales, the dotCYM campaign were initially promoting the potential use of .cym because it is the official ISO 639–2 alpha-3 code and the latest ISO 639–3 code for the Welsh language. The campaign was hence promoting the use of the .cym TLD as signifying a community (Welsh language, culture and interests) rather than a country. They believed that this sidestepped the problem ICANN has with including Wales as a country and draws on precedence established by the .cat TLD. In 2010 however, ICANN ruled that the TLD .cym was to be reserved for use by the Cayman Islands, even though they already have use of .ky. The dotCYM campaign is therefore currently canvassing for opinion on a number of other TLDs such as .cymru (cymru being the Welsh for Wales), .cwl (Cymru Wales) or .wales (dotCYM, 2010).

The campaign maintains that there would be a number of consequent benefits from having a TLD for the Welsh

CS

community. The prime focus is particularly one of promoting and supporting the Welsh language and it is claimed that the presence of an sTLD will serve to unite Welsh-speaking communities within Wales. It is also seen as a means of uniting other historic Welsh communities in other parts of the British Isles, as well as in North and South America, and Australia. The presence of having a domain name is seen as playing a pivotal role in promoting further the use of the Welsh language on the World Wide Web as a modern method of communication. However, in their campaign literature dotCYM also promote a larger vision for the domain name. They see it as enabling the creation of an online community of people, organisations and other stakeholders of all languages, ethnicity and diversity that have an interest in Wales and all things Welsh.

The dotCYM campaign took its initial inspiration from a successful campaign which has already established .cat as a sponsored top-level domain name through ICANN. The .cat domain was approved in September 2005 to serve the needs of the Catalan Linguistic and Cultural Community on the Internet. Catalan is an official language in Spain, and is widely spoken by an estimated 10 million first and second language speakers worldwide in many autonomous Spanish regions. The Charter for use of the .cat TLD states that 'the .cat TLD will be established to serve the needs of the Catalan Linguistic and Cultural Community on the Internet (the "Community")'. The definition of the Catalan Linguistic and Cultural Community refers 'to those individuals, groups, businesses, organisations, entities or initiatives, however constituted, eligible to register in the .cat TLD according to this Agreement and the .cat Charter. The Community includes those who use the Catalan language for their online communications, and/or promote the different aspects of Catalan culture online, and/or want to specifically address their online communications to this Community.'

PuntCAT comprised a private Catalonia foundation consisting of a coalition of around 98 organisations supporting the Catalonian language and culture. The registry operator selected the CORE (Internet Council of Registrars), to provide registry services. The establishment of the .cat TLD is seen as novel for ICANN, as the majority of countries and geographical territories all have domain names consisting of two letters and not three. As we have seen above, domain names consisting of three letters have previously been reserved for non-territorial domains which are largely under professional or national organisations like .com or .biz.

The Catalan government, soon after assignment, expressed its pleasure with the decision and expected that as a result of this decision many applications will be made to switch existing websites from .es (Spain) to .cat (Catalonia). The Catalonian Government itself announced that it would register its site under this new domain. During the sunrise period, there were around 11,400 .cat domain name applications, 9,300 of which were granted. Within 10 months, 19,000 domain names were registered under the sTLD, referencing 3.5 million Web pages.

As a sTLD, the .cym domain name must clearly signify a community. If successful, the sponsor is delegated the responsibility by ICANN of administering the domain in the sense that it decides if a person or legal entity can register for use of the domain. Most of the held benefits for the .cym domain relate to issues of signification. This is because a domain name is only useful in terms of what it signifies. To help unpack this it is useful to consider domain names in terms of the meaning triangle. Designation defines the symbol being used. In the case considered here this is the proposed string .cym. Intension refers to the concept for which the symbol is being taken to stand for. In this case, the campaign is proposing .cym to stand for some form of community. Extension refers to instances of the concept (intension) in question. In this case, the domain name will be used to stand for a community that, in practice, will consist of a body of organisations providing Web-based content addressed using the .cym domain.

In 2011 ICANN decided to end most restrictions on the names of generic top-level domains. This means that organisations are now able to bid for essentially any arbitrary top level Internet domain name and pay an annual fee for its registration. As a result of this the dotCYM campaign has changed tack and is now bidding for two new TLDs, .cymru and .wales. dotCYMRU is intended for use by websites based in Wales which have primarily Welsh language content while DotWales is intended for use by websites based in Wales, with primarily English language content and designed for use by international users.

Issues

- How important are domain names to the competitive performance of particular nations and regions?
- How important to an organisation's strategy is choosing and registering a domain name?
- What communities does the .cym or .cymru domain seek to signify, as compared to the .wales domain?
- How important is the registration of domain names to modern-day companies and other organisations?
- How important are domain names to nation-states?

8   eBay

See page: 162

Case description

eBay is one of the foremost examples of C2C eCommerce. Its dominance is due to early entry into what was a niche market at the time. Its business model relies on that used in familiar exchange and mart catalogues that have existed for decades. The competitive edge for the business lies in the way in which eCommerce enables mass customers to trade low-cost items efficiently through an auction process across the globe. eBay uses what is known as a Dutch auction model for its business. In this form of auction the seller places one or more identical items for sale at a minimum price for a set period. When the auction ends the highest bidder gains the item at their bid price. eBay also offers the ability for customers to pay for certain items offered through its website at a fixed price.

Pierre Omidyar created eBay in September 1995, using a website hosted by Omidyar's Internet service provider, and running the company in his spare time from his apartment. In its early guise eBay was little more than a simple marketplace where buyers and sellers could bid for items. The company took no responsibility for the goods being traded and gave no undertaking to settle disputes between parties.

By February 1996 so many people had visited the site that Omidyar decided to introduce a 10 Cent listing fee to recoup ISP costs. By the end of March 1996 eBay showed a profit. Eventually the volume of traffic to the site persuaded his ISP to ask him to move elsewhere. Omidyar decided to transfer the operation to a one-room office with his own Web server and he employed the services of a part-time employee. He also developed software capable of supporting a robust, scalable website as well as a transaction processing system to report on current auctions.

By August 1996 Omidyar had established one of his friends as the first president of eBay. In June 1997 the company approached venture capitalists for funding and secured $5 million. This enabled the company to establish a more extensive management structure for planned expansion. By the end of 1997 more than 3 million items (worth $94 million) had been sold on eBay amounting to revenues of $5.7 million and an operating profit of $900,000. eBay had an operating staff of only 67 employees at the time.

In its early days eBay undertook only limited marketing and relied on the loyalty of its customer-base and word-of-mouth referrals for its increased business growth. Eventually the company began to employ cross-promotional agreements, including banner advertising on Web portals such as Netscape and Yahoo!, as well as providing an auction service for AOL's classified section. This evolved into a conventional marketing campaign through traditional print and broadcast media in 1998.

In 1999 the company expanded internationally by creating communities in Canada and the UK. This was followed by expansion into Germany, Australia, Japan and France. During this year and into 2000 the company successfully held its position against strong new entrants into the online auctions market such as Amazon.com. The company also moved into the bricks and mortar area with the purchase of a San Francisco based auction house. eBay used this acquisition to move into the higher-price antiques sector of the market. By the end of June 1999 eBay had 5.6 million registered users and had conducted 29.4 million auctions during the previous 3-month period. In the third quarter of 2000 $1.4 billion worth of goods were traded on eBay in 68.5 million auctions, which generated $113.4 million in revenues. In 2012, eBay unveiled first-quarter profits of $725 million.

Millions of people join eBay each month from around the world and thousands of people around the globe earn a living as an eBay trader. Essentially, eBay's business model is a simple one of providing C2C auctions online. Much of the activity relies on collectors trading small-price items such as coins, stamps, militaria etc. Although the average item sold through these markets constitute no more than tens of dollars, as a whole, billions of dollars are traded every year in the US in C2C trading of this nature.

The concept is to provide a website where anyone wishing to buy or sell on eBay must register by providing personal and financial details. Every user of eBay is given a unique identifier. eBay offers a virtual tour of its services but people can start buying and selling straight away.

Sellers list items for sale by completing an online form. They pay a small listing fee for this privilege. The size of the fee depends on where and how the listing is presented and whether a reserve price is required for the item. Sellers also choose the duration they wish buyers to bid for the item. At the end of an auction, eBay notifies the seller of the winning bid and provides details of the successful bidder to the seller. The buyer and seller then make their own arrangements for payment and delivery of the goods, usually through email. Payment can be made by cash, cheque, and postal order or electronically through a payment service or financial intermediary such as Paypal (paypal.com), now a subsidiary of eBay. eBay charges a percentage of the final value of the transaction. For instance, suppose a seller listed a collection of stamps for sale at £24.00. The seller might

CS

pay approximately 50 pence to eBay to list this collection as a standard item on the website. If the collection was sold then the seller would pay 5% of the final sale price to the company.

Since buyers pay sellers before they receive items the business model runs on trust. The eBay feedback system is used to indicate problems with particular users. Users can file feedback about any user on the feedback site. This discourages trade with rogue participants. The only costs to eBay therefore amount to the costs of computing infrastructure and expenses associated with customer services. eBay keep no inventory, have no distribution network and does not have to maintain a large amount of staffing to make the company viable.

Most of eBay's sellers were serious collectors and small traders who used eBay as their shop-front. eBay enabled them to access a global marketplace for trading collectibles. For such a community eBay set up the eBay Café. This comprised a chat room where users of the site could communicate and exchange information. Such a facility proved useful to the company in being able to monitor customer reaction to various company initiatives. For instance, changes in pricing were frequently adversely commented on in such fora. eBay also used its customers to post answers to frequently answered questions (FAQs) on its bulletin boards and even employed some active and knowledgeable users of its site to provide email help to its new customers.

In an attempt to develop trust and loyalty among its customer community eBay established SafeHarbour in February 1998. SafeHarbour offered a certain verification and validation of customers, insurance associated with the selling and buying process and some regulation of sales activity. The company also created My eBay, a tool that customers could use to personalise the site in terms of keeping track of their favourite categories, view items they were selling or bidding on, or check their account balance.

Following a number of outages in 1999 the company decided to outsource its back-end infrastructure to an external supplier. It outsourced its Web servers, database servers and routers to these companies with the expectation of having excess capacity for preserving its service. Hence, periodic overhaul of the technical infrastructure of the company is critical to its success.

In 2012 eBay began an experiment in offline shopping. It occupied an empty shop in London's Soho district. Called the eBay boutique, the shop was stocked with 350 eBay bestsellers. Since the shop had no tills customers paid by smartphone, first selecting a product by pointing their smartphone at a QR code then paying via the ePayment section of the eBay website.

Issues

- Consider the issue of trust in relation to eCommerce transactions and how eBay attempts to build trust with its customers.
- How are electronic payments managed within eBay?
- Examine the issue of auction types. Try to identify the model for electronic auctions applied in eBay.
- Can eBay be considered a serious eProcurement hub?
- Investigate other ways of running auctions and search for any sites that run alternative auction models.
- eBay has been successfully sued by a number of companies for allowing traders to offer fake versions of their products through the website. Are problems with the trade in fake goods through eBay affecting eBay's long-term business model?
- Business analysts predict that many stores will start opening up offline outlets in collaboration with the online experience. Why do you think this is the case?

9   Facebook
See page: 253

Case description

Facebook was launched in February 2004 as a social networking website by Mark Zuckerberg, along with his fellow computer science students Eduardo Saverin, Dustin Moskovitz and Chris Hughes. The name of the company is taken from the name applied to a book commonly given to university students in the United States at the start of the academic year.

All Facebook users have their own personal profile. A Facebook profile usually consists of a profile picture, contact information, lists of interests, photos, notes and other personal data. To this profile other users may be added as friends. Facebook friends can interact in different ways: writing on profile walls, exchanging public or private messages, or using a chat feature. They may also receive automatic notifications when one of the friends in their network updates their profile. An additional facility for Facebook users is the creation of public or private groups formed around common interests. Public and private organisations can maintain their own pages (the so-called like pages) as a form of advertising.

The entry requirement for all Facebook users is to have a user's name and a profile picture that can be viewed by all the other users. The extent to which a profile can be accessed by other Facebook members, however, can be controlled through a number of specific privacy settings. For example, all Facebook profiles have their own Wall, that is, a space on which Facebook users can write short messages and post hyperlinks; however, Facebook users can decide who can see (and write on) their wall, and who cannot. One of the most popular applications in Facebook is the photos application that allows Facebook users to upload and share albums and photos.

Originally, Facebook was intended as a social network for Harvard students only. The website was later expanded to other colleges in the Boston area, the Ivy League, and Stanford University. Over time, students at other universities, as well as high school students, were gradually admitted to Facebook. Nowadays, membership is open to anyone aged 13 and over.

Facebook became a company in the summer of 2004. The first president of the company was Sean Parker, the creator of Napster. At the same time Facebook moved its base of operations to Palo Alto, California. The domain name facebook.com was purchased in 2005 for $200,000. In October 2008 Facebook set up its international headquarters in Dublin, Ireland. Facebook now has over 3,200 employees and offices in many countries.

The majority of the company's revenue comes from advertising, with Microsoft being the company's exclusive partner for serving banner advertising. In September 2009 the company first began to make a profit. Companies can create a page on Facebook with the aim of getting members to like their products or services. Clicking on the like button enables the company to add an advertisement, not only to the member's page but also to all of the member's friends.

In 2010 Facebook reshaped the way in which its users can interact introducing a new Facebook Messages service. This is a combination of text messaging, instant messaging (chat), emails, and regular messages. In terms of privacy policies, Facebook Messages is very similar to the other Facebook services. In 2011 the company announced a timeline feature which allows members to build an online record of their life history. Millions of websites now integrate with Facebook through social plug-ins that allow people to share things with other Facebook users, such as songs listened to or articles read.

It was estimated that Facebook reached 500 million users in 2010 and had 845 million users as of early 2012. This trajectory suggests that 1 billion users will be achieved in the 2013. Facebook ranks as the most popular social networking site in several English-speaking countries, including Canada, the United Kingdom, and the United States. However, it has failed to penetrate countries such as China and Russia.

In February 2012 the company announced an initial public offering in an attempt to raise $5 billion dollars for further investment. In 2011 the company generated $3.7 billion in revenue and $1 billion in net profits. Yet market analysts value the company as worth between $75 and $100 billion. This valuation is primarily based upon on its vast user-base and the data Facebook has about its user-base. It is hoped that the size and penetration of this social network will be a substantial platform for creating new business opportunities in areas such as social, or s-commerce, the buying and selling of goods through social networking sites. In May of 2012 Facebook was floated on the stock market with an initial share price of $38 a share. This meant that Facebook was initially valued at just over $100 billion. Within days the share price had fallen back because of fears investors had about the long-term profitability of the company.

In effect, some commentators caution that Facebook's strength is also a potential weakness and that the company will need to walk a tightrope over the next few years to strike the right balance (Economist, 2012a). The key strength of the company is reliant on the network effect; the value that members gain from having access to a large social network. In return for the free service which Facebook provides users implicitly provide the company with masses of data about themselves. This data is very valuable as a platform for commercial services such as advertising. But users may feel that certain uses of such personal data invade their personal privacy. At such a point users may decide to switch away from the service, removing the key value that the company provides to the market.

Issues

- Several governments have tried to block or even ban Facebook. This has happened in the People's Republic of China, Vietnam, Iran, Uzbekistan, Pakistan, Syria, and Bangladesh. Within certain Islamic states, claims have been raised that Facebook includes anti-Islamic content. Are sites such as Facebook a form of cultural imperialism?

- Sites such as Facebook are claimed to have played a major role in the organisation of political protest around the world, as in the case of the Arab uprising in Egypt and elsewhere. Investigate the role of such sites in political activity worldwide.

- Many young persons now prefer to use Facebook messaging over other forms of communication such as email. What are the long-term consequences for email and what do users of Facebook lose when they use such messaging?

- Use of Facebook has been banned within many workplaces in an attempt to prevent time-wasting. But how does this gel with professional social networking sites such as LinkedIn?

CS

- Difficulties of maintaining the privacy of content produced by Facebook users has been a continuing issue. The safety of user accounts has been compromised a number of times over the history of the site. Reflect upon this in terms of current thinking on data protection and data privacy.
- Some people have questioned the advertisement policy of Facebook. Should friends of a member who likes a company be advertised to by that company automatically?
- Facebook use has successfully moved onto mobile devices such as the smartphone. What part does a growing range of such mobile devices play in the growth of the company? What part will Facebook play in mobile commerce in the near future?

10 Failure in government ICT systems

See pages: 284, 294

Case description

Failure of ICT infrastructure can have a critical impact upon an organisation. For instance, in the concluding chapter of the book we covered the case of the London Ambulance Computer Aided Dispatch System. The failure of this system had drastic consequences for the London Ambulance Service. In this case we consider two examples of such a failure within UK government agencies. One such failure contributed to the closure of the agency concerned.

Child Support Agency

In the early 1990s, Electronic Data Systems (EDS) won the contract to develop an information system known as CS2 to support the work of the newly created Child Support Agency (CSA) in the UK. It is claimed that the failure of this information system contributed to the closure of the Child Support Agency and cost the UK taxpayer over a billion pounds sterling.

The Child Support Agency was a UK Government Executive Agency and was part of the Department for Work and Pensions in Great Britain and the Department for Social Development in Northern Ireland. The agency was launched on 5 April 1993 and was responsible for implementing the 1991 Child Support Act and subsequent legislation.

Child support, or child maintenance, is the contribution from a non-resident parent towards the financial cost of raising offspring. Maintenance is paid to the person with whom the child lives. The level and conditions of payment can either be mutually agreed between the two parties or, in case of disagreement, decided by legal means.

The CSA as originally conceived was a government organisation whose primary purpose was information-handling. For instance, the CSA was expected to:

- Receive and assess applications for child maintenance. This involved identifying and locating non-resident parents and confirming paternity.
- Calculate the payments to be made by non-resident parents. This involved establishing the non-resident parent's income or benefits status, determining the existence of children in the non-resident parent's current household and confirming levels of shared care.
- Maintain the accuracy of maintenance assessments. Any changes to the circumstances of the caring parent or the non-resident parent demanded recalculation of the maintenance payable.
- Collect money from non-resident parents and pay such money to the parent with care. This normally involved establishing a payment schedule with both parties.
- Enforce assessments. The agency was expected to chase missing payments and collect debt which may have built up.

After its creation in the early 1990s the CSA experienced difficulties in administering child support. This was apparently due to the complex rules embedded in the originating legislation that the agency was required to administer. In 2000 a new system of child support was introduced with the aim of simplifying the rules for child support and including a simplified calculation of maintenance. It was decided that the substantial business restructuring caused by these changes were to be supported by the introduction of a new ICT system.

In 2004, EDS was criticised by the UK's National Audit Office for its work on an ICT system for the CSA. This work ran seriously over budget and was over two years late in delivery, despite following the gateway review process mandated for the management of large projects of this nature and having spent over £91 million on external advice. These problems eventually led to the resignation of the CSA's head since the blame for this failure was laid partly at the door of the CSA. It was claimed that they did not have sufficient internal technical staff to be an 'intelligent customer' of EDS. Consequently, it took some time to establish an effective partnership between the CSA and EDS.

Following its introduction in March 2003 the CSA experienced problems with the operation of the new ICT system. The system somehow managed to overpay 1.9 million people and underpay around 700,000. This meant that the CSA was obliged to write off £1 billion in claims, while £750 million in child support payments from absent parents remained uncollected. An internal EDS memo was leaked that admitted that the system was 'badly designed, badly tested and badly implemented'.

Claims were made that this failure was partly due to the way in which a large and complex ICT system, at the upper end of what was achievable at the time, was introduced at the same time as attempts were being made to restructure the CSA.

In the period between 1993 and 2003 the CSA estimated that it had collected over £5 billion in maintenance payments and administered over 1.5 million live cases in 2006.

In December 2006, the Department for Work and Pensions released its Child Support white paper outlining its plans for the future of child support. It was announced by John Hutton MP that the CSA would be shut down, and replaced by the Child Maintenance and Enforcement Commission (C-MEC). This would be a non-departmental public body, therefore removed from the direct control of the Department for Work and Pensions.

The CSA case is part of a large programme of ICT adoption in government agencies in the UK. Much of this eGovernment change has been focused on enabling the customer chain with ICT. The CSA example demonstrates the importance of the effective implementation of back-end ICT infrastructure to eGovernment change.

The CSA was both an information-handling organisation and an enforcement organisation. Many of the operational difficulties the agency experienced appear due to the difficulties of capturing sufficient information in a timely manner about claimants and non-resident parents to make effective decisions quickly about enforcement actions.

The case is also an example of the difficulties of managing large-scale organisational change alongside considerable informatics change. The risk of failure in such situations is multiplied particularly when development is outsourced to an external supplier. Such sociotechnical change demands not only effective project management but also effective change management.

Passport Agency

The United Kingdom Passport Agency was established as an Executive Agency of the Home Office in April 1991. Its main aim was to provide passport services for British nationals in the United Kingdom promptly and economically. In 1998–99, the Agency employed an average of almost 1,800 staff in its passport offices in Belfast, Glasgow, Liverpool, London, Newport and Peterborough. The Agency's financial objective is to recover, via the passport fee, the full cost of passport services; the full cost includes the cost of non-fee bearing consular services provided by the Foreign and Commonwealth Office to UK citizens abroad.

In July 1996 the UK Passport Agency decided to introduce the idea of digital passports in an attempt to

minimise the risk of fraudulent use of passports. To do this the agency needed to replace its existing ICT system. It was envisaged that this would be done through a private finance initiative or outsourcing contract. The contractor bids were received in April 1997 and in June of that year a 10-year PFI contract was awarded to The Stationery Office (now Security Printing and Systems limited) for the printing and despatching of digital passports, valued at £120 million. In July of 1997 the Agency awarded a 10-year PFI contract for a similar value of £120 million to Siemens Business Services for the collection, storage and transmission of passport application data. This included the development of a new ICT system for this purpose.

In April 1998 an announcement was made that from October of that year children not already on their parents' passport would require their own passports to travel abroad.

In October 1998 the new information system (ICT system and procedures, including those outsourced) were introduced in the Agency's Liverpool office. One hundred Agency staff transferred over to Siemens. In November of the same year the new information system was rolled-out at the Newport office. 96 staff transferred over to Siemens at this office.

During the following summer of 1999 a number of problems were experienced by the Passport Agency. Over a half a million British citizens were less than happy to discover that their new passports could not be issued on time for them to take their holiday. In June 1999, processing times for passport applications were taking up to 50 working days. Emergency measures were introduced by the Home Office in July 1999, including free two-year extensions to passports. Coupled with a downturn in applications, these measures helped bring maximum processing times back within the Agency's 10 working day target by the end of August. However, the Home Office had to pay millions in compensation to citizens and in staff overtime required for managing the backlog of applications.

This information systems failure appears to have been due to a number of factors.

The change in the law on child passports was introduced at roughly the same time as the introduction of the new information system. The change in legislation caused a significant increase in the volume of applications for the summer of 1999. In May of that year, monthly output was 619,000 compared to a peak of 564,000 in the previous year. By June, the Passport Agency had around 565,000 applications still awaiting processing.

The introduction of a new passport processing system in two of the Agency's six offices was exacerbated by a failure to assess and test adequately the time needed by staff to learn and work the new passport processing system. The new system involved changes in clerical and administrative

CS

processes as well as computerisation. A four-month delay before the start of testing the new system, and testing its impact on productivity was not completed before it went live in late 1998

There was insufficient contingency planning in the event that implementation of the new system might not go according to plan. Despite the Passport Agency's experience of the flawed roll-out of its previous computer system in 1989, the agency launched the new system in its largest offices, Liverpool and Newport, which accounted for half its normal processing capacity

The strategy adopted by the Agency in early 1999 to get through the busy season rested on its past experience that it would be able to increase output by increasing overtime and hiring casual staff. A recovery plan was agreed between the Agency and the Home Office in March, including the recruitment of extra staff. However, the Agency did not foresee the loss in public confidence, which led to a sharp increase in applications and enquiries about them, once the delays attracted publicity.

The agency was also criticised for its failure to communicate effectively with the public, both at a personal level in dealing with calls from the public to its telephone enquiry bureau, and more generally via the media.

A National Audit Office Inquiry estimated that the cost of the additional measures taken by the Agency to deal with the failures during the year from October 1998 was around £12.6 million, including £6 million for additional staffing. The contract allowed Siemens to take responsibility for the risk associated with design and delivery of the system. However, the risk associated with business continuity remained with the Passport Agency. As a result, the agency incurred extra costs of £12.6m, with Siemens paying just £2.45m, spread over several years.

Not surprisingly, the Inquiry highlighted a number of important lessons. First, the need for proper testing of new systems before committing to live operation. Second, for staff to be adequately trained in the use of new ICT systems and in new procedures required. Third, the need to have realistic contingency plans in place. Fourth, the need, when service delivery is threatened, to have the capability to keep the public well informed.

For effective innovation organisations need to treat information systems change as a total package comprising both technical and social change. However, organisations frequently forget the need for effective management of project risks and effective change management practices, particularly user training.

Issues

- Both cases could be regarded as prominent examples of the continuing poor management of government ICT projects. There is a long history of public sector information systems failures in the UK, such as these cases. Why do you think this is?
- Evaluation of a number of public sector information systems failure (frequently through public inquiries) have expressed concerns over use of outsourcing providers for large-scale ICT projects. What sorts of concerns do you think might be raised in such evaluations, as, for instance in the case of the CSA? Why do you think these problems occur?
- Much of the information required for effective working of the CSA demanded integrated government information systems. Consider the effect of such integration on this example of information systems and organisational failure.
- The case of the change in passport legislation and its impact upon both the information system and its encompassing activity system, demonstrates the need to consider both activities and information jointly in any design. Why do you think this lesson is frequently ignored?

11   Google
See pages: 159

Case description

In a sense, although it developed merely as a search engine, Google as a company is now the most prominent example of an information brokerage on the Web. To google has become established as a verb in the English language and has become synonymous with searching for information on any particular topic. As such, the company is in an unprecedented position as a gatekeeper to information on the global scale.

Google Inc. is the most well-known of the companies specialising in Internet search and online advertising. The company is based in Mountain View, California, employing many thousands of full-time workers. Google's mission statement is, '*to organize the world's information and make it universally accessible and useful*'.

Google was co-founded by Larry Page and Sergey Brin while they were students at Stanford University, US on the back of research they were conducting on improvement to the algorithms underlying search engines. Traditionally, search engines worked in terms of matching a series of search terms entered by the user against the terms found in Web pages. The ranking of sites provided to the user was typically based on the number of times the searched for terms existed in the pages of the site.

Page and Brin produced an algorithm called PageRank which analyses the links emanating from and pointing to

Web documents and then assigns a numerical weighting to each element of a set of such documents with the purpose of measuring each document's relative importance within the set. In this sense, the PageRank algorithm treats links in a similar manner to academic citations. Generally, the larger the number of citations of an academic paper the more important the paper is considered by the academic community.

Google uses Web crawlers (also known as Web spiders or Web robots) to build and maintain its representation of links between Web documents. A Web Crawler is a type of software agent; a program or automated script which browses the World Wide Web in a methodical, automated manner. Web crawlers are mainly used to create a copy of all the visited pages for later processing by a search engine that indexes the downloaded pages to provide fast searches for users.

Google is best known for its web search service, which now gives it a dominant market share of the search engine market. Google indexes billions of Web pages through the process described above. Users search for Web content through the use of keywords and logical operators such as NOT and AND. The search engine ranks hits on the basis of the number of links a page receives, as well as the importance of the Web documents sourcing the links.

The company was first created in 1998 and went public in 2004. Through a series of new product developments, acquisitions and partnerships, the company has expanded its initial search and advertising business into other areas, including Web-based email, online mapping, office productivity, and video sharing, among others. Google has also employed its search technology in other services, including Image Search, Google News, the price comparison site Google Product Search, the interactive Usenet archive Google Groups and Google Maps.

As a value proposition, Google relies on the network effect, namely, that many people use its search engine to look for products and services. Google's application AdWords allows Web advertisers to display advertisements alongside Google's search results and the Google Content Network, through either a cost-per-click or cost-per-view scheme. This means that the company generates most of its revenue by displaying advertisements from the AdWords service that are tailored to the content of the email messages displayed on screen. The service is attractive to advertisers because it allows them to tailor eMarketing campaigns to specific searches and user profiles. The related service, Google AdSense, is also a key revenue stream. This allows website owners to display Google adverts on their own site, and earn money every time ads are clicked. Advertisers don't directly buy advertising space on Google. They bid on keywords associated with key terms and Website content. The bidding occurs through an AdWords auction service. Hence, the more popular a keyword, the more money an advertiser has to pay for it.

In 2004, Google launched its own free Web-based email service, known as Gmail which provides the capability to use Google technology to search email. Google has also developed several applications for the desktop, the most well-known probably being Google Maps. This consists of an interactive mapping program which allows users to locate places and pinpoint them against maps of the surrounding area at various scales of resolution. More recently, the application Picasa allows users to maintain an online photo album.

In an attempt to foster a culture of innovation Google encourages its employees to be creative. Personnel are allotted 20% of their time to pursue their own ideas. Several high visibility Google products such as Gmail and Google Earth emerged in this way. New ideas, at whatever stage of development are posted to the company's intranet, where they are evaluated and ranked by other personnel. Those ideas that collect the highest community ranking are pursued in more depth.

However, Google's sometimes aggressive expansion strategy has met with controversy. For example, in January 2006 Google agreed to censor its search service within China. Google.cn was highly regulated by the Chinese authorities and restricted access to thousands of terms and sites. As an instance, the BBC news website was made unavailable and searches for the banned Falun Gong spiritual movement produced only articles denouncing it. In January 2010 Google threatened to stop its censoring of search results in China and even to shut down its site completely in the country. This was in response to apparent hacking attacks on the company's Gmail service, targeting Chinese human rights activists.

Google introduced an application known as Street View in May 2007. This is a feature of Google Maps and Google Earth that provides panoramic views from a row of positions along a street. In March 2009, the service was launched in the UK amongst much controversy. Civil liberty groups cited it as a potential invasion of privacy. A number of images were taken off the site after requests from various people and organisation. These included an image of Number 10 Downing Street, an image showing some nude children playing in a garden, an image of a man drunk in the street and an image of a man leaving a sex shop.

In 2008 Google reached an agreement with representatives of authors and publishers in the United States to make millions of books in America searchable online. Under the terms of the agreement, Google is free to digitise most books published in America, including those that are out of print. It then makes chunks of text available through its search engine, sells individual eBooks, and offers libraries subscriptions to its entire database. Google keeps approximately one third of resulting revenue and gives the rest to a book-rights registry that pays copyright holders.

In 2011 the company launched Google+, a multi-lingual social networking and identity service. As of 2012, it has a total of 250 million registered users of whom 150 million are active. This is seen as a direct attempt to move into ground currently held by social networking sites such as Facebook.

Issues

■ Concern has been expressed over the dominance of Google in both the search engine market and the wider information brokerage market. As a reaction Microsoft proposed an alliance with the search engine Yahoo!, which came to nothing. What difficulties might ensue if Google becomes the monopoly player in this market?

■ For online businesses the issue of optimising the chance of the company website being retrieved early in the list of hits by search engine's such as Google is critical to online orders. This area of search engine optimisation is a specialist component of website design. How important is this optimisation to electronic marketing?

■ Google has come under fire for implicitly allowing censorship of Web content for users of the search engine in countries such as China. How healthy for individuals and organisations is the reliance on Google as a dominant gatekeeper to Web content?

■ Google has introduced a series of new privacy rules for users subscribing to its services. What impact will this have upon the continued growth of Google?

■ In its Google books application the company eventually intends to make all of the world's material published in English available in digital form. What are the pros and cons of this development?

12   Hollerith electronic tabulating machine

Case description

The founding fathers of the United States of America wrote into the constitution that a census of the population should be conducted every 10 years. The US Census Bureau was established for this purpose and can be considered as a major governmental activity system that has been emulated worldwide. The first US census was undertaken in 1790. The census was funded by Congress and conducted by assistant federal marshals from 1790 to 1890. During this century all data processing was conducted by hand. Figure C1 illustrates the major activities undertaken within the system of census-taking as evident in the 1890 US census.

For the 1880 census the Census Office received an increase in funding and was able to employ its own enumerators. Also, formal enumeration districts were defined for the first time. Over time, an increasing range of variables about the US population were collected (age, sex, race, place of birth, occupation etc.). Not surprisingly, it took almost 10 years to complete the data processing by hand for the 1880 census. With increasing population size

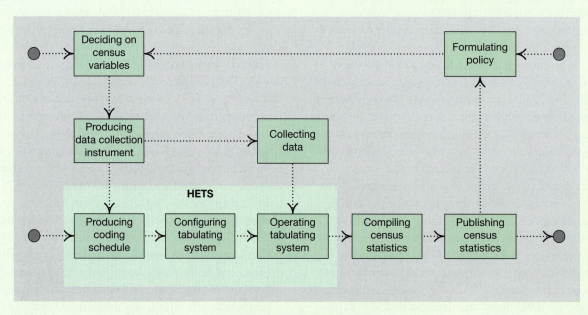

Figure C1 *The place of the Hollerith electronic tabulating system (HETS) within census-taking*

it was feared that the completion of the next census would overlap with the start of that immediately following.

A technological innovation supplied the solution to this problem. In 1890 the first automated census was conducted successfully due to an invention introduced by Herman Hollerith, known as the tabulating machine.

Herman Hollerith was born in 1860 of German immigrant parentage. He graduated from Columbia University School of Mines with a mining engineering degree in 1879 at the age of 19. That year, one of his former professors requested that he come to work for the US Census Bureau. After three years there, in 1882 Hollerith moved to Boston to teach mechanical engineering at MIT.

In 1886 the first test of Hollerith's tabulating machine took place in Baltimore's Department of Health. The test was conducted on recorded data about the deceased. The machine was then used in various ways such as the Surgeon General's office of the War Department and by the US Navy.

Data in the tabulating machine was recorded on punched cards and fed through an electro-mechanical device which sorted the cards according to a programmed characteristic. The use of punched cards for control purposes was originally pioneered in the Jacquard loom, a machine that automated the task of weaving complex patterns. In this loom, pasteboard cards with punched holes were used. Holes in the cards determined the passage of rods that controlled the operation of the loom.

Despite this history, Hollerith himself claimed that the idea of using punched cards was reputedly suggested when taking a train journey. He observed conductors using their punches to quickly code data about the characteristics of an individual onto a ticket, such as height, hair colour, size of nose. These codes, which were known to other conductors, could be used to detect any fraudulent use of tickets.

In the tabulating machine, each card recorded data about one individual. The card was made up of a number of columns and rows and holes punched through cells on the card would code data about that individual. Hollerith invented a punch to reduce the strain on operators in the production of punched cards. Each operator was able with this pantograph punch to produce approximately 500 cards per day.

An early version of the tabulating machine consisted of a press with a series of sprung pins. Pins passing through holes made contact with a mercury pan which established a circuit. Eventually the machine incorporated cards passed between a metal drum and a set of wire brushes. The brushes would briefly sweep through the holes making contacts. Relevant circuits would then be activated that would turn a dial – one dial for each variable – enabling

automatic tallying. After a certain number of cards were processed the operator took readings off the dials and set them back to zero.

Hollerith eventually improved this process by inventing a sorting machine. By means of switches the operator could instruct the machine to search for certain characteristics (what we would now refer to as a query). For example, the number of engineers living in a particular state that owned their own house and had two children. When a card with this characteristic was detected, the sorting mechanism would gather matching cards into a separate container for inspection.

The utility of using the tabulating machine as an information technology can be demonstrated in terms of the efficiency savings it generated. For the 1890 census an army of 50,000 census takers posed 235 questions. The original information system comprised making tally marks on small squares printed on rolls of paper and then adding the marks together by hand. Using this approach it was estimated that the 1890 census would take ten years to complete and would cover 62 million Americans.

On July 1st 1890 two thousand clerks began processing the US census assisted by Herman Hollerith himself. The use of Hollerith machines for this census brought the timescale down to three months saving tax-payers five million dollars, which at the time was a third of the census department's budget.

Hollerith combined the roles of inventor, entrepreneur and manager. Hollerith created his first prototype which he patented in 1884. His Tabulating Machine Company was founded in 1890. He established a near worldwide monopoly of his machines by using the business tactic of leasing rather than selling his machines.

Hollerith sold the company in 1911. The Computing-Tabulating-Recording Company was created in 1911 through a merger with two other companies. Thomas Watson became president of this company in 1924 and eventually changed its name to International Business Machines (IBM). Under his stewardship IBM became the dominant force in the data processing industry during the 1940s through to the 1980s.

Besides its importance as background to the formation of one of the global ICT companies, IBM, this historical case is useful in a number of ways. For instance, early information technology, such as the tabulating machine, had a massive impact upon government activities like conducting a census, the activity system. The tabulating machine caused significant improvements in the efficiency of conducting the data processing activities necessary for supporting its activity system. As such, the case can be considered a very early example of electronic government.

There is an inherent link between information and statistics. Statistics is fundamentally information collected about the attributes of some given population. Originally, such state-istics were collected solely by governments to aid in policy-making relevant to the nation-state. However, it did not take long for business organisations to recognise the value of collating statistics on populations of relevance to their activities, such as customers.

Issues

- Tabulating machines were used by businesses and governments worldwide up until the 1960s. In what way can such machines be considered the precursor of the modern ICT system?
- ICT is still critical to the compilation of national censuses. Investigate how organisations such as the UK Office of National Statistics undertake such exercises using ICT.
- IBM was the dominant player in the informatics industry up till the end of the 1980s, but eventually lost its dominance. Investigate the reasons why this occurred, particularly in relation to the rise of the personal computer.

13   Indian identity number

Case description

Modern India is a significant force in the global informatics industry, particularly in relation to its offshoring operations situated in Bangalore (see *Offshoring in Bangalore*). But India is also attempting a transformation in electronic government, part of which is the country's attempt to assign a unique code number to each of its estimated 1.2 billion citizens. This universal personal identifier is seen as important for Indian citizens in supporting their interaction not only with government but also with many aspects of the private sector on the sub-continent.

The attempt to enrol persons in this national personal identity management system is based upon a strategy of trying to alleviating poverty, improving access to government services and reducing corruption. India still suffers from high levels of poverty with some estimates claiming India has a third of the world's poor. The reasons for this poverty are complex but include the economy's high reliance on agriculture, the country's burgeoning population, poor penetration of market economy and government over-regulation.

In response, a number of government programmes have been established which attempt to distribute food, fuel and fertiliser to the poor. However, a substantial proportion of this distribution goes missing. For example, two thirds of

the subsidised grain that the government allocates to the poor in India is either stolen or adulterated by middlemen. The Indian government also spends 8 billion rupees a year on a scheme to create work for the rural poor. But much of this funding ends up in the pockets of middlemen who invent ghost workers to siphon off government payments. Registration for these government work programmes is also difficult for the poor because of its time-consuming nature and the need to obtain the necessary paperwork, frequently needing to bribe officials to gain access to the documentation. Also, this paperwork is needed every time a citizen moves between states in the sub-continent. The lack of personal identity is also seen as contributing to high levels of voter fraud, which is evident at regional and national elections.

One significant issue is seen to lie at the heart of these problems, the fact that many Indian citizens cannot prove who they are and where they live. India recognises at least twenty different proofs of identity, including birth certificates, caste certificates, tax codes, passports and driving licences. Universal personal identifiers are considered important in a country where many people lack such identity documentation. Many villagers in remote areas even have the same forenames and surnames and many lack skills in literacy. This lack of identification means that they cannot open bank accounts and find it difficult to access government welfare and private sector credit. Two thirds of Indian households lack access to a bank account.

In 2010 a scheme was created in which a number of public and private sector organisations were paid to enrol participants into the national personal identity register. Enrolment is entirely voluntary but has proven extremely popular among the rural poor. The enrolment process involves taking biometrics of the individual, such as iris scans and fingerprints. These biometrics are then associated with other personal data gathered about the individual and identified by a unique, assigned personal identifier. It is hoped that this will make the process of personal identification easier and faster for individuals in situations such as voter registration, applications for welfare and registration for work programmes. As a by-product it is hoped that national personal identification will help reduce the powerful position of corrupt middlemen in many areas of life. A positive side-effect of universal identification will hopefully be that a greater number of individuals and households will be encouraged to open bank accounts. Government will then be able to pay welfare payments directly, bypassing middlemen. This will then also make it easier to transfer any conditional payments that channel money in return for positive behaviours such as getting female children to attend school, persuading mothers to give birth in hospital and encouraging mothers to inoculate their infants against major diseases.

In early 2012 the identity scheme enrolled its 200 millionth member. It is hoped to enrol 400 million members by the end of 2012 and 600 million by the end of 2014. But the scheme is not without its critics. Some criticise the money spent on the scheme, which cost 32 billion rupees in its first phase and is estimated to cost 88 billion rupees in its second phase. Others cite the potential for data privacy infringement both by government and the private sector. Yet others fear the potential for a voluntary programme to turn into a compulsory one and for this to be the precursor to the next logical step, the inevitable reduction of the welfare budget and the attempt to direct welfare at the most needy in society.

Issues

- Why is authenticating personal identity so important in a country the size of India?
- India has experienced rapid economic growth over the last decade. Will this scheme play any part in sustaining such growth?
- What negative effects might emerge from having a national personal identity infrastructure in India?
- In the period between 2002 and 2010 the UK government attempted to introduce a national identity card for all UK citizens but failed. Investigate the reasons for this failure and contrast it with the Indian case. The case study by Beynon-Davies in the *Journal of information technology: teaching cases* is a good place to start.

14 Inka khipu

See pages: 76, 93

Case description

The Inkas were a sophisticated society which existed in the high Andes of South America for a comparatively short time (c.1200–1572 AD). This civilisation was remarkable in that it operated effectively without the benefits of a written language or any mode of transportation based on the wheel.

The Inka created their empire, which they referred to as *Tawantinsuyu* (meaning the four parts together), through conquest. This conquered territory stretched across modern-day Peru and Ecuador, reaching the coast of the Pacific Ocean, as well as extending into modern Colombia, Bolivia, Argentina and Chile. The four parts referred to were based on the Inkas' conception of the way in which their world was divided. The political and cosmic centre of the empire was the city of Cusco. Radiating from this centre were the lands and peoples associated with the four parts: Chinchaysuyu, Antisuyu, Kollasuyu and Cuntisuyu. *Chinchaysuyu* encompassed the lands and peoples of the

Peruvian coast, the adjacent highlands and the northern Andes. *Antisuyu* included the warm forests that lay to the north and north-east of Cusco. *Kollasuyu* formed the largest part of the empire and ran from Peru's central highlands through the altiplano area to central Chile and Argentina. *Cuntisuyu* was the smallest part and included the stretch of land that ran south-west from Cusco to the Pacific Ocean.

The Inkas were a highly ordered society. At the top of the society was the *Sapa Inka,* or emperor, who ruled by divine right as the son of the sun. Worshipped as a living god, the Sapa Inka's official wife was his full-blooded sister. The Sapa Inka also maintained a harem of concubines whose offspring held positions of power and influence in the Inka Empire. This hereditary aristocracy formed the upper class of Inka nobility, and was occasionally supplemented by Inkas assigned this rank through merit or exceptional service. Below the ruling class were the *curacas* who formed the lower echelons of Inka nobility. These individuals generally filled the administrative offices of government and supervised the large bureaucracy of the empire.

Officials called the *cacique* were placed at the head of agricultural communities made up of a group of individuals and families known as *ayllu*. Land was redistributed by the state among the ayllu every year according to the number of active people. Ayllu also had rights to water and herds. The land at the disposal of each ayllu was divided into three unequal parts: the largest of which was given to the community to farm. The other two land parts were consecrated to the cult of the sun and to the state. Communities also paid a tribute of textiles to the state and a periodic tax of labour. This labour tax, consisting of up to three months labour per calendar year for each active individual, was used for collective works such as building roads, monuments and irrigation canals.

Khipu, Khipucamayoq and Chaski

The organisation of activity within the Inka Empire relied on a number of critical elements: a large and efficient transport network, specialist information personnel (the chaskis and the khipucamayuq) and a method for recording data (khipu).

The Inka transport network consisted of thousands of kilometers of purpose-built roads and rope bridges which straddled Tawantinsuyu. Most of the roads were stone-lined and in places extremely narrow, allowing only foot travel and transport of goods using llamas. However, the roads could not be used by everyone. Only those on official business, the chaskis and the emperor and his armies were permitted to use the transport network.

The *chaskis* were highly trained runners employed purely to deliver messages throughout the Empire. A long series of small shelters, stocked with food and water and known as *tambos,* were arranged along the transport network. Individual chaski would transport messages by running between two such posts, and then pass them on to the next runner. A relay of chaski could transport a message in this manner up to 250 km in one day and it is claimed that a message could be delivered from Cusco to Quito, a distance of over 1500 km, within a week.

The Inka bureaucracy sent and received many messages daily in support of the activity of the empire. Typically, messages contained details of resources, such as items required or available in store houses, taxes owed or collected, census data, and the output of mines or the composition of particular workforces. Messages had to be clear, compact and portable. For this purpose an artefact known as the *khipu* was used, consisting of an assemblage of coloured, knotted cotton or camelid (llama or alpaca wool) cords.

The *khipucamayuq* (the keeper of the khipus) were responsible for encoding and decoding messages contained in the khipu. Encoding, or writing, a khipu involved tying together a complex network of cords of different materials and colours, and adding to them a series of different forms of knot. Decoding, or reading, a khipu involved a khipucamayuq in both visual inspection and running his fingers rapidly over the knots, rather like a Braille reader.

Khipu as a data system

Several hundred examples of khipu survive and typically vary from having a few cords to, in the largest case, being over 3 meters long with over 2000 cords. Andean scholars believe that there is sufficient evidence to suggest that khipu were true communication artefacts. This inference is based upon the historical record, which suggests that khipu were rolled up and transported by chains of chaski over long distances. The creator and sender of the khipu must therefore have been different from the reader, or receiver, of the khipu. This implies some form of encoding of data in these artefacts. This interpretation suggests that khipu were used by the Inka as a three-dimensional sign-system in which data was recorded by tracing figures in space with pieces of cord.

A number of facets have been identified within khipu for encoding the variety demanded of the construction of

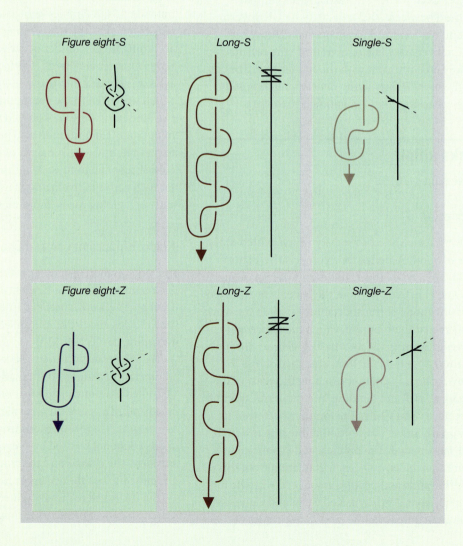

Figure C2 *Types of khipu knot*

messages with a significant meaningful content. Scholars of khipu suggest that these elements were used by a khipucamayuq in a sequence of decision-making related closely to the natural order of construction of khipu. This construction is regarded as being equivalent to writing, or encoding, a message in a khipu. First, the maker of khipu would consider the construction of cords. Then he would consider the placement of cords upon other cords. This would be followed by choices concerning the construction of knots as well as the placement of knots upon cords. We shall consider just two of these constructional elements to illustrate the point: the way in which knots were tied on khipu and the colour of cords.

Five distinct types of knots can be identified within khipu: loop hitch knots, single knots, long knots, figure of eight knots and figure of eight knots with an extra turn (Figure C2). Each type of knot may be tied in one of two ways. For instance, in terms of a hitch knot, the holding element of the knot may be either in front or behind the knot. The former is called a recto hitch knot and the latter a verso hitch knot. In terms of single, long and figure of eight knots the orientation of the dominant diagonal axis of these knots is used to distinguish between what are called 'S' knots and 'Z' knots.

A khipu thread has a particular colour. The threads and cords in khipu are frequently left in their natural cotton or camelid hues. However, a significant proportion of threads and cords, particularly those in cotton, are dyed a particular colour. It is possible to define a palette of some sixty or so colours from which the threads and cords of khipu were composed. Some of these colours are represented in Figure C3.

It is therefore possible to consider khipu as a data system: a system for encoding and decoding symbols. Khipu writing and reading rely on the human visual and tactile senses. The relative positioning of elements on khipu, such as pendant cords and knots, is readily perceived by expert khipu-makers. The colour of threads and cords are also clearly significant to a khipucamayuq. The writing of a khipu involved a khipucamayuq in constructing a complex network of coloured cords and knots. The reading of a khipu relied on visual inspection, as well as touching elements of the physical network.

Hence, there is evidence for the knot as being the fundamental symbolic element within khipu. The construction and positioning of knots relative to each other upon a pendant cord can be seen to constitute a datum. A related collection of knots upon a cord – a knot group – constitute a data item. The collection of knots within a knot group serves to value the data item. A group of pendant cords would constitute a data element and the entire assemblage of cords within a khipu constitute a data structure.

It is possible to use Backus-Naur Form (BNF) to express elements of a data model for khipu artefacts. Part of such a BNF specification is given below:

<khipu> ::= [<dangle cord>]<main cord>
<main cord> ::= <cord> <pendant group> [<knot group>] [<marker>] end knot
<dangle cord> ::= <cord> dangle knot [<knot group>]
<cord>::= <material><spin/ply> <cord colour> <cord length>
<material>::= cotton | alpaca wool | llama wool
<cord colour>::= <single colour> | <multi-colour>
<multi-colour>::= <colour 1> <colour 2> <combination type>
<colour1>::= <thread colour>
<colour2>::= <thread colour>
<single colour>::= <thread colour>
<thread colour>::= [<colour hue>]<colour grouping>
<colour grouping>::= <natural colour> | <dyed colour>

CS

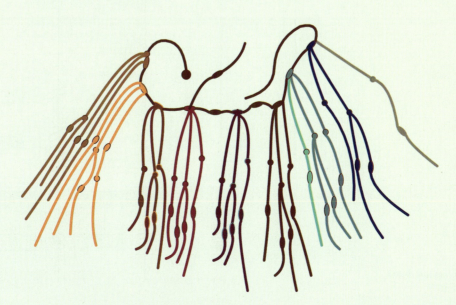

Figure C3 *An illustration of a khipu with typical colours*

<dyed colour>::= rose | yellow/orange | green | blue | plum/violet

<natural colour>::= neutral/white | yellowish brown | brown | grey | greyish brown | greyish olive | reddish brown

<colour hue>::= light | moderate | deep | dark | very dark

This BNF specification indicates how to build the structure of a khipu from basic elements. A khipu consists of an optional dangle cord, a main cord and an end knot. A main cord is built from one or more pendant cord groups. Each pendant cord group consists of one or more pendant cords and an optional top cord. Each pendant cord consists of a hitch knot and a possible subsidiary group and knot group. A subsidiary group consists of one or more subsidiary cords and a knot group consists of one or more knots. A subsidiary cord is also defined in terms of a hitch knot, possible knot groups and subsidiary groups. Top cords and dangle cords are also defined upon subsidiary groups and knot groups.

Khipu as an information system

The meaning of symbolic elements within khipu, such as the various types of knots described above, is still a matter of some debate. Researchers in the 1920s established that 100 or so of the remaining khipu were used to store the results of record-keeping, possibly in support of Inka imperial administration. Evidence suggests that knot groups tied on pendant cords within certain khipu represent numbers to the base 10 (decimal). Particular knot types such as single, figure of eight and long knots and their positioning upon pendant cords signify distinct numbers. The closer the knot to the top of a cord, the higher the

number. At the very top a single knot represented multiples of 10,000, then 1,000, then 100, then 10 (Figure C4). Some have proposed that the numbers on the cords of a khipu could also be used as labels to denote other referents. From this perspective, a given knot group on a khipu can be considered as similar in nature to a modern barcode, with individual knots substituting for the bars of the code.

Khipu and Inka activity systems

The Inkas were an ethnic group that conquered and subjugated many other ethnic groups in South America. They therefore faced the challenge of administering a populace who outnumbered them by about a hundred to one. Tawantinsuyu was divided into 80 provinces and was administrated by a provincial administration consisting of an umbrella of Inka officials supervising a hierarchy of ethnic lords appointed to state service.

As indicated above, various elements of tribute were collected from the provinces by the Inka state. The wealth of Inka society was based primarily upon agriculture and the herding of livestock. Mining, metalwork and textile weaving were also significant performative activities for the various ethnic groups subject to Inka control. Goods and artefacts produced from these activity systems were stored in vast storehouses distributed throughout the provincial areas. However, the main element of tribute paid to the Inka state was a labour tax in which each taxpayer had to work a specified number of days each year on state projects such as road construction.

Most taxpayers were appointed to tributary units of 10 to 10,000 households. At the lowest level, tributaries were

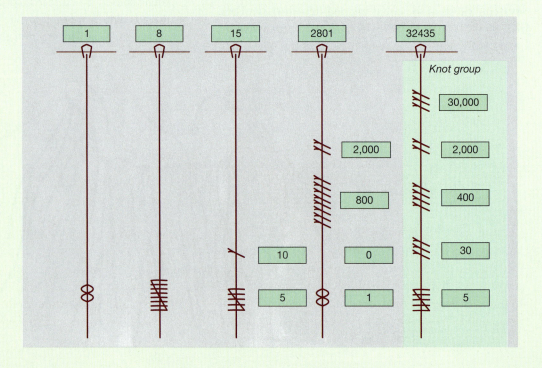

Figure C4 *Coding numbers with a khipu cord*

grouped into five accounting units of 10 members each. One person from each of these groups of 10 would serve as a *Chuka Kamayoq,* or organiser of 10. Five groupings of 10, making a group of 50 tribute payers, would be placed under the authority of a *Pichqa-Chunka-Kuraca,* or lord of the 50. Two groups of 50 would be combined into a unit of 100 tributaries led by a *Pachaka Kuraca,* or lord of 100.

This hierarchical system of tributary units would continue up to the head of one of the 80 provinces of the empire known as a *T'oqrikoq.* These provincial lords were normally ethnic Inka and had overall responsibility for administering the population and lands of the province, as well as ensuring that the roads and bridges were in good working order. Provincial lords were in turn placed under the control of an appropriate lord of the four quarters, called an *Apu,* who directly served the Inka emperor based in Cusco.

Therefore, a number of activity systems of the Inka Empire such as tax collection, the administration of workforces in the building of collective works and the distribution of goods within the Empire relied on an effective system of communication. There is clear evidence of the use of khipu for the keeping of records within wider communication systems. Using the data recorded in khipu, accountants in the Inka empire assessed levels of tribute due, recorded tribute paid and assigned aspects of performance to tributary units.

At the provincial level, the Inka also took censuses to keep track of the population. Census data included records of births, deaths, marriages, and other changes of a person's status. Individuals of each sex were assigned to one of ten categories corresponding not to their chronological age but to their stage in life and ability to perform useful work. Separate khipu were apparently kept for this purpose by each province.

Lower down the administrative hierarchy, two major communication channels were reliant on the use of khipu. Communication concerning tribute flowed up the administrative hierarchy and decisions detailing appropriate performance flowed down through the administrative hierarchy. Hence, local accountants would pass data as to completed tasks upward through the hierarchy. Data at each administrative level would represent the summation of accounts from the level immediately below. This data would eventually be used by imperial accountants based in the Inka capital of Cusco.

Cases such as that of the khipu are very useful to get us to think about some of the universal features of organisational informatics. In other words, much of the foundation material discussed within Chapters 1 to 3 of this book, is relevant to understanding many aspects of organisation beyond our modern institutions.

A number of performative patterns were important to sustaining the Inka empire such as activities of agriculture, textile manufacture, mineral extraction, road building and census taking. Each of these activity systems was reliant on a complex network of communicative or informative patterns. Hence, within the account detailed above, there is evidence to suggest that khipu were used to make persistent certain messages important to communicative acts. For instance, a particular pendant cord would be used to assert that a province had so many people of working age (⊢[this province has 2801 males of working age]). Alternatively, a pendant cord might be used to record the commitment of a defined amount of labour from a tributary unit for use by the Inka hierarchy (#[this ayllu will pay 54 units of labour tax over the next year in mining]). Khipu might also have been created in formative acts to record opinions about the performance of some group of workers (![this ayllu is under-performing in the growth of foodstuffs]), document orders to specific tributary units (?[185 workers from this province will work for three months on repairing a given stretch of road]) and to declare events, such as when tribute had been fully paid by a tributary unit (≡[all the textile tribute owed by this ayllu has been collected]). In each case, the data element produced by one khipucamayuq would be read by another khipucamayuq, normally displaced in time and space.

Issues

- Reread Chapter 2 and try to apply the idea of coding using knots to representing something like a record of a student's performance on a particular module.
- Do you think khipu could be used to convey more complex forms of communication such as stories? How do you think this might be achieved?

CS

15   Microsoft
See page: 337

Case description

Microsoft Corporation is a multinational business with its headquarters in Redmond, Washington State, USA. It has approximately 94,000 employees based in close to 120 countries and a global annual revenue in the billions of US dollars. The main activities of Microsoft are the development, manufacture, licensing, and support of a wide range of software products for computing devices. The best-selling Microsoft products are the Windows operating system series and the Microsoft Office suite of software.

The company was founded by Bill Gates in 1975, originally to develop and sell BASIC interpreters for the Altair 8800, an early micro-computer. Microsoft rose to dominate the personal computer market with another software product, its operating system MS-DOS, which rose to dominate the personal computer market by the mid-1980s. In 1985, Microsoft released its first retail version of Microsoft Windows, originally a graphical extension for its MS-DOS operating system. During the transition from MS-DOS to Windows, the success of the Microsoft Office suite allowed the company to gain ground on its competitors, such as WordPerfect and Lotus 1–2-3.

The company's official website is one of the most visited on the Internet. In the mid-1990s, Microsoft launched a major online service, MSN (Microsoft Network), as a direct competitor to America online (AOL). MSN became an umbrella service for Microsoft's online services. The company also released its web browser, Internet Explorer, with the Windows 95 Plus! Pack in August 1995 and subsequent Windows versions.

Microsoft has a foothold in other markets besides operating systems and office suites, with assets such as the MSNBC cable television network, the MSN Internet portal, and the Microsoft Encarta multimedia encyclopedia. The company also markets computer hardware products, such as the Microsoft mouse, and home entertainment products, such as the Xbox, Xbox 360 and MSN TV.

Throughout its history the company has been the target of criticism for various reasons, including monopolistic business practices. Both the US Justice Department and the European Commission have brought Microsoft to court for antitrust violations associated with software bundling.

Microsoft is currently organised as three core divisions: the Microsoft Platform Products and Services Division, the Microsoft Business Division and the Microsoft Entertainment and Devices Division.

The Platform Products and Services division produces the Windows operating system, Microsoft Visual Studio (a set of development tools) and enterprise software such as Microsoft SQL Server (a relational DBMS).

The Microsoft Business Division produces Microsoft Office, which includes Word (a word processor), Access (a relational DBMS), Excel (a spreadsheet program), Outlook (Windows-only groupware), PowerPoint (presentation software), and Publisher (desktop publishing software).

The Entertainment and Devices division produces software for mobile devices such as Windows CE for PDAs, gaming software for its own gaming console (the Xbox 360) and computer games that run on Windows PCs, including titles such as Age of Empires, Halo and the Microsoft Flight Simulator series. It also produces a line of reference works that include encyclopedias and atlases, under the name Encarta.

Microsoft is known for its developer-centric business culture. A large investment is made each year to recruit young, university-trained, software developers and to retain their services for the company. Key decision makers at every level within the company are either developers or former developers. Within Microsoft the expression 'eating our own dog food' is used to describe the policy of using the latest Microsoft products inside the company in an effort to test them in real-world situations.

Microsoft has historically given customer support over Usenet newsgroups and the Web. The company awards Microsoft Volunteer Partner status to volunteers who are deemed helpful in assisting the company's customers.

Technical references for developers and articles for various Microsoft magazines, such as Microsoft Systems Journal (or MSJ), are available through the Microsoft Developer Network, often called MSDN. MSDN also offers subscriptions for companies and individuals, and the more expensive subscriptions usually offer access to pre-release beta versions of Microsoft software.

In June 2008 Bill Gates stepped down from the board of Microsoft to spend his time managing his charity The Bill and Melinda Gates foundation.

Microsoft dominates the software industry, particularly in the areas of system and office software. In particular, its business tactics of 'embrace, extend and extinguish' have led to much controversy. Microsoft starts off by embracing a competing standard or product, then extending it to produce their own incompatible version of the software or standard, which in time extinguishes any competition that does not or cannot use Microsoft's new version.

Many have recently questioned whether Microsoft can maintain its dominance in the software market given a number of emergent trends such as open source software, software as services and cloud computing. Microsoft is already developing a strategy in light of such developments. For instance, it is investing in a network of data centres, writing new software and adapting its existing software to run in the cloud. It has also released a range of tablet devices which it hopes will compete with the likes of the Apple iPad.

In 2011 Microsoft paid $8.5 bn to takeover the voice over Internet protocol (VOIP) company Skype. Skype has over 650 million users worldwide. A number of technologists worry about the potential this gives Microsoft to monitor Internet traffic.

Issues

■ Business tactics employed by Microsoft have led to various companies and governments filing lawsuits against Microsoft. Consider whether this hinders the development of informatics.

- Concerns have been raised over the total cost of owner-ship associated with Microsoft products. In other reduce words, organisations spend lots of money maintaining and upgrading software licences for Microsoft products. Consider the implications of this for informatics infra-structure within organisations.
- Microsoft and the open source software movement have issue with each other over digital rights management. Consider this issue in light of the software industry as a value network.
- What impact will the Microsoft takeover have upon the viability of Skype? Will it enhance the business or will users switch to other offerings in this area?

16   Music industry

Case description

A key change to the music industry is generally attributed to the creation of an application known as Napster. The software application Napster is an important example of the way in which ICT impacts upon economic structures in an established industry. In Porter's terms such applications have begun to affect the competitive structure of the music industry.

This technology was created by Shawn Fanning when he was a freshman student at the North Eastern University in Boston, Massachusetts in the summer of 1999. It was initially produced as a fun application and Fanning originally released it to fifteen fellow students swearing them not to release it to others. Effectively Napster is a software application that enables users to locate and share digital music in MP3 format. It combined features of existing programs such as search engines, file-sharing systems and instant messaging and is generally regarded as a pioneer in what has become known as P2P (peer-to-peer) Internet software.

By August 2000 Napster had been used in a total of 6.7 million homes. By February 2001 Napster had 45 employees and by September 2002 had 60 million devotees worldwide. Napster threatened the traditional value-chain and business model of the music industry. The music industry encompasses many music-related businesses and organisations and is dominated by the major record groups or labels. Each of these record groups consists of many smaller companies and labels serving different regions and markets.

The traditional business model operated by the music industry involved musical artists recording for a recording company, which then mass-produced and marketed the musical material on media such as compact disks (CDs). This material was then sold by a number of retail outlets.

The consumer had to purchase the material from a retailer, plus an appropriate means of playing it, such as a CD player. In this value network artists got paid royalties on the sale and use of their musical material and therefore got a return on their creative investment.

One of the most significant forms of intangible good to benefit from digitisation is therefore music. The digitisation of music is most readily associated with a file format known as MP3. Developed by the Fraunhofer Institute in Germany in 1992, MP3 stands for Motion Picture Experts Group-1 Level 3. This format employs an algorithm to compress a music file, achieving a significant reduction of data while retaining near CD-quality sound. This means that a three-minute song, which would normally require 32Mb of disk space, can be compressed to 3Mb without a significant reduction in sound quality. Hence, using a standard connection the song can be transmitted over the Internet in a matter of a few minutes rather than the hours required if the file had not been compressed.

MP3 is not the only compression format available for digital music but it has become something of a de-facto standard. Its success is frequently attributed to the fact that it is open source and non-proprietary. The algorithm also employs an extremely efficient method of data compression. MP3 technology enables individuals to download and upload music to and from servers over the Internet efficiently and effectively. Individuals can easily rip (duplicate) MP3 files from CDs and can exchange files using technology such as email or more sophisticated peer-to-peer applications. Hence, it is relatively easy for users to build virtual libraries of music and listen to it either from their hard drives on their PC or from a growing range of portable MP3 players.

The recording of music in digital form means that it can be produced and distributed at much lower cost. The convergence of access devices and communication channels around IP-based standards means that it can also be delivered over a wide variety of access channels. Hence, using MP3 and Napster individuals could by-pass recording companies and retailers. This is essentially a form of disintermediation in the customer chain of the music industry. Essentially, Napster in its original form, and similar offerings, could be considered as a form of C2C eCommerce. Initially networks of enthusiasts used the application to share music at no cost.

Music can be quickly copied from CDs and stored as MP3 files. These files can then be freely distributed around the Internet using the Napster application. The music industry responded to digital music in general, and Napster in particular, on two fronts. First, the Recording Industry Association of America (RIAA) created the

Secure Digital Music Initiative (SDMI). This was an industry group that attempted to create a secure form of digital music format. The intention was to attempt to prevent the copying of digital music from CDs. Second, litigation was undertaken by various actors within the music industry which attempted to prove that the existence of Napster infringed US copyright law.

In 2002 Napster had to close down because of a judicial ruling in favour of the music industry. However, many P2P applications are still impacting upon sales of CD music. Napster was re-launched as a legally licensed download site in the US in 2003.

Apple Computers also launched its iTunes online music store in the same year. This stimulated the major record companies to begin to embrace digital downloading as the future of the music industry. Both Napster and iTunes, with the support of the major record labels are promoting digital music subscription as an attempt to reduce digital piracy. As of 2012 the number of digital music album sales continues to rise, while the number of CD purchases continues to fall.

Spotify is a Swedish company created in 2008 to offer streaming of Digitally Rights Managed music content from a set of major and independent recording companies. Users can register to listen to the music free, in which case they are targeted with visual and audio advertising. Alternatively, they pay a subscription using credit/debit cards or PayPal.

Issues

- Bands such as Metallica have fought back against peer-to-peer programs such as Napster. Is the issue of digital rights management a controversial reaction to such trends?
- The introduction of digital downloading is causing a fundamental change in the way music is consumed. In many ways it has become a utility that flows to a consumer rather than a commodity that is bought one-by-one. Hence, music is purchased like other utilities such as water. People effectively meter for their music or people may pay for their monthly consumption of music. Are all these trends positive for the music industry. What effect will this have long-term upon music production?
- On-going developments in the music industry have been proposed as a model for the future of other, so-called, content industries, such as the movie industry. What are the similarities and differences between the movie and music industries in this respect? For instance, what effect has freely available software for music production had upon the industry?

17   Offshoring in Bangalore

See page: 344

Case description

Offshoring stands for the relocation by an organisation of one or more of its business processes or activity systems, from one country to another. Offshoring might involve an operational process, such as manufacturing, or a supporting process, such as some aspect of informatics infrastructure. In recent years much informatics outsourcing has occurred through offshoring to geographical areas such as Bangalore on the Indian sub-continent.

Bangalore is the capital of the Indian state of Karnataka. In 1951 it had a population of only 800,000. This had grown to 5.6 million in 2001 and is estimated to be around seven million now, making it India's third most populous city. Nowadays, Bangalore is well-known as a hub for India's ICT sector; many local companies are involved in research and development and the production of electronics and software. Because of this, Bangalore is sometimes referred to as the Silicon Valley of India, since it is the base for the country's three largest ICT companies: Tata Consultancy Services, Wipro and Infosys. These three firms are now among the top ten companies in the world in terms of stock market capitalisation. Not surprisingly, some of the most well-recognised colleges and research institutions in India are located in this growing city. Bangalore alone accounts for approximately one third of India's software exports and some quarter of a million people are employed in ICT within the city boundaries.

One of the most significant companies working from Bangalore is Infosys Ltd, formerly Infosys Technologies. Infosys is a global company which provides business consulting, technology, engineering and outsourcing services. Infosys was founded in 1981 by seven young Indian entrepreneurs. It moved to Bangalore in 1983 and got its first foreign client, the US-based Data Basics Corporation, in 1987. The first Indian company to be listed on the US stock exchange, it now has offices in dozens of countries worldwide and development centres based in India, the US, China, Australia, the UK, Canada and Japan, amongst others.

ICT is key to enabling the offshoring of many business processes such as finance, sales, marketing and human resources. This process is the result of the increased availability of reliable and affordable worldwide communications during the late 1990s. This development has made possible the movement of service provision to low cost countries in a manner which is invisible (at least in principle) to the user of the service. For instance, many UK companies offshore their telephone marketing and after-sales service functions to Indian companies.

India benefited from the offshoring trend for a number of reasons. The country has a large pool of young people who speak English to a high standard and are technically proficient. Infosys, for instance, receives 1.4 million job applications per year. India's offshoring industry was originally rooted in low-end ICT functions in the early 1990s. Since then Indian companies have moved to provide back-office functions such as call centres and transaction processing. In the late 1990s, India's abundant pool of software engineers enabled companies to cope with increased demand caused by the millennium bug problem. This enabled companies such as Infosys to attract large-scale software development projects from Western companies, particularly those based in the US. Currently, India is the offshoring destination for global firms like HP, IBM, Accenture, Intel, AMD, Microsoft, Oracle Corporation, Cisco and SAP.

In recent times robust economic growth and rising inflation have caused a growth in wage costs for Indian firms. They are starting to worry that they may become too expensive in comparison with other destinations and have therefore attempted to diversify into high-end sectors beyond software and hardware engineering, for example, aerospace.

Issues

■ Many large Western banks have moved a considerable proportion of their back-office processes to India in general and Bangalore in particular. What management challenges arise from this form of remote operation through ICT?

■ There have been a small number of instances of lapses in data security, such as loss of personal data from customer databases held by Indian companies, and some instances of Indian employees engaging in identity fraud. How might such instances affect strategic decisions to offshore for Western companies?

---

18   Open source software
See pages: 186, 375

Case description

Open source software is computer software for which the source code is made available under a copyright license (or arrangement such as the public domain) that meets the Open Source Definition, a formal specification of what it means to be open source.

The aim of the open source movement is to make software easier to understand, modify and duplicate. Hence, an open source license permits users to use and change the software, and to redistribute it in a modified or unmodified form.

Open source software can be developed in traditional ways. However, such software has become associated with a particular model of software development, which sees itself as substantially different from traditional approaches.

Open source software is the most prominent example of open source development. Traditional software development is that promoted by people like Frederick P. Brooks in his book *The Mythical Man-Month*. In contrast, the open source guru Eric Raymond distinguishes between two different models of software development: the cathedral model and the bazaar model. In the cathedral model, development takes place in a centralised way. Roles are clearly defined and include people dedicated to designing (the architects), people responsible for managing the project, and people responsible for implementation.

Raymond suggests that all software should be developed using the bazaar model. This he describes as 'a great babbling bazaar of differing agendas and approaches'. Such a bazaar model tends to have features such as:

■ Users as co-developers. The users of open source software potentially become co-developers. Users are encouraged to contribute to the software with additions, code fixes for the software, bug reports, documentation etc. The general principle is that having more co-developers increases the rate at which the software evolves. One key claim is that the rate at which bugs are identified and fixed increases with open source production. Torvald Linus the originator of Linux states this as a law that, 'Given enough eyeballs all bugs are shallow'.

■ Early releases. Versions of software are released as early as possible so as to increase the chance of finding co-developers.

■ Frequent integration. New code is integrated as often as possible so as to avoid the overhead of fixing a large number of bugs at the end of the project life-cycle. Some open source projects have nightly builds where integration is done automatically on a daily basis.

■ Several versions. Open source software tends to have at least two versions. A development version is for users who want immediate use of the latest features, and are willing agree to accept the risk of using code that is not yet thoroughly tested. The users can then act as co-developers, reporting bugs and providing bug fixes, in fact acting as co-developers. The stable version offers users fewer bugs but usually fewer features.

CS

- High modularisation. Open source software tends to be highly modular. This allows for parallel development by a larger network of programmers.
- Dynamic decision-making structure. A decision-making structure, whether formal or informal, is needed. This structure makes strategic decisions as to the on-going design of the software.

The Open Source Initiative is an organisation dedicated to promoting open source software. The organisation was founded in February 1998 by Bruce Perens and Eric S. Raymond when Netscape Communications Corporation, published the source code for its flagship Netscape Communicator product (a Web Browser) as free software. This was due to lowering the profit margins and competition with Microsoft's Internet Explorer software.

A US federal court has ruled that anyone using the code distributed under an open source software licence must attribute the author of the software and acknowledge the source of the files, as well as explaining how the code has been modified in any way. This means that a commercial company cannot take some open source software, modify it and then sell it on as a commercial product.

The bazaar model of software development might be seen as an alternative to conventional approaches to information systems development. However, some maintain that the approaches promoted by the open source movement are not suitable for bespoke information systems development for a number of reasons. Perhaps the most important difficulty is that the requirements for such systems rely on a great deal of business domain knowledge, whereas open source production relies on a wide distribution of commonly accepted requirements for software. Hence, successful open source software products tend to be packaged or commoditised software products that can be used across a range of different industries, for example IS development tools. Two examples of such products are considered in the next section: MySQL and Linux.

MySQL and Linux

The data management layer of the typical ICT system normally relies upon a database management system, or DBMS. First released in 1995, MySQL is a multi-user relational DBMS which has more than 11 million installations worldwide. The applications software is considered to be one of the most prominent examples of open source software. MySQL is popular for web applications and acts as the DBMS component of the, so-called, LAMP stack for application development. DBMS has been used as part of the ICT infrastructure of organisations such as Wikipedia.

Linux is a computer operating system, which is based on a popular operating system created in the 1960s known as UNIX. An operating system is a piece of software that manages resources on a computing device and provides an interface used to access such resources. An operating system performs basic tasks such as controlling and allocating memory, prioritizing system requests, controlling input and output devices, facilitating computer networking and managing files.

The name Linux is attributed to the creator of this operating system's kernel or core facilities. Work on the kernel was started in 1991 by Linus Torvalds while he was a student at the University of Helsinki. Torvalds continues to direct the development of this kernel.

Although Linux is generally available free of charge, several large corporations have established business models that involve selling, supporting, and contributing to Linux and free software. These include Dell, IBM, HP, Sun Microsystems, Novell, and Red Hat. The free software licenses on which Linux is based explicitly accommodate and encourage such commercialisation. One common business model of commercial suppliers is charging for support, especially for business users. A number of companies also offer a specialised business version of their distribution, which adds proprietary support packages and tools to administer higher numbers of installations or to simplify administrative tasks. Another business model is to give away the software as a bundle in order to sell hardware. Many netbooks are sold in this manner, with Linux pre-installed.

Many free software titles that are popular on Windows, such as Pidgin, Mozilla Firefox, Openoffice.org, and GIMP, are available for Linux. A growing amount of proprietary desktop software is also supported under Linux, examples being Adobe Flash Player, Acrobat Reader, Matlab, Nero Burning ROM, Opera, RealPlayer, and Skype.

Issues

- Investigate the range of software produced using the open source model. For instance, is office software available as open source? Can you run an entire desktop computer using open source software?
- Investigate the similarities between open source software production and the collaborative production of Web content.
- The open source software movement has now been in existence for over a decade. Hence, one might argue that earlier critics of the movement who argued that it lacks a sufficiently robust revenue model have been silenced. But what of the software development industry. Does it undermine the business model of companies like Microsoft?
- Why do companies need to have DBMS such as MySQL in their ICT infrastructure? Why is MySQL preferred for use by companies such as Wikipedia?

- What advantages do organisations that adopt Linux achieve as compared to those that utilise Microsoft Windows as their dominant operating system?

19   SAP

See page: 190

Case description

SAP AG is the largest European software company. Known for its Enterprise Resource Planning software it has its headquarters in Walldorf, Germany.

SAP was founded in 1972 as Systemanalyse und Programmentwicklung by five former IBM engineers in Mannheim, Baden-Württemberg. The acronym was later changed to stand for Systeme, Anwendungen und Produkte in der Datenverarbeitung (Systems, Applications and Products in Data Processing). In 1976 SAP GmbH was founded and the following year it moved headquarters to Walldorf. SAP AG became the company's official name after the 2005 annual general meeting (AG is short for Aktiengesellschaft).

The company's main product is the SAP ERP package. This is an integrated suite of enterprise resource planning (ERP) software targeted at supporting the requirements of medium- to large-scale organisations in a number of industries and sectors.

Up until recently the SAP product was produced in three versions R/1, R/2 and R/3. The R stands for real-time, although the software is not normally what many would consider true real-time software. The number refers to the number of layers in the software architecture. Hence, R/3 refers to a three-tier client-server architecture whereas R/2 ran on a traditional mainframe architecture.

SAP R/1 was launched in 1972, SAP R/2 in 1979 and SAP R/3 in 1992, then a major overhaul of the package was undertaken culminating in the launch of SAP ERP in 2003.

SAP ERP includes four individual solutions that support key back-end functional areas:

- SAP ERP Financials
- SAP ERP Human Capital Management
- SAP ERP Operations
- SAP ERP Corporate Services

SAP ERP is one of five major enterprise applications in SAP's Business Suite. The other four applications, which support front-end functions, are:

- customer relationship management (CRM): helps companies acquire and retain customers, gain deep marketing and customer insight, and align organisations on customer-focused strategies
- product life-cycle management (PLM): helps manufacturers with a single source of all product-related information necessary for collaborating with business partners and supporting product lines
- supply chain management (SCM): helps companies enhance operational flexibility across global enterprises and provides real-time visibility for customers and suppliers
- supplier relationship management (SRM): customers can collaborate closely with suppliers and integrate sourcing processes with applications throughout the enterprise to enhance transparency and lower costs.

ERP software is an attempt to provide an integrated ICT infrastructure for a company. The software can be tailored to a specific company's mode of operation but this normally involves considerable investment.

The architecture of products such as SAP tends to emulate the distinctions made between core back-end information systems and front-end information systems discussed in Chapter 4 on infrastructure.

A vast industry has arisen around the implementation of ERP packages, such as SAP for companies. For instance, there is a vast range of informatics professionals and consultancies specialising in SAP work.

In 2012 SAP acquired US software producer, Ariba. Ariba makes Web-based software that connects suppliers and buyers online. This purchase is therefore seen as an attempt by SAP to consolidate its presence in cloud computing.

Issues

- ERP software is marketed as providing a complete solution for business. However, numerous companies have experienced difficulties with their ERP implementation. Why do you think this is?
- How is ERP software being affected by cloud computing?
- How does purchasing a large ERP strategy impact upon both business and informatics strategy?

20   Tesco

See pages: 38, 52, 59, 230, 286, 341

Case description

History

Tesco PLC is an international grocery and general merchandising retail chain. Founded in the UK it is the largest British retailer and the third-largest global retailer after Wal-Mart and Carrefour. In 2007, the supermarket chain announced over £2.55bn in profits, approximately the same amount as it declared in 2012. Tesco now controls just over 30% of the grocery market in the UK. Its declared mission is to 'create value for customers to earn

CS

their lifetime loyalty' and its declared strategy is based on offering a range of different types of stores, understanding its customers and treating its employees well.

The company originally specialised in food retail. It has now diversified into other areas such as discount clothes, consumer electronics, consumer financial services, selling and renting DVDs, compact disks and music downloads, Internet service provision, consumer telecoms, consumer health insurance, consumer dental plans and budget software.

The name Tesco was introduced in 1924, when the founder of the company Jack Cohen bought a shipment of tea from T. E. Stockwell. The product was branded Tesco Tea, merging the first three letters of the supplier's name (TES), and the first two letters of Cohen's surname (CO). In 1929 Cohen opened the first Tesco store in Burnt Oak, Edgware, Middlesex; the first self-service store opened in St Albans less than twenty years later, in 1947; the first supermarket store in 1956, in Maldon. Meanwhile, the company was floated on the London Stock Exchange in 1947, as Tesco Stores (Holdings) Limited.

The 1950s and the 1960s were years of growth for Tesco. By the end of this period, there were more than 800 Tesco stores. In 1973 Jack Cohen resigned and was replaced as Chairman by his son-in-law, Leslie Porter. Porter and managing director Ian MacLaurin changed the strategy of the company from a 'pile it high, sell it cheap' philosophy, which had left the company stagnating and with a bad brand image. In 1977 Tesco abandoned its discount savings scheme, Green Shield stamps, and implemented price reductions and centralised buying for all its stores.

During the 1970s and 1980s the company continued its strategy of acquiring new stores through the takeover of existing food retail chains. During the 1990s the company began diversifying in terms of its product range, its operating area and its delivery channels. Acquisition of Associated British Foods gave the company a major presence in Northern Ireland and the Republic of Ireland. A business alliance with the Esso Petroleum Company allowed the leasing of petrol stations under the Tesco Express format. Key developments in this period were the introduction of a loyalty card and an Internet shopping service. Tesco was one of the first UK retailers to be able to make a profit out of online shopping.

This process of diversification and expansion continued during the early 2000s as Tesco started to become a major international food retailer. In October 2003 it launched a UK telecoms division, comprising mobile and home phone services, to complement its existing Internet Service Provider business.

In the UK, there are four major formats for Tesco stores, depending on size and the range of products sold. The largest stores are called Tesco Extra, they are usually located out-of-town and offer the complete range of tangible products. A smaller range of non-food goods is available in Tesco superstores, that can be described as standard large supermarkets, stocking mainly groceries. Tesco Express stores cater to the convenience segment of the market (that is, small neighbourhood stores), while Tesco Metro stores are sized between Tesco superstores and Tesco Express stores and are mainly located in city or town centres.

Informatics infrastructure

Tesco uses ICT and information systems in a number of ways within its business. The company chairman, Terry Leahy, claimed in 2007 that if the firm's ICT failed the firm would fail.

In terms of its customer chain, Tesco introduced its loyalty card for customers, Clubcard, over twenty years ago. To get the loyalty card a customer must supply a range of personal details to the company. The customer can then use the Clubcard in all interactions with the company. Swiping the Clubcard through the EFTPOS terminals at checkouts associates the purchase of items against details held about the customer. For the customer regular use of the card accrues points, which can be redeemed via a voucher scheme discounting goods. 11 million UK loyalty card customers were reported in 2007. Capture of this data has become critical to company operation. Aggregation of this data in data warehouses allows the company to identify purchasing patterns and plan product and store operations accordingly.

In common with most other large retailers, Tesco draws goods from suppliers into regional distribution centres for preparation and onward delivery to stores. RFID technology is taking an increasing role in the distribution process.

Within the stores themselves the company's 'one in front' initiative, introduced in 1994 has been heavily reliant on ICT. The company uses thermal imaging technology to measure and predict customer arrivals at checkouts. This enables store managers to ensure that the right number of checkouts is open for every customer to receive a 'one in front' service.

In 2008 Tesco announced its intention to overhaul its ICT infrastructure, planning to replace a number of separate voice and data networks with a single communication network, which was eventually outsourced to Cable and Wireless. This network was used to standardise its key ICT systems in areas such as finance, human resources, payroll, in-store management, distribution and sales.

The intention was to manage these ICT systems centrally across the entire network from its ICT services centre in Bangalore, India (see *Offshoring in Bangalore*).

Informatics professionals based in countries of operation supply only front-line support. This standardisation is built upon an earlier effort by the company initiated in 2005, known as 'Tesco in a box'. This was a programme of standardisation based upon an Oracle ERP system, which was implemented in all countries of operation.

The rollout of these standard ICT systems is seen as a key enabler for standard business processes and standard management information across the Tesco group. This allows new stores opened in countries such as Malaysia or Japan to operate and be managed in exactly the same way as a store in the UK.

B2C eCommerce

Tesco made its major push into B2C eCommerce with a strategic move into online grocery retail. The tesco.com domain name and associated website was formally launched in 2000. Soon afterwards, in July 2001, the company attempted to become involved in Internet grocery retailing in the USA, when it obtained a 35% stake in GroceryWorks, a joint venture with American Safeway Inc., operating in the United States and Canada. However, GroceryWorks did not expand as fast as initially expected and Tesco sold its stake to Safeway Inc. in 2006.

Having said this, Tesco now claims to be the world's largest online grocery retailer. Tesco is reported as having 45.1% of the sales of online grocery sales followed by Sainsbury's (14.1%) and Asda (13.7%). Estimates of the percentage of online grocery sales within the British grocery market has placed this as much as 5%, with a doubling of growth over the next five years. In 2010 as much as 13% of grocery shoppers are reported as shopping online for their groceries regularly.

In 2006 Tesco was reported as having picked up two thirds of all online grocery orders in the UK and had over 750,00 regular users of its online grocery service, generating over 22,000 orders per week. This rose to 1 million active users in 2008 and a growth of 50% in online sales over the previous year. Internet sales were reported as contributing 4.2% of profits and 3.1% of overall sales. Tesco claimed in its 2005 annual report to be able to serve 98% of the UK population from its 300 participating stores. In the financial year ended 24 February 2007 it recorded online sales up 29.2% to £1.2 billion and profit up 48.5% to £83 million, with over 250,000 orders per week.

Not surprisingly, other online retailers have begun to look seriously at online grocery retail as a profitable market to explore. Amazon, for instance, announced in July of 2010 that it intended to compete with the major British supermarkets in offering online groceries. Of the available 22,000 products available to customers, 2,000 will be stocked in its normal warehouses, such as in Swansea. The additional products will be delivered direct from other suppliers. However, established online grocery retailers, such as Tesco, have a two hour delivery window for their groceries. This might prove difficult for Amazon to compete with given its current business model.

Grocery sales made online through the website are available to customers for delivery within a defined range of selected stores. Goods for each customer are hand-picked from goods held within each store. This is in contrast to other business models which pick items from the warehouse. The pick from store model allows rapid expansion with limited investment, but has led to a high level of substitutions when stock becomes unavailable.

Through its website, Tesco now offers a wide range of other products, including electronic goods, books, broadband and financial services. The company uses a content management system to maintain the content on its website, restricting content production itself to a limited range of users. More recently, Tesco have introduced the option within a limited range of stores for customers to pick up their crate of groceries from the store and thus deferring the delivery charge. Tesco launched its first home shopping catalogue in autumn 2006, as another channel for sales of its non-food ranges. This is integrated with the Internet operation, with both channels being branded as Tesco Direct. Tesco has also launched an advertising campaign for its VOIP product, marketing the service to customers by offering free calls to all other Tesco Internet phone customers.

In 2012 Tesco began trialling a mobile commerce application in the UK. For two weeks they trialled what they called an interactive virtual grocery store in the departure lounge at Gatwick Airport, UK. The fridge-sized machine displays four interactive screens that the customer can slide by hand to reveal shelves with an assortment of 80 products. If the customer wants to buy a product, they scan the barcode with their smartphone. The idea is that the customer will be able to use devices such as this to order a basket of essentials and have them delivered the day they get home from holiday.

Organisation

From an institutional perspective, Tesco would be considered a large multinational company, producing goods and services and competing within a number of markets. We would also be interested in the strategy of the organisation and ways of designing its activities in areas such as its supermarket operations to improve its performance. This would lead us to examine the place of information in support of activities such as decision-making about what products to stock where.

Considered from an action perspective we would be interested in how employees of Tesco PLC perform their work. Hence, for instance we would be interested in the experience of working as a checkout person for the company; in the established procedures for doing things such as operating checkouts, stocking shelves and receiving goods into the supermarket store. Some of the knowledge about how to do things will be formalised in the sense of being written down. Many other aspects of the everyday work of employees of the company will rely on tacit knowledge. We would also be interested in how such knowledge is communicated and how it is acquired.

System and environment

Tesco PLC can be considered in systems terms. As a food retailer the inputs to the organisation are the foodstuffs it receives from its suppliers. Outputs consist of foodstuffs sold on to customers. Its key transformation consists of those activity systems involved in supporting the sale of foodstuffs. These activity systems can be considered in a hierarchical fashion. Hence, the company will have systems of supply, supermarket operation and financial management that all contribute to the overall purpose of the organisation, which is making a profit for its shareholders.

The environment of the organisation consists of the retail industry generally and supermarket retail specifically. Within food retail in the UK the dominance of big supermarkets means that they have enormous power in determining pricing levels for key foodstuffs from their suppliers. However, the food retail industry is subject to quite heavy degrees of regulation in such areas as environmental health legislation. The food retail sector is still growing in the UK. In recent years the major supermarkets have increased their levels of technological deployment quite dramatically and have utilised their information systems in new areas such as financial services. The basis of competition has traditionally been on matters of pricing although other bases, such as the quality of foodstuffs (particularly in relation to organic foodstuffs), have recently come into play.

Value-chain and value network

The value produced by Tesco is primarily the sale of foodstuffs to customers. Its declared mission is to 'create value for customers to earn their lifetime loyalty'. Tesco introduced its loyalty card for customers a number of years ago. Value might therefore include the additional value services available to loyalty card customers such as discounted goods.

It is possible to consider the performance of Tesco in terms of the three Es of performance. Tesco efficacy measures are likely to include sales for product groups across different supermarkets. Efficiency measures are likely to include profit margins against product lines, or measures of stock fulfilment against orders in warehouses. In terms of effectiveness, measures might include the degree to which new customers are attracted to stores; old customers continue to come to their stores; and the levels of satisfaction expressed by customers with the level of service they receive.

Consider a supermarket chain in terms of the concept of the value-chain. It is possible to map some of the key processes from the internal value-chain onto this type of business. Inbound logistics involves the management of the purchasing of foodstuffs and the distribution of foodstuffs to warehouses. The process of operations involves the unpacking of bulk deliveries and the presentation of foodstuffs on supermarket shelves. Outbound Logistics involves the distribution of bulk foodstuffs from warehouses to supermarket stores. Marketing and sales involves the advertisement of product lines and the purchasing of foodstuffs from stores. After-sales service involves the handling of customer enquiries and complaints.

Tesco operate a number of information systems that contribute both to operational control through single-loop feedback and to strategic control through double-loop feedback. For instance, sales of products within their stores are recorded at checkouts that update information about stock levels in the service area of the store. This information triggers replenishment of products from stock held in the inventory area of the store. This is an example of operational control. Sales to loyalty card holders provide valuable information to the company, which is used for determining which products to sell at which stores at which times of the year. This is an example of strategic control.

eBusiness and eCommerce

Tesco is what we would refer to as a clicks-and-mortar company. It is primarily a physical operation but it has an online service as well. Tesco have made eCommerce work successfully and integrated it with its core business.

Tesco as a food retailer has relationships with its customers and suppliers. Revenue flows into its value-chain from its customers and on to its suppliers. Customers are mainly attracted to supermarkets by a combination of low prices and a large variety of goods on offer. Supermarket chains typically sell large volumes of their products and hence their business strategy is typically one of low-cost/high-volume operations with typically low margins on each product. Costs are minimised in a number of ways, such as buying in bulk from suppliers and letting customers bear the costs of selecting products from shelves, packing products and transporting goods to their homes. The critical success factor for a supermarket chain is therefore attracting sufficient customers to its store. This means that store location is critical, they need to be placed within easy reach of a catchment area with sufficient willing customers.

The provision of an eCommerce site such as Tesco.com changes the business model of a supermarket chain. Relationships with customers and suppliers change, as do costs and revenue. For example, if a supermarket fulfils online orders by having a member of staff walk around the store, picking and packing goods followed by transportation to customer's homes using delivery vans, then the costs of the operation can substantially increase. Hence, many supermarkets pass on this cost directly to the customer through a charge for delivery as Tesco does.

An alternative business model is to do away with stores entirely. Goods may then be stored in, and delivered from, low-cost warehouses. Hence, additional order fulfilment costs (picking, packing and transporting) can be balanced by lower operational costs (larger range, reduced inventory, larger volume, lower margins).

Technology clearly has had, and continues to have, an impact on organisational practices. The introduction of barcode scanners and electronic point of sale terminals at checkouts has rapidly improved throughput of customers. Tesco, like many other large retail companies, have also introduced automated self-service checkouts with the longer-term aim of reducing staffing costs. It is experimenting with the use of RFID tagging in its supply chain to automatically track its inventory, and intelligent trolleys in its stores which will automatically read the products purchased as they are dropped into the trolley.

Issues

- Supermarket chains such as Tesco have been criticised for the control they exercise over both their customer chain and their supply chain. Within food retail in the UK the dominance of big supermarkets means that they have enormous power in determining pricing levels for key foodstuffs from their suppliers. Criticism has also been voiced over the way in which companies such as Tesco have led to the decline in traditional smaller retail outlets on the high street. Examine this issue in greater detail.
- The food retail industry is subject to quite heavy degrees of regulation in such areas as environmental health legislation. This raises significant barriers of entry to the industry. How does Tesco's adoption of eBusiness act as a barrier to entry in these terms?
- The food retail sector is still growing in the UK. In recent years the major supermarkets have increased their levels

of technological deployment quite dramatically and have utilised their information systems in new areas such as financial services. How successful has this strategy been and how reliant is it upon technology?

- The basis of competition has traditionally been on matters of pricing, although other bases such as the quality of foodstuffs (particularly in relation to organic foodstuffs) have recently come into play. The value network in food retail shows signs of changing subtly. For instance, within the UK there has been significant growth in organic suppliers selling direct to customers through the Web, a form of disintermediation. Is this a challenge to a major online grocery retailer such as Tesco?
- Tesco have used information systems in a number of ways to help build customer loyalty and retention. Through use of its loyalty card scheme the company captures a lot of information about the consumer behaviour of its customers. Concerns have been raised over the potential dangers of using such transactional data and the questions it raises in areas of personal privacy. Examine the data stored on such cards and the uses to which it is put.

21 Twitter

Case description

Twitter is a website that was launched in July 2006 by Jack Dorsey. Dorsey came across the definition of the word twitter as '*a short burst of inconsequential information*', and felt that this was a perfect description of the type of product that his company wanted to create. The website is based in San Francisco, California, but Twitter also has offices and servers in other US cities, including San Antonio, Texas and Boston, Massachusetts.

Twitter is a social networking and micro-blogging website. Twitter users can write and read short, text-based messages (up to 140 characters), the so-called tweets; these messages are shown on the user's profile page. By default, tweets are visible to all. However, users can change their privacy settings and restrict delivery of tweets to their followers, that is, those users who subscribe to a particular user's tweets. Twitter users can mention or reply to other users by using the @ sign. In addition, the use of hashtags (#) as a prefix allows Twitter users to group tweets together.

Users send and receive tweets as posts via the website, through external applications such as those available on smartphones or through the short message service (SMS). The messages were initially set to the 140-character limit for compatibility with SMS messaging. This caused users to use shorthand notations in tweets in a similar manner to that used within SMS texts. For this reason, the company is sometimes described as the '*SMS of the Internet*'. It is estimated that Twitter has 190 million users, generating 65 million tweets a day and handling over 800,000 search queries per day.

In late 2010, Twitter began rolling out a new interface for the site with some additional aspects of functionality. Such functionality includes the ability to access images and videos by clicking on links embedded within individual tweets. These links direct to content held on a variety of supported websites, such as YouTube.

Twitter displays no advertising. Nonetheless, personal data about Twitter users is collected by the company, that can also be shared with third parties. This means that advertisers can target users by analysing their tweets and may also quote tweets in ads directed specifically to the user.

Sites such as Twitter appear to have played a major role in the organisation of political protest around the world, such as in the case of the Arab uprising in Egypt and elsewhere (see *Arab Spring and social media*).

Issues

- Twitter has suffered in the past from a number of security vulnerabilities causing several security breaches. What are the implications of this for data protection?
- Supporters of the site feel it is a good way to keep in touch with busy friends. Critics maintain that you can be too connected and that following the day-to-day activities of persons described on Twitter is part of the increasing cult of celebrity in modern societies. In this sense, is tweeting or following tweets a good or bad thing?
- Social media appears to be playing an increasing role within democratic processes. How will such technologies affect the political process within nation-states longer term?
- Companies have started using tweeting as a form of organisational communication. Examine the pros and cons of this technology for business communication.

22   UK Revenue and Customs

See page: 320

Case description

Large central government agencies such as the Inland Revenue have been subject to considerable computerisation, many such projects being financed by a mix of public and private sector investment over the last twenty years. In the UK, some 4 million people work in local government, central government and public administrations such as the National Health Service. It is therefore not surprising to find much of the rhetoric surrounding the expected benefits of eGovernment within the UK to be focused around efficiency and effectiveness improvements associated with the re-organisation and re-deployment of staff supported by integrated ICT systems.

In April 2000 the UK eGovernment Strategic Framework was published, requiring all central government departments to produce eBusiness strategies. These were intended to show how each department planned to implement eGovernment and to achieve electronic service delivery targets. The first draft was required in October 2000. From July 2001 departments were required to report progress against eBusiness strategies to the Office of the eEnvoy every six months. The Inland Revenue was, until 2005, the UK government department responsible for collecting and administering taxation. This government department has attempted to be at the forefront of eGovernment in the UK by transforming its performance using ICT. This is evident in much of the strategic thinking emanating from the leadership within the organisation.

For instance, at this time the organisation indicated four indicators that it would use to determine how well it has transformed itself. First, the receipt of clean data from customers would allow the Inland Revenue to remove work that added little value to the organisation and consequently release people to work at the front line of customer care. Second, increasing the organisation's capability to deliver services electronically and increasing the take-up of such services by customers. Third, it intended to increase use of knowledge management so that its staff had better guidance, which in turn would enhance its customer service capabilities. Finally, information and data management would enable it to progress towards the 'joined-up government' vision of developing seamless, quality services and making best use of the data it receives.

The department set out its first eBusiness strategy in 2000. The key feature of the strategy was the development of a number of access channels for different customer groups with clear incentives to encourage their use. As part of this strategy the organisation intended to offer improved e-services to the UK taxpayer, thus reducing the burden of compliance on individuals and organisations. The revenue also planned to use intermediaries, such as the National Association of Citizens Advice Bureau (see *Citizens Advice Bureau*), the Post Office and software suppliers, to provide bespoke services to the customers of the organisation. This transformation was predicated upon greater integration of its services with that of other departments and the provision of its services through commercial and government portals. It also required the transformation of staff roles to focus around support for the customer through the use of electronic tools.

In 2001 the Inland Revenue revised its strategy, keeping the fundamental principles above but making two additions: first, a transformation of the organisation around a focus on the customer; and second, a philosophy based on customer relationship management, creating a technical framework that would deliver e-services in a modular but integrated fashion. Within this strategy, the Inland Revenue established three targets. First, that 50% of services would be available electronically by 31 December 2002. By this time the organisation aimed to offer basic, secure e-services and have developed plans for organisational change based on such services. Second, it intended to have 50% take-up of its services by 2005. Third, all of its services would be available electronically by 31 December 2005. By this date the Inland Revenue aimed to have achieved significant business transformation with most customer transactions being conducted electronically.

However, subsequent to publication of the strategy, the Inland Revenue merged with Customs and Excise in 2006 to form Her Majesty's Revenue and Customs (HMRC). This was part of a wider attempt to improve the efficiency of UK government departments stimulated by a review of activity.

The newly formed HMRC, however, soon came into the spotlight in 2007 for its failings in data management.

In October of 2007 a junior official from Her Majesty's Revenue and Customs (HRMC) based in Washington, Tyne and Wear sent two compact disks (CDs) containing government records to the National Audit Office (NAO) based in London. The data was requested by the NAO in order to enable them to run their own independent survey of child benefit payments. The disks were password-protected but the data was unencrypted. The package was sent unrecorded and unregistered, using a courier company. The records on the disks contained the names, addresses, birth dates and national insurance numbers of all 25 million individuals dealt with by the HMRC in relation to child benefits. The records also contained details of partners, the names, sex and ages of children, as well as bank/savings account details for each claimant. This meant that details of 7.25 million bank accounts associated with families were stored on the disks.

The disks failed to arrive at the offices of the NAO and, following notification of this, a second package was sent by registered post and arrived safely. In November of 2007 senior managers at the HMRC were told that the first package had been lost. A week later the Prime Minister and other government ministers, most notably the Chancellor of the Exchequer were informed of the loss. Initially, government ministers were told that the CDs would probably be found, but when HMRC's search for the lost disks failed the Metropolitan Police were called in to investigate.

This data loss led the Chancellor to consult with the Information Commissioner, the person responsible for overseeing the implementation of data protection in the UK, and they agreed that consultation with UK financial institutions was required. At the request of these financial institutions the public was not informed of the data loss for some days in order to allow these institutions to monitor potential suspicious activity. Banks and other financial institutions tracked transactions back to the date at which the data was lost in an attempt to identify suspicious activity.

As a consequence of this data incident the HRMC Chairman resigned and the Chancellor made an announcement to the House of Commons. It was claimed that a junior civil servant at the HMRC had broken data security procedures in downloading the data to disks and sending them via unrecorded postal delivery. The Chancellor reassured the public that the police had no reason to suspect the data had got into the wrong hands. However, the public was urged to keep a close eye on their bank accounts for any unusual activity.

The possibility of criminals gaining access to the data and hence engaging in mass identity theft and identity fraud was raised in numerous quarters. This included not only criminals using data to gain access to existing bank accounts but also the possibility of such deviant groups using personal identity data to open new bank accounts or other financial products, such as credit cards, in the name of individuals. The issue of paedophile rings gaining access to the data on children and using it for grooming activities was also raised as a possibility.

A report into this incident was published in June 2008. The report concluded that the HMRC was woefully inadequate in its handling and managing of corporate data. It made a series of recommendations for tightening data security and improving data management practices across UK government.

Issues

- Managing channels of access is a significant issue for eGovernment. How is this issue relevant to the current case?
- In what ways do you think strategy in this area for private sector organisations differs from that for public sector organisations?
- The case highlights the importance of good data security and data management for organisations. With increasing

concern over identity theft and data privacy the reputation of organisations is increasingly reliant on good practice in this area. Investigate what the private sector is doing to ensure this.

23   Victorian railway clearing house

Case description

The British railway network first began to be developed during the 1830s. By 1840 some 1,500 miles of railway track had been laid and many problems, such as that associated with standardisation of railway gauge, had been resolved. It therefore became possible for railway passengers to embark upon long journeys, such as that between London and Newcastle. However, such journeys required passengers to use the railway lines belonging to several different railway companies. Such companies not only managed and operated their own trains, carriages and freight wagons; they also managed and operated their own sub-network of railway lines.

Hence, for long passenger, parcel or goods journeys that crossed the networks of two or more railway companies, the revenue from a journey had to be divided appropriately between the railway companies involved. Initially, private arrangements between companies for such through traffic enabled the division of a composite fare. However, as the number of railway operators grew, this accounting challenge proved monumental for individual companies. Also, companies were frequently unable to agree on the terms of a composite fare. This led to passengers being turned out of their railway compartments at the junctions between the networks of railway operators. Passengers then had to purchase tickets for the next leg of their journey. The same happened in the case of goods traffic. Philip Bagwell cites the case of a wealthy horse owner who had to send a servant to a station simply to lead his horse from one train to another.

The idea for a Railway Clearing House is generally attributed to George Carr Glyn and Kenneth Morrison. Glyn was the partner of a banking firm and chairman of the London and Birmingham railway. Morrison was chief accountant of the same railway and was to become the first executive secretary of the Railway Clearing House. The idea for this organisation appears to have been modelled on the Bankers' Clearing House, on whose executive committee Glyn sat.

In 1841, Glyn persuaded his own railway and that of eight others to jointly subscribe to a railway clearing system. The initial focus of the endeavour was upon establishing an intermediary organisation that would handle information associated with through passenger traffic. Under this system, passengers would be able to book a journey from any station to any other station in the network of participants. The Clearing House would then be responsible for distributing revenue from fares to the participants. In time, the Clearing House would also assume responsibility for clearing the transport of parcels and goods on the railway network. Parcels were carried in the goods van of passenger trains; the transport of goods demanded special freight wagons.

The Railway Clearing House began operations on 2 January 1842. Initially, its staffing consisted of George Carr Glyn as chairman, Kenneth Morrison as a part-time secretary and six full-time clerks. By 1845, 16 companies had joined the system and details of over a half a million passenger/journeys were being processed. By 1848, 43 companies had joined, raising the scale of the network to some 887 stations. This demanded an increase in staffing to 45 clerks and a change of accommodation to offices in Seymour Street, near Euston station in London. These offices were eventually substantially re-modelled and extended to create the famous long office, which was the largest single office in Britain at the time of its completion in 1855.

As the country's railway network continued to expand the Clearing House grew to meet the increased demand for its service. By 1861, 500 clerks worked in the Clearing House and were organised into a number of working divisions. In 1864, the Railway Clearing House had a total of 873 clerks and processed a total of 1.6 million settlements between participating railway companies. By 1874, the number of settlements totalled 4.9 million. However, staff numbers had not increased in proportion and comprised only 1,325 clerks. This was presumably because of increasing productivity among the workforce.

In 1876, the Railway Clearing House was at peak capacity and became an organisation that was respected worldwide. At this time, its staff comprised over 1,000 clerks and 500, so-called, number-takers, which we describe below. Staff were organised into three large divisions: the Coaching department with 352 clerks; the Mileage and Demurrage department with 276 clerks and 500 number-takers; and the Merchandise department with 720 clerks. In addition, there was a small Lost Luggage department with a complement of 16 clerks.

The Coaching department had responsibility for dividing up receipts from passenger and parcel traffic between member companies. The department was headed by an assistant secretary and divided into seven sections. Three passenger sections with 55 clerks each dealt with receipts from passenger traffic. Similarly, three parcel sections, again with 55 clerks each, dealt with receipts from parcels traffic. The final section was a ticket section with 25 clerks that processed passenger tickets. Each section was headed by a senior clerk and subordinates were graded and paid in a scale usually based upon experience. It took approximately three months for a clerk to achieve novitiate status and they were only considered experienced after five or more years of service.

The largest division in the Railway Clearing House was the Merchandise department, which was responsible for dividing revenues from goods traffic. It was divided into 16 sections each with 44 clerks.

The Mileage and Demurrage department was the smallest department but handled the most complex activities. By the 1870s it was possible for any railway company to transport a wagon-load of merchandise on any of the lines of the railway network using any suitable vehicle, whether or not the company actually owned the vehicle. The mileage function of this department divided the revenue between the many different actors who participated in this process: the company that organised the train, the company that owned the wagon, the companies that owned the railway lines and the companies that provided terminal facilities. A system of fines, known as demurrage, was enforced to ensure that unused rolling stock was returned promptly to its owner.

Clearly, the systems of the three departments of the Railway Clearing House worked differently. For our purposes, we shall focus on describing the systems underlying the work of the Coaching department, since they were the simplest of those used by the Clearing House.

The principle underlying the work of this department was straightforward. Any fare paid for a through-journey needed to be divided between the companies involved and a levy raised to help fund the operation of the Clearing House. The complexities lay in dividing up a given journey into its constituent parts and handling the vagaries of different fare structures. This took the monthly returns from booking offices and the tickets collected from passengers at the end of their journey and transformed them into payments made to railway companies.

The Railway Clearing House supplied all through-passenger tickets to member companies. These tickets were printed on 6 cm by 3 cm green card. Tickets were issued to each booking office on the railway network and were pre-printed with all the common destinations available on the network. Tickets were issued in batches of one hundred and within each batch an individual ticket was printed with a serial number by machine. Serial numbers continued between batches.

Tickets were sold in strict ascending serial number order from within a batch. At the end of each day, the booking office clerk would record the serial number of the lowest-numbered unsold ticket in each batch and send these numbers, with the cash collected, to the head office of the railway company. At head office these numbers were used to check the cash received against tickets sold. They were used to compile a monthly summary of tickets sales and receipts for the Railway Clearing House.

Tickets were collected at the end of each passenger's journey, usually at railway stations. These were sent on in batches to the head office of the railway where staff would sort them by destination. The batches of sorted tickets, along with a summary of ticket sales, constituted a monthly return from a railway company to the ticket section of the Coaching department.

In the ticket section 25 boy clerks would arrange the incoming tickets into serial order sequence and reconcile them with the monthly summaries of sales. Frequently, the reconciliation identified anomalies. For instance, there might be a missing half-fare ticket for a child within a batch. In such cases, a senior clerk was called in and a standard form was completed inviting explanation from the offending railway company. Ticket clerks were also responsible for determining the actual route taken by a passenger from a number of possible routes. This was determined by inspection of the punches made in a train ticket by train conductors. Each railway company used a distinctive set of snippers to make this possible. In 1876, there were approximately 3.3 million tickets processed in this manner.

After all the tickets from relevant batches had been verified the results would be tabulated on another standard form and passed on to the appropriate passenger section. In the passenger section the proceeds from an individual ticket needed to be divided between participating companies. To do this, clerks had to inspect a complex set of fare structures. The simplest fare structure was the ordinary fare, which consisted of the sum of local fares applicable to the individual legs of a passenger journey. In contrast, for certain discounted fares, a division had to be made on the basis of the total mileage between all the junctions in the railway network covered by a passenger journey. Hence, maps of the railway network detailing such junctions and the mileage associated with branches of the network had to be inspected.

In terms of each passenger ticket sold in the railway network, the company that sold the ticket was classed as the debtor of the transaction. All other companies involved in the passenger journey became creditors in the transaction. A month's worth of tickets generated thousands of debits and credits against each of the 80 companies in the railway network. Processing this volume normally took clerks a couple of weeks work. At the end of this activity, the total debits and credits were summed for each company and on this basis a single transfer of funds

CS

was made between the Railway Clearing House and the railway company. The aggregate result of these financial transfers had to balance. Hence, clerks normally worked in pairs, each checking the work of the other.

Issues

- How would you describe the primary activity system supported by the clearing house?
- In what way does the clearing house constitute an information system?
- What data was used within the clearing house and for what purpose?
- What do you think comprises information technology in the case of the clearing house?
- In 1993 British Railways, a public sector agency, was broken up and the operation of the UK railway network parcelled up among 25 railway franchises. This has meant that depending on where you travel the finance derived from ticketing has to be parcelled up between a number of railway operators. Is this similar to the situation in Victorian times or different?

24   Wikipedia

See page: 159

Case description

Wikipedia is cited as the pre-eminent example of the use of Web 2.0 technologies in collaborative production. The content is user-generated by a network of authors around the world for no financial gain. It thus has similarities with the production of open source software. Wikipedia was created by Larry Sanger and Jimmy Wales and launched as an English language project on 15 January 2001 and is now operated by the not-for-profit Wikimedia Foundation. Wikipedia is a multi-lingual project which offers a free encyclopaedia on the World Wide Web. The name Wikipedia is a combination of the words wiki and encyclopaedia. Wikipedia uses a type of software called a wiki which handles the construction of shared content that can be updated using easy to use tools through a Web browser.

Registered users of Wikipedia are able to create new articles. However, once an article is present on the site anyone with access to it can change its content and changes made to pages are instantly displayed. The consequence of this is that Wikipedia does not declare any of its articles to be complete or finished. This process of collaborative content production is built upon the premise that collaboration among users will improve articles over time, in much the same way that open source software develops.

Some of Wikipedia's editors have compared this process to Darwinian evolutionary processes where the fitness of content improves over time.

However, this collaborative content production model means that, so-called, vandalism and disagreements about content are common. Some take advantage of Wikipedia's openness to add nonsense to the encyclopaedia. Collaboration also sometimes leads to edit wars, which consist of prolonged disputes when editors do not agree.

Controversy has surrounded the project since its inception. Much criticism centres around the reliability and accuracy of the content on the site. Content has been criticised for uneven quality and inconsistency, systemic bias, and preference for consensus or popularity over credentials. The content of particular articles has been accused as being sometimes unconfirmed and questionable, lacking proper sources. The authors of articles need not have any expertise or qualification in the subjects that they edit, and users are warned that their contributions may be edited mercilessly and redistributed at will by anyone who wishes to do so.

Interestingly, a 2005 comparison performed by the science journal Nature of sections of Wikipedia and the Encyclopædia Britannica found that the two were close in terms of the accuracy of their articles on the natural sciences. However, this study was challenged by Encyclopædia Britannica, who described it as fatally flawed.

It is argued that there is a battle for the future of Wikipedia. Inclusionists would like all to have access to making content on whatever people choose to add to the encyclopaedia. The ideal would be to have as many articles on as many subjects as its contributors are able to produce. Deletionists believe that Wikipedia is more likely to be successful if it maintains both a relevance and quality threshold for its content. This implies a certain level of editorial control over content. Currently deletionists have the upper hand. Decisions as to whether to keep or delete articles are made after deliberation by some 1000 or so of Wikipedia's most ardent contributors. If a member of this group believes that your article fails to meet notability criteria it may be nominated for immediate deletion or to be removed after five days if no one objects. Notability criteria consist of a host of ever-changing rules. For instance, in terms of citations, articles in journals have a higher notability than an article in a newspaper; ten matches on Google is better than one match, and so on. Not surprisingly, debates about the merit of articles can drag on for weeks.

Some believe that the governance bureaucracy surrounding collaborative production deters people from contributing to Wikipedia. This is because to ensure that an article survives authors have to make sure their article is deletion-proof. This raises the threshold for writing articles to a level which deters many.

It is difficult to determine the precise number of articles held on the Wikipedia website. Analysis performed in 2012 suggests that Wikipedia has more than five million articles in many languages, including more than 1.4 million in the English language version. There are 250 language editions of Wikipedia, and 17 of them have more than 50,000 articles each. Wikipedia runs on a cluster of dedicated Linux servers located in Florida and four other locations around the world. It uses its own in-house created software, known as MediaWiki, which is an open source wiki system written in PHP and built upon MySQL.

Issues

- The Wikimedia foundation relies upon donations for its continuous operation. Is this a sustainable business model?
- Academics generally discourage students from citing Wikipedia articles. Why do you think they do this? Is this justified?
- In what sense is the collaborative production model of Wikipedia applicable to other domains? For instance, could you write a magazine in this way, or even a textbook?
- Wikipedia clearly sees itself as an encyclopaedia but many traditional encyclopaedias would beg to differ. Explain the main differences between these two forms of publication.

CS

Cases from the *Journal of Information Technology* (JIT) and the *Journal of Information Technology Teaching Cases* (JITTC) summarised in this section

		Learning goals of IS2010 curriculum											Page numbers in this section
		Organisations and systems	Data, information and knowledge	Infrastructure and information systems	Communication infrastructure	ICT systems infrastructure	Business environment	eBusiness, eCommerce and eGovernment	Use, impact and evaluation	Planning, strategy and management	Service, projects and operations	Information systems development	
1	Fixing the payment system at Alvalade XXI: a case on IT project risk management (JIT, 2007) *Ramon O'Callaghan*	✓	✓	✓	✓	✓		✓	✓		✓	✓	467
2	Modernisation of passenger reservation system: Indian Railways' dilemma (JIT, 2007) *Shirish C Srivastava, Sharat S Mathur and Thompson S H Teo*	✓	✓				✓			✓			467
3	Crafting and executing an offshore IT sourcing strategy: GlobShop's experience (JIT, 2007) *C Ranganathan, Poornima Krishnan and Ron Glickman*							✓		✓			468
4	Infosys Technologies: improving organisational knowledge flows (JIT, 2007) *Nikhil Mehta, Sharon Oswald and Anju Mehta*	✓					✓			✓			468
5	Constructing an e-Supply Chain at the Eastman Chemical Company (JIT, 2004) *Benjamin Yen, Ali Farhoomand and Pauline Ng*	✓		✓	✓	✓	✓						469
6	Lessons learned from the development and marketing of Mozilla Firefox 1.0 (JITTC, 2011) *Leigh Jin, Bruce Robertson and Huoy Min Khoo*				✓			✓					469
7	Finding the process edge: ITIL at Celanese (JITTC, 2011) *Ulrike Schultze*									✓	✓		470
8	Peak experiences and strategic IT alignment at Vermont Teddy Bear (JITTC, 2011) *Janis L Gogan and Mark O Lewis*						✓	✓		✓			470

Please see also the Case Study overview on pp. xviii–xx of the book for details of the CASE CHECKS and additional online support where available.

1 Fixing the payment system at Alvalade XXI: a case on IT project risk management

Case description

This case describes the implementation and subsequent failure of an innovative ICT system installed in the bars of Alvalade XXI, the recently built football stadium in Lisbon, Portugal. Casa XXI, the company running the bars, had entrusted the project to an ICT supplier who had limited experience with large systems. During the inauguration, the information system failed spectacularly, creating a chaotic situation for customers and employees. The failure meant not only a financial loss, but also a blow to the reputation of the company. The management blamed the ICT system supplier for the failure. The supplier, however, claimed that the problem was not technical but organisational, and was particularly due to the poor planning of operations. Subsequent tests were inconclusive and failed to restore trust. At the end of the case, the CEO at Casa XXI is considering the possibility of switching to an alternative ICT supplier. He also wonders what they could have done to manage the project and the associated risks more effectively.

Commentary

The case highlights the importance of considering the joint development of activity systems with ICT systems, and the exercise of good practice in these areas for successful implementation. Activity systems have to be designed and fully tested, as do ICT systems. The causes of information systems failure frequently lie in the space between activity systems and ICT systems. The case demonstrates that it is frequently difficult to assign blame purely to technology in such failures.

The case also highlights some of the difficulties of outsourcing information systems development; particularly decision-making relating to the selection of an outsourcing vendor. Considerations of risk assessment and cost/benefit analysis are clearly elements of such decision-making. There are also evident decisions relating to the degree of innovation desired and the most appropriate architecture for the ICT system.

Issues

The case particularly raises governance questions in relation to the outsourcing of information systems development.

- Who is responsible for the success of an outsourced project?
- How should the roles and responsibilities be apportioned between the company and the ICT supplier(s)?

- What mechanisms should be used to plan and execute ICT outsourced projects, and control their risks?

Access

See www.palgrave.com/business/beynon-daviesbis2e for further information and access to the article.

Visit www.palgrave-journals.com/jit for more information about the *Journal of Information Technology*, and the *Journal of Information Technology Teaching Cases*.

2 Modernisation of passenger reservation system: Indian Railways' dilemma

Case description

This teaching case discusses the challenges faced by technology managers at Indian Railways (IR) in endeavouring to modernise its central passenger reservation system. The old passenger reservation system (PRS) is a classic legacy information system. It has served the organisation for nearly two decades, is critical to the operation of the railway and has proven reliable. However, IR is facing increasing competition from road transport and from low-cost airlines for customers. As such, it wishes to change its rules of operation. However, the design of the PRS is inflexible in the face of such rapidly changing business requirements. The case describes the dilemma faced by the head of the Centre for Railway Information Systems (CRIS) – the informatics service of IR. Should IR continue using the old PRS with its inherent shortcomings, or should it take the risk and build a wholesale replacement with new state-of-art technology, which would make it easier to meet new changing business requirements through greater maintenance flexibility?

Commentary

The case describes a dilemma familiar to anybody concerned with developing informatics strategy, if and how an organisation should change core aspects of its informatics infrastructure. The case demonstrates the necessary interdependence of business activity and information systems. It highlights some of the dilemmas inherent in decision-making in this area and is an example of both business decision-making in general and of risk assessment in particular.

Issues

- The case describes a number of ways in which the passenger reservation system is critical to the operation

CS

of Indian Railways. How would one go about evaluating these as benefits to the organisation?

- Organisations do not stand still and their information systems have to change along with them. In what ways are information systems a brake on organisational change?
- Indian railways run a highly-centralised informatics service. Outline some of the advantages this has in terms of the project in question, as well as some of the disadvantages.
- If Indian Railways decide to build a new information system how would you recommend they handle implementation of this system?

Access

See www.palgrave.com/business/beynon-daviesbis2e for further information and access to the article.

Visit www.palgrave-journals.com/jit for more information about the *Journal of Information Technology*, and the *Journal of Information Technology Teaching Cases*.

3   Crafting and executing an offshore IT sourcing strategy: GlobShop's experience

Case description

This case discusses the decisions facing GlobShop, a global travel-retail company, in its efforts to offshore a significant portion of its ICT work. In response to the business challenges that arose due to the 11 September 2001 terrorist attacks, the company decided to outsource many of its ICT activities to a vendor on the Indian sub-continent. This case traces the key decisions made by the CIO and the challenges that were encountered during the planning and execution of the company's offshore sourcing strategy. These decisions relate to the choice of tasks to be offshored, decisions about the vendor and the nature of the sourcing arrangement, managing the vendor relationship and change management issues induced by offshoring. As GlobShop nears the completion of its 3-year agreement with the offshore vendor, the CIO is faced with decisions regarding continuing offshore outsourcing, extending the contract and the implications this has for the future of the informatics service at GlobShop.

Commentary

The case describes a generally successful arrangement where, over time, a multinational retailer outsourced major elements of its informatics service to a vendor on

the Indian sub-continent. GlobShop initially considered outsourcing as part of its attempt to centralise and standardise business processes and ICT infrastructure across many separate countries. Events in the environment, such as 9/11, caused a major re-orientation of this informatics strategy to one of cost reduction.

The case also highlights the important effort required in managing the relationship between the company and a partner handling major parts of the informatics infrastructure for a company. The issue of human resources and skills is particularly highlighted in this case.

Issues

In the latter part of the case study, issues relating to the future use of informatics outsourcing by GlobShop come to the fore. Like many companies, GlobShop is attempting to balance the cost/benefits it gains from offshoring elements of its informatics provision against the need to control such provision in the long-term, particularly in terms of future ICT developments.

Access

See www.palgrave.com/business/beynon-daviesbis2e for further information and access to the article.

Visit www.palgrave-journals.com/jit for more information about the *Journal of Information Technology*, and the *Journal of Information Technology Teaching Cases*.

4   Infosys Technologies: improving organisational knowledge flows

Case description

Knowledge is now seen as one of the most important organisational resources. But these resources exist in specialised pockets dispersed across the organisation, and dedicated knowledge management (KM) programs are required to improve their flow. However, high failure rates of such programs raise serious doubts about their ability to improve knowledge flows. This case traces the KM program of Infosys Technologies Ltd. The case describes how, in 1999, Infosys' top management detected a severe lack of organisational knowledge flows while implementing a program aimed at continuously improving their core business processes. A more detailed examination exposed that the lack of knowledge flows stifled the effectiveness of their organisational structure and their business model. Alarmed by these critical findings, Infosys initiated their KM programme. A five-stage knowledge maturity model (KMM) was conceptualized to aid KM implementation. With people, processes, and technology as the three pillars of Infosys' KM program, KMM identified the specific capabilities Infosys needed to develop in each of the five levels. Things worked fine till 2004 when Infosys began moving towards KMM Level 4, which required developing clear metrics to measure KM effectiveness, that is, improvements in knowledge flow. In the absence of such metrics, Infosys' Board of Directors started questioning the company's financial investment in the KM program. The CEO, who championed the KM program, knew that he faced two key challenges: to convince the Board of future revenue prospects of the KM program, and to identify metrics for assessing improvements in organisational knowledge flows.

Commentary

The case offers a practical example of the issue of knowledge management and how organisations approach the issue of managing knowledge.

Issues

- Tease out what knowledge means in terms of the organisation described in the case.
- What problems were identified in its management of knowledge?
- Were Infosys successful in their attempt to build better processes for managing knowledge?

Access

See www.palgrave.com/business/beynon-daviesbis2e for further information and access to the article.

Visit www.palgrave-journals.com/jit for more information about the *Journal of Information Technology*, and the *Journal of Information Technology Teaching Cases*.

---

5   Constructing an e-Supply Chain at the Eastman Chemical Company

Case description

The Asia Pacific Digital Business and Customer Services Manager of Eastman Chemical Company, was given a mandate to sell Eastman's philosophy for an integrated electronic supply chain, otherwise known as the Integrated System Solution (ISS), to its business partners in the region, and to encourage adoption. Having invested in a state-of-the-art ICT infrastructure that would support inter-connectivity with all parties along the supply chain, Eastman was keen to realise the full benefits to be gained from an integrated electronic supply chain on the global scale. Following numerous rounds of discussion with key

business partners in the Asia Pacific region, some progress had been made. One of these partners, Nagase & Co. Ltd. of Japan had agreed to progress electronic connections with Eastman. However, they had some reservations regarding the extent of the integration proposed, particularly the implications for their established business processes and corporate strategy.

Commentary

The case describes the environment of the chemical industry and key elements of the value network for Eastman. It outlines the key motivations for eBusiness at Eastman and some of the developments undertaken in formulating its eBusiness strategy. In the early 1990s Eastman adopted a SAP ERP system as the core element of its informatics infrastructure. The case details how this software architecture enabled Eastman to integrate some of its key business processes. The case particularly focuses upon the attempt to extend core infrastructure into its supply chain using XML technology.

Issues

- At a number of points in the case an attempt is made to evaluate the impact of eBusiness changes on the performance improvement of the company. Consider the benefits of information integration to organisational performance in terms of this case.
- ERP is a significant back-bone technology for Eastman. How important is this technology to the effective rollout of its eBusiness strategy?
- In terms of the case describe why XML is an important technology for supply-chain operations.

Access

See www.palgrave.com/business/beynon-daviesbis2e for further information and access to the article.

Visit www.palgrave-journals.com/jit for more information about the *Journal of Information Technology*, and the *Journal of Information Technology Teaching Cases*.

---

6   Lessons learned from the development and marketing of Mozilla Firefox 1.0

Case description

This case provides background in the form of a brief overview of the open source software development process and a description of the browser wars of the 1990s which saw Netscape Navigator fall from its place as the dominant

CS

Web browser in the marketplace. The case then goes on to describe the way in which developers of the open source browser Firefox established both a model of collaborative development and a strategy for marketing their product. Both the development and marketing model are seen as critical to the success of the product.

Commentary

Both Microsoft and Google offer Web browsers. One is bundled with the Microsoft operating systems, while the other is offered free but funded through advertising. In contrast, Firefox is a key example of open source software and, as such, is licensed under general public licenses.

Issues

- How will Firefox compete with other browsers in the coming decade?
- How are browsers adapted to the mobile market?

Access

See www.palgrave.com/business/beynon-daviesbis2e for further information and access to the article.

Visit www.palgrave-journals.com/jit for more information about the *Journal of Information Technology*, and the *Journal of Information Technology Teaching Cases*.

7   Finding the process edge: ITIL at Celanese

See page: 356

Case description

Celanese is a global leader in the chemical industry and spent years implementing an ERP solution and integrating its divisional IT functions into a shared services model. Around 2007, after years of growth in its ICT infrastructure, many within the informatics service at the company still believed that their internal operations would benefit from tighter coordination of business processes. They looked to ITIL to guide their effort at process integration. This case describes the first three years of experience with ITIL by Celanese's informatics service.

Commentary

ITIL enforces a strong process discipline on the informatics service. Some see this as important for justifying in-house provision of this service. Others see it as a constraint on the speed with which the service can respond to both business and technological change.

Issues

- Do you think Celanese eventually see ITIL as of benefit or not?
- Assess Celanese's approach to ICT service improvement. How effective was it? How might they have done things differently?

Access

See www.palgrave.com/business/beynon-daviesbis2e for further information and access to the article.

Visit www.palgrave-journals.com/jit for more information about the *Journal of Information Technology*, and the *Journal of Information Technology Teaching Cases*.

8   Peak experiences and strategic IT alignment at Vermont Teddy Bear

See page: 321

Case description

In 2010 the new CIO at Vermont Teddy Bear was of a mind to modernise the company's informatics infrastructure. He faced the considerable task of making explicit many implicit aspects of this infrastructure as a step towards developing the future informatics strategy for the company. The CEO of the company also sought new sources of revenue, which would impact upon decisions made by the CIO. Should the CIO have considered a long-term investment in enterprise systems or should he have taken immediate steps to produce tangible results, quickly?

Commentary

This case illustrates the complex decisions that help form informatics strategy. CIOs have to persuade their CEOs to invest in changes to informatics infrastructure. Some investment will be large-scale but will potentially deliver big dividends. Other changes are less costly but will only address short-term issues.

Issues

If you were CIO at this company would you invest in an ERP package and, if so, how would you justify this investment?

Access

See www.palgrave.com/business/beynon-daviesbis2e for further information and access to the article.

Visit www.palgrave-journals.com/jit for more information about the *Journal of Information Technology*, and the *Journal of Information Technology Teaching Cases*.

Further author-written cases available online

Please visit **www.palgrave.com/business/beynon-daviesbis2e** for access to the case studies and further supporting material.

		Learning goals of IS2010 curriculum										
		Organisations and systems	Data, information and knowledge	Infrastructure and information systems	Communication infrastructure	ICT systems infrastructure	Business environment	eBusiness, eCommerce and eGovernment	Use, impact and evaluation	Planning, Strategy and management	Service, projects and operations	Information systems development
1	Beer distribution game	✓	✓	✓								
2	Business motivation modelling	✓	✓						✓	✓		
3	Easyjet	✓		✓	✓	✓	✓	✓	✓		✓	
4	HiCar	✓	✓							✓		
5	IKEA *Written by Sharon Cox, Birmingham City University	✓		✓	✓	✓	✓	✓		✓		✓
6	MySpace				✓	✓	✓	✓				
7	OGC gateway process								✓	✓	✓	✓
8	Research information system				✓	✓					✓	✓
9	UK electoral system	✓	✓	✓			✓	✓	✓			
10	UK stock market		✓			✓	✓					✓
11	YouTube	✓			✓	✓						

Please see also the additional Case Study overview on pp. xviii–xx of the book for details of additional supporting material online.

CS

Further JIT and JITTC cases available online

Please visit **www.palgrave.com/business/beynon-daviesbis2e** for access to the case studies and further supporting material.

		Learning goals of IS2010 curriculum										
		Organisations and systems	Data, information and knowledge	Infrastructure and information systems	Communication infrastructure	ICT systems infrastructure	Business environment	eBusiness, eCommerce and eGovernment	Use, impact and evaluation	Planning, strategy and management	Service, projects and operations	Information systems development
1	Managing the Internet Payment Platform project (JIT, 2007) *Janis L Gogan and Ulric J Gelinas Jr*	✓						✓	✓	✓	✓	✓
2	Challenges in delivering cross-agency integrated e-services: the OBLS project (JIT, 2007) *K Pelly Periasamy and Siew-Kien Sia*	✓			✓	✓		✓		✓	✓	✓
3	Wireless technologies at Agriculture ITO (JIT, 2007) *Eusebio Scornavacca*	✓			✓	✓						✓
4	The ultimate bluff: a case study of partygaming.com (JIT, 2007) *Des Laffey*	✓					✓	✓				
5	E-business transformation at the crossroads: Sears' dilemma (JIT, 2004) *C Ranganathan, Analini Shetty and Gayathri Muthukumaran*	✓							✓	✓		
6	DCXNET: e-transformation and DaimlerChrysler (JIT, 2006) *Arnd Klien and Helmut Krcmar*	✓			✓	✓	✓	✓		✓		
7	Addressing the new regulatory landscape: IT compliance and E-Discovery at KMCO Gaming (JITTC, 2011) *Christina N Outlay, Poornima Krishnan and Chandrasekaran Ranganathan*											

Please see also the additional Case Study overview on pp. xviii–xx of the book for details of additional supporting material online.

Bibliography

Ackoff, R. L. (1967). Management Misinformation Systems. *Management Science* 14 (4): 147–156.

Alavi, M. and D. Leidner (2001). Knowledge Management and Knowledge Management Systems. *Management Information Systems Quarterly* 25(1): 107–136.

Alexander, C. (1964). *Notes on the Synthesis of Form*. Harvard, Mass., Harvard University Press.

Alter, S. (2006). *The Work System Method: Connecting People, Processes, and IT for Business Results*. San Francisco, Work System Press.

Ansoff, H. I. (1965). *Corporate Strategy*. New York, McGraw-Hill.

Applegate, L. M., R. D. Austin and and F. W. McFarlan (2009). *Corporate Information Strategy and Management: Text and Cases*. New York, McGraw-Hill.

Avison, D. E. and B. Fitzgerald (2006). *Information Systems Development: Methodologies, Techniques and Tools*. McGraw-Hill.

Avison, D. E., A. T. Wood-Harper, R. T. Vidgen and J. R. G. Wood (1998). A Further Exploration into Information Systems Development: The Evolution of Multiview2. *Information Technology & People* 11 (2): 124–139.

Bakos, J. Y. (1997). Reducing Buyer Search Costs – Implications for Electronic Marketplaces. *Management Science* 43 (12), 1676–1692.

Barrette, S. and B. R. Konsynski (1982). Inter-Organisational Information Sharing Systems. *MIS Quarterly* 6 (Fall): 93–105.

BBC News Online. (13/02/2003). ID Card Scheme Panned by Watchdog. Retrieved 22/10/2010.

BBC News Online. (06/03/2008). In Full: Smith ID Card Speech. Retrieved 22/09/2010, from www.bbc.co.uk/news.

BBC News Online. (12/05/2008). Update: Government Admits ID Cards Have No Business Case. Retrieved 22/10/2010, from www.bbc.co.uk/news.

BBC News Online. (25/05/2010). Identity Cards Scheme Will Be Axed 'Within 100 Days'. Retrieved 22/10/2010, from www.bbc.co.uk/news.

Bell, D. (1972). *The Coming of the Post-industrial Society*. Reading, Mass., Addison-Wesley.

Benbasat, I., D. K. Goldstein and M. Mead. (1987). The Case Research Strategy in Studies of Information Systems. *MIS Quarterly* 11 (3): 269–279.

Bentley, G. (2009). *Practical PRINCE2*. London, Stationery Office Books.

Berners-Lee, T. (1999). *Weaving the Web: The Past, Present and Future of the World Wide Web By Its Inventor*. London, Orion Business Publishing.

Berners-Lee, T., J. Hendler, and O. Lassilo. (2001). The Semantic Web. *Scientific American* 284 (5).

Beynon-Davies, P. (1995). Information Systems 'Failure': The Case of the London Ambulance Service's Computer Aided Despatch System. *European Journal of Information Systems* 4 (1): 171–184.

Beynon-Davies, P. (2004). *Database Systems*. Basingstoke, Palgrave Macmillan.

Beynon-Davies, P. (2005). Constructing Electronic Government: The Case of the UK Inland Revenue. *International Journal of Information Management* 25 (1): 3–20.

Beynon-Davies, P. (2007). Models for eGovernment. *Transforming Government: People, Process and Policy* 1 (1).

Beynon-Davies, P. (2011). *Significance: Exploring the Nature of Information, Systems and Technology*. Basingstoke, Palgrave Macmillan.

Beynon-Davies, P. (2012). *eBusiness*. Basingstoke, Palgrave Macmillan.

Beynon-Davies, P., I. Owens and M. D. Williams (2004). IS Failure, Evaluation and Organisational Learning. *Journal of Enterprise Information Management* (formerly Logistics and Information Management) 17 (4): 276–282.

Biles, G., A. A. Bolton and B. M. DiRe. (1989). Herman Hollerith: Inventor, Manager, Entrepreneur – A Centennial Remembrance. *Journal of Management* 15 (4): 603–615.

Black, E. (2002). *IBM and the Holocaust*. London, Time Warner.

Bott, F. (2005). *Professional Issues in Information Technology*. London, British Computer Society Publications.

Bratton, J., M. Callinan, C. Forshaw and P. Sawchuk. (2010). *Work and Organisational Behaviour*. Basingstoke, Palgrave Macmillan.

Brooks, F. P. (1997). *The Mythical Man Month and Other Essays on Software Engineering*, Boston, Mass., Addison-Wesley.

Brynjolfson, E. (1993). The Productivity Paradox of Information Technology. *Communications of the ACM* 36 (12): 67–77.

B

Brynjolfson, E. and L. Hitt (1998). Beyond the Productivity Paradox. *Communications of the ACM* 41 (8): 49–55.

Burnham, D. (1983). *The Rise of the Computer State*. New York, Random House.

Burton Swanson, E. (1992). *Maintaining Information Systems in Organisations*. Chichester, John Wiley.

Bush, V. (1945). *As We May Think*. Atlantic Monthly, New York.

Button, G. and R. H. R. Harper (1993). Taking the Organisation into Accounts. In G. Button (ed.), *Technology in Working Order: Studies of Work, Interaction and Technology*. London, Routledge.

Cabinet Office (2002). *Privacy and Data Sharing: The Way Forward for Public Services*. London, Performance and Innovation Unit.

Carroll, J. M. (ed.) (1995). *Scenario-Based Design: Envisioning Work and Technology in Systems Development*. New York, John Wiley.

Cash, J. I., F. W. McFarlan and J. L. McKeney (1992). *Corporate Information Systems Management*. Homewood, Ill., Richard Irvin.

Cassidy, J. (2002). *Dot.Con*. London, Allen Lane/Penguin Press.

(Castells, 1996)

Chaffey, D., R. Mayer, K. Johnston and F. Ellis-Chadwicj (2009). *Internet Marketing*. Harlow, Pearson.

Chan, Y. E. and B. H. Reich (2007). IT Alignment: What Have We Learned? *Journal of Information Technology* 22 (4): 297–315.

Checkland, P. (1999). *Soft Systems Methodology: A Thirty Year Retrospective*. Chichester, John Wiley.

Christakis, N. and J. Fowler (2010). *Connected: The Amazing Power of Social Networks and How They Shape Our Lives*. New York, Harper Press.

Clarke, R. (1988). Information Technology and Dataveillance. *Communications of ACM* 31 (5): 498–512.

Coase, R. H. (1937). The Nature of the Firm. *Economica* 4 (16): 386–405.

Cohen, A. (2002). *The Perfect Store: Inside eBay*. New York, Little, Brown and Co.

Copeland, J. B. (2004). *The Essential Turing*. Oxford, Oxford University Press.

Cordella, A. and F. Iannacci (2010). Information Systems in the Public Sector: The e-Government Enactment Framework. *Journal of Strategic Information Systems* 19 (1): 52–66.

Crosby, J. (2008). *Challenges and Opportunities of Identity Assurance*. London, HM Treasury.

Cusumano, M. A. and R. W. Selby (1995). *Microsoft Secrets: How the World's Most Powerful Software Company Creates Technology, Shapes Markets and Manages People*. New York, Free Press.

D'Altroy, T. N. (2002). *The Incas*. Oxford, Basil Blackwell.

Darwin, C. (1998). *The Expression of Emotions in Man and Animals*. Oxford, Oxford University Press.

Davenport, T. H. and L. Prusak (2000). *Working Knowledge: How Organisations Manage What They Know*. Boston, MA, Harvard Business School Press.

DeLone, W. H. and E. R. McLean (1992). Information Systems Success: The Quest for the Dependent Variable. *Information Systems Research* 3(1): 60–95.

DeLone, W. H. and E. R. McLean (2003). The DeLone and McLean Model of Information Systems Success: A Ten Year Update. *Journal of Management Information Systems* 19 (4): 9–30.

Dreyfus, H. L. (2001). *On the Internet*. London, Routledge.

Drucker, P. F. (1994). The Theory of the Business. *Harvard Business Review* 72 (5): 95–104.

Drummond, H. (1994). Escalation in Organisational Decision-Making: A Case of Recruiting an Incompetent Employee. *Journal of Behavioural Decision-Making* 7: 43–55.

Earl, M. J. (1989). *Management Strategies for Information Technology*. Hemel Hempstead, Prentice Hall.

Earley, S. (2010). *DAMA-DMBOK Guide: The DAMA Guide to the Data Management Body of Knowledge*. LLC, Technics Publications.

Eason, K. D. (1988). *Information Technology and Organisational Change*. London, Taylor and Francis.

(Economist, 2008)

Economist (2012a). A Fistful of Dollars. London, *Economist Magazine*, 402: 9.

Economist (2012b). The Value of Friendship. London, *Economist Magazine*, 402: 20–22.

Emery, F. E. and E. L. Trist (1960). Socio-Technical Systems. In C. W. Churchman and M. Verhulst (eds), *Management Science, Models and Techniques*. New York, Pergamon.

Ewusi-Mensah, K. and Z. H. Przasnyski (1994). Factors Contributing to the Abandonment of Information Systems Development Projects. *Journal of Information Technology* 9 (3): 185–201.

Ewusi-Mensah, K. and Z. H. Przasnyski (1995). Learning from Abandoned Information System Development Projects. *Journal of Information Technology* 10 (1): 3–14.

Farrington, B. and K. Lysons (2012). *Purchasing and Supply Chain Management*. London, Financial Times/Prentice Hall.

Fitzgerald, B. (2006). The Transformation of Open Source Software. *Management Information Systems Quarterly* 30 (3): 587–598.

Fitzgerald, G. (2000). *Adaptability and Flexibility in IS Development*. In R. Hackney and D. Dunn (eds), *Business Information Technology Management: Alternative and Adaptive Futures*. London, Macmillan: 13–24.

Fitzgerald, G. and N. L. Russo (2005). The Turnaround of the London Ambulance Service Computer-Aided Dispatch System (LASCAD). *European Journal of Information Systems* 14 (3): 244–257.

Floridi, L. (2007). A Look into the Future Impact of ICT on Our Lives. *The Information Society* 23 (1): 59–64.

Fountain, J. E. (2001). *Building the Virtual State: Information Technology and Institutional Change*. The Brookings Institution, New York.

Fortune, J. and G. Peters (2005). *Information Systems: Achieving Success by Avoiding Failure*. Chichester, John Wiley.

Friedman, A. L. and D. S. Cornford (1989). *Computer Systems Development: History, Organisation and Implementation*. Chichester, John Wiley.

Galliers, R. D. (2006). On confronting some of the common myths of information systems strategy discourse. In R. Mansell, D. Quah and R. Silverstone (eds), *The Oxford Handbook of Information and Communication Technology*. Oxford, Oxford University Press.

Galliers, R. D. and W. L. Currie (eds) (2011). *The Oxford Handbook of Information Systems: Critical Perspectives and New Directions*. Oxford, Oxford University Press.

Galliers, B. and D. Leidner (2003). *Strategic Information Management: Challenges and Strategies in Managing Information Systems*. New York, Butterworth-Heinemann.

Gillenson, M. L. (1991). Database Administration at the Crossroads: The Era of End-user-Oriented, Decentralised Data Processing. *Journal of Database Administration* 2 (4): 1–11.

Gladden, G. R. (1982). Stop the Lifecycle I Want to Get Off. *Software Engineering Notes* 7 (April) (2): 35–39.

Graham, I. (2006). *Business Rules Management and Service Oriented Architecture: A Pattern Language*. London, John Wiley.

Granovetter, M. (1973). The Strength of Weak Ties. *American Journal of Sociology* 78 (6): 1360.

Gray, I. (1984). *General and Industrial Management*. New York, IEEE Press.

Hay, D. C. (1996). *Data Model Patterns: Conventions of Thought*. New York, Dorset House.

Heeks, R. (1999). *Reinventing Government in the Information Age: International Practice in IT-enabled Public Sector Reform*. Routledge, London.

Hevner, A. R., S. T. March, J. Park and S. Ram (2004). Design Science in Information Systems Research. *Management Information Systems Quarterly* 28 (1): 75–105.

Hirschheim, R. A. (1983). Assessing Participatory Systems Design: Some Conclusions from an Exploratory Study. *Information and Management* 6: 317–327.

Hirschheim, R. and H. Klein (2003). Crisis in the IS Field? A Critical Reflection on the State of the Discipline. *Journal of the Association for Information Systems* 4 (5): 237–293.

Hirschheim, R. and M. Newman (1988). Information Systems and User Resistance: Theory and Practice. *Computer Journal* 31 (5): 398–408.

Hofstede, G. (1991). *Cultures and Organisations*. McGraw-Hill, New York.

Holwell, S. and P. Checkland (1998a). An Information System Won the War. *IEE Proceedings Software* 145 (4): 95–99.

Holwell, S. and P. Checkland (1998b). *Information, Systems and Information Systems*. Chichester, John Wiley.

Holzner, S. (2008). *How Dell Does It*. New York, McGraw-Hill Professional.

Hunt, T., C. Humby, et al. (2006). *Scoring Points: How Tesco Continues to Win Customer Loyalty*. London, Kogan Page.

Ives, B. and G. P. Learmonth (1984). The Information System as a Competitive Weapon. *Communications of the ACM* 27 (12): 1193–1201.

Jackson, M. C. (2003). *Systems Thinking: Creative Holism for Managers*. Chichester, John Wiley.

Johnson, G., K. Scholes and R. Whittington (2007). *Exploring Corporate Strategy: Text and Cases*. Englewood-Cliffs, Prentice-Hall.

Kaplan, R. S. and D. P. Norton (1992). The Balanced Scorecard: Measures That Drive Performance. *Harvard Business Review* January–February: 71–79.

Keen, P. (1981). Information Systems and Organisational Change. *Communications of the ACM* 24 (1): 24–33.

Keen, P. G. W. (1980). Reference Disciplines and a Cumulative IS Tradition. *International Conference on Information Systems*, Philadelphia.

Kirkpatrick, D. (2011). *The Facebook Effect: The Real Inside Story of Mark Zuckerberg and the World's Fastest Growing Company: The Inside Story of the Company That is Connecting the World*. London, Virgin Books.

Kling, R. and J. P. Allen (1996). Can Computer Science Solve Organisational Problems? The Case for Organisational Informatics. In R. Kling (ed.), *Computerisation and Controversy: Value Conflicts and Social Choices*. San Diego, Academic Press.

Kling, R. and W. Scaachi (1982). The Web of Computing: Computer Technology as Social Organisation. *Advances in Computers* 21: 1–90.

Kraemer, K. L. and J. Dedrick (2002). Strategic Use of the Internet and e-Commerce: Cisco Systems. *Journal of Strategic Information Systems* 11 (1): 5–29.

Kumar, K. (1990). Post Implementation Evaluation of Computer-based Information Systems: Current Practices. *Communications of the ACM* 33 (2): 236–252.

B

Lacity, M. and L. Wilcocks (2006). *Information Systems and Outsourcing*. Basingstoke, Palgrave Macmillan.

Lacity, M. C., S. A. Khan and L. P. Wilcocks (2009). A Review of the IT Outsourcing Literature: Insights for Practice. *Journal of Strategic Information Systems* 18 (3): 130–146.

Landauer, T. K. (1995). *The Trouble with Computers: Usefulness, Usability and Productivity*. Cambridge, Mass., MIT Press.

Le Guin, U. (1974). *The Dispossessed*. New York, Harper and Row.

Lenk, K. and R. Traunmuller (2002). Preface to the Focus Theme on e-Government. *Electronic Markets* 12 (3): 147–148.

Lyytinen, K. (1988). The Expectation Failure Concept and Systems Analysts View of Information Systems Failures: Results of an Exploratory Study. *Information and Management* 14: 45–55.

Lyytinen, K. and R. Hirschheim (1987). Information Systems Failures: A Survey and Classification of the Empirical Literature. *Oxford Surveys in Information Technology* 4: 257–309.

Malinowski, B. (1922). *Argonauts of the Western Pacific: An Account of Native Enterprise and Adventure in the Archipelagoes of Western New Guinea*. London, Routledge Kegan Paul.

Malone, T. W., J. Yates and R. I. Benjamin (1987). Electronic Markets and Electronic Hierarchies. *Communications of the ACM* 30 (6): 484–497.

Marchand, D. A., W. J. Kettinger and J. D. Rollins (2000). Company Performance and Information Management: The View from the Top. In D. A. Marchand, T. H. Davenport and T. Dickson (eds), *Mastering Information Management*. Harlow, Essex, Pearson.

Martin, J. (1996). *Cybercorp*. New York, American Management Association.

Maslow, A. (1954). *Motivation and Personality*. Cambridge, Mass., Harper and Row.

Mason, R. O. (2004). The Legacy of LEO: Lessons Learned from an English Tea and Cake Company's Pioneering Efforts in Information Systems. *Journal of the Association for Information Systems* 5 (5): 183–219.

Mason, R. O. and I. I. Mitroff (1981). *Challenging Strategic Planning Assumptions: Theory, Cases and Techniques*. New York, John Wiley.

McGrath, K. (2002). The Golden Circle: A Way of Arguing and Acting About Technology in the London Ambulance Service. *European Journal of Information Systems* 11 (1): 251–256.

McGregor, D. (1960). *The Human Side of the Enterprise*. New York, McGraw-Hill.

McKenzie, D. (1994). Computer-Related Accidental Death: An Empirical Exploration. *Science and Public Policy* 21(4): 233–248.

Menn, J. (2003). *All the Rave: The Rise and Fall of Shawn Fanning's Napster*. New York, Crown Business.

Monk, E. and B. Wagner (2012). *Concepts in Enterprise Resource Planning*. Boston, Mass., South-Western College Publishing.

Morgan, G. (1986). *Images of Organisation*. London, Sage.

Moritz, M. (2009). *Return to the Little Kingdom: Steve Jobs, the Creation of Apple, and How It Changed the World*. Oxford, Gerard Duckworth.

Mumford, E. (1983). *Designing Participatively*. Manchester, Manchester Business School Press.

Mumford, E. (2006). The Story of Socio-Technical Design: Reflections on Its Successes, Failures and Potential. *Information Systems Journal* 16 (4): 317–342.

Newell, S. M., M. Robertson, H. Scarbrough and J. Swan (2009). *Managing Knowledge, Work and Innovation*. Basingstoke, Palgrave Macmillan.

Nielsen, J. (1993). *Usability Engineering*. Boston, Academic Press.

Nonaka, I. and H. Takeuchi (1995). *The Knowledge-Creating Company*. New York, Oxford University Press.

Norris, M. and West, N. (2001). *eBusiness Essentials*. John Wiley, Chichester, UK.

(O'Connell, 1996)

O'Connell, F. (2001). *How to Run Successful Projects II: The Silver Bullet*. Hemel Hempstead, Prentice Hall.

OGC (2005). *Introduction to ITIL*. London, Stationery Office Books.

OGC (2009). *ITIL V3 Foundation Handbook*. London, Stationery Office Books.

O'Neill, M. G. (2010). *Green IT: For Sustainable Business Practice*. Swindon, British Computer Society.

Orlikowski, W. J. (1996). *Realising the Potential of New Technologies: An Improvisation Model of Change Management*. Business Information Technology, Manchester Metropolitan University.

Orlikowski, W. T. and T. C. Gash (1994). Technological Frames: Making Sense of Information Technology in Organisations. *ACM Trans. on Information Systems* 12 (2): 17–207.

Oshri, I., J. Kotlarsky and L. Wilcocks (2008). *Outsourcing Global Services: Knowledge, Innovation and Social Capital*. Basingstoke, Palgrave Macmillan.

Osterwalder, A. and Y. Pigneur (2010). *Business Model Generation*. Hoboken, New Jersey, John Wiley.

Oz, E. (1994). When Professional Standards are Lax: The Confirm Failure and Its Lessons. *Communications of the ACM* 37 (10): 29–36.

Paolini, C. (1999). *The Value Net: A Tool for Competitive Strategy*. Chichester, John Wiley.

Parker, M., R. Benson and H. Trainor (1988). *Information Economics: Linking Business Performance to Information Technology*. New Jersey, Prentice-Hall.

Pierce, C. S. (1931). *Collected Papers*. Cambridge, Mass., Harvard University Press.

Pinker, S. (2001). *The Language Gene*. Harmondsworth, Middx, Penguin.

Polanyi, M. (1962). *Personal Knowledge*. New York, Anchor Day Books.

Porter, M. E. (1985). *Competitive Advantage: Creating and Sustaining Superior Performance*. New York, Free Press.

Porter, M. E. (2001). Strategy and the Internet. *Harvard Business Review* 79 (3): 63–78.

Porter, M. E. and V. E. Millar (1985). How Information Gives You Competitive Advantage. *Harvard Business Review* 63 (4): 149–160.

Putnam, R. D. (2000). *Bowling Alone: The Collapse and Revival of American Community*. New York, Simon and Schuster.

Raymond, E. S. (1999). The Cathedral & the Bazaar. *Knowledge, Technology and Policy* 12 (3): 23–49.

Rheingold, H. (1995). *The Virtual Community: Finding Connection in a Computerised World*. London, Minerva.

Sachs, P. (1995). Transforming Work: Collaboration, Learning and Design. *Communications of the ACM* 38 (9): 36–45.

Sauer, C. (1993). *Why Information Systems Fail: A Case Study Approach*. Henley-On-Thames, Alfred Waller.

Sawhney, M. and D. Parikh (2001). Where Value Lies in a Networked World. *Harvard Business Review* 79 (1): 79–86.

Shneiderman, B., C. Plaisant, M. Cohen and S. Jacobs (2009). *Designing the User Interface: Strategies for Effective Human-Computer Interaction*. New York, Pearson.

Searle, J. R. (1970). *Speech Acts: An Essay in the Philosophy of Language*. Cambridge, Cambridge University Press.

Senge, P. M. (2006). *The Fifth Discipline: The Art and Practice of the Learning Organisation*. New York, Doubleday.

Shannon, C. E. (1949). *The Mathematical Theory of Communication*. Urbana, University of Illinois Press.

Silver, M. S., M. L. Markus, and C. M. Beath (1995). The Information Technology Interaction Model: A Foundation for the MBA Core Course. *MIS Quarterly* 19 (3): 361–390.

Singh, S. (2000). *The Science of Secrecy*. Fourth estate, London.

Stacey, R. D. (2003). *Strategic Managment and Organisational Dynamics: The Challenge of Complexity*. Harlow, Pearson Education.

Stamper, R. K. (1973). *Information in Business and Administrative Systems*. London, Batsford.

Stamper, R. K. (2001). Organisational Semiotics: Informatics without the Computer? In L. Kecheng, R. J. Clarke, P. Bøgh Andersen and R. K. Stamper (eds), *Information, Organisation and Technology: Studies in Organisational Semiotics*. Dordecht, Netherlands, Kluwer.

Stapleton, J. (1997). *DSDM – Dynamic Systems Development Method: The Method in Practice*. Addison-Wesley, Harlow, England.

Tapscott, D. and A. D. Williams (2006). *Wikinomics: How Mass Collaboration Changes Everything*. London, Atlantic Books.

Timmers, P. (1998). Business Models for Electronic Marketplaces. *Electronic Markets* 8 (1): 3–8.

Urton, G. and C. J. Brezine (2005). Khipu Accounting in Ancient Peru. *Science*: 1065–1068.

US (1985). US Government Accounting Office Report. FGMSD-80-4. *ACM Sigsoft Software Engineering Notes* 10 (5).

Vannevar Bush (1945)

Venkatesh, V., M. G. Morris, F. D. Davis and G. B. Davis (2003). User Acceptance of Information Technology: Toward a Unified View. *MIS Quarterly* 27 (3): 425–478.

Vickers, G. (1965). *The Art of Judgement*. London, Chapman and Hall.

Vidgen, R. T., D. E. Avison, B. Wood and A. T. Wood-Harper (2002). *Developing Web Information Systems: From Strategy to Implementation*. London, Butterworth-Heinemann.

Vise, D. A. (2005). *The Google Story*. New York, Random House.

Von Baeyer, H. C. (2003). *Information : The New Language of Science*. London, Weidenfeld & Nicolson.

W3C. (2000). *XML 1.0*. 2nd edition. World-Wide-Web Consortium.

Walsham, G. and C.-K. Han (1991). Structuration Theory and Information Systems Research. *Journal of Applied Systems Analysis* 18 (1): 77–85.

Ward, J. and J. Peppard (2012). *Strategic Planning for Information Systems*, 4th edition, New York, John Wiley.

Ward, J., P. Taylor and P. Bond (1996). Evaluation and Realisation of IS/IT Benefits: An Empirical Study of Current Practice. *European Journal of Information Systems* 4 (1): 214–225.

Weill, P. and J. Ross (2004). *IT Governance: How Top Performers Manage IT Decision Rights for Superior Results*. Boston, Harvard Business School Press.

Whyte, W. H. (1956). *The Organization Man*. New York, Simon & Schuster.

Wilcocks, L. and H. Margetts (1994). Risk Assessment and Information Systems. *European Journal of Information Systems* 3 (2): 127–138.

Womack, J. P. and D. T. Jones (2003). *Lean Thinking: Banish Waste and Create Wealth in Your Corporation*. London, Free Press Business.

Worthington, I. and C. Britton (2009). *The Business Environment*. Englewood Cliffs, NJ, Prentice Hall.

Wright, R. (1989). *Systems Thinking: A Guide to Managing in a Changing Environment*. Dearborn, Michigan, Society of Manufacturing Engineers.

Yeates, D., D. Paul, T. Jenkins, K. Hindle and C. Rollason (2007). *Business Analysis*. London, BCS Publications.

Zuboff, S. (1988). *In the Age of the Smart Machine: The Future of Work and Power*. London, Heinemann.

B

Glossary

An online version of the glossary is available at www.palgrave.com/business/beynon-daviesbis2e

A

Acceptance testing Conducting any tests required by the user to ensure that the user community is satisfied with the system.

Access A pre-condition for the electronic delivery of services and goods. Stakeholders must have access to remote access devices.

Access channel A means of accessing the goods and services provided by an organisation. Consisting of an access device plus an associated communication channel.

Access device A device that enables access to organisation ICT systems.

Accounting information system That part of the information systems infrastructure involved in managing information concerning the financial state of some organisation.

Action perspective The perspective on organisations that focuses on the process of organising.

Activity system A coherent collection of inter-related and coordinated activities performed by some group of people.

Activity systems infrastructure The entire set of activity systems performed by an organisation.

Activity-based planning A form of project management in which planning and control is conducted in terms of project activities.

Actor Any entity which is able to act.

Adaptation The process of ensuring that a system continues to sustain itself in the face of environmental change.

Adaptive maintenance Changes made to the information system to provide a closer fit between an information system and its environment, the activity system.

Adjunct community Forms of virtual community that focus around the development of relationships between customers and the business.

ADSL Asynchronous Digital Subscriber Line. A broadband communication channel for the local loop.

After-sales service A primary process in the internal value-chain. These are services that maintain or enhance product value by attempting to promote a continuing relationship with the customer of the company. It may involve such activities as the installation, testing, maintenance and repair of products.

Aggregation The relationship between a class treated as a part and its containing class.

Analogue signal A signal modulated with a continuous range of values.

Analysis See *Systems analysis*.

Application A term generally used as a synonym for an ICT system or some other piece of software designed to perform a particular function.

Application service provider A company supplying a software service as an application.

Application software Software designed for a particular set of tasks in an organisation.

ASCII American Standard Code for Information Interchange – a standard coding scheme for characters on computing devices.

Assertive A communicative act that explains how things are in a particular organisational domain.

Association The relationship between instances of one object class and another object class.

Attribute A property of some class.

Attribution The relationship between an object class and an attribute.

Auction A form of commercial exchange involving bidding.

Authentication The process of identifying some actor to a system.

Authorisation The facilities available for enforcing database security.

Awareness A pre-condition of electronic delivery. Stakeholders must be aware of the potential benefits of electronic delivery.

B

B2B Business to business. *See Supply Chain*.

B2B eCommerce The use of *eCommerce* in the supply chain.

B2C Business to customer. *See Customer Chain*.

B2C eCommerce The use of *E-Commerce* in the customer chain.

Back-end ICT infrastructure The ICT systems used to support the core information systems of the business.

Back-end ICT system A core ICT system involved in manipulating the key data for the organisation.

Back-end information system A core transaction processing information system concerned with supporting the internal processes of some organisation.

Back-end information systems infrastructure The core set of inter-related information systems supporting business operations.

Backus-Naur Form A notation for specifying the data structures of a data model.

Balanced scorecard A popular performance measurement system for organisations.

Bandwidth A measure of the amount of data that can be transmitted along a communication channel in a unit of time. Normally measured in bits per second.

Banner advertisement Adverts typically displayed across the top of a Web-page.

Benchmarking Sometimes called competitive practices benchmarking. The process of comparing performance against other comparable organisations or processes.

Bespoke development The development style in which an organisation produces a new information system to directly match the organisation's requirements.

Bit An abbreviation of binary digit, one of the two digits (0 and 1) used in binary notation.

Blog A Web-site where entries are written in chronological order and commonly displayed in reverse chronological order.

Branding The process of using some form of sign to identify a product or service provided by some organisation.

Bricks and mortar business Businesses that have a physical presence usually in terms of some buildings where they are located.

Broadband A term generally used to describe a high bandwidth communication channel.

Browser A program that allows users to access and read Web-documents.

Bulletin board Web facilities that permit users to post items to a central access area.

Business analysis The analysis of business systems.

Business case The case made for the utility of an information system.

Business intelligence Business intelligence broadly refers to a number of techniques for identifying and analysing patterns in business data.

Business layer That part of an ICT system involved with the management of update functions, transactions and business rules.

Business model An organisation's core logic for creating value.

Business process See *Organisational Process*.

Business process re-engineering An *organisational analysis* approach to redesigning business processes.

Business rule A rule which specifies how a particular part of an ICT system should behave.

Business sign A sign of interest in a business domain.

Business strategy See *Organisation Strategy*.

Buyer-oriented B2B A consumer opens an electronic market on its own server and requests bids.

Byte A collection of eight bits.

C

C2C eCommerce Consumer to Consumer eCommerce. ICT enablement of aspects of the community chain.

C2C eGovernment Citizen to citizen eGovernment. Enablement of the community chain with eGovernment.

C2C exchange An ICT enabled facility that involves trade between complex networks of individual actors.

CAISE See *Computer Aided Information Systems Engineering*.

Capacity See *Bandwidth*.

Cardinality Cardinality establishes how many instances of one information class are related to how many instances of another information class.

Cash commerce The exchange of low-price goods in irregular exchanges between actors.

Cash's taxonomy A taxonomy of organisations which indicates the value that informatics planning will have for the organisation.

Cellular network A wireless network supporting mobile phones.

Channel strategy A set of choices for the organisation about how, and through what means, services and goods will be delivered.

Character set A scheme for representing symbols in binary notation.

Chat Technology enabling near synchronous many-to-many communication over the Internet.

Chief information officer CIO – a term for an executive level manager in the organisation responsible for informatics.

CIO See *Chief information officer*.

Class See *Information class*.

Classification The relationship beween a class and an object or instance.

Clicks and mortar business Businesses that still maintain a physical presence but also offer services and products accessible by clicking online.

Clicks-only business Businesses that have emerged entirely in the online environment.

Client A key type of organisational stakeholder. Clients sponsor and provide resources for the construction and continuing use of an information system. Also, the computer that requests services from servers.

Client-server An applications architecture in which processing is distributed between machines acting as clients and machines acting as servers.

Closed system A system that does not interact with its environment.

Cloud The idea of computing power being delivered to the user in much the same way as electricity or water is delivered as a utility over the Internet.

G

Cloud computing A term used to refer to a number of technologies that support remote computing such as SOA, data centres and virtualisation.

COBIT Control Objectives for Information and related Technology, a method for ICT governance.

Coding The translation of a signal from one medium into the same pattern expressed differently in some other communication medium.

Command language interface An interface in which the user enters statements in a formal language.

Commerce That process which deals with the exchange of goods and services between actors.

Commissive A communicative act that commits an actor to some future course of action.

Communication The accomplishment of meaning between actors.

Communication channel The medium along which messages travel.

Communication network A set of devices connected with communication channels.

Communication software Software enabling the inter-connection of computer systems.

Communication subsystem That part of an ICT system enabling distribution of the processing around a network.

Communication technology Technology used for communication.

Community chain The chain of social networks within which the organisation sits.

Comparator A process that compares signals from sensors with control inputs.

Competitive position An organisation takes up a particular position in a market defined by its activities and relationships with its competitors, suppliers, customers and regulators.

Competitor A key type of organisational stakeholder. Key organisations in the same industrial sector or market that compete with an organisation.

Complex data Data structures using complex data types such as images, video and audio.

Computer Aided Information Systems Engineering CAISE. Information technology used to automate aspects of the information system development process.

Concept The idea of significance. The collection of properties that in some way characterise a phenomena.

Conception See *Systems Conception*.

Configuration A version of some development product.

Configuration management The process of controlling the changes made to an information system over time.

Construction That part of the development process devoted to building information systems.

Content A term now used to refer to any media stored in digital form.

Content management The process of ensuring that content is accurate, relevant and timely.

Control The process that implements regulation and adaptation within systems.

Control Inputs Special types of input to a control process that define levels of performance for some system.

Control process See *Control Subsystem*.

Control Subsystem That subsystem which regulates the behaviour of a system it is monitoring. Also known as a control process or mechanism.

Cookie A data file placed on a user's machine by a Web browser. Used by an organisation's ICT system to monitor interaction.

co-option?

Coordination cost A cost incurred in making an economic exchange. Also known as a transaction cost.

Copyright Copyright law enables authors of an intellectual property to prevent unauthorised copying of their material. The law applies to physical transactions of written material regardless of its country of origin.

Cost advantage An organisation strategy. This essentially aims to establish the organisation as a low-cost leader in the market.

Cost per acquisition A form of revenue generation in which the advertiser pays for new acquisitions such as new customers, prospects or leads achieved through online adverts.

Cost-benefit analysis Critical to assessing whether or not the process of developing an IS is a worthwhile investment.

Create (formative act) A formative act that brings a new data structure, element or item into existence.

Credit commerce Where irregular transactions occur between trading partners and the processes of settlement and execution are separated.

Critical path An activity within a project whose float is zero.

Critical success factor A factor which is deemed crucial to the success of a business.

CRM See *Customer relationship management*.

Customer A key type of organisational stakeholder. Consumers of an organisation's products or services.

Customer acquisition Consists of that set of activities and techniques used to gain new customers.

Customer chain The chain of activities that an organisation performs in relation to its customers.

Customer extension Consists of the set of activities and techniques used to encourage existing customers to increase their level of involvement with a company's products and services.

Customer-facing information system A type of information system supporting interaction with the customer of the organisation.

Customer profiling and preferencing A mechanism of customising online products and services for the customer based on detailed information captured about them.

Customer relationship management The set of activities devoted to managing the customer chain.

Customer relationship management system That information system devoted to managing all interactions of a customer with an organisation.

Customer resource life-cycle A strategic planning framework due to Ives and Learmonth. Also useful in defining elements of the *customer chain*.

Customer retention Refers to the set of activities and techniques used to maintain relationships with existing customers.

D

Data Symbols used to represent something. See *Forma*.

Data administration That function concerned with the management, planning and documentation of the data resource of an organisation.

Data element A collection of data items.

Data flow A pipeline through which data of known composition flow. Also referred to as information flow.

Data format A format for the structure of data.

Data infrastructure The set of inter-related data models that define the data needs of the organisation.

Data integrity Ensuring that the data stored in an ICT system remains an accurate reflection of the state of the activity system it describes.

Data item A physical structure which can store some value.

Data layer See *Data management layer*.

Data management The set of facilities needed to manage a data resource.

Data management layer That part of an ICT system involved with the storage and maintenance of data.

Data mining The process of extracting previously unknown data from large databases.

Data model A model representing the structure of data appropriate to a domain, or a blueprint of data requirements for an application.

Data privacy Ensuring the privacy of personal data.

Data protection The activity of ensuring data privacy.

Data security The process of ensuring the security of stored and transmitted data.

Data store See *Information store*.

Data structure A collection of data elements.

Data subsystem That part of an ICT system concerned with managing the data needed by the application.

Data system Physical patterns which can be combined into structures and manipulated to produce new structures.

Data type A definition which constrains the data appropriate to a data item.

Data validation Ensuring that data captured and stored remains an accurate reflection of its domain.

Data verification Ensuring that data is both entered and transmitted correctly.

Data warehouse a type of contemporary database system designed to fulfil decision-support needs.

Data warehousing The process of building and managing data warehouses.

Database An organised repository for data.

Database administration Involves technical implementation of database systems, managing the systems currently in use and setting and enforcing policies.

Database management system An organised set of facilities for accessing and maintaining one or more databases.

Database system A term used to encapsulate the constructs of a *data model*, *DBMS* and *database*.

Database/website integration The technologies associated with integrating database systems with websites.

Datum A unit of *data*.

DBMS See *Database management system*.

Decision A selection between alternative courses of action.

Decision strategy A set of rules that implement control inputs.

Decision support database Databases used to support organisational decision-making.

Decision support system DSS. See *Executive information system*.

Decision-making The activity of deciding on appropriate action in particular situations.

Declarative A communicative act that changes the state of an organisational domain.

Decomposition The relationship between a class treated as a whole and its parts.

Delete (formative act) A formative act that removes an existing data structure, element or item from existence.

Demand chain See *Customer chain*.

Design See *Systems design*.

Designation See *Symbol*.

Developer See *Producer*.

Development failure Failure of an information system project while in development.

Development information system That information system designed to support the development process.

Development method A specified approach for producing information systems.

Development organisation The group of people involved in a particular development effort.

Development process That activity system concerned with developing an information system

G

Development technique Normally used to guide activity within one phase of the development process.

Development toolkit The methods, techniques and tools available to the development organisation.

Differentiation strategy The organisation undertaking this strategy aims to differentiate its product or service from its competitors.

Digital cash A type of non-credit-based payment system.

Digital certificate Sometimes referred to as digital signatures, they are used to authenticate parties in e-Commerce transactions.

Digital convergence The convergence around digital standards allowing interoperability of a variety of digital technologies.

Digital divide The phenomenon of differential rates of awareness, interest, access, skills and use of ICT among different groups in society.

Digital signal A signal modulated with a limited range of values.

Direct conversion An implementation approach in which the new system directly replaces the old system.

Direction A property of a communication which refers to the direction of the data flow between sender and receiver.

Directive A communicative act that attempts to influence action.

Disintermediation The process by which intermediaries are removed from parts of the value network.

Division of labour This is the way in which tasks and responsibilities are assigned to members of the organisation.

Document management An ICT system devoted to manage the collection, storage and distribution of organisational documentation.

Domain integrity That the values in a column of a table are defined on a pool known as a domain.

Domain name A hierarchical naming convention for identifying host computers on the Internet.

Double-loop feedback A type of feedback which monitors both an underlying control process and the environment and makes adjustments to the control inputs of lower-level controllers if needed.

E

eBusiness Electronic Business. The conduct of any business using information and communication technology. A superset of *eCommerce*.

eBusiness strategy The development of strategy for the electronic business.

eCommerce Electronic Commerce. The conduct of business commerce using information and communication technology.

eCommunity Term used to describe either a traditional community enabled with ICT or a virtual community.

Economic actor An agency which engages in economic exchange.

Economic environment That part of the environment concerned with material provisioning.

Economic relationship The relationships of exchange between economic actors.

Economic system See *Economic environment.*

eDemocracy Electronic democracy. The application of ICT to support democratic processes and systems.

EDI Electronic data interchange. A set of standards for the transfer of electronic documentation between organisations.

Effectiveness A measure of the extent to which the system contributes to the purposes of some higher-level system.

Effector A process that cause changes to a system's state.

Efficacy A measure of the extent to which a system achieves its intended transformation. See also *Utility.*

Efficiency A measure of the extent to which a system achieves its intended transformation with the minimum use of resources.

EFT Electronic funds transfer is a means for transferring money electronically between financial repositories (such as banks or bank accounts).

EFTPOS Electronic funds transfer at point of sale is a form of EFT where the purchaser is physically at the point of sale.

eGovernment Electronic government. The application of ICT within government organisations

EIS See *Executive information system.*

Electronic community A community supported through ICT.

Electronic delivery The use of ICT to deliver goods and services to customers.

Electronic government See *eGovernment.*

Electronic hierarchy A form of managerial control in which exchanges on a one-to-many basis are conducted using ICT.

Electronic payment system A system for the electronic transfer of monetary data.

email Electronic mail. The transmission and receipt of electronic text messages using communication networks.

email protocol A communication protocol for the transfer of electronic mail.

eMall A collection of eShops.

eMarket A market in which economic exchanges are conducted using information technology and computer networks.

eMarketing The process of planning and executing the conception, pricing, promotion and distribution of ideas, goods and services using electronic channels.

eMarketing strategy A strategy for electronic marketing.

Employee-facing information system A type of information system supporting interaction with employees of the organisation.

eNabled Community A traditional community supported by ICT.

Encryption The process of securing data through the application of a security algorithm.

End-user That stakeholder group which uses an information system to conduct work.

Enterprise resource planning system ERP system. A package that implements an enterprise architecture for an organisation.

Enterprise system A system that integrates data and processes across the organisation.

Entity integrity That each table must have a primary key.

Environment Anything outside the organisation from which an organisation receives inputs and to which it passes outputs.

Environment Anything outside the organisation with which the organisation interacts and which influences the behaviour of the organisation.

eProcurement A term used to refer to ICT enablement of key supply chain activities.

Equifinality The idea that a system can be designed to fulfil its purpose in a number of different ways.

eShop A single firm selling their products or services online.

ETHICS Mumford's sociotechnical design method.

Evaluation Assessing the worth of something.

Executive information system EIS. That type of information system designed to support high-level, strategic decision-making in organisations.

Expectation failure The inability of an information system to meet a specific stakeholder group's expectations.

Explicit knowledge Readily accessible, documented and organised knowledge.

Expressive A communicative act that reflects an actor's feelings towards a proposition.

Extension See *Referent*.

Extranet A network established such that external users can gain access to specified parts of the internal network of an organisation.

F

Feasibility study That part of systems conception concerned with assessing the feasibility of developing an information system.

Feedback The way in which a control process adjusts the state of some system being monitored to keep it within defined limits.

File An element of *physical data organisation*; a collection of records.

Firewall A collection of hardware and software placed between an organisation's internal network and an external network such as the Internet.

Five forces model A strategic planning framework based on Porter and Millar.

Foreign key An attribute or attributes within a table which cross-relate to data held in other tables within a database.

Forma The physical representation of signs.

Formative act Formative acts amount to the enactment of forma: acts of data representation and processing.

Formative action Action directed towards representation.

Formative evaluation Assessing the shape of an information system within the development process itself.

Formative pattern A coherent collection of related, formative acts.

Formative system An organised collection of formative patterns. See *Activity system*.

Fragmentation A measure of the degree to which data and processing is fragmented across information systems.

Front-end ICT infrastructure The organised collection of ICT systems interacting with key stakeholders.

Front-end ICT system An ICT system that supports a front-end information system.

Front-end information system An information system which interacts with internal or external stakeholders of the organisation.

Front-end information systems infrastructure The set of related information systems that interact with the major stakeholders of the organisation.

FTP File Transfer Protocol. A communication protocol for transferring files over communication networks.

Functionality What an ICT system is able to do.

G

General systems theory See *Systemics*.

Generalisation The relationship beween a class and a sub-class.

Gestural interface An interface controlled by forms of bodily gesture such as hand gestures.

Giga-byte 1,000,000,000 bytes (billion).

Globalisation The process by which organisations are operating across the globe.

Good Any product or commodity which is valued and exchanged.

GPRS General Packet Radio System. A form of radio communication channel for data transmission with high bandwidth.

Grammar Rules that control the correct use of a language.

Green ICT Considering and managing the impact ICT has upon sustainability.

H

Hardware The physical aspects of ICT consisting of processors, input devices and output devices.

Hierarchy An important systems concept in which a system can be de-composed to form various levels of detail.

Holistic thinking Thinking which studies the properties of whole systems rather than its parts.

Homeostasis The process of ensuring that a system remains regulated within defined limits.

Horizontal portal These portals attempt to serve the entire Internet community, typically by offering search functions and classification for all Web content.

HTML Hypertext Markup Language. a standard for marking up documents for publishing on the Web.

HTTP Hypertext Transfer Protocol. a communication protocol designed for the transfer of hypertext documents.

Human resource management A secondary process in the internal value-chain. This involves the recruiting, hiring, training and development of the employees of a company.

Hybrid implementation This form of implementation phases in particular components as replacements or pilots major modules of the system.

Hypermedia The technology supporting the construction of documents of multiple media associated together with links.

Hypertext A subset of *hypermedia* focusing on the construction of network text.

Hypertext Markup Language See *HTML*.

I

ICT Information and communication technology. Any technology used to support data gathering, processing, distribution and use. A term used to encapsulate hardware, software, data and communications technology.

ICT governance A subset of the discipline of corporate governance, focused on ICT systems and their performance.

ICT infrastructure The set of inter-related ICT systems used by an organisation.

ICT management Concerned with the maintenance of the ICT infrastructure, developing new applications and maintaining existing ICT applications.

ICT service delivery Delivering services, monitoring operations and costing services.

ICT service improvement Managing the process of improving aspects of ICT infrastructure.

ICT service strategy Defining a strategy for the ICT service.

ICT service support Supporting users in the use of the ICT service.

ICT services management The management of ICT as a service.

ICT strategy A specification of the hardware, software, data, communication facilities and ICT knowledge and skills needed by the organisation to support its information systems.

ICT system A technical system sometimes referred to as a 'hard' system. It is a system of data representation and processing. In the modern organisation it generally consists of an organised collection of hardware, software and communications technology designed to support aspects of an information system.

Impact The effect of information systems on individuals, groups and organisations.

Implementation See *Systems implementation*.

Implicit knowledge Knowledge accessible through querying and discussion but needing communication.

Inbound logistics A primary process in the internal value-chain involving the receipt and storage of raw materials and the distribution of such materials to manufacturing units.

Inconsistency A measure of the degree to which data is held or processed differently across information systems.

Inference Bringing new knowledge from existing knowledge.

Informa The meaning of signs within communication.

Informatics The study of information, information systems and ICT applied to various phenomena.

Informatics consumer A consumer of aspects of informatics, such as hardware or software.

Informatics field The academic study of informatics issues and problems.

Informatics industry A vast industry developed worldwide to service the informatics needs of organisations, groups and individuals.

Informatics infrastructure The sum total of information, information systems and ICT resources available to an organisation at any one time.

Informatics management The process of putting information, information systems and information technology plans into action.

Informatics operations That process devoted to the successful operation of existing informatics infrastructure.

Informatics outsourcing The use of external agents to perform some aspect of informatics.

Informatics planning The process of defining informatics strategy.

Informatics practice The practical application of informatics knowledge and skill within organisations.

Informatics profession The bodies exercising control over informatics practice.

Informatics provider A producer of hardware, software or communication technology.

Informatics service That organisational function devoted to the delivery of informatics.

Informatics strategy A definition of the structure within which information, information systems and information technology is to be applied in an organisation.

Information Data interpreted in a meaningful context.

Information and communication technology ICT, any technology used to support information gathering, processing, distribution and use. Information technology consists of hardware, software and communications technology.

Information and communication technology infrastructure See *ICT infrastructure*.

Information and communication technology system See *ICT system*.

Information centre A structure for the informatics service in which the service acts as a centre of expertise for other business units.

Information class A category that defines something of interest. A key element of an information model.

Information economics Information economics attempts to include the evaluation of intangible as well as tangible benefits into the process of IS evaluation.

Information economy An economy in which information is both important and essential to effective performance.

Information infrastructure The set of inter-related information models describing the information needs of the organisation.

Information management That part of informatics management concerned with the management of information.

Information model A model of the things of interest relevant to some area of business.

Information security The process of protecting information systems from criminal or unwanted activity.

Information society A term very loosely used to refer to the effect of ICT, information systems and information generally on modern society.

Information store A place where records are kept (sometimes referred to as a data store).

Information strategy That part of an informatics strategy concerned with specifying the information need for the future within an organisation.

Information system A system of communication between people, that supports coordinated and purposive activity.

Information system model A representation of an information system.

Information systems development

  That activity system devoted to the creation of a new information system or the maintenance of an existing information system.

Information systems development method A specified approach for producing information systems.

Information systems development technique Development techniques are normally used to guide activity within one phase of the development process.

Information systems development tool The hardware, software, data management and communication technology used to construct information systems.

Information systems evaluation Assessing the worth of an information system.

Information systems failure The development or use failure of an information system.

Information systems infrastructure The entire set of information systems supporting activity in an organisation.

Information systems management Concerned with the management of information-handling applications, both computerised and non-computerised.

Information systems planning The process of defining some *information systems architecture*.

Information systems portfolio A list of current systems in the *information systems architecture* or future systems in the *information systems strategy*.

Information systems strategy A specification of the information systems needed to support organisational activity.

Informative act Informative acts constitute the enactment of informa: acts of decision-making and communication involving message-making and interpretation.

Informative action Action involving communication, directed towards coordination.

Informative pattern A coherent collection of related, communicative acts.

Informative system An organised collection of informative patterns. See *Information system*.

Infrastructure Systems of activity, communication and technology that create organisation.

Input The things that a system takes from its environment.

Input device A device concerned with the input of data.

Input subsystem That part of a computer system concerned with the input of data.

Instantiation The relationship between an object or instance and its class.

Institutional perspective The perspective on organisations that treats them as wholes or units.

Instruction set A list of instructions understood by a computer system's processor.

Intangible good A good that can essentially be represented as data and hence can be delivered over data communication channels.

Intangible service A service that effectively can be represented as data and hence delivered over data communication channels.

Integration testing At some point the system has to be assembled as a complete unit and testing conducted of all related systems together.

Intension See *Concept*.

Interaction failure The argument is that if a system is heavily used it constitutes a success; if it is hardly ever used, or there are major problems involved in using a system then it constitutes a failure.

Interactive content Interactive content is two-way content. It allows users both to retrieve information as well as to

G

communicate with internal organisational stakeholders and/or systems.

Interactive digital television IDTV. A remote access device. A combination of digital television and an up-channel using conventional telephony.

Interest A pre-condition of electronic delivery. Stakeholders must be interested in using remote access channels for electronic delivery.

Interface layer That part of an ICT system devoted to the management of the user interface.

Intermediary Sometimes known as a channel organisation. An organisation which mediates between other organisations in the value-chain.

Intermediary-oriented B2B Intermediaries run electronic markets for buyers and sellers in a specific area.

Intermediation The process by which intermediate actors establish themselves within the value network.

Internet A set of inter-connected computer networks distributed around the globe that adopt the TCP/IP standard.

Internet auction An auction conducted over the Internet.

Internet service provider ISP. A company supplying connections to the Internet.

Interoperability A measure of the degree to which information systems are able to coordinate and collaborate.

Inter-organisational information system That form of information system that is developed and maintained by a consortium of companies in some cognate area of business for mutual benefit.

Intra-business eBusiness The use of ICT to enable the internal business processes of the firm.

Intranet The use of Internet and Web technology within the confines of a single organisation.

IP Address Internet Protocol Address. A unique identifier for computers on a communication network using TCP/IP.

ISDN Integrated Service Digital Network. A broadband communication channel for the local loop.

ISP Internet service provider, a company supplying connections to the Internet for customers.

Iterative development In this model systems conception triggers an iterative cycle in which various versions of a system (prototypes) are analysed, designed, constructed and possibly implemented.

ITIL Information Technology Infrastructure Library, a method for ICT services management.

J

Job analysis Involves the analysis of the content and relationships of current jobs in terms of both organisational and individual objectives.

K

Kilo-byte 1000 bytes.

Knowledge Building and using patterns of inference from data and information.

Knowledge codification The representation of knowledge for ease of retrieval.

Knowledge creation The acquisition of knowledge from organisational members and the creation of new organisational knowledge.

Knowledge management Consists of knowledge creation, knowledge codification and knowledge transfer.

Knowledge transfer The communication and sharing of knowledge among organisational members.

L

LAN See *Local Area Network*

Legacy ICT system An aging ICT system that is important for the organisation but which constrains infrastructure change.

Linear development The phases of development are strung out in a linear sequence with outputs from each phase triggering the start of the next phase.

Local area network LAN. A type of communication network in which the nodes of the network are situated relatively close together.

Local loop The communication channel between the local telephone exchange and customer premises.

Location strategy Involves the organisation attempting to find a niche market to service.

Logical design The attempt to specify the design of an ICT system independent of any implementation detail.

M

Maintenance See *Systems maintenance.*

Management The process through which organisations are controlled.

Management information system MIS. A type of information system supporting management activities, particularly tactical decision-making.

Management-facing information system A front-end information system used by management. See *Management information system, Executive information system.*

Managerial hierarchy Organisations coordinate the flow of value by controlling and directing it at a higher level in management structures.

Manual information system A term used to refer to an information system relying upon the technology of paper-based forms and other types of business documentation.

Market A medium for exchanges between buyers and sellers.

Marketing and sales A primary process in the internal value-chain. Marketing is the process of planning and executing the conception, pricing, promotion and distribution of ideas, goods and services to create exchanges that satisfy individual and organisational goals. Sales is the associated activity involved in the management of the customer's purchasing activities.

Marketing channel A channel for the communication of marketing messages.

Mega-byte 1,000,000 bytes (million).

Mega-package See *Enterprise resource planning system.*

Method See *Information systems development method.*

MIS See *Management information system.*

Mobile commerce The use of mobile access devices such as smartphones to conduct eCommerce.

Mobile device Any access device that can be used for access on the move.

Modelling approach Consists of constructs, notation and principles of use.

Modelling notation A way of representing the constructs of a model.

Modulation The process of introducing variety into a physical pattern such a signal.

MP3 Stands for Motion Picture Experts Group-1 Level 3. This format employs an algorithm to compress a music file, achieving a significant reduction of data while retaining near CD-quality sound.

Multi-channel access centre A centre that integrates various access channels into the organisation.

Multimedia kiosk A remote access device. Specialist access points to services provided on the Internet.

N

Natural language interface An interface in which the user enters statements in a natural language, such as English.

Negative feedback A type of feedback in which the control process takes action to reduce the variation between control inputs and sensed inputs.

Newsgroup Technology for enabling threaded discussions between many-to-many users.

Non-credit-based payment systems Non-credit-based payment systems are designed to encourage the electronic exchange of micro-payments.

Non-repudiability A user of an ICT system should not be able to deny that they have used it for a commercial transaction.

N-tier client–server architecture A layered model of an ICT system in which N layers of the system interact.

O

Object An instance of something of interest to some domain.

Object class A grouping of similar objects.

Object-oriented A term applied to programming languages, design methods and database systems to mean providing support for constructs such as objects, classes, generalisation aggregation etc.

OLAP Online analytical processing. Supports complex analytical operations such as consolidation, drilling down and pivoting.

Ontology That branch of philosophy concerned with theories of reality. Also used to describe a systematic model of some area of existence.

Open system A type of system that interacts with its environment.

Operating procurement Procurement conducted to support all the operations of the business.

Operating system That piece of system software concerned with the management of all other applications on a computer system.

Operational management The lowest level of management involved with making structured decisions with detailed data.

Operational research A discipline devoted to applying scientific methods to the problems of management.

Operations A primary process in the internal value-chain involving the transformation of raw materials into finished products.

Optionality Rules that specify whether all instances of classes participate in a relationship.

Organisation A social system consisting of activity, communication and representation.

Organisation culture The set of behavioural expectations associated with an organisation.

Organisation data model A high-level map of the data requirements for an organisation.

Organisation information model Provides detail of the structure of the major information classes used by the organisation, and the relationships between them.

Organisation planning Organisation planning is the process of formulating an organisation strategy.

Organisation process A set of activities cutting across the major functional divisions within organisations by which organisations accomplish their mission.

Organisation process model A high-level map of organisational processes.

Organisation strategy The general direction or mission of an organisation.

Organisation structure The set of objects of relevance to an organisation, plus the relationships between such objects.

Organisation theory That body of knowledge concerned with defining the key features of organisations.

Organisational analysis The process of analysing and redesigning key business processes or human activity systems.

Organisational informatics Another term for the discipline of information systems. The application of informatics within and between organisations.

Outbound logistics A primary process in the internal value-chain involving the storage of finished products in

G

warehouses and the distribution of finished products to customers.

Output The things that a system provides to its environment.

Output device A device that outputs data.

Output subsystem That part of a computer system that outputs data to the user or some other device.

Outsourcing The strategy in which the whole or part of the informatics service is handed over to an external vendor.

P

P2P eCommerce Partner to partner eCommerce. ICT enablement of aspects of the partnership chain.

Package development In package development an organisation purchases a piece of software from a vendor organisation and tailors the package to a greater or lesser extent to the demands of a particular organisation.

Packet switching The process of breaking up message data into packets that are disseminated over a communication network by routers.

Parallel implementation An implementation approach in which two systems, the old and the new, run in parallel.

Partner A key type of organisational stakeholder. Key organisations in the same industrial sector or market that participate in a partnership arrangement with an organisation.

Partnership chain The chain of activities conducted with partners in delivering value to a common customer.

Pattern Elements which repeat across situations.

Payback period Payback is calculated on the basis of:

Payback = Investment – cumulative benefit (cash inflow).

Payroll information system That back-end information system dealing with the payment of employees.

Perfective maintenance Changes made to the information system which make improvements but without affecting its functionality.

Performa The use of signs in support of coordinated activity.

Performance The degree to which a system reaches specified levels.

Performative action Action which involves actors transforming objects with tools.

Performative pattern A coherent collection of related, performative acts.

Performative system An organised collection of performative patterns. See *Activity system*.

Personal computer A desktop computer used as a remote access device.

Personal identity management A term used to encompass all those issues involved with authenticating, identifying and enrolling individuals.

Physical design The design of the implementation of a system, a blueprint for its construction.

Physical environment The ecological environment within which an organisation sits.

Physical flow This represents the flow of tangible or physical goods and services such as foodstuffs and automobiles.

Piecemeal ICT systems ICT systems that lack integration.

Podcast A series of digital media files such as audio or video files that are released episodically to users.

Political environment That part of the environment concerned with power and its exercise.

Polity A political system centred on a geographical area.

Portal A portal is designed to be an entry point for users into the World Wide Web.

Post-mortem evaluation Examining the reasons for an information systems failure.

Power Power is the ability of a person or social group to control the behaviour of some other person or social group.

Pragmatics The study of the general context and culture of communication.

Pre-conditions for electronic service delivery A range of social factors, expressed in a sequence, which affect the likely uptake of the electronic delivery of goods and services.

Preventative maintenance Changes aimed at improving a system's maintainability such as documentation or improving the flexibility of the information technology system.

Primary activities Activities that constitute the core competencies of an organisation.

Primary key A unique identifier for each of the rows in a table.

Privacy See *Data privacy*.

Problem situation A situation in organisational life that is regarded by at least one person as a problem.

Process A set of activities that transforms inputs into outputs.

Process design Specifying how a new activity system should work for a domain.

Process failure This type of failure is characterised by unsatisfactory development performance.

Process map See *Organisation process model*.

Process mapping See *Process modelling*.

Process modelling Specifying how the activity system in some existing area works.

Process redesign See *Process re-engineering*.

Process re-engineering The process of analysing, redesigning and implementing organisational processes.

Process/information matrix A matrix which indicates which information class on the organisation information model is used by which organisational process.

Procurement A secondary activity in the internal value-chain. Procurement is the process of purchasing goods and services from suppliers at an acceptable quality and price and with reliable delivery.

Producer A key type of organisational stakeholder. Teams of developers that have to design, construct and maintain information systems for organisations.

Product-based planning A form of project management in which project planning and control is focused around information systems products.

Production That set of activities concerned with the creation of goods and services for human existence.

Production cost The cost of producing something.

Production database A type of database designed to support standard organisational functions.

Production-related procurement Procurement designed to support manufacturing operations.

Productivity paradox The paradox that those organisations that have invested significantly in ICT do not appear to have experienced significant improvements in productivity.

Programme management The management of a suite of linked projects.

Programming language A language for instructing a computer system.

Project control Concerns ensuring that a project remains on schedule, within budget and produces the desired output.

Project escalation The process in which decision-makers become locked in an irrational course of action.

Project management The process of planning for, organising and controlling projects.

Project organisation Concerns how to structure staff activities to ensure maximum effectiveness.

Project planning Determining as clearly as possible the likely parameters associated with a particular project.

Prototyping The development approach in which prototypes are produced.

Public Internet access point Specialist access points to services provided on the Internet.

Public key infrastructure An infrastructure for ensuring the security of electronic transactions that includes ensuring that digital keys are used only by legitimate holders and procedures for managing the assignment and storage of digital keys.

Publish content One-way content. It allows the user to retrieve general information placed on the website or Webpage.

Purchase order processing information system The information system that records details of purchase orders to suppliers.

Q

QUIS Questionnaire for user interface satisfaction – a means of assessing user satisfaction with an interface.

R

Read (formative act) A formative act that decodes the values associated with one or more data items.

Record An instance of persistent forma or a data element of a file.

Redundancy A measure of the degree to which data is unnecessarily replicated across information systems.

Referent That which is being signified. The range of phenomena referred to.

Referential integrity That a foreign key must refer to a primary key value or be null.

Regulation The process of ensuring that a system remains viable.

Regulator A key type of organisational stakeholder. These are groups or agencies that set environmental constraints for an information system.

Re-intermediation The process in electronic markets of new intermediaries developing between buyers and sellers

Relationship An *association* between classes.

Repeat commerce The pattern in which regular, repeat transactions occur between trading partners.

Representation The process of denoting something with a physical pattern.

Representative participation A design group is formed made up of representatives of all grades of staff with systems analysts. The representatives however are selected by management.

Requirements analysis Negotiating and agreeing requirements with the various stakeholders.

Requirements elicitation The process of identifying requirements for the system from stakeholder groups.

Requirements specification Representing the requirements established in the requirements elicitation process.

Return on investment The return on investment (RoI) associated with an IS project is calculated using the following equation:

RoI = average (annual net income / annual investment amount).

RFID tag Radio Frequency Identification tag, an access device that can be incorporated into an object.

Rich picture A graphical representation of key elements of a problem situation.

Ring network A network topology in which network devices are connected in a loop.

Risk analysis The identification, estimation and assessment of risk.

Role A package of behaviour associated with particular social situations.

Root definition A way of representing the perspectives of key stakeholders as to the core purpose of an activity system.

Router Hardware and software that direct packets to their indicated destination along a communication network.

Rules subsystem That part of an ICT system concerned with application logic.

G

S

Sales order processing information system The information system that records details of customer orders.

Satisficing The term used by Herbert Simon to describe the characteristics of human decision-making.

Scenario A narrative description of what people do and experience as they try to make use of computer systems and applications.

Search engine A system that allows users to locate websites matching keywords.

Secondary activities Activities that are critical to supporting primary activities.

Secure socket layer SSL, Netscape's attempt to offer a secure channel of communication. It is a framework for transmitting sensitive information, such as credit card details, over the Internet.

Security See *Data security*.

Semantic Web An attempt to build semantics into the links used in associating Web content.

Semantics The study of the meaning of signs.

Semiosis The process of using signs.

Semiotics The discipline devoted to the study of signs and sign-systems.

Sensor A mechanism that monitors changes in the environment of a system.

Server The computer that supplies services to clients.

Service Some form of valued activity that is exchanged between actors.

SGML Standard Generalised Markup Language is used for describing the formatting of electronic documents.

Sign A pattern of significance. Something which stands to somebody for something.

Sign-system An organised collection of signs and relations between signs.

Single-loop feedback A type of feedback involved in regulating the behaviour of an underlying operational process.

Social capital A feature of social networks that facilitates coordination and cooperation among actors.

Social environment That part of the environment concerned with the cultural life of some grouping.

Social infrastructure The social infrastructure for eBusiness consists of those human activity systems central to supporting the conduct of eBusiness. These include competencies in planning, management, development and evaluation.

Social network A network of people joined together by social relations.

Social networking site A website that facilitates social networking.

Sociotechnical design The parallel design of both technical and social systems.

Sociotechnical system A system of technology used within a system of activity.

Soft system A social system that is designed to meet certain objectives.

Soft systems methodology The approach to organisational analysis created by Peter Checkland and associates.

Software Programs of instructions for controlling hardware.

Software metric A number extracted from a software product.

Spamming The process of sending unsolicited emails to large numbers of people.

Specialisation The relationship between a sub-class and its super-class.

SQL See *Structured Query Language*.

Stakeholder A person or group that has some claim on an organisational problem and its solution.

Stakeholder analysis Analysing the types and impact of stakeholders on information systems.

Stakeholder identification Identifying the group of people to which an information system is relevant.

Stakeholder involvement Involvement of stakeholder representatives in the development of an ICT system.

Stakeholder participation Involvement of stakeholders both in the development of the IT system and the work surrounding its use.

Stakeholder resistance The resistance of stakeholder groups to the introduction of an information system.

Stakeholder satisfaction The state of satisfaction expressed by a stakeholder group in an information system.

Standard data Data structures using common data types such as text, numbers or unit of time.

Star network A network topology in which network devices are connected to a central computer.

State The set of all values assumed by the properties of a system at one point in time.

Stock control information system An information system for recording details of inventory.

Storage That part of a system concerned with the representation of data.

Storage device A device that persistently represents data.

Storage subsystem That part of the computer system concerned with the persistent representation of data.

Strategic analysis Strategic analysis involves determining the organisation's mission and goals.

Strategic choice This involves generating strategic options, evaluation of such options and the selection of a suitable strategy to achieve the selected option.

Strategic decision-making Making less structured decisions, with summary information about courses of action with a long timescale.

Strategic evaluation The evaluation of the strategic benefit of an information system.

Strategic implementation Comprises determining policies, making decisions and taking action.

Strategic information system An information system that delivers competitive advantage.

Strategic management The top-level of management concerned with making unstructured decisions with heavily summarised data.

Strategy The process of directing future activity.

Strong link A relationship between two actors in regular contact with each other.

Structuration The process by which human action both produces and reproduces social structure and also how social structure both informs and constrains human action.

Structured Query Language SQL. A database programming language designed for use with relational databases.

Subculture The set of behavioural expectations associated with some part of a larger social grouping.

Sub-optimisation The idea that optimising the performance of a particular subsystem will not necessarily optimise the performance of the whole system.

Subsystem A coherent part of a system that can be treated as a system itself.

Summative evaluation Assessing a delivered information system against its strategic evaluation.

Supplier A key type of organisational stakeholder. Organisations that supply goods and services to an organisation.

Supplier relationship management The management of supply-chain activities. Sometimes referred to as supply chain management.

Supplier-facing information systems A type of information system supporting interaction with the suppliers of the organisation.

Supplier-oriented B2B Producers and consumers use the same electronic marketplace. Essentially the same as B2C eCommerce.

Supply chain The chain of activities that an organisation performs in relation to its suppliers.

Supply chain management The collection of an organisation's activities devoted to the management of the supply chain.

Symbol A pattern of energy or matter used to denote something.

Synchronisation A property of a communication channel. The degree to which the sender and receiver of messages are synchronised.

Syntax The operational rules for the correct representation of terms and their use in the construction of sentences of the language.

System An organised set of interdependent elements that exists for some purpose, has some stability, and can be usefully viewed as a whole.

System documentation This describes the structure and behaviour of the IT system for developers.

System lag A delay between the issuing of a control signal and the adjustment of the system process to the signals.

System software That collection of programs which coordinate the activities of hardware and all programs running on a computer system.

System testing Testing of an entire system as a unit.

Systemics See *General systems theory*.

Systemics The study of systems.

Systems analysis That part of the development process devoted to eliciting and representing the requirements for systems.

Systems conception That part of the development process devoted to assessing the investment potential and feasibility of systems.

Systems construction That part of the development process devoted to constructing systems.

Systems design That part of the development process devoted to designing the functionality of systems.

Systems engineering A systems discipline concerned with the production of large, complex physical artefacts.

Systems implementation That part of the development process devoted to delivering the system into its context of use.

Systems maintenance That part of the development process devoted to maintaining systems.

Systems thinking See *Systemics*.

T

Table The major data structure in the relational data model.

Tacit knowledge Knowledge accessible only with difficulty through elicitation techniques.

Tactical management Middle management which interfaces between strategic and operational management.

Tactics Belong only to the mechanical movement of bodies set in motion by strategy.

Tangible good Goods that have a physical form and cannot be delivered to the customer electronically.

Tangible service A service that has to be performed physically by one actor for another.

Target advertisement One-to-many active advertisements.

Task analysis Specifying the precise organisation of tasks associated with the use of a computer system.

TCP/IP Transmission Control Protocol/Internet Protocol is the communications model underlying the Internet.

Technical infrastructure The supporting infrastructure of ICTs for eBusiness.

Technique Some systematic activity within the development process.

Technological frame A collection of underlying assumptions, expectations and knowledge that people have about technology and its use.

G

Telecommunication carrier An organisation which provides the telecommunication infrastructure for communications.

Telecommunication device A piece of hardware that permits electronic communication to occur.

Telecommunication media Media used for the transmission of data in communication networks.

Telecommunication service See *Telecommunication carrier*.

Telephony A category of access device which includes fixed audio and video telephones as well as mobile telephones and fax machines.

Tera-byte 1,000,000,000,000 (trillion) bytes.

Testing Part of *systems construction*; ensuring that an information system is working effectively.

Theory X According to this theory the average human being is perceived as disliking work and hence avoiding it wherever possible. The average human being avoids responsibility and has little ambition.

Theory Y According to this theory physical and mental effort are important and natural human functions. If humans are committed to certain objectives they will exercise self-direction and self-control. The capacity to exercise imagination, ingenuity and creativity are widely distributed in the population.

Three-tier architecture A client-server architecture divided into three layers: interface, business and data.

Timebox An agreed period of time for the production of a deliverable.

Tool Software used to aid the development process.

TPS See *Transaction processing system*.

Transaction A logical unit of work which transforms a database, or more generally a data structure, from one state to another.

Transaction processing system TPS. A type of information system supporting the operational activities of an organisation.

Transaction subsystem That part of an IT system concerned with communicating between the interface and rules subsystem and the data subsystem.

Transactional data Data that records events taking place between individuals, groups and organisations.

Trust The glue that binds organisations together into a single cohesive unit and keeps them functioning. Trust is also critical to economic transactions between buyers and sellers. It is defined in the Oxford English Dictionary as, 'a firm belief that a person or thing may be relied upon'.

Tunnelling technology Involves the transmission of data over the Internet using lines leased to the local ISP. With the use of encryption, authentication and other security technologies such an approach can be used to produce a virtual private network (VPN) over a wide area network.

Tweet A text-based post of up to 140 characters.

U

Unit testing Testing of individual programs or software modules.

Universal resource locator URL. A unique identifier for a document placed on the Web.

Update (formative act) A formative act that changes the values associated with one or more data items of some data element.

Update function Individual components of functionality that are triggered by events in the interface and change the state of data structures.

URL See *Universal resource locator*.

Usability An information system's usability is how easy a system is to use for the purpose for which it has been constructed.

Use A pre-condition of electronic delivery. Stakeholders must regularly use remote access mechanisms in core areas of life.

Use case A use case model provides a high-level description of major user interactions with an information system.

Use failure Failure of an information system after a period of use.

Use setting The setting within which a particular interface is used.

User documentation A source of reference for users to turn to when puzzled about aspects of use.

User interface That part of an ICT system that allows users to control the functionality of the system.

Utility Utility refers to the worth of an information system in terms of the contribution it makes to its human activity system and to the organisation as a whole.

V

Value A general term used to describe the worth of something such as the output from some organisation or ICT system.

Value added network VAN. A type of communication network in which a third-party creates and maintains a network for other organisations.

Value-chain A collection of interrelated activities that delivers value to the customer.

Value network The network of actors within which an organisation sits and with which the organisation exchanges value.

Value-network analysis The analysis of the value network appropriate to that organisation.

Variety A measure of the complexity of a system; the number of states a system can assume.

Vertical portal These normally provide the same functionality as horizontal portals but for a specific market sector.

Viable system A term used by Stafford Beer to describe a system capable of surviving in a volatile environment.

Viral marketing The idea of spreading product referrals through a social network in a similar manner to the way in which a virus might spread through a population.

Virtual community A community consisting of a network of actors on a communication network.

Virtual organisation An organisation built on an ICT infrastructure that enables collaborative e-Working among members. Also referred to as network organisations. Organisations characterised by flat organisational hierarchies, formed around projects and linked together by ICT.

Virtual Private Network See *VPN*.

Vocabulary A complete list of the terms of a language.

Volume testing Testing the application with large amounts of data and use.

VPN Virtual Private Network. A form of network which employs tunnelling technology to secure data transmission over the Internet.

W

WAN See *Wide area network*.

WAP Wireless Application Protocol.

Weak link A relationship between two actors in irregular contact.

Web 2.0 A collection of Web-based communities and hosted services which facilitate collaboration.

Web analytics Can be seen as a subset of business analytics and refers to a battery of techniques employed to measure website traffic.

Web page A term generally used to refer to the presentational aspect of a Web document.

Web portal A portal is designed to be an entry point for users into the World Wide Web.

Web service A component piece of an ICT system that implements a limited piece of functionality which can be distributed over the Web.

Website A collection of HTML documents stored on a Web server.

Wicked problems Complex problems in which the problem itself is open to interpretation.

Wide area network WAN. A type of communication network in which the nodes of the network are geographically remote.

WiFi A series of standards supporting short range, high bandwidth communication networks.

Wiki A wiki is a shared web page or site that can be updated with easy-to-use tools through a browser.

WiMax A related technology to WiFi but designed to provide communication over longer distances.

Word One or more bytes treated as a unit.

Worldview A set of underlying assumptions held by a particular stakeholder group.

World Wide Web An application that runs over the Internet supporting the use and transmission of hypermedia documentation.

WWW See *World Wide Web*.

X

XML Extensible markup language is a meta-language for the definition of document standards.

G

Index

I

I

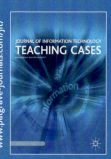

Printed in China